History of Universities

History of Universities
Editor:
Mordechai Feingold (California Institute of Technology)

Managing Editor:
Jane Finucane (Trinity College, University of Glamorgan)

Editorial Board:
R. D. Anderson (University of Edinburgh)
L. J. Dorsman (Utrecht University)
Thierry Kouamé (Université Paris 1 Panthéon-Sorbonne)
Mauro Moretti (Università per Stranieri di Siena)
H. de Ridder-Symoens (Ghent)
S. Rothblatt (University of California, Berkeley)
N. G. Siraisi (Hunter College, New York)

Birkbeck

*200 Years of Radical Learning
for Working People*

JOANNA BOURKE

Great Clarendon Street, Oxford, OX2 6DP,
United Kingdom

Oxford University Press is a department of the University of Oxford.
It furthers the University's objective of excellence in research, scholarship,
and education by publishing worldwide. Oxford is a registered trade mark of
Oxford University Press in the UK and in certain other countries

© Joanna Bourke 2022

The moral rights of the author have been asserted

First Edition published in 2022

Impression: 2

All rights reserved. No part of this publication may be reproduced, stored in
a retrieval system, or transmitted, in any form or by any means, without the
prior permission in writing of Oxford University Press, or as expressly permitted
by law, by licence or under terms agreed with the appropriate reprographics
rights organization. Enquiries concerning reproduction outside the scope of the
above should be sent to the Rights Department, Oxford University Press, at the
address above

You must not circulate this work in any other form
and you must impose this same condition on any acquirer

Published in the United States of America by Oxford University Press
198 Madison Avenue, New York, NY 10016, United States of America

British Library Cataloguing in Publication Data

Data available

Library of Congress Control Number: 2022939624

ISBN 978–0–19–284663–1

DOI: 10.1093/oso/9780192846631.001.0001

Printed and bound in the UK by
Clays Ltd, Elcograf S.p.A.

Links to third party websites are provided by Oxford in good faith and
for information only. Oxford disclaims any responsibility for the materials
contained in any third party website referenced in this work.

Contents

List of Illustrations	vii
Preface	xiii
1. Introduction	1

PART I. FROM MECHANICS TO GRADUATES

2. The Crown and Anchor Tavern	11
3. Education for Whom?	29
4. Useful Knowledge	49
5. The Birkbeck Schools	67
6. Ravenscroft's Birkbeck Bank	78
7. Governing the College	95
8. What Is a University?	122

PART II. PLEASURE AND PREFERENCES

9. Art and Architecture	143
10. Dancing the Polka	160
11. The New Woman	174
12. Minoritized Communities	204

PART III. STUDENT LIFE

13. 'Tea and Kippers'	233
14. Hares versus Rabbits; Or, Social Lives	247
15. 'Man versus Rabbits'	286
16. The Students' 'Joy-Night'	304

PART IV. WAR AND POLITICS

17. Worlds at War, 1914–1918	317
18. Worlds at War, 1939–1945	335
19. Reds in the Classroom	359
20. Radical Intellectuals	381

PART V. CLASSROOMS

21. Science in the World	407
22. Disciplines	431
23. Numerical Automation; Or, Computing	456
24. Paranormal Sciences	469
25. Teaching	496

PART VI. BATTLES FOR BIRKBECK

26. 'Birkbeck's Unique Mission?'	527
27. Containing the Crisis	547

PART VII. CONCLUSION

28. Into the Twenty-First Century	573

Bibliography	595
Acknowledgements	617
Index	619

List of Illustrations

2.1. St Clements in the Strand and the Crown and Anchor Tavern in the foreground on the right. — 12
2.2. Page from the minutes of the first meeting of the founders of the LMI, in which their aims are outlined, 8 November 1823. — 15
2.3. Announcement of the first public meeting to discuss founding the LMI, November 1823. — 16
2.4. Francis Place. — 17
2.5. Portrait of George Birkbeck by Samuel Lane, *c.*1830. — 20
2.6. 'Institutions for Instruction of Mechanics. Proposals for a London Mechanics Institute', *Mechanic's Magazine, Museum, Register, Journal & Gazette*, 11 October 1823. — 23
2.7. A ballad sung at the 4th Anniversary Dinner of the LMI in 1828. — 24
2.8. The Order of Procession for the funeral of George Birkbeck. — 26
2.9. The Crown and Anchor Tavern on fire in December 1854. *Illustrated London News*, 9 December 1854. — 27
3.1. Engraving from a sketch of the theatre of the LMI, *c.*1825. — 36
3.2. The LMI's Student Register for 1824. — 40
3.3. Engraving of the London Mechanics' Institution façade in 1865. — 44
5.1. The proposed advertisement for a new schoolmaster, in the LMI's minutes, 27 May 1833. — 69
5.2. The 1849 Prospectus for the Birkbeck School, in the *Mechanics' Magazine, Museum, Register, Journal and Gazette*, 23 December 1848. — 72
6.1. Bust of Francis Ravenscroft in Birkbeck's Council Room. — 79
6.2. Advertisement for the Birkbeck Bank, in *The British Women's Temperance Journal*, 1 November 1889. — 82
6.3. An advertisement for the Birkbeck Bank and Building Society. — 84
6.4. A surviving Birkbeck pub. — 86
6.5. The list of subscribers to Bream's Building, 'Windsor House, Bream's Buildings & Cursitor Street', plans, *c.*1880s. — 89
6.6. A photograph of Bream's Building, 'Windsor House, Bream's Buildings & Cursitor Street', plans, *c.*1880s. — 90
6.7. Crowds gathering outside the Birkbeck Bank during the 1911 crisis. — 93
7.1. Resolution by Hume and Richardson for election to the Board of Governors, 1913–14. — 106

viii   LIST OF ILLUSTRATIONS

7.2. Minutes of the General Meeting of the Birkbeck Students' Union on 22 January 1914 recommending that the College becomes part of the University of London. 107

7.3. The most powerful women at Birkbeck, c.1997. Front row: Professor Josephine Labanyi (Spanish); Christine Mabey (College Secretary 1988–99), Philippa Dolphin (Library). Back row: Professor Julia Goodfellow (Crystallography); Professor Nicola Lacey (Law); Tessa Blackstone (Master); Professor Jennifer Hornsby (Philosophy); Professor Isobel Armstrong (English). 113

7.4. Baroness Smith of Gilmorehill (Elizabeth Margaret Smith), 1998–2002. 118

7.5. An advertisement for an 'Addressograph', purchased by Birkbeck. It shows a blonde, fashionably dressed 'secretary' addressing envelopes, making sure she does not disturb the clearly more important, formally dressed man making a telephone call. Birkbeck's addressograph was only replaced in August 1990. 120

8.1. The library at Bream's Building c.1923, complete with log fire. The library moved to Greystoke Place in around 1935. 123

8.2. Portrait of George Armitage-Smith by Amy Armitage-Smith. 127

8.3. 'Vivat Academia', the College's anthem. 135

8.4. Ragging during the Centenary Celebrations of 1923. 137

8.5. Stanley Baldwin delivering the Foundation Oration at the College's Centenary in Bream's Building on 20 March 1924. 138

8.6. The Court of Electors' centenary dinner at Princes Restaurant on 31 March 1924. 139

9.1. Art class at the Birkbeck Literary and Scientific Institution in the early 1900s. 148

9.2. The Birkbeck Cinema, 2007. 159

10.1. The College theatre in Bream's Building in the 1920s. 161

10.2. Letter from Oscar Wilde. 166

10.3. The English Department's Christmas party in the Tillotson Room during the early 1980s. 172

11.1. Edith Lanchester. 175

11.2. John Manger Fells, friend of G. B. Shaw and Sidney Webb, Secretary of the Zetetical Society, and the leading cost accountant in Britain in the late nineteenth century. 194

12.1. James Julian Ben ('Sammy') Samnadan-Pillai in 1952. 209

12.2. 'National Uncle Toms Organisation', a leaflet criticizing the Post-Conference Constituent Committee, 1975. 221

13.1. 'Ma' Francis in her youth (with her husband, Alfred) and in old age (with her daughter, L. A. Wilson, and dog). 234

13.2. The Student Bar in 1970. 244

LIST OF ILLUSTRATIONS ix

14.1. A satirical cartoon captioned 'Professor Voelkickups school for the instruction of Gentlemen of all ages in the arts of Running, Tumbling, Leaping, Scrambling, Crawling, Creeping, Climbing, Pushing, Poking, and Hobby-horsemanship'. 251
14.2. Female students competing in tug-of-war at Paddington Green playing fields in 1914. 253
14.3. The opening of the new pavilion at Greenford in May 1928. 254
14.4. The notice for the 8th Annual Excursion of the London Mechanics' Institution in 1858. 256
14.5. *The Lodestone*'s cover for 1906. 257
14.6. 'Mr Can't, Mr Can'. *The Lodestone*, 1933. 259
14.7. The 'Old' Common Room, photographed by physicist B. D. H. Watters. 260
14.8. The Students' Common Room 1943. 266
14.9. Two Birkbeck students preparing the house for Hungarian refugees. 278
14.10. Stills from the Pathé film, showing the railway sign telling refugees where to get off the train, the first young refugees arriving at the Birkbeck house, and a drawing of St Teresa. 279
14.11. Problems with the boilers at Greenford in 1969, resulting in months with very limited supply of hot water. 'Occasional Showers!', *Spectrum*, 1969. 281
15.1. The zoology laboratory at Birkbeck College, *c*.1920s–1940s. 291
15.2. The Master Lockwood and his wife at the 'Chimpanzee Tea Party' in the London Zoological Gardens in 1956. 294
15.3. A Home Office pamphlet sent to Birkbeck College advising how to deal with the new threat from animal liberationist activists, *c*.1980s–1990s. 302
16.1. Ragging during the 1923 Centenary Celebrations. 306
17.1. Louis Raemaeker's cartoon 'The Spring Song', *The Studio*, 1918. 321
17.2. Photographs of Clements and his gravesite. 322
17.3. A roll of some of the student refugees from Belgium to whom the College offered a free education. 323
17.4. Photograph of M. G. Varwell, President of Birkbeck Students' Union, in a trench, *c*.1914–18. 324
17.5. Special classes taught at Birkbeck during the war. 327
17.6. Portrait of Helen Gwynne-Vaughan by the Hungarian Philip de László, *c*.1910. 328
17.7. Helen Gwynne-Vaughan's election poster when she stood as a Unionist candidate in the 1922 general election. 329
17.8. The unveiling of the First World War memorial in Bream's Building on 11 December 1921. 332
17.9. Reginald Francis Clements' name on the scroll of honour. 334

x   LIST OF ILLUSTRATIONS

18.1. Lena May Chivers (more widely known as Lena May Jeger), President of Birkbeck Students' Union and later prominent Labour Party politician, 10 November 1953.   337
18.2. Detail from a student poster near the end of the war, protesting the persecution of the Jews.   342
18.3. Books drying outside the destroyed Birkbeck College library in Greystoke Place during the Blitz in May 1941.   346
18.4. Bomb damage to the College's library, May 1941.   347
18.5. Dame Gwynne-Vaughan in the uniform of the Auxiliary Territorial Service with Queen Elizabeth, Queen Mother, in 1939.   350
18.6. Students sent hundreds of letters to the College Secretary, Troup Horne.   351
18.7. Telegram from Buckingham Palace dated 10 May 1945.   354
18.8. The steel frame of the Malet Street building under construction, 1947.   355
18.9. The Second World War memorial.   357
19.1. Nikita Khrushchev, General Secretary of the Communist Party of the Soviet Union, addressing the World Conference for General Disarmament and Peace, Moscow, July 1962.   375
20.1. Heads of department in the Council Room, 1972–3.   385
20.2. The library at Gresse Street in the 1970s.   389
20.3. Portrait of Baroness Blackstone by Peter Douglas Edwards.   390
20.4. Costas Douzinas, critical legal theorist and co-founder of the Birkbeck Law Department and the Birkbeck Institute for the Humanities.   396
21.1. Female students working in one of Birkbeck's laboratories.   410
21.2. J. D. Bernal, Irene Joliot-Curie, Frederic Joliot-Curie, and C. V. Ramon.   414
21.3. J. D. Bernal and the Crystallography Department at the Royal Institution Faraday Laboratory, 1946.   415
21.4. J. D. Bernal and Dorothy Hodgkin.   417
21.5. Chemistry laboratory in Bream's Building, 1923.   426
22.1. Vera Evison, who carried out the first excavations on the West Stow Anglo-Saxon village site from 1957 to 1961.   454
23.1. Kathleen Britten (later, Booth), Xenia Sweeting (Research Assistant), and Andrew Booth working on ARC, December 1946.   459
23.2. A demonstration of the Computer Science Department during the 1973 Open Day, Birkbeck's 150th anniversary.   468
25.1. Cover of C. E. M. Joad's *More Opinions by Joad* (1946).   499
25.2. Oil painting of C. E. M. Joad by artist J. M. Clark, 1947.   502
25.3. J. D. Bernal with his students on a field trip to Stonehenge, Wiltshire, to study mineral crystallography.   509
25.4. Oil painting of C. A. Mace, unknown artist.   510

25.5.	Marjorie Daunt. *The Lodestone*, 1956.	513
25.6.	Thorndike's 'Back at Birkbeck Again!' *Spectrum*, 1970.	521
25.7.	Map of student residences, 1920–1.	523
26.1.	Temporary, prefabricated classrooms for geography and psychology classes on a bombed site beside Bream's Building.	529
27.1.	An oil portrait of H. Gordon Jackson, Master of Birkbeck during the Second World War, by Sam Morse-Born, *c*.1940.	549
27.2.	The Master, Ronald Tress, showing Margaret Thatcher, Secretary of State for Education and Science, a set of rocks used for teaching in the Geology Department during her visit to Birkbeck during the 150th anniversary, 14 July 1973.	551
27.3.	'Government Threats + Government Cuts = Our Misery'. Cover of *Spectrum*, January 1985.	553
28.1.	A member of staff uses the library card catalogue in the building at Gresse Street in the 1970s.	580
28.2.	Professor David Latchman during the graduations, 2003.	586
28.3.	Letter from Ramsay MacDonald in 1935.	588

Preface

If you walk along the south side of Birkbeck, starting from Torrington Square and heading towards Malet Street, and look right, you might catch a glimpse of our current Vice Chancellor, Professor David Latchman, conducting meetings in his office. As befits a hard-working head of a college of the University of London, his rooms are an austere workplace. They are located at the end of a sombre corridor lined by portraits (all male, except for one wife perching precariously on the arm-rest of the chair where her husband sits), in which the College's senior administrators work. These are said to be the most important rooms in College.

This was where I was summoned in late 2016. Latchman sat me down and wasted no words: would I write the history of Birkbeck for our bicentenary in 2023? This request was unexpected: I am primarily historian of interpersonal violence and the emotions it engenders. I have worked in universities all my adult life, but I have never really thought historically about Higher Education. For nearly thirty years, my intellectual home has been Birkbeck. The students have been inspiring; governmental assaults on our 'unique mission', frustrating. But the truth is: I love the place.

Latchman interrupted my thoughts: what was my decision? Could my history be 'warts and all', I asked. I would not have considered undertaking the project if there had been any restrictions on my research. 'Yes,' he replied. I accepted.

It was a rather intimidating assignment. There are many perils in writing the history of an institution. The most important question is: who are my readers? Many will be current or former students who will, inevitably, turn immediately to the index to see if their departments, disciplines, or favourite lecturers are mentioned. My fellow-academics will surely look for their own names, so I must state here that I have been extremely parsimonious in mentioning current colleagues. There is also the fact that I am an actor in this history, having arrived in the Department of History, Classics, and Archaeology at Birkbeck in October 1992. And I remain a devoted Birkbeckian. How could I maintain a cool eye when examining a college of which I am so proud? Most importantly: how could I ensure that my book was not a dry chronicle of an educational institution? I wanted to write a book that people would enjoy reading.

I knew I would not please everyone. Some readers would want more on administrative structures. Others, on the bricks-and-mortar. More could have been said about certain disciplines. The history of a living institution has no tidy 'end'. I sent the final version of the book to Oxford University Press at the end of September 2021, so, when it is published, lots more history will have occurred. The College's bicentenary website will be filling in some of the gaps. Writing a history of the present is even more problematic. Historians inevitably rely on hindsight. I can only apologise for any failings and omissions.

In the end, this book is animated by the conviction that Birkbeck is its people. Their thoughts and ambitions, hopes and dreams, labours and laughter, are what this book describes, celebrates, and occasionally laments. The journey took me from Birkbeck's classrooms to its refectories and sports fields. I was required to navigate theatrical extravagances and political intrigues. Radical working men and women appear in these pages; they strove to 'better themselves'. We will meet a free-thinking, suffragette student who was incarcerated in a mental asylum in the 1890s on the grounds that she had been 'over-educated' in the college; a woman who, in 1936, stole food and cigarettes from the canteen and was living with her son's 'pal'; academics who bonded over haggis and whisky; intellectuals who squabbled over facts and interpretations; and men and women struggling to change their worlds. Most of all, this is a book about their ideas. What does it mean to be educated? Why have Birkbeck's students been prepared to give up so much to study for a higher degree? What does it mean to be fully human, exploiting our faculties in order to become better people?

In the end, the story of Birkbeck contains some blood, oceans of scholarly sweat, and not a few tears. But it is also a story of intellectual excitement, scholarly eccentricity, collective as well as personal ambition, and, most of all, the quirky passions and personalities that make up our community. It is a story of a unique university but also of Higher Education in Britain.

1
Introduction

Names matter. Today, the College is known as Birkbeck, University of London. This was not always the case, nor was it inevitable. It started life as the London Mechanics' Institution (LMI). In 1850, there was an unsuccessful attempt to rename it 'Birkbeck College'. In 1866, it became politically expedient to rename it 'The Birkbeck Literary and Scientific Institution', then simply the Birkbeck Institute. Most people called it 'The Birkbeck'. In 1891, financial benefit made the college join up with the Northampton Polytechnic and the City of London College to form the City Polytechnic. This was always a union of convenience, rather than anything more substantive, and was formally dissolved in 1907 when it was renamed 'Birkbeck College'. After years of lobbying and restructuring, the College finally became a college of the University of London in 1920. Today, it is simply called 'Birkbeck, University of London.'

It could have been otherwise. Coincidence, luck, and happenstance all played their parts. A small change in the dynamics of power or personality had dramatic consequences. As we will see in the next chapter, the LMI/Birkbeck was founded by patent agent and editor Joseph Clinton Robertson, journalist and economist Thomas Hodgskin, tailor and professional radical Francis Place, prominent Whig politician Henry Brougham (who would become the controversial Lord Chancellor of England), and physician and philanthropist George Birkbeck. Birkbeck could have been called the 'Robertson and Hodgskin's Institute', 'Robertson's Temple of Science', 'Brougham's Palace of Education', or even 'Place's Place'. It could have become the 'Birkbeck Technical College' or even 'London's Evening University'. If one Master had had his way, Birkbeck would have deserted the metropolis altogether, setting itself up in the fields of the Home Counties. For the purposes of this book, I will simply call the college the LMI or Birkbeck, although occasionally I will employ the name used at the time as a reminder that the future was (and is) never certain.

* * *

Birkbeck College started as the London Mechanics' Institution in 1823. At the time, the term 'mechanic' had many meanings. Mechanics were not the 'labouring poor' or paupers. Nearly three quarters (72 per cent) were 'operatives,' men who worked with their hands or identified as members of the 'working class'.[1] In the

---

[1] Helen Hudson Flexner, 'The London Mechanics' Institution: Social and Cultural Foundations', PhD thesis (London: University College London, 2014), 129.

LMI's early Rules, members signing the Registers were required to declare whether they were 'of the working class' or 'not of the working class' (the term 'middle class' was never used). The majority identified as workers.

The LMI was born in the Crown and Anchor Tavern at the junction of the Strand and Arundel Street, before moving to its current location in Bloomsbury. Today, the Strand and Bloomsbury are occupied by twenty-first century shrines to urban conviviality, including numerous coffee houses and restaurants, as well as university premises, fashionable hotels and apartments, and expensive shops. In 1823, it was a very difference scene. London was the largest city in the world, the capital of the British empire, and a global financial, trading, and political centre. But it was also a city of immense poverty. Cholera, typhoid, and typhus killed thousands each year. In the poorest parts of the city, a labourer's life expectancy was only 29 years. The air was thick with soot; the River Thames was polluted with human and animal excrement. Sheep grazed in nearby Regent's Park. The roads were made of stone, lit with newly installed gas lights, and punctuated at intervals by turn-pike gates exacting tolls from carriages pulled by horses. The first 'locomotive' (railway carriage) had been built only two decades earlier and it travelled at 5 miles per hour. There were no police; order was kept by parish constables and night watchmen. Working men and women had little access to basic education. Illiteracy was widespread. As late as 1841 (that is, nearly two decades after the establishment of the LMI), one third of men and nearly one half of women who signed marriage registers in England and Wales were unable to write their names.[2]

This was the context in which George Birkbeck and the other founders of the LMI decided to establish an institution for the education of 'mechanics'. It is important to recall just how radical this proposal was. It was only from the late eighteenth century that there had been powerful movements to educate 'the people'. The most important precedent to the LMI was 'Anderson's Institution' established in 1796 by John Anderson, a Professor of Natural Philosophy in Glasgow. This was where George Birkbeck (whose name, contacts, respectability, and money were to ensure the survival of the LMI) had given his first lectures. Anderson's model of adult education spread. By the middle of the nineteenth century, there were 610 mechanics' institutions in England alone, with over 100,000 members.[3] Indeed, bragged one proponent, mechanics' and literary institutes ('humble temple[s] of knowledge') had been established 'in every quarter of the world'.[4]

---

[2] Frances Hawes, *Henry Brougham* (London: Jonathan Cape, 1957), 163.

[3] James William Hudson, *The History of Adult Education, in Which it Comprised a Full and Complete History of the Mechanics' and Literary Institutions, Athenæums, Philosophical, Mental and Christian Improvement Societies, Literary Unions, Schools of Design, Etc., of Great Britain, Ireland, America, Etc. Etc.* (London: Longman, Brown, Green and Longmans, 1851), vi.

[4] Ibid., xiii.

The rapid establishment of mechanics' institutions occurred despite vehement elite hostility to educating working people. Few people opposed teaching 'the masses' to read and write but educating them in anything more substantial incited anxiety. These fears were in part rooted in the religious monopoly over schools and universities. Churchmen and their adherents feared that any education that was primarily 'scientific and philosophical' rather than 'moral and religious' was risky, as conservative Anglican biblical scholar Edward William Grinfield warned in 1825.[5] The National School system, which was associated with the established Church, was committed to safeguarding the souls of its pupils. In its schools, workers would learn not only the basics of reading and writing but also 'their duties towards God and man' together with 'a strong attachment to the laws and institutions of their country'. National Schools 'taught that knowledge and science' were 'of very secondary value when compared with piety and virtue'.[6] Grinfield firmly believed that

> it would be far better that the common people of this country should remain totally illiterate, than they should thus be furnished with *tools* by which they would inevitably work out their own and the public ruin.[7]

Even as late as 1860, Charles Langdale (one of the first Roman Catholic MPs in Parliament) was heard warning that mechanics' institutions posed a 'danger to the moral well-being' of members: their 'course of reading' and the 'subject-matter' required 'close supervision' lest they end up propagating 'infidel principles'.[8]

Opponents of workers' education were also anxious that a more educated population would not be sufficiently awed by the achievements of their 'superiors'. One of the arguments against the mechanics' institutions was that they would bolster the self-esteem of working people—a risky thing. In Grinfield's view, while the 'superior classes' possessed a legitimate sense of pride in mastering 'Chemistry and Mathematics', when this knowledge was acquired by working men it would make them 'conceited' and 'inflated' by their 'supposed acquirements'.[9] As a result, the 'self-conceit and self-importance' of educated working men would 'tempt them to look down upon others with disdain'.[10] Grinfield was alarmed that this would include a disdain for their alleged 'superiors'.

---

[5] Edward William Grinfield, *A Reply to Mr. Brougham's 'Practical Observations Upon the Education of the People; Addressed to the Working Classes and Their Employers'* (London: C. & J. Rivinton, 1825), iv.
[6] Ibid., 27.   [7] Ibid., 10–11.
[8] Evidence by Charles Langdale, in *Education Commission: Answers to the Curriculum of Questions, 1860*, vol. V (London: Her Majesty's Stationery Office, 1861), 290.
[9] Grinfield, *A Reply to Mr. Brougham's 'Practical Observations Upon the Education of the People'*, 14.
[10] Ibid., 16. Also see Evidence from Miss Carpenter, founder of the Red Lodge Girls' Reformatory, in *Education Commission: Answers to the Curriculum of Questions, 1860*, vol. V, 111.

Educating male workers could entice them to seek pursuits and entertainments outside the moral shelter of the domestic hearth, encouraging drunkenness and other dissolute behaviour. Evidence disputing this claim was presented by numerous commentators, most notably in the Select Committee of Inquiry into Drunkenness in 1834, but it was a common sentiment nonetheless, complicated by questions of sex.[11] Because workers toiled during the day, they would attend the institutions at a time when 'both mind and body crave[d]...relaxation'. 'Is it not likely', the Rector of Faldingworth (Lincolnshire) warned in the 1860s, that the 'enforced strain' involved in attending the lectures 'would lead to physical degeneration', at least for some members?[12] Opponents were convinced that 'When seven or eight hundred mechanics meet together in the evening after their daily occupations', it was obvious that 'all the allurements of science' would be unable to 'prevent them adjoining afterwards to the tavern or the ale-house'. Instead of reading 'by his fire-side, and in company with his wife and family', the working man who attended the meetings would 'return home quite unfitted to join in the domestic circle'.[13]

An extreme version of this argument can be seen in the evidence given by Archibald Alison to the 1838 Select Committee on Combinations of Workmen. Alison was a prominent Crown Counsel, historian, and former enslaver. Benjamin Disraeli was to satirize him in *Conningsby* (1844) as the character 'Mr. Wordy', who sought to prove that 'Providence was on the side of the Tories.'[14] Alison believed that educating working men was 'a very great cause of the depravity of the times'. He argued that

> the pleasure of intellectual exertion, or the pleasure to be derived from books of science, history, philosophy or literature, is of a sort which nature has given to a limited number only in society.

Indeed, he estimated that only about one quarter of all people 'derive serious pleasure from literary, philosophical pursuits'. However, he warned, since '*all* men...derive pleasure from animal gratification, or from excitement, emotion, and passion', the inevitable result of extending educational provision would be to give these men 'the means of the gratification of the animal or the sensual propensity'. The effect would be to 'aggravate the evil'.[15]

---

[11] Evidence from John Twells, in 'Report from the Select Committee on Inquiry into Drunkenness, with Minutes of Evidence and Appendix', 5 August 1834, 298 and 412. Similar evidence was given to this select committee by Francis Place, p. 173.

[12] Evidence by Rev. Irvin Eller, in *Education Commission: Answers to the Curriculum of Questions, 1860*, vol. V, 173.

[13] Grinfield, *A Reply to Mr. Brougham's 'Practical Observations Upon the Education of the People'*, 16.

[14] Benjamin Disraeli, *Conningsby*, vol. 1 (London: Henry Coulburn, 1844), 265.

[15] Evidence from Archibald Alison, in 'First Report from the Select Committee on Combinations of Workmen; Together with Minutes of Evidence and Appendix' [488], *British Parliamentary Papers* (1838), 187.

The moral anxiety and status-based pride expressed by opponents of mechanics' institutions were predicated by contempt for working people and other members of the 'lower orders'. Grinfield was condescending about the ability of the poor to understand 'abstract truth' about, for example, political economy. He scoffed that no insight into the theoretical principles of Malthusianism would deter working men from 'premature or imprudent marriage'.[16] What use, he asked, were geometry, algebra, mathematics, chemistry, astronomy, geology, and natural philosophy to men who work with their hands?[17] In his evidence to the Education Commission in 1860, Chief Rabbi Adler went so far as to argue that the lectures provided by mechanics' institutions were 'beyond the sphere of the young men's intellect'. Members were 'either lulled into sleep' or left with 'undigested notions' and 'half matured ideas'. The result was that the members became 'dreamers, talkers, [and] vague reasoners'.[18] A member would become unhappy 'in that station to which Providence has called him'.[19]

It was easy to mock the ambitions of working men and women who sought to educate themselves. William Mattieu Williams was a chemist and prominent figure in the LMI. Looking back on his long career in the Institution, he recalled that 'in the windows of every print shop of London' there used to hang

> caricatures of working men of different trades engaged in studying the sciences, and their wives and daughters practising the operatic music of Rossini and Bellini. The mere imagining of such a thing was then considered so absurd, that its representation constituted a broad caricature.[20]

One critic even quipped that educating working men was as useless to society as educating animals. 'Suppose', he wrote, that 'some friend to humanity were to attempt to improve the condition of *the beasts* of the field; – to teach the horse his power, and the cow her value'. Wouldn't that make the animal less 'tractable and useful' and not 'so profuse of her treasures' (that is, milk) 'to a helpless child?' This scenario was not 'one jot more ridiculous than teaching tailors and cobblers "the beautiful system of geometry"'.[21] The popular periodical *John Bull* went even

---

[16] Grinfield, *A Reply to Mr. Brougham's 'Practical Observations Upon the Education of the People'*, 19.
[17] Ibid., 21.
[18] Evidence by Rev. Dr Nathan Marcus Adler, in *Education Commission: Answers to the Curriculum of Questions, 1860*, vol. V, 19.
[19] Grinfield, *A Reply to Mr. Brougham's 'Practical Observations Upon the Education of the People'*, 25. Also see Evidence from Moses Angel of the Jews' Free School, in *Education Commission: Answers to the Curriculum of Questions, 1860*, vol. V, 48.
[20] William Mattieu Williams, *The Intellectual Destiny of the Working Man; An Address Delivered on the 28th May, 1863, to the Members of the 'Institute Chemical Society'* (Birmingham: Cornish Brothers, 1863), 12.
[21] 'The Consequences of a Scientific Education', *Edinburgh Review* (1 December 1826), 194. This witty quote was repeated in the 'Ministry of Reconstruction. Adult Education Committee. Final Report' [Cmd. 321], *British Parliamentary Papers* (1919), 14.

further, claiming that it was an 'absurdity' to hear the 'lower orders' learning to speak French. The only predictable result was that the aristocracy would need to distinguish themselves from the now-French-speaking *'canaille'* (or riff-raff) by speaking 'Hebrew, Sanscrit, Cingalese, or Malabar'.[22]

These ugly prejudices culminated in concerns that the entitlements of the 'higher classes' to unquestioned rule were being undermined. Although *supporters* of the mechanics' institutions reminded their critics that 'ignorance did not ensure obedience and order' (as the radical politician Sir John Hobhouse put it in 1830), mechanics' institutions were regularly accused of 'working mischief'.[23] Education would make working men 'impatient, fantastic and mutinous', warned *Bell's Weekly Messenger* in 1823; it would 'excite an inordinate vanity' and 'not render him a better workman'. At worse, it would spread that 'unhappy skepticism' seen in France. The paper recommended that the LMI confine its teaching to 'practical aid and instruction', since anything higher would 'incur the peril of much eventual mischief'.[24] In 1825, the *Saint James' Chronicle* was similarly alarmed by the possibility that mechanics' institutions might have been 'invented by the author of evil himself' (that is, the Devil) to bring about the 'destruction of this Empire'. The spread of mechanics' institutions was already responsible for the establishment of a couple of radical newspapers aiming to 'resist the legitimate and natural authority of employers'. He dismissed analysts who claimed that 'Mr. Brougham, or Doctor Birkbeck, or Mr. Huskisson' were not capable of 'design[ing] the ruin of the country'. Instead, he maintained that

> whatever their motives may be, every step which they take in setting up the labourers *as a separate or an independent class* is a step taken, and a large one too, towards that fatal result.... They are all three [men] ... scattering the seeds of evil.[25]

Or, in the words of yet another critic, the LMI could even lead to the creation of 'tumultuous assemblies'.[26]

Grinfield also warned against 'encouraging restless or self-interested individuals' who roamed throughout the UK 'distracting the minds of our mechanics by lecturing on civil or political economy, or by giving them a smattering in the higher branches of abstract science'.[27] He worried that, instead of letting people

---

[22] Richard White, 'To John Bull', *John Bull* (3 December 1827), 381.
[23] This was the seventh anniversary: see 'The Mechanics' Institution', *Bell's Life in London and Sporting Chronicle* (12 December 1830), n.p.
[24] 'London Mechanics' Institute', *Bell's Weekly Messenger* (16 November 1823), 2.
[25] 'Postscript', *Saint James' Chronicle* (2 August 1825), 4.
[26] Grinfield, *A Reply to Mr. Brougham's 'Practical Observations Upon the Education of the People'*, 20.
[27] Ibid., 15.

with 'superior knowledge'[28] choose what workers should read, this choice was being made by 'chance and accident' or even by 'the tricks of wandering lecturers who shall harangue them on subjects little fitted to their rank and condition in society, and still less fitted to promote their private and domestic happiness'.[29] The involvement of prominent Whig politician Brougham was viewed as particularly dangerous, since Brougham had 'identified himself with those who are habitually opposed to the measures of government'[30] and had 'defamed' the National Society for the Education of the Poor in the Principles of the Established Church.[31] Grinfield agreed that education of the masses was inevitable, but warned that

> restless and artful men are attempting to pervert it to their own mischievous purposes; some under the mask of diffusing science are teaching them a species of knowledge which may give them power but will not furnish them with the means or desire of self-government; others under the pretence of the love of liberty, are inviting them to discuss questions of politics, and to attend lectures on moral and political science.[32]

In 1860, Moses Angel of the Jews' Free School was similarly worried that the mechanics' institutions would 'convert half-educated men into ill-formed politicians,' perhaps 'revolutionist[s]' but definitely 'democrats'.[33]

* * *

This was the context in which the LMI/Birkbeck was established. Opponents of workers' education were consumed by moral anxieties, pride, disdain, and fear that their privileges would be eroded. These were not simply worries held by elites in the 1820s but, as we have seen, were prominent well into the 1860s. The fact that the LMI was established and flourished despite such opposition is a testament to the widespread aspirations of working people.

It also flourished in a context in which Higher Education more generally was the preserve of a small minority. As late as the mid-nineteenth century, British universities were 'part seminary and part finishing school for the sons of the aristocracy and the gentry', with only 3,000 students in total, as historian Thomas William Heyck reminded us.[34] In 1921, at the time when Birkbeck became part of the University of London, universities throughout England educated only 0.09

---

[28] Ibid., 17.   [29] Ibid., 18.   [30] Ibid., 2.   [31] Ibid., 2–3.   [32] Ibid., 18.
[33] Evidence from Moses Angel of the Jews' Free School, *Education Commission: Answers to the Curriculum of Questions, 1860*, vol. V, 48–9.
[34] Thomas William Heyck, 'The Idea of a University in Britain, 1870–1970', *History of European Ideas*, 8.2 (1987), 205.

per cent of the total population and only 1 per cent of those aged 20 to 24.[35] The LMI/Birkbeck was not only a pioneer in Higher Education but was providing this education for people who were multiply excluded by reasons of class, gender, ethnicity, religion, age, disability, and employment status.

The rest of this book seeks to explore the establishment of the LMI/Birkbeck and trace its life over 200 years. The hostility that it incited from some parts of British society in its early decades was unique—Higher Education has since been generally regarded as a societal 'good'. The Higher Education sector is considered as second only to health care in promoting the welfare of British citizens.[36] In 1823, however, university-type education was reserved for men (only men) who were charged with running the country. Deeply embedded ideas about class differences—including fundamental beliefs about the innate superiority and inferiority of the different social 'orders'—encouraged elites to believe not only that working people were incapable of imbibing knowledge but that, when they did so, it could only result in societal chaos. This was why, when the founders of the LMI/Birkbeck drew up their plans to widen access, they were considered revolutionaries. Their instincts were good, however: as we shall see next, mechanics and others who worked with their hands were ready and keen.

---

[35] Roy Lowe, 'The Expansion of Higher Education in England', in Konrad H. Jarausch (ed.), *The Transformation of Higher Learning 1860–1930: Expansion, Diversification, Social Opening, and Professionalization in England, Germany, Russia, and the United States* (Chicago: University of Chicago Press, 1983), 52.

[36] Universities UK, at https://www.universitiesuk.ac.uk/facts-and-stats/Pages/higher-education-data.aspx, viewed 20 July 2021.

PART I
FROM MECHANICS TO GRADUATES

2
The Crown and Anchor Tavern

Birkbeck College was born in the Crown and Anchor Tavern in 1823. The area surrounding the tavern was the centre of government and religion. It was close to the luminous church of St Clement Danes, designed by Christopher Wren between 1680 and 1682. Only a short walk away was the political powerhouse of government, the Palace of Westminster. It was a medieval royal palace used as the home of the British Parliament before it was razed to the ground on 16 October 1834. The construction of the current Parliament didn't start until 1840 and took thirty years to be completed.

But the area had a more sordid side. The radical tailor Francis Place, who had grown up there in the 1780s, later recalled that there used to be an alehouse called the Crooked Billet close by. In his old age, Place would tell people that two women used to sing risqué songs in the open space between the godly St Clement, the respectable Crown and Anchor Tavern, and the disreputable Crooked Billet alehouse. One of these songs was 'Sandman Sam', a ballad about a seller of sand who finds escape from the harshness of his life through gin and sex with his 'flash girl Sally'. The culmination of this song required the singers to 'sham dying away' (that is, faking the 'little death' of orgasm) 'amidst roars of Laughter' from their audience.[1] Of course, as Place (who was to become one of the founders of the London Mechanics' Institution) hastened to insist, he and his radical colleagues spurned the debauched attractions of the Crooked Billet for the politically radical yet eminently respectable confines of the Crown and Anchor.

The Crown and Anchor Tavern (see Fig. 2.1) was well known. A fairly modest tavern had existed in the spot since the early 1730s. Originally, it was simply 'The Crown Tavern' but, at some stage, an Anchor had been added to the sign, possibly because this was the emblem of the St Clement Church or because the Lord High Admiral once resided there.[2]

Between 1787 and 1790, the building was transformed.[3] Charles Howard, the corpulent 11th Duke of Norfolk, wanted something more impressive. The tavern was dramatically expanded, eventually stretching behind the shops along the Strand from Milford Lane to Arundel Street. Visitors could access the tavern from

---

[1] Cited and analysed in Ian Newman, 'Civilizing Taste: "Sandman Joe", the Bawdy Ballad, and Metropolitan Improvement', *Eighteenth-Century Studies*, 48.4 (summer 2015), 437–56.
[2] 'Fire in the Strand—Site of Arundel House', *Illustrated London News* (9 December 1854), 584.
[3] Christina Parolin, *Radical Spaces: Venues of Popular Politics in London, 1790–c.1845* (Canberra: ANU Press, 2010), 108.

Fig. 2.1 St Clements in the Strand and the Crown and Anchor Tavern in the foreground on the right. The sign of the crown and anchor hangs over the two lampposts. Birkbeck Image Collections: Birkbeck History BH0320.

a narrow passageway between the shops off the Strand,[4] but the main entrance was in Arundel Street.

The building was typical of Georgian architecture at that time. It was four storeys high, with seven windows on each floor. The windows on the first floor had iron balconies. Inside, different spaces catered for various activities, including an impressive dining room, a library, lecture halls, drawing rooms, reading rooms, and classrooms, as well as a room for smoking and another for reading the newspapers. One room was simply designated the 'ladies' room', set aside to facilitate decorous discussions between respectable persons of that sex.[5]

Customers walking through the stone-paved entrance in Arundel Street would enter a foyer framed by four large, plain columns, in the style of the classical Greek Doric order. Much of the ground floor, however, was dedicated to dining. A spacious kitchen could provide food and drinks for more than 500 diners at any one time. The dining hall itself was elaborately decorated with a frieze of eight panels, two marble and wooden fireplaces, and chandeliers hung from carved cornices from the ceiling. The attention paid to eating facilities was calculated. In this period, dinners were at the heart of political networking; and there was no place more acclaimed for scheming than the Crown and Anchor.

The second most important room was on the first floor. A grand stone staircase flanked by an ornamental iron and mahogany handrail led from the ground floor

[4] Ibid., 110.   [5] Parolin, *Radical Spaces*, 110–12.

to the 'Great Assembly Room'. In summer, natural light would be streaming through the skylight but in the evenings or on wintery days, the space was lit by a huge lantern. The 'Great Assembly Room' was one of the largest rooms in all of London: it measured 25.6 metres long by 11 metres wide, which means that it was almost as large as the House of Commons Chambers in the Palace of Westminster.[6] It was truly 'great', with an ornate ceiling, elaborately carved window frames, majestic chandelier, marble fireplaces, and a raised music gallery. The walls were covered with ornamental panels and festoons.[7] This was where Birkbeck College—or, as it was then called, the London Mechanics' Institution—was founded.

* * *

The Crown and Anchor Tavern was a unique institution. Coffee houses and taverns had been centres for public debate and conviviality since the twelfth century. But the Crown and Anchor was nothing short of an unorthodox political space, renowned for its radical politics. At one time, it had been seen as an alternative parliamentary space, even symbolically mimicking the forms, structures, and rituals of Westminster by appointing chairmen (they were all men), debating resolutions, and voting on outcomes. Visitors to the Crown and Anchor did not just *mimic* the official political sphere; they took it to another level by undercutting notions of higher and lower orders. It was a space in which a working-class radical could sit next to a 'Prince of the Blood'.[8] Because it encouraged commentary from 'the floor', political debates often became rowdy, even disorderly. Although not the openly seditious space of the Rotunda on Blackfriars Road, members of the Spensean Philanthropists (who had been responsible for the Cato Street conspiracy) had chosen the Crown and Anchor as the place where they plotted to assassinate the entire UK cabinet. The tavern had also hosted grand dinners to celebrate the Fall of the Bastille. Guests regularly toasted 'The Liberty of the Press', 'The People, The Source of Power', Catholic emancipation, and the Great Reform Bill.

The Crown and Anchor was a cosmopolitan forum, proudly European. The tavern welcomed politicians, radicals, and public speakers from all over the world, but particularly Europe. The same year that LMI was established, the tavern hosted speakers arguing for the 'defence of rights' of Spain, calling upon those who love 'liberty and independence' to show their support.[9] In 1823, it hosted a committee responsible for gathering funds to help the Greeks fighting for independence from the 'tyrannical Turks'. The Greek Committee lauded 'the valour

---

[6] 'Fire in the Strand—Site of Arundel House', *Illustrated London News* (9 December 1854), 584. That is, 25.6 metres by 11 metres (281.6 square metres) or 84 feet long by over 35 feet wide. The House of Commons Chamber is 14 metres by 20.7 metres or 289.8 square metres in size.
[7] Parolin, *Radical Spaces*, 110–12.
[8] 'There is a Difference between Hume and Brougham', *John Bull* (11 July 1825), 220.
[9] Joseph Joachin De Mora, 'Appeal to the People of Great Britain' (London: Richard Taylor, 1823), 1 and 8–9.

and the virtue of the heroic descendants of the great masters of art and science' and their 'extraordinary successes in the midst of incredible privation and active suffering'. They were optimistic that 'the classic land of Greece' would be freed from 'those usurping barbarians, whose tyranny had for centuries degraded and desecrated the soil'. To support this democratic revolution, they asked all freedom-loving Britons to rally behind the Greeks.[10] For 1823, this was radical cosmopolitanism at its height.

* * *

Who were the leading people in the College's foundation? In 1823, the five men responsible for establishing the LMI could be found inside the Crown and Anchor: they were Joseph Clinton Robertson, Thomas Hodgskin, Francis Place, Henry Brougham, and George Birkbeck (see Figs. 2.2 and 2.3). All five had expansive personalities, with powerful egos and preoccupations. Differences, even bitter confrontations, were inevitable.

Robertson had been born into a comfortable nonconformist family and had chosen a career as a patent agent and editor. He was a tricky character, however: easily offended, undeterred by legal threats and bankruptcy courts, and with a proclivity for fraud and blackmail. He was also a talented editor and passionate about the empowerment of working men. In 1823, in his mid-thirties, Robertson founded the popular *Mechanics' Magazine*, printed by John Knight and Henry Lacey.

Hodgskin's background was considerably more modest. His father worked at the Chatham Naval Dockyards, which explains why he was sent to sea at the tender age of 12. The Napoleonic Wars between England and France were under way and Hodgskin moved quickly up the ranks to become First Lieutenant. He hated the brutality of the Navy, however, and was eventually court-martialled and dismissed for 'losing' (probably purposefully) a prisoner who was to be flogged. His first book, with the expansive title *An Essay on Naval Discipline, Shewing Part of its Evil Effects on the Minds of Officers, on the Minds of Men, and on the Community; with an Amended System by which Pressing be Immediately Abolished* (1813), was a searing indictment of the Navy.[11] His second publication was equally political. It was an account of a walking tour through Germany, in which he contended that the 'landlord and the capitalist produce nothing. Capital is the produce of labour, and profit is nothing but a portion of that produce.'[12]

---

[10] 'Appeal from the Greek Committee to the British Public in General, and Especially to the Friends of Religion' (London: The Greek Committee, 1823), 1.

[11] Thomas Hodgskin, *An Essay on Naval Discipline, Shewing Part of its Evil Effects on the Minds of Officers, on the Minds of Men, and on the Community; with an Amended System by which Pressing be Immediately Abolished* (London: The Author, 1813).

[12] Thomas Hodgskin, *Travels in the North of Germany; Describing the Present State of the Social and Political Institutions, the Agriculture, Manufactures, Commerce, Education, Arts and Manners in that Country, Particularly in the Kingdom of Hannover*, vol. 2 (Edinburgh: Archibald Constable and Co., 1820), 97.

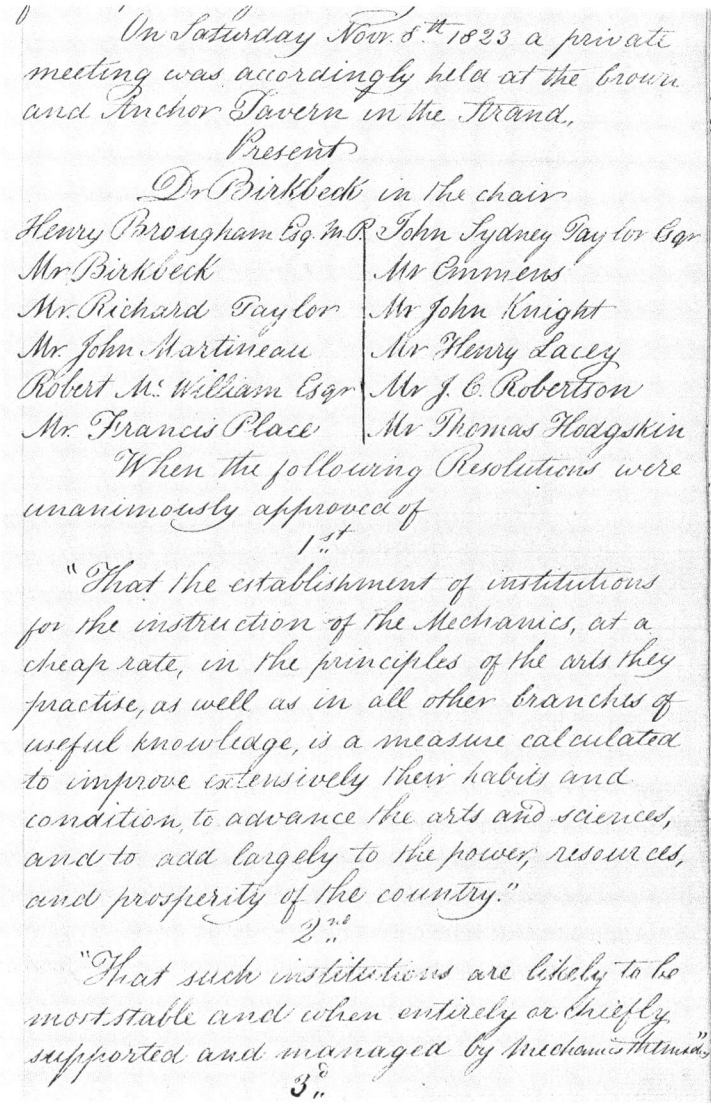

Fig. 2.2 Page from the minutes of the first meeting of the founders of the LMI, in which their aims are outlined, 8 November 1823. Birkbeck Image Collections: Birkbeck History BH0203.

In 1823, Hodgskin returned to London to work as a journalist and quickly joined Robertson on the *Mechanics' Magazine*. This began an intellectually productive period of his life. He published three other books in quick succession: *Labour Defended against the Claims of Capital* came out in 1825 and was based on his first lectures at the LMI; *Popular Political Economy: Four Lectures Delivered at*

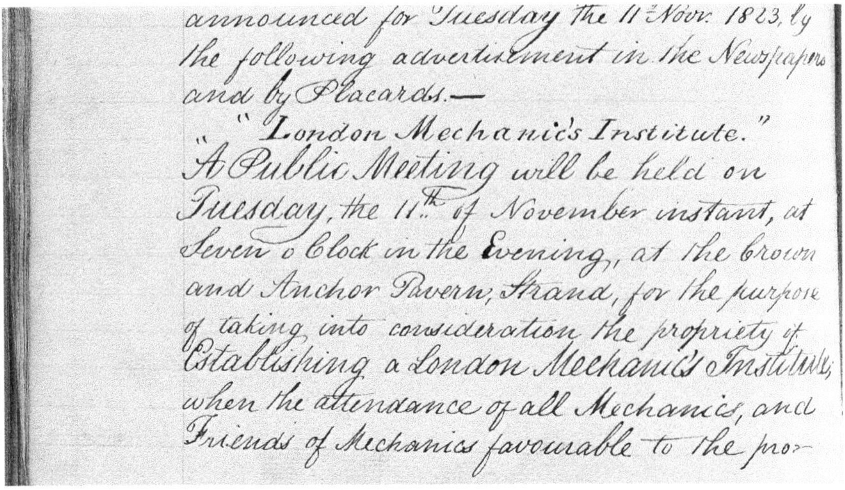

announced for Tuesday the 11th Nov: 1823, by
the following advertisement in the Newspapers
and by Placards.—
"London Mechanic's Institute."
"A Public Meeting will be held on
Tuesday, the 11th of November instant, at
Seven o Clock in the Evening, at the Crown
and Anchor Tavern, Strand, for the purpose
of taking into consideration the propriety of
Establishing a London Mechanic's Institute;
when the attendance of all Mechanics, and
Friends of Mechanics favourable to the pro-

Fig. 2.3 Announcement of the first public meeting to discuss founding the LMI, November 1823. Birkbeck Image Collections: Birkbeck History BH0201.

the London Mechanics' Institution followed two years later, and, in 1832, *The Natural and Artificial Right of Property Contrasted*. He argued that machines were the property of workers, and they should therefore reap all benefits from their use. Karl Marx admired him, claiming not only that Hodgskin was 'one of the most important modern English economists'[13] but also that *Popular Political Economy* had been important in developing his own labour theory of value in the third volume of *Capital*. Although relatively unknown today, Hodgskin deserves to be recognized as one of the founders of British socialism.

The third protagonist is Francis Place (see Fig. 2.4). He is often ignored in discussions about the establishment of the LMI, even though Place had been responsible for drafting the first plan and constitution for the Institution. He was the one who raised funds, approached working men's organizations for support, and enlisted the patronage of Utilitarian, Whig, and Radical politicians.

Place's familial status was as modest as that of Hodgskin. He was born in 1771, the son of a tavern-keeper at the King's Arms in Arundel Street, close to the Crown and Anchor. As Place later admitted, his father was a 'Drinking, Whoring, Gaming, Fishing, and Fighting' type of man. Unlike his father, Place worked hard and read widely. At the tender age of 17, he became an independent journeyman breeches-maker, eventually setting himself up in Charing Cross. Despite living in poverty with his wife, a former servant called Elizabeth Chadd, Place believed in education and self-improvement. He would work from 7 a.m. until 9 p.m., after

[13] Karl Marx, *Capital: A Critique of Political Economy*, vol. 1, trans. Ben Fowkes (Harmondsworth: Penguin in association with the New Left Review, 1976), 1000.

Fig. 2.4 Francis Place. Birkbeck Image Collections: Birkbeck History BH0012.

which he would spend two to three hours reading the most radical authors of his time, including Tom Paine's *Rights of Man* and William Godwin's *Political Justice*. Place, who was known as the 'Radical Tailor of Charing Cross', was also an atheist and political activist. His beliefs cost him business and friends. He was controversial: the middle classes regarded him as a dangerous extremist while working men thought he kowtowed too much to the bourgeoisie. Place promoted causes such as birth control (his much-loved wife was in poor health because of frequent childbearing), free love, equality between the sexes, sex for pleasure, and regular sexual intercourse for young people. This was heady stuff indeed for the 1820s.

The fourth main founder is Brougham. Although Brougham had not been present at the first meetings of the LMI and never served on any of its committees, he was the Institution's leading orator and played a significant role in its establishment and survival. He was also active in a wide range of educational initiatives. In 1826, he founded the Society for the Diffusion of Useful Knowledge and, a few years after that, published the Library of Entertaining Knowledge, which was responsible for the *Penny Magazine* and the *Penny Cyclopedia*.

Brougham's interest in educational reform followed from his more general radical politics. As a lawyer by profession, he came to public notice because of his role as chief adviser to Queen Caroline, the estranged wife of King George IV. The King was attempting to divorce the Queen by persuading the government to introduce a 'bill of pains and penalties' in the House of Lords. Brougham's and Thomas Denman's spirited defence of the Queen was widely supported by the public. By the 1830s, Brougham was Lord Chancellor of Great Britain, where he was an active supporter of the 1832 Reform Act (which radically transformed the electoral system in Britain) and, as passionate abolitionist, the 1833 Slavery Abolition Act.

Crucially, however, his book on education—published just two years after the founding of the LMI—became the 'Bible' for everyone involved in educating working people. Dedicated to George Birkbeck, *Practical Observations Upon the Education of the People. Addressed to the Working Classes and their Employers* was a popular success. It went through nineteen editions in the first year alone.[14] According to one admirer, not since 'the Scriptures were first printed and circulated in the common tongue' had there been such an important text.[15]

In *Practical Observations*, Brougham argued that only 'tyrants' and other 'bad rulers' should be terrified by 'the progress of knowledge among the mass of mankind'.[16] He maintained that 'the time is past and gone when bigots could persuade mankind that the lights of philosophy' were 'dangerous to religion' and when despots could stigmatize lecturers 'as enemies to their power'. Quite the contrary: knowledge of science would promote awareness of God. Civic society, too, had a lot to gain from the spread of education. If there was ever an 'interruption...in the commercial prosperity of the country' causing wages as well as profits to plummet, people's ignorance about the relationship between labour and capital might see the 'two classes' mobilizing 'in opposition to each other'. The 'peace of the country, and the stability of the government, could not be more effectually secured than by the universal diffusion' of knowledge about the 'true principles and mutual relations of population and wages'.[17]

In Parliament, too, Brougham was a tireless champion of workers' education. One of the most famous of his speeches was given in 1828, on the occasion of the Duke of Wellington (Arthur Wellesley) becoming Prime Minister. Wellesley had made his name as the Commander-in-Chief who had helped defeat

[14] These sale figures were according to 'A Reply to Mr Brougham's "Practical Observations Upon the Education of the People, Addressed to the Working Classes and Their Employers"', a response to Grinfield's article, *Edinburgh Review*, 42.83 (1 April 1825), 212.

[15] Review of Brougham's tract entitled '"Practical Observations Upon the Education of the People; Addressed to the Working Classes and Their Employers" (London, 1825)', *Edinburgh Review*, 41.82 (1 January 1825), 508. For another extreme response, see the review of Brougham's book in "'Practical Observations Upon the Education of the People; Addressed to the Working Classes and Their Employers' (London, 1825)", *Edinburgh Review*, 41.82 (1 January 1825), 508.

[16] Henry Brougham, *Practical Observations Upon the Education of the People: Addressed to the Working Classes and their Employers*, 1st pub. 1825 (Manchester: E. J. Morten, 1971), 31.

[17] Ibid., 4.

Napoleon at Waterloo. Brougham disapproved of Wellesley's appointment as PM on constitutional grounds but contended that he did not fear that Wellesley's military background would cause violence to be 'directed against the liberties of the country'. After all, there had been times when the British public 'heard with dismay' that 'the soldier was abroad'. This was 'not the case now', Brougham contended, adding:

> Let the soldier be ever so much abroad, in the present age he could do nothing. There was another person abroad, – a less important person, – in the eyes of some[,] an insignificant person.... The schoolmaster was abroad [cheers!] and he trusted more to the schoolmaster, armed with his primer, than he did to the soldier in full military array, for upholding and extending the liberties of the country.[18]

The phrase 'the schoolmaster is abroad!' was to become the catchphrase of workers' educational movements everywhere.

As this speech suggests, Brougham was a brilliant orator, described as having the entire Parliament 'visibly agitated at times by the splendour of his eloquence'.[19] Less sympathetic commentators noted that he was also a man 'stern and repellent...whose opinions must be received with the most respectful deference; whose mental superiority would be somewhat overwhelming'.[20] Vain and deceitful, he certainly was. Even his biographer admitted that he could be 'the most amiable of men' when his 'spleen was rested', but it was more common to find him 'combative' and 'ill-mannered'.[21] Karl Marx famously maintained that Brougham's writings were those of a 'windbag' and should be avoided on the grounds of their 'superficiality'.[22] Whatever the assessment, Brougham was tireless in his defence of mechanics' institutions throughout the UK and the London-based one in particular.

The final main protagonist in our story is, of course, George Birkbeck (Fig. 2.5). He was born into a Quaker family in North Yorkshire and trained as a doctor at the University of Edinburgh Medical School. It was at this time that he became friends with fellow-student Brougham and was elected President of the Royal Medical Society.[23] He also made friends with philosophical radicals such as Sydney Smith and Francis Horner as well as prominent men like chemist Thomas Thomson, optics expert David Brewster, and historical novelist Walter Scott. In

---

[18] 'Commons Sitting of Tuesday, January 29, 1828', *House of Commons Hansard*, 2nd series, vol. 18 (1828), 58.
[19] Knight, cited in Robert Stewart, *Henry Brougham 1778–1868: His Public Career* (London: The Bodley Head, 1985), 189.
[20] Stewart, *Henry Brougham 1778–1868*, 189.   [21] Ibid., 260.   [22] Marx, *Capital*, 1000.
[23] 'Memoir of George Birkbeck, M.D.', *The Imperial Magazine; or, Compendium of Religious, Moral, and Philosophical Knowledge* (January 1825), 21.

Fig. 2.5 Portrait of George Birkbeck by Samuel Lane, *c*.1830. Birkbeck Image Collections: Birkbeck History BH0107.

1799, George Birkbeck was invited to teach 'natural philosophy and chemistry' in the Anderson Institution, Glasgow. His interest in the education of working men started when he wanted a particular machine to be made for his classes. He visited the workshop of some workmen and was struck, first, by their ignorance of the basics of engineering and, second, by their hunger for knowledge. He promptly opened his classes to mechanics, offering classes on Saturday evenings. By the fourth class, there were 500 men in attendance and, as Birkbeck put it, 'an audience more orderly, attentive, and apparently comprehending, I never witnessed'. George Birkbeck issued a statement, setting out the rationale for these classes. As he put it, his lectures on the 'Mechanical Affections of solid and fluid Bodies' were

> solely for persons engaged in the practical exercise of the mechanical arts: men, whose situation in early life, has precluded even the possibility of acquiring the smallest portion of scientific knowledge, and whose subsequent pursuits, not always affording more than is necessary for their own support and that of their dependent connexions, have not enabled them to *purchase* that information,

which curiosity, too active for penury wholly to repress, or the prevailing bias of their natural genius, might prompt them to obtain.[24]

He admitted that a mechanic attending his lectures might not discover wholly new forms of knowledge but was convinced that he would gain much 'pleasure...in the exercise of his art', due to being able to 'meditate' on 'systematic philosophical ideas' in those hours after 'bodily toil'.[25] He noted the

> greater satisfaction in the execution of machinery [that] must be experienced, when the uses to which it operates, are well understood, than when the manual part alone is known.[26]

The aim was to ensure that a working man would 'cease to be a mere machine, toiling on from day to day', but would 'understand the laws on which his operations were based' and therefore 'perfect himself in his calling'.[27]

It was a short-lived experiment, however. By 1804, Birkbeck had decided to leave Glasgow for work as a doctor in London, and his classes were taken over by Dr Ure. In London, he was elected one of the presidents of the Physical Society of Guy's Hospital and set up a fashionable medical practice, in addition to working as a physician to the General Dispensary for the Relief of the Poor in Aldersgate Street, which provided home-visiting and outpatient treatment for paupers and the working class in that area of London. He was also active in the Medical and Chirurgical Society, the Chemical Society, and the Meteorological Society, as well as being one of the founders of the London Institution, established in 1809 for the diffusion of science, literature, and the arts. It was during this stage in his life that he forged friendships with radicals and economists including Ricardo Hume, John Hume, William Cobbett, Jeremy Bentham, George Grote, James Mill, and John Stuart Mill.[28]

Within this milieu, George Birkbeck was well placed to throw his energies into a wide variety of social causes. Amongst many, these included medical insurance for the working classes, improving conditions for 'climbing boys' (that is, chimney sweepers), life-belts for use at sea, and promoting mechanical inventions that would enhance people's lives. He was a keen supporter of the Reform Act of 1832, which reformed the electoral system, including dramatically expanding the number of men who could vote. Most prominent was his fight to repeal the duty on paper and the tax on newspapers, which severely limited the ability of people to contribute to political debate and disseminate knowledge. The respect he roused

---

[24] Ibid., 24.   [25] Ibid., 24.   [26] Ibid., 24.
[27] John George Godard, *George Birkbeck: The Pioneer of Popular Education—A Memoir and a Review* (London: Bemrose and Sons, 1884), n.p.
[28] Ibid., n.p.

among people from all walks of life and political persuasions meant that he was the ideal President of the new Institution.

This is the all-male cast of the fledgling-Birkbeck. There is no point seeking out female protagonists: there were many, but they were sequestered in 'ladies' reception rooms', or in the kitchens, parlours, drawing rooms, and bedrooms of the Great White Men. When women do enter the LMI's earliest history, it is generally in jest. As the editor of *John Bull* (a fierce opponent of the mechanics' institutions) sneered at the opening of the LMI, there were 'a *great many ladies!*' present in a 'little gallery, appropriated to them'. He sarcastically repeated that the mechanics and distinguished founders should be '*honoured* with the presence of a *great many Ladies!*'[29]

* * *

On 11 October 1823, Robertson (along with his collaborator Hodgskin) published the first call for the establishment of a London Mechanics' Institution in the *Mechanics' Magazine* (see Fig. 2.6). One thousand copies of the journal advertising the event were printed, guaranteeing a wide circulation. Robertson (along with Hodgskin and Francis Place) were then responsible for managing the first public meeting of the Institution on 11 November. At this stage, Robertson claimed never to have 'even heard' the name of George Birkbeck.[30] Significantly, on the LMI's inaugural Code of Laws, Robertson's name is listed first; Hodgskin's, second. However, the relationship between Robertson, the LMI, and the publishers of the *Mechanics' Magazine* quickly became antagonistic. Within three years, Robertson was being accused of 'mad hostility' to the LMI and 'conspiring to ruin' the magazine financially.[31] The conflict was so acrimonious that, at one stage, two different versions of the *Mechanics' Magazine* were being published each week.

On 11 November 1823, Robertson, Hodgskin, Place, and George Birkbeck, along with around 2,000 supporters, met in the Crown and Anchor Tavern's 'Great Assembly Room' to establish the LMI. A few drunk men had to be tossed out, but the rest of the assembly were said to be sober and serious about establishing a working man's institution that would be managed by working men themselves. The Rules were drafted, ensuring that mechanics would hold 'the principal share' in the management of the new institution. 'Independence' was essential. The list of Committee members includes three who are not given occupations: George Birkbeck, lawyer Robert M'William, and John Vallance, who built the first

---

[29] 'There is a Difference between Hume and Brougham', *John Bull* (11 July 1825), 220.

[30] 'Explanation of the Charge of Misrepresentation Brought by the Editor of the Mechanics' Magazine Against Lord Broughton, in Regard to the Rise of the Mechanics' Institutions in England', *Mechanics' Magazine, Museum, Register, Journal, and Gazette*, 606 (21 March 1835), 458.

[31] John Knight and Henry Lacey, 'Preface to Volume the Fifth', *Mechanics' Magazine*, 5 (London: Knight and Lacey, 1826), v.

> INSTITUTIONS
> FOR
> Instruction of Mechanics.
>
> *Proposals for*
> A LONDON MECHANICS INSTITUTE.
>
> "———— still to employ
> The mind's brave ardour in heroic arms,
> Such as may raise us o'er the grov'ling herd,
> And make us shine for ever—that is life."
>
> "KNOWLEDGE," says one of the wisest of men, Lord Bacon, "IS POWER;" and the first step, probably, towards the mechanics of this great empire obtaining the power to raise themselves to their proper station in society, is to acquire knowledge. Notwithstanding all that has been yet done to diffuse the blessings of education, the great mass of our people are still, comparatively speaking, sunk in a state of great ignorance; and it is only because so many are ignorant, that so many are poor and miserable. Even in the arts which mechanics themselves practise, most of them have much to learn. With the various modes by which the hand exercises its cunning, they are, of course, well acquainted; but of the principles of the operations they know little or nothing, and are proportionally incapable of discovering how they may be simplified and improved.
>
> England, though the first manufacturing country in the world, is singularly deficient in schools for instructing people in the mechanical arts. In Paris there is a celebrated institution called the *Conservatoire des Arts et Métiers*, where instruction is liberally dispensed by professors appointed and paid by government, on most subjects connected with mechanics. Similar institutions are in existence, we believe, both at Berlin and Vienna. The British government has hitherto been always so much occupied in devising means to secure its power, that it has been able to pay but little attention to the instruction of the people: nor do we wish that it should. The education of a free people, like their property, will always be directed most beneficially

Fig. 2.6 'Institutions for Instruction of Mechanics. Proposals for a London Mechanics Institute', *Mechanic's Magazine, Museum, Register, Journal & Gazette*, 11 October 1823.

atmospheric railway in 1826.[32] The others included a printer, tailor, carpenter, shoemaker, oilman, coachmaker, painter, two smiths, and five engineers.[33] Indeed, this was what made the LMI *particularly* radical, because it was led by the mechanics

---

[32] Joseph Brennan, 'The Atmospheric Road. Explorations in England, Ireland, and France', at http://www.columbia.edu/~brennan/atmo/24_EXP.html, viewed 1 September 2021.
[33] 'London Mechanics' Institution', *Mechanics' Magazine, Museum, Register, Journal, and Gazette* (15 November 1823), 189.

themselves, as opposed to the top-down model that had previously prevailed. Later, Brougham would maintain that it would be better if workers' education failed altogether than it fostered 'dependence upon their superiors'.[34] Admittedly, Brougham conceded, wealthy people could help lay 'the foundations' for educational reform, but if they took over the provisions and management, the purpose of knowledge acquisition would never take 'deep root' amongst the labouring

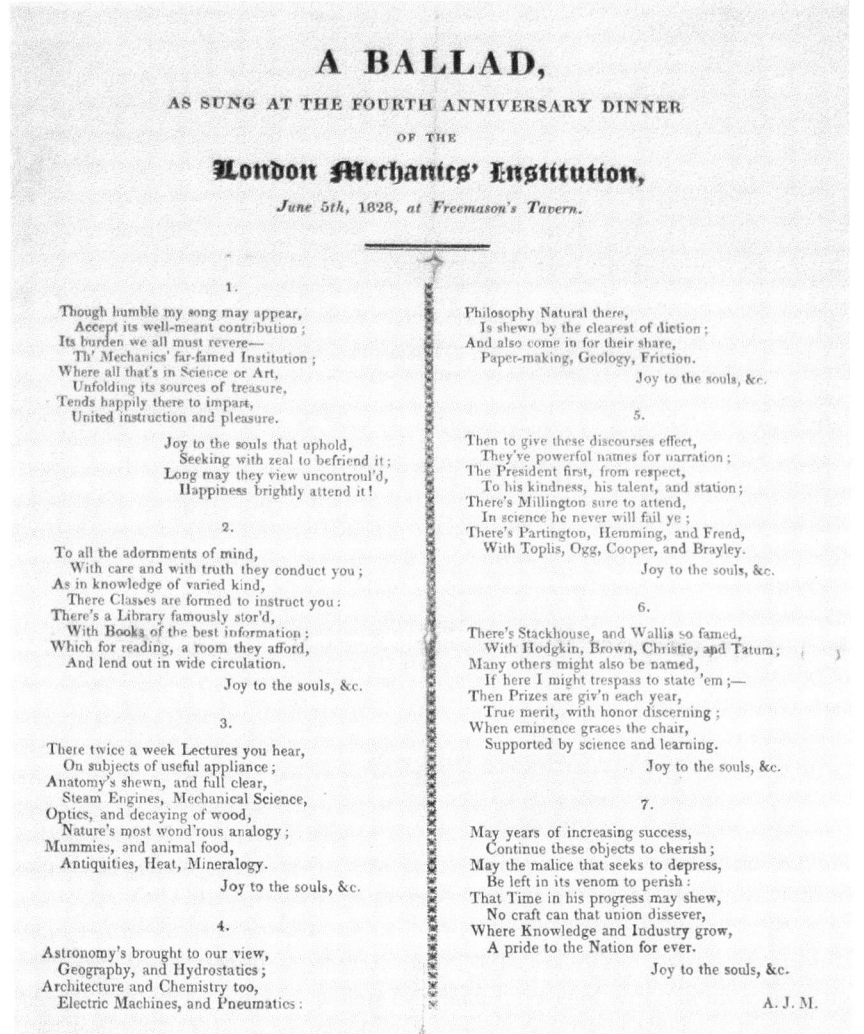

Fig. 2.7 A ballad sung at the 4th Anniversary Dinner of the LMI in 1828. Birkbeck Archive, 'A4 Black Ring Binder 1', 76.

[34] Brougham, *Practical Observations Upon the Education of the People*, 16.

people.[35] Nevertheless, the assembly acknowledged that patronage was needed. George Birkbeck was unanimously elected President and a committee was established. On 2 December that year, the London Mechanics Institution was declared founded, and 656 members signed up.

Once the Institution was established, however, the Crown and Anchor Tavern was no longer thought to be a suitable venue. Instead, the lectures were given in the private homes of members and in Monkwell Street Chapel (also known as Lamb's Chapel) in Clerkenwell. It was noted that the transfer of classes from 'the Bar of the Crown and Anchor tavern to more academic surroundings' did not result in any decline in the number of enrolments, which 'says much for the thirst for knowledge prevailing at the time'.[36] On 20 February 1824, the inaugural lecture was given by John Millington, patent lawyer, Professor of Mechanics at the Royal Institution, and one of the vice-presidents of the LMI. Its theme? The 'elementary principles of mechanical science'[37] (see Fig. 2.7). Offices were rented at 15 Furnival's Inn for £55 annually. When these premises proved too small, more permanent accommodation was found just west of Furnival's Inn in the Southampton Building, Chancery Lane.[38] This move was to have far-reaching consequences: it changed the type of workers attending the classes. As Samuel Vallentine, a member of the management committee of the LMI for fourteen years, noted in 1853, the new home in Southampton Buildings was 'the reverse of a working neighbourhood, being entirely surrounded by the inns of court'. As a consequence, 'the working men fell from the ranks of our members'.[39] The LMI was to stay in the Southampton Buildings, supplemented by renting rooms in the neighbourhood, for a century.

* * *

These were the first steps in the history of Birkbeck. The founders had mixed motives. For George Birkbeck, the Institution was a political as well as philanthropic project. He moved in politically radical circles. Although he was a middle-class liberal, he was the friend of working-class agitators and labour leaders, especially those working for the abolition of newspaper tax, the corn laws, and tithes. He personally knew William Lovett, a leading Chartist and member of the LMI, and frequently visited the radical printing shop of Henry Hetherington, a Chartist, Owenite, freethinker, and editor of the *Poor Man's Guardian*. George Birkbeck was also impelled by a profound sense of social service. His experience with the mechanics of Glasgow, followed by his medical work ministering to the

---

[35] Ibid., 11–12.
[36] Minutes of the Governors, 26 January 1824, 'This Time Last Century', *The Lodestone*, xix.2 (spring, 1924), 97.
[37] 'Literary and Scientific Institutions of the Metropolis: London Mechanics' Institution', *London Saturday Journal*, 1.26 (29 June 1839), 407.
[38] Evidence from Samuel Vallentine, member of the LMI and on the management committee for the past 14 years, in 'Report from the Select Committee on Parliamentary Papers; Together with the Proceedings of the Committee, Minutes of Evidence, Appendix, and Index' [720] (London: HMSO, 1853), 115.
[39] Ibid., 115.

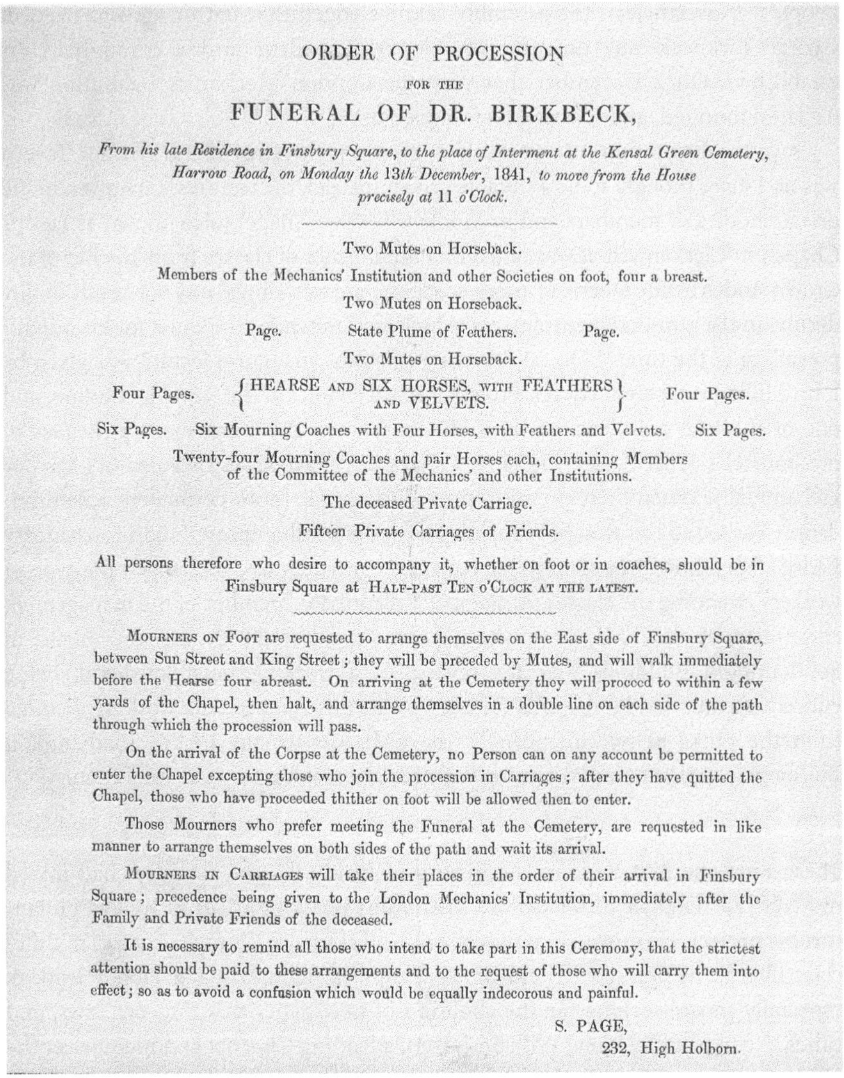

> ORDER OF PROCESSION
> FOR THE
> ## FUNERAL OF DR. BIRKBECK,
> *From his late Residence in Finsbury Square, to the place of Interment at the Kensal Green Cemetery, Harrow Road, on Monday the 13th December, 1841, to move from the House precisely at 11 o'Clock.*
>
> Two Mutes on Horseback.
> Members of the Mechanics' Institution and other Societies on foot, four a breast.
> Two Mutes on Horseback.
> Page.   State Plume of Feathers.   Page.
> Two Mutes on Horseback.
> Four Pages.   { HEARSE AND SIX HORSES, WITH FEATHERS AND VELVETS. }   Four Pages.
> Six Pages.   Six Mourning Coaches with Four Horses, with Feathers and Velvets.   Six Pages.
> Twenty-four Mourning Coaches and pair Horses each, containing Members of the Committee of the Mechanics' and other Institutions.
> The deceased Private Carriage.
> Fifteen Private Carriages of Friends.
>
> All persons therefore who desire to accompany it, whether on foot or in coaches, should be in Finsbury Square at HALF-PAST TEN O'CLOCK AT THE LATEST.
>
> MOURNERS ON FOOT are requested to arrange themselves on the East side of Finsbury Square, between Sun Street and King Street; they will be preceded by Mutes, and will walk immediately before the Hearse four abreast. On arriving at the Cemetery they will proceed to within a few yards of the Chapel, then halt, and arrange themselves in a double line on each side of the path through which the procession will pass.
>
> On the arrival of the Corpse at the Cemetery, no Person can on any account be permitted to enter the Chapel excepting those who join the procession in Carriages; after they have quitted the Chapel, those who have proceeded thither on foot will be allowed then to enter.
>
> Those Mourners who prefer meeting the Funeral at the Cemetery, are requested in like manner to arrange themselves on both sides of the path and wait its arrival.
>
> MOURNERS IN CARRIAGES will take their places in the order of their arrival in Finsbury Square; precedence being given to the London Mechanics' Institution, immediately after the Family and Private Friends of the deceased.
>
> It is necessary to remind all those who intend to take part in this Ceremony, that the strictest attention should be paid to these arrangements and to the request of those who will carry them into effect; so as to avoid a confusion which would be equally indecorous and painful.
>
> S. PAGE,
> 232, High Holborn.

Fig. 2.8 The Order of Procession for the funeral of George Birkbeck. Birkbeck Image Collections: Birkbeck History BH0205.

poor in some of the most deprived areas of London, had made him exquisitely aware of social inequalities. Education was a way to bring greater happiness to the people. For others—especially Place, Hodgskin, and Brougham—politically radical ideas fired their enthusiasm for workers' education while for Robertson the enterprise had probably as much to do with propagating his magazine and patent work as with any political objective. These differences were to contribute to disputes in the subsequent decade.

George Birkbeck had worked incredibly hard to establish the LMI. On 1 December 1841, on the eve of the anniversary of the founding of the LMI eighteen

Fig. 2.9 The Crown and Anchor Tavern on fire in December 1854. *Illustrated London News*, 9 December 1854.

years earlier, he died. He was only 65 years of age. His funeral procession left his residency at Finsbury Square at 11 a.m. on Monday, 13 December 1841, making its way to Kensal Green Cemetery. The 'Order of Procession' (see Fig. 2.8) tells us that at the front were 'two mutes on horseback', followed by members of the LMI and other societies on foot, four a breast. They were followed by a Page carrying a 'state plume of feathers'; another 'two mutes on horseback'; the hearse and six horses decorated with feathers and velvet; six mourning carriages with four horses (also decorated); twenty-four mourning coaches, each with two horses and containing members of the LMI; George Birkbeck's private carriage; and fifteen carriages of friends. On arriving at the cemetery, those who had accompanied the funeral procession on foot were sternly told that only those who arrived by carriage would be allowed to enter the Chapel (although they could enter after everyone else had departed). Any 'confusion', mourners were told, would be 'indecorous and painful'. Henry Buss, a member of the Committee of the LMI, observed that

> So well known and respected was Dr. Birkbeck, that as the procession slowly wended its way through the streets, the passers-by were, as a rule, observed to lift their hats as a token of respect.[40]

What happened to the Crown and Anchor Tavern after the LMI moved out? As a centre of urban conviviality, the tavern thrived for another three decades. In 1847, it was taken over by the charismatic journalist and dramatist Douglas Jerrold and renamed the Whittington Club. Disaster struck at 5.30 a.m. on Saturday, 2 December 1854, after a fire broke out in the kitchen. It quickly spread. According to the *Illustrated London News*, the fire 'swept furiously through the great room' and burst 'through the large windows at the east end, across Mitford-Lane'; it had 'a most alarming appearance' (see Fig. 2.9).[41] The roof of the

---

[40] Henry Buss, *Eighty Years Experience of Life* (London: Thomas Danks and Sons, 1893), 63.
[41] 'Fire in the Strand—Site of Arundel House', *Illustrated London News* (9 December 1854), 585.

enormous building collapsed. The servants who were living in rooms near the top of the building escaped in their night-clothes by climbing out of the parapet windows and making their way gingerly along the stone coping of the building to climb on to the roof of the *London Illustrated News*'s printing offices, next door. It turns out that a large quantity of the *London Illustrated News*'s paper had been stored in a vault beneath the club's ball-room. They feared it had been destroyed but 'on clearing away the ruins of the fire, only the edges of the paper were found to be slightly discoloured'. The editors asked for the 'indulgence of our subscribers' for the discolouration of their paper.[42] The tavern was no more.

---

[42] Ibid., 586.

3
Education for Whom?

By the end of 1824, the LMI was comfortably ensconced in the Southampton Building, and its management committee was eyeing up a vacant plot of land next door. Wouldn't it be perfect for a large lecture theatre?

The decision made was to have major repercussions for decades. Instead of relying on a slow trickle of subscriptions from mechanics and other members, George Birkbeck made a 'handsome and liberal offer' to advance the cost of building the lecture theatre. Believing that workers should retain their independence, George Birkbeck offered the money as a *loan*, not a gift. An interest rate of 4 per cent was agreed.[1] This decision was to become the spark for a bitter dispute between, on the one side, Robertson and (briefly) Hodgskin, and, on the other side, Place, Brougham, and George Birkbeck.

On the afternoon of 2 December 1824, the first stone was to be laid at the building site of the proposed lecture theatre. The elaborate ceremony was attended by a large group of 'very genteelly-dressed and respectable'[2] members of the LMI, along with their families and other interested people. One of the reading rooms in the Southampton Building had been set aside for the 'reception of ladies' wishing to attend the ceremony, but unfortunately the 'disagreeable state of the weather deprived the occasion of the ornament of many female beauties'.[3] Only the most intrepid women braved the 'dripping showers'.[4]

At three o'clock precisely, the all-male procession began. Stewards dressed in black suits and carrying white wands kept the path clear for the official party as they paraded from the Committee room of the Crown and Anchor, down the 'grand staircase', through the hall, and onto a temporary broad-way.[5] The march was led by a member of the Building Committee carrying a silver trowel and carpenter's square, decorated by a gold plume.[6] The Clerk of Works followed, holding the plans for the theatre, then the Chairman of the Building Committee, and the Institution's Secretary holding a sealed bottle. Inside this bottle were: the 'Rules and Orders' of the LMI; the 10th edition of the *Mechanics' Magazine*, which had an account of the first meeting of the LMI; a 'beautifully embellished' calfskin

---

[1] 'Mechanics' Magazine. London Mechanics' Institution. Fourth Quarterly Meeting, 11 December 1824', in Francis Place's papers, vol. xxxv, 188.
[2] 'Ceremony of Laying the First Stone', *London Mechanics' Register*, 5 (4 December 1824), 67.
[3] Ibid., 67.   [4] Ibid., 67.   [5] Ibid., 67.   [6] Ibid., 67.

parchment listing the officers of the LMI; and a portrait of George Birkbeck.[7] Following behind these men were the trustees (Henry Brougham and John Walker), the Treasurer, Sheriff Key, the Secretary (holding the Book of the Laws on a crimson velvet cushion), and solicitor William Tooke. Then came the President, George Birkbeck, the four Vice-Presidents (Professor Millington, John Gilchrist, John Martineau, and Robert M'William), and finally members of the Apparatus, Library, and General Committees.[8] They all solemnly mounted the scaffolding. After explaining the meaning of the various objects to the assembled crowds, these were laid down and the stone was lowered. The names of Place, Brougham, and George Birkbeck were engraved on the stone; there was no mention of Robertson or Hodgskin. This foundation stone can still be seen in a small alcove in Birkbeck's Malet Street building.

The ceremony marked the importance of estates and buildings in the life of the College. In the words of Nikolaus Pevsner, architectural historian at Birkbeck, 'Every building creates associations in the mind of the beholder, whether the architect wanted it or not. The Victorian architect wanted it. Nineteenth century architecture is evocative architecture.'[9] This was true of the LMI/Birkbeck. Many future reforms and changes were associated with the appropriation of new buildings. Buildings are an important part of a university; its destiny is often determined by spatial considerations.

As the audience fell silent, George Birkbeck walked to the front of the stand and began speaking. The first thing he wanted to impress on his listeners was his belief that the new theatre would be a 'Temple' of knowledge. As a Quaker and a supporter of working people, George Birkbeck said that he hoped, one day, that all of humanity—from 'the highest and the humblest, alike and equal (applause)'— would be 'freed from the deformity of ignorance and vice'. Once this happened, God would 'confer upon us a portion of his powers'.[10]

If George Birkbeck's first theme was about the confirmation of Higher Powers, his second was about the contribution of secular powers in *this* world. The early seventeenth-century philosopher Francis Bacon had declared that 'knowledge is power', George Birkbeck reminded his audience. So true!, he exclaimed, but knowledge was also 'wealth...comfort...security...enjoyment...happiness'. Knowledge 'gives a charm to social life, it makes morals more upright; it supports religion, and purifies politics'. Even more: education was 'an avenue and a

---

[7] 'Mechanics' Magazine. London Mechanics' Institution. Fourth Quarterly Meeting, 11 December 1824', in Francis Place's papers, vol. xxxv, 188, and 'Ceremony of Laying the First Stone', *London Mechanics' Register*, 5 (4 December 1824), 66.

[8] 'Ceremony of Laying the First Stone', 66.

[9] Nikolaus Pevsner, *A History of Building Types* (London: Thames and Hudson, 1976), 293.

[10] This speech is reported slightly differently in the *Mechanics' Magazine* and the *London Mechanics' Register*: see 'Ceremony of Laying the First Stone of the Mechanics' Theatre', *London Mechanics' Register*, 5 (4 December 1824), 67, and 'Mechanics' Magazine. London Mechanics' Institution. Fourth Quarterly Meeting, 11 December 1824', in Francis Place's papers, vol. xxxv, 189.

road-way to the temple that is made without hands—to eternity in heaven!'[11] The applause was deafening. When it died down, the patrons and members processed back to the Crown and Anchor Tavern to celebrate the pleasures of the flesh over those of their immortal souls.

Just before five in the afternoon, 300 invited guests entered the Crown and Anchor Tavern from Arundel Street, moved into the large dining room on the ground floor, and an evening of food and wine began.[12] Noisy toasts started the proceedings. George Birkbeck toasted the King, whose 'health was then drank... three times three'.[13] This was followed by toasts to the Duke of York, then the Duke of Sussex, who was 'described as the friend of the Mechanical Society and the patron of all that contributed to the dissolution of the distress and ignorance of mankind'. It was reported that 'this toast was received with an enthusiasm which it would be impossible to describe'.[14] The guests then toasted 'The rest of the Royal Family', followed by a cry of 'Prosperity to the London Mechanics' Institution'.

Brougham—the great orator—could not stay silent. After toasting George Birkbeck and providing the assembled supporters with a potted history of mechanics' institutions (in which he gave George Birkbeck rather than Robertson or Hodgskin the credit), he turned political. He encouraged the guests—including those 'of every sex'—to support the establishment of workers' institutions. It was important for democracy itself, he contended. Admittedly, Brougham continued, 'honest men' could be found arguing on *both* sides of the question of whether 'the people' possessed 'a sufficient share in the government of this country'. Whatever their view, though, the more educated working people were, the 'more capable were they of participating in the affairs of Government'.[15] 'Knowledge was power', Brougham cried, to enthusiastic applause.[16]

George Birkbeck then had something to say. 'Amid general cheering', he declared that it was his honour and pleasure

> to have contributed to the extension of knowledge among a class, where there existed intelligence without education—intelligence without means—intelligence smothered in the difficulties of disorganization and distress.

---

[11] This speech was reported slightly differently in the *Mechanics' Magazine* and the *London Mechanics' Register*: see 'Ceremony of Laying the First Stone of the Mechanics' Theatre', *London Mechanics' Register*, 5 (4 December 1824), 67, and 'Mechanics' Magazine. London Mechanics' Institution. Fourth Quarterly Meeting, 11 December 1824', in Francis Place's papers, vol. xxxv, 189.

[12] 'Fourth Quarterly Report of the Committee of Managers of the London Mechanics' Institution', in 'Ceremony of Laying the First Stone', 72.

[13] Ibid., 72.   [14] Ibid., 72.

[15] 'Mechanics' Magazine. London Mechanics' Institution. Fourth Quarterly Meeting, 11 December 1824', in Francis Place's papers, vol. xxxv, 190, and 'Fourth Quarterly Report of the Committee of Managers of the London Mechanics' Institution', in 'Ceremony of Laying the First Stone', 73.

[16] 'Fourth Quarterly Report of the Committee of Managers of the London Mechanics' Institution', 73.

However, he insisted that it was the mechanics themselves who had answered the appeal for a mechanics' institution.[17] Probably feeling embarrassed at having been proclaimed the *founder* of the London Mechanics' Institution by Brougham, George Birkbeck therefore proposed a toast to the 'enlightened Editor of the *Mechanics' Magazine*'—that is, Robertson—who had been responsible for publishing the original appeal. Although Robertson had become 'estranged' from the movement, George Birkbeck admitted, his 'great services' to the Institution deserved recognition.[18] It was a position echoed in the next speech, where Hodgskin gently contended that George Birkbeck 'had already too many claims to the gratitude of mankind', so would not begrudge giving a 'little honour' for establishing the Institution to 'much humbler individuals'—that is, Robertson and himself as editors of the *Mechanics' Magazine*.[19]

The final prominent person to speak was the radical MP John Hume who railed against the 1799 Combination Laws, which made it illegal for workers to join together to press their employers for shorter hours or better pay. These laws were contrary, Hume said, to the 'true spirit of English law, which dealt out equal justice to the rich and poor'. He proclaimed that their recent repeal was a victory for fairness, enabling workers to enjoy 'all the advantages which their skill and industry entitled them to receive'.[20] Hume contended that 'Much has been said of the wealth of this country, but it did not consist in its gold or silver, but in the industry of its mechanics'.[21] And so the speeches and toasts continued throughout the evening, greeted with 'mixed bursts of applause and laughter' and not a little drunkenness.[22]

* * *

For all the *bonhomie*, this ceremony marked a bitter breach between the main protagonists. Robertson had boycotted both the ceremony and the dinner,[23] but when he heard about the speeches proclaiming George Birkbeck the founder of the London Mechanics' Institution, he was livid. Rather disingenuously, he insisted that his animosity towards the LMI was not due to 'private pique'. Nevertheless, he was angry that his role in establishing the LMI had not been sufficiently recognized.[24] He accused George Birkbeck and Brougham of being charlatans who were purposefully demolishing his dream of a truly '*mechanics*' institution'. It was 'ridiculous' to call the LMI representative of the working classes of London,

---

[17] Ibid., 74.
[18] 'Mechanics' Magazine. London Mechanics' Institution. Fourth Quarterly Meeting, 11 December 1824', in Francis Place's papers, vol. xxxv, 190.
[19] Ibid., 191.   [20] Ibid., 192.   [21] Ibid., 74.   [22] Ibid., 75.
[23] 'London Mechanics' Institution', in Francis Place's papers, vol. xxxv, no. 33, handwritten date of 18 November 1824, v.
[24] Ibid., v.

he spluttered, when fewer than half of the 750 members were mechanics.[25] Furthermore, the original intention of the scheme—that the Institution was to provide education *for* the workers, run *by* the workers—had also been smothered by the deceitful leadership. He blamed George Birkbeck for plunging the Institution into a state of serious debt and 'dangerous subserviency' [*sic*] through his loan of money. Since George Birkbeck's demand of 4 per cent interest was higher than they could have got elsewhere,[26] what should have been a 'public cooperation and utility' had become nothing less than 'a private speculation'.[27] According to Robertson, his dream of workers' independence had been ruthlessly crushed.[28]

There were more recriminations to come. Robertson accused Birkbeck of reneging on his promise to ensure that working men themselves would have a prominent role in the management of the LMI. Written into the rules was a pledge that the management of the LMI would have a two-thirds majority of working mechanics. This had not happened. At this point, Robertson's bile turned away from George Birkbeck and towards his old ally Francis Place, whose son had recently been elected to the Committee of the LMI. Robertson noted that Place's son had been elected as a '*common workman*', even though he was actually 'a master tradesman at the head of a large establishment'. This, Robertson claimed, was 'an illegal usurpation' of the rights of ordinary mechanics.[29] An additional insult was the fact that Place's son had the audacity to adopt the title of 'Esquire' on the final list of members.[30] How could a man be *both* a member of the working classes and an 'Esquire', Robertson sneered?

A mild and conciliatory response to Robertson's diatribe came from his colleague on the *Mechanics' Magazine*. Hodgskin *had* attended the 'laying of the foundation stone' ceremonies. Indeed, in his speech on that occasion, Hodgskin had been fulsome in giving credit to Robertson (and himself) for originating the idea of a mechanics' institution in London. The difference between the two men lay less in their radical vision for working men, and more in tactics and personality. Hodgskin was not particularly upset about the violation of the rule requiring a two-thirds majority of mechanics on the management committee. Admittedly, he contended, it was 'more manful to propose the abrogation of the rules than secretly violate them', but, always true to his anarchist sentiments, he had 'never set any value on the rules, and care not how much they are violated'. Furthermore,

---

[25] 'Mechanics' Magazine. London Mechanics' Institution. Fourth Quarterly Meeting, 11 December 1824', v.
[26] Ibid., 192.
[27] 'Mechanics' Magazine. London Mechanics' Institution. Fourth Quarterly Meeting, 11 December 1824', 192.
[28] 'London Mechanics' Institution', in Francis Place's papers, vol. xxxv, no. 33, handwritten date of 18 November 1824, v.
[29] Ibid., v.   [30] Ibid., v.

Hodgskin noted, although a 'gentleman' had been elected (that is, Place's son), there was no suggestion that he had not been 'properly chosen' by the members. Of course, it was an 'absurdity' that Place's son claimed to be *both* a working mechanic *and* an 'Esquire', but this infraction of social conventions was 'so trifling…that I will not quarrel with it'.

This did not mean that Hodgskin was complacent. He was deeply despondent that the LMI had not become the *mechanics'* institution that he and Robertson had 'hoped for, struggled for'. Nevertheless, the Institution was still 'calculated to do some good' and was therefore deserving of support. In the final reckoning, Hodgskin was pragmatic. He told Robertson that 'If, as you think, *the proceedings of the Doctor* [George Birkbeck] *are calculated to ruin the Institution*, that ruin will not be stopped by my presence' at the ceremonies. Hodgskin professed himself to be committed to 'instructing the people of every class', not just mechanics, so 'do not think I am at all bound to stay away from the anniversary dinner, because the President and Committee do not act on my ideas'.[31] Hodgskin's matter-of-fact response only further enraged Robertson.

The *Mechanics' Magazine* was not the only place where the open hostility towards George Birkbeck and Brougham was being expressed. Throughout September and December 1824, a sustained attack was conducted in the pages of the *Literary Chronicle and Weekly Review*. The *Chronicle's* criticisms were threefold. First, it challenged the management of the LMI to show how they had 'substantially benefitted the mechanics of England a single jot'.[32] On the contrary, the *Chronicle* contended, the managers had tied 'a millstone of debt' around the Institution's neck.[33] Was it any wonder that membership was in steep decline?[34] The Institution was being ineptly managed, resulting in a situation where members were being 'led a confused dance from one science to another, at the caprice of the managers, or as vanity or *interest* may suggest'. It was also not catering to its members. As they exclaimed, the Institution was offering lectures on 'astronomy and short-hand writing!! short-hand writing for mechanics! Was there ever such an absurdity?'[35]

Second, the *Chronicle* believed that the independence of mechanics was being usurped by other classes and political interest groups.[36] George Birkbeck was

---

[31] 'Sequel to the Brougham Correspondence', *Mechanics' Magazine, Museum, Register, Journal, and Gazette*, 607 (28 March 1835), 475. The emphasis was added by Robertson, not Hodgskin.
[32] 'London Mechanics' Institution', *Literary Chronicle and Weekly Review*, 6.277 (4 September 1824), 573.
[33] Ibid., 573.
[34] 'London Mechanics' Institution', *Literary Chronicle and Weekly Review*, 6.278 (11 September 1824), 589.
[35] Ibid., 588.
[36] 'London Mechanics' Institution', *Literary Chronicle and Weekly Review*, 6.277 (4 September 1824), 573.

hardly impartial, it contended.[37] Both he and the LMI more generally had become 'tools for an odious faction'.[38] The *Chronicle* even accused the LMI leadership of 'recent flirtations' with their 'old political loves', with the intention of 'making a noise and clatter along the streets at the anticipated parliamentary election?'[39] Finally, it claimed that George Birkbeck and Brougham were taking credit for being the founders of the LMI when they both 'knew better'.[40] Robertson's message was getting across.

When George Birkbeck responded to these criticisms, the *Chronicle* either dismissed his comments or refused to publish them on the grounds that they were both 'very long and very dull' as well as being 'very angry, and very ungentlemanly'.[41] They boasted about having made George Birkbeck 'betray...a want of temper'[42] and joked that he had recently published books called *Triumphs of Temper* and *Polite Letter-Writer*.[43]

* * *

All this acrimonious ink was spilt well before the lecture theatre had even opened. That day finally arrived on 8 July 1825. The lecture theatre, which could comfortably seat over 1,000 people, was described as a 'plain, unadorned building', in which 'nothing has been given up to vanity and ostentation' (see Fig. 3.1).[44] This did not inhibit a crowd of supporters, amongst whom were 'a great many ladies' who (once again) had a 'little gallery appropriated to them'.[45]

The more important guests at the opening were named. They included representatives of royalty (the Duke of Sussex, the sixth son of King George III), Whig and Liberal statesmen (the Marquis of Lansdowne, Sir Robert Wilson, Joseph Hume, and Henry Brougham), and other dignitaries, such as the Sheriff for the City of London (Sir Peter Laurie) and local aldermen.

Once again, the star of the event was the LMI's President, George Birkbeck. His speech was heavily peppered with lush metaphors. He insisted that the new lecture theatre would 'cultivate' the mind, 'fertilize a wilderness of intellect', and act like a 'beam of heaven glimmering through the darkness of the storm'. Rather

---

[37] Ibid., 573; 'The Rambles of Asmodeus', *Literary Chronicle and Weekly Review*, 6.280 (25 September 1824), 621; 'Mechanics' Institution', *Literary Chronicle and Weekly Review*, 6.290 (4 December 1824), 782.

[38] 'London Mechanics' Institution', *Literary Chronicle and Weekly Review*, 6.278 (11 September 1824), 588.

[39] 'Dr Birkbeck and Mechanics' Institution', *Literary Chronicle and Weekly Review*, 6.279 (18 September 1824), 605, and 'Mechanics' Institution', *Literary Chronicle and Weekly Review*, 6.290 (4 December 1824), 782.

[40] 'Mechanics' Institution', *Literary Chronicle and Weekly Review*, 6.290 (4 December 1824), 782.

[41] 'Dr Birkbeck and Mechanics' Institution', *Literary Chronicle and Weekly Review*, 6.279 (18 September 1824), 603.

[42] 'The Rambles of Asmodeus', *Literary Chronicle and Weekly Review*, 6.280 (25 September 1824), 621.

[43] Ibid., 765.

[44] 'London Mechanics' Institution', *Bell's Life in London and Sporting Chronicle* (10 July 1825), 221.

[45] Ibid., 221.

Fig. 3.1 Engraving from a sketch of the theatre of the LMI, *c*.1825. Birkbeck Image Collections: Birkbeck History BH0034.

than being 'confined within certain privileged' classes, the knowledge acquired by working people in the theatre would be like a 'flood of light' that 'blazes with meridian splendour'. Linking his main two metaphors of barren land becoming fertile and darkness turning to light, George Birkbeck observed that stumbling upon 'fertile places in the wide-spreading deserts' would make the 'long period of darkness more visible, and the vast regions of barrenness more conspicuous'.

Birkbeck also heaped praise on Brougham, claiming that his *Practical Observations upon the Education of the People, Addressed to the Working Classes and Their Employers* was responsible for convincing 'the wavering' and 'the ignorant' about the value of 'scientific education of the artisan'. And what was the value of this education? It was both theological and utilitarian. God had endowed humans with 'habits of patient and profound inquiry which are necessary to elicit the truth to be disclosed'. Knowledge would make people 'prosperous, virtuous, and happy'.

Brougham—who stepped up to the podium next—maintained a similar level of grandiloquence. Having been praised so highly by George Birkbeck, it was his duty to reciprocate. Brougham commended the President for having encouraged the establishment of mechanics' institutions throughout the UK, as well as having 'laid down the necessary funds' to pay for 'this convenient and beautiful theatre'. The lecture theatre would be a temple to the pleasures of knowledge acquisition. Because working men were 'obliged to steal an hour' from tiresome work 'to come here and listen to the instruction of our tutors', they would find 'refined and exquisite pleasure' in learning. The joy of 'moral and intellectual' knowledge would never be understood by those who 'yield themselves to mere brutal and sensual enjoyments'. The audience erupted in 'Immense cheers'.

But the most controversial part of Brougham's speech came next. He admitted that

> Some will tell us that it is dangerous to teach too much to the working classes, for, say they, it will enable them to tread on the heels of their superiors—(Cheers)—Now this is just the sort of treading on the heel that I long to see—(Laughter).

Brougham warned that some of 'these self-nominated superiors' have heels armed with spurs, so 'let the toe of the mechanic be also armed with a spur, and I think it will prove a stimulus to the heel of the other—(Much laughter)'.

Wary of being accused of encouraging rebellion amongst the people, Brougham addressed the fears of some establishment commentators that 'if science were taught to the lower orders, there would be an end to the government of the country'. On the contrary. He insisted that 'it is my firm belief that, so far from science being inimical' to good governance, 'the more knowledge, the more learned, and the more moral, that the people become, the safer and more sure will the Government be—(Loud cheers)'. It was a rhetorical strategy that the promoters of workers' education routinely employed in their speeches: asserting the *radical* consequences of education while simultaneously reassuring critics that education would stifle *revolutionary* inspirations. Crucially, *both* sentiments were loudly cheered by the audience.

Given the vitriol that had been poured upon Birkbeck and Brougham after the laying of the stone ceremony, it was not unexpected that this would be repeated when the theatre was opened. The Editor of *John Bull*, a vigorous defender of High Toryism, was livid about what he regarded as attempts to fan an 'incendiary' flame.[46] *John Bull* claimed that Brougham 'not only knows that he is sowing the seeds of anarchy and revolution' but was so vain as to *boast* that it would have a pernicious effect.[47] The periodical warned that 'to see Squire Brougham active, is to know that mischief is busy' and to witness him 'inflaming the minds of the lower orders, under false pretences' is proof that he is a 'squalid hypocrite' with a

---

[46] 'We Have Heard', *John Bull* (1 August 1825), 245.
[47] 'There is a Difference between Hume and Brougham', *John Bull* (11 July 1825), 220.

'crooked mind'.[48] *John Bull* was vexed about the effect of taking so many 'journeymen...away from their homes and families to sit as *Members of an Assembly*, in which political speeches are delivered to them'.[49] In other words, *John Bull* believed that the opening of the lecture theatre was a thinly disguised political event; it was a plot by 'Revolutionists'[50] to inculcate radical thought. Although, the journal sneered, 'some of the contributors to the scheme are tottering on the verge of the grave', nevertheless, they were invigorated with a 'zeal which prompts men to sow acorns that their descendants may fell oaks'. These 'hoary profligates' knew only too well that 'the results will be terrible and fatal to the peace and happiness of the country'.[51]

If *John Bull* sounded enraged, it was met many times over by the fury of Robertson. His critique echoed that of eight months earlier. 'Through deception and manœuvre', he declared, London's mechanics have been 'deprived of that share in the management, which it was stipulated in the laws of the Institution they should always possess'. Moreover, the Institution was in debt and therefore 'necessarily more dependent on its creditor than it is fitting such a public establishment should be'. Instead of independence and self-governance, the mechanics

> have been taught to place their chief hope on the benevolent assistance of the great and wealthy, and to applaud, to the very echo, every announcement of a new subscription from Lord this and Sir that.

Robertson concluded by stating that it was simply not true that the mechanics could never have afforded to erect a 'Temple of Science' solely '*with their own savings*, and *with their own hands*'. Instead, their enthusiasm for such a project had been 'nearly extinguished, by disappointments and discouragements'.[52]

Robertson's bile was to continue for another decade. Although the old gripes remained, including his claim that George Birkbeck had saddled the Institution with an unmanageable debt which gave him the powers of a 'perpetual dictator', Robertson increasingly focused on the question of who founded the LMI.[53] He was furious that Hodgskin had dedicated his book *Political Economy* (1827) to George Birkbeck. Hodgskin had written that 'from the beginning' it was his and George Birkbeck's 'common pride to have originated, and supported' the

---

[48] 'We Have Heard', *John Bull* (1 August 1825), 245.
[49] 'There is a Difference between Hume and Brougham', *John Bull* (11 July 1825), 220.
[50] Ibid., 220.
[51] Ibid., 220. Even reports not hostile to the LMI noted the political motives behind those on the platform and subscribers: for example, see 'Mechanics' Institution', *Bell's Life in London and Sporting Chronicle* (23 January 1825), 28.
[52] 'London Mechanics' Institution', *Mechanics' Magazine, Museum, Register, Journal, and Gazette*, 99 (16 July 1825), 232–40.
[53] For example, see 'Sequel to the Brougham Correspondence', *Mechanics' Magazine, Museum, Register, Journal, and Gazette*, 607 (28 March 1835), 475, and 'Members of the London Mechanics' Institution of Five Years Standing', *Mechanics' Magazine, Museum, Register, Journal, and Gazette*, 607 (28 March 1835), 480.

LMI.⁵⁴ Robinson had also heard that, on 7 March 1835, Brougham had told members of the Marylebone Literary and Scientific Institution that George Birkbeck was 'the Founder'.⁵⁵ While Robertson went ballistic,⁵⁶ Brougham was unrepentant. Writing from his grand residence in 48 Berkeley Square, Mayfair, Brougham claimed that he always had 'thought…and he still thinks, that to Dr Birkbeck belongs the praise of first establishing Mechanics' Institutions'.⁵⁷

Robertson's former ally, Hodgskin, joined the fight.⁵⁸ Hodgskin was piqued by the fact that Robertson had described him as being 'employed as *an assistant* in conducting some of the earlier numbers of the Magazine'. While denying 'idle vanity', Hodgskin was insulted, reminding Robertson that he had been a joint-editor and 'equal co-operator' in the creation of the *Mechanics' Magazine*. Although he agreed that Robertson had been the person who sketched out the original idea for the LMI, he reminded readers that 'before it was well established' Robertson had 'deserted it' and had constantly sought to 'disparage it to the utmost of his means'.⁵⁹ Hodgskin argued that George Birkbeck was much more deserving of the honour of having founded the Institution because it was Birkbeck who put all his energies into promoting its success 'by unwearied exertions', including 'eloquent and seducing lectures' in addition to providing publicity and financial help.⁶⁰ In other words, Robertson might be given 'the somewhat barren praise of having projected an institution' but to George Birkbeck 'belongs the more fruitful praise of its being chief promoter and preserver'.⁶¹

* * *

How valid was Robertson's complaint that the Institution was 'a Mechanics' one in *name* only' (see Fig. 3.2)?⁶² This is not a straightforward question. Not only is the occupational affiliation (let alone, 'class') of members difficult to assess, but the term 'mechanics' turns out to be a very fluid one. 'Mechanic' did not necessarily mean employee rather than employer, since it was not unusual for successful 'mechanics' to employ other workmen. Furthermore, the benefits of belonging to the LMI were such that members who wished to have a say in the governance of the LMI might even be evasive about their occupation: a shopkeeper, for example, would enter his name 'as a worker of fabric or a manufacturer of the article he may sell'.⁶³

---

⁵⁴ 'Sequel to the Brougham Correspondence', *Mechanics' Magazine, Museum, Register, Journal, and Gazette*, 607 (28 March 1835), 475.
⁵⁵ 'Lord Brougham', *Mechanics' Magazine, Museum, Register, Journal, and Gazette*, 604 (7 March 1835), 432.
⁵⁶ 'Explanation of the Charge of Misrepresentation Brought by the Editor of the Mechanics' Magazine Against Lord Broughton, in Regard to the Rise of the Mechanics' Institutions in England', *Mechanics' Magazine, Museum, Register, Journal, and Gazette*, 606 (21 March 1835), 457–63.
⁵⁷ Ibid., 460.
⁵⁸ 'Sequel to the Brougham Correspondence', *Mechanics' Magazine, Museum, Register, Journal, and Gazette*, 607 (28 March 1835), 474–5.
⁵⁹ Ibid., 474.   ⁶⁰ Ibid., 475.   ⁶¹ Ibid., 475.   ⁶² Ibid., 475.
⁶³ James William Hudson, *The History of Adult Education, in Which it Comprised a Full and Complete History of the Mechanics' and Literary Institutions, Athenæums, Philosophical, Mental and*

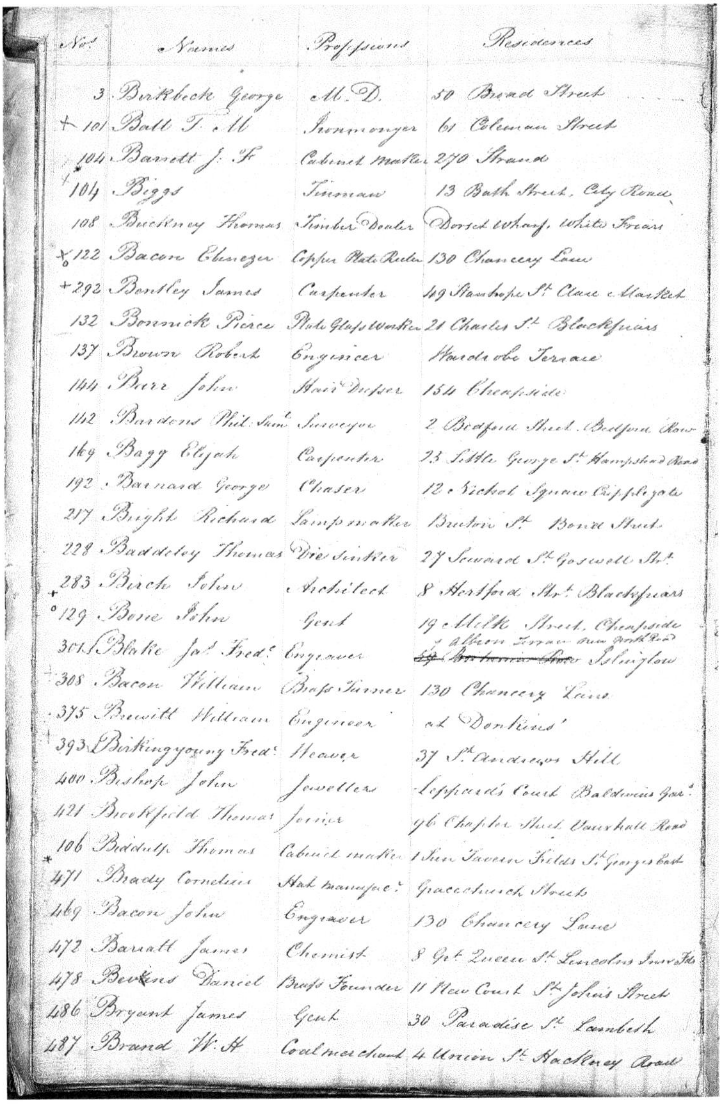

No.	Names	Professions	Residences
3	Birkbeck George	M.D.	50 Broad Street
+ 101	Ball T. M	Ironmonger	61 Coleman Street
104	Barrett J. F	Cabinet maker	270 Strand
+ 104	Biggs	Tinman	13 Bath Street, City Road
108	Buckney Thomas	Timber Dealer	Dorset Wharf, White Friars
+ 122	Bacon Ebenezer	Copper Plate Ruler	130 Chancery Lane
+ 292	Bentley James	Carpenter	49 Stanhope St. Clare Market
132	Bonnick Pierce	Plate Glass Worker	21 Charles St. Blackfriars
137	Brown Robert	Engineer	Wardrobe Terrace
144	Burr John	Hair Dresser	154 Cheapside
142	Bardens Phil. Saml.	Surveyor	2 Bedford Street. Bedford Row
169	Bagg Elijah	Carpenter	23 Little George St. Hampstead Road
192	Barnard George	Chaser	12 Nichol Square Cripplegate
217	Bright Richard	Lampmaker	Bruton St. Bond Street
228	Baddeley Thomas	Die Sinker	27 Seward St. Goswell Str.
+ 283	Birch John	Architect	8 Hertford Str. Blackfriars
° 129	Bone John	Gent	19 Milk Street, Cheapside
301	Blake Jas. Fredc.	Engraver	7 Albion Terrace New North Road ~~54 Britannia Row~~ Islington
+ 308	Bacon William	Brass Turner	130 Chancery Lane
375	Brewitt William	Engineer	at Donkins'
+ 393	Birkingyoung Fred.	Weaver	37 St. Andrews Hill
400	Bishop John	Jeweller	Leppard's Court Baldwins Gar.
421	Brookfield Thomas	Joiner	96 Chapter Street Vauxhall Road
* 106	Biddulph Thomas	Cabinet maker	1 Sun Tavern Fields St. Georges East
471	Brady Cornelius	Hat manufac.	Gracechurch Street
469	Bacon John	Engraver	130 Chancery Lane
472	Barratt James	Chemist	8 Gt. Queen St. Lincolns Inn Flds
478	Bevkins Daniel	Brass Founder	11 New Court St. Johns Street
486	Bryant James	Gent	30 Paradise St. Lambeth
487	Brand W. H	Coal merchant	4 Union St. Hackney Road

Fig. 3.2 The LMI's Student Register for 1824. Birkbeck Image Collections: Birkbeck History BH0204.

Contemporary commentary is not always helpful. In the early years of the LMI, the various mechanics' institutions were often conflated with other educational bodies, such as scientific and literary societies. Other commentaries adopted a

Christian Improvement Societies, Literary Unions, Schools of Design, Etc., of Great Britain, Ireland, America, Etc. Etc. [*sic*] (London: Longman, Brown, Green and Longmans, 1851), 52.

UK-wide perspective, ignoring major regional variations, especially the contrast between the London Institution and provincial ones. The most important of these differences include the fact that the LMI was particularly successful. It was based at the heart of a diverse metropolis, so was more likely to contain men and women from different 'stations' in life, as well as presenting greater opportunities for upward social mobility.

Equally important, any analysis of membership must also take account of the fact that joining a mechanics' institution might be a route *out of* that occupation: education meant social mobility. This was acknowledged at the time. For example, in 1829, a stone mason named Henry Poole won the LMI's prize for the best essay on a mechanical topic. He was described as 'an operative' who, prior to joining the LMI, 'had hardly a definite idea of what was meant by geometry, and knew nothing of the philosophic meaning of mechanics'. However, the mathematician judging the prize said that Poole's essay was 'the work of an accomplished scientific man' and Poole maintained that he intended to become a 'teacher of mathematics'.[64] In other words, one indication that mechanics' institutions were successful might actually be a *reduction* in the proportion of working mechanics, as its members used that education to 'rise' in the world.

Indeed, upward social mobility through education was the experience of Francis Place, who had started adult life as an impoverished journeyman breeches' maker but, through self-education, became the owner of a flourishing business. Place was proud of this achievement and saw the LMI as facilitating upward social mobility for other working men. As he informed readers of *The Republican* on 28 July 1826, from the age of 18, when he was employed as a journeyman, he 'experienced the terrible evils of poverty' due to the 'uncertainty of constant employment' as well as low wages. It looked likely that he faced a 'life of misery' and would be 'turning loose into the world a large number of wretched children'. He was 'saved' from such a fate 'by precisely such teaching as journeymen may receive in Mechanics' Institutions'. His success had taken place through *self*-education because the LMI had not existed at the time. But Place testified that, had the Institution existed, 'our poverty would have been of short duration—our success earlier, and more certain—our cares, anxieties, and fears would have been lessened, and our families benefitted much earlier'.[65] This helps to explain why Place's son claimed to be *both* a working mechanic as well as an 'Esquire'. Robertson and Hodgskin found this incongruous, but the other members of the LMI who voted him onto the management committee of the LMI presumably did not. Social mobility was an educational aim.

The most cited analysis of the employment status of members of mechanics' institutions was carried out by James William Hudson in a book, published in

---

[64] 'London Mechanics' Institution', *The Examiner* (6 December 1829), 774.
[65] 'F. P.' [Francis Place], 'Mechanics' Institutions', *The Republican*, 14.3 (28 July 1826), 91–3.

1851, exploring 'Mechanics' and Literary Institutions, Athenæums, Philosophical, Mental and Christian Improvement Societies, Literary Unions, [and] Schools of Design'. Hudson claimed that nearly all the first 500 members of the LMI were master mechanics, shopkeepers, and dealers in hardware and their workmen, cabinet makers, and housepainters but, within a short period, 'the attorney's clerk out-talked and ultimately, out-voted the working mechanic'.[66] He claimed that the LMI became 'an association of shopkeepers and their apprentices, law copyists and attorneys' clerks'.[67]

Hudson's view that a shift had taken place in the occupational status of members in the first decade of its existence was shared by many others. In the mid-1830s, one of the Vice-Presidents of the LMI estimated that only one third of the members of the LMI were mechanics.[68] A report in 1839 maintained that members were primarily 'persons in business, clerks, shopmen, &c., comparatively few artisans'.[69] One explanation for the change in the class status of members can be found in a casual comment made in 1853 by Samuel Vallentine, a long-standing member of the LMI. Having served on the management committee since 1839, Vallentine believed that the character of the members changed once the LMI moved out of working-class Clerkenwell and into the Southampton Buildings. This new location was 'exactly the reverse of a working neighbourhood, being entirely surrounded by the inns of court', he observed. As a consequence, 'the working men fell from the ranks of our members, and now we have few, if any'.[70] He added that, although 'many of the sons and relatives of working men' became members, there were many more 'clerks and the middle class of tradesmen and their relatives', as well as those 'employed in light avocations'.[71]

With the shift in membership came changes in the topics being taught. After all, mechanics' institutions in general were supposed to respond to the needs of their members. Even in London, different institutes offered varied courses. As Charles Topliss, one of the Vice-Presidents of the LMI, explained in the mid-1830s, the mechanics' institutions diverged. Depending on 'the wishes or wants of the particular class forming the society', some institutes 'pursue more literary subjects' while others focused on 'matters of science or matters of

---

[66] Hudson, *The History of Adult Education*, 52.   [67] Ibid., 52.
[68] Evidence from Charles Toplis, in *Report from Select Committee on Arts and Manufactures: Together with the Minutes of Evidence, and Appendix*, [598] (London: HMSO, 1835), 115.
[69] 'Literary and Scientific Institutions of the Metropolis', *London Saturday Journal*, 2.32 (10 August 1839), 94.
[70] Evidence from Samuel Vallentine, in *Report from the Select Committee on Parliamentary Papers; Together with the Proceedings of the Committee, Minutes of Evidence, Appendix, and Index* [720] (London: HMSO, 1853), 115.
[71] Ibid., 115. When pushed on the question of whether the decline in working-class membership was due to 'the inconvenience of the situation', Vallentine prevaricated. 'No,' he responded, 'I rather think under any circumstances they would have fallen off.' He thought the main reason was simply exhaustion.

[artisan] taste'.[72] The statement was an early manifestation of the 'two cultures' of the arts and the sciences.

When the LMI was young, there was a strong emphasis on the sciences. For example, in 1824, lectures included topics such as mechanics, pneumatics, hydrostatics, hydraulics, chemistry, astronomy, electricity, and mathematics.[73] There is some evidence, however, that the curriculum quickly moved away from this strong focus on the sciences. At the Select Committee on Arts and Manufactures in 1835, Topliss noted that the class on the study and practice of music was regularly attended by 90 people; other popular classes included those on English grammar, shorthand, French language, literary composition, natural history, and geography. The only mechanically orientated class that attracted over thirty members was practical geometry.[74] Topliss' assessment was supported by a report in the *London Saturday Journal* a few years later that observed that 'When a lecture on "Music, with *numerous* illustrations", is to be delivered, the theatre, which can contain within its walls a thousand persons, is usually filled to overflowing.' In contrast, students attending the classes in sciences were 'comparatively small'. The Editor of the *London Saturday Journal* hastened to add that they mentioned this fact 'not because we are averse to the cultivation of that which "softens men's manners and suffers them not to become brutal", but as showing in a striking manner what is and what is not "popular"'.[75] In the words of another commentator, lectures on mechanics and chemistry were 'not so well attended…when they get beyond the attractive experiments'.[76]

* * *

Between the 1840s and the 1860s, the Institution (see Fig. 3.3) was in trouble.[77] In the words of George Senter (Master of the College between 1918 and 1939), it was in 'very low water' because 'the early enthusiasm had evaporated and it seemed probable that its period of usefulness was nearing an end'. Senter accurately contended that 'the situation was saved by the younger members', by whom he meant George Morris Norris and James C. N. White, who served in the top positions in the Institution for fifty-nine and sixty-nine years, respectively (see Chapter 7).[78]

---

[72] Evidence from Charles Toplis, in *Report from Select Committee on Arts and Manufactures*, 115.
[73] 'Fourth Quarterly Report of the Committee of Managers of the London Mechanics' Institution', in 'Ceremony of Laying the First Stone of the Mechanics' Theatre', *London Mechanics' Register* (4 December 1824), 67.
[74] 'Paper Delivered in [sic] by Charles Toplis, Esq', in *Report from Select Committee on Arts and Manufactures*, 140.
[75] 'Literary and Scientific Institutions of the Metropolis. London Mechanics' Institution, *London Saturday Journal*, 1.26 (29 June 1839), 408.
[76] Evidence from Samuel Vallentine, in *Report from the Select Committee on Parliamentary Papers*, 118.
[77] George Senter, 'George Morris Norris', *The Lodestone*, 19.2 (spring 1924), 83.
[78] Ibid., 83.

Fig. 3.3 Engraving of the London Mechanics' Institution façade in 1865. Over the door and at the top of the lower two right-hand windows (as well as across the façade) can be read 'London Mechanics' Institution'. However, on the lower left-hand window this is replaced by 'Birkbeck School founded 1848'. Inscribed across the centre of all three windows is 'Birkbeck Building and Freehold Land Society' and, below this, 'Birkbeck Deposit Bank'. Courtesy of Richard Clarke.

The crisis could be traced back to George Birkbeck's 1824 loan. Twenty-nine years after the loan, Samuel Vallentine (who had been a member of the LMI's management committee since 1839) lamented the fact that

> We commenced with a heavy debt to Dr. Birkbeck, and it is exactly the amount of interest, or nearly so, that we find ourselves deficient in at the close of the year.... For the last 10 or 12 years I do not think one shilling has been paid off; indeed we have increased the debt by having to add the interest upon it.[79]

Not everything could be blamed on the original debt, however. The Institution was also in trouble because of its dependency on subscriptions. In the 1840s,

---

[79] Evidence from Samuel Vallentine, in *Report from the Select Committee on Parliamentary Papers*, 116.

members could be heard complaining loudly about the LMI's inadequate library and reading rooms: membership plummeted from 1,000 to 600. In May 1845, Brougham appealed for funds to improve the library, and was rewarded by donations of between £20 and £25 from Prince Albert (Queen Victoria's husband), the Marquess of Landsdowne, and the publisher Charles Knight.[80]

More radical change would be needed if the Institution was to survive. In 1850, John Rüntz (of the Birkbeck School: see Chapter 5), along with a W. H. Carpenter and T. Moring, published a pamphlet entitled 'Can the London Mechanics' Institution Be Made Self-Supporting and How?'[81] They argued that the LMI should transform itself into 'Birkbeck College', with a Council elected by subscribing members. This College would be 'essentially collegiate' and educational; 'entertainment' would be resolutely excised! The leading British literary magazine *The Athenæum* was favourable. It pronounced the idea of turning the Institution into 'a place of education, instead of a mere refuge for idleness and daily gossip' a good one. After all, 'Men who want amusement will always prefer the theatre to the lecture or class room; they who want instruction are not willing to be put off with anything inferior.' *The Athenæum* did warn, however, against placing too much emphasis on *lectures* as opposed to *classes*. It pointed out that lectures were 'dead burdens.... They are scantily attended—and they rarely pay expenses.' Nevertheless, the magazine recognized that converting the nearly moribund Institution into a 'Birkbeck College' was 'a great stride forward'.[82]

Unfortunately for Rüntz, Carpenter, and Moring, their 'new scheme' failed to gain wider support. Worse: their attempts were lampooned. A post began circulating, in which Rüntz was cruelly mocked. It read:

> Birkbeck College. £167 reward. Lost or strayed in an unsound state of mind, two Mechanics, a Carpenter and a Moring, supposed to have been lost or led astray in the neighbourhood of the London Mechanics' Institution; last seen in the hands of J. R...z, Esq., F. B. A., A. S. S.[83]

In 1858, immediately before Norris joined the Institution as a student, it was in such a serious state of collapse that it appealed to the government for help. Dr Lyon Playfair, who had been appointed Secretary to the Department of Science five years earlier, was charged with investigating the situation. His warning was stark: unless the 'heavy debt' was 'cut from the neck of the Institution', it 'may

---

[80] 'London Mechanics' Institution', *John Bull* (10 May 1845), 296. Also see 'The London Mechanics' Institution', *Friendly Companion and Illustrated Instructor* (1 February 1857), 54.
[81] W. H. Carpenter, T. Moring, and J. Runtz, 'Can the London Mechanics' Institution Be Made Self-Supporting and How?'
[82] 'Our Weekly Gossip', *The Athenæum: Journal of Literature, Science, and the Fine Arts for the Year 1850* (7 December 1850), 1281–2.
[83] Cited in C. Delisle Burns, *A Short History of Birkbeck College (University of London)* (London: University of London Press, 1924), 73.

rapidly sink'.[84] The main problem, he maintained, was that working men and women could 'only pay low fees'. Playfair required more assurances that the Institution's classes were being run efficiently. At present, he found, the classes were 'cumbrous and inefficient'.[85] Teachers were inadequately paid—indeed, many were paid nothing at all. Playfair noticed that the Committee 'can scarcely be said to superintend the classes, or to be responsible for their efficiency'. In fact, each class operated as 'a little independent republic, appointing its own teacher, and electing a secretary for its especial management'.[86] The result was a hotchpotch of 'disjointed' lessons. Classes were being given on topics as diverse and unrelated as

> 'The Atlantic and Ocean Telegraph'; A Gossiping Concert; Christmas Books of Charles Dickens; A Second Peep at Scotland; A Broad Stare at Ireland; Characters in Imaginative Literature; the Romance of Biography; Concert by the Vocal Music Class; On the Apparent Contradictions of Chemistry; Gems of Scottish Song; On Explosive Compounds; Entertainment by Elocution class.[87]

The Institution also had to contend with the problem that members 'appear to relish amusement more than instruction' and, although the Institution has 'tried to keep by its original scheme of class instruction', it has been 'unable to resist the demand for novelty and amusement'.[88]

Playfair argued that there were three options available to the Institution: wealthy benefactors, subscriptions, or state aid. If the government was going to contribute, it would need to be assured that pupils were receiving 'instruction of an efficient character', sufficient to pass examinations and allay the anxieties of inspectors.[89] Even then, the sum required to save the 'parent Institution' would be £8,100: it owed a debt of £4,000; purchasing the premises would cost £3,500; and £600 would be needed for repairs. Playfair proposed that the government pay half this sum; the rest could be collected through public subscription.[90]

The LMI's Committee had no clear response to Playfair's damning report. In July 1858, they lamely defended their courses by stating that it was

> important that the wants of the large class whose daily avocations involve mental care and anxiety should be met by useful studies of a less severe kind—music, elocution, drawing, etc.[91]

---

[84] 'London Mechanics' Institution. Return to an Order of the Honorable The House of Commons, Dated 26 March 1858;—for, Copy of the Report of Dr Lyon Playfair, as to the State of the London Mechanics' Institution in Southampton Buildings', [170], *House of Commons Parliamentary Papers* (1857), 2.
[85] Ibid., 1. [86] Ibid., 2. [87] Ibid., 2.
[88] Ibid., 2. [89] Ibid., 3. [90] Ibid., 3.
[91] Committee's response to Playfair's report in July 1858, cited in Burns, *A Short History of Birkbeck College*, 75.

They blamed their decline on 'the extensive and continued alterations in the city and its neighbourhood, and the increased occupation of its houses for business only'. In other words, residents (who mighty become members) were moving out and the area was becoming one for the conduct of business. There was also the fact that the LMI faced increasing competition from 'evening classes at colleges and governmental institutions'.[92] It was a weak riposte that only further emphasized the inertia at the heart of the college's management committee.

This was the context in which Norris and White arrived in the Institution in 1859 and 1862, respectively. Both were aware that, in 1859, the Education Commission was hearing evidence that the LMI had 'begged for assistance from the Government to save it from sinking into a mere place for concerts and dancing'.[93] They energetically set about reforming the Institution. In 1866, the college was renamed 'The Birkbeck Literary and Scientific Institution'.

* * *

Today, the bitterness, hatred, and resentment of the main protagonists (particularly Robertson) seems out of proportion. Robertson dedicated more than a decade of his life to a struggle for recognition which he initially *did* receive and (arguably) then lost primarily because, out of pique, he refused to have dealings with the Institution he had promoted. As a patent agent and the Editor of, amongst others, the *Mechanics Magazine*, Robertson had a major stake in ensuring that *mechanics* made up the bulk of the membership. This was not merely a personal feud, however. The passions stemmed from conflicting notions about the roles of social elites in acting in solidarity with their poorer brothers and sisters. Would the involvement of men like George Birkbeck or Brougham 'water down' any radical agenda or were their endeavours necessary for societal change? More broadly, detractors of the LMI had very different ideas to the founders of the purpose of educational institutions catering to working men and women: cementing the 'status quo' or promoting the greatest happiness of the greatest number?

Finally, debates about who founded the Institution never really died. In 1875, more than half a century after its foundation, the Lord Chief Justice offered a substantial prize of 20 guineas to the best English essay about whether George Birkbeck had a legitimate claim to having founded the LMI.[94] Histories of Birkbeck are also ambivalent. In some texts, Robertson, Hodgskin, and Place are entirely ignored, while most commentaries limit their role to one

---

[92] Ibid., 75.
[93] Evidence by Rev. F. D. Maurice, in *Education Commission: Answers to the Curriculum of Questions, 1860*, vol. V (London: Her Majesty's Stationery Office, 1861), 299.
[94] 'A Third Meeting', *John Bull* (13 November 1875), 776.

or two sentences.[95] My view is that all five men share responsibility for the inauguration of the Institution: Robertson and Hodgskin for the original ambition; Place for mobilizing radical supporters; Brougham for harnessing the 'great and the good'; and George Birkbeck for giving his name, respectability, and money to the entire project. Nevertheless, the Institution was never really about these five men. Rather, what became Birkbeck was always due to the intellectual aspirations and ambition of its members and students. As we shall see in the next chapter, though, these supporters first had to survive a tsunami of still more ugly feelings.

---

[95] Ronald K. Huch, *Henry, Lord Brougham: The Later Years, 1830–1868—The 'Great Actor'* (Lewiston: Lampeter, 1993), 24; Frances Hawes, *Henry Brougham* (London: Jonathan Cape, 1957), 164; Bernard Becker, *Scientific London* (London: Henry S. King and Co., 1874), 203. In Huch's book, only Hodgskin and Place are mentioned, although Hodgskin is misspelt 'Hodgskins'.

4
Useful Knowledge

The eager students who congregated inside the LMI in the first few decades of its existence were politically as well as socially receptive. The question on their minds was: what do we want to learn and why is this knowledge important to us? Many proponents of workers' education also debated the content and context of 'useful knowledge'. Was knowledge important for its own sake? Was it required in the struggle towards personal fulfilment and familial prosperity? Was it necessary for social stability or economic development? Was it a civic duty or a way of promoting a particular political agenda? As we shall see, these questions have also interested historians of the mechanics' movements.

* * *

Many supporters of the LMI believed that the Institution was a way to guide working people morally. In the words of John Robert Taylor, who had attended lectures in the LMI from the beginning, it was a great misfortune to the nation as well as to individuals that so many people 'enter into this world, and pass through the portals of death, without their minds being even so much attended to as the treatment bestowed upon the inferior animals'. Like 'inferior animals', he complained, Britons were exposed to a multitude of bestial entertainments. London had 'casinos, concerts, and other places for the allurement of youth' and they were 'crowded nightly almost to overflowing, with all their demoralising influences'. He lamented that 'many a simple-minded youth' flocked to such places and, therefore, 'the seed is … sown of a miserable manhood'. Taylor believed that the lack of education was 'one of the chief and paramount causes of ignorance, poverty, pauperism, and crime'.[1] The solution was the establishment and growth of mechanics' institutions like the LMI.

Taylor's ambitious hopes for the education of working people were, perhaps, unrealistic. In the words of an unnamed author of an 1860 article in the *Literary Gazette*, when the LMI was established, idealists fantasized that

> Public houses would, if not closed, be at least restricted to their original and legitimate purposes; tippling [that is, imbibing alcohol] would receive a heavy blow and sore discouragement; homes would be cleaner and more comfortable;

---

[1] John Robert Taylor, *The Rise and Progress of Mechanics' Institutes in England: An Address Delivered at St. Pierres-Les-Calais, France, to The St. Pierre's Young Men's Mutual Improvement Society on Saturday Evening, the 15th December, 1860* (London: Simpkin, Marshall, and Co., 1860), 14–15.

wives more tidy and careful; education would be the lot of children, and a new *avatar* of Minerva was to take place.²

The Victorian belief in the reforming potentialities of 'useful knowledge', particularly that focused on engineering, technology, and design, was widely held. This was why George Birkbeck, the LMI, and the exhibition movement (especially the National Repository) had strong ties. George Birkbeck was even the Chairman of the National Repository, which invited 'manufacturers, artisans, patentees, modellers, mechanical draftsmen, and other inventors to send their new inventions for improved production to the annual exhibition'.³ The Repository later became the Museum of National Manufactures and of the Mechanical Arts, with Charles Toplis, who was also Vice-President of the LMI, as its Director. Its focus and function were identical to those of the LMI. As *Percival's Annual Guide to the Principal Exhibitions of London* (1835) explained, the Museum provided 'youthful minds' with 'highly instructive' knowledge, which would be 'interesting to all who feel that the conveniences, the comforts, and the enjoyments of civilised life have sprung and have expanded with the cherished cultivation of productive industry'.⁴ In this way, the benefits of 'useful knowledge' would expand outwards from the individual, to the community, then to the nation, and even the globe.

However, some commentators asked, might the *kind* of 'useful knowledge' offered by mechanics' institutions actually thwart 'the conveniences, the comforts, and the enjoyments of civilised life'? Might they be 'traps to catch the people … and prevent their attaining a knowledge of the true cause of their miserable and degraded state', wondered the *People's Magazine* in 1841, before advising workers to 'shun all this as a pest'.⁵ This was the fear of people like Robertson, as we saw in the previous chapter. It was an anxiety shared by Lord Byron. Although Byron was said to have promised to subscribe £50 to the fledging LMI, the *Mechanics' Magazine* (edited by Robertson) claimed that he was nevertheless 'apprehensive' that the LMI would 'dupe' or 'deceive' its members. If the LMI

> permit any but mechanics to have the direction of their affairs, they will only become tools of others. The real working man will soon be ousted, and his more cunning pretended friends will take possession, and reap all the benefits.⁶

---

² 'Literary and Scientific Institutions', *Literary Gazette: A Weekly Journal of Literature, Science, and the Fine Arts* (7 April 1860), 433.
³ *Percival's Annual Guide to the Principal Exhibitions of London* (London: Percival, 1835), 6.
⁴ Ibid., 6.
⁵ *The People's Magazine*, cited in Chase Malcolm, *Chartism: A New History* (Manchester: Manchester University Press, 2007), 144.
⁶ 'Lord Byron's Opinion of Mechanics' Institutions', *Mechanics' Magazine, Museum, Register, Journal, and Gazette* (6 May 1825), 68, citing from William Parry, *The Last Days of Lord Byron; With His Lordship's Opinions on Various Subjects, Particularly on the State and Prospects of Greece* (Paris: The Author, 1826). This is also cited in Joseph Cowen, Jr, 'Mechanics' Institutions', in *Chambers's Papers for the People* (London: William and Robert Chambers, 1850), 13.

Ostensibly quoting Bryon, this statement sounds much more like Robertson. Their unease, however, was shared by Friedrich Engels in *The Condition of the Working Class in England* (1844). As a co-founder of Marxism, Engels reproached the mechanics' institutions for being 'organs for the dissemination of the sciences useful to the bourgeoisie'. Their teachings were 'tame, flabby, subservient to the ruling politics and religion'. Engels denounced the institutions for propagating a 'constant sermon upon quiet obedience, passivity, and resignation to his fate'.[7] Of course, Engels was a firm proponent of workers' education, but believed it should be conducted in proletarian reading-rooms, run by the workers themselves, rather than being sponsored by wealthy men such as George Birkbeck and Brougham.

* * *

I have briefly rehearsed these radical critiques of the mechanics' institutions because some historians from the late 1970s onwards have argued that they inhibited workers' militancy. In particular, they have lamented the absence in the LMI of an explicitly revolutionary rhetoric or radical ideology.

Marxist or Marxist-inspired historians keen on 'recovering' the history of the working class have been at the forefront of these arguments. In the words of Adrian Desmond, writing in the history of science journal *Osiris* in 1987, the mechanics' institutions were an attempt to 'curb the insurrectionary tendencies of a targeted elite amongst the working classes'; they were engaged in 'camouflaging capitalism's alienating features'.[8] For such historians, 'autonomous expressions of working class culture' could be found instead in the Owenites' 'Halls of Science', which had a short life between 1839 and 1841.[9]

The key argument of historians critical of mechanics' institutions is that their aim was 'social control'.[10] This was succinctly expressed by historian Richard Johnson in an influential article in *Past and Present* in 1970. According to him,

> the early Victorian obsession with the education of the poor is best understood as a concern about authority, about power, about the assertion (or the re-assertion?) of control. This concern was expressed in an enormously ambitious attempt to determine, through the capture of educational means, the patterns of thought, sentiment and behaviour of the working class.[11]

---

[7] Friedrich Engels, *Condition of the Working Class in England*, 1st pub. 1844 (London: Panther, 1969), at https://www.marxists.org/archive/marx/works/1845/condition-working-class/ch10.htm, viewed 1 August 2021.
[8] Adrian Desmond, 'Artisan Resistance and Evolution in Britain, 1819–1848', *Osiris*, 3 (1987), 77.
[9] Ibid., 84.
[10] For example, see Lawrence Stone, 'Literacy and Education in England, 1640–1900', *Past and Present*, 42 (February 1969), 91.
[11] Richard Johnson, 'Educational Policy and Social Control in Early Victorian England', *Past and Present*, 49 (November 1970), 119.

The most systematic 'social control argument' was made in 1977 in an article by Steven Shapin and Barry Barnes, historians of science. Their concern was less to prove that the mechanics' institutions *were* primarily about social control—this they took as a generally accepted fact—but rather '*how* the founders of the British Mechanics' Institutions thought a scientific education would aid in the social control of those artisans'. They asked how education in mechanics' institutions would make workers 'more docile, less troublesome, and more accepting of the emerging in structure of industrial society'.[12] They regarded as significant that the education provided by organizations like the LMI was *scientific*, which they explained in terms of the close relationship in the nineteenth century of science, religion, and morality. In their words,

> The study of the natural world would point out laws, relationships and the presence of design of which the worker would otherwise be unaware. And in being thus brought to perceive this rational organization of nature, he [a working man] would perceive (metaphorically or directly) the rational organization of society also, in its harmonious relationship with the natural world. The effect of this perception would be to render behaviour and values more stable.[13]

If the aim of the founders of mechanics' institutions was to render workers more accepting of the status quo, why didn't they turn instead to the 'useful knowledges' doled out by clerics and moralists, Shapin and Barnes asked? This was because the 'objectivity and value-neutrality' of science was free from the taint of party and class.[14] This was very different from 'crude attempts at coercion or suppression'. In contrast, the 'liberalizing strategies' adopted by founders of mechanics' institutions embraced a policy of 'cultural aggression'. They argued that 'by bribe or indoctrination', these policies ensured that 'natural leaders' amongst working men 'identified with and affiliated to those above them rather than those below'. It was done in two different ways. The first was 'divide and rule', or 'splitting the lower orders and preventing the growth of a common consciousness among them'. The second was by emphasizing the 'dominant position of artisans *within* the working classes' and ensuring that 'other workers were influenced by them'.[15]

Shapin and Barnes' arguments are complex and systematically articulated. But they do not allow for high levels of inconsistency in the actual practices of the men and women within the various mechanics' institutions and they over-state the degree of conscious manipulation of working people by the managers. Their arguments also place considerable weight on the importance of *scientific*

---

[12] Steven Shapin and Barry Barnes, 'Science, Nature and Control: Interpreting Mechanics' Institutes', *Social Studies of Science*, 7.1 (February 1977), 32.
[13] Ibid., 36–7.   [14] Ibid., 37.   [15] Ibid., 40.

knowledges. However, science in the LMI was often secondary to other intellectual and social pursuits. Members of the LMI pursued a wide range of 'useful knowledges', which were largely demand-led. Mechanical, engineering, and other scientific pursuits gradually took second place to music, singing, art, debating, elocution, chess, and gymnastics. I will return to this latter point in the final half of this chapter. Suffice to say here that one of the most long-standing (pseudo-) scientific knowledges that flourish at the LMI—that is, phrenology—can be seen as politically and socially radical.

Perhaps the most persuasive evidence for the LMI being intended as a pacifying instrument within working-class radicalism is its directive forbidding the discussion of politics or religion.[16] There are also arguments that working-class education was co-opted by the Victorian doctrine of 'self-help'. In 'The Victorian Gospel of Success' (1957), historian J. F. C. Harrison maintained that the doctrine of self-help underwent a subtle transformation after the 1840s. He claimed that 'what had been originally a working men's device to try to grasp some of those cultural and material benefits which were denied to them in the new industrial society' turned into 'a middle-class reply to workers' demands for better social conditions'.[17]

These critiques are only partly convincing. First, it is important not to minimize the extent to which early supporters of the movement fought vigorously for radical causes. This was not incompatible with a belief that 'combinations' (that is, trade unions), strikes, mass protests, and popular violence against property or persons had proven ineffectual in the face of the formidable economic and political powers wielded by the state of early capitalism. The founders and early members of the mechanics' institutions were not proposing to abandon aggressive political tactics. They believed it was strategically important to pursue them *alongside* more pacific activities, including workers' education. The LMI provided its members with vital organizational and administrative skills, which encouraged their participation in political movements and radical causes—indeed, it gave them the necessary skills to do so effectively. As historian Emma Griffin argues, they were the main conduit for channelling working men and women into politics.[18] Many members also continued to adhere to Robertson's principle that the LMI should be run by mechanics. This was what George Foggo referenced in his evidence to the Select Committee on Arts and Manufactures of 1835. Foggo was

---

[16] 'The Members of the London Mechanics' Institution', *Bell's Life in London and Sporting Chronicle* (4 December 1825), 389.

[17] J. F. C. Harrison, 'The Victorian Gospel of Success', *Victorian Studies*, 1.2 (December 1957), 163. Also see Malcolm Chase, *Chartism: A New History* (Manchester: Manchester University Press, 2007); Richard Clarke, 'Really Useful Knowledge and 19th [sic] Century Adult Workers Education—What Lessons for Today?', unpublished (c.2016), 8.

[18] Emma Griffin, 'The Making of the Chartists: Popular Politics and Working-Class Autobiography in Early Victorian Britain', *English Historical Review*, 129.538 (June 2014), 583 and 587.

an artist who founded a society for obtaining free access to English museums, art galleries, and other public buildings. He informed the Committee that while 'political and religious discussions are generally excluded from the laws of mechanics' institutes', nevertheless, there was 'strong aversion in the leading institutions to the Government having any thing to do with them'.[19] Excluding potentially controversial political and religious beliefs (including atheism) was one thing; handing over workers' control, quite another.

Second, the LMI was founded at a time of intense political turmoil. As suffrage campaigner Richard Carlile bluntly noted in his *Address to Men of Science* (1821), they were living in an age of revolution, suppressed only by the force of 'fixed bayonets and despotic laws'.[20] On 16 August 1819, only four years before the establishment of the LMI, the Peterloo massacre had taken place. A crowd of 60,000 protestors had peacefully assembled in St Peter's Fields in Manchester, demanding universal suffrage and the repeal of the Corn Laws. The yeomanry had drawn their sabres and (in the words of Samuel Bamford, who was present) had 'hew[ed] a way through naked held-up hands, and defenceless heads'. The yeomanry 'then chopped limbs, and wound-gaping skulls were seen, and groans and cries were mingled with the din of that horrid confusion'.[21] Up to twenty people were killed and hundreds wounded. Dubbed the 'Peter-loo massacre' by the *Manchester Observer* (the appellation was a reference to the fact that the Hussars were wearing their medals from the battle of Waterloo), it was a grim reminder to working men and women of the lengths to which the Royalists who had triumphed at Waterloo would go to suppress dissent.

In 1820, 8 months after Peterloo, radicals and other working people received another reminder of the vigour of tyranny in Britain. Government spies goaded members of a revolutionary organization called the Spensean Philanthropists (after Thomas Spencer) to conspire to assassinate the entire cabinet and then overthrow the government—an event known as the Cato Street conspiracy. Many of the plotters had hatched their plans in the Crown and Anchor Tavern, the birthplace of the LMI. Five of the conspirators were sentenced to transportation for life. Another five were sentenced to be hanged, drawn and quartered, although this sentence was later commuted to hanging with posthumous decapitation. On 1 May 1820, 100,000 people gathered outside Newgate Prison to watch Arthur Thistlewood, Richard Tidd, James Ings, William Davidson, and John Brent

---

[19] Evidence from George Foggo, historical painter, in *Report from Select Committee on Arts and Manufactures: Together with the Minutes of Evidence, and Appendix* [598] (London: HMSO, 1835), 51.
[20] Richard Carlile, *An Address to Men of Science; Calling Upon Them to Stand Forward and Vindicate the Truth from the Foul Grasp and Persecution of Superstition; and Obtain for the Island of Great Britain the Novel Appellation of the Focus of Truth; Whence Mankind Shall be Illuminated, and the Black and Pestiferous Clouds of Persecution and Superstition be Banished from the Face of the Earth; as the Only Sure Prelude to Universal Peace and Harmony Among the Human Race, in which a Sketch of a Proper System for the Education of Youth is Submitted to their Judgment* (London: R. Carlile, 1821), 21.
[21] Samuel Bamford, *Passages in the Life of a Radical*, 1st pub. 1839–41 (Oxford: 1984), 231.

executed. According to radical politician John Hobhouse, who was there, 'the men died like heroes', although when Ings began singing 'Death or Liberty', Thistlewood stopped him with the words, 'Be quiet, Ings; we can die without all this noise.'[22] After death, the men's bodies were decapitated with a knife wielded by a man in a black mask. The noise of the crowd was deafening when their heads were held up for display. This outrage took place only three years before the establishment of the LMI and just a mile from the Crown and Anchor Tavern where the rule prohibiting political debate had been agreed.

With the memory of Peterloo and the execution of the Cato Street conspirators still raw, it might be argued that it was a reasonable assumption for men and women who wanted radical change to believe that more aggressive forms of radicalism had failed: why not try other ways of changing the world? In hindsight, the new model based on workers' education failed to challenge capitalist modes of production effectively. But the radical men and women who placed hope in education, self-improvement, and developing organization skills and experience were not lily-livered for being wary of the reactionary, bellowing mobs that they would have heard from their lodgings.

The third point, however, is more pragmatic: *in practice*, political debates continued. The managing committee of the LMI was worried about a political backlash and resolved not to rent rooms to radical groups, but pragmatic financial needs trumped these anxieties. Newspaper reports noted that members of the LMI had to be 'repeatedly' warned to avoid politics, implying that they routinely ignored the ban.[23] There is also evidence that, although members sometimes shouted down speakers who crossed a party-political line, this was generally done in a good-humoured and fairly tolerant fashion. An example of this can be seen during the 1833 anniversary of the LMI when the radical, utilitarian MP John Arthur Roebuck, also known as 'tear 'em' for his vehemence in debate, told the members that 'what they desired to have in the way of education they must get themselves' and they 'could expect nothing from the Government'. He was scolded for being 'so indiscrete as to enter upon political topics' and members of the LMI treated him to 'a torrent of hisses'. However, Roebuck made 'an apologetic explanation', which the members 'took in good part'.[24]

In fact, the LMI rented out its rooms and lecture theatre to some of the most radical organizations of the time. As *John Bull* observed in September 1828, the LMI's theatre was regularly 'let out for the purpose of political discussion and

---

[22] John Hobhouse, diary for 1 May 1820, in '1820: Newgate Diary, the 1820 Westminster Election, Byron's Ballad *My Boy Hobby, O*, the Execution of the Cato Street Conspirators, and the Trial of Queen Caroline', 750, British Library Add. Mss. 56,540 and 56,541.
[23] 'The Members of the London Mechanics' Institution', *Bell's Life in London and Sporting Chronicle* (4 December 1825), 389.
[24] 'London's Mechanics' Institution', *Bell's Life in London and Sporting Chronical* (24 February 1833), n.p.

party assemblies'.[25] In the 1820s, its premises were used by the Friends of Civil and Political Liberty[26] and the Owenite London Co-operative Society.[27] In the 1830s, various trade unions and other 'combinations' used the premises.[28] In one of the meetings held by the Society for Promoting Radical Reform in February 1830, 800 people turned up to hear the notorious agitator Henry Hunt lecture them on the 'deep distress' he had recently witnessed in the west of England: his audience noisily responded with 'groans, and cries of "Shame!"' against the government.[29] There were also meetings about 'the present DISTRESS among the LABOURING CLASSES',[30] the working conditions of engineers and builders,[31] the injustice of the newspaper tax,[32] and the need to repeal the Corn Laws.[33] In the 1830s and 1840s, members were often able to hear the formidable radical Robert Owen holding forth on socialism.[34] In the 1840s, there were meetings of not only the Metropolitan Total Abstinence Society,[35] which was socially conservative, but also the Anti-Corn Law League[36] and various trade organizations, none of which can be accused of conformism.[37] In the 1850s, the LMI hosted meetings of working men supporting strikes and the introduction of more labour protections.[38]

It was the members who pushed for a change in the policy. Indeed, the management committee of the LMI would have found it difficult to prohibit debate categorically. Its early founders—including George Birkbeck—did not think there

[25] 'Partridge Shooting Began Monday', *John Bull* (8 September 1828), 285. Note that it called George Birkbeck 'Brickbat': 'The Rambles of Asmodeus', *Literary Chronicle and Weekly Review*, 6.322 (16 July 1825), 460.
[26] 'Partridge Shooting Began Monday', *John Bull* (8 September 1828), 285.
[27] 'London Co-Operative Society', *Bell's Life in London and Sporting Chronicle* (2 October 1825), 314.
[28] 'Reform Meeting', *Bell's Life in London and Sporting Chronicle* (21 February 1830), n.p.
[29] Ibid., n.p.
[30] The LMI sold 'Correspondence between the Right Hon. W. Wilmot Horton and a Select Class of the Members of the London Mechanics' Institution, Formed for Investigating the Most Efficient Remedies for the Present DISTRESS among the LABOURING CLASSES in the United Kingdom. Also a Letter from the Right Hon. R. Wilmot Horton to Dr Birkbeck, President of the Institution, and his Answer': reported in 'Correspondence', *Bell's Life in London and Sporting Chronicle* (12 December 1830), n.p.
[31] 'Meeting of the Operative Engineers', *Bell's Life in London and Sporting Chronicle* (9 October 1836), n.p., and 'Meeting of the Builders and Operatives', *Bell's Life in London and Sporting Chronicle* (14 September 1834), n.p.
[32] 'The Mechanics' Institution', *Bell's Life in London and Sporting Chronicle* (12 December 1830), n.p., and 'Taxes Upon Newspapers', *Bell's Life in London and Sporting Chronicle* (3 May 1835), n.p.
[33] 'Colonel Thompson and the Corn Laws', *Bell's Life in London and Sporting Chronicle* (30 September 1838), n.p.
[34] 'On Easter Monday', *John Bull* (19 April 1830), 124, and 'Lectures on Socialism', *Penny Satirist* (28 March 1840), 4.
[35] 'Olla Podrida', *Bell's Life in London and Sporting Chronicle* (17 July 1842), n.p.
[36] 'From the Newspapers', *John Bull* (3 December 1842), 582, and 'The Leisure', *John Bull* (15 April 1843), 223.
[37] 'The Bookbinders Pension Society', *English Gentleman* (3 May 1845), 18; 'The Bible Society and Cheap Bibles', *John Bull* (29 September 1849), 610; 'Dissent', *John Bull* (3 November 1849), 690.
[38] 'Typefounders' Strike', *John Bull* (24 August 1850), 533; 'Protection of Labour', *John Bull* (9 February 1850), 94.

was anything to fear from lively yet respectful debate. Furthermore, the Institution prided itself on its educational policy of 'mutual instruction': in other words, students were regarded as 'active searchers after knowledge, rather than passive recipients of the information of others', as one commentator put it in the 1830s.[39] This meant that questions of politics, class, and morality were in fact widely discussed in classes. Even if members were discouraged from directly pontificating on political matters, the nature of the classes meant that such topics inevitably arose.

Finally, did the membership of the LMI become less 'working class' and more socially conformist? Robertson certainly believed so, complaining that the classes increasingly served not 'mechanics' but other working people such as clerks and shopkeepers. These members demanded more 'entertaining' subjects. This critique masks a masculinist bias. After all, the classes offered as evidence of conventionality tended to be the ones attracting female members. They included the predominantly female singing and art classes. Yet admitting women as students was a pioneering step; offering classes that appealed to those women was important, especially since such classes allowed them to earn an independent income—for instance, as tutors. In a highly gendered as well as classed society, the relative decline in topics that attracted working *men* and the relative rise in those attracting working *women* should be seen not as evidence of conservatism but rather as an expression of different gender options.

It is also worth asking why working men and women should be expected to attend only 'serious' lectures. I was charmed by a report about a concert that took place in the theatre of the LMI in 1843 that promised 'an evening with Charles Dibdin': audiences were promised music 'interwoven with anecdote and repartee', which would 'amuse without wearying'. The *Theatrical Journal* reported that

> In these days of repeal agitation, and when our minds are excited by the feverish discord of the times, nothing has a greater tendency to exhilarate, and promote tranquillity than the soft sounds of sweet music; an irresistible charm, which falls upon our ears like oil upon the agitated waters.[40]

Those critics of the LMI who applauded 'feverish discord' and 'agitated waters' would disagree, but it is surely the 'condescension of posterity', as historian E. P. Thompson would have called it, to be suspicious of the pleasures of 'sweet music'.

At different times and for pragmatic reasons, members of the LMI would emphasize their moderation or their desire for radical changes to a society based on class and gender hierarchies that harmed their interests. They often disagreed

---

[39] *Phrenological Journal*, 7 (1831–2), 479.
[40] 'London Mechanics' Institution', *Theatrical Journal* (October 1843), 342.

with the policies promoted by the Institution's management and pushed the LMI away from its stated moderation. At times, instrumental goals (such as securing financial support from wealthy patrons) encouraged them to emphasize the more pacifying aims of education; at other times, members acted according to personal priorities and concerns. They might also express weariness with the demands of endless revolt or their desire to relax after a long day's work. There was nothing in these positions which excluded political engagement and activism.

* * *

In the second half of this chapter, I want to return to the comment made earlier about the potentially pacifying function of science teaching within mechanics' institutions. It is possible to explore this contention by looking at two debates: the education of women in anatomy and the education of men and women in phrenology.

In 1827, George Birkbeck did a bold thing: he decided to give a series of lectures on human anatomy at the LMI. That same year, he was a member of the Council of the University of London, which was to become University College London. It stated as one of its aims to provide the 'youth of England' with a university education that was not restricted to members of the established Church or students with considerable income.[41] One of the subjects to be taught was anatomy, which, we will see, was seen as a direct attack on theological precepts.[42] It was a logical move, therefore, for George Birkbeck to offer anatomy lectures at the LMI. He even used a human cadaver to illustrate his arguments.[43] The talks were an immediate success, with *The Lancet* noting that the lecture room was 'always crowded'.[44] *The Lancet* also approvingly reported that 'one of the most gratifying scenes' was 'the introduction of the human subject [that is, corpse] before so numerous and mixed an audience without the slightest mark of disapprobation'. This, it claimed, was 'striking proof of the good sense of the members' of the LMI.[45] On the surface, the study of human anatomy was a kind of 'useful knowledge' for working people.

However, something scandalous happened: women were attending the lectures. Their presence was revealed in a letter to the *Mechanics' Magazine* on 8 May 1827, signed by 'Aurum'. He announced that the presence of women in anatomy classes was 'to say the least ... grossly indelicate'. He had been unnerved by the fact that the number of female attendees had increased between the first and the second lectures. This was worrying since it suggested that 'in proportion as the doctor proceeds to explain the secrets of our conformation'—that is, the intimate

---

[41] *Statement by the Council of the University of London, Explanatory of the Nature and Objects of the Institution* (London: Longman, Rees, Orme, and Green and John-Murray, 1927), 7.
[42] Ibid., 11, 19, and 25.
[43] 'London Mechanics Institution', *The Lancet*, 8.198 (16 June 1827), 349.
[44] Ibid., 349.   [45] Ibid., 349.

'secrets' of the deity's creation—so will female curiosity grow. He was determined to prevent this travesty to social decency. Aurum sought to remind women of their need to act according to '*decent* procedure[s]' in the presence of 'the sex which they were born to please', meaning, men. He continued, asserting that he wanted to

> prevent the attendance of those who have had a taste of the sweets of Anatomy, and banish the eyesore of their presence from our walls. I could 'launch out', and go into a variety of illustrations and arguments on the gross impropriety of such conduct, but I hope a 'broad hint' will suffice to prevent its recurrence.

If gentle persuasion did not work, he declared that he would be forced to appeal to 'the good sense and feeling of the [Institution's] Committee, positively to deny them admission; in which case they would have only to thank themselves for the degradation'.[46]

Aurum's letter excited a rapid response from 'Platinum'. In a letter dated 12 May, Platinum teased Aurum for having such 'exquisitely sensitive...nerves'. He reassured Aurum that, before the start of the lectures, George Birkbeck and the LMI had been asked whether women could attend. Birkbeck had answered that 'in the three or four first lectures there would be nothing to render their absence at all necessary'. 'Platinum' challenged Aurum to point to a single sentence or display of an object that could be 'calculated to raise a blush on the cheek of the most delicate female'. He pointed out that the inaugural lecture simply consisted of

> a masterly survey of the animal, vegetable, and mineral kingdoms; the distinguishing characteristics of organic and inorganic bodies, the circulation of the blood, and some general remarks on the human structure.

This was followed by two lectures that focused on the human skeleton, explaining 'the construction of the skull, the spine, the ribs, the bones and joints of the arm and hand, and the articulation of the hip'. George Birkbeck took great care when illustrating such parts of the anatomy, giving 'the most scrupulous attention to delicacy'. The introductory content of the lectures, together with the 'high character' of George Birkbeck, were sufficient guarantees of propriety. Platinum informed readers that women would not be present at future lectures: their absence had nothing to do with Aurum's 'broad hint' or threat to have them disciplined by the Institution's Committee. Rather, it had been decided from the onset that women would be excluded from any lectures where 'impropriety' might be risked.[47]

---

[46] 'Aurum', 'Female Attendance on [*sic*] Anatomical Lectures', *Mechanics' Magazine*, vii (1827), 296.
[47] 'Platinum', 'Female Attendance on [*sic*] Anatomical Lectures', *Mechanics' Magazine*, vii (1827), 310.

Platinum's response did not satisfy Aurum. He pedantically responded that the women who had attended the lectures did not *know in advance* that there would be nothing immodest about the first few lectures: so, they still deserved his 'severe censure'.[48] The editors of the *Mechanics' Magazine* had something to contribute to this discussion too. They claimed that one of the female attendees reported that she 'knew nothing of *the subject* to be discussed' by 'the Doctor', until 'I saw it before me'. She blamed the 'male attendants' who accompanied her, claiming that she would 'never forgive the *stupid fool* who invited me to be the spectator of such a spectacle'.[49]

Why did the presence of women in elementary anatomy classes incite such passions? Anatomists had an unsavoury reputation in Britain at the time. Concerns had been expressed about the procurement of corpses for medical education. These concerns resulted in a scandal the following year, 1828, when it was revealed that William Burke and William Hare had been murdering people to donate their corpses to the anatomy lectures of surgeon Robert Knox, whom George Birkbeck knew. Furthermore, executions such as those of the Cato Street conspirators, which took place in 1820 close to the LMI, had seen anatomists skilfully decapitating the men's heads in public.

But there were more fundamental reasons for anxiety. Human anatomy was a radical science in this period, largely because it substituted providential design for a naturalistic framework which could easily become anti-clerical. The idea of allowing women, as well as working men, to gaze upon the mechanisms of the human body was therefore morally dangerous.[50] The study of 'nature' encouraged a materialist philosophy of 'matter' that was blasphemous. When this philosophy was made available to women, the potentials for disrupting hierarchies of power were even more manifest. As we will see in Chapter 11, in the early nineteenth century the LMI/Birkbeck was a hotbed of radicalism for women in many other contexts in addition to anatomy classes.

* * *

The other lens for examining the pacifying function of science is the most prevalent and long-standing science that was taught in the LMI: phrenology. A forgotten proponent of the LMI, William Mattieu Williams, a prominent figure in the Institution from the 1830s through to the late nineteenth century, gives an insight.

Williams was born in 1820 and, at the age of 14, had been apprenticed to a mathematical and optical instrument maker in Lambeth. In 1834, he became keenly aware of his own educational deficiencies so, after working from seven in

---

[48] 'Aurum', 'Female Attendance on [sic] Anatomical Lectures', *Mechanics' Magazine*, vii (1827), 351.
[49] Editors quoting one of the women who attended the lecture, in 'Female Attendance on [sic] Anatomical Lectures', *Mechanics' Magazine*, vii (1827), 352.
[50] For a discussion, see Adrian Desmond, 'Artisan Resistance and Evolution in Britain, 1819–1848', *Osiris*, 3 (1987), 92.

the morning to eight at night, he ran 2½ kilometres to Southampton Buildings to attend classes in the LMI.[51] The 1830s were a stimulating time to be involved with the Institution. George Birkbeck was still President and he had the talented support of luminaries such as Lord Brougham, Sir Francis Burdett (reformist politician), Joseph Hume (doctor and radical MP), and Connop Thirlwall (liberal bishop and historian of Greece). It is no wonder that Williams was inspired by the LMI, throwing his energies into the promotion of learning. Like the proponents discussed at the beginning of this chapter, Williams believed that education would 'ultimately wash away ninety-nine hundredths of all the vice, the misery, the poverty and the disease which it was the misfortune of the average thinker of the time to regard as inseparable from our social system'.[52]

It wasn't easy. After all, Williams' daytime job was as an electrical instrument maker and electrotyper. He also advised on a number of patents, including those related to electric light, a more economical way of tanning leather, improvements in the steam engine, and railway engineering.[53] His social life was hectic as well: he was a painter, operatic singer, and enthusiastic traveller.[54] Williams had to juggle all these jobs and hobbies with attending the regular series of lectures at the LMI as well as classes in mathematics, chemistry, natural philosophy, French, literary composition, and, crucially, phrenology.[55]

In his book entitled *The Intellectual Destiny of the Working Man* (1863), published three decades after he joined the LMI, Williams reflected on one of the first classes he had attended, which was on 'Chemistry and Natural Philosophy'. He admitted that the class was not perfect: the 'absence of a regular teacher' meant that the subject was not taught as systematically as it should have been. Nevertheless, Williams contended that LMI classes were of 'great value in training their members in independent and vigorous habits of thought, and fitting them to communicate to others any knowledge they possessed'.[56] Williams exemplified such an ethics, eventually giving lectures himself at the Institution and becoming a long-term member of the LMI's management committee.

Williams' lectures were heterodox. They included topics such as: 'On the Relative Character of the French and English', 'Would it be Advantageous for Railways to Become National Property?', and, the most relevant one for this chapter, 'Should Political Questions be Discussed at Mechanics' Institutions?' But his real passion was teaching the 'science' of phrenology (from the Greek *phrenes*,

---

[51] John Angell, 'Memoir', in William Mattieu Williams, *A Vindication of Phrenology* (London: Chatto and Windus, 1894), vii.
[52] Ibid., viii.   [53] Ibid., xii.   [54] Ibid., xiii.   [55] Ibid., viii.
[56] William Mattieu Williams, *The Intellectual Destiny of the Working Man; An Address Delivered on the 28th May, 1863, to the Members of the 'Institute Chemical Society'* (Birmingham: Cornish Brothers, 1863), 4.

meaning 'mind').[57] Phrenology, he freely confessed, was his 'first love'.[58] Williams admitted to an 'ever-increasing conviction of the solid truth of the great natural laws' that phrenology represented. Its 'pre-eminence as the highest and most important of all the sciences' was assured because it was 'the only philosophy of mind that rests upon a strictly inductive basis'.[59] He was convinced that phrenology would 'contribute… to the moral and social progress of man'.[60]

What was this new 'science'? Phrenology was founded by German physician Franz Joseph Gall and, from 1813, popularized in England by Gall's pupil Johann Caspar Spurzheim. Williams noted that

> When Gall and Spurzheim wrote their first great work, wild and baseless theories still prevailed, even among men of high official scientific standing, concerning 'the seat of the soul', the residences of the passions.

Williams observed that some commentators at that time believed that important 'intellectual and emotional functions' resided in organs such as 'the spleen, the liver, the abdominal viscera, the heart, etc.' They also contended that the 'seat of the soul' was the pineal gland, since it was 'a neat little cone snugly ensconced nearly in the middle of the brain'. It was the responsibility of phrenologists to

> seriously and laboriously refute these absurdities, and to show that the brain was something more than a sponge whose function was to attract the humidity of the body, or to temper the heat of the heart.[61]

Phrenology was a battering ram that would 'refute these absurdities'. It maintained that the brain is the organ of the mind. By examining the contours or 'bumps' of the skull, phrenologists claimed that they could identify dominant 'faculties' of that person's mind, including 'Benevolence', 'Combativeness', and 'Philoprogenitiveness' (love of children). These 'faculties' had an identifiable location in the brain. Crucially: the larger the region of the brain, the more dominant the 'faculty'.

The LMI actively promoted this popular, early Victorian science. In January 1826, Spurzheim caused a stir by accepting an invitation to lecture at the Institution. He attracted so many people that there was 'not room enough on the benches to sit' and around 100 people had to stand.[62] By the 1840s, other phrenological lecturers at the LMI attracted audiences of up to 800 people.[63] The LMI

---

[57] Phrenology was also known (each with distinctive variations) as craniology, cranioscopy, and zoonomy.
[58] John Angell, 'Memoir', in William Mattieu Williams, *A Vindication of Phrenology* (London: Chatto and Windus, 1894), ix.
[59] Williams, *A Vindication of Phrenology*, 2.   [60] Ibid., 2.   [61] Ibid., 10.
[62] *Phrenological Journal*, 3 (1825–6), 824.   [63] *Phrenological Journal*, 20 (1847), 308.

was well equipped to demonstrate phrenological principles, being the owner of a collection of 150 illustrative casts and skulls, in addition to an impressive library of between forty and fifty phrenological books and pamphlets.[64] The Phrenological Society even succeeded in persuading the LMI's library to classify these books under 'Phrenology', rather than by name of the author, on the grounds that 'by being placed together, the works would excite more attention than they receive when scattered'.[65] At this time, more than one third of the directors of the LMI as well as one third of the lecturers openly espoused the science of phrenology.[66]

It was a useful science. Phrenology could be used to learn about and judge other people: everything from individual character to personal propensities was visible to the 'knowing eye'. The science claimed to explain everything. For example, in the late 1830s, LMI classes explored phrenology in relation to free will, education, philosophy, sound, happiness, music, national characteristics, dreaming, moral conduct, nervous physiology, novels, the fine arts, drunkenness, and 'the degenerating tendency of the Military Profession'. One lecturer based his class on 'the benefits derivable by Females from the Study of Phrenology', addressed to women seeking to understand their lovers.[67] In other words, phrenology was as useful in diagnosing illness as in choosing a spouse.

It was also a potentially radical science. Although Gall identified a faculty of the brain that he labelled 'evil', Spurzheim's more popular version of phrenology was optimistic, offering the possibility of human perfection. As Spurzheim argued in *A View of the Philosophical Principles of Phrenology* (1825), 'no faculty in itself can be bad and...all the innate powers of man have some aim'.[68] In other words, negative 'faculties' could be treated, while positive ones could be encouraged to grow. This directly challenged religious dogma: it jettisoned ideas about original sin, substituting a philosophy that opened up a wealth of possibilities for human renewal. Through the kind of education provided by the mechanics' institutions, people could better understand and change both themselves and their worlds. This is why the Phrenological Society praised the LMI for its long-term commitment to providing classes on phrenology. In the words of the *Phrenological Journal* in 1842, by professing 'obedience to its injunctions', the study of phrenology by members of the Institution would contribute to 'the happiness of man'.[69] A similar message had been propagated a decade earlier by J. L. Levison at the LMI. He informed members of the Institution that the science of phrenology would

---

[64] *Phrenological Journal*, 12 (1839), 107, and *Phrenological Journal*, 14 (1841), 193.
[65] *Phrenological Journal*, 14 (1841), 194.   [66] *Phrenological Journal*, 15 (1842), 185.
[67] See *Phrenological Journal*, 11 (1837–8), 338, and *Phrenological Journal*, 12 (1839), 107.
[68] Johann Caspar Spurzheim, *A View of the Philosophical Principles of Phrenology*, 3rd ed. (London: Charles Knight, 1825), 133.
[69] *Phrenological Journal*, 15 (1842), 185.

'place happiness and moral good within the reach of all, and make the earth, instead of a scene of vice and bloodshed, comparatively a terrestrial Paradise'.[70]

It is not surprising, therefore, that such rhetoric inflamed critics. Williams observed that critics were outraged by the phrenologist's comparisons between human and nonhuman animals.[71] Others were 'shocked' when they heard phrenologists arguing that 'cerebral functions' were localized. Theological critics believed that the 'metaphysical soul' was 'one and indivisible'. Therefore, they reasoned, it was nothing less than 'sacrilegious' to 'break up the pure entity into different faculties and locate them separately in different parts of the brain'.[72]

Most importantly, critics accused phrenologists of promoting atheism. Members of the LMI were used to this accusation. As John Robert Taylor explained, the fact that Jews, Catholics, and Protestants 'sit down together in the same class room and theatre' was 'considered inimical to the cause of Christianity!'[73] Teaching phrenology took godlessness to an even more perilous level. In Williams' words, religious commentators regarded it as a 'dangerous heresy involving the denial of the separate existence of an immortal soul'.[74] Of course, the critics had a point: after all, this was precisely what attracted radicals such as Richard Carlile to the young science. The same year that Spurzheim addressed hundreds of students at the LMI, Carlile wrote an article for *The Republican* contending that phrenology was

> centred in Materialism, and annihilates by demonstrative proofs all ideas of spirit or human soul.... It strikes at the very source of religion, and is a new and invincible proof of the good foundation of the science called Atheism or Materialism.[75]

The difference between the critics and supporters of phrenology was that the latter regarded materialism as a positive force.

Many attacks on phrenology classes at the LMI focused on its use of George Combe's *The Constitution of Man Considered in Relation to External Objects* (1828).[76] This was one of the best-selling books of the nineteenth century, with over 100,000 copies printed in Britain alone and selling at prices that even working men and women could afford.[77] Indeed, Williams was so fond of Combe that he named his son after him.

---

[70] 'Cases by Mr J. L. Levison of London', *Phrenological Journal*, 7 (1831–2), 383.
[71] Williams, *A Vindication of Phrenology*, 10.   [72] Ibid., 10.
[73] Taylor, *The Rise and Progress of Mechanics' Institutes in England*, 16.
[74] Williams, *A Vindication of Phrenology*, 10.
[75] Richard Carlile, 'Phrenology', *The Republican*, 13.15 (14 April 1826), 451.
[76] George Combe, *The Constitution of Man Considered in Relation to External Objects*, 1st ed. 1828 (Edinburgh: John Anderson jun., 1835).
[77] A. R. Wallace, *The Wonderful Century: Its Successes and Failures* (London: Swan Sonnenschein and Co., 1898), 164. Also see Hewett C. Watson, *Statistics of Phrenology: Being a Sketch of the Progress and Present State of that Science in the British Isles* (London: n.p., 1836).

But Combe was a lightning rod for anti-phrenology ideologues. In 1840, the author of 'George Combe and the Philosophy of Phrenology' set out his opposition to this dangerous philosophy in *Fraser's Magazine for Town and Country*. He noted that Combe 'regards the material philosophy as all sufficient—as able to effect the perfection and felicity of mankind without any assistance from spiritual sources'. This was nothing less than a rejection of 'the doctrine of the atonement'. It also meant that the LMI was promoting the ungodly 'theory of man's competence to raise his own nature by the cultivation of human wisdom to a state of perfect knowledge and happiness on earth'. Consequently, Combe's book 'cannot be adopted without renouncing the very principles of the New Testament… We *know* that it has made some infidels'.[78]

The same year that *Fraser's Magazine for Town and Country* published its attack on phrenology's godless doctrines, lecturers at the LMI were forced to address explicitly whether their classes were responsible for creating 'infidels'. In a series of lectures on phrenology, a special session had to be added, entitled 'On the Propriety of Studying Religion in Connection with Phrenology'.[79] Then, in September that year, an unnamed 'Reverend Gentleman' complained that the 'Discussion Class' that took place after a lecture on phrenology at the LMI had debated whether Combe's *Constitution of Man* was 'presumptuous, fallacious, and anti-Christian'.[80] Given the way the journal of the Phrenological Society reported what then took place—alternatively defensive and bullish—it is obvious that a heated debate took place. The *Phrenological Journal* accused the reverend of 'mysticism, deficient logic, misconception, and mis-statement', adding that 'the manner in which his views were supported supplied an apt illustration of dogmatic "zeal without knowledge"'. It claimed that, except for the vote cast by the 'Reverend Gentleman', the class was unanimously of the view that 'the phrenological portion' of Combe's book was 'based upon truth, and is in entire accordance with the *spirit* of Christianity'.[81]

In fact, the Phrenological Society was grateful to the LMI for taking its science seriously. After all, the middle classes could increasingly be heard lampooning phrenology as absurd. *Punch* joked about introducing 'stomachology'.[82] The Society was also extremely sensitive to accusations of quackery. In an 1842 report on the LMI's lectures, the Society's journal reiterated their belief that 'the essence of phrenology does not consist in mere "bump-feeling"'. Rather, the focus on the serious science behind phrenology—as promoted by the LMI—was responsible for attracting 'men of moral and intellectual capacity to our ranks'. These new members were not discouraged by the

---

[78] 'George Combe and the Philosophy of Phrenology', *Fraser's Magazine for Town and Country*, cxxxi.xxi (November 1840), 511–13.
[79] *Phrenological Journal*, 13 (1840), 185.   [80] Ibid., 185.   [81] Ibid., 185.
[82] 'Punch's Stomachology', *Punch, or the London Charivari* (27 November 1841), 232, and 'Punch's Stomachology', *Punch, or the London Charivari* (n.d., probably issue 20, 1842), 50.

quackery of advertising bump-feelers, whose lavish flattery has made manliness revolt and whose ignorance or distortion of the plainest doctrines of the science has made it appear a mass of incongruous absurdity.[83]

By establishing classes on phrenology, the LMI was conferring a degree of respectability on the science: newspapers 'no longer disgrace themselves by paltry jokes' but were forced to report seriously on the lectures at the LMI.[84]

* * *

The teaching of 'science' in all its forms, including anatomy and phrenology, directly challenged some of the moral pieties and ideological principles of the time. The teaching of 'science' at a period when it was developing fast was itself radical, especially since science was the main adversary of religion. By disseminating scientific views to the working class, the LMI was part of the radical enlightenment.

William Mattieu Williams died suddenly of cerebral apoplexy on 28 November 1892, aged 72 and a phrenologist to his last breath.[85] This case study on phrenology at the LMI illustrates the complexity of life at the Institution in its early decades. 'Useful knowledge' was contested: but, crucially, the definition of both 'useful' and 'knowledge' was largely dictated by the Institution's members. It was their subscriptions, small though they were, that dictated which classes went ahead and which quietly folded. Of course, enthusiasts such as George Birkbeck and Williams led the way, but members did not passively soak up their offerings. They argued about whether phrenology was inherently atheistic; they danced to the music of Charles Dibdin; they joined the political agitation inspired by the repeal movement. What they did not do is passively acquiesce to the manipulative machinations of self-ordained 'betters'.

---

[83] *Phrenological Journal*, 15 (1842), 185.   [84] *Phrenological Journal*, 3 (1825–6), 824.
[85] Geo. Combe Williams, 'Memoir', in Williams, *A Vindication of Phrenology*, xiii.

5
The Birkbeck Schools

'Very well', said this gentleman, ... 'Now, let me ask you girls and boys, Would you paper a room with representations of horses? ... I'll explain to you, then. ... Do you ever see horses walking up and down the sides of rooms in reality—in fact? Do you? ... You are to be in all things regulated and governed', said the gentleman, 'by fact. We hope to have, before long, a board of fact, composed of commissioners of fact, who will force the people to be a people of fact, and of nothing but fact.'

Charles Dickens in *Hard Times*[1]

This was the way Charles Dickens lampooned one of the educational innovations that emerged out of the LMI in its early years. They were eventually called the 'Birkbeck Schools', in honour of George Birkbeck, who died seven years before they were named after him. The first Birkbeck School opened in the theatre in the LMI's Southampton Buildings on 17 July 1848. It was the creation of William Ellis, one of the original founders of the LMI. His name was carved in the 1824 Foundation Stone. For a small fee, the LMI's Birkbeck School offered elementary education to the children of working parents. In its time, it had a radical approach to education and not just for admitting the children of working- and lower-middle-class parents. It also espoused an educational philosophy that prohibited rote learning, focusing instead on Socratic dialogues between pupils and schoolmasters; equally unusual, it rejected the common practice in schools at that time of caning disobedient or 'dull' students. For Dickens, however, the LMI's Birkbeck School, together with the numerous other ones that imitated it, was just another example of utilitarian thinking and dogged self-interest run riot. As we shall see, introducing the Birkbeck School into the LMI mirrored the radical political economy espoused by the Institution's founding economists like Hodgskin, who sought to give working men and women ways to *critique* and *change* society. Although Ellis' vision was of a school that taught conciliation to the emerging industrial capitalism, it provided the skills with which less well-off children and their families could change their worlds.

* * *

---

[1] Charles Dickens, *Hard Times* (London: Chapman and Hall, 1905), chapter 2, at https://www.gutenberg.org/files/786/786-h/786-h.htm#page4, viewed 1 August 2021.

1848 has rightly been heralded as the year when the first Birkbeck School was founded. It did have an important predecessor, however, that has been entirely forgotten. Seventeen years before Ellis persuaded the managing committee of the LMI to establish their school, a builder called Pierre Barthelemy Guinebert De Bac had approached the Committee with an almost identical proposal. Very little is known about De Bac. He had been granted a patent for 'Improvements Relating to Rail Roads'. In 1831, he was reported to be a London-based builder who lived in Tavistock Square and had filed for bankruptcy.[2] Only five months after being declared bankrupt, however, De Bac persuaded the Committee of the LMI to lend him two rooms on the second floor of their Southampton Buildings to establish a day school for boys. Du Bac promised to draw up the plans and help with all the administration of the school 'free of expense'.[3] Junior pupils would be charged 1 guinea each quarter, while senior pupils would be charged £1 7s. Crucially, parents or wards who were already members of the LMI would be charged 7s. less than 'the sons of Strangers'.[4] Two thirds of the fees would go to pay for the schoolmaster, who was Samuel Preston, while the LMI would retain the final third.[5]

The school grew rapidly, from only five boys when the first class met on 2 January 1832 to fifty within six months. Their ages ranged from 6 to 16 years,[6] with more than 80 per cent attending the 'junior' class.[7] Like its successor, Du Bac and Preston's day school was a significant departure from other educational opportunities at the time. After all, it would be another forty years before the 1870 Elementary Education Act authorized local authorities to provide money for the schooling of children aged between 5 and 12 years. Most importantly, the school had a different attitude to discipline. Preston bragged that 'the discipline is wholly moral, neither external punishments nor external rewards being employed as stimuli either to the acquirement of knowledge or the practice of virtue'.[8] Pupils could learn Greek and Latin.[9]

Within a year of opening, however, the day school at the LMI was in trouble. Local residents wrote to complain about 'injurious annoyance' caused by 'the noise

---

[2] Also spelt Debac. 'Bankrupts', *Worcester Journal* (28 April 1831), 2; 'Bankrupts', *Bath Chronicle and Weekly Gazette* (28 April 1831), 3; 'Bankrupts', *Reading Mercury* (2 May 1831), 2; 'Bankrupts', *Morning Post* (23 April 1831), 1; 'Bankrupts', *The Globe* (27 April 1831); 'Bankrupts', *London Courier and Evening Gazette* (27 April 1831), 4.

[3] 'Birkbeck College (University of London). Extracts from Minutes', dated 19 September 1831, in Birkbeck Archive, Box 13, file 'Miscellaneous'.

[4] 'Birkbeck College (University of London). Extracts from Minutes', dated 7 November 1831, in Birkbeck Archive, Box 13, file 'Miscellaneous'.

[5] Ibid.

[6] 'Birkbeck College (University of London). Extracts from Minutes', dated 2 January and 4 June 1832, in Birkbeck Archive, Box 13, file 'Miscellaneous'.

[7] 'Birkbeck College (University of London). Extracts from Minutes', dated 4 June 1832, in Birkbeck Archive, Box 13, file 'Miscellaneous'.

[8] Ibid.

[9] 'Birkbeck College (University of London). Extracts from Minutes', dated 12 November 1832, in Birkbek Archive, Box 13, file 'Miscellaneous'. They did have to pay a slightly higher fee.

and improper conduct of the boys as they come to and go from the day school'.[10] On more than one occasion, pupils were reported to have 'assailed' members of the LMI with 'a shower of peas'.[11] The Committee responded promptly. 'While it must be observed that the conduct of boys outside of the school cannot come within the absolute control of the Committee', they began their letter, they promised to act if anyone could identify any of the boys who had been 'prominent for their misconduct'. They particularly wanted to know the names of students who had been 'running into all sorts of excesses and using language most disgusting and offensive'. The Committee would 'make such examples' of the offenders 'as will deter others from offending in a similar manner'.[12]

The day school did not survive these complaints. It is impossible to know whether schoolmaster Preston was fired on account of his inability to control the pupils or if he resigned upon hearing that his policy of not punishing pupils was to be abandoned. All we know is that Preston's job was re-advertised (see Fig. 5.1). The advertisement asked for a schoolmaster to teach

> Writing, Mercantile and Mental Arithmetic, the English Language comprehending Pronunciation, Grammar and Composition, Mathematics, Drawing and Lessons in objects of Nature and Art.[13]

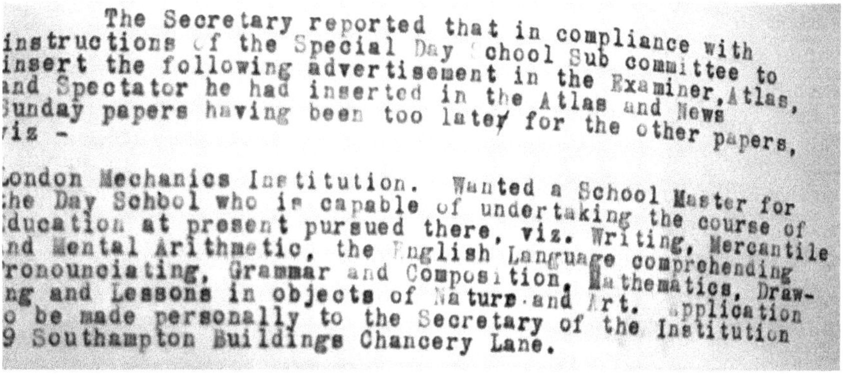

The Secretary reported that in compliance with instructions of the Special Day School Sub committee to insert the following advertisement in the Examiner, Atlas and Spectator he had inserted in the Atlas and News Sunday papers having been too later for the other papers, viz -

London Mechanics Institution. Wanted a School Master for the Day School who is capable of undertaking the course of education at present pursued there, viz. Writing, Mercantile and Mental Arithmetic, the English Language comprehending Pronounciating, Grammar and Composition, Mathematics, Drawing and Lessons in objects of Nature and Art. Application to be made personally to the Secretary of the Institution 29 Southampton Buildings Chancery Lane.

Fig. 5.1 The proposed advertisement for a new schoolmaster, in the LMI's minutes, 27 May 1833. Malet Street Archive.

[10] 'Birkbeck College (University of London). Extracts from Minutes', dated 28 January 1833, in Birkbeck Archive, Box 13, file 'Miscellaneous'. The person making the complaint on behalf of himself and others was Henry Chitty.

[11] 'Birkbeck College (University of London). Extracts from Minutes', dated 29 April 1833, in Birkbeck Archive, Box 13, file 'Miscellaneous'.

[12] 'Birkbeck College (University of London). Extracts from Minutes', dated 27 May 1833, in Birkbeck Archive, Box 13, file 'Miscellaneous'.

[13] Ibid.

No one applied. The LMI's first 'day school' was discontinued.

We don't know what job Preston took after the day school's closure, but the bankrupt De Bac seems to have flourished. By 1837, he was living in Brixton (Surrey) and claiming to be a civil engineer as well as a 'professor of languages and mathematics'. De Bac had also filed a patent for an invention of 'certain improvements applicable to railroads', specifically 'an improved machine for weighing, with the means of keeping a register of the operations of the instrument'.[14] In this transition from a bankrupt builder to school administrator to enterprising engineer and 'professor' of languages and mathematics, De Bac exemplified one model of the mechanics' movement.

* * *

The second episode in the education of children at the LMI had a longer and more successful life. Fourteen years after the closure of De Bac and Preston's day school, William Ellis, who had been a part of the mechanics' movement from its start and had made his money managing the Marine Indemnity Society, approached the Committee of the LMI with another proposal to establish a day school. He even pledged £1,000 from his own purse to get it off the ground.

Recalling the debacle of the previous initiative, the Committee was reluctant. Fourteen years earlier, their minutes had contended that 'If on a future occasion the Institution should be in a condition to provide accommodation for such school... the undertaking may be resumed', but only if they could be confident that it would not 'produc[e] the inconvenience now complained of'. They reminded themselves of the need to reflect on 'the experience of the present Class... in making a new arrangement'.[15] Ellis' offer gave them such an opportunity.

We have different versions of what happened after the governing committee received Ellis' offer. What is clear, however, is that they stalled. The Committee accepted that there was a need to offer 'a good secular education to the Children of members, as well as to children in general',[16] but they then failed to inform the wider membership that a concrete proposal, with a significant sum of money attached, had been made.

By September 1847, still nothing had happened. A small group of LMI members, including William Mattieu Williams (the keen phrenologist, electrical instrument maker, and electrotyper mentioned in the previous chapter), John Angell (chemist and ardent follower of phrenologist and philosopher George Combe), David William Mitchell (zoologist), and Chas. Aason (subsequently of

---

[14] 'New Patents', *Morning Adviser* (3 September 1837), 2. Also see 'List of New Patents', *Morning Adviser* (6 June 1837), 3, and 'Patents', *Mechanic's Magazine, Museum, Register, Journal and Gazette* (18 November 1837), 112.

[15] 'Birkbeck College (University of London). Extracts from Minutes', undated but between 27 May and 10 June 1833, in Birkbeck Archive, Box 13, file 'Miscellaneous'.

[16] 'Birkbeck College (University of London). Extracts from Minutes', 20 April 1847, in Birkbeck Archive, Box 13, file 'Miscellaneous'.

the W. H. Smith and Son railway booksellers) decided to press matters.[17] When the LMI's Committee submitted its annual report to the members, and failed even to mention Ellis' generous offer, for the first time in its history the report was 'not accepted by the members, but was, in consequence of the omission, sent back to the Committee for reconsideration'.[18] They persuaded forty members of the LMI to call for a Special General Meeting of the members to discuss Ellis' proposal and to make 'the necessary arrangements, if accepted, for its establishment'.[19] Five hundred copies of Ellis' offer were distributed. According to Williams, this started a 'revolutionary battle between the old Directors and the Members who supported the quartett [sic] group'.[20] The members won and a Birkbeck School Committee (which included Ellis) was established to manage the project. In honour of George Birkbeck, they agreed to call the school 'The Birkbeck School'.[21]

In the months before the first class in July 1848, Ellis appointed his friend John Rüntz to the post of schoolmaster with a £100 annual salary as well as a fee of 2s. per pupil.[22] Rüntz proved an inspired choice. He was a cabinet maker by trade but was an active member of the Metropolitan Board of Works and a campaigner for London's open spaces. He had attended evening classes to learn about music and art, followed by a course at the Training School of the British and Foreign School Society. He also had teaching experience and had ambitions for himself and his pupils.[23] It was decided that the sons or brothers of members would pay 4s. a quarter while other pupils were charged an additional 2s. (see Fig. 5.2).[24] The second day school was significantly cheaper than the earlier one.

The Birkbeck School flourished. Within two years, it was teaching 340 pupils, the maximum that could be accommodated, and a girls' school had been opened.[25] In addition, the school was being used to train future teachers in Ellis' methods, leading to the establishment of other Birkbeck Schools throughout the country.[26]

---

[17] 'A Pioneer Educator. W. Mattieu Williams', *The Character Builder: Devoted to Personal and Social Betterment*, ed. John T. Miller (February 1919), 47. This is identical to the text in John Angell, 'Memoir', in Williams, *A Vindication of Phrenology*, x.
[18] Angell, 'Memoir', in Williams, *A Vindication of Phrenology*, x.
[19] 'Birkbeck College (University of London). Extracts from Minutes', 27 September 1847, in Birkbeck Archive, Box 13, file 'Miscellaneous'.
[20] 'A Pioneer Educator. W. Mattieu Williams', *The Character Builder*, 47. This is identical to the text in Angell, 'Memoir', in Williams, *A Vindication of Phrenology*, x.
[21] 'Birkbeck College (University of London). Extracts from Minutes', 26 April 1847, in Birkbeck Archive, Box 13, file 'Miscellaneous'.
[22] 'Birkbeck College (University of London). Extracts from Minutes', 1 May and 12 June 1848, in Birkbeck Archive, Box 13, file 'Miscellaneous'.
[23] Edmund Kell Blyth, *Life of William Ellis (Founder of the Birkbeck Schools) with Some Account of his Writings and of his Labours for the Improvement and Extension of Education*, 2nd ed. (London: Kegan Paul, Trench, Trübner and Co. Ltd, 1892), 89. Rüntz's campaigns for open spaces is commemorated by a drinking fountain and a lake in Clissold Park in Hackney: Runtzmere.
[24] 'Birkbeck College (University of London). Extracts from Minutes', 15 July 1847, in Birkbeck Archive, Box 13, file 'Miscellaneous'.
[25] Letter from Ellis to Hodgson, 10 November 1850, in Blyth, *Life of William Ellis*, 79 and 85.
[26] Ibid., 85.

> **The Birkbeck School.**
> LONDON MECHANICS' INSTITUTION (Patron the Earl of Radnor) will recommence its Studies on Monday, January 8, 1849. The course of Instruction pursued in the above School is purely Secular, and includes Reading, Writing, Arithmetic, English Grammar, Composition, History, Geography, *Model and Inventive Drawing*, and Vocal Music, also the Elements of Algebra, Geometry, Mensuration, Mechanics, and of the Natural Sciences. The *Laws of Health*, and the Principles of Social and Political Economy. Terms. To Sons and Brothers of Members of the Institution,
>
>   4s. per Quarter or 4d. per week.
> Non Members 6s.   ditto   6d.   ditto.
>
> Prospectuses containing further particulars may be obtained at the Institution, 29, Southampton Buildings, Chancery-lane.
>
>   J. ANGELL, Hon. Sec.

Fig. 5.2 The 1849 Prospectus for the Birkbeck School, in the *Mechanics' Magazine, Museum, Register, Journal and Gazette*, 23 December 1848. Birkbeck Archive.

The schools attracted the interests of a diverse array of political and social reformers, including Lady Byron and Florence Nightingale. According to Nightingale, Ellis was providing

> the best and most effective teaching I have ever heard, bringing what are called the most difficult subjects in an absolutely clear and most *living* way to the understanding of a child, so as to make them practical and practicable.[27]

Leading British phrenologist George Combe also praised the schools and proposed setting up one in Edinburgh which would follow Ellis' principles while also emphasizing his pet 'science'. When Combe visited the school in the LMI and attended one class given by a 14-year-old 'monitor' to a group of sixty boys, he observed that 'One-half of the House of Commons might listen to these lessons with advantage'.[28] When Combe established his school in Edinburgh, he appointed Williams of the LMI as the first headmaster. The school was called the Williams Secular School in his honour.[29] Including the word 'secular' in the title was provocative. After all, as Combe worried, 'evangelical religion is strong, active,

---

[27] Personal communication to Edmund Kell Blyth from Florence Nightingale, cited in ibid., 98.
[28] Angell, 'Memoir', in Williams, *A Vindication of Phrenology*, xii.   [29] Ibid., xiv.

and penetrating' in Edinburgh, and 'it uses *all means* to command every class of the inhabitants'. He lamented that the Church

> will oppose our school, and vilify it and ourselves by every possible endeavour. Now it is so powerful that scarcely any person of the middle, and none of the upper ranks here will lend his name or countenance to our school, through sheer fear of the theological outcry, although many wish us well…This 'fear of folk' operates irresistibly in the class of persons from whom you desire to draw the pupils, viz., clerks and superior mechanics. They tremble before their evangelical masters and clergymen.[30]

Despite such opposition, the Williams Secular School opened in December 1848 and flourished.

Back in London, Ellis was becoming increasingly disgruntled. The school's balance sheet for 5 August 1848 hints at the tensions. While Ellis had personally donated £100 to the school fund and had collected an additional £177 from sponsors, the entire Committee of the LMI had only managed to raise £36.[31] Clearly, the Committee was still not fully committed. Ellis was also indignant when he was asked to pay rent for using the LMI's premises, even though (he claimed) the school was a net *gain* to the Institution because it attracted members.[32]

There is evidence that the Committee was still mulling over the 1832–3 debacle. They insisted that the pupils would only be allowed to enter the building via a door in Northumberland Court, rather than from the front entrance.[33] Sensibly, they ruled that pupils 'labouring under any contagious or infectious disease' should be refused entry, but they also barred pupils of 'uncleanly habits, or ragged appearance'. The schoolmaster was not only 'authorised' but '*required*' to 'prevent the attendance of such objectionable Pupils; and also to suspend any disorderly, mischievous, or improper character, who may have obtained admission'.[34] The respectability of the mechanics' institution had to be sustained at all costs.

Some of the more traditional members of the LMI's managing committee also looked askance at Ellis' educational philosophy. It was anything but conventional. The education was thoroughly secular: the Bible would not be studied, either as scriptural text or even as simply a reading book. This upset those in charge of Church schools. Ellis also argued against 'stuffing' pupils 'with dead languages,

---

[30] Ibid., xiv–xv.
[31] 'Birkbeck College (University of London). Extracts from Minutes', 7 August 1848, in Birkbeck Archive, Box 13, file 'Miscellaneous'.
[32] 'Birkbeck College (University of London). Extracts from Minutes', 28 January 1850, in Birkbeck Archive, Box 13, file 'Miscellaneous'.
[33] 'Birkbeck College (University of London). Extracts from Minutes', 15 July 1847, in Birkbeck Archive, Box 13, file 'Miscellaneous'.
[34] 'Birkbeck College (University of London). Extracts from Minutes', 15 July 1847, in Birkbeck Archive, Box 13, file 'Miscellaneous'. Emphasis added.

obsolete dogmas, or the discarded husks and refuse of science'.[35] He had quirky views about the study of subjects such as classics, history, and poetry. He argued that the study of classics taught pupils 'the filth and superstition of by-gone days', while history writing was typically of low quality and so should also be omitted from the curriculum. Poetry came in for an equally trenchant critique on the grounds that it was a dishonest art. As Ellis explained in *Conversations Upon Knowledge, Happiness, and Education Between a Mechanic and a Patron of the London Mechanics' Institution*, published during the first year of the Birkbeck School, the poet's aim was to 'excite intense feeling, to interest his reader warmly'. To do this, 'there is no degree of exaggeration that poets will not sometimes practice' and exaggeration 'is disregard of truth, and a disregard of truth is always mischievous'.[36] These aspects of his philosophy were what Dickens was lambasting in *Hard Times*: the Birkbeck School encouraged pupils to be 'people of fact, and of nothing but fact'.

Ellis was passionate about the teaching of what he called (at various times) 'political economy', 'social economy', 'economical science', the 'science of conduct', and the 'science of human well-being'. The Birkbeck School's prospectus even boasted that the emphasis on 'Human Well-Being' was what gave the school 'so distinctive a character'.[37] An understanding of 'social economy', Ellis argued, was the solution to the 'great evil' of poverty. It imparted three lessons. The first was knowledge about 'the means by which wealth or the comforts and necessities of life are produced', thus emphasizing the need for 'industry, skill, economy, and security to property... in order that this production may be abundant'. Second, a recognition of the 'advantages of the division of labour' and the 'co-operation of labour and capital', which would 'demonstrate beyond all doubt, how honesty, sobriety, punctuality, and moral discipline must obtain amongst a people for these arrangements to be fully serviceable'. Finally, 'social economy' would provide lessons in the importance of 'parental forethought or of parental improvidence'.[38] These three objectives would teach pupils

> how much their health, general energy, physical happiness, and length of life are dependent on their own conduct, also with the laws of social economy, that they may properly understand their own position in society, and their duties towards it.... The moral training is based on the principle that the moral feelings, like the physical and intellectual powers, can only be strengthened by actual exercise.[39]

---

[35] William Ellis, *Education as a Means of Preventing Destitution; With Exemplifications from the Teaching at the Birkbeck Schools* (London: Smith, Elder, and Co., 1851), 15.
[36] William Ellis, *Conversations Upon Knowledge, Happiness, and Education Between a Mechanic and a Patron of the London Mechanics' Institution* (London: Baldwin and Cradock, 1829).
[37] 'Birkbeck Schools. Prospectus', Howell Collection 12.27–374.5, at Bishopsgate Library.
[38] Ibid.   [39] Prospectus for the Birkbeck School, cited in Blyth, *Life of William Ellis*, 92.

The content of the classes was not the only uniqueness of Ellis' Birkbeck School. The other was the mode of teaching: dialogue rather than rote learning. This was the thing Dickens was lampooning in *Hard Times*. As a member of the LMI's management committee, Williams was a fan. He disparaged the conventional way of educating children by 'forcing the Boys to commit long sentences to memory' and hoped to create a school which would be 'a place of amusement and happiness instead of tears and trembling'.[40] Williams noted that classes would begin by Ellis or Rüntz telling the pupil what 'general principle' would be discussed. This would be followed by a series of questions and answers, starting with the most basic and gradually becoming more complex. The questions were merely suggestive, encouraging the pupils to 'reason for themselves as far as possible'. Definitions were 'amended' time and again,

> until the best and most concise definition was arrived at. Thus[,] they were not merely taught the definitions dogmatically, but were led to invent and agree to them and practically to learn why certain particular limitations or directions of definition were necessary.[41]

A concrete example of this 'Socratic' method of teaching was given by literary editor Henry Morley in an article published in Dickens' *Household Words* in 1851. To get a sense of this mode of teaching, the dialogue needs to be quoted in full. It went:

> 'What are wages?' Answers vary in form; 'The reward of labour', 'Capital employed to purchase labour', and so forth. 'When you become men, and work, and receive wages, will you all receive the same amount of money for your labour?'—'No, very different.'—'Why different?'—'The price paid for labour will depend among other things upon the value of it, and that differs in different people'—'How?'—'Some are more skilful than others.'—'Why so?'—'Because they have spent more time and pains, and perhaps money, to become able to do something; and they must be paid more for the more that they have spent.'—'Then the rate of wages that a man can earn in any business will depend upon his skill?'—'Yes, and on other things; men must be industrious. If two men are equally skilful, and one is more industrious than another, the one that is more industrious will give more valuable labour, and the price obtained by labour depends on the value of it.'—'The rate of wages depends then on the skill and industry of the labourer. On anything else?'—'Yes, he must be sober. He may be

---

[40] William Mattieu Williams, 'The Birkbeck School, London Mechanics' Institution. Under the Patronage of the Right Hon. The Earl of Radnor' (Edinburgh: n.p., 1848), 1, at https://iiif.wellcomecollection.org/pdf/b28749169, viewed 1 August 2021.
[41] William Mattieu Williams in a paper read to the Social Science Association in 1857, cited in Blyth, *Life of William Ellis*, 94.

very skilful and work hard, but he may get drunk and be unable to turn his skill and industry to full account. If he does that, he lessens his own value.'—'The best wages then go to the man who is skilful, industrious, and sober; are there any other qualities concerned in the contract between employer and employed?'... 'He must be honest.... If he is skilful, industrious, and sober without being trustworthy, his value to the employer is destroyed.' Honesty was, therefore, added to the list. 'He must be skilful, industrious, sober, and honest, yet, if he be nothing more', said the teacher, 'there is a workman who may beat him yet'.—'Yes', half-a-dozen cried, 'he must be punctual'.[42]

Morley's account of the dialogue was later ridiculed by Dickens, but Morley believed that such an education would transform the lives of working-class boys by emphasizing the need for self-help. The pupils in the Birkbeck School were 'learning what work means', Morley enthused, adding that pupils who underwent such training would never become part of 'the unhappy crowd' who act 'to its own hurt under the guidance of pot-house orators and pot-house prints'.[43] In other words, by lauding traits such as skill, hard work, sobriety, honesty, and punctuality, these pupils would become compliant workers in a hierarchically ordered labour market. As Ellis argued in *Education as a Means of Preventing Destitution; With Exemplifications from the Teaching at the Birkbeck Schools* (1851), the boys at the Birkbeck School in the LMI would be taught that competition was 'one of the most efficient agents for diffusing the benefits of industrial enterprise over the whole world'.[44] The pupils would learn that 'wages, profit, rent, prices, &c. adjust themselves harmoniously with well-being' and when something goes 'wrong in regard to these instruments of distribution', the solution was 'not to run riot in interminable gabbling [sic] and wrangling' but to 'confirm the social qualities'.[45] In sum, they would know 'their place' in the world.[46]

Some commentators did not think that the Birkbeck School in the LMI—and the ten similar schools that followed their model in London and elsewhere in the UK (including Manchester, Edinburgh, and Glasgow)—went far enough. John Robert Taylor, Secretary at the LMI, believed that the schools were so valuable in helping working people cope with 'inadequate wages, precarious and uncertain employment, and the great increase in the price of provisions since 1850' that he wanted to establish a fund to enable those families who could not afford the modest fees to attend. In an open letter addressed to Lord Brougham, Taylor made the

---

[42] Anon. [Henry Morley], 'Rational Schools', *Household Words* (25 December 1851), 339.
[43] Ibid., 340.   [44] Ellis, *Education as a Means of Preventing Destitution*, 113.
[45] Ibid., 153.
[46] It is important to observe, however, that William Mattieu Williams was willing to publish his tract on the Birkbeck School in the LMI alongside an exceptionally radical tract by William Lovett. See 'Letter from Mr William Lovett, In Explanation of the National Hall School, London', which is in the same book as Williams' 'The Birkbeck School, London Mechanics' Institution'.

case for providing the poorest of children with 'gratuitous instruction', once a certificate had been 'signed by an authorised person' bearing witness to their poverty.[47] He contended that the 'voluntary principle' was failing the poorest children, so steps were needed to educate *all* children through public subscription or local government grants.[48] It was a vision that would not come to fruition for another twenty years. When the 1870 Elementary Education Act was finally passed, establishing the London School Board and regulating teaching standards using public funds, it sounded the death knell for the Birkbeck Schools. The school at the LMI was finally closed in 1873.

Despite the end of the LMI's experiment in the education of children, the schools remain a living part of Birkbeck's history, with Birkbeck's Vice Chancellor appointing a governor to the William Ellis School, in Highgate (London), supported by the William Ellis and Birkbeck Schools Trust. The original Birkbeck School, however, was a radical one, despite Ellis' advocacy of a conservative economic ideology and his belief that competition was the way to create a balanced economy and peaceful coexistence between the different classes—each of whom accepted their 'place' in the world. The school's educational philosophy, refusal to appeal to theological texts, and 'Socratic' method of teaching, which makes pupils think critically for themselves, is still regarded as progressive. The Birkbeck School's aims—which were the 'acquisition of knowledge...not as a laborious task-work, but as the most agreeable as well as the most elevating pursuits' and 'active and intelligent citizens'—remain central to the College's mission today.[49]

---

[47] John Robert Taylor, 'Letter to the Right Honorable Lord Brougham and Vaux on Instituting Special Evening Classes, In Connection with the London Mechanics' and Other Similar Institutes' (London: n.p., 1857), 2.
[48] Ibid., 2.   [49] Williams, 'The Birkbeck School, London Mechanics' Institution', 1.

6
Ravenscroft's Birkbeck Bank

As we saw in the previous chapter, Charles Dickens enjoyed making fun of the earnest schoolmasters at the Birkbeck Schools, the first of which was established in the London Mechanics' Institution in the Southampton Buildings. Educational reformers such as Ellis and Rüntz, however, have generally been ignored, with the exception of some historians of elementary schools. The same can be said about two other businesses that operated from the Southampton Building: the Birkbeck Building Society and the Birkbeck Bank.

Like the Birkbeck Schools, these societies also regularly appeared in fiction. Baroness Orczy's *The Old Man in the Corner* is a case in point. Emma Magdolna Rozália Mária Jozefa Borbála 'Emmuska' Orczy de Orci was a popular Hungarian-born British novelist, celebrated for her play and novel depicting the adventures of the Scarlet Pimpernel.

The Old Man in the Corner, published in 1909, is a detective story in which an unprepossessing man sitting in a corner uses his keen reasoning powers to identify murderers. The last person to be killed in this novel was Mrs Owen, the caretaker of the small Rubens Studios for artists. She died after receiving a blow to the head followed by exposure to the cold. Mrs Owen was described as a 'quiet, respectable woman' who lived with her cockatoo and 'eked out her scanty wages by sundry—mostly very meagre—tips doled out to her by impecunious artists'.[1] Mrs Own was extremely thrifty. She 'lived on her wages; and all the tips added up, and never spent, year after year, went to swell a very comfortable little account at interest in the Birkbeck Bank'. Gradually, the tips 'mounted up to a very tidy sum', which was why the young artists in her studios referred to her as a 'lady of means'.[2] Shortly before her untimely death, Mrs Owen had been seen with a young man, whom she referred to as her 'nephew'. One day, the prudent Owen approached the cashier at the Birkbeck Bank and withdrew her entire savings, amounting to £827. She seemed 'exceedingly happy', the cashier later maintained. He warned her to be careful not to part with her money 'injudiciously', since he feared that was what 'women of her class are apt to do'. The novel's narrator followed this comment with the patronizing statement that 'women of that class are apt at times to mistrust the Bank of England', which was why he believed that the 'nephew'

---

[1] Baroness Emma Orczy, *The Old Man in the Corner* (London: Greening and Co., 1908), at http://www.gutenberg.org/ebooks/10556.
[2] Ibid.

must have used threats to convince Mrs Owen that 'her money is no longer safe even in the Birkbeck Bank'.[3]

The credibility of Baroness Orczy's plot relied on common beliefs about the type of person who banked with the Birkbeck Bank. They tended to be working- and lower-middle-class men and women who possessed small savings. Their customers distrusted large banks, such as the Bank of England, which were thought to be serving the interests of affluent depositors. The Birkbeck Bank was promoted as the institution which would protect thrifty women like Mrs Owen.

* * *

The Birkbeck Land and Building Society and Birkbeck Bank were the creations of Francis Ravenscroft (see Fig. 6.1). Today, Ravenscroft is known for the company 'Ede and Ravenscroft', the famous wig and gown makers, founded in 1689, whose robes Birkbeck students still wear on ceremonial occasions such as

Fig. 6.1 Bust of Francis Ravenscroft in Birkbeck's Council Room. Photograph courtesy of Sasha Dovzhyk.

---

[3] Ibid. Spoiler alert: in a twist to the story, it turned out that the 'old man in the corner', not the 'nephew', was responsible for her death.

graduations. Unsurprisingly, Francis Ravenscroft was a stylish man-about-town. According to William Bull (a keen Birkbeck art student who went on to become a leading solicitor and Conservative politician), Ravenscroft could often be seen strolling around the LMI in 'a curious suit of deep blue-black broad-cloth... with a waistcoat cut in a clerical manner, with a row of little buttons on one side, and black velvet skull cap'.[4] Some sense of his grandeur is evident in the bust of him which is on display in Birkbeck's Council Room.

Ravenscroft's early working life gave little sign that he would become a rich businessman. Although he belonged to a distinguished wig-making family, at the age of 15, Ravenscroft had been apprenticed to a tea taster. After only four months, he quit. Because he was bound into a five-year apprenticeship, this meant, as he explained in later years, that 'I ran away, thus rendering myself liable to be sent to Bridewell [prison], where all refractory apprentices were at that time imprisoned.'[5] Fortunately, his parents convinced the master to cancel the indenture. Ravenscroft then pursued a career in law, being appointed to work for a barrister and then a solicitor for seven years.

It was during this period that 19-year-old Ravenscroft joined the LMI. It was June 1848 and the Institution was in what looked like terminal decline. It had never fully recovered from the death of George Birkbeck in 1841. Not only did William Lloyd Birkbeck (George's son, who inherited the Presidency) have none of his father's fervour for the education of working people, but other educational organizations and libraries were now in direct competition with the LMI.[6] Indeed, the 1851 Census lists over 1,000 'literary and scientific' institutions in England and Wales. It also claims that there were more than 1,500 evening schools for adults, catering for nearly 40,000 pupils. There were twenty-eight mechanics' institutes in London alone.[7] As one long-standing member of the Institution's managing committee later recalled, 'public enthusiasm' for the LMI was dying. The Institution was 'hopelessly in debt, was badly housed, and dirty, and apparently at its last gasp'.[8]

Ravenscroft helped reverse its fortunes. Within a few months of his joining, William Ellis (whom we met in the previous chapter) managed to get Ravenscroft elected to the LMI's management committee; a month later, he was its Chair. Ravenscroft served the LMI from 1849 until his death in 1902. In fact, as Ravenscroft later admitted at a public meeting, when he was first nominated to become a member of the Committee, candidates were required to 'make a solemn

---

[4] Rt Hon. Sir William Bull, 'Forty Years Back', *The Lodestone*, 20.2 (1925), 6.
[5] 'The Two Birkbecks', *Building Societies' Gazette and Land Companies Record* (1 March 1899), 43.
[6] Ibid., 44.
[7] Sean Glynn, 'The Establishment of Higher Education in London: A Survey', in Roderick Floud and Sean Glynn (eds), *London Higher: The Establishment of Higher Education in London* (London: Athlone Press, 1998), 17.
[8] 'The Two Birkbecks', *The Building Societies' Gazette and Land Companies Record* (1 March 1899), 42.

declaration' that they were at least 21 years old. He wasn't. 'At that time I was in the eyes of the law an infant—(laughter)—and consequently was not entitled to serve', he admitted. However, 'being ambitious I recklessly signed the printed form—(laughter and "Oh, Oh")—and I am pleased to find that the institution has suffered no harm'.[9] In 1893, the *Birkbeck Institution Magazine* quipped that 'there is only one thing that Mr Ravenscroft has ever refused to do for our Institution, that is to make a speech'. When asked to, he would reply, 'I am a man of figures, not of words'.[10]

Around this same time, two other events changed Ravenscroft's life. First, his father died in 1851, which meant that he came into an inheritance. Second, the solicitor he worked for asked him to deal with a case involving 'a building society in difficulties' due to 'the misconduct of the manager and the society being unable to meet its liabilities'.[11] Ravenscroft explained that this gave him the opportunity 'of thoroughly investigating and properly understanding the general routine and intricacies of building societies'. He concluded that, if 'properly and honestly managed, with resources to meet withdrawals', building societies could be a 'safe and profitable investment'.[12] Ravenscroft's problem was 'providing a fund wherewithal to pay withdrawals upon demand'. This gave him the idea of also opening a deposit bank linked to the building society, promising that at least three quarters of the money would be invested in Consols (that is, government bonds), or other 'convertible securities'.[13] He drew up a set of rules and a prospectus for his 'proposed new society', which he then 'christened Birkbeck', due to his admiration of George Birkbeck.[14]

* * *

From the start, the Birkbeck Building Society and the LMI were closely linked. Ravenscroft initially based the building society and bank in a cupboard in the secretary's office of the LMI. Within less than a decade, he had taken over the entire ground floor, except for the lecture theatre in which Ellis and Rüntz taught pupils of the Birkbeck School.[15] Members of the Institution, therefore, had to walk through the public part of the bank in order to enter the LMI.[16] In the evening, the bank managers simply pulled down 'two vertical revolving shutters, extending from the floor to the ceiling', cutting off the counters.[17] The bank and the Institution even published their prospectuses in the same booklet. Most of the directors of the building society were members of the LMI, as was its President

---

[9] Ibid., 43.
[10] 'Birkbeck Men. Mr Francis Ravenscroft', *Birkbeck Institution Magazine* (January 1893), 34.
[11] 'The Two Birkbecks', 43.   [12] Ibid., 43.   [13] Ibid., 43.   [14] Ibid., 43.
[15] Bernard Becker, *Scientific London* (London: Henry S. King and Co., 1874), 209.
[16] A. Gavin Burns, 'Reminiscences of the Birkbeck Literary and Scientific Institution', *The Lodestone*, 19.2 (1924), 59.
[17] Ibid., 59.

(William Lloyd Birkbeck), Trustee (William Eward, Vice-President of the LMI), and Treasurer (Andrew MacFarlane, Secretary of the LMI). In 1852, Ravenscroft also co-opted Rüntz (whom we heard about in the previous chapter). Rüntz had valuable experience, having been associated with the British Empire Mutual Life Assurance Society since 1847. By 1860, Rüntz was a trustee of the Birkbeck Building Society and, eight years later, its Chairman. Ravenscroft believed that these links were 'a great advantage' to the fledging society.[18] It was one of the first 'permanent' building societies in the world.

Both the bank and the building society required a vast investment of time and energy: Ravenscroft boasted that he worked sixteen hours every day. Both flourished.[19] Within only a few years, Ravenscroft was turning over £20 million a year as a private banker.[20] This was an extraordinary sum at the time. By 1890, the Birkbeck Bank had more than 40,000 depositors.[21] It was the heyday of the 'penny banks', of which the Birkbeck was the largest.

Ravenscroft's building society and bank were unusual for their time. They set out to help men and women belonging to the working and lower middle classes, women like Mrs Owen in Orczy's *The Old Man in the Corner*, to buy their own homes through principles of mutual cooperation. Customers could also save

```
            ESTABLISHED 1851.
    BIRKBECK BANK,
       Southampton Buildings, Chancery Lane.
  THREE per CENT.INTEREST allowed on DEPOSITS,repayable on Demand.
  TWO per CENT. INTEREST on CURRENT ACCOUNTS, calculated on the
      minimum monthly balances, when not drawn below £100.
  STOCKS, SHARES, and ANNUITIES purchased and sold, and Letters of
      Credit and Circular Notes issued.
                  SAVINGS DEPARTMENT.
      For the encouragement of Thrift the Bank receives small sums on deposit,
  and allows Interest at the rate of THREE PER CENT. per Annum, on each
  completed £1. The Interest is added to the principal on the 31st Mar. annually.
      The BIRKBECK ALMANACK contains full particulars, and may be
  obtained post free, on application.    FRANCIS RAVENSCROFT, Manager.
  HOW TO PURCHASE A HOUSE FOR TWO GUINEAS PER MONTH, or
       a PLOT of LAND for FIVE SHILLINGS per MONTH, with immediate
  possession.
      The BIRKBECK ALMANACK contains full particulars, and may be had
  post free on application to       FRANCIS RAVENSCROFT, Manager.
      Southampton Buildings, Chancery Lane.
```

Fig. 6.2 Advertisement for the Birkbeck Bank, in *The British Women's Temperance Journal*, 1 November 1889.

---

[18] 'The Two Birkbecks', 43.   [19] Ibid., 43.
[20] G. F. Troupe Horne, 'Birkbeck', *The Lodestone*, 46.1 (autumn 1954), 11.
[21] Matthew Hollow, 'Strategic Inertia, Financial Fragility and Organisational Failure: The Case of the Birkbeck Bank, 1870–1911', *Business History*, 56.5 (2014), 752.

small sums of money in 'current' (or 'drawing') accounts. Unlike similar institutions at the time, the bank allowed customers to withdraw their money at any time. Perhaps more importantly, women were specifically targeted as customers, with advertisements placed in the *British Women's Temperance Journal* (see Fig. 6.2) and the *Woman's Herald*.[22]

* * *

A detailed exposition of the ambitions of the Birkbeck Building Society and Bank can be seen in a pamphlet published in 1855 and called *The Birkbeck Building and Freehold Land Societies Simplified and Explained in a Conversation between a Manager and a Person Desirous of Becoming a Member*, which was published by the LMI. The pamphlet was written in the form of a 'dialogue', similar to Ellis' Socratic method of education discussed in the previous chapter. It featured a married man simply called 'Stranger', who has six children. Stranger criticizes benefit societies on the grounds that members conducted their meetings in pubs and 'spent too much in drinking' as well as enjoying 'bands, and flags, and such-like amusements'.[23] The Manager of the Birkbeck Building and Freehold Land Society agrees with Stranger, informing him that pub landlords make money from benefit societies and 'instead of teaching men habits of economy, they in reality do the reverse'.[24] The Manager then recommends the Birkbeck Building Society, reasoning that

> Suppose, for instance, you occupy a small house and pay for it £10 a year rent, and that you can buy that house for £100. Well, you borrow the money of [*sic*] the Society, and by paying a small extra sum for interest beyond the rent, in about 19 years you make that house your own.[25]

The Stranger worries, stating that he had read in *Chambers's Journal* (a serious magazine of the time) that

> The working man is a migratory character—that his capital is his ability to move himself from one place to another, and that, therefore, a bit of ground or a house will do the working man more harm than good, as he will thus be tied down to a particular spot.[26]

---

[22] For example, see *British Women's Temperance Journal* (1 July 1889), 1, (1 November 1889), iv, and 1 December 1890, 144. Also see *Woman's Herald*, (20 July 1893), iv, (3 August 1893), iv, and (24 August 1893), ii.
[23] *The Birkbeck Building and Freehold Land Societies Simplified and Explained in a Conversation between a Manager and a Person Desirous of Becoming a Member* (London: London Mechanics' Institution, 1855), 5.
[24] Ibid., 6.   [25] Ibid., 6.   [26] Ibid., 16.

The Manager rejects this argument, maintaining that it was 'not at all desirable that the working man should be a migratory character'.[27] Instead, by cultivating habits of saving, the working man would 'never be a burden upon his friends or the parish, his expenditure will always be within his income—he will be a better citizen—a better father of a family—and a better friend than another man'.[28] He tells the Stranger that 'land is the best bank—it cannot run away—no fraudulent manager can escape with it to America or Australia'.[29] This was a reference to the Liberator Building Society, run by the Liberal politician Jabez Balfour, who left thousands penniless through fraud, and who fled to Argentina.

There was more to these arguments than financial security and the respectability of owning a home. Citizenship rights were involved (see Fig. 6.3). Crucially, according to the Representation of the People Act of 1832, the first of the great electoral Reform Acts, all male landowners living in properties worth at least £10 had the right to vote. Men who owned a home were granted suffrage. The Manager agreed that a working man 'desires to have a vote—it is quite right that he should

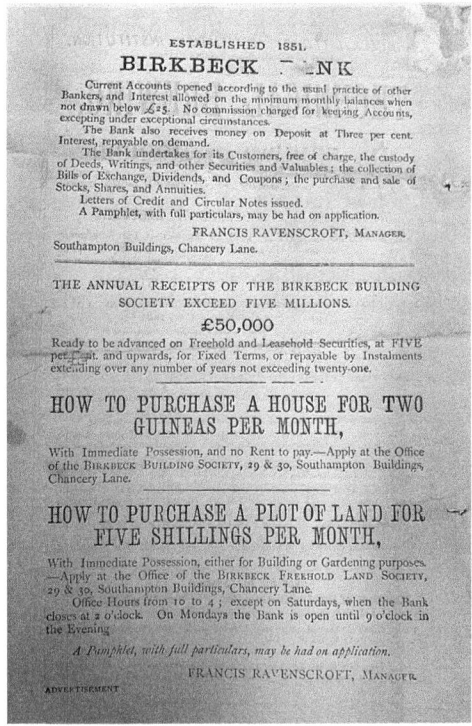

Fig. 6.3 An advertisement for the Birkbeck Bank and Building Society. Birkbeck Archive, 'Small Black Ring Binder', p. 7.

---

[27] Ibid., 16–17.   [28] Ibid., 17.   [29] Ibid., 22.

do so—it is a natural object of laudable ambition'. Together with 'the pecuniary advantages', it was irresistible. As the Manager reiterated, by

> belonging to the BIRKBECK LAND SOCIETY, you can have a nice piece of ground at Highgate or Holloway, which will make you a freeholder of the country of Middlesex; and then by means of the BIRKBECK BUILDING SOCIETY you will be able to build on it, and thus have the privilege and pride of living in a house of your own.[30]

In the last sentence of the pamphlet, the Stranger is convinced and gives the Manager 11s. to start his investment. Readers are informed that 'with a smile of satisfaction on his face', the working man then 'goes home to tell his wife that he will soon have a vote, and that she will soon have a house of her own to live in'.[31] The gender message was clear: prudent working men would win the right to vote; their thrifty wives, the duties of a home. All would be well in the world.

* * *

These societies were part of a move towards a different—more 'self-help'-orientated—form of moral control. In the words of *The Working Man's Friend* (1853), 'Savings banks make HAPPY HOMES.' They encouraged working people to exercise 'providence', or astute planning for the future. The 'steady worker', it declares, saves money in the Birkbeck Bank in order to gain 'Self-respect, true Independence, and Political Equality'.[32]

The Birkbeck Building Society and the Birkbeck Bank also played leading roles in the spread of a property-based citizenry as well as suburbanization. In the words of historian Richard Clarke, the Birkbeck Bank 'was a major element in the English property-based financial system and contributed significantly to the suburban growth of London'.[33] Many of their projects still exist today: the name 'Birkbeck' appears in the names of numerous estates and roads. Furthermore, despite the emphasis on temperance in pamphlets like the one involving a 'Conversation between a Manager and a Person Desirous of Becoming a Member', the Birkbeck estates also included pubs (see Fig. 6.4). Four Birkbeck pubs still survive, including the Highgate Birkbeck Tavern, which is now called the Boogaloo; it retains the Birkbeck mosaic in its entrance.[34]

However, not everyone was impressed by the bank's emphasis on self-help as opposed to more fundamental political and social reforms. Friedrich Engels, for

---

[30] Ibid., 23–4. [31] Ibid., 24. [32] *The Working Man's Friend* (19 February 1853), 333–4.
[33] Richard Clarke, 'Self-Help, Saving and Suburbanization: The Birkbeck Freehold Land and Building Societies, Their Bank, and the London Mechanics' Institute, 1851–1911', *London Journal*, 40.2 (2015), 123.
[34] Richard Clarke, 'Birkbeck Boozers', unpublished MSS, c.2016.

Fig. 6.4 A surviving Birkbeck pub. Richard Clarke, 'Birkbeck Boozers', unpublished MSS, *c*.2016.

example, pointed to a Birkbeck Land and Building Society advertisement that compared buying a house on a mortgage with the hire-purchase of a piano. He regarded this as proof that the bank's main customers were 'petty bourgeois and those who would like and are able to become petty bourgeois'.[35] Engels argued that

> These building societies are not workers' societies, nor is it their main aim to provide workers with their own homes…their chief aim is always to provide a more profitable mortgage investment for the savings of the petty bourgeoisie, at a good rate of interest and the prospect of dividends from speculation in real estate.[36]

There were more positive interpretations. In its early years, the building society was an attempt to extend the manhood franchise: an increase in the number of men who held property meant an increase in the number entitled to vote under

---

[35] Friedrich Engels, *The Housing Question* (Moscow: Co-operative Publishing Society of Foreign Workers, 1872), 67, at http://www.hlrn.org/img/documents/Engels%20The%20Housing%20Question.pdf, viewed 20 January 2021.
[36] Ibid.

the 1832 Reform Act. In the words of their prospectus of 1855, the Birkbeck Building Society aimed to

> facilitate the acquisition of Freehold land, and the erection of houses thereon, to enable such of its Members as are eligible to obtain the county franchise, and to afford a secure and profitable investment for money.[37]

It was also a recognition that the more radical plans of the Chartists had failed. In 1845, the Chartists had sold shares in their Land Company to working people. These shares were sold to fund the purchase of estates, which were then split up into smallholdings, and distributed via a ballot. In 1848, a House of Commons Select Committee declared the practice illegal, and the company was wound up in 1851—the same year that Ravenscroft established the Birkbeck Bank. In effect, this represented a shift *from* full workers' ownership *to* a more individualistic, self-help and (crucially) a profit-making approach to the politics of citizenship. As the Manager in that earlier pamphlet explained, the Birkbeck Building and Freehold Land Societies originally 'had a political bearing; but they have now lost that altogether'.[38]

* * *

Ravenscroft never gave up working for the LMI. He remained an active governor of the Institution for half a century. Indeed, Ravenscroft was largely responsible for changing the name of the London Mechanics' Institution to the Birkbeck Literary and Scientific Institution (BLSI) in 1866, commonly known as 'The Birkbeck'. Nevertheless, the building society and bank were his dominant enterprises. In the 1870s, 'the word Birkbeck to most people meant the Birkbeck Building Society and Bank, whose commercial activities had quite overshadowed the educational work of its parent'.[39] Ravenscroft created 'The Birkbeck' in the image of his building society and bank, not the other way round.

Nevertheless, the LMI would have been dissolved if Ravenscroft and his businesses had not given regular as well as generous support. This was the point James C. N. White (who was associated with the Institution for over thirty years as a member of the Committee and later its Chair) made during a speech in 1899. He maintained that, after the death of George Birkbeck, the

> majority of those responsible for the management gave up the struggle and resigned in a body. A few staunch friends remained for a time, but for various reasons retired soon afterwards, and then Mr. Ravenscroft, the only one to stick

---

[37] 1855 Prospectus, cited in Clarke, 'Self-Help, Saving and Suburbanization', 128. This point was made by Clarke, 'Self-Help, Saving and Suburbanization', 124.
[38] *The Birkbeck Building and Freehold Land Societies Simplified*, 23.
[39] 'F. A. W.' [Frederick A. Wright], 'Birkbeck in the Past', *Lodestone*, 30.3 (summer 1935), 122.

to the ship, was left with new associates. Of the 20 committee men, Mr. Ravenscroft was the only one of any age or position.... We went to him whenever we required assistance, and we never went in vain. (Cheers).[40]

This was never more the case when Ravenscroft provided the BLSI with a new building. The Southampton Buildings had been inadequate for decades. As A. Gavin Burns recalled of his time there in the 1870s, in the evenings 'the staircases and landings were packed full with people coming in and going out of the class rooms. The result was a good deal of delay in starting instruction.'[41] Clearly, new premises were urgently required. The autonomy of the Institution and its members was as important to the management committee in the 1880s as it had been for the LMI's founders, so they sought to raise money for a building through public subscriptions. White recalled that 'we badgered the Corporation very much; we badgered the City Companies; and we pestered our private friends' but they still failed to raise the necessary funds.[42] Ravenscroft stepped in—in much the same way that George Birkbeck had done in 1824. According to the *Birkbeck Institution Magazine*, Ravenscroft 'agreed to play the part of the Good Fairy'. He 'personally guaranteed the entire cost of the new building; he also undertook, at a later stage, to obtain an advance from his bank on favourable terms'. He collected subscriptions for the Building Fund and collected just under £4,000 (that is, around £500,000 today). Subscribers included royalty, William Lloyd Birkbeck, numerous guilds and corporations (including the City of London), and London's most prominent citizens, including many of Ravenscroft's friends and family (see Fig. 6.5).[43]

The building they acquired was Bream's Building (see Fig. 6.6), located near Fleet Street and formerly the home to publishers and printers. The surveyors boasted that 'Every part of the building is light: there are no dark corners.'[44] In short, it was perfect for the Institution. The Duke of Albany (Prince Leopold, the youngest son of Queen Victoria and Prince Albert) laid its foundation stone but, by the time the building opened, the Duke had died. On 4 July 1885, therefore, it was the Prince of Wales (later, King Edward VII) who opened the building. In his opening address, the Prince expressed his 'heartfelt satisfaction...in visiting an Institution with which my lamented brother's name will ever be associated'. He noted that

[40] 'The Two Birkbecks', 42.
[41] A. Gavin Burns, 'Reminiscences of the Birkbeck Literary and Scientific Institution', *The Lodestone*, 19.2 (1924), 60.
[42] 'The Two Birkbecks', 42.
[43] 'Birkbeck Men. Mr Francis Ravenscroft', *Birkbeck Institution Magazine* (January 1893), 34.
[44] 'Windsor House, Bream's Buildings & Cursitor Street', plans (London: Cuthbert Lake and Sutton, n.d., c.1880s), in Birkbeck Archive.

Amongst the Donors to the Building Fund are the following:—

Donor	£	s.	d.	Donor	£	s.	d.
Her Majesty the Queen	50	0	0	The Worshipful Company of Joiners	15	15	0
H.R.H. the late Duke of Albany	50	0	0	The Worshipful Company of Vintners	10	10	0
The Corporation of London	420	0	0	W. Lindley, Esq.	205	0	0
The City and Guilds of London Institute	150	0	0	Samuel Morley, Esq., the late	200	0	0
The Worshipful Company of Clothworkers	205	0	0	F. Ravenscroft, Esq.	1700	0	0
The Worshipful Company of Goldsmiths	175	0	0	W. Lloyd Birkbeck, Esq., (including legacy)	450	0	0
The Worshipful Company of Fishmongers	157	10	0	J. Vernham, Esq.	200	0	0
The Worshipful Company of Grocers	125	0	0	Dr. Leggatt	126	0	0
The Worshipful Company of Drapers	105	0	0	The Right Hon. The Baroness Burdett-Coutts	100	0	0
The Worshipful Company of Mercers	105	0	0	Proceeds of Reading by Henry Irving, Esq.	212	5	10
The Worshipful Company of Carpenters	50	0	0	W. Burdett-Coutts, Esq., M.P.	100	0	0
The Worshipful Company of Cordwainers	26	5	0	His Grace The Duke of Westminster	100	0	0
The Worshipful Company of Salters	26	5	0	The Right Hon. The Earl of Northbrook	100	0	0
The Worshipful Company of Leathersellers	25	0	0	T. E. Knightley, Esq.	78	15	0
The Worshipful Company of Merchant Taylors	21	0	0	Messrs. Clayton & Aston	78	15	0
The Worshipful Company of Skinners	21	0	0	The Right Hon. The Earl of Derby	70	0	0
George Palmer, Esq.	52	10	0	Alderman Sir Thomas Dakin	10	10	0
His Grace The Duke of Bedford	50	0	0	John Walter, Esq.	10	10	0
J. Passmore Edwards, Esq.	50	0	0	Sir H. W. Peek, Bart.	10	10	0
Trustees of the Mitchell Charity	50	0	0	General Sir George Balfour, M.P.	10	10	0
H. Ravenscroft, Esq.	52	10	0	Sir Samuel Wilson, M.P.	10	10	0
Messrs. Smith, Payne & Smiths	35	10	0	F. D. Mocatta, Esq.	10	10	0
Warren De la Rue, Esq., the late	31	10	0	Octavius E. Coope, Esq., the late	10	10	0
His Grace The Duke of Devonshire	25	0	0	Professor Charles Tomlinson	10	10	0
The Right Hon. Lord Carlingford	25	0	0	F. T. Mappin, Esq., M.P.	10	10	0
Henry Vaughan, Esq.	25	0	0	R. B. Lloyd, Esq.	10	10	0
George M. Norris, Esq.	26	5	0	Stuart M. Samuel, Esq.	10	10	0
Proprietor of the "Daily Chronicle"	25	0	0	Arthur Pease, Esq.	10	10	0
The Right Hon. The Earl of Shaftesbury, the late	20	0	0	H. R. Williams, Esq.	10	0	0
The Right Hon. Lord Aberdare	20	0	0	Miss Soames	10	10	0
Sir Julian Goldsmid, Bart., M.P.	21	0	0	Messrs. Barclay, Bevan, & Co.	10	10	0
J. W. Zambra, Esq.	21	0	0	Messrs. Barnetts, Hoares, & Co.	10	10	0
Alderman Sir Reginald Hanson, Bart.	21	0	0	Messrs. Hoares	10	10	0
Alderman Sir J. Whittaker Ellis, Bart., M.P.	21	0	0	Messrs. Donald Currie, & Co.	10	0	0
Messrs. Thomas De la Rue & Co.	21	0	0	Messrs. Rothschilds	10	0	0
The Prudential Assurance Company	21	0	0	Messrs. Eyre & Spottiswoods	10	10	0
Elizabeth, Countess of Harrington	20	0	0	F. Nettlefold, Esq.	10	0	0
E. J. Watherson, Esq.	21	0	0	J. H. Fordham, Esq.	10	10	0
John Runtz, Esq.	21	0	0	J. L. Ohlson, Esq.	10	10	0
A. W. Mason, Esq.	20	0	0	Messrs. Thomas Taplin & Co.	10	10	0
J. C. N. White, Esq.	20	0	0	H. Harben, Esq.	10	10	0
W. Simpson, Esq.	16	16	0	G. Chaloner, Esq.	10	10	0
The Right Hon. The Earl of Lytton	15	15	0	G. A. Smith, Esq.	10	0	0
J. Corbett, Esq., M.P.	15	15	0	Wm. J. Bull, Esq.	10	10	0
J. B. Birkbeck, Esq.	15	15	0	Dr. J. H. Gladstone	10	10	0
Messrs. Shaw & Sons	15	15	0	Cecil S. Judd, Esq.	8	8	0
E. J. Ravenscroft, Esq.	15	15	0	Rev. G. Henslow	7	0	0
W. H. Congreve, Esq.	15	15	0	H. Wells Eames, Esq.	6	6	0
Messrs. Brown, Gould, & Co.	15	5	0	The Right Hon. The Earl of Milltown	5	0	0
Dr. Wendt	15	5	0	The Right Hon. The Earl of Aberdeen	5	0	0
The Hon. Dudley Campbell	13	13	0	The Right Hon. Viscount Harberton	5	5	0
His Grace The Archbishop of Canterbury	10	0	0	The Right Hon. The Earl of Meath	5	0	0
The Most Hon. The Marquis of Lansdowne	10	0	0	The Hon. Mr. Justice Denman	5	5	0
The Right Hon. Viscount Cranbrook	10	0	0	Sir Frederick Pollock, Bart., the late	5	5	0
Lady Wantage	10	0	0	Alderman Sir William M'Arthur, the late	5	5	0
The Right Hon. W. H. Smith, M.P.	10	10	0	Sir Frederick Leighton	5	5	0
Viscountess Ossington	10	10	0	The Right Hon. Sir Thomas Dyke Acland, Bart.	5	0	0
T. C. Baring, Esq., M.P.	10	10	0	Sir David Salomons, Bart.	5	5	0
Lady Goldsmid	10	10	0	Isaac Braithwaite, Esq.	5	0	0
Lord Edmond Fitzmaurice	10	10	0	Sir C. W. Siemens, the late	5	0	0
Alderman Sir Polydore De Keyser	10	10	0	Dorabjee Pestonjee Cama, Esq.	5	5	0
Alderman Sir J. C. Lawrence, Bart.	10	10	0	John Penn, Esq.	5	5	0

Fig. 6.5 The list of subscribers to Bream's Building, 'Windsor House, Bream's Buildings & Cursitor Street', plans (London: Cuthbert Lake and Sutton, n.d., c.1880s). Birkbeck Archive.

Fig. 6.6 A photograph of Bream's Building, 'Windsor House, Bream's Buildings & Cursitor Street', plans (London: Cuthbert Lake and Sutton, n.d., c.1880s). Birkbeck Archive.

> Sixty years ago the Duke of Sussex performed the inaugural ceremony of your old building, and it speaks much for the vitality of your Institution, that after so lengthened a period a member of my family should be again invited to declare a building open so extensive as this one.... An Institution in which provision is made for 6000 Students, and to which both sexes are invited, must exert a very beneficial influence on the young men and women of the metropolis.[45]

Ironically, the man who had been central to the creation of the new building—Ravenscroft—appeared nowhere in the opening ceremony except in the list of 'donors' to the Building Fund. The list reveals, however, that Ravenscroft's donation of £1,700 was nearly four times larger than the second largest donation, which was made by George Birkbeck's son, William Lloyd Birkbeck.

What did this mean for the Birkbeck Bank? In 1896–7, the old Mechanics' Institute in Chancery Lane was torn down. By 1902, the Birkbeck Bank had

---

[45] 'Opening of the Breams Buildings' (1885), 1–2, in Birkbeck Archive, Box 3a.

reopened in what the *Architectural Review* dubbed 'the greatest single extravaganza of central London'.[46] The building had a huge hall which was six floors high, culminating in a gilded dome larger than that of the Bank of England. The inside was all carved wood, yellow tiles, and iron balustrades. There were large, naked children in white china; and the banking hall had black-and-white tiles. One of the symbols repeated throughout the build was 'B', for Birkbeck. Around the outside were reliefs of Birkbeck, as well as poet Lord Alfred Tennyson, essayist Charles Lamb, engineer Isambard Kingdom Brunel, artist Michelangelo, and steel-maker Sir Henry Bessemer. Its grandiose style did not impress Nikolaus Pevsner, Birkbeck's first Professor of the History of Art: for him, the style should be condemned as a 'phantasmagoria'.[47]

Crisis came in two waves. The first was on 12 September 1892. Corruption had been uncovered at the Liberator Building Society, leaving thousands of investors penniless. As a response to the scandal, depositors belonging to the Birkbeck Bank panicked. Ravenscroft later recalled that Chancery Lane was 'blocked with thousands of hungry-looking, anxious depositors, all anxiously waiting their turn to be paid'.[48] The *Illustrated London News* had more exciting things to say. It claimed that

> the doors of the Birkbeck were besieged by a frantic throng, chiefly women, with only one thought—that of saving the small store which, in many cases, represented the savings of years.... Vendors of provisions, chiefly bread and hard-boiled eggs, drove a roaring trade among the famished depositors, many of whom had bitter reason to repent their distrust of the bank. The pickpockets were busy, and it is said that in some instances hundreds of pounds were stolen.[49]

In other words, these were women like the Baroness's Mrs Owen, except that the cost of not trusting The Birkbeck was being targeted by pickpockets, not murderers.

Ravenscroft responded quickly, extending opening hours to allow customers to withdraw their money and even printing additional withdrawal forms. Nearly £1.6 million was withdrawn from the bank in a few days.[50]

Even a distinguished medical journal, *The Lancet*, reported the event, linking the financial panic to wider fears about degeneration, reverse evolution, and societal collapse. *The Lancet* claimed that such panics should only occur in 'savage existence', not 'civilised' societies. It reminded its readers that the evolutionary biologist and political theorist Herbert Spencer had observed that the 'chief

---

[46] Nicholas Taylor, 'Ceramic Extravagance', *Architectural Review*, 138 (1965), 320.
[47] Nikolaus Pevsner, *The Buildings of England: London I. The Cities of London and Westminster* (Harmondsworth: Penguin, 1973), 477.
[48] 'The Two Birkbecks', 43.
[49] 'The Run on the Birkbeck Bank', *Illustrated London News* (17 September 1892), 355.
[50] Hollow, 'Strategic Inertia, Financial Fragility and Organisational Failure', 754.

distinction between the human being and the brute' was the ability of the human to 'cultivate the faculty of self-control'. In contrast, 'maniacal excitement', along with the 'other symptoms of derangement, loss of appetite, watchful and sleepless nights and a total inability to think soberly on any subject', would result in 'an insane rush of selfish impetuosity'. Furthermore, the effects of panics tended to linger: the spooked depositors in the Birkbeck Bank could be expected to suffer from 'nervous exhaustion and prostration'; some might even have to be incarcerated in lunatic asylums. Physicians had a duty to inspire calm by helping people cultivate 'the all-important moral attributes of self-control, self-restraint, self-government'.[51] In effect, *The Lancet* was pathologizing bank panics as an illness.

The crisis was averted in 1892, but the Birkbeck Bank had less luck in 1911. Ravenscroft, with his calm, intuitive business acumen, had died in 1902, and his successors were less canny. This second panic began after an anonymous letter was sent to all depositors of the Birkbeck Bank on 8 November 1910. It read:

> Dear Sir or Madam—For your personal information I beg you to withdraw your deposits from the Birkbeck Bank as I have heard on sound authority that the company are in very low water, and there may be a run on the bank any day. This has occurred through the failure of the Charing Cross Bank. There may be no cause for anxiety, but it is well to be on the safe side—Yours, A Friend.[52]

Once again, hundreds of depositors streamed into Chancery Lane (see Fig. 6.7); the bank's managers responded in the same way they had in 1892. But this time, the fall in the value of government bonds and other gilt-edged securities, which made up over 80 per cent of its total assets, meant that the Bank suffered significant loses. Its chief problem had been its failure to adapt quickly enough to changing market conditions.[53] It turned out that Orczy's 1909 novel, *The Old Man in the Corner*, was two years too early: Mrs Owen's money really was 'no longer safe even in the Birkbeck Bank'.[54]

The fall of the bank—which occurred on 11 June 1911—was inevitable. There was nothing to be done and the bank was taken over by the London and Westminster. The splendid building, with its golden dome, was finally demolished in 1962 to make way for a modernist-style office block in which the Chancery Lane branch of the Westminster Bank is now housed.

The run on the Birkbeck Bank was immortalized in Walt Disney's 1962 film *Mary Poppins*, which was set in 1911. In the film, some elderly bankers (including Grubbs Fidelity Fiduciary Bank) attempt to persuade young George Banks to

---

[51] 'The Birkbeck Panic: A Maniacal Excitement', *The Lancet* (24 September 1892), 732. For a response, see 'The Birkbeck Panic: A Maniacal Excitement', *The Lancet* (8 October 1892), 859.
[52] For a detailed analysis, see Hollow, 'Strategic Inertia, Financial Fragility and Organisational Failure', 758.
[53] Ibid., 746–64.   [54] Orczy, *The Old Man in the Corner*.

Fig. 6.7 Crowds gathering outside the Birkbeck Bank during the 1911 crisis. Getty Images.

invest his tuppence. Even small investments, they claim, will yield great wealth. As one verse puts it,

> If you invest your tuppence wisely in the bank,
> Safe and sound,
> Soon that tuppence safely invested in the bank,
> Will compound.
> And you will achieve that sense of conquest,
> As your affluence expands...[55]

George resists but has the coin taken from him. When others in the bank hear him crying out, 'Give me back my money!', there is a run on the bank. The cultural memory of what happened to the Birkbeck Bank inspired the scene.

* * *

The closure of Ravenscroft's Birkbeck Bank was a sad end to a business that had flourished for sixty years. The bank had been an integral part of the pioneering spirit that characterized the life of the LMI/Birkbeck. Although, unlike the

---

[55] *Mary Poppins*, the run on the bank scene at https://www.youtube.com/watch?v=GW-22ZtfhBU.

Birkbeck School, the bank remained removed from the main vocation of an educational institution, it nevertheless bridged the two activities that can be seen as important instruments of social control: education and finance. As with the earlier controversies, education became part of a much wider canvas that aimed at social peace and mobility through the educational and financial improvement of the working class.

In 1911, the Birkbeck Literary and Scientific Institution paid homage to the bank, admitting that the bank had been responsible for the Institution's survival. Ravenscroft, too, was grateful to Birkbeck. Four years before his death at the age of 73, Ravenscroft boasted that he was the 'oldest continuous manager of any building society and bank in the world'.[56] He tirelessly praised the BLSI for his successes in life. His 'gratitude', he maintained,

> knows no bounds, for it is very largely to my association with the Birkbeck that I owe my success in life. This obligation I can never forget, and the sense of it increases as the years go by. Any efforts of mine, therefore, to promote the interests of the institution I regard as but a poor and inadequate return for the benefits that I have myself received.[57]

It was a generous remark from a brilliant and benevolent man.

---

[56] 'The Two Birkbecks', 43.   [57] Ibid., 43.

7
Governing the College

There would be no university community without effective governance. It requires skilled management, cautious financial control, astute estate and classroom planning, and an executive that inspires confidence among the teaching, research, and administrative staff as well as the students. It increasingly demands sensitivity to state policies and priorities, in addition to shrewdness with respect to externally imposed benchmarks.

This chapter traces some of the most important shifts in the governance of LMI/Birkbeck in the past 200 years. It argues that, after the initial struggles in the 1820s, which have been explored in earlier chapters, the College and its management went through four major periods of transformation: the student revolt of the 1880s, the creation of the City Polytechnic in the 1890s, the upheavals of federalism in the 1920s, and the imposition of 'new managerialism' associated with state neoliberal policies from the 1970s onwards. There were two other major transformations in governance—introduced as a response to the crises of 1986 and 2008—but these are discussed separately in Chapter 27 entitled 'Containing the Crisis'. This chapter will conclude by providing a sketch of the types of men and women who have held the most influential leadership roles in the College. What does an analysis of changes in their personal and political characteristics add to debates about the nature of the university?

* * *

In 1823, the LMI was a 'small Democracy' or 'little Republic' with fewer than 2,000 subscribing 'members', as they were called, not 'students'.[1] During the first few decades of its existence, it was dependent on the charity of generous benefactors such as George Birkbeck, Francis Ravenscroft, and the expansive political and social networks mobilized by Francis Place and Henry Brougham. Financial stability was also (and increasingly) dependent on annual subscriptions paid by members of the Institution. Members were charged 5s. per quarter, the equivalent of one day's wage for a skilled tradesman.[2] For this sum, members were given free admission to weekly lectures and entertainments, half-price tickets to any of the special classes, and admission to the reading room and library of 7,000 volumes.[3] Library

---

[1] Henry Buss, *Eighty Years Experience of Life* (London: Thomas Danks and Sons, 1893), 43.
[2] John George Godard, *George Birkbeck, the Pioneer of Popular Education: A Memoir and a Review* (London: Bemrose and Sons, 1884), 64.
[3] Bernard Becker, *Scientific London* (London: Henry S. King and Co., 1874), 206.

access was a powerful incentive. At a time when few unskilled workmen earned more than 10–12s. a week, most books cost between 6s. and 10s.; the average price of books listed under 'Novels, Biography, Travel, and Poetry' was over 14s. Books on art or law were significantly more expensive.[4] Many members joined the LMI solely for the pleasure of reading.

At the beginning of the LMI, the President was George Birkbeck, although the day-to-day administration of the Institution was carried out by a General Committee, elected by the members. As we saw in Chapter 2, according to its Charter, the managing Committee consisted of a two-thirds majority of working mechanics. The President chaired the Committee when in attendance. When he was absent (as was frequently the case when William Lloyd Birkbeck, George Birkbeck's son, inherited the presidency in 1841), the Committee would elect a member to preside. Smaller subcommittees were formed to deal with specific issues, such as financial management, decisions about the subjects to be taught, and the appointment of lecturers. These subcommittees would make recommendations to the General Committee, which, through its Secretary, would make the final decision.[5]

Effectively, then, the most powerful person in the Institution was the Secretary. In the LMI's early years, the longest-standing Secretary was Andrew MacFarlane. Unfortunately, we know little about him except for the fact that he served as Secretary for thirty-three years between 1830 and 1863. He was also Treasurer for the Birkbeck Bank and may have been the inventor of MacFarlane's Circular Interest Rate and MacFarlane's Cylindrical Slide Rule.[6]

Arguably, the most influential of the early secretaries was George M. Norris. His importance lies not only in his secretaryship (which lasted only six years) but also in the fact that he occupied every important managerial post within the Institution/Birkbeck for forty-two years. Norris joined the Institution in 1859 as a 17-year-old student.[7] Within seven years, he had been appointed Secretary. At that stage, Norris was working as a civil servant for the Board of Education, which wasn't a problem because the post at the LMI was part time: he was expected to be present for one hour in the morning and then from 7.10 p.m. until 10 p.m., six days a week.[8] Norris served in this post from 1866 to 1872. It was under Norris' stewardship that the declining fortunes of the LMI were reversed. He argued that the London Mechanics' Institution had to change its name. In a 'great commercial

---

[4] Frances Hawes, *Henry Brougham* (London: Jonathan Cape, 1957), 165.
[5] Buss, *Eighty Years Experience of Life*, 43–4.
[6] See Florian Cajori, *A History of the Logarithmic Slide Rule and Allied Instruments* (London: Archibald Constable and Co., 1909), 51, at http://cs.furman.edu/~chealy/cs273e/A_History_of_the_Logarithmic_Slide_Rule.pdf, viewed 12 April 2021. Also see Florian Cajori, 'The Slide Rule', at www.sliderules.info/pdf/cajori.pdf, 26, viewed 12 April 2021. Cajori is unsure whether this is MacFarlane of the LMI or Donald McFarlane [sic], laboratory assistant to Lord Kevin at Glasgow University.
[7] George Senter, 'George Morris Norris', *The Lodestone*, 19.2 (spring 1924), 83.
[8] Ibid., 83–4.

city', he contended, the word 'mechanics' was inappropriate if they were to 'attract a wider range of students'.[9] In 1867, less than one year after he became Secretary, he persuaded the Committee, by twenty-nine votes to seventeen, to change the name of the LMI to the Birkbeck Literary and Scientific Institution (BLSI).[10] Norris resigned as Secretary in 1872 and the following year was made Chair of the Committee. Committee members no longer voted for the Chair at their meetings in the absence of the President. This role was given to Norris, making him responsible for the 'general supervision of the Institution'.[11]

In 1885, William Lloyd Birkbeck, who was the President, had largely withdrawn from governance of the Institution after he became the Downing Professor of Laws of England in 1860 and was appointed Master of Downing College. After forty-four years as President (and he served for another three years), William Birkbeck was relieved to be able to hand over the day-to-day running of the college to Norris. Norris became the Institution's first 'Manager', the title of which was later changed to 'Principal'. In today's nomenclature, this makes Norris the College's first Vice-Chancellor. He was to serve in this position until 1896, when he was replaced by George Armitage-Smith, even though Norris remained a governor until 1908.[12]

Norris' tenure in the LMI/Birkbeck lasted nearly fifty years between 1859 and 1908. During that time, he held all the most senior positions, in turn. His length of service was only exceeded by that of James Charles Napoleon White, who joined the Birkbeck Institute in 1862, as Secretary of Classes. White was a young man who had excelled in art at the St Martin's School of Art, but was keen to join the Institution's elocution classes, in which he won prizes. By 1866, White had been elected a member of the Committee. He was only 21 years old, the minimum age a person could be elected.[13] He became Treasurer in 1887[14] and Chair of the governing body from 1891 until he retired in 1921. In other words, White had held senior important roles at the LMI/Birkbeck for nearly sixty years.[15]

The other long-serving Secretary at the LMI/Birkbeck was William Henry (W. H.) Congreve who succeeded Norris in 1872 when Norris left to become Chair of the Committee, then Principal. Congreve was Secretary for thirty-four years between 1872 and 1906. His father had been a progressive printer and friend of the anti-slavery activist MP George Thompson. Congreve had followed

---

[9] 'Ourselves', *Birkbeck Institution Magazine* (October 1892), 10.
[10] Letter from the Secretary to Delisle Burns, dated 25 September 1923, and citing from the minutes in 1866–7, in 'Birkbeck College letters 1923.2', Birkbeck Archive, Box 65.67.
[11] Resolution of the General Committee of 16 June 1873: cited in C. Delisle Burns, *A Short History of Birkbeck College (University of London)* (London: University of London Press, 1924), 83.
[12] George Senter, 'George Morris Norris', *The Lodestone*, 19.2 (spring 1924), 84.
[13] 'Birkbeck Men. Mr James C. N. White', *Birkbeck Institution Magazine* (March 1893), 53.
[14] Or 1878 according to 'Birkbeck Men. Mr James C. N. White', 54.
[15] George Senter, 'James C. N. White', *The Lodestone*, 19.2 (spring 1924), 82.

in his father's footsteps.[16] He had started the magazines *Diogenes* and the *Comic Times*, both in opposition to *Punch*.[17] Like White, Congreve had joined the elocution class at the Institution in 1851, aiming to improve his performances in comedies and farces. From the 1850s, Congreve served as Secretary to the elocution as well as Latin classes, he was appointed to a seat on the Committee of Management, then served as librarian. By 1872, he was both Secretary and Librarian or, as the *Birkbeck Institution Magazine* admitted in 1893, he was 'expected to know everything, to remember everything, and to do everything'. No wonder, they explained, he often appeared to be 'ruffled'.[18]

At least some of these men were supported by the considerable behind-the-scenes emotional and social labour of their wives. This was rarely acknowledged. One of these exceptional admissions can be found in the *Birkbeck Institution Magazine* in 1893 where the author observed that there were 'many duties in an Institution attended by both sexes which must be undertaken by a lady'. 'Mrs White' was said to perform these tasks 'in the most perfect manner'. The 'rare grace and charm with which she receives distinguished personages on ceremonial days, and her amiable acquiescence in the demands made upon her leisure, call forth…admiration'.[19] Unfortunately, this admiration did not extend to telling readers her name.

* * *

MacFarlane, Norris, White, and Congreve contributed to the Institution's governance in various capacities for thirty-three, forty-two, fifty-nine and thirty-four years, respectively. There was considerable overlap in tenure between Norris and White, but these four men essentially ran the Institution for ninety-one of its first 108 years in existence.[20] Is it any wonder that their longevity caused one of the most serious rifts in the Institution's governance?

Norris, White, and Congreve were young men when they arrived at the College, keen to improve their own lives, as well as others', through the acquisition of 'useful knowledge'. By the 1880s, they were middle aged and, when they retired, elderly. Their views were increasingly at odds with the new generation who were politically progressive in mentality. Their seeming permanency in positions of power in the Institution, together with what was euphemistically called White's 'strength of character' (remember, one of White's middle names was Napoleon),[21] riled many members or, as they increasingly began calling themselves, students.[22] They began criticizing the Committee for its remoteness. Even a laudatory biography

---

[16] 'Birkbeck Men. Mr W. H. Congreve', *Birkbeck Institution Magazine* (May 1893), 77.
[17] Ibid., 78.   [18] Ibid., 78.   [19] Ibid., 54.
[20] MacFarlane 1830–63; Norris 1866–1908, not including his time as a student from 1859; White 1862–1921; Congreve 1872–1906.
[21] 'F. A. W.' [Frederick. A. Wright], 'Birkbeck in the Past', *The Lodestone*, 30.3 (summer 1935), 124.
[22] George Senter, 'James C. N. White', *The Lodestone*, 19.2 (spring 1924), 82.

of Congreve in 1893 (when he was twenty-one years into his term as Secretary) admitted that 'If our members were asked to describe the Secretary, it is probable that some would refer to him as being rather curt in his manner and unsympathetic in temperament.'[23] As William Bull, who went on to become a leading solicitor and Conservative politician, recalled,

> We did not speak of the Governors in those days, but of the Committee—an august body the members of which did not mix much with the students.... They never spoke to us or said an encouraging word. On reflection, I do not think it was haughtiness but shyness on their part. They were vaguely unpopular, as I suppose most governing bodies are with constituents who do not know the nature and extent of their duties.[24]

There was another sticking point: these younger students had ambitious plans for the Institution. They wanted a 'university'.[25] In contrast, Norris, White, and Congreve were conscious that they had worked extremely hard from the 1860s to save the Institution from shutting its doors permanently. One way they had done this was by introducing more 'popular' and 'entertaining' classes. They understandably resisted their legacy being side-lined.

Student dissatisfaction came to a head in 1880, led by 20-year-old Sidney Webb. He was one of the Institution's most enthusiastic students. In 1879–80 alone, he won the Institution's English Essay Prize, Mednyansky Essay Prize, Henken Prize in correspondence, Ravenscroft Prize for English grammar, Chester Prize in political economy, and the Birkbeck Prize for mental science, as well as prizes for logic and geology.[26] Four years after leaving Birkbeck, Webb was to become one of the founding members of the socialist Fabian Society and he later co-established the London School of Economics (LSE).

On 8 January 1880, however, he was angry. Along with sixteen other students, including Bull and W. [William] Pett Ridge (who went on to become a prominent philanthropist, novelist who was often said to be a successor to Charles Dickens, and friend of H. G. Wells), he sent a memorandum demanding representation of students on the Committee. The immediate pretext for their protest was a proposal to require a two-thirds majority for decisions of the Committee. The students argued that 'unanimity of opinion' could only be achieved by 'the sacrifice of

---

[23] 'Birkbeck Men. Mr W. H. Congreve', *Birkbeck Institution Magazine* (May 1893), 77. The author goes on to claim that, in fact, Congreve was 'a warm and steadfast friend' with a 'kindly heart, a keen sense of humour, a shrewd intellect, and most artistic feeling'.
[24] Sir William Bull, 'Forty Years Back', *The Lodestone*, 20.2 (spring 1925), 4. He exempted George Norris and 'gentle Herbert Wells Eames' (successor to William Henry Congreve as Secretary) from this criticism.
[25] George Senter, 'James C. N. White', *The Lodestone*, 19.2 (spring 1924), 82.
[26] Royden J. Harrison, *The Life and Times of Sidney and Beatrice Webb: 1858–1905—The Formative Years* (Basingstoke: Macmillan, 1999), 10.

either invaluable individuality, or of that healthy general interest in the affairs of the institution, which is the best guarantee for its stability'.[27] They maintained that a two-thirds majority would mean that

> No measure opposed by the Committee will have a chance of being passed: the Committee alone will practically be able to reject any alteration brought forward by the body of members.

They complained that the Committee on which Norris, White, and Congreve sat held too much power: after all,

> through its official position—its organisation—the numerous acquaintances of its members and their esprit de corps—[it] necessarily commands great power in a meeting. This power is now rendered irresistible.

They were also irritated by a change in rules that would 'prevent lady subscribers from acquiring the full privilege of members'.[28]

Their fundamental objection, however, was that elections to the Committee were a sham.[29] Norris and White were accused of negating the Institution's foundational tradition of students ('members') playing a prominent role in the government of their college.[30] As George Senter, Master of Birkbeck between 1918 and 1939, later admitted, White

> had little respect for the tradition of the College that the Governors should be elected by the members, and during practically his whole period of office the College was governed by a permanent Committee, vacancies, as they occurred, being filled by the Committee itself.[31]

The students' petition failed to elicit a positive response. In October 1880 and February 1881, they put forward three names for election to the Committee; once again, their bid failed.[32] Their attempt at 'radical democracy' was judged 'very unpalatable to the governing committee'.[33] It took until 1885 for 22-year-old Bull and 26-year-old Ridge finally to be elected to the Committee, albeit after 'infinite

---

[27] Ibid., 10.
[28] 'Representations of the Birkbeck Student Committee (S. Webb, Secretary)', 8 January 1880, 'Minutes of the Committee of the Birkbeck Literary and Scientific Institution', Birkbeck Archives.
[29] Burns, *A Short History of Birkbeck College*, 94–5.   [30] Ibid., 96.
[31] George Senter, 'James C. N. White', *The Lodestone*, 19.2 (spring 1924), 82.
[32] Burns, *A Short History of Birkbeck College*, 95.
[33] E. H. H., 'In Memoriam. W. Pett Ridge', *The Lodestone*, 26.2 (spring 1931), 93.

difficulties'.³⁴ It was an important moment, cementing the College's commitment to student representation in all decision making.³⁵

Their bid to give equal privileges to 'lady subscribers' also had an impact. Birkbeck's archive contains a hand-edited issue of the *Rules and Orders of the Birkbeck Literary and Scientific Institution* for 1881 in which phrases such as 'members, students, and lady subscribers' had been crossed out in red ink and replaced by 'members and students'. 'Committee-men' had been changed to 'Committee members', and 'he' changed to gender-neutral words or 'he or she'. Cheaper subscription rates for 'lady members' were retained, however, with women paying 12s. annually compared with 18s. for men.³⁶

Forty years after being elected, a more mellow Bull recollected the campaign launched by the younger members. He admitted to having been dismayed by the Committee's 'hatred of new blood or fresh ideas'. He claimed that

> They said to themselves, 'We are the trustees of this priceless institution. Do you think for one moment we are going to allow a lot of hairbrained young men to interfere with and perhaps wreck the sacred work of our lives?'

To prevent that happening, 'every kind of rule or bye-law was made which would keep the new men at bay' was invoked by the Committee.³⁷ Contrary to the rules, which allowed potential candidates to put their name forward for election, Congreve informed Bull that

> I presume your intention was not to oppose the election of any of the present Committee and only to stand if there was an actual vacancy...but as the whole of the present members were willing to continue their services, no vacancy really existed, and the trouble and loss of time of a contested Election has been saved.³⁸

However, Bull was bullish. He noted that

> The Committee presented a solid and iron front when they sat in a row at the Annual General Meeting—but, as a matter of fact, they were timid men—lath

---

³⁴ Ibid., 93. In 1907–8, White and his fellow governors attempted again to reconstitute the governing committee but were defeated by the students. A further protest was made in 1920.
³⁵ Burns, *A Short History of Birkbeck College*, 96.
³⁶ *Rules and Orders of the Birkbeck Literary and Scientific Institution* (London: J. C. Larrance, 1881), 7–8.
³⁷ Sir William Bull, 'Forty Years Back', *The Lodestone*, 20.2 (spring 1925), 4. He exempted George Norris and 'gentle Herbert Wells Eames', successor to William Henry Congreve as Secretary, from this criticism.
³⁸ Ibid., 5.

painted to look like iron. They had nothing of which to be ashamed—on the contrary, everything to be proud of, and yet they did all they could to prevent fresh prying eyes interfering in what they considered was their more than private affairs.[39]

In the end, the 'walls of Jericho' fell fast. The sudden resignation of a few members of the Committee freed up places for younger men, which Bull and Ridge promptly took.

This was a crucial shift for the College's governance. It entrenched the principle of student representation in all important committees in the College—a tenet enshrined in Birkbeck's governing structure to the present. The ramifications were immense. All early student governors were described as being 'of the University type'. They were 'bent on steering the institution out of the somewhat frivolous course of evening pastimes in which it was then engaged into the broader sea of university study'.[40] They were no longer content with makeshift classes, thrown together in response to the whim of lecturers and student appetites. They were hungry for higher knowledge and university standards.

Norris and White—the titans of Birkbeck for nearly sixty and seventy years respectively—died within a year of each other in 1922 and 1923, respectively. Even their foes acknowledged that these two men, along with Congreve, had dragged a dying LMI back to life between the 1860s and the 1880s. Norris and White also lived to see the LMI and the Birkbeck Scientific and Literary Institution become part of the University of London. But, as we shall see in the next chapter, it was Principal George Armitage-Smith who would get the credit.

* * *

The crisis of governance in the 1880s was led by politically and socially progressive students such as Webb, Ridge, and Bull. The one that occurred in the early 1890s was purely financial. The City Parochial Charities Act of 1883 had decreed that a proportion of the money distributed by the city's charities was to be devoted to education. By claiming that they were an 'old City institution and a pioneer in education', the LMI won an annual endowment of £1,000.[41] But this was not going to save the Institution, which was faced by declining student fees due in part to increased competition from the School Board, which had begun offering free classes in modern languages, elementary science, and commercial subjects.

In 1891, Birkbeck partnered up with the City of London College and the Northampton Institute to form the City Polytechnic. This triangular union was

---

[39] Ibid., 5. [40] E. H. H., 'In Memoriam. W. Pett Ridge', *The Lodestone*, 26.2 (spring 1931), 93.
[41] Evidence by G. Armitage-Smith to the *Royal Commission on University Education in London. Appendix to Third Report of the Commissioners. Minutes of Evidence, November 1910–July 1911; with Appendices and Index* [Cd. 5911] (London: His Majesty's Stationery Office, 1911), 242 and *Birkbeck Literary and Scientific Institution. Report 77th Session, 1899–1900* (London: Witherby and Co., 1900), 5.

solely pragmatic: it made Birkbeck eligible to receive grants from the London County Council (LCC). From the start, the coalition was uncomfortable. Indeed, Birkbeck's annual report often omitted to include any mention of belonging to the 'City Polytechnic'![42] There were good reasons for this omission. After all, unlike other 'polytechnics' which offered technical or commercial training, by the turn of the century Birkbeck prided itself on providing more intellectually demanding classes. Admittedly, Birkbeck's students reaped some benefits from the coalition. The College's premises were extremely 'limited' in terms of 'social and recreative facilities'. By becoming federated with the new Northampton Institute in Clerkenwell, members of Birkbeck were able to 'enjoy the almost unparalleled recreative facilities of the Northampton Institute with its magnificent swimming bath, gymnasium, and great assembly hall'.[43] Conversely, the Northampton Institute was less pleased. As the Educational Adviser of the Technical Education Board of the LCC rather dryly put it, the Northampton Institute risked 'hypertrophy of the social and recreative department'.[44] They had also been forced to promise 'not to establish...any classes in science, art, or commercial subjects of the same kind as those conducted by the sister institutions' (that is, Birkbeck and City of London College). For the Northampton Institute, this meant an increased focus on building, engineering, and metal trades as well as artistic crafts and (for women) domestic economy.[45] Meanwhile, Birkbeck was experimenting with daytime courses, especially in science subjects such as physics, biology, chemistry, and mathematics, but also in Latin, Greek, and French.[46] In the end, no one was happy with the union. In 1907, it was quietly dissolved, although the College continued to receive financial assistance from the LCC. Freed from the uncomfortable shackles of the City Polytechnic, the Birkbeck Literary and Scientific Institution changed its name to 'Birkbeck College', although the name had been used unofficially since 1903.[47]

* * *

The third important shift in governance occurred when Birkbeck became part of the University of London in 1920. This story is told in the next chapter. For our purposes in this chapter, however, the movement resulted in two seismic shifts in the College's governance. The first related to the way student attempts to move the College in a university direction encouraged them to lobby for greater student

---

[42] Burns, *A Short History of Birkbeck College*, 111.
[43] William Garnett [Secretary and Educational Advisor of the Technical Education Board of the London County Council], 'The Work of the Polytechnics', *Journal of the Society of Arts* (23 July 1897), 864.
[44] Ibid., 867.   [45] Ibid., 867.
[46] 'Report of the Birkbeck Literary and Scientific Institution (City Polytechnic) for the Seventy-Fourth Session 1896–97', in the Birkbeck Archive.
[47] 'The City Polytechnic', *The Times* (6 February 1906), 9, and 'Birkbeck College, 1823–1923', *The Lodestone*, 19.2 (spring 1924), 73.

representation in the government of the College; the second, the entry of the college into the University of London, a federation of colleges, meant ceding certain powers.

The first of these shifts started as early as 1904, when Birkbeck students decided that they needed a Students' Union.[48] They met their first major challenge three years later with the move to the 'new scheme', which would see the Birkbeck Literary and Scientific Institution eventually becoming Birkbeck College. Like the earlier fight for student representation in the 1880s and 1890s, which was led by Webb, Bull, and Ridge, the dissent was also led by students, the most prominent of whom were Henry Gerald Richardson and Charles Wesley Hume. Richardson was only 15 years old when he entered the Civil Service in 1899 and, by 1905, his passion for medieval history led him to take part-time classes in Latin and Old French at Birkbeck. At Birkbeck, he was called a 'fire-brand', although later in life he calmed down, becoming a 'highly respectable and rather conservative Civil Servant'. Only two years after Richardson joined Birkbeck classes, Hume arrived and, by 1913, had been elected President of the Birkbeck Student Union. Hume found his 'spiritual home' in the Physics Department,[49] quickly becoming friends with physicist Albert Griffiths as well as F. A. Wright, the head of Classics, who was accustomed to holding 'open house for all Birkbeckians'. It was in Wright's garden that the 'plot was hatched' to transform the College into a university.[50]

When Richardson and Hume arrived at Birkbeck, they identified a similar problem to that complained about by the previous cohort of student-rebels: the governors were 'old buffers devoted to the moribund regime'.[51] As part of the new scheme, the governing body was to be reformed: crucially, it was proposed that governors would be co-opted from *within* the governing body rather than being elected. Worse: student representation would be eliminated.[52] This was anathema to the Students' Union. In October 1908, they protested directly to the Board of Education. They complained that abolishing 'the students' privilege of electing the Governing Body' would

> prevent the accession of persons to power who are in sympathy with the aspirations and desires of the students, and earnestly support modern progressive movements, especially that for the further development of University work.[53]

---

[48] Originally, there were three unions—the Students' Union, Men's Athletic Union, and Women's Athletic Union—which merged into a single union in 1923. It was not an easy decision (indeed, it was said to have emerged from 'much discussion and possible a little heart-burn') but was made in the interests of efficiency: 'Birkbeckian', *The Lodestone*, 19.1 (1923), 38.

[49] C. W. Hume, 'Quorum Pars Parva Fui: Some Random Reminiscences', *The Lodestone*, 32.2 (spring 1935), 71.

[50] Ibid., 73.   [51] Ibid., 71.

[52] 'Birkbeck College New Scheme', no newspaper title given, in 'Extracts from Newspapers for General Reference', in the Birkbeck Archive.

[53] Cited in 'Your Heritage', *The Lodestone*, 46.2 (spring and summer 1955), 5.

S. W. Hood (President of Birkbeck's Student Union) and K. M. Hearn (Secretary) drafted a petition and sent a letter of protest to the press. They protested voraciously against the 'new scheme of government for Birkbeck', saying it met with the 'strong disapproval of students and past students of the college'. They reminded people that the 'work of the college is to provide courses of instruction for the [external] degree of the University of London, and it is not...a polytechnic of low order and rather frivolous aims'. They were especially upset by the proposal that governors should be co-opted, insisting that government of the College should be vested mainly in current and former students and that provision should be made for the representation of women as well. They were anxious that the new proposals would hamper attempts to have Birkbeck recognized as a college of the University of London.[54]

The students put up a strong fight (see Figs. 7.1 and 7.2). Hume and Richardson discovered that by paying just £1, any student could vote at the annual elections. Richardson proposed using this as a weapon to 'turn out the old gang and put in progressives'.[55] Of course, this process of substitution was slow so, in the meantime, the Students' Union simultaneously campaigned for other reforms, including the establishment of a larger and more academic library as well as the development of other facilities necessary if they were to achieve their goal of transferring the College into the University of London. Under the penname of 'Catilinarius' (that is, one who conspires against the government), Richardson set out a programme of reform. The governors were outraged: indeed, one governor was 'so much upset that he had to take to his bed'.[56] Richardson was 'sent down'— that is, expelled from the College.[57]

Increasingly the students' attention focused on the new constitution that the College required to join the federal University of London. In 1917, the proposal for the constitution included four representatives of the Court of Electors on the Board, but no representatives of the students. In 1920, when the governors, academic staff, and Senate of the University of London prepared to implement this change, the students rebelled. The Birkbeck Students' Union protested that the amended scheme 'virtually destroys the democratic basis on which the College was originally built and on which it has stood securely for nearly a century'.[58] As one student explained, while there were many benefits of becoming a full member of the University of London, the change should not mean that Birkbeck students would lose 'some of her ancient privileges'. As he put it, in reorganizing the governing body the College should 'not sacrifice to expediency, all the self-governing traditions which have so long distinguished Birkbeck democracy'. He maintained that

---

[54] S. W. Hood and K. M. Hearn on behalf of the Students' Union of Birkbeck, '[Letter to the Editor] Birkbeck College', *The Academy* (24 October 1908), 401. Also see 'Birkbeck College', *The Times* (24 October 1908), 2, and 'Birkbeck College New Scheme', *London Evening Standard* (22 October 1908), 5.
[55] Hume, 'Quorum Pars Parva Fui', 72.   [56] Ibid., 73.   [57] Ibid., 72–3.
[58] Cited in 'Your Heritage', *The Lodestone*, 46.2 (spring and summer 1955), 5.

BIRKBECK COLLEGE.

Annual Election of Members of Governing Body, 1913-14.

SIR,

By the Scheme of the 23rd June, 1891, under which the College is governed, it is provided that male members of the College of not less than 21 years of age, who have attended for at least one Session some class or course of instruction at the College, shall annually elect from among themselves seven ordinary members of the Governing Body. YOU ARE THEREFORE ENTITLED TO VOTE AT THE FORTHCOMING ANNUAL MEETING, which has been fixed for Wednesday, the 7th January next. We have had the honour to be duly nominated for election, and venture to solicit your support and vote.

In accordance with the customary practice in such circumstance, we submit a statement of our policy and aims.

We are, and have been for many years, enthusiastic supporters of the movement for the continued development of Birkbeck College as a seat of university education, and, with that end in view, and having regard to the recommendations of the Royal Commission upon University Education in London, we desire to see the following objects attained at the earliest possible date.

In the first place, we desire to see a radical change in the constitution of the College, and we believe it desirable that an endeavour should be made to secure a new scheme of government on the following lines :—

Graduates (without regard to sex) of the College (together with a limited number of persons who may have rendered conspicuous service to the College) to be formed into a permanent body with powers analogous to those possessed in the University by Convocation, viz. :—
to elect representatives to the Governing Body ; to be consulted in regard to the policy of the College ; to advise as to the management and policy of the College :

The Governing Body of the College to consist of :—
(a) Representatives of the organised body of graduates (and others as indicated above) ;
(b) Representatives of the lecturers of the College (as in the delegacies appointed for the Colleges already incorporated in the University of London) ;
(c) Representatives of the Students' Union (as in the case of the Scottish Universities and the proposed Court of the University of London) ;
(d) Representatives of the Senate, the London County Council, and any other body or persons to whom it may be desirable to accord representation (e.g., the headmasters of Secondary Schools in London).

Further, we are of opinion that the College, having made itself responsible for providing university education, must not stop half-way, but must accept full responsibility for the welfare of its students. We consider it self-evident that an adequate reference library should be immediately provided ; equally necessary, in our opinion, are an adequate refectory, adequate common rooms, and permanent playing-fields. The rectification of existing defects in these respects would do much to secure the present welfare of the students who are now members of the College ; but to secure their continued welfare and to provide for the educational needs of London students, the College must adopt a policy of expansion and development. We believe that the time has come when large provision should be made for advanced and post-graduate work to be pursued during the evening. That there is a need for this our knowledge of the College and of the University fully warrants us in asserting. Moreover, it is hopeless to expect Birkbeck to take that exalted place in the University which we hope and believe it will take, unless it can be seen that the College is actively and largely pursuing the search for new truth, that it is earnestly endeavouring to widen the bounds of knowledge—ends, which, no less than the calm and learned discipline of everyday life, are the crown and flower of university education.

It may be urged that such a policy as we have outlined entails expense, extended premises, and much labour. We are fully conscious of these difficulties, but we are equally confident that they are not in any way insuperable obstacles ; and we rest unshaken in the belief that the college is worthy of all the endeavours which may be within the power of any of its members.

In the hope that our ideals and purpose will meet with your sympathy and support,

We are, Sir,
Your faithful servants,
C. W. HUME.
H. G. RICHARDSON.

December, 1913.

IF YOU DESIRE TO REGISTER YOUR VOTE IT IS ABSOLUTELY NECESSARY THAT YOU SHOULD ATTEND THE ANNUAL MEETING. VOTING IS BY BALLOT.

Fig. 7.1 Resolution by Hume and Richardson for election to the Board of Governors, 1913–14. Birkbeck Archive, '5 Student Affairs Misc'.

> At a GENERAL MEETING of BIRKBECK COLLEGE STUDENTS' UNION, at 7.30, Thursday, 22nd January, 1914, the President in the Chair, the following MOTIONS were carried:-
>
> 1. "That this Meeting emphatically welcomes the recommendation that Birkbeck College be made a constitutent College of the University of London, under the educational and financial control of the proper authorities thereof."
>
> 2. "That under any future scheme of government the Graduates of the College, irrespective of sex, should elect representatives to serve on the Governing Body, and should have the right to advise the Governing Body in regard to matters affecting the general interests of the College."
>
> 3. "That under any future scheme of government the Students' Union should be represented on the Governing Body."
>
> 4. "That this Meeting regrets the proposal entirely to exclude whole time stduents from the College and desires that no effect be given thereto."
>
> 5. "That it is desirable that full courses in Economics and Laws be maintained at Birkbeck College."
>
> 6. "That a copy of these Resolutions be sent to the Governing Body of the College and to the Board of Education."

Fig. 7.2 Minutes of the General Meeting of the Birkbeck Students' Union on 22 January 1914 recommending that the College becomes part of the University of London. Birkbeck Archive, '5 Student Affairs Misc', p. 1.

the direct representation of students on the governing body is a right which should not be allowed to vanish in blind deference to rather undiscoverable views of even the Senate. The price of recognition should not be made too heavy.[59]

The Senate made the necessary concessions. Not only were four of the representative governors to be appointed by the Board of Electors (which was made up of

---

[59] 'The Recognition of the College as a School', *The Lodestone*, 16.2 (Lent 1921), 79.

governors, former governors, and Birkbeck graduates), but the Student Union was also allowed two representative governors. These were usually the current and most recent former President. The College's report for the year 1920-1 boasted that 'no other London College concedes such representation' but the history of the Institution and College had 'shown its value'.[60] In effect, Birkbeck was the only college in the country in which students had an effective voice in its governance. As the Editor of *The Lodestone* boasted in 1923, from its foundation, the College was

> the most democratic of institutions.... The rawest recruit, if he [sic] will take the trouble, may raise his voice in the exercise of a controlling influence. Through the Principal, as a member of the Senate, he may guide the steps of the university itself.[61]

In the end, both Hume and Richardson became governors and their programme 'seemed to have rosy prospects' of leading to the College's admission to the University of London. Crucially, Norris stepped down and the students found that they had a strong advocate in the Master, Armitage-Smith—but that story is told in the next chapter.

If the first seismic shift between 1904 and 1920 involved student representation, the second was the implications of joining the governing structure of the University of London. The University of London was a federal body which, at its height, consisted of over fifty colleges, institutes, and centres spread from Mile End to Hammersmith and from Hampstead to Tooting.[62] There were even colleges in Egham (Surrey) and Wye (Kent). As a price of joining this expansive federation, Birkbeck had to surrender some of its autonomy to a federal Court, whose administrative centre was Senate House. The union rendered the College dependent for much of its finances on the University Grants Committee (UGC), which had been established in 1919 to facilitate the distribution of the government's 'grant-in-aid'. The UGC largely consisted of senior academics who negotiated with the Treasury over the amount of money that would be allocated to the universities. The UGC's grant would then be given to the federal Court in Senate House, which would then distribute it to the various colleges, schools, institutes, and centres. Senate House was also responsible for all syllabuses, as well as the setting and marking of examinations. This was only devolved to individual colleges in 1965 and 1969, respectively.

---

[60] *Birkbeck College (University of London). Report from 98th Session 1920-21* (London: Birkbeck College, 1921), 1. Also see *The University* (summer 1929), in 'Newscuttings. June 1926 to March 1935', in the Birkbeck Archive.

[61] 'Editorial', *The Lodestone*, 19.1 (1923), 2.

[62] Rosalind M. O. Pritchard, 'Has the Federation a Future? The Case of the University of London', *Oxford Review of Education*, 21.1 (March 1995), 47.

From the 1960s, however, the two governing bodies of the University of London—the Court and the Senate—were coming under pressure. The Court had been established in 1929 and was responsible for controlling *finances*.[63] The Senate was the governing body for *academic* matters. Problems arose because only a few heads of colleges, schools, institutes, and centres were members of the Court, which meant that many of them had no control over how the UGC's grant-in-aid was distributed. The tensions reached crisis point in 1972 with the publication of the Murray Report. It criticized the 'secrecy and mystique which are thought to envelop the operations of the Court'. It encouraged the Court to 'strive to make itself better known among the Schools of the University'.[64] The Court slowly became more open but financial stringencies were gradually encouraging colleges to withdraw from centralized services. They started to procure these services separately. From the 1980s, the University of London began to break up, with the individual colleges eventually becoming independently financed as opposed to being dependent on Senate House. By 1991, the Court was abolished.

Birkbeck's admission to the University of London also resulted in the introduction of a Board of Governors, consisting of twenty-four people. In addition to the President and the Principal/Master (now, Vice-Chancellor) of the College, it included eighteen representative governors of whom four were appointed by the University of London, four by the London County Council, four by the Court of Electors (which consisted of governors, ex-governors, and graduates of the College), two by the Academic Board, one by the City Parochial Foundation, one by the Corporation of London, and two by the Students' Union. There were also four co-optative governors.[65] It was the only college in the University of London that allowed for direct representation of present students. It was perhaps no surprise that the change led to the departure of a number of people who had led the College for decades, including White (who had been active in the government of the College for fifty-five years, including over thirty years between 1890 and 1921 as Chair of the governing committee), A. Ernest Fisher, Frank Gossling, G. Druce Lander, James Woodward, William Garnett, M. F. Levey, Clement A. Ravenscroft, Alfred B. Rendle, and Alfred M. Shiner.[66] It also meant a change of status from an 'Aided Institution' financed by the LCC (which would be reimbursed of half its expenditure from the Board of Education) to one eligible for a grant from the Treasury as well as a maintenance grant from the LCC.

* * *

---

[63] This was introduced because of the Hilton Young Report.
[64] Pritchard, 'Has the Federation a Future?', 55. Murray Report, paras 255 and 319.
[65] *Birkbeck College (University of London). Report from 98th Session 1920-21* (London: Birkbeck College, 1921), 1–2.
[66] Ibid., 2–3.

The final dramatic shift in governance was not unique to Birkbeck or the University of London but was common to Higher Education nationally. It emerged from the 1980s in response to increased governmental intervention into research and teaching under the guise of reductions in state funding and increased emphasis on taxpayer accountability. National policies were imposed upon every aspect of Higher Education.

To appreciate what an enormous shift this entailed, it helps to turn to the 1950s. In 1956, the independence of universities from direct state interference was celebrated by John F. Lockwood, Master of Birkbeck but also the newly appointed Vice-Chancellor of the University of London. In a talk entitled 'The Universities and Modern Life', he observed that, except for Oxford and Cambridge, most university funding came from the state in the form of a quinquennial grant to meet normal recurrent expenditure (for the University of London, this amounted to £7 million) along with large capital grants for new buildings. Lockwood admitted that many university managers and academics were worried that this dependency would result in 'interference by the government in the conduct of our affairs and possibly in our academic policy'. That had not happened. 'A few members of parliament have begun to show an interest in the way in which we spend our grants', he observed, but 'successive governments have protected us. The universities have not been put under the authority of the Minister of Education'.[67] Lockwood quoted an unnamed 'head of one of the colleges in London' as saying that the UGC was a

> characteristically English and most happy device for mediating between the Government and the academic institutions. Its members are all university graduates, as are also the Treasury and other departmental officials with whom it has to negotiate, and all of them, as well as most Cabinet Ministers, understand university problems and are sympathetic to academic ideals.[68]

University autonomy was qualified, however. The 'condition of autonomy' was 'responsibility', Lockwood pontificated. This was why it was important that the federation of the University 'keep our hands free from any close ties to particular [political] interests, because the consequent limitations upon our independence would all too certainly create "a weakening of the very qualities which originally made" our "services so desirable to secure"'.[69] Lockwood believed that it was fortunate that

> Both Labour Government and Conservative Government alike have given a sympathetic hearing to the universities' difficulties and a generous response to

---

[67] John F. Lockwood, 'The Universities and Modern Life' (April 1956), unpaginated.
[68] Quoting the unnamed head of a college in the University of London, in ibid.
[69] Lockwood, 'The Universities and Modern Life'.

their needs, and such is the temper of our people as a whole that one may feel reasonably confident that this attitude of mutual understanding and respect will continue.[70]

Lockwood spoke too soon. Change came slowly but started in 1964 when the new Labour government set up the Department of Education and Science (DES). The DES took over responsibility for overseeing the UGC. From 1988, state educational interventions accelerated. The UGC was abolished and replaced by the Universities Funding Council (UFC). It was a significant shift because, instead of senior academics making their case for funding, members of the UFC were largely drawn from business. As Stefan Collini put it in *Speaking of Universities* (2018), it was a 'deliberate attempt to make the funding of universities more directly responsive to government priorities' and the interests of 'business, trade, and employment'.[71]

These changes led to the strengthening of hierarchical models of management. This represents a shift from the university of George Birkbeck and the post-Second World War universities. These were designed according to Enlightenment principles of a collegiate and self-managed community. One of the biggest shifts caused by the neoliberal 'new management' was the weakening of deliberative bodies such as Academic Board, which is made up of the academic staff of the College and student representatives. The Academic Board is important because no final decision on an academic matter may be taken by the governors until they have sought and considered their opinion. The lack of enthusiasm shown by many Birkbeck lecturing staff for the Board is a serious blow to George Birkbeck's radical democracy.

* * *

The final third of this chapter turns away from the four main shifts in governance of the College to ask about broad shifts in those who *do* the governing. We have already been introduced to some of these men—Norris, White and Congreve, among others—but is it possible to discern *general* trends in the make-up of the men and women who have guided the Institution and College through these changes in governance?

Although the governing body or governors are responsible for the College overall, the most prominent person is the Principal/Master, to whom the governors delegate executive management. Since Norris became the Institution's first Principal in 1885, the College has been run by three Principals, nine Masters, three Acting Masters (one of whom, the classicist Eric Herbert Warmington, valiantly served two separate terms), and one Vice-Chancellor. None served as

---

[70] Quoting the unnamed head of a college in the University of London, in ibid.
[71] Stefan Collini, *Speaking of Universities* (London: Verso, 2018), 94–5.

long as the first three Principals.[72] Indeed, as we have already seen, one of the notable features in the early LMI/Birkbeck is the longevity of many of the officeholders. Norris served forty-two years in the most influential posts in the College—six years as Secretary, thirteen years as Chair of the executive Committee, eleven years as Principal, and twelve years as a governor. His replacement as Principal was George Armitage-Smith, who held the position of Principal for 22 years. When he left in 1918, he was replaced by George Senter who failed by just one year to beat Armitage-Smith's time in post. In the year of the College's bicentenary, David Latchman will have served as Master/Vice-Chancellor for twenty years.

In 1939, the title 'Principal' was changed to 'Master'. The first (and, so far, only) woman in the post was Tessa Blackstone, who retained that title for a decade between 1987 and 1997 (see Fig. 7.3). As a philosophy student complained in the student magazine, *Spectrum*, 'To call a woman "Master" is surely wrong—grammatically and indeed semantically—as it would be to call a man "mistress".' The designation 'Master' implied that any woman in the role was 'an intruder in an otherwise all-male post' or that she was being allowed to hold the post as an 'honorary' man. These were offensive propositions, but since 'the alternative "mistress" sounds ridiculous because of its totally inappropriate connotations', she proposed that 'Principal' should be used.[73] It was a fair point. However, Blackstone felt no need to change the title: and so the title of 'Master' prevailed until 2020, when the University of London voted to allow its constituent colleges to become separate universities within the University of London. This vote had to be ratified by the Department of Education and then the Privy Council, which would need to amend the Royal Charter. Unfortunately, this process was stalled due to the COVID-19 pandemic. In 2021, then, Latchman began using the title 'Vice-Chancellor', making him the first VC in the College's history.

Principals/Masters served for a wide range of years. On average, they stayed in post for eleven years, although this does not take into account the fact that the current VC is still in post.[74] This average of eleven years is also deceptive because some Masters served as little as two years. If we exclude the first three long-serving Principals as well as the current serving VC, Masters are in post for an average of seven years. Acting Masters only serve for an average of eight months. On only two occasions did an Acting Master become a Master: William George Overend and Harold Gordon Jackson. In the case of Jackson, his ascension from Acting

---

[72] The second and third Principals (George Armitage-Smith and George Senter) served twenty-two and twenty-one years, respectively, while the first Principal (Norris) served eleven years. Admittedly, John Lockwood served more years than Norris (fourteen years), but Norris served in all the top positions prior to the invention of the position of 'Principal'.

[73] Oliver Mahler, 'Master, Mistress, Principal', *Spectrum*, 5 (April 1988), 5.

[74] Note that this does not include the years that Norris spent as Secretary and then Chair of the Executive Council.

Fig. 7.3 The most powerful women at Birkbeck, c.1997. Front row: Professor Josephine Labanyi (Spanish); Christine Mabey (College Secretary 1988–99), Philippa Dolphin (Library). Back row: Professor Julia Goodfellow (Crystallography); Professor Nicola Lacey (Law); Tessa Blackstone (Master); Professor Jennifer Hornsby (Philosophy); Professor Isobel Armstrong (English). Birkbeck Image Collections: Birkbeck History OBC0004.

Master to Master was due to the exceptional circumstance of the Second World War. On that occasion, in 1939, John Primatt Redcliffe Maud had been appointed Master but the College 'lent' him to the Ministry of Food where he became a leading figure in establishing and implementing the wartime rationing system.[75] As a consequence, Jackson was appointed as an interim Master. By 1943, however, Maud recognized that it was time for him to resign. His resignation letter was written on notepaper of the Ministry of Food where he had just been appointed second Secretary.[76] It read:

---

[75] 'Head of Civil Service', *The Times* (9 February 1945), 4, and 'High Commission in S. Africa. Sir John Maud's Appointment', *The Times* (20 May 1958), 10.
[76] 'Food Expert to Help Lord Woolton', *The Times* (15 January 1944), 4. In 1944, he was transferred to the Ministry of Reconstruction: 'Head of Civil Service', *The Times* (9 February 1945), 4.

You will remember that when, after two wartime sessions, I had to relinquish the hope of being able to do my work at Birkbeck as well as my work in this Ministry. I asked the Governors to accept my resignation. At that time the Governors asked me to withdraw my resignation, and remain Master, with an Acting Master to do the work. I of course fell in with the wishes of the Governors and I feel confident that the Governors were right in what they then did. But I believe the time has now come when the Governors should proceed to appoint a Master who is not prevented by wartime duties from giving his whole time to the College and who will be in the saddle when there is a European armistice.[77]

Maud went on to become Permanent Secretary to the Ministry of Education and Jackson remained in post until he died in 1950.

Tracing trends in the *type* of person who served in the highest offices of the Institution/College is difficult because information about some of the early Principals is minimal. We know surprisingly little about Norris, for example. We do know that he applied for the post of Secretary when it became vacant due to fraud. The librarian, who also worked for the London and South-Eastern Railway Company, had 'misappropriated monies... to the extent of thirty pounds' (that is, around half a year's salary) and the Secretary, Thomas J. Pearsall (in post between 1863 and 1866), had been aware of the fraud. The librarian was 'threatened with exposure if he did not refund the money', while Pearsall was 'allowed to resign'.[78] Norris started by teaching history and geography courses in the Institution before taking up administrative posts.[79] As he aged, his politics changed. In 1892, the *Birkbeck Institution Magazine* acknowledged that 'the members of the governing body represent every shade of political and theological thought'. It noted that when Norris first arrived in the Institution in the late 1850s, he was 'an advanced Liberal'. But 'time... has mellowed his political ideas, and while still advocating every Liberal reform, he supports the moderate Conservative Party'. It observed that Norris was

> a sound churchman, but ever tolerant of dissent; a warm advocate of temperance, but never intemperate in his advocacy; a strict moralist; and while possessing a strong individuality, and holding decided views on all things appertaining to our work, he is ever ready to consider the opinions of his colleagues.[80]

The dominant characteristic of Principals/Masters of Birkbeck is that they were academics by profession. The early Principals had all taught at the Institution.

---

[77] Letter from Maud to the Deputy Chairman of the Governors, dated 30 August 1943, in Birkbeck Archive, Box 43-44.
[78] Letter from the Secretary to Delisle Burns dated 25 September 1923, in 'Birkbeck College letters 1923.2', Birkbeck Archive, Box 65.67. The librarian was called Berry.
[79] 'Birkbeck Men. Mr George M. Norris, LL.B.', *Birkbeck Institution Magazine* (November 1892), 17.
[80] Ibid., 18.

An academic/teaching background was also a characteristic of post-1960s Masters. This was not typical of university governance elsewhere. From the mid-twentieth century, universities have increasingly been governed by senior civil servants or business notables. At Birkbeck, however, all Masters had distinguished academic careers prior to their appointment at the College. Birkbeck has been run by learned individuals who can draw on their earlier international research and often administrative experience in other institutions of Higher Education. This has meant that they have a clear sense of the university's interests and the way it operates. Many had even been lecturers or professors at Birkbeck before accepting the highest post in the College. For example, George Armitage-Smith (1896–1918) had lectured in Economics and Mental Science in the College, while George Senter (1918–39) had been head of the Department of Chemistry. Harold Gordon Jackson, an expert on crustacea, was appointed to Birkbeck in 1921 as Reader and then head of the Zoology Department before becoming Acting Master and then Master (1943–50).

While Acting Masters had always come from within the College, which is not surprising since they were often required to 'step in' at short notice to deal with unexpected departures or the death of the incumbent Masters, all of Birkbeck's Masters had been professors or served as heads of departments elsewhere. Masters with the most extensive administrative experience in Higher Education before Birkbeck were John P. R. Maud (1939–43) who had been Dean of University College; John Lockwood (1951–65) who had been Dean of the Faculty of Arts at the University of London; F. Kenneth Hare (1966–8) who had been Dean of Arts and Science at McGill University. A similar background is held by the VC at the time of the College's bicentenary. Latchman (2003–) is one of the country's leading geneticists. Educated at the University of Cambridge, where he completed a PhD entitled 'Control of Alpha-Fetoprotein Gene Expression in the Mouse' (1981), he went on to become Professor of Human Genetics at UCL, Director of the Windeyer Institute of Medical Science at UCL, and Dean of the Institute of Child Health. In 2010, he was appointed CBE for Services to Higher Education.

The academic credentials of Masters had all been forged in distinguished universities. A large proportion had been educated in Cambridge, Oxford, and the various colleges of the University of London. Senter and Hare had degrees from German and Canadian universities. With the expansion of Higher Education from the 1960s, however, Masters started to come from 'newer' universities, including University College Southampton (Ronald C. Tress, 1968–77) and the universities of Sussex and Leeds (Timothy M. M. O'Shea, 1998–2002, went to both). Nearly all were Fellows of distinguished societies and academies; some held titles such as Baron (Maud), Baroness (Blackstone), and Sir (Lockwood and Acting Master Evans), although in some cases these titles were bestowed after they left Birkbeck. They were also relatively young when they took the post.

Maud was only 33 years of age. Even the oldest Master (William George Overend, 1979–87) was only 57 years old when he was appointed.

If there is a *general* trend in terms of politics, the College has been increasingly represented by Principals/Masters on the Liberal/Labour spectrum. The only Masters who went on to have a political career were Maud (Permanent Secretary to the Ministry of Education) and Blackstone (Minister for Education, then Minister for the Arts), both under Labour governments. Rather than political careers, the mastership at Birkbeck has tended to be a stepping stone to other jobs in Higher Education. F. Kenneth Hare (1966–8) went on to be President of the University of British Columbia; O'Shea became Principal of the University of Edinburgh; Ronald Tress became the Director of the Leverhulme Trust; and Richard Evans, who was Acting Master in 1997, became Regius Professor of Modern History at the University of Cambridge and then President of Wolfson College and Provost of Gresham College.

* * *

What about the characteristics of other senior people in the College's administration? Second in importance to Principals/Masters is the Secretary and Clerk to the Governors, head of administration and professional services. As with Principals/Masters, in the first half of the College's history, they were characterized by their longevity in the post. Although the first of the College's thirteen Secretaries (James L. Flather, a tin and iron plate worker)[81] lasted less than one year (he fled London 'in order to avoid imprisonment for debt'),[82] 30 per cent served for between twenty-seven and thirty-four years each. These were Andrew MacFarlane (1830–63), William Henry Congreve (1872–1906), George Francis Troup Horne (1919–52), and Arnolfo John Caraffi (1952–79). Since 1979, the average time spent as Secretary has been significantly shorter—an average of eleven years, although the current incumbent (Keith Harrison) has already been in post for sixteen years.

The characteristics of Secretaries are markedly different from those of Principals/Masters. Although a large majority have higher degrees, including PhDs, their careers have been in administration rather than academia. The one exception is Thomas J. Pearsall (1863–6), who contributed to the science of optics. He was first person to create colour centres in colourless crystals by exposure to radiation.[83] A relatively high number had experience in colonial administration. These include William Henry Congreve (1872–1906), who had been awarded the

---

[81] Minutes of the Governors, 26 January 1824, 'This Time Last Century', *The Lodestone*, 19.2 (spring 1924), 97.

[82] Minutes of the Governors, 22 November 1824, 'This Time Last Century', *The Lodestone*, 20.1 (Michaelmas 1924), 32.

[83] See Stephen R. Wilk, *How the Ray Gun Got Its Zap: Odd Excursions into Optics* (Oxford: Oxford University Press, 2013), 84.

Imperial Service Order. It is no coincidence that during his period as Secretary, a number of speakers were invited who 'rejoiced' in the fact that many men 'now occupy important positions in our colonies and received their education in the Birkbeck Institution', as Lord Aberdare put it in 1880.[84] But a background in colonial administration also includes more recent Secretaries, such as Robert E. Swainson (1979–88) and Brian Roberts (1999–2005). At least one Secretary (Caraffi) was an artist, who twice exhibited at the Royal Academy Summer Exhibition; while another (Roberts) was a reverend.

What about Presidents and Vice-Presidents, who are the most senior *individuals* in the College's hierarchy, even though their role is primarily ambassadorial? Vice-Presidents are largely invisible in the College: whoever is the Lord Mayor of the City of London automatically becomes the College's Vice-President. In contrast, Presidents play important ceremonial roles, including during graduations and other formal events.

Presidents are appointed on an annual basis, although, as Overend admitted, 'the governors temper their caution with loyalty and so re-appointment is our custom'.[85] On average, Presidents have served for eleven years. This masks huge differences. Aside from William Lloyd Birkbeck, who inherited the post from his father George and held the title for forty-seven years (and, in reality, should be considered a Principal/Master), the longest serving President was Baron Denning, who held the post for thirty-one years from 1953. Not surprisingly, Presidents have been significantly older than Principals/Masters. On average, they have been in their early sixties when appointed, although Albert Frederick Arthur George Windsor, HRH Duke of York, was only 40 years old and stayed in the post for just one year in 1935–6. Many Presidents have been very elderly. Nearly one-third were over the age of 80 when they retired. Hobsbawm was an exception: he was 85 when *appointed* and retired aged 95 years, the year he died.

While Principals and Masters have almost entirely come from university positions, Presidents have all been leading members of the establishment. For example, Thomas Baring (1888–97) was Viceroy of India, the representative of the monarchy. Neither George Birkbeck nor his son William Lloyd Birkbeck had royal titles, but nearly all others did. They were HRH (Duke of York), Duke (once), Earl (twice), Viscount (three times), Baron (three times), Baroness (three times), and Order of the Companions of Honour (once). As this implies, many were politically conservative. This was notably the case with Baring (the 1st Earl of Northbrook, 1888–97), Richard Webster (1st Viscount Alverstone, 1903–15), and Tom Denning (Baron, 1952–83). Only one President did not have a royal title: this was William Temple (1942–4), who was the Archbishop of Canterbury.

[84] 'The Birkbeck Institution', *Morning Post* (4 February 1880).
[85] *Birkbeck College (University of London). Master's Report on the One-Hundred-and-Sixtieth Session 1982/83* (London: Birkbeck College, 1983), 4.

As a generalization, however, the Presidents of Birkbeck have *increasingly* been left-wing. Temple was a socialist, as were Baron Young of Dartington (1989–93), Lord Healey (1993–8), and Eric Hobsbawm (2002–12). The three female Presidents have also been either strong Liberals or Labourites. The first female President was Betty Lockwood (Baroness, 1983–9), a leading feminist and Labour Party activist. The second woman was Elizabeth Margaret Smith (Baroness, 1998–2002), who heads the John Smith Fellowship Trust (see Fig. 7.4). The trust is named after her husband, who was the leader of the Labour Party, and it promotes principles of democracy and good government. The third woman is Joan Bakewell (Baroness, 2012 to the present), a distinguished journalist and broadcaster as well as Labour Party peer.

Finally, two important actors in the College's governance must be mentioned—and they are at the two extremes in terms of privilege: royalty and what used to be called 'Secretaries'. The College has long received the patronage of the royal family. The Duke of Sussex laid the foundation stone of the London Mechanics' Institution. Nearly sixty years later, in 1883, the Duke of Albany (formerly Prince Leopold, the youngest son of Queen Victoria) laid the foundation stone of Bream's Building in Fetter Lane.[86] Two years later, on 4 July 1885, the building was opened by the Prince of Wales.[87] In 1920, the Queen became a patron of the College.[88] During the College's centenary in 1924, King George V, his mother Alexandra, and Queen Mary were patrons. King George V contended that throughout the life of the LMI/Birkbeck 'there has been a personal association between the college and successive members of my family'.[89] In 1926, a Royal Charter was granted to the College. In 1935, their Royal Highnesses the Duke and Duchess of York

Fig. 7.4 Baroness Smith of Gilmorehill (Elizabeth Margaret Smith), 1998–2002. Birkbeck Image Collections: Birkbeck History OBC0016.

---

[86] 'F. A. W.' [Frederick A. Wright], 'Birkbeck in the Past', *The Lodestone*, 30.3 (summer 1935), 123.
[87] Bull, 'Forty Years Back', 6.   [88] 'News in Brief', *The Times* (1 July 1920), 13.
[89] 'University Life in London', *The Times* (1 April 1924), 12.

launched an appeal for funds for the new Malet Street building at the Mansion House, although the completion of the building was delayed because of the war. Such appeals—then, as now—depended heavily on the support given by individuals (often alumni), charitable trusts and foundations, corporate organizations, and legacy gifts, all of which contribute significantly to widening access and student support, academic research and PhD scholarships, and capital projects and facilities.

The final group of administrators are routinely overlooked, yet nothing would happen without them. These are the Secretaries. Departmental and School administrators are discussed in Chapter 25, but in the context of executive-level management, the most valued people in this role are those who work alongside Principals/Masters. In the College's 200 years, no one fulfilled this post with more dedication, skill, and sensitivity than Miss Hilda Keet, who worked for the College under four different Principals/Masters. Her career at Birkbeck started in 1906, when she became the first woman in the College to be appointed to an administrative role. Her job title was 'typewriter'—a term that used to refer to the *person* who typed, not the machine—in the College's office (see Fig. 7.5). When she retired in 1949, after forty-three years of service, an article in her honour was published in *The Lodestone*. Its patronizing tone probably echoed the way 'Miss Keet' had been treated all her working life. The author reported that, although Miss Keet's job was 'normal office routine work', the 'meticulous care' she 'lavished' upon the academic staff, especially in the Departments of Mathematics and Science, meant that 'they began to think of more and more things that they wanted to have done'. Keet also made herself indispensable to the Students' Union and the many clubs and societies. When George Armitage-Smith encouraged her to spend her evenings taking a degree in the College, Keet's day was lengthening even further. For four years during the First World War, it was said to be 'natural and even inevitable' that Miss Keet would take over the duties of the College Secretary, Hubert Wells Eames, when he left for war-work. Near the end of that war, when the Principal, Armitage-Smith, lost most of his sight, *The Lodestone* informed its readers that it became 'one of Miss Keet's self-imposed duties and, no doubt, incidentally, pleasures...to see him safely on his homeward journey through the darkened streets'. However, once the war was over and a new College Secretary (George Francis Troup Horne) was appointed, Miss Keet was unceremoniously stripped of her duties as the unofficial College Secretary and reverted to the usual chores of being the 'typewriter' to the new Principal, George Senter. 'Oceans of paper work' piled upon her desk as the College transformed itself into a constituent part of the University of London.[90]

---

[90] S. H. W. E., 'Hilda Keet', *The Lodestone*, 41.3 (summer 1949), 47–8.

Fig. 7.5 An advertisement for an 'Addressograph', purchased by Birkbeck. It shows a blonde, fashionably dressed 'secretary' addressing envelopes, making sure she does not disturb the clearly more important, formally dressed man making a telephone call. Birkbeck's addressograph was only replaced in August 1990. Birkbeck Archive.

Although we have no idea how Keet felt about the demands made upon her, officially, at least, it seems that she was uncomplaining. Her physical working conditions were perhaps her most legitimate gripe. Miss Keet worked from a small, curtained compartment just inside Bream's Building. As one College Secretary recalled, since there was no space for a door[,] her privacy was secured by a heavy velvet curtain drawn over the opening. Miss Keet sat in that wretched cubbyhole without daylight and little ventilation for much of her life giving sound and telling advice, to all who cared to seek it, in a quiet and devotional manner.

The space was more like a 'confessional from which one emerged feeling shriven and ready to face the ongoing struggle', than a working office.[91] Keet retired before the move to the new Malet Street building. It was an inglorious way to end more than four decades of service to the College.

* * *

In conclusion, the governance of the LMI/Birkbeck has undergone significant shifts in the 200 years of its existence. Some of these changes were responses to the College's traditions—student representation, for example, was important since, like the medieval universities of Bologna and Pavia as well as universities in Scotland, the LMI/Birkbeck was a corporation of students rather than teachers. This democratic idea of education was a feature of the Institution from its conception and another pioneering, progressive policy. Many shifts in governance became necessary for financial reasons and, increasingly, they have been influenced by party-political shifts in Higher Education more generally. What is not in question, though, is the fact that the College would not have survived without effective management. These aspects of the College were summarized in part of a song sung by R. L. Oakeshott in 1908:

> Here's to the Principal, dear to our hearts,
> There's never a man to approach him...
> Here's to the Council that make our good name
> Grow greater and better and sounder...
> Here's to the Principal's lost millionaire,
> And here's to his finding him quickly.
>   Let the toast, etc.[92]

---

[91] Arnolfo John Caraffi, 'Memories of Breams II', in Birkbeck Archive, Box 15.
[92] 'The Union Dinner', *The Lodestone*, 3.2 (Lent 1908), 52–3.

8
What Is a University?

Walking into Bream's Building at the turn of the century could be a dispiriting experience. Student Charles Westley (C. W.) Hume deemed the place 'depressing'. To the left of the entrance, he recalled, there was a reading room, which was generally 'occupied by very aged proletarians' reading newspapers. On the right, there was a small office where the librarian 'doled out...some old volumes of early-Victorian fiction' from 'an alleged library'.[1] It was more like a club than an institution of higher learning. For a small fee, men could use the reading and magazine rooms and, following lunch, 'it was always possible to see the "regulars" having their afternoon nap'.[2] Indeed, during the Boer War, on the day Mafeking was relieved, 'by 9 a.m. the porter was so overcome with alcohol that it was necessary to lock him in the...Students' Common Room' until he had sobered up.[3]

Hume's criticisms were sharp but judicious. His acerbic views about the library (see Fig. 8.1) were especially valid, given that access to high-quality books and journals are central to any institution seeking to educate its members. This fact was recognized by the founders of the LMI, one of whose first acts was to approve the investment of £50 (approximately £5,000 today) for books.[4] But the LMI's library remained primarily dependent on donations—which were of variable quality (for example, in November 1824, the LMI's solicitor donated several publications by the Society for the Relief of Climbing Boys).[5] The College's history as a *mechanics'* institution, specializing in practical instruction, can be seen by looking at magazine subscriptions. In 1908, these included *Building News*, *English Mechanic and World of Science*, *Electrical Engineering*, *Electrical Review*, *Woodworker*, *Marine Engineer*, and *Gardening*. As an indication of the College's more progressive socio-politics, it also stocked *The Animal's Friend* and *Vegetarian Messenger*.[6]

The problems faced by the LMI went much deeper than that of the library, as Hume knew. By the turn of the century, the entire Institution was at risk of

---

[1] C. W. Hume, 'Quorum Pars Parva Fui: Some Random Reminiscences', *The Lodestone*, 32.2 (spring 1935), 71.
[2] H. G. B., 'A Fire-Watcher's Interview with his Own Memory', *The Lodestone*, 36.3 (summer 1944), 12.
[3] Ibid., 12.
[4] Burns, *A Short History of Birkbeck College*, 55. For the conversion, see CPI Inflation Calculator, at https://www.in2013dollars.com/uk/inflation/1820, viewed 1 August 2021.
[5] This was Mr Tooke: Burns, *A Short History of Birkbeck College*, 55.
[6] Olim Civis, 'To the Editor', *The Lodestone*, 4.1 (December 1908), 23.

Fig. 8.1 The library at Bream's Building c.1923, complete with log fire. The library moved to Greystoke Place in around 1935. Birkbeck Image Collections: Birkbeck History BH0223.

closure. This was lamented by George MacDonald Davies, whose memories of those early days were like Hume's. Davies had first entered the Institution's buildings in Chancery Lane and Bream's Building in 1903; he returned seventeen years later as the College's first full-time head of the Geology Department.[7] Indeed, Davies would become a prolific author, with books on 'elementary crystallography' and the geology of London, south-east England, and the Dorset coast. In 1932, he even published a book of French–English vocabulary for ecologists attempting to read French texts. However, when Davies first arrived at the College at the turn of the century, he recognized that Birkbeck was struggling. Its library contained 'a few dingy volumes of standard novels, with a few popular books of science and travel'; the reading room was frequented by elderly men; vocational subjects such as 'steam, metallurgy, photography and…art' dominated.[8] More important for this young, aspiring geologist, the equipment for teaching his discipline was appalling. The College owned 'one petrological microscope', an 'inefficient micro-projector', a 'poor collection of rocks', and a collection of books on geology that consisted of 'barely a dozen volumes'.[9] Pedagogically, things were

---

[7] 'G.M.D.' (George MacDonald Davies), 'Forty Years On', *The Lodestone*, 35.2 (Easter 1943), 10.
[8] Ibid., 8.   [9] Ibid., 8.

not great either. The main lecturer in geology was George F. Harris, a specialist on granites. According to Davies, Harris had a

> rotund style of lecturing: 'You will ask me... My reply to you is...' was a favourite mode of expression. He discoursed expansively, not without interest, but with little idea of covering a syllabus.[10]

Students were not helped by the fact that Harris 'despised' lecture notes and, as a consequence, his lectures 'were very dry... requiring beer as an antidote'.[11] The only good thing that could be said about Harris was that he occasionally revealed a very dry wit. When one disgruntled student looked down a microscope and said, 'You tell us that that mineral is hornblende, but how do you know it is hornblende?', Harris responded, 'How do you know I am Harris? You see me day after day till you recognise me.'[12]

Davies also complained that systematic instruction was lacking. In the annual reports, each course was listed individually, as opposed to being grouped under broad, academic disciplines. The majority of classes were technical in nature: they included 'Practical Electric Lighting', hygiene, steam and the steam engine, building construction, machine construction, drawing (including model, ornamental, perspective, figure, and landscape drawing), watercolour and oil painting, debating, elocution, chess, theory of music, elementary singing, and advanced singing.[13] From 1880 to 1883, students could even attend classes on 'Blowpipe Analysis'.[14]

Intellectually, the College had clearly lost its vigour. Under an 'obsolete scheme', the Institution was expected to provide courses in subjects such as 'Emigration' as well as 'needlework and various other useful arts'.[15] Throughout the 1880s, between one quarter and 38 per cent of students were studying subjects such as music, art, debating, elocution, chess, and gymnastics.[16] Indeed, between 16 and 27 per cent of all students were taking courses in music and singing alone.[17] In the contemptuous words of one commentator, it was

> a little disappointing to find [that] the number of students of 'fancy' subjects exceed so largely that of those pursuing the severe branches of knowledge; but it must not be forgotten that lady scholars are admitted to the Birkbeck Institution, and that the demand for musical instruction is in a considerable degree referrible [sic] to this fact.[18]

This disparagement of 'lady scholars' was indicative of an institution that cared little for the ambitions of its students.

---

[10] Ibid., 8. [11] Ibid., 8. [12] Ibid., 9.
[13] From the annual reports. [14] Ibid. [15] Hume, 'Quorum Pars Parva Fui', 71.
[16] From the annual reports. [17] Ibid. [18] Becker, *Scientific London*, 207.

Students were dissatisfied, complaining that there was 'no provision for higher education'. Admittedly, Birkbeck did have lecturers who were 'recognized' by the University of London. This meant that their courses were considered of sufficiently high standard to be part of the University of London's curriculum. This was important because, in 1858, the University of London had introduced a new Charter allowing anyone to sit their examinations for degrees. The Charter was confirmed in 1863. Henceforth, candidates no longer had to take a minimum of two years' study in one of the colleges of the University.[19] Overnight, LMI students were able to sit the examinations.

There were many obstacles, however. Many students attended classes 'for knowledge without any intention, however, of submitting themselves to the test of University examinations', explained the annual report for 1911–12. These students were

> not necessarily less serious in their pursuit of knowledge which they require for culture and as equipment for the practical affairs of life.... Some are teachers seeking to extend their acquaintance with subjects in which they are interested; others are in the civil or municipal employ, and many are business men.[20]

The number of students who were trainee-teachers (from the LCC's teachers training college opposite in Greystoke[21] Place) or candidates for the Patent Office and other Civil Service examinations were particular problems. As 'H. R. N.', a physics demonstrator, explained, this 'non-University work was the chief source of revenue and could not be discontinued on the then slender chance of our ultimate destiny as a University College'.[22]

In addition, students had to pass compulsory courses in two ancient languages to be awarded an Arts degree by the University of London. However, Birkbeck refused to guarantee a salary to lecturers in Classics on the grounds that the subject was 'a superfluous luxury'.[23] This is where Classics scholar Frederick A. Wright stepped in. He offered to teach Latin and Greek in exchange for a share of the fees. As a result, the first Birkbeck graduate of the University of London was a woman who had enrolled for the University's Internal BA in 1897. Wright dryly noted that she was 'rewarded for her efforts by a post as teacher in a school for the mentally deficient'.[24]

Despite these attempts to integrate Birkbeck into a university system, progress was limited. Most students did not take degree courses but only individual classes.

---

[19] Burns, *A Short History of Birkbeck College*, 79.
[20] *Birkbeck College: Report 89th Session, 1911–12* (London: Geo. Barber, 1912), 7.
[21] It is often spelt 'Graystoke'.
[22] H. R. N., 'Dr B. W. Clack', *The Lodestone*, 32.4 (autumn 1937), 16.
[23] 'F. A. W.' [Frederick A. Wright], 'Birkbeck in the Past', *The Lodestone*, 30.3 (summer 1935), 123.
[24] Ibid., 124.

For example, Henry Buss (who became a physician) was a subscriber to the LMI for twenty-five years, during which time he had 'profited by taking copious notes of between two and three thousand lectures'.[25] Although Buss was unusual in the number of years he took classes at the LMI, it was typical for students to 'drop in and out' of classes. As late as 1911–12, for example, there were only 340 students at Birkbeck studying for the University of London degree. This represented one third of the total number of students.[26] Furthermore, these 'University of London' courses were not fully integrated into the College.[27] Hume rightly observed that Birkbeck in 1906 was 'a cross between a mortuary and a maternity hospital'. The Birkbeck Institution 'was dying by inches', but Birkbeck College had not quite been born.[28]

* * *

This was to change with the appointment of George Armitage-Smith as Master (see Fig. 8.2). He arrived in 1896, and when he left twenty-two years later, the College had been transformed. Known as a 'shrewd and practical North Countryman' who possessed 'an abundant stock of nervous energy',[29] Armitage-Smith did more than any other administrator (except the original founders) to transform the fortunes of the College.

On the surface, Armitage-Smith was an unlikely revolutionary. He was a political economist. His books on taxation and in the defence of free trade make for dry reading today. A 1901 lecture suggests a man of solid tastes: he warned students against 'the vice of desultory reading', which he believed was 'one of the frailties in an age of cheap paper, when everyone can read and too many write'.[30] Nevertheless, he was a popular teacher and talented administrator.

His legacy was the transformation of the Birkbeck Literary and Scientific Institution into Birkbeck College, University of London. It was not an easy task. As discussed in the previous chapter, since 1891, Birkbeck had belonged (with the City of London College and the Northampton Institute) to the City Polytechnic. This triangular union was purely pragmatic: it made Birkbeck eligible to receive grants from the County Council. Although it was always an artificial union, with each institution pursuing its own work independently, it had a deadening impact on College life and academic aspirations.

Armitage-Smith initiated a massive programme of restructuring. He was spurred on by a new generation of students and staff, including Hume and classicist

---

[25] Buss, *Eighty Years Experience of Life*, 24.
[26] *Birkbeck College: Report 89th Session, 1911–12*, 7.
[27] Hume, 'Quorum Pars Parva Fui', 71.
[28] Ibid., 71.
[29] Fred A. McKenzie, 'The Birkbeck Institute: The Story of London's Evening University', *Windsor Magazine: An Illustrated Monthly for Men and Women*, 7 (December 1897), 376.
[30] George Armitage-Smith, *Inaugural Address by the Principal G. Armitage-Smith on the Opening of the Seventy-Ninth Session. Monday, 30th September, 1901* (London: Birkbeck College, 1901), 12.

Fig. 8.2 Portrait of George Armitage-Smith by Amy Armitage-Smith © The Artist's Estate.

Wright, who were clamouring for reform, as discussed in the previous chapter. Armitage-Smith was the first Principal to be paid as a full-time head of the College and he reciprocated by introducing a system of salaries for lecturers. As College historian Delisle Burns explained, until Armitage-Smith arrived, 'teachers received a proportion of the fees paid by students as part of their remuneration'. Armitage-Smith believed that 'benevolent amateurs lecturing when they could spare time or energy are no more likely to teach well than amateur carpenters are likely to build well'. He introduced salaries based on the academic status of the teachers.[31]

In his first year as Principal, Armitage-Smith also grouped the dozens of individual classes into five 'faculties': these were English and Commercial; Languages; Law; Mental and Moral Science; and Science and Technology.[32] For the first time, Birkbeck's annual reports listed which University of London degree courses were being offered. By 1900, the Faculty of 'Science and Technology' had become

---

[31] Burns, *A Short History of Birkbeck College*, 117.   [32] From the annual reports.

simply 'Science'.[33] In 1907, the list was streamlined even further, with courses appearing under four headings: the School of Art; Arts; Law; and Science.[34] Classes in elocution, debating, vocal music, and pianoforte disappeared.[35] By 1912, the 'School of Art' had been dropped.[36] In the words of Viscount Haldane of Cloan (President of Birkbeck between 1919 and 1928), the College was changing from 'a place where knowledge had the aspect of fragments, into a place where it has become a living whole of the University standard'.[37]

By 1905, the campaign to have Birkbeck recognized as a college in the University of London was in full force. When Sir Edward Busk, the Vice-Chancellor of the University of London, was invited to open the College's 1905-6 session, he expressed his 'cordial acknowledgement of the efforts the Birkbeck College has always made to satisfy in all respects the requirements of the University'.[38] Busk contended that university-quality education had to be driven by research. Rather than knowledge based on 'authority, or work by rule', each student had 'to see and realize for himself [sic] the truth of what he learns'. Above all, education was concerned with 'the acquisition and extension of knowledge and the training of the mind in true culture, so that it may be free from prejudice and cultivated for the patient investigation of truth'.[39] This was precisely, he concluded, what Birkbeck was providing. It was no coincidence that the College's annual report for 1905-6 included a list of all staff publications for the first time.[40]

The Royal Commission on University Education in London, which sat between 1909 and 1912, was the perfect opportunity for Armitage-Smith to make his case. However, before he was called to give evidence, he had to endure condescending arguments against Birkbeck made by Robert Blair (Education Officer of the London County Council) and the Rev. Arthur Cayley Headlam (Principal and Dean of King's College, London). Blair believed it would be a better strategy to enlarge *existing* colleges of the University of London, rather than adding new ones. He worried that if Birkbeck were given 'University of London' status, the competition would have an adverse effect, especially on the geographically close King's College.[41]

Blair's tone was courteous; not so, Headlam's. He derided 'polytechnics' that wanted to become universities, saying that this would 'hamper them in doing their own proper work, which is that of technical education, and of intermediate

---

[33] Ibid. [34] Ibid. [35] Ibid. [36] Ibid.
[37] Viscount Haldane of Cloan (Richard Haldane), 'Preface', in Burns, *A Short History of Birkbeck College*, 5.
[38] Sir Edward Busk, cited in *Birkbeck College: Report, 83rd Session, 1905-1906* (London: Witherby and Co., 1906), 9.
[39] Ibid., 9. [40] Ibid., 16-17.
[41] Evidence by Mr R. Blair to the *Royal Commission on University Education in London. Appendix to First Report of the Commissioners, Minutes of Evidence, July 1909-April 1910; with Appendices and Index* [Cd. 5166] (London: His Majesty's Stationery Office, 1910), 17.

education...for those who have not had a complete secondary school education'.[42] Naturally, he contended, teachers at Birkbeck were 'ambitious', but it would be 'far more economical' if the money were spent providing students with scholarships to cover the higher university fees than 'inefficiently' supporting 'a *quasi*-University Staff'.[43] However, Headlam also revealed that King's College was feeling vulnerable. Birkbeck, he fretted, was half a mile from King's and 'does everything cheaper than we do'. Such competition was unfair.[44] He proposed that Birkbeck retain its lowlier status and take on the education of those 'who have not had a proper school education up to the Matriculation or Intermediate standard'. At King's, he noted, there was 'a very large amount of work not of a university standard, which we are anxious to get rid of'. It would be advantageous if Birkbeck was 'a place to which the University could recommend anyone to go who is not yet fit for University work'.[45]

The comments infuriated Armitage-Smith. In 1911, when he was called to give evidence, he launched a counterattack on Headlam for knowing 'nothing of polytechnics from the inside'. The idea that 'King's College should hand over its inferior students to Birkbeck College' and periodically cream off its best students was offensive.[46] He was 'indignant' that Headlam had even suggested turning Birkbeck into 'a preparatory school' for King's. After all, Armitage-Smith reminded the Commissioners, King's College had been established later than Birkbeck College and was 'chiefly known...as a theological institution, and as an evening coaching establishment for the lower Civil Service examinations'. In contrast, Birkbeck College

> has steadily developed during the 87 years of its existence, carefully adapting itself to the continual changes that have been proceeding in metropolitan education, and it now takes its place as a college of university character.[47]

Armitage-Smith noted that here were two models for a metropolitan university. The first was a restrictive one: only a few colleges would be members and the education would be made available to only a small proportion of people. These students would be admitted because they could either afford high fees or compete for a few bursaries. The second model was open, welcoming all educational establishments that met a certain standard. These colleges would be 'easily

---

[42] Evidence by the Rev. Arthur Cayley Headlam to the *Royal Commission on University Education in London. Appendix to First Report of the Commissioners*, 88.
[43] Ibid., 88.   [44] Ibid., 99.   [45] Ibid., 88.
[46] Evidence by G. Armitage-Smith to the *Royal Commission on University Education in London. Appendix to Third Report of the Commissioners*, 244.
[47] Ibid., 244.

accessible to all classes capable of profiting by its aid and willing to make some sacrifice of labour and money to that end'.[48]

This second model was superior. After all, London was a vast metropolis, as well as the centre of government, administration, commerce, trade, and banking. Consequently, Higher Education was 'a necessity' for a large number of people.[49] Indeed, Armitage-Smith contended, facilities for university education were proportionately much lower in London that in Scotland, Ireland, Wales, and the north of England.[50] He believed that it was important to distinguish the University of London from Oxbridge, not only on the grounds that those universities were residential but also because Oxford and Cambridge were

> the educational homes of the sons of the wealthy and of the fortunate (though not wealthy) few who can obtain scholarships; they are more or less uniform in tradition, atmosphere, tone, and training. They serve a section or stratum of the whole country and even the empire.[51]

This was the opposite of what a metropolitan university needed. It had to be non-residential; it was required to 'satisfy the diverse educational needs of a vast city and its suburbs'. Most importantly, it

> must be adapted to the needs of a large body of persons engaged in every branch of professional work, many of whom, while earning their own subsistence, have, nevertheless, sufficient time, energy, and desire to demand facilities for advanced instruction and research in subjects that have a bearing upon their own employments.[52]

The University of London should be a 'people's university'.[53]

The University of London would gain a great deal from including Birkbeck. This was because Birkbeck was primarily an evening institution. The city could not afford to ignore the educational needs of people who were employed during daylight hours: these students were 'drawn from classes of considerable culture' whose 'influence counts for much in social affairs'. It was unjust to deny such students university training. It was insulting to offer them only an 'inferior kind of degree or diploma'.[54] Armitage-Smith believed strongly in a common standard for degrees and was only pleading for flexibility in 'the details of hours, fees, and regulations to meet different conditions and circumstances'.[55] Finally, Birkbeck had been preparing students for the University of London's examinations for

---

[48] Ibid., 241. [49] Ibid., 241. [50] Ibid., 241. [51] Ibid., 241.
[52] Ibid., 241. [53] Ibid., 241. [54] Ibid., 241. [55] Ibid., 241.

degrees ever since the 1858 Charter, when the University started allowing it. The College was already part of the University of London 'in everything but name'.[56]

Armitage-Smith did have to address one major problem: the perception that the College was a polytechnic that taught practical trades rather than academic subjects. With exemplary patience, Armitage-Smith explained that the College's link to polytechnics had only been one of convenience. And, anyway, the grants the College received from the County Council 'were not made with a view to equipping [students] for trade or engineering classes, as those subjects were relegated to the new Northampton Institute'. It was understood at the time that 'the College would not develop in a technical direction, but would confine itself to the advance of scientific and general education, which had become its characteristic work'. The alliance with the City of London College and the Northampton Institute had always been minimal and their union had been 'dissolved a few years ago by mutual consent'.[57]

Armitage-Smith further noted that very little 'elemental work' was now taught at Birkbeck. Indeed, he pointedly announced, the proportion of non-university level courses at Birkbeck was actually smaller than at King's.[58] Birkbeck's teaching staff were 'recognised teachers' with high academic qualifications, strong publication records, and memberships in scientific councils and institutions.[59] He reminded the Commissioners that in June 1908, the governors of Birkbeck had made an application to be recognized as a school in the University of London on the grounds of 'the high standard of instruction, the large staff of "recognised teachers", and the great success achieved in examinations'.[60]

Armitage-Smith knew that he had to do more than merely promote the College; he also had to demolish King's key challenges.[61] The argument that Birkbeck was acting in an unfair, competitive fashion because its students paid lower fees was ridiculous, Armitage-Smith asserted. First, the objection referred to day pupils, who were only one fifth of Birkbeck's students. Second, Birkbeck's day fees were nearly double those of East London College. Third, Birkbeck provided an education for students who could not afford the higher fees. 'If the University is not to be a preserve of the rich or the endowed', Armitage-Smith declared, the existence of colleges like Birkbeck was essential. Birkbeck would 'not compete with the more expensive colleges' in the same way that 'modest shops of one street' do not compete 'with more fashionable and expensive shops in another street'.[62] The only relevant factor was quality of education. In this, Birkbeck excelled.

Armitage-Smith also disputed the proximity argument, noting that Birkbeck's students were 'drawn from a very wide area', a circuit of 30 miles (or 48 kilometres) around London. Fewer than 8 per cent of students lived within a

[56] Ibid., 242. [57] Ibid., 242. [58] Ibid., 242. [59] Ibid., 243.
[60] Ibid., 243. [61] Ibid., 243. [62] Ibid., 244.

1-mile radius.⁶³ Furthermore, most of the teaching at Birkbeck occurred in the evening. He was forced to admit that the College did some daytime teaching—something he wanted to preserve since it enabled the College to employ 'superior staff' at higher salaries and it was prudent that expensive equipment and rooms were not left 'idle' during the day.⁶⁴ But if there were to be any accusations of poaching students, then *King's* was to blame, not Birkbeck, since King's had recently attempted to introduce evening classes.⁶⁵ Armitage-Smith insisted that Birkbeck had 'always been a people's college, democratic in the truest sense of the term'; King's College, he bitingly noted, 'has a different tradition'.⁶⁶

At the end of hours of gruelling evidence, the chief message was Armitage-Smith's pride in Birkbeck students. 'The evening student has more stamina and greater capability of work than the younger day student', he contended, adding that such students are 'earnest, eager, intellectually alert'. Not content to simply regurgitate facts, Birkbeck students were 'anxious to understand principles' and were not shy about 'brac[ing] up to the lecturer' with 'inquiries and illustrations'. Birkbeck students were nothing less than 'the *élite* of the day worker; they represent not the average nor the many, but are the chosen few'.⁶⁷

Armitage-Smith was impressive. When the Royal Commission on University Education in London issued its final report in 1913, it recommended that Birkbeck College should become a 'Constituent College in the Faculties of Arts and Science for evening students' in the University of London.⁶⁸ It imposed two stipulations: Birkbeck had to abandon day-time teaching and it was to cease teaching economics (on the grounds that this was the prerogative of the London School of Economics).⁶⁹ Both were major concessions. After all, around one fifth of Birkbeck students were 'day students'⁷⁰ and Birkbeck's teaching in economics was distinguished. Indeed, Birkbeck was where Fabian Sidney Webb learnt economics. Unfortunately, Sidney and Beatrice Webb had co-established in 1895 (along with Graham Wallas and George Bernard Shaw) the LSE, so were probably partly responsible for the stipulation that competition in teaching economics was not allowed.

Unfortunately, the First World War intervened. As a consequence, it wasn't until 1920 that Birkbeck was officially granted University of London standing for a probationary period of five years. In 1925, when the governors applied for University of London recognition without time limit, they were informed by the Senate that, 'while the character and extent of the work performed by the College

---

⁶³ Ibid., 243.   ⁶⁴ Ibid., 244.   ⁶⁵ Ibid., 244–5.   ⁶⁶ Ibid., 244.   ⁶⁷ Ibid., 245.
⁶⁸ *Royal Commission on University Education in London. Final Report of the Commissioners* [Cd. 6717] (London: His Majesty's Stationery Office, 1913), 79.
⁶⁹ Ibid., 68 and 97.
⁷⁰ From the annual reports 1908–21. Note that the proportion varied from a low of 12 per cent in 1913–14 (probably because of the closure of the Art Department) to a high of 25 per cent in 1919–20 (probably because of ex-service students).

were sufficient to justify its continuation as a School of the University without time-limit', recognition was granted for only another five years pending the acquisition of buildings 'worthy of the College'.[71] A major period of building began.

* * *

Birkbeck's membership of the University of London dramatically raised its profile and intellectual standing. For the first time, the College could promote lecturing staff to the positions of reader and professor, and therefore to the highest echelons of academia. One of the first to gain such a title was the formidable Helen Gwynne-Vaughan, who became the first female professor in the College. In the History Department, Arthur Jones was promoted to a Readership, as was the German poetry enthusiast Jethro Bithell.[72]

In the flurry of activity leading up to the College's entrance into the University of London, the library was overhauled, effectively dealing with Humes' and Davies' complaints at the start of this chapter. In 1914, *The Lodestone* reported on these changes. It admitted that large sums of money used to be 'diverted to the purchase of rubbishy fiction and ephemeral publications of all kinds'. This would no longer be the case. All fiction, except 'that which can be termed classical', was 'cast out'. Individual departmental libraries (except for some specialist science ones) were amalgamated and housed in the old Reading Room, Study, and Students' Common Room. Books were no longer 'circulating' (a system that 'makes books filthy, shatters bindings, tears leaves and plays havoc with sets') but for reference only. Above all, students were requested never to return the books to the shelves. Instead, 'competent persons will kindly (but firmly)' put the books back in their 'proper places' in alphabetical order.[73] By the time of the declaration of the Second World War, the library held around 42,000 books, although a large proportion would be destroyed by bombs in May 1941.[74]

Armitage-Smith had many reasons to feel proud for having safely steered the College into the University of London. This did not stop commentators (even proud Birkbeckian ones) from repeating disparaging, and gender-offensive wisecracks: Birkbeck was a child who had become 'a companion of a lusty University'; the College was 'the Cinderella of London University Colleges' who had 'done her work in the kitchen of the Hall of Learning'; Birkbeck's admission into the University of London 'made an honest woman' out of the College.[75]

---

[71] *Birkbeck College (University of London). 102nd Session, Ended 31 July, 1925* (London: Birkbeck College, 1925), 12.

[72] *Birkbeck College (University of London). Report for 98th Session, 1920–21* (London: Birkbeck College, 1921), 7.

[73] H. G. R., 'Under Entirely New Management', *The Lodestone*, 10.1 (Michaelmas 1914), 3–4.

[74] 'Academic Board Minutes. October 1949 to July 1951', 'Minutes of the Meeting of the Academic Board, 2nd May 1950', in the Birkbeck Archive.

[75] Editorial, *The Lodestone*, 1.19 (1923), 2–3, and 'Birkbeck', *The Lodestone*, 46.1 (autumn 1954), 13.

More accurately, Birkbeck had won her place as a distinguished institution of Higher Education.

* * *

The entry of Birkbeck into membership of the University of London coincided neatly with the College's centenary three years later. In 1923, therefore, there was a great deal to celebrate. The proud chorus of Birkbeck's anthem—'Vivat Academia' (see Fig. 8.3)—reverberated around Birkbeck's lecture halls, theatre, and the Council Room in commemoration of the College's foundation. The chorus went:

> At the hub of all the world,
> London surging round us,
> Keep we Birkbeck's flag unfurl'd:
> Nothing shall confound us.

The music had been composed in 1908 by the wife of Armitage-Smith and the words written by George Francis Troup Horne, former student then Secretary and Clerk to the Governors for thirty-three years from 1919.[76] The words were platitudinous. At least one critic lamented the way that singers were 'rather inclined to draw out [the refrain] like a lot of villagers singing a hymn in chapel'.[77] But in 1923–4 it was sung exuberantly during the College's celebrations of its 100 years of existence.

Staff and students threw themselves into the festivities. Student societies, including those dedicated to drama, opera, science, politics, sport, and French language and literature invited members and their guests to attend special lectures and galas. Birkbeck's theatre company produced the Elizabethan tragedy *Arden of Feversham*,[78] which had recently been revived from obscurity thanks to the 'scholarly enthusiasm' and 'very pretty wit' of John Hay Lobban, Professor of English Language.[79] The Students' Union even published a book of poems that had previously appeared in *The Lodestone*, although even the Editor admitted that the verses were neither 'noteworthy' nor 'outstanding'. Indeed, he conceded, many were 'half-articulate'![80] Nevertheless, the volume was intended to pay tribute not only to Birkbeck's apprentice-poets but also to those student poets who, ten years

---

[76] *Birkbeck College, 1823–1913. Reception at Grafton Galleries, Grafton Way, W., 27th October, 1913, in Celebration of the Ninetieth Anniversary of the College* (London: Birkbeck College, 1913). The song was chosen from a number submitted for a prize: 'College Song', *The Lodestone*, 4.1 (December 1908), 30–1, which also gives the lyrics for the song in second place.

[77] Letter to Principal from Arthur Sorren, 30 January 1935, in 'Miscellaneous', in the Birkbeck Archive, Box 13.

[78] It is also spelt 'Faversham'.

[79] 'J.M.B.', 'The Way of the World', *The Graphic* (15 December 1923), 20.

[80] 'H. B.', 'Preface', in *Birkbeck College (University of London) Centenary 1823–1923. Verse Book. Being an Anthology Compiled from Poems which have Appeared in the Pages of the 'Lodestone', the Magazine of the Students' Union* (London: Birkbeck College, 1923), 1.

WHAT IS A UNIVERSITY? 135

Fig. 8.3 'Vivat Academia', the College's anthem. Birkbeck Archive, 'A3 Black Folder 1', pp. 11–12.

earlier, 'left their studies for France and those other battlefields from which there was no returning'.[81]

At the College level, eminent men (and they were all men) were invited to contribute to a series of public lectures, grandly themed 'Progress in…' They included: Labour Party grandee Richard Haldane ('Progress in Philosophy'); Michael Sadler, Master of University College, Oxford ('…Education'); Nobel laureate in Physics, Joseph John Thomson ('…Physical Science'); William Bateson, the scientist who coined the word 'genetics' ('…Biological Science'); diplomatic historian George Peabody Gooch ('…Historical Studies'); and economic historian William Ashley ('…Evolutionary Economics').[82] These orations were later bound together in a volume entitled *Birkbeck College Centenary Lectures* (1924) and prefaced by an elegant essay by Prime Minister and former Birkbeck student, Ramsay MacDonald.[83] Students were also invited to listen to Conservative statesman Arthur Balfour pontificate on politics, as well as Percy Moore Turner, art dealer and friend to the Bloomsbury Group, speaking about 'The Evolution of Modern Painting'.

Keen for Birkbeck's history to be more widely celebrated, the Master of the College had commissioned Cecil Delisle Burns to write the College's history. Burns was well known in progressive circles. As a young man, he had studied to join the priesthood but, by the time of the centenary, was one of Britain's most fervent atheists. He had also been appointed as the first lecturer in Birkbeck's Department of Philosophy when it was established in 1920. As a prolific author, Burns wrote the book very quickly. Nevertheless, a reviewer in the *Journal of the Royal Society of Arts* praised it for having 'thrown a curious—almost incredible—light on the manner in which popular education was regarded a hundred years ago'.[84] The College could not have hoped for more.

Burns' history was prefaced by an essay from Viscount Haldane of Cloan, the College President. He praised the College for the fact that 'a large part of the motive force which impelled' the transition from an institution which merely taught 'fragments' to one of 'university standard' was due to 'the students themselves'. These students 'have taken that education, not as a mere external advantage, but as what they aspire to incorporate with their souls'.[85] They have embraced learning because 'they have found that life is not complete without it'.[86]

Esteemed lectures, theatrical productions, and the publication of books could not compete with the key event in the centenary calendar, however.

---

[81] Ibid., 1.

[82] *Birkbeck College (University of London). Report. The 101st Session, 1923–24* (London: Birkbeck College, 1924), 6.

[83] *Birkbeck College Centenary Lectures* (London: Birkbeck College, 1924). Also see 'Books in Brief', *Aberdeen Press and Journal* (19 December 1924), 2.

[84] 'Notes on Books', *Journal of the Royal Society of Arts*, 73.3774 (20 March 1925), 430. For similar praise, see 'Notes on Books', *British Medical Journal* (5 April 1924), 634.

[85] Viscount Haldane of Cloan, 'Preface', in Burns, *A Short History of Birkbeck College*, 5–6.

[86] Ibid., 6.

This undoubtedly occurred on 20 March 1924 when former Prime Minister Stanley Baldwin gave the Centenary Foundation Oration. For Birkbeck students, this meant one thing: a 'ragging' (see Fig. 8.4). An 'uproarious' group of male and female students wearing make-up, dressed in 'fantastic costumes', and excited to a 'fever pitch', pounced on Baldwin outside of Chancery Lane, noisily shouting, 'Where's your pipe!' The students 'chaired' Baldwin to the Birkbeck theatre, where he was 'reminded of his affection for the juicy and consoling briar by a huge representation of a pipe which nearly concealed the top balcony of the theatre from view'. There, they presented him with a 'couple of pipes and a pound of tobacco'.[87] As many of the students 'sucked at empty churchwardens' (that is, long-stemmed tobacco pipes), Baldwin rose to give the 'centenary oration' (see Fig. 8.5).

He began by denying that his talk would be an 'oration' at all, since he disliked the word. Rather, he wanted to speak to them plainly about the greatness of being British. No other race, he proclaimed, had 'more ability, latent though it might be, than our own'. In particular, 'there was a higher aptitude for mechanical genius' in

Fig. 8.4 Ragging during the Centenary Celebrations of 1923. Birkbeck Archive.

---

[87] 'Gaining Marks', *Aberdeen Press and Journal* (21 March 1924), 7; 'Birkbeck', *The Lodestone*, 46.2 (spring/summer 1955), 26; 'Odd Moment Education', *Birmingham Daily Gazette* (21 March 1924), 5.

Fig. 8.5 Stanley Baldwin delivering the Foundation Oration at the College's Centenary in Bream's Building on 20 March 1924. He served three terms as Prime Minister in the 1920s and 1930s. Birkbeck Image Collections: Birkbeck History BH0218.

British people 'than there is in any other'.[88] Baldwin also lauded the values of a British education. He admitted that 'many people had tried to educate him, and the reaction was not always successful'.[89] Like most people, he contended, much of his education took place as he 'went about his business, in the evening, or on railway journeys, and at odd moments'.[90] The chief value of a good education, however achieved, was that it enabled a person not only to be 'the master of his own job' but also to know 'enough of other men's jobs to be able to understand the part they are playing in life'. Only this skill enabled people to practise 'humanity' and 'urbanity', which Baldwin defined as

> the way of going among your fellows as a brother man or a sister woman ready to help, ready to sympathize with people, and not to go through life as a perpetual blister.

At this point, the students began loudly cheering.[91] Perhaps in an attempt to calm them down, Baldwin closed his speech with a warning. 'Pride of intellect', he

---

[88] 'Odd Moment Education', *Birmingham Daily Gazette* (21 March 1924), 7. Also see 'The Student at Odd Moments', *Belfast News-Letter* (21 March 1924), 10.
[89] 'Odd Moment Education', *Birmingham Daily Gazette* (21 March 1924), 5.   [90] Ibid., 5.
[91] 'The Educated Man', *The Scotsman* (21 March 1924), 6.

lectured, was 'more vulgar than the pride of the *nouveau riche* in his wealth, for the simple reason that the *nouveau riche* has made his own money, whereas your intellect is a gift of God'.[92] On that pompous note, Baldwin sat down.

After the applause had faded away and the audience had started to disperse, Baldwin left the theatre, smoking one of his newly acquired pipes. In their excitement, however, Birkbeck students had nearly forgotten the 'final item in the Union programme'. As Baldwin's car was pulling out of Fetter Lane, they remembered: a large crowd of students ran after his car, finally overtaking it outside the Law Courts. Then, 'surrounded by a cheering mob', a breathless Master of Ceremonies presented the former Prime Minister with a 'sucking [sic] pig'.[93]

The dramatic highpoint of the centenary was the 'ragging' of Baldwin; a much more formal celebration took place eleven days later. On 31 March 1924, nearly 250 people gathered in the grand dining room at Princes Restaurant in Piccadilly to dine on some of London's best food and to soak up flattery (see Fig. 8.6).[94] This was organized by Birkbeck's Court of Electors—alumni who elected four representatives to the College's governing body. Sound engineers from the BBC were present to broadcast the event live from 9.45 p.m. Reports from listeners as far afield as Chester and Manchester declared that the 'audition was perfect'.[95]

Fig. 8.6 The Court of Electors' centenary dinner at Princes Restaurant on 31 March 1924. Birkbeck Image Collections: Birkbeck History BH0220.

[92] Ibid., 6.
[93] 'Birkbeck', *The Lodestone*, 46.2 (spring/summer 1955), 26.
[94] For a grand image, see https://www.agefotostock.com/age/en/Stock-Images/Rights-Managed/MEV-10578849 and http://collections.britishart.yale.edu/vufind/Record/3803618.
[95] 'The Court of Electors', *The Lodestone*, 20.3 (1924), 149.

With the Vice-Chancellor of the University of London chairing the event, the guests and thousands of people throughout the UK heard eloquent speeches from the French ambassador, the Lord Chancellor, the Secretary General, politician William Bull, industrialist William Lionel Hichens, scientist David Owen, and businesswoman and suffragette Margaret Mackworth. King George V was unable to be present in person, but he sent a message in which he listed the close ties between the College and the royal family. He boasted that the Duke of Sussex had laid the Foundation Stone for the London Mechanics' Institution in 1824, his father (then, the Prince of Wales) had opened its new building in 1885, and he, his wife, and Queen Alexandra (his mother) were all patrons.[96]

Not to be outdone, Archibald Primrose, the 5th Earl of Rosebery and Chancellor of the University of London, also sent a moving tribute, praising Birkbeck students for their 'perseverance over difficulties'. He lamented that there was a great deal of 'apathy and indifference displayed in general towards Education in England'. This meant that it was incredibly important that, despite the 'myriad distractions' of metropolitan life, there existed an educational establishment like Birkbeck. Only at such a place could

> hundreds of men and women who, engaged during the day in earning the wherewithal to live, spend their leisure hours in seeking that knowledge which...tends so much to increase the pleasure of life and the value of the individual to the community.[97]

The most florid response, though, came from Prime Minister J. Ramsay MacDonald. After recalling his own 'happy memories' of studying at Birkbeck, he noted that the College was a 'gateway', enabling people who were 'walled in by the limits of their own occupations' to 'adventure into the wide fields of Learning and Opportunity'.[98] Speeches over, wine was imbibed, followed by more wine and food.

By the end of the year-long celebrations, was it any wonder that centenary fatigue set in? Students and staff alike could be seen wandering the corridors of Birkbeck with 'haggard faces and lustreless eyes'.[99] In the words of an unnamed 'genial gentleman' speaking at the 'Rugger Supper', 'any further mention of the word "Centenary" would...gravely accelerate the ordinarily dignified human progress towards lunacy'.[100] The centenary over, the College settled down to consolidating its vision and status.

---

[96] Ibid., 149.   [97] Ibid., 149.   [98] Ibid., 149.
[99] 'Centenary Orations', *The Lodestone*, 20.3 (1924), 147.   [100] Ibid., 147.

PART II
PLEASURE AND PREFERENCES

9
Art and Architecture

In the corridor leading to the Vice-Chancellor's office at Birkbeck is a glass cabinet containing a wooden palette. The inscription states:

THE PALETTE OF
BENJAMIN ROBERT HAYDON
Which he used when painting
'MACBETH'
'THE JUDGMENT OF SOLOMON'
'CHRIST'S ENTRY INTO JERUSALEM'
'LAZARUS'
1786–1846

'Presented to the London Mechanics' Institute, May 16, 1836, by B. R. Haydon as a memento of respect for the conduct of its honourable President, Dr Birkbeck, and its Members, in opening their doors to him when every other institution had the moral cowardice to close them.'[1]

Benjamin Robert Haydon is not famous today but in the first half of the nineteenth century he was a celebrity painter, celebrated for his enthusiasm for reviving British history painting on vast canvases. His themes were imposing. His oil paintings depict scenes from the Bible and Shakespeare; he indulged in dramatic portraits of classical history, royalty, and battle. Haydon's warm dedication to George Birkbeck was due to the fact that, in the 1830s, the LMI gave him a platform to spread his ideas when, as Haydon put it, other institutions (by which he primarily meant the Royal Academy) had the 'moral cowardice' to attempt to silence him. The palette that he donated to the LMI had been 'used in the execution of his most celebrated works', and Haydon wanted it 'to remain over the Chimney Piece in the Committee Room, between the Drawings of his Pupils' as 'evidence of his affectionate regard for the cheering reception he met with during his lectures'.[2] Birkbeck no longer has a chimney over which Haydon's palette can hang, and his pupils' drawings have long disappeared, but George Birkbeck's commitment to artistic and intellectual freedom remains central to the College's ethos.

* * *

---

[1] Burns, *A Short History of Birkbeck College*, 53.
[2] Cited in a letter from the Secretary to Denisle Burns, 2 November 1923, in 'Birkbeck College Letters', in Birkbeck Archives, Box 65.67.

In his time, Haydon was greatly admired. He was friend to some of the most illustrious writers, critics, and social commentators of the time, including Romantic poets such as John Keats, William Wordsworth, Samuel Taylor Coleridge, Robert Southey, Joanna Baillie, and Elizabeth Barrett; essayists Leigh Hunt, William Hazlitt, and Charles Lamb; actresses Maria Foote and Sarah Siddons; and author Mary Russell Mitford. He inspired Keats to write the 'Ode on a Grecian Urn'. These connections, as well as his mesmerizing lectures on the theory of painting and design, made him a real asset for the LMI.

However, Haydon was a profligate character, always in debt. This explains why, when he was invited in September 1835 to give lectures at the LMI, for which he would be paid a share of the audiences' fees, he eagerly accepted. Admittedly, he was forced to use a gift of 5 guineas to get his black dress-coat out of the pawn shop in time for his first lecture.[3] However, Haydon confessed in his diary, 'after all my humiliations', this lecture was 'at first a rather nervous affair', but had been warmly received. 'I laid down principles which must reform English Art', Haydon boasted, and his audience had 'gloriously comprehended them'. They

> paid me keen and intense attention, and ultimately were enthusiastic. One man said my delivery was perfect; another, who was deaf, said my delivery was the only thing wanting. Dr. Birkbeck said, as we went out, 'You have got 'em: it is a hit'; and I think it was.[4]

In his second lecture in January 1836, Haydon became even more daring: he spoke about the nude figure. We don't know if it happened at that lecture, but at some future ones he rather audaciously had a nude posing on the stage.[5] Haydon was defiant, telling the assembled members and students at the LMI that

> if they did not get rid of every feeling of indelicacy in seeing the naked form, and did not relish its abstract beauty, [then a] taste for Grand Art would never be rooted amongst them.

He reported that this statement 'was received with applause, and I broke the ice for ever. I always said the middle classes were sound, and I am sure of it.'[6]

As this suggests, Haydon was not shy of expressing his views including his politics. Although he could never be said to be a democrat, he was a strong

---

[3] Journal entry for 13 January 1836, in Benjamin Robert Haydon, *The Autobiography and Journals of Benjamin Robert Haydon*, ed. Malcolm Elwin, 1st pub. 1853 (London: MacDonald, 1950), 539.

[4] Journal entry for 8 September 1835, in Haydon, *The Autobiography and Journals of Benjamin Robert Haydon*, 536.

[5] Eric Warmington, 'Students of Birkbeck. I. From Institution to College', *The Lodestone*, 53.3 (summer 1963), 4.

[6] Journal entry for 13 January 1836, in Haydon, *The Autobiography and Journals of Benjamin Robert Haydon*, 539.

supporter of the Reform Act of 1832, which led to major changes in the electoral system including dramatically increasing the number of people entitled to vote in elections to one in five men. Late in his life, he was also a convert to the anti-slavery cause, producing a painting to commemorate the World Anti-Slavery Convention in 1840.[7]

His real obsession, though, was the politics of the art world. Echoing the ethos of the LMI but applying it to the fine arts, Haydon argued that 'Government has a responsibility to the public in art as much as in education.'[8] He campaigned vigorously for the wider appreciation of art: in particular, he contended that governments had a responsibility to buy works of artistic merit and to allow the general public, as opposed to patrons and connoisseurs only, to view them.[9] This was an unusual, even radical, idea at the time.

Haydon was not an easy character, however. Like George Birkbeck, he was enthusiastic about anatomy and had once assisted the famous physiologist Sir Charles Bell in dissecting a lioness.[10] He was also fanatical, egotistical, combative, and a relentless self-promoter.[11] At one stage, Haydon was so convinced that the LMI's fee of 5 guineas per lecture was proof of his popularity that he decided to offer his lectures independent of the Institution. Haydon hired the theatre from the LMI but, when he turned up to give his first lecture, he was 'sadly grieved' to find the room almost empty.[12] Humbled, he returned his name to the LMI's roster of lectures, where he attracted crowds in the hundreds. Haydon worked sixteen or more hours a day[13] and believed himself to be brilliant. In his diary, he even maintained that 'genius' (by which he primarily meant his own) 'will arise and make its way, if born at the bottom of the Indian Ocean'.[14]

Unfortunately, artists in the early nineteenth century relied almost entirely on the patronage of royalty and extremely rich families to make a living. And not everyone agreed with Haydon's self-assessment of painterly genius. A childhood illness had left him with very poor eyesight, so he struggled with the large canvases that he so admired.[15] Whig politician Thomas Babington Macaulay dismissed

---

[7] For a complex discussion of Haydon's changing views on race, see David Higgins, 'Art, Genius, and Racial Theory in the Early Nineteenth Century: Benjamin Robert Haydon', *History Workshop Journal*, 58 (autumn 2004), 17–40.

[8] 'Benjamin Robert Haydon (1786–1846)', *Burlington Magazine for Connoisseurs*, 88.519 (June 1946), 133.

[9] William Vaughan, 'Higher Education and the Visual Arts', in Roderick Floud and Sean Glynn (eds), *London Higher: The Establishment of Higher Education in London* (London: Athlone Press, 1998), 268.

[10] Theodore Dalrymple, 'A Painter's Writings', *British Medical Journal*, 343.7830 (5 November 2011), 961.

[11] For example, see Clarke Olney, 'John Keats and Benjamin Robert Haydon', *PMLA*, 49.1 (March 1934), 258–75.

[12] Buss, *Eighty Years Experience of Life*, 24.   [13] Dalrymple, 'A Painter's Writings', 961.

[14] Benjamin Robert Haydon, *The Diary of Benjamin Robert Haydon*, ed. William Bissell Pope, vol. 1 (1960), 241.

[15] Buss, *Eighty Years Experience of Life*, 25.

his works as 'painted signs'[16] and Charles Dickens contended that 'all his life, [Haydon] had utterly mistaken his vocation... he most unquestionably was a very bad painter'.[17]

Given such assessments, is it any wonder that Haydon was paranoid? He believed that members of the artistic establishment were persecuting him. He was 'gravely mortified' that the Royal Academy was 'ignoring his masterful talent and refusing to hang his pictures'.[18] His vigorous fights with the Royal Academy were the stuff of legend, as he accused academicians of being nothing short of a corrupt clique of low-grade portrait painters.[19] He believed that the fine arts consisted of more than ostentatious portraits and grand historical narratives (although these were his themes) but also included those artistic skills essential for designers and manufacturers. He lobbied the government to establish a National Art School.[20] Such a school, he bullishly noted, would do the job that the Royal Academy was neglecting.

None of this detracted from the mesmerizing nature of his lectures. Henry Buss, a member of the Committee of the LMI, attended Haydon's lectures in the 1830s. In later years, Buss recalled that between 100 and 200 eager students would crowd the lecture theatre, awed by 'being in pupilage under so grand a subject-painter'.[21] Buss observed that Haydon's diagrams were nothing short of 'masterful in precision, firmness and quickness' and his knowledge of 'literature and oratory [was] very good'.[22] Buss contended that

> Few men were better qualified to lecture on the fine arts than Haydon. In treating of Greek sculpture, he reminded his hearers that the frequent display of athletes and gladiators, almost nude, in the public arenas, sufficed to educate the artistic eye of the period, to realise in sculpture and painting, the necessary prominence of the superficial muscles, resulting from the varied movements of the body, as dictated by the will of the models.

Even more thrilling, Buss recalled that Haydon would illustrate his arguments by bringing life-guardsmen into the lecture theatre, where they 'stripped to the waist, wrestling together, and otherwise going through strained exertions'.[23] Was it any wonder that members and students were entranced?

Lecturing at the LMI would never provide enough money to pay off Haydon's debts, which exceeded £3,000. His appeals for money from Lord Brougham (the

---

[16] G. O. Trevelyan, *The Life and Letters of Lord Macaulay* (London: Longman, Green, and Co., 1881), 597.
[17] Charles Dickens, cited by Dalrymple, 'A Painter's Writings', 961.
[18] Buss, *Eighty Years Experience of Life*, 25.   [19] Higgins, 'Art, Genius, and Racial Theory', 21.
[20] Vaughan, 'Higher Education and the Visual Arts', 269.
[21] Buss, *Eighty Years Experience of Life*, 25.   [22] Ibid., 24.   [23] Ibid., 25.

great patron of the LMI) were met with silence. Buss observed that Haydon was becoming increasingly bitter about his failure to 'obtain the patronage which he believed he merited, because of his exclusion from the Royal Academy'. He fell into 'fits of morbid mental depression'.[24] The end came painfully. On 22 June 1846, his daughter found him slumped next to a blood-splattered easel on which he had been painting a portrait of 'Alfred and the first British Jury': he had shot himself in the head with a low-calibre bullet and, when the end didn't come quickly enough, slashed his throat with a razor. Next to his body lay a piece of paper, on which was written:

> In the name of my God I hope for forgiveness for the step I am about to take—a crime, no doubt; but if I am judged immediately hereafter, I have done nothing all my life that will render me fearful of appearing before the awful consciousness of my invisible God, or hesitate to explain my actions.... I am sure He will be just, however awfully displeased, at the wickedness of my conclusion. I forgive my enemies and slanderers from my heart, and hope my worthy and *unworthy* creditors will forgive me. I meant all in honour.[25]

He was only 61 years of age.

* * *

A year before Haydon's inglorious suicide, art lectures at the LMI had been regularized by the founding of an Art School in the basement of the Birkbeck Bank in the Southampton Buildings (see Fig. 9.1).[26] In his account of 'scientific London' in 1874, Bernard H. Becker described descending to the basement of the LMI where 'in a semi-circular cavern, hung round with plaster casts, and lighted with flaring gas, is crowded together a large number of pupils busy over their drawing boards'. Becker was impressed by the students' intense concentration, contending that such 'persistence [is] generally observed in those who pay for their instruction out of their own hardly-earned wages'. There was

> no dawdling and no 'larking' visible, and the spirit of work which apparently inspires every department of the Birkbeck is clearly dominant in this ill-lighted cellar where, in spite of every disadvantage, valuable knowledge and technical dexterity can be acquired by those who seek for them.[27]

---

[24] Ibid., 25.
[25] Haydon, *The Autobiography and Journals of Benjamin Robert Haydon*, 653.
[26] 'City School of Art to Cease', *The Standard* (10 July 1913), and 'A.E.R.', '[Obituary] Mr A. W. Mason', *The Times* (10 August 1933), 12.
[27] Becker, *Scientific London*, 213.

Fig. 9.1 Art class at the Birkbeck Literary and Scientific Institution in the early 1900s. The use of naked or semi-naked models in the 'life class' was lampooned in a novel by William Pett Ridge (a famous novelist who had been a student in the LMI) entitled *Three Women and Mr Frank Cardwell* (1898). In the novel, a 'grim lady' kept the register for the art classes, keeping a 'very stern and careful eye' on the 'life class'. Birkbeck Image Collections: Birkbeck History BH0099.

Haydon would have approved.

Except for Becker's description, we know almost nothing about this Art School until 1878 when the classes were taken over by Alfred William Mason, together with Childs Pocock and around seven assistants.[28] As a friend of John Seymour Lucas (the distinguished Victorian historical and portrait painter) and Sir George Frampton (a leading member of the New Sculpture movement), Mason was at the heart of 'London of the "artistic eighties"'.[29] He held his position at Birkbeck at the same time as he was Assistant Art Master at Eton.[30] He was only 30 when he was appointed to the LMI and brought with him immense energy. His Art School was the only one in the City of London and was the first in London to accept female students.[31] Perhaps this helps explain the emphasis on commercial art, such as

---

[28] 'City School of Art to Cease', *The Standard* (10 July 1913).
[29] 'A.E.R.', 'Mr A. W. Mason', *The Times* (10 August 1933), 12.
[30] 'Birkbeck Men: Mr Alfred W. Mason', *Birkbeck Institution Magazine* (July 1893), 98.
[31] 'City School of Art to Cease', *Standard* (10 July 1913).

the drawing of fashion plates.[32] The Art School was so respected that, when the students' artistic works were exhibited in the galleries of the Institution, they merited reviews in *The Times*.[33]

Famous students included John Henry Amschewitz, who, in 1911, created the famous fresco at the Royal Exchange, entitled *Henry VI Battle of Barnet 1471, the Trained Bands Marching to the Support of Edward IV*. It also included Hanslip Fletcher (illustrator and painter specializing in architectural studies on London) and Thomas Maybank (surveyor and painter, publishing in *Punch*).[34] William James Bull, who became a leading solicitor and Conservative politician, was a student. In 1883, he recalled, the class resembled a 'picturesque scene' with 'lighted furnaces' housed in a 'large old-fashioned building'. After class, he and his fellow art students would visit the iron foundries and other manufacturing workshops in Hatton Gardens and the surrounding streets around Holborn. They would 'watch men making all kinds of things in glass—vases, fancy-wares, test-tubes, and the like' and, occasionally, would be allowed to blow 'glass ourselves', turning out 'fancy shapes on the lathes with the help of the workmen'.[35] This was the time before the mass factory production of such things, when even the most intricate scientific equipment had to be produced individually and by hand.

The most notable student was Isaac Rosenberg, who won the Mason Prize in 1917 for his 'time-studies from the figure'. His art career was disrupted by the 1914–18 war, which saw him thrown into the front line. From the trenches on 28 March 1918, just four days before he was killed,[36] he reflected that

> during our little interlude of rest from the line I managed to do a bit of sketching—somebody had colours—and they werent [sic] so bad. I dont [sic] think I have forgotten my art after all.

He also began writing poetry, although he admitted with characteristic understatement that 'we are very busy just now and poetry is right out of our scheme'.[37]

Rosenberg was one of millions of talented young men killed in their prime. Today, he is not known for his art, but for his bitter, posthumously published war poems. In one, entitled 'Dead Man's Dump', Rosenberg described

> The wheels lurched over sprawling dead
> But pained them not, though their bones crunched,

---

[32] 'The Birkbeck School of Art', *The Times* (25 September 1912), 8.   [33] Ibid., 8.
[34] Chas. W. F. Goss, 'Birkbeck Art School. L.C.C. Criticised', *The City Press* (18 October 1913).
[35] Bull, 'Forty Years Back', 3.
[36] 'The Birkbeck School of Art', *The Times* (2 October 1907), 2. Also see 'Birkbeck School of Art', *Morning Post* (30 September 1907), in the Birkbeck Archive.
[37] Isaac Roseberg, *The Collected Works of Isaac Rosenberg: Poetry, Prose, Letters, and Some Drawings*, ed. Gordon Bottomley and Denys Harding (London: Chatto and Windus, 1937), 322.

> Their shut mouths made no moan,
> They lie there huddled, friend and foemen,
> Man born of man and born of woman,
> And shells go crying over them
> From night till night and now...
> A man's brains splattered on
> A stretcher-bearer's face;
> His shook shoulders slipped their load,
> But when they bent to look again
> The drowning soul was sunk too deep
> For human tenderness.[38]

In the foreword to these poems, Siegfried Sassoon recognized Rosenberg's sensibilities as a British-Jew and artist. He noted how Rosenberg's poems encapsulated the 'hateful and repellant, unforgettable and inescapable' realities of life in the front line. Rosenberg was 'naturally empowered with something of the divine spirit', Sassoon contended, 'which touches our human clay to sublimity of expression'. But his death in war denied the world of his full artistic brilliance.[39]

Mason's classes were not only renowned because of their students. They became famous for introducing the novel practice of including architecture in the syllabus. By the end of the 1890s, architecture students eagerly joined the classes in order to hear lectures on topics such as classical design.[40] This explains why Albert Edward Richardson came to the Institution to be taught by both Mason and Pocock. Richardson went on to become a leading English architect as well as President of the Royal Academy. His fastidious sensibilities can be judged by the fact that he refused (initially, at least) to install electricity in his eighteenth-century townhouse on the grounds that it was not in harmony with its Georgian style. Richardson praised the LMI for being one of the first in London to 'recognize art to be necessary to social attainment'.[41]

Mason worked at the Art School for thirty-four years and oversaw the move of the school from the basement of the LMI to sunny, spacious, upper-floor studios next door. However, the school was closed in 1912–13.[42] The lease on the building had come to an end and the London County Council refused to renew the annual grant. The Birkbeck Art School was also facing competition from the new London

---

[38] Ibid., 81 and 83.   [39] Siegfried Sassoon, 'Foreword', in ibid., ix–x.
[40] Sir Albert Edward Richardson, 'Scholarship and the Fine Arts' (London: Birkbeck College, 1955), and 'A.E.R.', '[Obituary] Mr A. W. Mason', *The Times* (10 August 1933), 12.
[41] Richardson, 'Scholarship and the Fine Arts'.
[42] Fred A. Mackenzie, 'The Birkbeck Institution: The Story of London's Evening University', *Windsor Magazine: An Illustrated Monthly for Men and Women*, 7 (December 1897), 378, and 'Report of the Birkbeck Literary and Scientific Institution (City Polytechnic) for the 69th Session 1891–92', 5, in the Birkbeck Archive.

County Council School of Arts and Crafts.[43] Perhaps just as relevant in explaining the school's demise was the fact that the Master, George Armitage-Smith, was keen to remove all non-university subjects from the College's curriculum in his campaign to have Birkbeck admitted as part of the University of London. As Bull lamented, 'the Powers-that-Be' sought to 'divorce Art from a university education'.[44]

In the end, the remaining students and alumni presented Mason with a volume of 'illuminated addresses', along with a 'purse of gold'.[45] Unsurprisingly, Mason was proud of the reputation he had built at The Birkbeck. He set up his own private School of Art, advertising it as 'formerly the Birkbeck School of Art', until forced by the College to give up this form of advertising.[46] Mason died in 1933, aged 85 years. To the regret of many in the College today, the Birkbeck School of Art has still not been resuscitated.

* * *

Mason's emphasis on architecture as an important part of a fine arts training returned to the College nearly thirty years later. Nikolaus Pevsner, the first Professor of Art History at Birkbeck and the most influential architectural historian of the twentieth century, was following in a very strong Birkbeck tradition. Like Haydon and Mason, Pevsner sought to bring the fine arts to wider audiences; he was passionate about widening the definition of the 'fine arts' to include manufacturing design and architecture (something that was usual in Germany where he studied); and he believed in the power of the arts to transform lives. As historian Paul Crossley explained in the introduction to *Reassessing Nikolaus Pevsner* (1998), Pevsner 'almost single-handed' dragged 'English architecture into public consciousness, and elevated it into an art form to be studied, enjoyed, and protected alongside the other "fine arts"'. Pevsner sought to teach Englishmen and women about 'the glories of their architectural past and to convert them to a Modernist aesthetic in tune with what he held to be the deepest impulses of the twentieth century'.[47] This emphasis on 'Englishness' is important because Pevsner was especially attuned to English (rather than 'British') identities in artistic expression. He was a proponent of *Kunstgeographie*, a form of environmental and climatic determinism, and vigorously celebrated the Englishness of English art and architecture. This was a rare thing at a time when European styles were regarded as superior.

---

[43] *Birkbeck College. Report. Ninetieth Session, 1912–13* (London: Geo. Barber, 1913) and 'City School of Art to Cease', *The Standard* (10 July 1913).
[44] Bull, 'Forty Years Back', 3.   [45] 'City School of Art to Cease', *The Standard* (10 July 1913).
[46] 'Minutes of Meeting of Governing Body, 19th January, 1914', in *BC Minute Book. 16th Sep., 1912 to 29th July, 1919*, in the Birkbeck Archive.
[47] Paul Crossley, 'Introduction', in Peter Draper (ed.), *Reassessing Nikolaus Pevsner* (London: Ashgate, 2004), 1.

The fact that Pevsner was not English was an advantage. He had been born in Leipzig into a wealthy Jewish family of Russian origin. Although he had converted to Lutheranism as a young man, in 1933 the Nazis dismissed him from his lectureship at the University of Göttingen, despite his early sympathy for German nationalism and even Reichsminister Josef Goebbel's programme of interfering in art.[48] The following year, he emigrated to Birmingham, but his parents remained in Germany. His father died in 1940 and, shortly afterwards, his mother committed suicide rather than be transported to a concentration camp.[49]

Pevsner was a prodigious writer, editor, and broadcaster, as well as chairing numerous organizations, including the Victorian Society. However, he was most famous for his forty-six volumes (of which he wrote thirty-eight and contributed substantially to others) called *Buildings of England* (1951–74).[50] Each volume focused on one county and sought to be a comprehensive account of all buildings of architectural interest in that area from the Saxon period to the present.

Pevsner was a familiar figure in London as well as the College. Birkbeck historian Eric Hobsbawm remembered seeing him 'perambulating the area for his great *Buildings of England* like an examiner giving marks to the past'.[51] Pevsner would probably not have liked being caricatured as a kind of scolding schoolmaster. His own metaphors were much more combatant. As he told one journalist, he was engaging in an architectural 'blitzkrieg raid on each target county'. He explained that he and his wife would start their travels early in the morning. Equipped with 'the day's schedule, maps, gazettes, official list, clipboard and midday break sandwiches', his wife would drive the car while Pevsner scribbled 'on the trot around the next Norman church or Victorian public lavatory'. Evenings were spent 'in the hotel transcribing accumulated notes, planning tomorrow's foray, plotting the navigation, writing letters and making appointments'.[52] Pevsner admitted that, when he first started the project, he had little idea of how to find 'the right things', but (like Haydon) he worked a '90-hour week, cramming two weeks into one'. He later reflected that he

> managed to live two lifetimes.... It was done by starving the rest of my existence. I never went to the theatre, a concert, a film. Always working. That's not right. It is not good for one's humanity.... I don't regret it. There was nothing I could do about it. That's the way I was made.[53]

---

[48] Stephen Games, *Pevsner: The Early Life—Germany and Art* (London: Continuum, 2010).
[49] Peter Murray, 'Nikolaus Bernhard Leon Pevsner', *Proceedings of the Royal Academy* (1985), 501.
[50] Alec Clifton-Taylor, 'Address Given at the Memorial Service in the Church of Christ the King, Bloomsbury, for Nikolaus Pevsner: 6 December 1983', *Architectural History*, 28 (1985), 5.
[51] Eric Hobsbawm, *Interesting Times: A Twentieth Century Life* (London: Allen Lane, 2002), 176.
[52] 'The Professor's Doomsday Odyssey', *Sunday Times* (25 February 1973), in 'Newscuttings 1971–3', in the Birkbeck Archive.
[53] Ibid.

The invitation for Pevsner to lecture on architecture and art history at Birkbeck was initially made in February 1940. The College was losing most of its male lecturers to war-work. George Francis Troup Horne, the College Secretary, not only was deeply impressed by Pevsner's scholarship but also saw an opportunity to help alleviate a serious staffing crisis. Pevsner's first lecture was a success but did not translate into a more regular job.

From the end of 1940, the war came home. German planes started bombing London and other cities. Pevsner joined other refugees and émigrés in helping local authorities to clean up the mess after the bombing. Pevsner became one of the 'rubble-shovellers'. He asked himself:

> Why shouldn't a man like me—a creature of luxury, author, lecturer—try to earn my money honestly and usefully, try to offer some help to England this way, if England wasn't ready to let me help in the way to which I was most suited?

He reflected that it was 'dirty work.... One is not digging the garden, after all, God's own earth, but broken tiles, decoying cement, bent and rusty pieces of iron, fragments of furniture, suits thick with filth and damp.'[54] The job still had to be done.

On 29 December 1940, an incendiary raid on the city of London led to what was called the 'second Fire of London'.[55] In panic, the government rapidly introduced compulsory fire-watching duties on all men on the home front aged between 16 and 60. Troup Horne employed Pevsner to join him in protecting Bream's Building in Chancery Lane from fire during the night. They were joined by Count Nicholas Egon, who had read physics, chemistry, and psychology at Birkbeck from 1937, but was to become a renowned portrait painter.[56] Pevsner combined fire-watching with giving occasional lectures on topics such as the 'decline and fall of Roman art' and 'the spirit of Roman as against Greek art' during daylight hours.[57] As Pevsner wrote in a letter to Esther Simpson at the Society for the Protection of Science and Learning (now the Council for At-Risk Academics):

> I have received promotion and am now fire-spotter at Birkbeck College. It is by no means the kind of return to academic surroundings that one would fancy, but it is a decided improvement.[58]

---

[54] Cited in Susie Harries, *Nikolaus Pevsner* (London: Vintage Digital, 2011), 186–7. Pevsner wrote two articles about this under the pen-name 'Ramaduri', a contraction of the emphatic utterance 'Räumen tu ich!', pronounced in a heavy Bavarian accent. They were called 'My Colleagues the Rubble-Shovellers' and 'The Psychology of the Rubble-Shoveller'. They were written in German and published in *Die Zeitung*.
[55] Harries, *Nikolaus Pevsner*, 291.
[56] 'Count Nicholas Egon: Diminutive, Philanthropic Czech Count Who Worked as a War Artist Before Becoming a Portrait Painter', *The Times* (20 October 2017), 48.
[57] Harries, *Nikolaus Pevsner*, 325.   [58] Ibid., 292.

The two men watched for fires on the roof of Bream's Building: Troup Horne also used the time on the roof to trap pigeons for his famous pigeon-pies, while Pevsner sat on a bucket and wrote the first draft of *Outline of European Architecture* (1943). This was his first major best-seller: it sold over 1 million copies, was published in seven editions, and translated into sixteen languages.[59] Troup Horne and Pevsner became friends. This was why the first London volume of *The Buildings of England* was dedicated 'To the memory of G. F. Troup Horne and the nights of 1941–1944 at the old Birkbeck College in Bream's Building'.

After the war, the College finally issued Pevsner with a regular contract. He lectured not only to students on art history courses but also to students of English literature (for example, lectures on art in George Eliot's *Romola*) and those of modern languages (architecture in the age of Goethe, for instance). Pevsner's method was simple: he would approach lecturers in the Departments of History, English, French, and German, and, after inquiring about their teaching, would offer to 'provide them with a few lectures dealing with art and architecture from their specific point of view'.[60]

Pevsner was a driven man. He was impelled by the belief that art is a form of cultural history, a visual codification of the times in which it was produced. In his words, art is the 'visual expression of the history of man's mind'.[61] For example, the 'informality of the English garden' reflected English laissez-faire democracy, while the more formal Continental gardens were 'ascribed to French-inspired absolutism'.[62] As he wrote in his lecture notes,

> It is this spirit of the ages which I want to define.... Not in the childish way of the sworn Marxist who thinks it is all just social changes, causing the others. Something much subtler, less material, less clumsy. You can call it irrational. I believe in its existence, see in it the deepest cause of evolution, and find this belief confirmed in thousands of details which once you follow the method dictated by this belief, fall into their proper places and reveal their true meaning.[63]

It was such an approach that led him to the view that the modernist style, with its functionalist ethic, was in tune with the democratic, anti-hierarchical character of British society.

Pevsner was also a fervent believer in the value of teaching art and architectural history as full university subjects. For him, art history is not a form of moral

---

[59] Murray, 'Nikolaus Bernhard Leon Pevsner', 505.
[60] Nikolaus Pevsner, '[Letter to the Editor] Study of Art History', *The Times* (5 November 1952), 9.
[61] Nikolaus Pevsner, 'Reflections on Not Teaching Art History', in Stephen Games, *Pevsner: The Complete Broadcast Talks—Architecture and Art on Radio and Television, 1945–1977* (London: Ashgate, 2014), 198. Radio talk for the BBC Third Programme on 19 October 1952.
[62] Crossley, 'Introduction', in Draper (ed.), *Reassessing Nikolaus Pevsner*, 13.
[63] Harries, *Nikolaus Pevsner*, 426.

or aesthetic 'uplift'; neither does it merely provide 'background' context that runs 'parallel to history and modern languages'. Rather, it is a set of knowledges in its own right.[64] The eyes, he contended, 'should help to enlighten the mind on matters of *style* as they apply to drama and poetry and even to social history, as much as to painting'.[65] Pevsner argued that people should 'look at a Victorian villa in the same way one approaches a Syrian church of the 6th century'.[66] Both are worthy of serious contemplation.

Consequently, Pevsner fought for art history to become a standard part of the university curriculum. He believed that

> Studies in the history of art are as scholarly and as disciplined a pursuit as social and constitutional history or history of thought, though many people seem still inclined to deny that.[67]

In his Reith Lectures on the BBC Home Service on 16 October 1955, Pevsner repeated this theme, lamenting the fact that 'the history of art is not a universally accepted academic subject in this country, as it is on the Continent and America'. He insisted that

> an understanding and appreciation of the work of the artist adds to the truly valuable pleasures and therefore enhances one's life. That poetry or music can do that, no one denies. The revelations which can reach us through the eye are less familiar.[68]

Like Haydon and Mason before him, Pevsner's views were innovative. All three men took industrial and domestic design seriously. Pevsner believed that 'ninety per cent of British industrial art' was 'devoid of any aesthetic merit'.[69] For him, the 'fight against the shoddy design of those goods by which our fellow-men are surrounded' was 'a moral duty'.[70]

All three men also sought to remove architectural history from the province of antiquarians, connoisseurs, and biographers. Although in a much less cantankerous fashion, Pevsner was as critical as Haydon of self-appointed elites with 'taste'. Unlike Plymouth-born Haydon, however, Pevsner had an additional gripe: these elites believed that English art was 'an elusive, hermetic thing, perceptible only to

---

[64] Pevsner, 'Reflections on Not Teaching Art History', 204. Radio talk for the BBC Third Programme on 19 October 1952.
[65] Ibid.   [66] Cited in Harries, *Nikolaus Pevsner*, 339.
[67] Nikolaus Pevsner, '[Letter to the Editor] Study of Art History', *The Times* (5 November 1952), 9.
[68] Pevsner's Reith Lectures, BBC Home Service, 16 October 1955, in Games, *Pevsner: The Complete Broadcast Talks—Architecture and Art on Radio and Television, 1945–1977*, 254.
[69] Cited in Colin MacInnes, 'The Englishness of Dr Pevsner', *Twentieth Century* (January 1960), in 'Newscuttings', in the Birkbeck Archive.
[70] From *Industrial Art in England*, and cited in ibid.

the native-born'.[71] Therefore, they resented the highly scholarly yet popular interventions of the German-born émigré.

It was no coincidence, then, that Pevsner's first lecture at Birkbeck College combined these themes: his belief in the democratic knowledge of art and architecture, together with his conviction that education and artistic appreciation are central to the flourishing of humanity. His lecture was entitled 'Enjoyment of Architecture'. Pevsner admitted that

> there are not many among us who can say that they really enjoy architectural values, and of those who do, a good many would not know what they are, and what exactly it is they are enjoying.

This was because architecture was an abstract art, like music. Education in the appreciation of architecture was therefore necessary. After all, he continued,

> In drama your intellect is kept busy, in painting too. But in architecture and music it is left to ramble unless you can by instinct or effort keep it silent and let other spiritual faculties be on the alert.... It is my aim... to put into words—very sketchily, of course—what it is we feel in looking at architecture.[72]

It helped that Pevsner was a brilliant lecturer. Stories circulated about him not pausing in his lecture even after falling off the stage or setting the projector cloth on fire.[73] He was also demanding. At that time, some of the students were 'occasional students'—that is, they were taking individual classes rather than pursuing a coherent degree programme. He told them: 'I don't mind you being an occasional student, as long as you don't just come occasionally.'[74] He could be withering in his feedback on written work: 'Was this written under examination conditions, or with the help of books? In the latter case, p.1 is inexcusable', he wrote on one essay, and 'No-one need draw quite so badly', on another.[75] Students were understandably awed by him but mesmerized, nonetheless.

* * *

Haydon, Mason, and Pevsner were very different characters, but they shared a belief in the power of art and architecture to enhance people's lives. This was why they argued for an enhanced role of government in fostering the arts. As Haydon expressed it in the early decades of the nineteenth century, 'a state which has lost a sense of civic and patriotic values inherent in High Art is a state that has lost

---

[71] Crossley, 'Introduction', in Draper (ed.), *Reassessing Nikolaus Pevsner*, 21.
[72] Harries, *Nikolaus Pevsner*, 255.   [73] Ibid., 426.
[74] Cited in ibid., 427.   [75] Cited in ibid., 430.

everything worth having'.⁷⁶ Although Haydon and Pevsner had major careers outside the College, it is no coincidence that all three were dedicated teachers in the LMI/Birkbeck, with its ethos of exposing working men and women to forms of understanding that had previously been kept from them by self-appointed, elite gatekeepers.⁷⁷ In this sense, the title of one of Pevsner's books is revealing: *Visual Pleasure from Everyday Things: An Attempt to Establish Criteria by which the Aesthetic Qualities of Design can be Judged* (1946). All three men believed that 'ordinary' people, and not just elites and self-appointed cultural tsars, were capable of appreciating beauty—even if they needed to be educated or given 'criteria' with which to judge.⁷⁸

Although teaching of the fine arts disappeared with the departure of Mason and the entry of Birkbeck into the University of London, the teaching of art history and architecture has flourished. When Pevsner retired in 1967, the Department of History of Art was formally inaugurated and Renaissance scholar Peter Murray appointed the first Pevsner Professor.

Debates continued about how the discipline should be defined. In the 1970s, there were discussions about the balance between the history versus the theory of art.⁷⁹ What about the contribution that computing could make to the analysis of paintings? And film? In 1999, the history of film was incorporated into the History of Art Department, bringing in the talents of Laura Mulvey, Ian Christie, and Mike Allen. Today, it is a separate Department of Film, Media, and Cultural Studies, encompassing the study of film and television, journalism, artistic practice and arts management, and digital media, culture, and design.

The range of approaches adopted by lecturers in both the Department of History of Art and the Department of Film, Media and Cultural Studies is immense, but lecturers have forged powerful intellectual alliances with psychoanalysis, feminism, and critical theory. One of the most prominent exponents is Mulvey, who was appointed to the College from the British Film Institute (BFI) in 1999. This was an unsurprising move. After all, links between Birkbeck and the BFI were long established: the first film studies course in the UK was a collaboration between Birkbeck's Extra Mural Department and the BFI's Education Department. Mulvey's teaching focused on film in the late 1920s and early 1930s—that is, the late silent film period—tracing the impact of the transition to synchronized sound. But her theoretical research has had a similarly powerful impact. In 1975, she had published a paradigm-changing article entitled 'Visual

---

[76] John Barrell, 'Benjamin Robert Haydon: The Curtis of the Kyber Pass', in John Barrell (ed.), *Painting and the Politics of Culture* (Cambridge: Cambridge University Press, 1992), 263.
[77] 'Benjamin Robert Haydon (1786–1846)', *Burlington Magazine for Connoisseurs*, 88.519 (June 1946), 133.
[78] For example, see Nikolaus Pevsner, *Visual Pleasure from Everyday Things: An Attempt to Establish Criteria by which the Aesthetic Qualities of Design can be Judged* (London: B. T. Batsford, 1946), 2.
[79] Letter to the Vice-Master dated 14 December 1978 and signed by Peter Draper, Francis Ames-Lewis, and Katherine (Kit) Galbraith, in 'Review of the History of Art Department', in Birkbeck Archives, Box 48.

Pleasure and Narrative Cinema', in which she used Sigmund Freud and Jacques Lacan to reflect on scopophilia (the 'love of looking') and the 'male gaze'. She argued that psychoanalytic theory could be useful 'as a political weapon, demonstrating the way the unconscious of patriarchal society has structured film form'.[80] 'In a world ordered by sexual imbalance,' she maintained, 'pleasure in looking has been split between active/male and passive/female. The determining male gaze projects its fantasy on to the female figure which is styled accordingly.' Women 'connote *to-be-looked-at-ness*'.[81] Hers is the kind of radical approach that pays attention to the unconscious, as it is determined by dominant structural conditions. The interplay between image and word, erotic desires, and psychic tensions is woven together in the interests of exploring alternative, even utopian, visions.

The two departments have also been moulded by their environments. They are located in the School of Arts in Gordon Square, buildings that were developed in the 1820s. It is celebrated for the 'Bloomsbury Group' who were residents from 1904. This is where Virginia Stephens (later, Woolf), Vanessa Stephens (later, Bell), Toby Stephen, Lytton Strachey, and John Maynard Keynes lived. Paintings by Vanessa Bell and Duncan Grant still grace the walls of the Keynes Library, thanks to a loan by Bell's daughter, Angelica Garnett. Virginia Woolf used the upstairs room in 46 Gordon Square as her writing room. It was the 'room of one's own' that Virginia Woolf wrote about so powerfully in her essay of 1929. 'A woman must have money and a room of her own if she is to write fiction', Woolf maintained, insisting on the need to shake off the shackles of domesticity and discrimination, in order to find room (a gender-free space) to explore the world in all its complexities.[82]

The Birkbeck Cinema, which was opened in 2007 at 43 Gordon Square, is another part of the environment that would have astounded even Pevsner (see Fig. 9.2). The designers drew on their reading of the Bloomsbury Group. In the words of the lead architect Andy MacFee,

> We became very interested in the writings of Virginia Woolf, in particular her narratives of streams of consciousness. That inspired us with the project. The narrative that we created was of a tumbling block that moved through the space and changed its characteristics as it moved, so it changed its shape, its colours, and its material. And like a stop-frame animation, we analysed the motion of a tumbling block at certain stages and the imprint (or the residue) that it left on the existing space or the existing block conceptually. And that process carved a series of interlocking forms and spaces that you see.[83]

---

[80] Laura Mulvey, 'Visual Pleasure and Narrative Cinema', *Screen*, 16.3 (autumn 1975), 6.
[81] Ibid., 11.
[82] Virginia Woolf, *A Room of One's Own/Three Guineas*, 1st pub. 1929 (Harmondsworth: Penguin, 1993), 3.
[83] Andy MacFee, 'Birkbeck's School of Arts at 43 Gordon Square', from 6:43 to 7:54, at www.bbk.ac.uk/schools/arts/buildings-and-facilities, viewed 1 August 2021.

Fig. 9.2 The Birkbeck Cinema, 2007. Birkbeck Image Collections: Birkbeck History BH0057.

The design won a Royal Institute of British Architecture (RIBA) Award in 2008. The Birkbeck Cinema (as part of the Institute for the Moving Image), Peltz Gallery, and the various theatre and performance spaces enable students and staff to stage creative exhibitions, films, and theatrical performances.

* * *

Art and architecture—and, more recently, film and photography, and related creative fields—have been central to the College since its foundational years. Haydon's bloody demise should not mask the fact that he was crucial in bringing 'high art' to working men and women, encouraging them both to experience and to experiment with artistic forms. This was followed by artist-scholars such as Mason, Pevsner, the various Pevsner Professors, and other distinguished members of the Departments of Art History and Film, Media and Cultural Studies. In teaching art, architecture, and film, and the history and theory of art, Birkbeck has maintained its pioneering tradition, while maintaining that art and culture are living entities. It is a tradition that continues to animate the various artistic components of life at Birkbeck.

10
Dancing the Polka

> You should see me dance the Polka,
> You should see me cover the ground,
> You should see my coat-tails flying,
> As I jump my partner round;...
> For a rollicking romping Polka,
> Is the jolliest fun I know.
> George Grossmith, 'See Me Dance the Polka', c.1886[1]

The theatre at the 'old Birkbeck Lit. and Sci. Inst.', as it was affectionately called,[2] was one of London's great attractions (see Fig. 10.1). In the 1880s, it was renowned for hosting entertainers such as George Grossmith and George Grossmith, Jr. 'G. G. Senior' would begin the programme by reciting popular verse and reminiscing about his experiences as a reporter. His performance was followed by 'G. G. Junior' who would dance and sing droll songs.[3] As art critic C. Lewis Hind later recalled, he spent 'many happy hours' in Birkbeck's theatre, revelling in the ebullient 'Evenings with Dickens' that were presented by Grossmith, Senior, a 'smiling, rubicund elderly gentleman'. At the end of Grossmith's recitation of 'Boots at The Holly Tree Inn', he would hand proceedings over to his son, the 'slim, alert, dry, delightful G. G.', who would later become famous in the Gilbert and Sullivan operas.[4] Grossmith, Junior, would sit at the piano and, as Hind remembered it, would

> Delight[ ] us...with 'You should see me dance the polka'; and when he rose from his seat and illustrated the song, with a chair as partner and coat-tails flying, the excited and delighted audience clamoured for a triple encore. It may have been then that George Grossmith said in his quick, bird-like way, 'It is my

---

[1] George Grossmith, *See Me Dance the Polka. Humorous Song Written, Composed, and Sung by George Grossmith* (London: J. Bath, 1886), 5.
[2] C. Lewis Hind, 'Life and I. No. 48. Doughty Street', *Daily Chronicle* (17 June 1925), in 'Newscuttings June 1926 to March 1935', in the Birkbeck Archive.
[3] A. Gavin Burns, 'Reminiscences of the Birkbeck Literary and Scientific Institution', *The Lodestone*, 19.2 (1924), 62.
[4] C. Lewis Hind, 'Life and I. No. 48. Doughty Street', *The Daily Chronicle* (17 June 1925), in 'Newscuttings June 1926 to March 1935', in the Birkbeck Archive.

Fig. 10.1 The College theatre in Bream's Building in the 1920s. Birkbeck Image Collections: Birkbeck History BH0097.

ambition to play in a farce wherein, at the beginning, I place a bandbox upon a chair—and never sit upon it.[5]

The Grossmith father-and-son were two of the most popular performers in London at the time.

What did theatrical extravaganzas have to do with an institution dedicated to scholarly pursuits? Despite George Birkbeck's insistence that the LMI's mission was to provide scientific instruction at a level equivalent to what was offered to middle- and upper-class men at the ancient universities of St Andrews, Oxford, and Cambridge, the Institution also recognized that students needed a social life. 'Innocent amusements' and 'systematic teaching' could take place in adjacent rooms. At least, this was the observation of one commentator writing in *The Englishwoman's Review and Home Newspaper* in 1858. The author admitted that George Birkbeck had insisted that the mission of the Institution was to 'instruct the artizan [sic] in the science of his daily work', but contended that, in recent years, this 'work of instruction' had 'been subordinated to that of amusement'. The reason was simple: 'people pay cheerfully for their amusement, but they pay

---

[5] C. Lewis Hind, 'Looking Back at the Eighties', *The Sphere* (18 June 1925), 74, in 'Newscuttings June 1926 to March 1935', in the Birkbeck Archive. Also see C. Lewis Hind, *Naphtali: Being Influences and Adventures While Earning a Living by Writing* (London: John Lane, 1926), 38.

grudgingly for education'. After all, 'working men and apprentices do not always want to be bored with reading difficult books and learning difficult subjects'. Although critical of the ascendancy of entertainment, the *Englishwoman's Review* conceded that working-class men and women had a right to 'laugh as well as look serious' and it was neither 'very dreadful' nor 'wicked' for the management committee to provide entertainment by hiring 'Ethiopian serenaders or Christy's Minstrels'. Indeed, these American blackface minstrel groups were a long-standing distraction for members of the LMI, performing in the LMI's theatre from the 1840s.[6]

The belief that serious study was not antithetical to entertainment and amusement could be heard throughout the College's history. Entertainments attracted students to the Institution; they might also help over-worked brains become more receptive to the acquisition of knowledge. This was the point made during a lively 1835 debate about whether chess ought to be taught at the LMI. *Bell's Life in London and Sporting Chronicle* responded with an enthusiastic 'Yes!' Chess would be 'just the relief wanted in Southampton-buildings between the intervals of severe study'.[7] Some commentators even sought to elevate chess into something much more esoteric. In his speech at the fifty-fifth anniversary of the College, Prince Leopold (youngest son of Queen Victoria) claimed that the study of chess taught important lessons. He observed that the syllabus for chess at Birkbeck paid 'particular attention...to the study of openings', since 'is it not true that in life, as in chess, it is often the opening, and the opening only, which is under our control?' 'Later in the game,' he admitted, 'the plans and wishes of others begin to conflict unpleasantly with your own', and so chess enthusiasts quickly learnt that it might 'repay us to sacrifice a pawn or a piece so as to gain at once a position which may give us a decided advantage throughout the whole game'. This was an important lesson for anyone wanting to prosper in life. To triumph socially, Birkbeck students needed

> to sacrifice some pawn of present pleasure or profit to gain a vantage ground which may help us to that success which self-indulgence would never win...self-denial and conscientiousness form at least one-half of the real benefit of education.[8]

He contended that 'amongst the bright young faces I see around me there are many who have known what it is...to begin a lesson when they would rather

---

[6] 'Dempster's Original Ballad Soirees', *The Satirist; or, the Censor of the Times* (27 December 1846), 414.

[7] 'To Correspondents', *Bell's Life in London and Sporting Chronicle* (26 July 1835), n.p.

[8] Prince Leopold, cited in 'Birkbeck Literary Institution', *Daily Telegraph* (26 February 1879).

have gone to the theatre'.⁹ At Birkbeck, they could study studiously *and* enjoy the lighter offerings of the College's theatre.

Prince Leopold's oration had been vigorously applauded, but even the most austere observers contended that entertainment was good for students—albeit, on *moral* grounds. In 1863, the Central Society of Education observed that teaching mechanics the intricacies of music and the art of singing were 'our strongest allies in improving the recreations of the working men'.¹⁰ It noted that in some neighbourhoods, music was enjoyed in 'the public-house, the small theatre, and the casino', which was why it was important to 'present it in an innocent form' at places such as Birkbeck.¹¹ It was 'surprising how much time may be spent in a harmless and pleasurable way through a taste in music', the Central Society pointed out, since it involved 'learning and practising' as well as 'an occasional performance before friends and neighbours'. Because of this, 'singing-classes, and classes for instrumental music' were 'strongly insisted upon by all who have much experience of the pursuits of English mechanics'.¹²

Entertainment and instruction coincided during important occasions, such as College anniversaries. Members and guests were subjected not only to highbrow speeches but also to music, singing, recitations, and theatrical performances. At the twenty-ninth anniversary of the Institution in 1852, for example, *The Lady's Magazine* observed that the celebrations began with a speech 'showing the advantages of mechanics' institutions in diffusing a knowledge of literature and arts'. This was followed, however, by music and recitations by members of the elocution class. Songs included 'Slave Girl's Love', 'Bid me Discourse', and 'Tight Little Ireland'.¹³ There was also an exhibition, which showcased such diverse objects as 'a gold digger's tent, gold-washing apparatus, revolvers, drawings by members of the institution, rugs, carpets, models of yachts and other vessels, gas stoves, &c.&c.', all of which were said to have given 'universal satisfaction'.¹⁴ The choice of entertainments reflects the racialization of empire and an emphasis on colonizing and exploiting other regions of the world.

However, the College's performances also had an important influence on the dramatic arts in London during most of the nineteenth and early twentieth centuries. For decades, the Institution's lecture theatre hosted weekly lectures and entertainments: these were free to members, but available at a reasonable price for the general public. It quickly gained a reputation for its elocution lessons and performances. Elocution was intended to 'civilize' working men and women. As Bernard Henry Becker conceded during a visit in the 1870s,

---

[9] Ibid.
[10] 'Paper by the Central Society of Education', *Quarterly Review*, 113.225 (January 1863), 47.
[11] Ibid., 47.   [12] Ibid., 47.
[13] 'London Mechanics' Institution', *Lady's Newspaper* (18 December 1852), 382.
[14] Ibid., 382.

elocution is a good thing, if only for its use in teaching some little respect for the letter *h*, a hapless aspirate utterly disregarded by thorough-bred Londoners [that is, 'Cockneys'].

The 'absurdly vulgar Cockney dialect... absolutely flays "ears polite"', so this 'striving to inoculate the untutored mind with some little taste and accuracy in speaking or reading a plain sentence' was a worthy one.[15]

Becker was being patronizing. In contrast, C. Lewis Hind was a fan who claimed that his life had been transformed by such lessons, especially since he suffered from speech difficulties.[16] In the 1880s, he fondly recalled Professor Olsson's elocution lessons.[17] Hind would wake at six in the morning and make his way to a disused house where he would 'practise long and short vowel sounds such as Cǎr, Bāre, Bǎt, Bāte', as well as 'tricky elocutionary sentences', including 'Though the rough cough and hiccough plough me through'.[18] In the evenings, he would make his way to The Birkbeck, where he learnt to recite scenes from Shakespeare, William Pitt's 1741 speech in the House of Commons (which started with the 'The Atrocious Crime of Being a Young Man'), and Alexander Pope's 'Vital Spark of Heavenly Flame' ('Vital spark of heavenly flame,/Quit, O quit this mortal frame!/Trembling, hoping, lingering flying,/O the pain, the bliss of dying!').[19]

The Birkbeck theatre also hosted concerts, poetry readings, musical recitations, and performances by members of the College as well as professional actors.[20] Well-known speakers included Samuel Brandram (who could recite entire plays by Shakespeare from memory),[21] explorer Henry Morton Stanley, war correspondent Archibald Forbes, Sir Squire Bancroft (reported to be the instigator of 'drawing-room comedy' or 'cup and saucer drama'), author William Pett Ridge, and editor Charles Dickens Jr, who was famous for his 'Dickens Dictionaries'.[22] Gladys Cooper appeared as well, and was described as 'the most attractive lady that ever appeared on the College stage'. Her 'make-up was superb—a perfect blending of soft tones, seldom seen in these days of harsh contrasts'.[23] In contrast, the 'finest actor' was said to be Forbes Robertson, whose stage whisper could be 'heard distinctly at the back of the top gallery'.[24] When, in 1881, Lord Northbrook (who later became President of Birkbeck) started a movement to raise voluntary subscriptions in order to build new premises (the building was estimated to cost

---

[15] Becker, *Scientific London*, 211–12.

[16] G. G. Wells, *Experiment in Autobiography: Discoveries and Conclusions of a Very Ordinary Brain, Since 1866* (London: Victor Gollancz, 1934), online in Gutenberg.

[17] Hind, *Naphtali*, 35.   [18] Ibid., 36.   [19] Ibid., 37.

[20] Burns, 'Reminiscences of the Birkbeck Literary and Scientific Institution', 62.

[21] Hind, *Naphtali*, 37.   [22] See *Hampstead and Highgate Express* (25 September 1886), 2.

[23] H. G. B., 'A Fire-Watcher's Interview with his Own Memory', *The Lodestone*, 36.3 (summer 1944), 12.

[24] Ibid., 12.

£23,000),²⁵ the famous actor-manager Henry Irving became involved. Bull recalled that Irving

> gave us a reading in aid of the Building Fund. He took infinite trouble, lent us his splendid black velvet curtain from the Lyceum, paid all expenses and sold or gave half the seats to his friends, handing over the whole of the receipts, without deduction, although the expenses must have been considerable. Everything he did was on a generous and princely scale.²⁶

When Irving recited *Hamlet* in the theatre, both Ellen Terry (the leading Shakespearean actress in Britain) and the tall, blond Bram Stoker (the author of *Dracula*) were in the audience.²⁷

Oscar Wilde, a close friend of Stoker, also made occasional appearances (see Fig. 10.2). In November 1884, for example, Wilde spoke in the Birkbeck theatre on 'The Value of Art in Modern Life'. The *Morning Post* reported that Wilde 'illuminated his remarks by a series of costumes expressive of his views on the correct principles of dress'. He attracted 'an unusually large audience' and was 'frequently applauded'.²⁸ Two years later, Wilde was back. On 24 November 1886, Wilde (calling himself a 'Professor of Aesthetics') stood in the Birkbeck theatre and, 'leaning against a table...with his hands in his pockets and a lily in his buttonhole', gave a lecture in the theatre on Thomas Chatterton.²⁹ The lecture on the 'marvelous boy' was an attempt by Wilde and the Editor of *Century Guild Hobby Horse* to build a Chatterton monument at the poet's school in Bristol.³⁰ This eighteenth-century poet and forger had killed himself at the tender age of 17 after having been refused the patronage which would have enabled him to devote his life to poetry. Wilde's choice of subject was ideally suited to the general obsession at the time with misunderstood romantic genius. Despite the appalling weather, 800 people turned up to hear him.³¹ The chairman at the event—William Bull (later, solicitor and Conservative MP)—recalled Wilde's 'fat, puffy face, an enormous bosom of shirt front and white feminine hands'. As he walked Wilde to the theatre, he noticed that Wilde was trembling. When asked 'if he was all right', Wilde simply replied, 'I am nervous.'³²

---

²⁵ Evidence by G. Armitage-Smith to the *Royal Commission on University Education in London. Appendix to Third Report of the Commissioners*, 242.
²⁶ Bull, 'Forty Years Back', 6.   ²⁷ Hind, *Naphtali*, 38.
²⁸ 'Mr Oscar Wilde at the Birkbeck Institution', *Morning Post* (20 November 1884), 2.
²⁹ This is according to A. M. Somerville Story's *Twenty Years in Paris with a Pen* (London: Alston Rivers, 1927), 156–7.
³⁰ 'The Memorial to the Men of Letters of the Lake District', *Century Guild Hobby Horse* (January 1887), 41.
³¹ Oscar Wilde, 'To Herbert P. Horne', 7 December 1886, in Merlin Holland and Rupert Hart-Davis (eds), *The Complete Letters of Oscar Wilde* (London: Fourth Estate, 2000), 289–90.
³² Bull, 'Forty Years Back', 6.

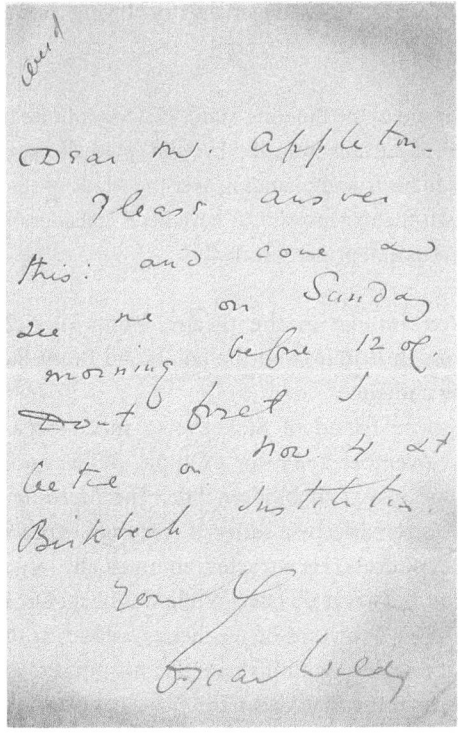

Fig. 10.2 Letter from Oscar Wilde. Birkbeck Image Collections: Birkbeck History BH0208.

Other speakers included George Bernard Shaw, talking about education. The College's annual report noted that 'the theatre proved far too small to accommodate those anxious to hear his views on "The Failure of Education"'.[33] W. R. Wooldridge, Secretary of the Students' Union and a student studying the sciences, recalled watching him deliver his speech, 'without a note', to an audience of around 1,200 people:

> He stood erect, wearing a grey Norfolk jacket and knickerbockers, with his hands thrust into his side pockets, with just the thumbs showing and projecting forwards. It was an erudite lecture and influenced me as much as anything I heard during my student years.[34]

---

[33] *Birkbeck College (University of London). Report for Ninety-Ninth Session 1921–22* (London: Birkbeck College, 1921), 7.

[34] W. R. Wooldridge, 'Birkbeck Reminiscences', *The Lodestone*, 53.2 (spring 1963), 9.

Although no script remains of his speech, this was probably like the witty one he published in the *Journal of Education* in 1919. In it, he characterized the schoolmaster as

> the person who takes the children off the parents' hands for a consideration. That is to say, he establishes a child prison; engages a number of employee schoolmasters as turnkeys; and covers up the essential cruelty and unnaturalness of the situation by torturing the children if they do not learn.

The schoolmaster had the audacity to 'call[ ] this process...by the sacred name of Teaching'.[35] Shaw exhorted teachers to allow young people to freely 'walk out of a classroom where they are bored by a dull teacher', just as 'grown-up people are to walk out of a theatre where they are bored by a dull play'. Until this happened, 'we shall remain the barbarians we are at present'.[36]

Given the fame of such speakers, was it any wonder that The Birkbeck was reputed to possess the 'best college theatre in London' and The Birkbeck Players were adored?[37] Some even claimed that, until Birkbeck moved to its Malet Street premises in the early 1950s, its theatre was 'one of the seven Wonders of London University'.[38]

* * *

Exaggeration or not, the College's theatre undoubtedly attracted aspiring actors and producers. Arthur Wing Pinero was another luminary of the arts who was regularly seen at Birkbeck's theatre. He later became one of the most distinguished dramatists and stage directors of the late nineteenth and early twentieth centuries.

As a studious, stocky 15-year-old, Pinero first walked into the Birkbeck Literary and Scientific Institution in Southampton Buildings, Chancery Lane, in 1870. Although he signed up to four years of legal classes, his real reason for choosing Birkbeck was for its magnificent theatre and unrivalled reputation for dramatic performances.[39] It was a perfect home for him. During his time in the College, not only did he write plays such as *Achilles*, *Heir at Law*, *The Hundred Thousand Pounds*, and *The Castle Spectre*, but he also organized performances, to which he would drag his family and friends.[40] As he wrote to his Aunt Eliza on 8 November 1872, enclosing a 'Programme of next Wednesday's Entertainment',

---

[35] 'George Bernard Shaw on Education', *Journal of Education*, 89.11 (13 March 1919), 289.
[36] Ibid., 289.
[37] 'The Birkbeck Players', *The Observer* (4 December 1927), in 'Newscuttings June 1926 to March 1935', in the Birkbeck Archive.
[38] Sylvester Savigeas, 'The Next Stage', *The Lodestone*, 26.2 (spring 1931), 56.
[39] 'D.J.F.', 'B.D.B. (Birkbeck Dictionary of Biography)', *The Lodestone*, 32.2 (spring 1935), 57.
[40] John Dawick, *Pinero: A Theatrical Life* (Niwot: University Press of Colorado, 1993), 14.

It has been said that the anticipation of an event is more pleasing than the event itself, and as I am certain it will be so in the present instance, I beg of you to expect a very great deal of us on Wednesday next, because the delight you experience in so doing, will in a great measure compensate for yr. discovery that we are a miserable set of people who can do next to nothing.[41]

Within only a couple of years, Pinero had won the College's prize for dramatic technique (which earned him a 'handsome set, bound in half calf, of three Dickens' novels')[42] and was making monthly appearances as an amateur actor in Birkbeck student productions.[43] Audiences at The Birkbeck remembered his final performance as an amateur: it was a stunning performance of *Hamlet*, which was played without scenery.[44] Along with other Birkbeck theatre buffs, he even went on tour, putting on performances and recitals in Ilfracombe, Gravesend, and Bristol.[45] They weren't always a resounding success. As he confessed in a letter dated 1 October 1873, on at least one occasion, they had barely any audience since 'the evening being fine...everybody went on the promenade'. He quipped: 'Why are we like the lady whose remains were found in the Thames?' The answer: 'Because we are cut up, but in excellent spirits.'[46]

Upon completing his legal training, Pinero decided he could not bear the thought of life as a City solicitor, so he accepted a job as an actor in the Edinburgh Stock Company, first appearing at the Theatre Royal in Edinburgh on 22 June 1874.[47] Two years later, he returned to London as part of the Lyceum Company, beginning a distinguished career as a writer for the theatre. In later years, he reflected on the dire state of English theatre when he first became involved at The Birkbeck. It was a theatre 'of faded outworn tradition', he later recalled, in which Shakespeare was acted 'in a plodding, uninspired way' and anyone interested in modern drama was subjected to 'the jog-trot rhetoric of James Sheridan Knowles and to the claptrap of Edward Bulwer Lytton'.[48] It was at The Birkbeck that Pinero first set out to change that situation. He became a prolific dramatist, producing over fifty dramas, some of which had over 1,000 performances.[49]

Despite his subsequent fame, Pinero never forgot that it was The Birkbeck that gave him his first start in theatrical life. From the early 1890s onwards, he visited the College frequently and even read his work there. Since British playwrights had not done this before, the College was subjected to 'murmurings against the

---

[41] Ibid., 14.   [42] Ibid., 14.
[43] 'D.J.F', 'B.D.B. (Birkbeck Dictionary of Biography)', *The Lodestone*, 32.2 (spring 1935), 57.
[44] Hamilton Fyfe, *Sir Arthur Pinero's Plays and Players* (London: Ernest Benn Ltd, 1930), 3.
[45] Dawick, *Pinero*, 19.   [46] 1 October 1873: from ibid., 19.
[47] 'D.J.F', 'B.D.B.', 57.   [48] Dawick, *Pinero*, 17.
[49] Heather Anne Wozniak, 'The Play with a Past: Arthur Wing Pinero's New Drama', *Victorian Literature and Culture*, 37 (2009), 391.

novelty'.⁵⁰ Pinero also accepted the position of Honorary Examiner for students of drama from 1893 to 1904 and, from 1899, was a vice-presidential member of The Birkbeck's Council. Colleagues fondly remembered seeing him 'playfully "fencing"' with friends and colleagues in the College's library, wielding 'a long bladed knife'.⁵¹

* * *

Today, Pinero's plays don't seem to be particularly subversive, but at the time they represented a seismic shift in theatrical theme and performance. Previously, Victorian theatre and art had emphasized the inextricable link between beauty and goodness. Its aesthetics was self-consciously moral, hoping to raise audiences to a higher pitch of virtue. In contrast, as critic Tori Moi explains, modernist theatre was 'built on the negation of idealism': it was amoral and lauded freedom as well as independence.⁵² It drew attention to the tension between free will and fate. It also rejected conventions such as the soliloquy and the 'aside', as being 'destructive of verisimilitude', as Pinero put it.⁵³

This new theatre also portrayed women in a different way. Pinero's 'New Women', for example, were emancipated and edgy. They were sexually liberated, politically astute, and career-minded. They espoused the rights of women. The tabloids labelled such women 'mannish' because they smoked, rode bicycles, and read serious books.⁵⁴ Of course, it is important not to exaggerate Pinero's role in bringing the 'New Woman' to the British stage. Birkbeck scholar Sally Ledger rightly argued that *that* accolade must go to Henrik Ibsen.⁵⁵ Nevertheless, *The Profligate* (one of Pinero's most influential plays) preceded the first production of *A Doll's House* in the UK⁵⁶ and Pinero denied knowing about Ibsen prior to writing his play.⁵⁷ Written in 1887, *The Profligate* was first performed in 1889 and, on 16 May 1890, Pinero gave a solo reading of *The Profligate* at Birkbeck in aid of its Library Fund.⁵⁸ In the words of a reviewer writing in the journal *Theatre*, 'from the opening of the reading…to the close, Mr Pinero was very successful', ensuring that 'each character was individualised by excellent dramatic effect'.⁵⁹ The main

---

⁵⁰ Hamilton Fyfe, *Sir Arthur Pinero's Plays and Players* (London: Ernest Benn Ltd, 1930), 110.
⁵¹ 'D.J.F.', 'B.D.B', 58.
⁵² Toril Moi, *Henrik Ibsen and the Birth of Modernism: Art, Theatre, Philosophy* (Oxford: Oxford University Press, 2006), 67.
⁵³ T. Carlo Matos, *Ibsen's Foreign Contagion: Henrik Ibsen, Arthur Wing Pinero, and Modernism on the London Stage, 1890–1900* (London: Academica Press, 2012), 118.
⁵⁴ Wozniak, 'The Play with a Past', 392.
⁵⁵ Sally Ledger, 'Ibsen, the New Woman, and the Actress', in Angelique Richard and Chris Willis (eds), *The New Woman in Fiction and in Fact: Fin-de-Siècle Feminisms* (New York: Palgrave, 2001), 79–93.
⁵⁶ Matos, *Ibsen's Foreign Contagion*, 118. Pinero's other two most influential plays are *The Second Mrs Tanqueray* (1893) and *The Notorious Mrs Ebbsmith* (1895).
⁵⁷ Letter to H. H. Küther, 10 May 1932, in Arthur Wing Pinero, *The Collected Letters of Sir Arthur Pinero* (Minneapolis: University of Minnesota Press, 1974), 288.
⁵⁸ Matos, *Ibsen's Foreign Contagion*, 117, and Dawick, *Pinero*, 166.   ⁵⁹ Dawick, *Pinero*, 166.

character in *The Profligate* was a 'New Woman'. As we will see in the next chapter, Pinero's 'New Woman' appeared not only on stage at The Birkbeck but also in the classrooms.

* * *

But all was not well with the theatre. The first signs of problems appeared as early as the 1920s, when Birkbeck began shedding its less 'academic' programmes in its bid to become a member of the University of London. By the middle of that decade, a student could complain that, while Birkbeck formerly had 'a reputation for showing good plays well-produced', in more recent years its actors had become 'as awkward as children performing a little cantata at their Sunday School'.[60] The theatre was also specializing in Elizabethan revivals,[61] which no longer appealed to the tastes of more progressive students. Worse: the Dramatic Society was accused of having 'a weakness for Galsworthy and a habit of producing Shaw'.[62] In a letter to the Editor of *The Lodestone*, 'Cicerone' claimed that

> before every production, the committee solemnly discusses some score of other playwrights, and a couple of hundred plays or so. Then, having unburdened themselves of all superfluous authors' works, they proceed to decide which of their two favourite authors' works shall be played.[63]

Another critic agreed, observing that the most honest thing that could be said about one of the theatre's productions was 'another Shaw (or Galsworthy) play. How long, oh Lord, how long!'[64] Admittedly, this critic continued, the chief function of theatrical productions was social. They

> act as one of the many links whereby individuals undergoing a University education may get to know each other, and relationships established behind and across the footlights are just as valuable as those formed in Common Rooms, the playing fields, or in class rooms and lectures.[65]

This was no excuse, however. He joked that there was a 'small earthquake in the neighbourhood of Windsor on Friday, 22nd February', due to 'the Kings of England turning in their graves at the rendering of the National Anthem which the orchestra gave'.[66]

---

[60] 'Cicerone', 'To the Editor', *The Lodestone*, 20.2 (1925), 29.
[61] 'The Birkbeck Players', *The Observer* (4 December 1927), in 'Newscuttings June 1926 to March 1935', in the Birkbeck Archive.
[62] 'Cicerone', 'To the Editor', *The Lodestone*, 20.2 (1925), 29.   [63] Ibid., 29.
[64] 'Contra Bono Publico', 'The Skin-Game', *The Lodestone*, 20.3 (1924), 134. Note: this sounds very much like 'Cicerone'.
[65] Ibid., 134.   [66] Ibid., 137. Note: this sounds very much like 'Cicerone'.

The glories of modernist theatre were also being edged out by Gilbert and Sullivan operas. When Wooldridge joined the College's Operatic Society in 1919, he recalled that the Birkbeck theatre was dominated by three men:

> George Robey's son, now a Metropolitan Magistrate, who took the part of Ko-Ko in the Mikado, Rex Palmer of B. B. C. fame, who took the part of Pish-Tush, and as Nankie-Poo, Norman Kipling (now Sir Norman), the busy director of the federation of British Industries.[67]

Even the support of Harold Gorgon Jackson, Professor of Zoology and, later, Master of the College, failed to revive the theatre in the longer term. Jackson was passionate about music, opera, and collecting Georgian silver. He gave public talks in the theatre on the music of Bach, 'illustrated with gramophone and epidiascope' (an early version of the overhead projector) and, between the wars, was the Musical Director of the Operatic Society. In this role, the society

> jumped from Gilbert and Sullivan to Mozart in one year and the performance of 'The Magic Flute' was the highlight in the Society's history.... Even the Music Critic of the *Times*, who usually ignores amateur performances, gave notice to these productions.[68]

However, the Second World War forced Jackson to accept the role of Acting Master (then, Master) of the College, obliging him 'to relinquish the direction of the Operatic Society', which then petered out.[69] The Birkbeck Players struggled on, encouraged by well-known actors. In the 1930s, these included Franklyn Kelsey, known for *Knight Without Armor*, *Once in a Blue Moon*, and *Little Miss Molly*.[70] In the 1950s, Derek Birch (famous for his 1950s performances of *Treasure Island* and *Sherlock Holmes*) produced plays for the Birkbeck Players, including Henry Fielding's *The Miser*.[71] But the excitement and glamour had gone.

Worse was to come in the 1950s. Plans for a new building in Malet Street did not even include a theatre. In 1944, one student reflected on what this would mean. Simply signing herself 'Arts Student', she wrote that the new building 'fills me with alarm and despondency'. The theatre was associated with the 'Freshers' Social', foundation orations, the 'ribald mirth of students who saw a joke where none was intended, the French plays with their audiences of solemn school children, the performances of operas, and the one-act plays and sketches enjoyed at Court reunions'.[72] All this would be gone. Was the College reorientating itself

---

[67] Wooldridge, 'Birkbeck Reminiscences', 10.
[68] 'The Master', *Lodestone*, 41.1 and 41.2 (autumn and spring 1948–9), 24.   [69] Ibid., 24.
[70] 'Birkbeck Players in "The Witch"', *Sunday Mirror* (15 November 1936), 4.
[71] 'Birkbeck Players', *The Stage* (10 March 1949), 8.
[72] 'Arts Student', 'Letter to the Editor', *The Lodestone*, 36.2 (spring 1944), 7–8.

towards the sciences, leaving the arts to flounder, she asked?[73] Student protests failed. The Malet Street building was erected without a theatre, effectively ending a distinguished theatrical tradition at The Birkbeck.

The Birkbeck theatre saw a temporary reprieve in the 1980s, due to the enthusiastic labours of Paula Neuss, Michael Slater, Steve Connor, and Barbara Hardy. In 1982, the medievalist Neuss, who was based in the English Department, reawakened the Birkbeck Players. In the open-air space of Torrington Square, she put on a production of *The Crooked Rib*, a series of short medieval plays or 'pageants' about women. In it, Slater played Herod, who 'rageth, in the pageant and in the street also' among the audience seated on the grass. In the square and the unglamorous setting of Malet Street's Harkness Hall, they set out to revive interest in medieval romances, Shakespearean farces, and Dickens' less well-known plays.

Fig. 10.3 The English Department's Christmas party in the Tillotson Room during the early 1980s, where the staff (including Michael Slater as Ebenezer Scrooge, Miriam Allott, Andrew Saunders, Steve Connor, and Paula Neuss) performed Dickens' *A Christmas Carol* (1843) for students. Photograph courtesy of Professor Michael Slater.

---

[73] Sylvester Savigeas, 'The Next Stage', *The Lodestone*, 26.2 (spring 1931), 56.

It was no coincidence that the inaugural performance of the (new) Birkbeck Players took place at the annual Dickens' Days, which celebrated the 150th anniversaries of the first publication of successive Dickens novels.

* * *

The LMI/Birkbeck had a distinguished tradition of theatrical performances and public speaking. These aspects were especially influential in the late nineteenth and early twentieth centuries when the Birkbeck theatre was the hotbed of modernist plays. It was attractive to students, not only in its own right but also because training in acting and elocution could forge careers in the theatre, law, and politics. There were increasingly criticisms about the more conservative productions staged in the Birkbeck theatre, but it flourished nevertheless until the move to the Malet Street building in the early 1950s. A revival in the 1980s and 1990s was led by a small group of Birkbeck staff based in the Department of English, the heart of Dickens' studies at the time (see Fig. 10.3). From its beginning, however, the theatre and other entertainments were caught up in debates about the purpose of education. What was the role of sociability in fostering intellectual engagement? How could scholars understand literature through the written word only? Was the university a collection of individuals or a community of scholars seeking to advance knowledge? They are questions that continue to be debated today.

11
The New Woman

> In every battle some must bravely fall,
> 'Tis only thus great victories are won!
> The dash of blood and brains upon the wall—
> A woman's too—may make the conq'ring call...
>   Gerald Massey, 1895, written in honour of Edith Lanchester [1]

In the 1890s, the Birkbeck Literary and Scientific Institution was a magnet for the 'New Woman'. Radical young women keen to assert their independence while trampling on conventional mores could find within its walls a place to display their talents and expand their horizons. Indeed, the Institution had championed female education for the previous sixty years. In 1830, the LMI first admitted women to its classes. There were concerns about the 'undesirable consequences' of female membership and the 'governing body was solemnly warned of the downfall it was inviting'.[2] The Committee also continued for at least three years to debate 'the propriety of admitting females attending lectures through the front entrance',[3] and women were not able to become full members until 1896.[4] Nevertheless, allowing women to attend classes was extremely progressive. Birkbeck provided higher education for women long before other institutions in the UK: Queen's College in Harley Street was not founded until 1848 and Bedford College the following year.[5]

One of these female students was a self-styled 'New Woman' called Edith ('Biddy') Lanchester (see Fig. 11.1), who put her name down for classes in botany and zoology.[6] Lanchester was no ordinary student. Although born into a wealthy middle-class family, headed by the architect Henry James Lanchester, she was socially and politically radical. Since 1892, she had been galvanized into political activism by the Social Democratic Federation (SDF), Britain's first socialist party, with members that included H. M. Hyndman (its founder), William Morris (designer), James Connolly (Irish republican), and Eleanor 'Tussy' Marx (activist

---

[1] 'Battersea Romance', *South Wales Echo* (1 November 1895), 2.
[2] Fred A. Mackenzie, 'The Birkbeck Institution: The Story of London's Evening University', in *Windsor Magazine: An Illustrated Monthly for Men and Women*, 7 (December 1897), 377.
[3] Burns, *A Short History of Birkbeck College*, 43.
[4] 'Sex Equality. Lord Balfour or Burleigh and Married Women Ban', *Daily Herald* (28 May 1928), 7.
[5] Burns, *A Short History of Birkbeck College*, 43.
[6] 'A Socialist Romance', *Lloyd's Weekly Newspaper* (27 October 1895), 1.

Fig. 11.1 Edith Lanchester. Birkbeck Archive.

and youngest daughter of Karl Marx). Lanchester not only stood for the London School Board but also was an SDF candidate for West Lambeth. One commentator remembers the way she heckled candidates in Liberal Party meetings. On one occasion, she

> asked the candidate at least a dozen questions, which he answered with studied politeness. The aspirant for Parliamentary honours was a very young man, and the questioner being a charming young lady, the audience watched the duel for a time with interest. However, when Miss Lanchester reached seventhly [sic] there were manifestations of impatience, and when, twelfthly [sic], she asked the candidate whether he would vote against vivisection the audience refused to control themselves any longer. A storm of yells arose and Miss Lanchester had to subside.

Nevertheless, she returned the following night and 'harangued the crowd from a friendly tradesman's cart'.[7] Another party comrade observed that Lanchester was a 'fluent out-of-door speaker, never dismayed however turbulent a crowd may be'. He added, however, that her 'eloquent speeches' were sometimes 'marred for the general hearer by her abundant use of what I may call the "slang" of Socialism'.[8] In 1895, as a member of the SDF Executive during the general election, she could be seen canvassing the residents of Walworth on behalf of the socialist-feminist George Lansbury, dressed splendidly in 'a vivid red "Garibaldi"' (a wool shirt named after the Italian political hero).[9]

---

[7] 'Our Capital Letter', *Tower Hamlets Independent and East End Local Advertiser* (2 November 1895), 3.

[8] 'The Strange Case in London. The Effect of Unwholesome Literature', *Dublin Evening Telegraph* (29 October 1895), 2. Also see 'The Remarkable Abduction Case', *Glasgow Evening Post* (29 October 1895), 2.

[9] 'The Strange Case in London. The Effect of Unwholesome Literature', *Dublin Evening Telegraph* (29 October 1895), 2 and 'The Walworth Election', *South London Press* (18 May 1895), 5.

Although Lanchester's background meant that she was economically self-sufficient, she insisted on earning her own money. Admittedly, a stint as a teacher at the Maria Grey College (the first and very progressive teacher training school for women in England) had not gone well: her views were judged 'rather too strong' and she was asked to leave.[10] But by the mid-1890s, however, she was employed as a clerk for the Cardiff (New South Wales) Gold Mining Company[11] while also acting as secretary to 'Tussy' Marx. For a few years, she had even been living independently, renting rooms from Mrs Mary Gray, a prominent woman in the SDF and a guardian for the Wandsworth and Clapham Union in Battersea (south-west London).[12]

Lanchester's early education was typical of her sex and class: in her childhood, she had 'learnt scarcely anything but drawing'.[13] She joined Birkbeck, keen to learn about science while also taking more practical classes in typewriting and shorthand.[14] In 1894, she was interviewed for an article on 'new employment for women', published in the *Aberdeen Press and Journal*. She had told the journalist that, when she was a child, art was considered to be the most important acquisition for a girl, which is why 'as she grew older she went through the more usual educational curriculum, attending classes at the Birkbeck'.[15] This provided her with the skills required to earn a living by drawing 'diagrams for lecturers on scientific subjects, especially anatomy'.[16] The journalist concluded that

> So long as the lecture continues to be the general vehicle of instruction, it was likely that Miss Lanchester or any other lady pursuing this career will find that lecturers furnish the majority of her patrons.[17]

Other 'New Women' were encouraged to take note.

Lanchester's educational achievements, combined with her intelligence, politics, and self-confidence, meant that she was widely regarded as an eccentric. In 1895, the *South London Press* described the way she would 'stalk through the Battersea streets on her way to the City', where Birkbeck was based.[18] She was 'picturesque', according to *Lloyd's Weekly Newspaper*, with

---

[10] 'A Socialist Romance', *Lloyd's Weekly Newspaper* (27 October 1895), 1.
[11] 'The Extraordinary Alleged Abduction. One of Grant Allen's Disciples', *Gloucester Citizen* (28 October 1895), 3.
[12] 'Edith Lanchester', *South London Press* (2 November 1895), 1.
[13] 'A New Employment for Women', *Aberdeen Press and Journal* (6 June 1894), 5. Lanchester's daughter maintains that she learnt shorthand and typing at Birkbeck and also went to the University of Cambridge and the College of Preceptors: Elsa Lanchester, *Elsa Lanchester Herself* (New York: St Martin's Press, 1983), 1.
[14] 'A Socialist Romance', *Lloyd's Weekly Newspaper* (27 October 1895), 1.
[15] 'A New Employment for Women', *Aberdeen Press and Journal* (6 June 1894), 5.   [16] Ibid., 5.
[17] Ibid., 5.   [18] 'Edith Lanchester', *South London Press* (2 November 1895), 1.

her slim form, loosely-clad in hodden grey, her child's face, rich colour, and sparkling eyes, her dark hair cut short like a boy's, surmounted with a little polo cap, and her ringing voice, she was able to command attention, even among a hostile crowd.... [She] possesses an independent spirit.[19]

Still others described her as 'tall and slim, with a masculine gait, closely cropped hair, and a kind of pea-jacket',[20] and claimed (in the words of a journalist for the *Dublin Evening Telegraph*) that she was fond of wearing 'a golf cap on her head, and a kind of pilot jacket[,] in the pockets of which she always tucks her hands as she walked'.[21] She 'looks more like an overgrown boy in petticoats than a young girl'.[22] As these descriptions suggest, there was something not quite feminine about Lanchester. Commentators regularly noted her 'masculine gait', 'weird and uncanny' eyes: she looked as though she had 'a whole hive of bees in her bonnet'.[23] In other words, she was the archetypical 'New Woman'.

In 1895, however, she was 24 years of age and in love. Her beau was the handsome, large-moustached James ('Shamus') Sullivan, working-class clerk, and active member of the Battersea branch of the SDF. He spoke with a strong cockney accent, enjoyed reading dictionaries and encyclopedias, and was highly respected in the neighbourhood.[24] He had learned shorthand and was known for his 'elegant, scriptlike [sic] handwriting'.[25] It is likely that they originally met in those shorthand classes at Birkbeck.

Lanchester was besotted. She announced to friends and family that, on 26 October 1895, she intended to move in with Sullivan. Marriage was ruled out. As one newspaper coyly put it, Lanchester was going to make Sullivan her 'chum'.[26] The issue at stake was clear—at least to Lanchester. She told her mother that if she married, 'I should lose all my self-respect, and to lose self-respect is not good for anyone.'[27]

Lanchester's announcement was met with incredulity, followed by horror. Her parents accused 'The Birkbeck', as well as membership of the SDF, of having 'unhinged her mind'.[28] Her mother blamed the 'painful affair' on the fact that she was 'an intelligent young woman'.[29] 'My opinion, and that of the family', explained her father, was that 'the girl is, for the time being, not of sound mind', adding that the 'effects of overstudy [sic] have predisposed her naturally impressionable

---

[19] 'A Socialist Romance', *Lloyd's Weekly Newspaper* (27 October 1895), 1.
[20] 'Edith Lanchester', *South London Press* (2 November 1895), 1.
[21] 'The Strange Case in London. The Effect of Unwholesome Literature', *Dublin Evening Telegraph* (29 October 1895), 2.
[22] Ibid., 2.   [23] Ibid., 2.   [24] Lanchester, *Elsa Lanchester Herself*, 2.   [25] Ibid., 2.
[26] 'Edith Lanchester', *South London Press* (2 November 1895), 1.
[27] 'A Socialist Romance', *Lloyd's Weekly Newspaper* (27 October 1895), 1.
[28] 'Edith Lanchester', *South London Press* (2 November 1895), 1.
[29] 'Her Incarceration in an Asylum', *Sheffield Independent* (30 October 1895), 5. Also see 'A Socialist Romance', *Grantham Journal* (2 November 1895), 7.

temperament'.³⁰ Birkbeck's commitment to the education of women was poisoning the morals of a generation of women.

The day before Lanchester had intended to move in with her lover, all hell broke loose. She was having breakfast at 8.30 a.m. in the back parlour of 72 Este Road, Battersea, when her father, three brothers, and an 'alienist' (the term used at the time for a psychiatrist) called George Fielding Blandford burst in. They were furious. Blandford fumed that Lanchester was 'advocating promiscuity and community in everything', which Lanchester hotly denied.³¹ He noted that Lanchester

> could give no reason for this conduct beyond saying that marriage was immoral.... She also said that if she married she would lose her independence. I pointed out that if she had children and was deserted she would have very little independence, but she only replied that he would not desert her. She could, she said, earn her own livelihood if he did. I reminded her that if she had the incumbrance of a family she would not be able to do this.³²

He was bewildered about what to do, noting that

> She seemed quite unable to see that the step she was about to take meant utter ruin. If she had said that she contemplated suicide a certificate might have been signed without question. I considered that I was equally justified in signing one when she expressed her determination to commit this social suicide.³³

As he left the room, he tutted, 'Dear, dear, I can do nothing with her',³⁴ then he signed papers committing her to an insane asylum.

Her brothers did the rough work: they tied her up and dragged her kicking and screaming into the street. Gray attempted a rescue but was rewarded with a black eye. Lanchester was bundled into a brougham (a carriage named after Lord Brougham, one of the men responsible for the existence of 'The Birkbeck' in the first place). In her struggles, she broke one of its glass windows.³⁵ As the brougham approached the asylum—the notorious Priory in south-west London—her broth-

---

³⁰ Henry Jones Lanchester, '[Letter to the Editor] The Case of Miss Lanchester', *The Times* (31 October 1895), 10; 'An Alleged Abduction', *Tenbury Wells Advertiser* (5 November 1895), 6; 'An Alleged Abduction', *East and South Devon Advertiser* (2 November 1895), 2; 'An Alleged Abduction', *Exmouth Journal* (2 November 1895), 2.

³¹ 'Edith Lanchester', *South London Press* (2 November 1895), 1.

³² 'The Lanchester Case', *British Medical Journal*, 2.1818 (2 November 1895), 1127. Also see 'An Alleged Abduction', *Exmouth Journal* (2 November 1895), 2.

³³ 'The Lanchester Case', *British Medical Journal*, 2.1818 (2 November 1895), 1127. Also see 'An Alleged Abduction', *Exmouth Journal* (2 November 1895), 2.

³⁴ 'Edith Lanchester', *South London Press* (2 November 1895), 1.

³⁵ 'The Socialist and His Would-Be Wife', *Faringdon Advertiser and Vale of the White Horse* (2 November 1895), 2.

ers tried to reassure her that it was simply 'a private house, and that I should be comfortable there' but 'I told him that I knew perfectly well the kind of place it was'.[36] Dr Chambers, the Superintendent of the Priory, reluctantly noted that all the paperwork was in order, so he was 'obliged to receive me as a patient'.[37] Lanchester was to be detained there for the next four days.

When Lanchester's lover and other members of the SDF[38] eventually found out where she had been confined, they did what every good socialist organization does: they organized a solidarity campaign and set up a committee to coordinate it. They employed a cornet-player, gathered together the musical scores for 'The Roll Call', 'All For the Cause' (words by William Morris), and 'The Marseillaise', and took a train to the Priory. Taking up positions outside its gates, they began singing loudly. It was intended to be 'a serenade' to boost the spirit of their free-loving heroine.[39] Alas: Lanchester was 'entirely unconscious of the attentions, being sound asleep in another part of the building', perhaps under sedation.[40] The committee then missed their last train home, so were forced to 'trudge all the way back to Battersea' by foot, arriving at a quarter to two in the morning.[41]

John Burns, the MP for Battersea, was more effective. He visited the Priory with some members of the Lunacy Commission, who concluded that Lanchester was 'no doubt very foolish, but not mad'.[42] She was released and never spoke to her family again.

* * *

The saga incited a media frenzy. The case—dubbed 'The Lanchester Kidnapping Case'—generated hundreds of excitable comments in the UK, Germany, America, South Africa, and India.[43] Lanchester's 'abduction' by her father provoked arguments about some of the most heated questions of the time, including the power of psychiatry, the social status of the 'New Woman', and the dangers of female education. Blandford defended his decision to sign the warrant for Lanchester's incarceration by claiming that she was suffering from 'monomania on the subject of marriage'.[44] He pointed to the fact that there was insanity in her family, although (as one journalist reminded readers) having a grandmother who was 'imbecile in old age' was 'a condition not unknown in the best regulated families'.[45] Blandford was adamant that he had

---

[36] 'Edith Lanchester', *South London Press* (2 November 1895), 1.   [37] Ibid., 1.
[38] Including Harry B. Rogers, Mary Gray, Hyndman, and Herbert Burrows.
[39] 'The Woman Who Would', *Gloucester Citizen* (30 October 1895), 3.   [40] Ibid., 3.
[41] Ibid., 5.   [42] 'Edith Lanchester', *South London Press* (2 November 1895), 1.
[43] Lanchester, *Elsa Lanchester Herself*, 4.
[44] 'An Alleged Abduction', *Tenbury Wells Advertiser* (5 November 1895), 6. Also see 'Miss Lanchester's Rescue', *Hull Daily Mail* (31 October 1895), 4, and 'An Alleged Abduction', *Exmouth Journal* (2 November 1895), 2.
[45] 'The Lanchester Case. Some Curious Documents', *Totnes Weekly Times* (23 November 1895), 3.

signed the certificate...entirely for her own good. I thought it such a terrible thing that an educated young woman in this good position should go and do such a thing as this. The only cause for detention was to stop her from doing it.[46]

He believed that she was committing 'social suicide'.

Blandford didn't come out of the furore well. He was disparaged for being a 'well-meaning and kindly medical despot'.[47] A journalist of the *Cardiff Times* reported that he was

> an elderly gentleman, of grave and benevolent aspect, who would combine most admirably the traditional *role* of physician and 'friend of the family', with a proper horror for new-fangled ideas, especially on such a sacred subject as that of marriage.[48]

He was definitely 'not one of those for whom the holder of advanced views can hope to obtain anything in the nature of sympathy'.[49] After the scandal settled down, a deputation (including Lanchester and members of the SDF) petitioned the Lunacy Commissioners to prosecute Blandford for 'having wilfully issued a false certificate of lunacy'.[50] The Commissioners agreed that Blandford had made a 'mistake' but, although he had been paid 'his fee of a guinea, or perhaps three guineas', they 'could not see any evidence of a corrupt motive'.[51] In other words, Blandford's fellow-alienists closed ranks behind him.

Public commentators were divided. Some regarded Lanchester as a heroine who had '"with noble soul" brought the emancipation of woman much nearer'.[52] In the *Labour Leader*, Lily Bell argued that Lanchester's brave act would 'do more than anything else to strengthen the feeling of revolt amongst women, and to hasten the time when they shall be able to hold themselves in freedom'.[53] 'Women in a

---

[46] 'Miss Lanchester's Rescue', *Hull Daily Mail* (31 October 1895), 4.

[47] 'Medical Lettres de Cachet', *Saturday Review* (2 November 1895), 569.

[48] 'The Kidnapping Case', *Cardiff Times* (2 November 1895), 4. [49] Ibid., 4.

[50] 'The Lanchester Case. Appeal to the Lunacy Commissioners', *Sheffield Daily Telegraph* (9 January 1896), 7.

[51] Ibid., 7. Also see 'General', *Manchester Courier and Lancashire General Advertiser* (11 January 1896), 12, and 'Miss Lanchester and the Marriage Laws', *London Evening Standard* (9 January 1896), 2. For a critique of the Lunacy Commissioners' response, see 'Edith Lanchester', *Woman's Signal* (16 January 1896), 14.

[52] 'Edith Lanchester', *South London Press* (2 November 1895), 1. Also see 'Our Capital Letter', *Tower Hamlets Independent and East End Local Advertiser* (2 November 1895), 3.

[53] Lily Bell in *Labour Leader* (2 November 1895), cited in Karen Hunt, *Equivocal Feminists: The Social Democratic Federation and the Woman Question* (Cambridge: Cambridge University Press, 1996), 103. There are disputes about the identity of Lily Bell. Some argue it was Keir Hardie but there is stronger evidence for it being Isabella Bream Pearse: see June Hannam, 'Women and the ILP, 1890–1914', in David James, Tony Jowitt, and Keith Laybourne (eds), *The Centenary History of the Independent Labour Party* (Edinburgh: Edinburgh University Press, 1992), 205–28.

middle-class position' were reported to have 'urged her to keep firm'.[54] Poet, spiritualist, and expert on ancient Egypt, Gerald Massey, even sent her the poem with which I started this chapter, lauding her for being one of those bloodied women who 'bravely fall' in the battle for freedom.[55]

* * *

For social radicals, the 'kidnapping' of Lanchester provided an opportunity to reflect on activist practice. The Marquis of Queensberry (after whom the Queensberry Rules for boxing were named, but also the father of Alfred Douglas and therefore responsible for the trial of Oscar Wilde) publicly thanked Sullivan for taking a stand against marriage, adding that he would 'like to know you and your brave wife'. However, he ruefully contended that Lanchester's actions had been premature: society was not ready for such zealotry. He reminded Sullivan that it was

> not fair to the woman to place her in such a cruel position—to say nothing of the children of such marriages. What we want is a protest; change of laws follow, do not precede, change of opinion. We want change of opinion first.... it is no use knocking your head against a brick wall. To bring that wall down[,] undermine it—don't crack your own skull.

He offered the lovers £100 if they married and then immediately 'protest[ed] against it and repudiate[d] it, saying it was naught to you, and that if mutual love and affection cannot bind you together as man and wife nothing else could'. Since 'every one's [sic] attention is attracted' to the case, this 'public protest' was likely to have more impact than defiantly choosing to cohabit outside of marriage.[56] Indeed, what the Marquis was proposing was already a practice in radical circles of the time. Not long before the Lanchester furore, a couple belonging to the Bradford socialists had married in a registry office but then immediately issued a circular stating that they were in 'entire disagreement with the present marriage laws'.[57] The Marquis wanted Lanchester and Sullivan to do likewise. It was too much of a compromise, so they ignored him.

The Marquis' pragmatic response was supportive, although ultimately conservative. The SDF proved similarly ambivalent. Party leaders worried about headlines sporting titles such as 'A Socialist Romance'. Recruitment could be hampered, they feared, if people thought the party was hell-bent on destroying

---

[54] 'Battersea Romance', *South Wales Echo* (1 November 1895), 2.   [55] Ibid., 2.
[56] 'Edith Lanchester', *South London Press* (2 November 1895), 1. Also see 'An Alleged Abduction', *Exmouth Journal* (2 November 1895), 2, and 'The Kidnapping Case', *Cardiff Times* (2 November 1895), 4.
[57] 'From Our London Correspondent', *Lancashire Evening Post* (29 October 1895), 2.

the family.⁵⁸ Even the *British Medical Journal* reported that 'the very last thing which practical Socialists would desire' was any 'popular association of their ideas with a loosening of the marriage tie'.⁵⁹ Keir Hardie, founder of the Labour Party, warned that the 'enemies of Socialism know that such an escapade...tends to discredit it among all classes'.⁶⁰ Despite the feminist credentials of many of their members, the leadership of the SDF were much more concerned with the status of *male* workers and the eight-hour day than anything that upset sexual conventions.⁶¹ In the words of a member writing in the SDF's newspaper *Justice*,

> though we are as much opposed to the present marriage laws...as the most vehement 'new woman' can be, we have the right to ask that the question shall not be publicly raised in an acute form by an official member of the SDF, without any conference whatever with other comrades.⁶²

Lanchester's mistake, then, was not to have convened a committee in advance of announcing her intentions.

Non-comrades were much harsher, deriding Lanchester for being a 'silly' young woman who 'thought to cast aside all pretensions to decency in order to shew [sic] her contempt for the marriage laws'.⁶³ She was nothing more than a 'strong-minded but ignorant young lady', concluded another commentator.⁶⁴ *Blackwood's Edinburgh Magazine* published an account by 'The Looker-On' which was particularly misogynistic. The author was exasperated by Lanchester's confidence. He claimed that 'a girl with opinions' was 'the most hopeless member of society, and more wholly beyond the reach of conviction than any other human creature conceivable'. Such women believed that they could act however they chose and would 'not pay the penalty'. He sneered that Lanchester has 'the unalterable conviction that amid all the unfaithful heroes of the world her particular man will be the one who will never forsake the woman of his choice'. This was also the conviction of 'poor Mary Wollstonecraft', he contended, who similarly

> would not marry, not believing in or approving of marriage; and the end of it was that she was left stranded in Paris with an unfortunately baby, and a very miserable time of it till Godwin...took her up.

---

⁵⁸ 'A Socialist Romance', *Nottinghamshire Guardian* (2 November 1895), 4.
⁵⁹ 'The Lanchester Case', *British Medical Journal*, 2.1818 (2 November 1895), 1127.
⁶⁰ *Labour Leader* (2 February 1896), cited in Karen Hunt, *Equivocal Feminists: The Social Democratic Federation and the Woman Question* (Cambridge: Cambridge University Press, 1996), 102.
⁶¹ Hunt, *Equivocal Feminists*.   ⁶² *Justice* (2 November 1895), cited in ibid., 99.
⁶³ 'Weekly London Letter', *Leeds Times* (9 November 1895), 3.
⁶⁴ 'A Socialist Romance', *Grantham Journal* (2 November 1895), 7.

What more could be expected, 'Looker-On' exclaimed, from someone 'who is at once a Socialist and a Woman'.[65]

Very few journalists commented on the role of James Sullivan. Since he was neither insane and nor anti-marriage, he had no excuse for encouraging Lanchester, argued the *Dublin Evening Telegraph*.[66] Another newspaper castigated him for lack of 'chivalry' and a 'sense of honour' in being unable to persuade Lanchester to give up her dangerous views.[67] The *Saturday Review* blandly noted that 'A man can deliberately dispense with the ceremony of marriage without the slightest interference; in a woman it seems to be regarded virtually as madness.'[68]

More typical commentary focused on the fact that Sullivan was 'lower on the social ladder' than Lanchester.[69] This roused widespread indignation. Lanchester was making a 'silly decision to cohabit with a man socially her inferior', concluded the *Leeds Times*, alarmed that class distinctions were being violated.[70] Even worse, it wasn't as if Lanchester did not have other options, either: she was said to have 'attracted many admirers' but 'gave them no encouragement, though many...were in a much better station of life than Sullivan'.[71] Lanchester herself refused to grant the argument any legitimacy, pointing out that 'I do not recognise the question of station. He is a clerk, and I am a clerk; we are both earning the same salary, so I don't see the inequality.'[72] This progressiveness left most readers speechless.

* * *

What could have led Lanchester to think of breaching public morals in this way? Some commentators blamed the effect of 'Penny or Shilling Shockers upon the mind of the time'.[73] The *Dublin Evening Telegraph* was brutal, stating that the 'misguided young lady' had 'apparently been unhinged by the study of "New Woman" literature'.[74]

The chief culprit was Grant Allen's *The Woman Who Did*, which was published that same year of Lanchester's protest and had already gone through eighteen

---

[65] 'The Looker-On', *Blackwood's Edinburgh Magazine*, 158.963 (December 1895), 915–16; 'Pernicious Literature', *Newcastle Courant* (7 December 1895), 2. Parallels to Wollstonecraft and George Eliot were also made by 'Medical Lettres de Cachet', *Saturday Review* (2 November 1895), 569.
[66] 'The Strange Case in London. The Effect of Unwholesome Literature', *Dublin Evening Telegraph* (29 October 1895), 2.
[67] 'A Socialist Romance', *Grantham Journal* (2 November 1895), 7.
[68] 'Medical Lettres de Cachet', *Saturday Review* (2 November 1895), 569.
[69] 'Edith Lanchester', *South London Press* (2 November 1895), 1. Also see 'An Alleged Abduction', *Exmouth Journal* (2 November 1895), 2, and 'The Lanchester Case', *British Medical Journal*, 2.1818 (2 November 1895), 1127.
[70] 'Weekly London Letter', *Leeds Times* (9 November 1895), 3.
[71] 'A Socialist Romance', *Nottinghamshire Guardian* (2 November 1895), 4. Also see 'A Socialist Romance', *Lloyd's Weekly Newspaper* (27 October 1895), 1.
[72] 'The Case of Miss Lanchester', *Lloyd's Weekly Newspaper* (12 January 1896), 6.
[73] 'Pernicious Literature', *Newcastle Courant* (7 December 1895), 2.
[74] 'The Strange Case in London. The Effect of Unwholesome Literature', *Dublin Evening Telegraph* (29 October 1895), 2.

editions.[75] Indeed, the Marquis of Queensberry claimed that Allen's novel taught why 'at present such marriages must not be made'.[76] The chief character in the novel was another highly educated young woman called Herminia, who dedicated her life to the pursuit of moral independence and social freedom. Herminia was particularly opposed to marriage. It was 'vile slavery'[77] and

> an assertion of man's supremacy over woman. It ties her to him for life, it ignores her individuality, it compels her to promise what no human heart can be sure of performing; for you can contract to do or not to do, easily enough, but to contract to feel or not to feel,—what transparent absurdity!... If I love a man at all, I must love him on terms of perfect freedom.[78]

Herminia chose to live with her lover, as well as bear his child, outside of marriage. Like Lanchester, the fictive Herminia had also been employed as a teacher and, despite attempting 'so hard unobtrusively to train up' the schoolgirls 'towards a rational understanding of the universe', her radical views forced her to resign.[79] That was not the worse tragedy: just before Herminia's daughter was born, her lover died, leaving her penniless. Herminia was rejected by both her family and her lover's; was forced to work for a living; and was scorned for being 'scarcely short of sheer madness'.[80] Herminia never gave up the battle, however. She became involved in radical, left-wing politics and firmly believed that her daughter would follow in her footsteps, then 'regenerate humanity' and herald in a utopia of absolute freedom.[81]

The connections between Allen's heroine and Lanchester's life were apparent to everyone, even though Lanchester claimed never to have read the book.[82] She was widely said to have adopted the 'anti-marriage cult' preached by Allen.[83] Allen's philosophy was 'cheap and rather nasty' but had seduced Lanchester, decreed the *Dublin Evening Telegraph*.[84] At least one journalist subtitled his article 'The Woman Who Would But Was Prevented'.[85] Like the Marquis of Queensberry, the author of 'A Socialist Romance' maintained that

---

[75] This was a common statement. For a few examples, see 'Singular Abduction Case', *Middlesex and Surrey Express* (2 November 1895), 7. The number of editions is from 'Herminia in Real Life', *Western Daily Mercury* (29 October 1895), 4.

[76] 'Edith Lanchester', *South London Press* (2 November 1895), 1.

[77] Grant Allen, *The Woman Who Did* (London: John Lane, 1895), 41.   [78] Ibid., 43.

[79] Ibid., 83.   [80] Ibid., 87.   [81] Ibid., 179.

[82] 'A Socialist Romance', *Grantham Journal* (2 November 1895), 7.

[83] This phrase is used in many places, including 'The Extraordinary Alleged Abduction. One of Grant Allen's Disciples', *Gloucester Citizen* (28 October 1895), 3; 'The Socialist and His Would-Be Wife', *Faringdon Advertiser and Vale of the White Horse* (2 November 1895), 2; 'A Socialist Romance', *Nottinghamshire Guardian* (2 November 1895), 4; 'A Socialist Romance', *Lloyd's Weekly Newspaper* (27 October 1895), 1.

[84] 'The Strange Case in London. The Effect of Unwholesome Literature', *Dublin Evening Telegraph* (29 October 1895), 2.

[85] 'The Kidnapping Case', *Cardiff Times* (2 November 1895), 4.

It is a pity for Miss Lanchester's sake that she has not studied the book: for if she had read it she would have realised some of the grave perils that may attend the course of conduct which she seems determined to pursue.[86]

This journalist was referring to the way Grant's book ended. In the novel, Herminia fails. Her daughter discovers that she is illegitimate and, therefore, cannot marry the man she loves. In order to free her daughter from this burden, Herminia 'put on a fresh white dress' and drank a phial of prussic acid.[87]

The only other fictional characters that Lanchester was compared with were those in the novels of Alec Nelson. In the words of the *South London Press*, Lanchester 'has not lived long, but, like one of Alec Nelson's characters, she has lived "much"'.[88] It was an astute comment because Lanchester would have known 'Alec Nelson'—his real name was Edward Bibbins Aveling, lover of 'Tussy' Marx and the prototype of Dubedat in *The Doctor's Dilemma* by Shaw, for whom Lanchester worked as a secretary. Together, Aveling and Marx wrote a pamphlet entitled *The Woman Question* (1886), in which they registered strong support for those activists campaigning for female suffrage as well as access of women to Higher Education and the professions. However, these were reforms that benefited primarily middle- and upper-class women. Of much greater importance was to free women from the tyranny of men and marriage. Like the labouring classes, women are 'in an oppressed condition' and, in terms of the 'sex relation', in a position of 'merciless degradation': 'Women are the creatures of an organized tyranny of men, as the workers are the creatures of an organized tyranny of idlers'—that is, capitalists.[89] Marriage in the capitalist world was based on 'commercialism' and weddings are nothing more than 'business transactions'.[90] This leaves a terrible toll on women. Aveling and Marx drew on physiognomic theory to make their argument. They pointed out that

> Every one [sic] knows the effect that certain callings, or habits of life, have on the *physique* and on the face of those that follow them. The horsy man, the drunkard, are known by gait, physiognomy. How many of us have ever paused, or dared to pause, upon the serious fact that in the streets and public buildings, in the friend-circle, we can, in a moment, tell the unmarried woman, if they are beyond a certain age?... But we cannot tell a man that is unmarried from one that is wedded.... How is it that our sisters bear upon their brows this stamp of

---

[86] 'A Socialist Romance', *Grantham Journal* (2 November 1895), 7.
[87] Allen, *The Woman Who Did*, 222–3.
[88] 'Edith Lanchester', *South London Press* (2 November 1895), 1.
[89] Edward Aveling and Eleanor Marx Aveling, *The Woman Question* (London: Swan Sonnenschein, 1886), 6.
[90] Ibid., 8.

lost instincts, stifled affections, a nature in part murdered? How is it that their 'more fortunate brothers' bear no such mark?[91]

The answer was that unmarried women bear the 'stamp of eternal virginity' because they are economically dependent upon men and are denied the 'means of gratifying [their] sex instinct' outside of marriage, in the way men were allowed to do, without becoming a 'pariah'.[92] They hoped for a day when women 'shall no longer be man's slave, but his equal' in education, economics, and marriage.[93] It was Lanchester's dream.

Ironically, however, it was 'Tussy' Marx, not Lanchester, who was to follow in the footsteps of the fictional Herminia. When 'Tussy' discovered that her lover had secretly married another woman, she committed suicide. Years later, Lanchester recalled that

> If a person must commit suicide, Eleanor Marx did it well. She had a bath and cleaned herself thoroughly inside and out, wrapped herself in a sheet, and took prussic acid.... Not at all messy.[94]

It was a death eerily close to the one Grant Allen staged for Herminia. There could be no clearer warning to 'New Women' who defied convention.

* * *

In contrast, Lanchester survived the scandal. On returning to her lodgings in Gray's home, she found herself besieged by well-wishers. A friend from 'The Birkbeck' accompanied her to a 'retreat' to enjoy 'a much-needed rest'.[95]

Not surprisingly, detention in an insane asylum had not changed her views. Quite the opposite, Lanchester insisted that she 'held to them more firmly than before'.[96] Unlike the 'New Woman' of Pinero's plays (discussed in the previous chapter) or Grant Allen's novels, in which the heroines ultimately fail (they commit suicide or they return, defeated, to conventional morality), Lanchester threw herself back into the political affray, lecturing on economics in Leigh and on 'Socialism and Progress' in Blackburn.[97] As one journalist noted with admiration, socialists like Lanchester 'never shirk a discussion'.[98] She could also be seen on a boat trip with more than sixty socialists and feminists (including the suffragette Emmeline Pankhurst), loudly singing 'The Marseillaise', much to the bemusement

---

[91] Ibid., 7–8.   [92] Ibid., 8–9.   [93] Ibid., 15.
[94] Lanchester, *Elsa Lanchester Herself*, 16.
[95] 'The Kidnapping Case', *Cardiff Times* (2 November 1895), 4.
[96] 'The Case of Miss Lanchester', *The Times* (30 October 1895), 10.
[97] 'Notes of the Week', *Leigh Chronicle and Weekly District Advertiser* (27 March 1896), 5, and 'Lecture on "Socialism and Progress"', *Preston Herald*, 1896.
[98] 'Notes of the Week', *Leigh Chronicle and Weekly District Advertiser* (27 March 1896), 5.

of 'hundreds of holiday-making aristocrats' lining the banks of the river.[99] Lanchester remained a prominent warrior for women's rights and freedoms: she waved the suffragettes' green, white, and purple flag in Trafalgar Square and was even imprisoned for her role in a protest.[100] Although the *Saturday Review* contended that Lanchester's rejection of marriage was morally wrong, it also viewed the saga as teaching an important lesson: 'public opinion' still did not think that a woman was capable of 'thinking for herself and deciding for herself', even though that woman might be 'grown up, educated, self-supporting, and intellectually the superior of the average male'.[101] In contrast to 'public opinion', Birkbeck encouraged thinking women, whether 'New Women' or not.

The 'Socialist Romance' of the two overeducated lovers lasted until Sullivan's death in 1945.[102] They never married but had a son and daughter together. Their daughter was Elsa Lanchester, a talented actress, who starred as the *Bride of Frankenstein* (1935). Edith Lanchester died aged 94, a fervent socialist to her last breath.[103]

* * *

Lanchester's outrageous proposal to remain unmarried and her 'abduction' by her father raised questions about the role played by 'The Birkbeck' in the education of women. Two contradictory views appear time and again. On the one hand, people commenting on the Lanchester scandal were aghast that a woman who possessed 'a good education' would be able even to *contemplate* doing such a foolhardy thing as living with a man outside of marriage.[104] It was 'social suicide', precariously close to prostitution. On the other hand, the same commentators blamed 'over-education' for *inevitably* leading women into immorality.[105] Educated women would come to resemble men: they cut their hair short, 'stalked' the streets, and walked with a 'masculine gait', hands in pockets.

This contradiction was present throughout the early days of the London Mechanics' Institution. As early as 1827 (that is, three years *before* women were officially allowed to attend classes at the Institution), the fact that some women could be seen in the audience of major lectures drew protest. The governing body of the LMI was 'solemnly warned of the downfall it was inviting' by admitting women to all classes and the potential for 'undesirable consequences'.[106] As we saw in Chapter 4, 'Useful Knowledge', George Birkbeck's decision in 1827 to allow women to attend his anatomy classes was regarded as scandalous. These classes

[99] 'Socialism', *Reynolds's Newspaper* (9 August 1896), 1.
[100] Lanchester, *Elsa Lanchester Herself*, 17.
[101] 'Medical Lettres de Cachet', *Saturday Review* (2 November 1895), 569.
[102] Hunt, *Equivocal Feminists*, 98.   [103] 'Remarkable Women', *The Stage* (15 March 1984), 26.
[104] 'Weekly London Letter', *Leeds Times* (9 November 1895), 3.
[105] 'The Lanchester Case. Some Curious Documents', *Totnes Weekly Times* (23 November 1895), 3.
[106] Mackenzie, 'The Birkbeck Institution', 377.

were an affront to religious mores as well as subverting 'natural' social hierarchies. Six decades later, Lanchester's attendance at anatomy classes was still scandalous, although it enabled her to earn a living by drawing 'diagrams for lecturers on scientific subjects, especially anatomy'.[107]

Crucially, though, in its early decades the LMI/Birkbeck was welcoming not only to female students but also to progressive, early feminists. The LMI/Birkbeck provided platforms for dozens of women to speak. Today, these women are known as 'first-wave feminists'. Allowing women to give public lectures was extremely progressive. In the words of one journalist, reviewing the lectures made by one of the LMI's most popular female lecturers, 'In former times lady lecturers were only expected to be found in the dull drab atmosphere of a quakers' conventicle [sic].' But, he continued, they were now living in an 'age of progress' and 'utilitarianism advances' where 'such attractions are becoming less rare'.[108] A similar comment was made by another journalist, writing in 1845 about 'Lectures and Lecturers at the Mechanics' Institution'. He contended that the 'appearance of a lady as a lecturer at any of our public institutions is something new, and, therefore, will by many be considered as an improper thing'. However, it was pointless arguing with those who believed women should remain silent in public, since 'you will never convince a man whose mind has prejudged a question'. He noted that the Institution attracted large audiences of women as well as men: 'surely if so many ladies are here to *hear*, why may not one lady be there to *speak?*', he asked.[109]

Who were these female lecturers in the LMI? They included people like Mrs Thomas Cooke Foster, who gave lectures not only on the Elizabethan court but also on female dress reform;[110] Miss Clara Seyton was invited to speak about 'English Comedy';[111] and members of the class on literary composition (a predecessor to 'creative writing') debated the question: 'Should National Education Include Political Economy, and Instruction to Females?'[112] Many of these mid-nineteenth-century female lecturers on women's rights were extremely popular. Three are particularly noteworthy: Mrs C. L. (Clara Lucas) Balfour, Mrs John Darcus, and the poet Miss Georgiana Bennett.

Balfour was lauded for her views on the position of women in Christianity and the female sovereigns of Europe, as well as her lectures on women's literature,

---

[107] 'A New Employment for Women', *Aberdeen Press and Journal* (6 June 1894), 5.
[108] He was referring to Georgiana Bennett: 'Mechanics' Institution', *Coventry Standard* (2 December 1853), 4.
[109] 'Lectures and Lecturers at the Mechanics' Institution', *Liverpool Mercury* (14 November 1845), 1.
[110] See the leaflet entitled 'London Mechanics' Institution' (London: London Mechanics' Institution, 1852), 2–3, and Don Chapman, *Wearing the Trousers: Fashion, Freedom, and the Rise of the Modern Woman* (Stroud: Amberley Publishing, 2017).
[111] Leaflet entitled 'London Mechanics' Institution' (London: London Mechanics' Institution, 1844), 2.
[112] Leaflet entitled 'London Mechanics' Institution' (London: London Mechanics' Institution, 1848), 3.

history, and social status.[113] She was not only an opponent of socialism but also a leading temperance reformer, serving as President of the British Temperance Association from 1877. The titles of some of her lectures reveal their extremely progressive politics. They include 'The Obligations of English Literature to Female Writers', 'Enquiries into the Mental Condition and the Educational Privileges of the Women of the Middle Classes', and 'Historical Testimony in Reference to the Influence of Superior Female Education on National Advancement'.[114] Balfour's book, *Working Women of the Last Half Century: The Lessons of Their Lives* (1854), celebrated female achievements,[115] while a central theme in all her work was the crucial role played by women in the history of 'great men'.[116] To critics who 'brought as an objection to the so-much-talked-of capabilities of women, that among them there had never arisen a Shakspere [sic], a Milton, and a Newton', she reminded them that 'these illustrious beings stood supreme, not only over the female sex, but over the male also'.[117]

To make her arguments, Balfour drew on the Bible. She contended that the 'Women of Scripture' were 'not degraded or oppressed' but shared an 'identity of interests and feelings' with their menfolk, with whom they lived in a state of 'affectionate equality'. She claimed that the biblical Sarah, for example, could be heard 'giving counsel, uttering directions, and sharing the authority of her husband [Abraham] over their vast household'. This was proof of woman's 'spiritual and intellectual privileges, her social influence, authority, and rights'.[118]

So why were women considered inferior to men, she asked? For Balfour, the problem was inadequate education, which focused on 'showy results' and 'the acquisition of a certain routine of fashionable acquirements laid down irrespective of capability'.[119] Female degradation was due to the 'shameful state into which, in consequence of neglected education, the sex had sunk'.[120] She called on women in

---

[113] Leaflet entitled 'London Mechanics' Institution' (London: London Mechanics' Institution, 1845), 3; leaflet entitled 'London Mechanics' Institution' (London: London Mechanics' Institution, 1848), 3; leaflet entitled 'London Mechanics' Institution' (London: London Mechanics' Institution, 1849), 3; leaflet entitled 'London Mechanics' Institution' (London: London Mechanics' Institution, 1850), 2.
[114] Leaflet entitled 'London Mechanics' Institution' (London: London Mechanics' Institution, 1842), 4; leaflet entitled 'London Mechanics' Institution' (London: London Mechanics' Institution, 1844), 3; leaflet entitled 'London Mechanics' Institution' (London: London Mechanics' Institution, 1845), 2; leaflet entitled 'London Mechanics' Institution' (London: London Mechanics' Institution, 1853), 2.
[115] Clara Lucas Balfour, *Working Women of the Last Half Century: The Lessons of Their Lives* (London: W. & F. G. Cash, 1854).
[116] 'Proceedings of Institutions', *Journal of the Society of Arts* (8 May 1857), 370.
[117] 'Mrs. C. L. Balfour's Lectures on the Influence of Woman on Society', *Manchester Times* (24 October 1846), 7.
[118] 'The Women of Antiquity', *Lady's Newspaper and Pictorial Times* (3 January 1863), 14.
[119] 'On the Moral and Intellectual Influence of Woman', *Huddersfield Chronicle* (17 November 1855), 6.
[120] 'Mrs. C. L. Balfour's Lectures on the Influence of Woman on Society', *Manchester Times* (24 October 1846), 7.

her audience to contribute to the 'march of human improvement', since 'every one had a duty to perform in furthering the cause of truth and knowledge'.[121] The LMI was one place where women could develop an 'intellectual culture'.[122]

It was a message echoed by Mrs John Darcus, another popular LMI lecturer on elocution, poetry, Shakespeare, and female education.[123] She believed that women were 'of the most vital importance to the nation at large, and the rising generation'.[124] Her 1847 lecture on the 'Rights of Women' attacked the 'little estimation' females were too often held' by men who clung to 'the idea that *woman* must be subservient to them'. If women were 'placed on a level with the male part of the human family', she contended, 'the effect would be the happiness and prosperity of the rising generations'.[125] However, such a revolution in human affairs would require an educational philosophy 'based upon good and upright principles'. If the 'female mind' was 'well cultivated, and the proper principles formed', then

> society would wear a must happier aspect, the condition of mankind would be greatly improved, and vice would be nearly extinct: in a word, the world would almost become heaven[,] and hell would be nowhere found.[126]

It was a radical vision that was precariously close to declaring a secular heaven *on earth*.

Finally, Georgiana Bennett was giving lectures at around the same time as Balfour and Darcus. Although she lectured on literature, her argument was that women should read female poets, rather than reading novels, which she believed were 'unfitting the minds of ladies for encountering the stern realities of life'.[127] She also had strong views about the custom of women making 'morning calls' (that is, brief visits to other women in the mornings) on the grounds that it was a 'sad waste of time, the conversation being generally on some frivolous subject'. Instead, women had a duty to visit the poor in order to impart 'kind and wholesome advice', rather than merely alms.[128] Although she was unmarried, she insisted that marriage was women's 'proper sphere'. This was not a call for female

---

[121] Sheffield Athenæum and Mechanics' Institution', *Sheffield Independent* (9 October 1847), 6.

[122] 'On the Moral and Intellectual Influence of Woman', *Huddersfield Chronicle* (17 November 1855), 6.

[123] Leaflet entitled 'London Mechanics' Institution' (London: London Mechanics' Institution, 1846), 3; 'The Weekly Record', *Howitt's Journal of Literature and Popular Progress* (1847), 15; 'The Weekly Record', *Howitt's Journal of Literature and Popular Progress* (1846), 25.

[124] 'Newbury', *Reading Mercury* (11 September 1847), 2.   [125] Ibid., 2.   [126] Ibid., 2.

[127] 'Lectures "On Woman"', *Staffordshire Adviser* (22 February 1851), 4. Also see the leaflet entitled 'London Mechanics' Institution' (London: London Mechanics' Institution, 1852), 2; 'Lecture on the Female Poets of Great Britain', *Yorkshire Gazette* (28 October 1848), 5; 'Rugeley', *Staffordshire Advertiser* (25 October 1851), 4; 'Potteries' Mechanics' Institutions', *Staffordshire Advertiser* (12 October 1850), 4.

[128] 'Lectures "On Woman"', *Staffordshire Adviser* (22 February 1851), 4.

'submission', however. As she put it, 'a right-minded man would require nothing more than what a right-minded woman could very properly acquiesce in'.[129]

While marriage might be women's 'proper sphere', this did not mean it should be her *only* one. Similar to all the other female lecturers at the LMI, Bennett was a fervent advocate of female education as emancipatory. Women needed 'more solid and useful acquirements, instead of, as at present, what are termed accomplishments'.[130] In 'Woman and Her Duties', Bennett lamented the fact that women were 'unfitted by education from many situations'. This was a tragedy since there were

> few ways in which a woman can earn her daily bread, and those few are dependent on the caprice of man. If she undertakes some, man censures her for stepping out of her sphere, or for being actuated by wrong motives.

In her words, 'it is about time that there should be more ways open to us to earn our own living'.[131]

The prominent and powerful arguments made by Balfour, Darcus, and Bennett for female education and rights were radical for their time. All three women adhered to 'separate spheres feminism'—that is, they believed that the sexes were 'separate but equal'. As Balfour expressed it, 'as providence had given to woman duties that differed from those of men, so had it probably intended that her capabilities should have a different development'.[132] Rather than being 'conservative' feminists, historian Kristin G. Doern explains that these women used issues such as temperance, religion, and morality, to justify their 'transgression into the public sphere'.[133] And they did so in ways that enabled them to make independent livings. They passionately believed that the reason women were *not* regarded as equal was because of lack of educational opportunities. This was why they lectured at the LMI: to ensure that the 'shameful...neglected education' (as Balfour expressed it) of the female sex was remedied.

* * *

There was hostility to the prominence of women in the LMI/Birkbeck. Educated women were a threat to male students as well, especially when the two sexes sat in the same lecture rooms. This was what worried Nathan Marcus Adler, Orthodox Chief Rabbi of the British Empire, when he gave evidence to the Education

---

[129] Ibid., 4.   [130] 'Nantwich Mechanics' Institution', *Chester Chronicle* (13 December 1851), 8.
[131] 'A Woman's Position', *Stroud News and Gloucestershire Advertiser* (27 May 1887), 10.
[132] Mrs. C. L. Balfour's Lectures on the Influence of Woman on Society', *Manchester Times* (24 October 1846), 7.
[133] Kristin G. Doern, 'Equal Question: The "Woman Question" and the "Drink Question" in the Writings of Clara Lucas Balfour, 1808–78', in Sue Morgan (ed.), *Women, Religion, and Feminism in Britain, 1750–1900* (Basingstoke: Palgrave Macmillan, 2002), 159.

Committee in 1861. He was concerned that the mechanics' institutions would 'lead to intercourse with the other sex, which cannot always be beneficial to morality'.[134] Moses Angel of the Jews' Free School shared these fears. He was strongly opposed to the institutions on the grounds that they bred 'revolutionists, or at least democrats', and warned that there was a risk that the institutions would encourage a tendency to 'indulge in company-keeping, and, thus, in extravagant habits'.[135] Nevertheless, he admitted, the institutions were

> a vast improvement on the tavern, the billiard-room, the cheap theatre, and the casino. Your men had better meet young persons of the opposite sex whom they believe to be respectable, because they are assembled for the cultivation of the mind, than find themselves associating habitually with females whose presence is no restraint on the deterioration of morals.[136]

Although women's presence in the classes might promote 'company-keeping', it might also encourage men to desert drinking dens, nudging men into more decorous habits. This was also the view of Armitage-Smith, Master of Birkbeck at the time Lanchester would have been attending classes. He believed that educating men and women together was

> beneficial to both, and had a refining influence.... The women as eager and industrious as the men... The hardworking tone of the Institute is not favourable to frivolity, and there is little opportunity for it in an Institution so entirely educational and with no recreative [sic] elements.[137]

Such tensions—educating women, on the one hand, risked encouraging liberationist ideals and, on the other hand, would promote respectability amongst both sexes—were evident during another scandal that occurred only a few years before the Lanchester abduction. On this occasion, College officials were directly involved. It was set in the context of the 1881 funding campaign aimed at raising money for a new building in Fetter Lane. Acutely sensitive of the need to ensure that potential funders understood that 'The Birkbeck' was a place of high repute, the President of the College was dismayed to discover that they had in their midst a decidedly radical student: 33-year-old Annie Besant, who studied 'Electricity and Magnetism', 'Sound, Light, and Heat', and 'Biology' under James Wilson. Besant's presence threatened Birkbeck with scandal. After all, three years before

---

[134] Evidence by Rev. Dr. Nathan Marcus Adler, in *Education Commission. Answers to the Curriculum of Questions, 1860. Vol. V* (London: Her Majesty's Stationery Office, 1861), 19.
[135] Evidence from Moses Angel of the Jews' Free School, in ibid., 48.   [136] Ibid., 48.
[137] Mackenzie, 'The Birkbeck Institution', 377.

joining Birkbeck in 1880, Besant had published *The Gospel of Atheism* with Freethought Publishers.[138] In it she made the startling statement that 'ignorance... imagined the supernatural, and knowledge would bring all things within the reason of common sense'. She claimed that

> Atheism alone made science possible. No science was possible so long as we believed in a personal God who might intervene at any moment and overthrow all calculations.... The one true God was that of humanity, and manifest in the flesh.[139]

Even worse: she was a leading advocate of 'neo-Malthusianism', or birth control, a revolutionary doctrine that cost her dearly: she lost custody of her two children. Besant had also been tutored by Lanchester's friend, Edward Aveling, and championed by George Lansbury, the socialist politician on whose behalf Lanchester was to campaign vigorously fourteen years later.[140] That such a woman could be associated with 'The Birkbeck' was unthinkable; the Birkbeck Committee failed to send her a 'notice of the public distribution of certificates' and removed her name from their list of successful students.[141]

They had not reckoned on Besant's fury. Like Lanchester, she was not a woman to be silenced. Besant understood why they had acted in such a censorious manner. It was her views on the 'population question', which were not thought to be 'a fitting subject for discussion at this Institution'.[142] She believed that the Committee also 'feared that if my name appeared as a successful student it might induce rich people to withdraw their subscriptions from your Building Fund'.[143] This was unacceptable. 'I readily admit the full right of the Birkbeck Institute to refuse admission to any person who offers himself or herself as a student', she acknowledged in a letter. However, she challenged

> the right of any body of honest and respectable persons to take the money of a student, and then to omit the student's name from the list of successful candidates, and to shut her out from the public award of certificates, thus publicly

---

[138] Annie Besant, *The Gospel of Atheism: A Lecture* (London: Freethought Pub. Co., 1877).
[139] 'Mrs Besant and Mr Bradlaugh in Middlesbrough', *Daily Gazette for Middlesbrough* (5 May 1876), 3.
[140] Asa Briggs, *Communications and Culture 1823–1973: A Tale of Two Centuries—An Oration Delivered at Birkbeck College, London, 4th December 1973 in Celebration of the 150th Anniversary of the Foundation of the College and the Commencement of the 151st Session* (London: Birkbeck College, 1974), 13.
[141] 'G. F. T. H.', 'B.D.B.', 85.
[142] Resolution in the Minutes on 20 September 1880, cited in a letter from the Secretary to C. Delisle Burns, 2 November 1923, 'Birkbeck College Letters', in Birkbeck Archives, Box 65.67 [sic].
[143] 'G. F. T. H.', 'B.D.B.', 85.

implying that she has failed in the examinations.... I leave you to judge whether you desire to obtain contributions from 'rich people' by a deliberate fraud.[144]

Her protest was back by the Students' Union. A stern letter from J. M. Fells (see Fig. 11.2) to the College Secretary W. H. Congreve insisted on the 'desirability of inserting Mrs Besant's name in the syllabus next printed, with an explanation as to its being an omission'.[145] 'The Birkbeck' backed down.

Besant left a mark on Birkbeck—but only because it elected to discriminate against her on the grounds of her radical social politics. Many other women have passed through the College, unremembered, because no historical trace remains to record their discriminatory treatment. One of these students who lacks a prominent *Birkbeck* entry but is as famous as Besant is Marie Stopes. She took zoology night classes at Birkbeck while studying at University College London during the day. This enabled her to complete a University of London BSc (first-class) in only two years in 1902, with honours in botany, with geology as a subsidiary subject. In her subsequent academic career, Stopes made significant contributions to plant palaeontology and coal classification, as well as becoming the first female academic on the faculty of the University of Manchester. Like Besant, she was a prominent eugenicist, founding the first birth control clinic in Britain, and editing the explicit advice-newsletter 'Birth Control News'. Today, Stopes is most famous for her sex manual *Married Love* (1918), which brought the subject of birth control and the Stopes' clinics into wide public discourse.

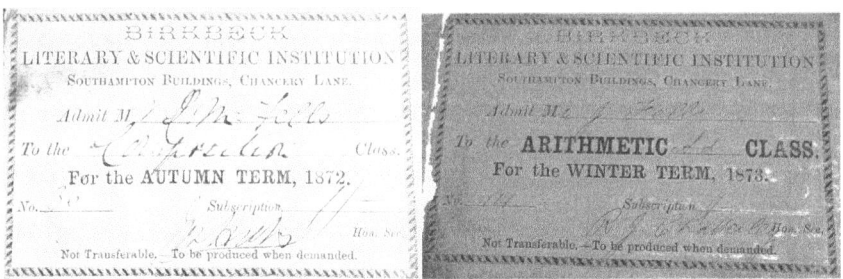

Fig. 11.2 John Manger Fells was a friend of G. B. Shaw and Sidney Webb (whom he may have met at Birkbeck) and, in 1872 and 1873, took classes in intermediate arithmetic, mathematics, dictation, English history, and composition. He was Secretary of the Zetetical Society, a free-thinking society founded in London in 1878 to facilitate debate on social, political, and scientific questions, and went on to become the leading cost accountant in Britain in the late nineteenth century. Birkbeck Archive.

---

[144] Ibid., 85.
[145] Letter from J. M. Fells to the College Secretary W. H. Congreve, undated (c.19 April 1882), in Birkbeck Archive, 'A4 Blue Ring Binder', 29.

Lanchester, Besant, Stopes, and numerous radical yet unnamed women who attended lectures at Birkbeck were exceptional women. Until the twentieth century, women were a relatively small proportion of the College's students. In 1841, they made up only 2 per cent of its 850 members.[146] By the time Lanchester went to Birkbeck, women constituted between one quarter and one third of students. The First World War saw this proportion shoot up to over half (peaking at 56 per cent in 1915) before dropping in the 1920s to around 40 per cent.[147] Today, women constitute 55 per cent of students and 48 per cent of staff.[148]

Female students as well as female lecturers also tended to take what were widely considered at the time as 'feminine' or 'lighter' subjects, such as elocution, music, and art. For example, in the 1840s and 1950s, a Mrs S. Butler gave a series of lectures entitled 'Readings, Dramatic, Historical, and Original, illustrative of elocutionary expression',[149] while Mrs E. F. Grosvenor (also known as Fanny Healy) taught 'Rare Songs and Ballads'.[150] Grosvenor was a well-known romantic English opera singer and described as 'one of the First Vocalists of the day'.[151] Other women accompanied men on the piano, provided 'Vocal Illustrations' for male lecturers, and taught dressmaking.[152] By the end of that century, they could also be found teaching pianoforte and piano,[153] while Miss Lilian Wright and Miss Alice Wright regularly taught art alongside Alfred W. Mason and H. C. Pocock. When Bernard Becker visited Birkbeck in the 1870s, he observed that 727 students attended the music and singing classes. He lamented as 'disappointing' that 'the number of students of "fancy" subjects exceed so largely that of those pursuing the severe branches of knowledge'. However, he condescendingly concluded, 'it must not be forgotten that lady scholars are admitted to the Birkbeck Institution, and that the demand for musical instruction is in a considerable degree referrible [sic] to this fact'.[154]

---

[146] Eric J. Hobsbawm, 'Birkbeck and the Left', *Times Change: Quarterly Political and Cultural Review*, 21 (spring/summer 2001), 15.

[147] See my Excel file called 'Women-Students-Percentage'. The data are taken from the annual reports. The 1841 data are from Hobsbawm, 'Birkbeck and the Left', 2001, 15. The 1906 data are from 'Birkbeck College', *The Times* (27 September 1906), 4. The 1926 data are from 'Landmark in Education', *The Times* (8 December 1927), 11.

[148] Rachel Hewitt, 'Mind the Gap: Gender Differences in Higher Education' (7 March 2020), at https://www.hepi.ac.uk/2020/03/07/mind-the-gap-gender-differences-in-higher-education/, viewed 1 August 2021.

[149] Leaflet entitled 'London Mechanics' Institution' (London: London Mechanics' Institution, 1847), 3.

[150] Ibid., 2.

[151] *Western Courier* (7 September 1853). See 'Fanny Healy', at https://www.englishromanticopera.org/singers/fanny_healy.htm, viewed 1 October 2021.

[152] Miss Emily G. Hillyer in the leaflet entitled 'London Mechanics' Institution' (London: London Mechanics' Institution, n.d., c.1850s), 2.

[153] Miss E. M. Andrew in the leaflet entitled 'London Mechanics' Institution' (London: London Mechanics' Institution, 1896), 3–4.

[154] Becker, *Scientific London*, 207.

Many of the managers of early Birkbeck generally shared such prejudices. They assumed that female education was important as much, if not more, for the way it benefited the future of the 'race' (which helps explain their antipathy to Besant), as for its advantages in individual women's intellectual growth and economic independence. In the words of a lecturer giving evidence to the Select Committee on Education in 1835, female students 'derived great advantage' from the classes, and this was important because of their 'influence on the present and future generations'.[155] During the prize-giving ceremony in 1897, Lord Russell of Killowen (the Lord Chief Justice of England and Wales) put it more outrageously. He told Birkbeck students that he

> did notice several prizes received by three or four attractive young ladies, of the utility of which I had little doubt; they were elocution prizes—(*cheers*)—and I took the liberty of whispering into the ears of one or two of the recipients of those prizes that I hoped they would not try their elocutionary powers too much or too often upon their future husbands (*cheers and laughter*).[156]

It would take three quarters of a century before such boasts would become evidence of boorishness rather than wit.

Or perhaps it was evidence of male insecurity. After all, as we have already seen, the LMI/Birkbeck had been a hotbed of feminism in its many incarnations. One former student who was particularly favourable to the presence of 'New Women' at Birkbeck was William Pett Ridge. In the early 1880s, he took classes in the college in order to catapult himself from a dull job as a city clerk to that of a novelist. He eventually became a friend of H. G. Wells, a major philanthropist and popular novelist who was widely thought to be a successor to Charles Dickens. Although he is now widely thought of as belonging to the 'Cockney School',[157] many of his ninety books focused on the 'New Woman'. One of these novels is set at the LMI/Birkbeck. In *Three Women and Mr Frank Cardwell* (1898), Ridge describes Birkbeck's female students as 'new women', keen to discuss 'abstruse questions'.[158] Instead of 'asking each other for an opinion of the new large hats turned up at the back', these women wanted to know 'how acetobenzoic anhydride be obtained from acetyl chloride, and other riddles of a scientific nature'.[159]

---

[155] A. J. D. Dorsey, in *Report from the Select Committee on Education in England and Wales Together with the Minutes of Evidence, Appendix, and Index*, [465], (London: HMSO, 1835), 38.

[156] Lord Russell of Killowen, *Address by the Right Honorable Lord Russell of Killowen, Lord Chief Justice of England, to the Students of the Birkbeck Institution, on the Occasion of the Annual Distribution of Prizes and Certificates, January 14th, 1897* (London: J. C. Larrance Printer, 1897), 5.

[157] P. J. Keating, *The Working Classes in Victorian Fiction* (London: Routledge and Kegan Paul, 1971), 199–222.

[158] W. Pett Ridge, *Three Women and Mr Frank Cardwell* (London: C. Arthur Pearson Ltd, 1898), 39.

[159] Ibid., 40.

Ridge maintained that The Birkbeck boasted that 'scandal had never whispered a word against it', but claimed that 'this was not odd, because when young people are improving their minds they leave their hearts alone'.[160] More acidly, he noted that scandal had been avoided because 'the young lady students were not for the most part dazzlingly beautiful, being as a fact partial to spectacles and barbaric fashions in the dressing of hair'.[161] In other words, they wore their hair short, as did Lancaster. One of the main characters in the novel was Mary Willis, who had come to the LMI to learn shorthand because her family had fallen on hard times. She mused that 'life would necessitate work on her part', but rather than regard this as a misfortune, Mary Willis was 'really pleased at this'.[162] She was the archetypical 'New Woman'.

This is not to say that the College dissolved gender divisions. Indeed, they could be policed enthusiastically; in 1920, for example, a male-only 'smoking room' was approved.[163] However, staff, lecturers, and students fought passionately over political issues such as female suffrage. Harold Redmayne (H. R.) Nettleton, who conducted physics research into the determination of thermal conductivities of liquids and the Thomson effect from 1906 until he retired in 1952, was an ardent champion of women's suffrage, as was J. D. Bernal, his head of department.[164] The Students' Union also provides many forums for debates about the rights of women. For example, on 18 December 1908, Miss H. F. Carter moved that 'in the present state of Society Womanhood Suffrage would be beneficial to the State', which she won by fourteen votes to nine.[165] Two years later, a motion that 'the business girl makes the best wife' was carried, a far cry from earlier anxieties that the education of women would wreck marriage chances and conduct.[166] Anger towards those who continued to deny women their rights was polite but firm. For example, when it became known that a politician belonging to the anti-female suffrage Liberal Party of H. H. Asquith would be present at the graduation ceremony, students registered their protest. One of these was James Small, who studied pharmacy at Birkbeck, before the subject was discontinued in 1905,[167] and went on to become a prominent botanist. On 7 December 1913, Small wrote to the College's Principal, declaring that he was a member of the Men's Political Union for Women's Enfranchisement, which was the militant male equivalent to

---

[160] Ibid., 40.   [161] Ibid., 40.   [162] Ibid., 41.
[163] 'B.C. Minute Book. 22nd Sep., 1919 to 25th July, 1922' in 'Minutes of Meeting of Governing Body. Monday 26th January 1920'.
[164] W. Ehrenberg, 'Obituaries. Dr. H. R. Nettleton', *Nature*, 217 (20 January 1968), 296.
[165] Students' Union debate on 18 December 1908, in 'Minutes of Debates and Literary Discussions Including "Birkbeck Parliament", 1908–1920', in Birkbeck Archive, 'A4 Black Ring Binder 2', 9. They returned to the topic on 25 October 1910, but this time the motion was lost (pp. 36–7).
[166] Students' Union debate on 22 November 1911, in 'Minutes of Debates and Literary Discussions Including "Birkbeck Parliament", 1908–1920', in Birkbeck Archive, 'A4 Black Ring Binder 2', 47.
[167] *Birkbeck College. Report. Eighty-Second Session, 1904–1905* (London: Witherby, 1905), 5.

the Women's Social and Political Union (WSPU). He informed Armitage-Smith that his 'intense sympathy with the advanced section of suffragists' meant that

> I could not conscientiously allow myself to be presented to any member of the present Government without making a protest against the shameful treatment of those who are fighting for what is conceded on every hand to be their rights.

Because any protest he made would have to be 'more emphatic than polite' (that is, his protest would be aggressive), he believed that it 'would be against the interests of the college' for him to attend and 'therefore I hope you will pardon me for refraining from taking an active part on Wednesday's ceremony'.[168] It was a fierce yet principled course of action.

Lanchester was far from being the only prominent member in the suffrage movement. Annie Somers, for example, took a degree in 'Mental and Moral Science' as well as mathematics at Birkbeck, which also elected her as a governor. She went on to become an accountant, leading member of the National Union of Clerks and Administrative Workers, and the London Women's Organiser for the Labour Party. In 1914, Somers was elected President of the London University Suffrage Society and became leading member of the United Suffragists.[169]

Students could be found selling suffragette pamphlets and newsletters in the College and on nearby street corners. One of these students simply signed herself 'Pethpank' (after Frederick and Emmeline Pethick-Lawrence, whose home was the London headquarters of the WSPU, and the Pankhursts, leading suffragette family). In 1913, Pethpank sold radical suffragist newspapers on a kerb at Holborn Circus, on her way to classes at the College. She recognized that 'public feeling runs very high' about the women's movement, especially since newspapers reported that a bomb that had been placed in St Paul's. One 'unpleasant individual' told her she ought to be burnt at the stake, while another muttered 'Go 'ome and mind the biby [sic]'. One 'tall cadaverous' man yelled, 'You ought to be ashamed of yourself! You're no good to man or beast!' Pethpank was relieved when she spotted another Birkbeck student on his way to class: he not only bought a paper but kept her company for a while. Women, too, would purchase copies, treating her 'with the cheery comradeship which distinguishes the adherents of our cause'.[170]

* * *

So far in this chapter, I have focused on female students: the 'New Woman' Lanchester, the taboo-busting Besant and Stopes, and numerous named and

---

[168] Letter from James Small, to the Principal Armitage-Smith, dated 7 December 1913, in Birkbeck Archive, '5 Student Affairs Misc.', 54–5.
[169] A. Somers, 'London University Suffrage Society', *The Lodestone*, 9.3 (summer 1914), 93.
[170] 'Pethpank', 'On the Kerb', *The Lodestone*, 9.1 (Michaelmas 1913), 8–10.

unnamed suffragettes. But Birkbeck rebels also include its lecturers. Some of these will be discussed in greater depth in the next chapter, which turns to more recent decades in Birkbeck's history. But this chapter ends with the remarkable life and career of Lillian Penson, who was the first person of any sex in the University of London to be awarded a PhD, the first woman to become a Professor of History at any British university, and the first woman in the UK and Commonwealth to become a vice-chancellor of a university. She owed her undergraduate and doctoral education as well as her start as a university lecturer to the History Department at Birkbeck in the 1910s and early 1920s.

At the time, opinions about Penson were divided. Was she the 'foremost woman in the academic life of our day' (*The Scotsman*)[171], a 'remarkable woman' (*The Times*),[172] and someone who exuded 'charm, tolerance, and a sense of humour'?[173] Or was she an 'imperious *grande dame*',[174] '*très autoritaire*',[175] and 'too trenchant'?[176] Perhaps 'a mixture'. Although Penson 'could on occasion be brusque and even intimidating', she 'had a happy knack of getting to know people quickly', was 'an excellent judge of wine and loved good company', and projected 'a wealth of genuine kindness'.[177] In other words, Penson was probably trapped in that familiar double-bind experienced by powerful women in male-dominated fields: she was admired for her intellect and determination, yet disparaged for being a woman possessing those same traits. One newspaper report on the achievements of 'the professor' even referred to Penson using the masculine pronoun 'he'.[178]

Who was Penson? She was born in Islington on 18 July 1896. Her father worked as a wholesale dairy manager and her family were of the Plymouth Brethren persuasion.[179] Indeed, one colleague observed that the 'marks of a puritanical upbringing were never effaced' and her 'belief in work and duty' meant that she was always made uncomfortable by 'flippant talk'.[180] She never married.

From her youth, Penson was intrigued by diplomatic history, colonial policy, and foreign affairs. Her intellectual talents were obvious. In 1917, at the age of 21 years, she graduated from Birkbeck with a BA in History (first class). The war was at its height, so she joined the Ministry of National Service as a junior administrative officer before moving to the war trade intelligence department. At the end of the

---

[171] 'Graduation Day', *The Scotsman* (1 July 1950), 4.
[172] Alan Pifer, Richard Taylor, and William Gaines, 'Letter to the Editor', *The Times* (2 May 1963), 23.
[173] 'Making History', *Dundee Evening Telegraph* (4 October 1948), 2.
[174] Lewis H. Gann, 'Ex Africa: An Africanist's Intellectual Autobiography', *Journal of Modern African Studies*, 31.3 (1993), 482. He wrote that there were three: the other two were Margery Perham and Lucy Mair.
[175] Robert Greaves, 'Penson, Dame Lillian Margery', in H. C. G. Matthew and Brian Harrison (eds), *Oxford Dictionary of National Biography*, vol. 43 (Oxford: Oxford University Press, 2004), 620–1.
[176] Ibid., 620. [177] 'Obituary. Dame Lillian Penson', *The Times* (20 April 1963), 12.
[178] '"Give Nurses More Leisure" Plea', *Torbay Express and South Devon Echo* (31 January 1949), 1.
[179] Greaves, 'Penson, Dame Lillian Margery', 620. [180] Ibid., 620–1.

war, Penson returned to her studies of history at Birkbeck and became, in 1921, the first person in the University of London to be awarded a PhD. Birkbeck must have been delighted to have beaten University College London and King's College London to this honour.

Penson's achievement was even more remarkable because of her gender. Between 1921 and 1990, only one fifth of PhD students in history were female.[181] Penson was also young. The average age for history students to complete their doctorates was the mid-thirties; Penson was only 25 years old.[182] Birkbeck immediately offered her a job as a part-time lecturer, during which time she also taught part time at the East London Technical College, now Queen Mary University of London. In 1925, she was given a full-time lecturing post at Birkbeck.

Penson was ambitious. In 1930, she left Birkbeck for a Chair in Modern History at Bedford College for Women. She was following in the footsteps of Bedford's Professor of English, Caroline Spurgeon, who had been the first female professor in the University of London and only the second in the UK. Newspaper reports dwelt on the fact that Penson was only 34 years old when she was awarded her professorship (Spurgeon had been 54, which had also been considered young). Female academics faced significant misogynistic barriers to being promoted to the top rank of their profession.

She was a formidable intellectual. At Birkbeck, Penson had been trained in the kind of diplomatic history promulgated by the titans of her day: men like George Peabody Gooch, Arthur James Grant, and Harold William Vazeille Temperley.[183] Her Birkbeck PhD focused on colonial politics in the West Indies. Published by the University of London Press in 1924, it had the matter-of-fact title, *The Colonial Agents of the British West Indies: A Study in Colonial Administration, Mainly in the Eighteenth Century*.[184] In it, Penson stated that her intention was not to investigate whether the West India Company was responsible for the 'revolt of the mainland colonies'. She admitted that if the agents did play a role 'in causing the alienation of the mainland colonies, that alienation in time brought about their downfall'. However, she maintained that her research would focus resolutely on 'investigat[ing] the character and workings of this powerful interest'.[185]

By the time Penson became a professor, her interests had widened. Her inaugural lecture, on 15 October 1930, developed her ideas about the 'close connection

---

[181] Irena Nicoll, 'A Statistical Profile of the London PhD in History 1921–1990', *Oxford Review of Education*, 22.3 (1996), 279.
[182] Ibid., 279.
[183] J. Mordaunt Cook, *Bedford College University of London: Memories of 150 Years* (London: Royal Holloway and Bedford New College, 2001), 217.
[184] Lillian M. Penson, *The Colonial Agents of the British West Indies: A Study in Colonial Administration, Mainly in the Eighteenth Century* (London: University of London Press, 1924).
[185] Ibid., v.

between colonial interests and foreign policy'.[186] She warned that these connections were waning due to sea power. Perhaps just as importantly, the growing international status of the colonies also 'gives them the power of independent action even in foreign affairs'.[187] The last sentence of her lecture predicted that the 'power of the air' (that is, the aeroplane) was challenging the 'distinction between sea and land'. Where it would lead, no one could predict. Any 'new system' was 'still hidden in the clouds', she wittily concluded.[188]

Penson went on to publish many books, including several co-written or co-edited with Temperley, the distinguished Cambridge diplomatic historian. She also published in the *English Historical Review* (1925), the *Cambridge Historical Journal* (1935), and the *Transactions of the Royal Historical Society* (1943). From 1928 until a year before her death in 1963, Penson ran a seminar on diplomatic history at the Institute of Historical Research: these were dubbed 'legendary'.[189] She also took a leading role in the creation and development of the Institute of Commonwealth Studies, the Courtauld Institute, the Warburg Institute, the School of Slavonic and East European Studies, and the School of Oriental and African Studies.[190]

Her leadership responsibilities in education expanded from simply managing the History Department at Bedford College to the top positions University-wide. She became Dean of the Faculty of Arts (1938–44), a member of the Senate from 1940 (which, one journalist observed, she won 'in a straight fight with a male professor),[191] and in 1945 was elected chair of the Academic Council. In 1946, she became a member of the Court of the entire University of London and, two years later, was unanimously elected Vice-Chancellor of the University of London, the most powerful university in the world. As the first woman in that post, and from the age of only 52, she served until 1951. The second female Vice-Chancellor would not be appointed for another twenty-seven years—this was Dr Alice Rosemary Murray who was appointed Vice-Chancellor of Cambridge in 1975.[192] *The Times* observed that Penrose conquered the 'citadel[s] of male exclusivity'.[193]

In 1948, the University of Cambridge finally agreed to award degrees to women. The last time it had tried this, in 1897, there had been a riot. In 1948, however, the Queen, pianist Myra Hess, and Penson became the first women to be awarded honorary Cambridge degrees, in Penson's case, a LL.D or Doctor of

---

[186] Lillian M. Penson, *The Colonial Background of British Foreign Policy* (London: G. Bell and Sons, 1930), 1.
[187] Ibid., 48–9.   [188] Ibid., 50.
[189] Mordaunt Cook, *Bedford College University of London*, 217.
[190] 'Obituary. Dame Lillian Penson', *The Times* (20 April 1963), 12.
[191] 'Making History', *Dundee Evening Telegraph* (4 October 1948), 2.
[192] 'A Woman to be Vice-Chancellor of Cambridge', *The Times* (24 May 1924), 4.
[193] 'Obituary. Dame Lillian Penson', *The Times* (20 April 1963), 12.

Laws. *The Scotsman* decreed Penson's academic and administrative talents to be 'unsurpassed even in the annals of that great institution'.[194]

Further honours followed. In 1956, Penson was awarded an honorary doctorate (DCL or Doctorate of Civil Law) by the University of Oxford. The other recipient that year was Harry S. Truman, the former US President. She was also presented with honorary degrees from the universities of St Andrews, Leeds, Sheffield, Southampton, Belfast, McGill, and Western Ontario.[195] In 1951, she was awarded a DBE (Dame Commander of the Most Excellent Order of the British Empire). *The Scotsman* ranked her as 'the first woman historian of our time'.[196] Penson made history as well as teaching it.

Whether in London or the British colonies, where Pension expended much labour advancing universities, Penson believed that if people had to choose between pursuing 'on the one hand what is true and on the other hand what is useful', then 'I think we should all agree that it is what is true that is the prior importance'.[197] It was a restatement of the aims of the founders of the LMI/Birkbeck, who believed in pursuing 'really useful knowledge' or truth, rather than 'merely useful' kinds. Penson observed that

> There are people who would have us study history because it is so useful in the understanding of the present. If we accept this view, we are liable indeed to falsify the past, and not only so, but to falsify the future. Any restriction of this kind in our approach to what has characterized past ages may falsify the future simply because of the very many characteristics of those past ages, which may not seem important at the present moment, but which will seem important to our successors.[198]

Penson regularly urged educationalists, politicians, and policy-makers to safeguard 'freedom in the field of learning', which included the 'freedom of men of learning to follow in their research wherever the research itself leads'.[199] She contended that it was 'hardly an exaggeration to claim that the future of humanity is to a very large extent' dependent on upholding 'freedom in research'.[200]

Many of the values that Penson promoted were those at the heart of the Birkbeck mission. She spoke eloquently on the need to offer university education to 'virtually all comers', with no restriction based on religion, race, or sex.[201] She was keen to insist that the job of the university teacher was to 'do something more

---

[194] 'Graduation Day', *The Scotsman* (1 July 1950), 4.
[195] 'Obituary. Dame Lillian Penson', 12.   [196] 'Graduation Day', *The Scotsman* (1 July 1950), 4.
[197] Penson's speech at the Royal Society of London, in Herbert Morrison, 'Anniversary Dinner 1948', *Notes and Records of the Royal Society of London*, 6.2 (May 1949), 101.
[198] Ibid., 101.   [199] Ibid., 101.   [200] Ibid., 102.
[201] Lillian Penson, 'University Ventures Old and New', *British Medical Journal*, 2.4683 (7 October 1950), 831.

than impose upon the memories of our students masses of detailed information'.[202] She encouraged people to think anew about old problems.

* * *

The life-stories of Lanchester and Penson deserve to be told in full because they exemplify the earth-shattering impact of university education on female students. Both used their time at 'The Birkbeck' to forge exceptional careers in ways that broke important 'ceilings' in the possibilities for women. The LMI/Birkbeck was committed to educating women from its early years, as we also saw in Chapter 4, although some male members and official representatives of the College often shared the prejudices of their wider communities. Female students and their male allies fought against the injustices they faced: they had to be twice as good as their male co-students and many times more tactful in negotiating their rights. As we will see in the next chapter, though, they were not the only group fighting discrimination: racially and sexually minoritized communities also struggled to achieve educational justice.

---

[202] Ibid., 830.

12
Minoritized Communities

> You never fully understand the Other...
> Les Back and Avtar Brah, 2012[1]

The LMI/Birkbeck has always been a diverse community of scholars, students, and staff, all of whom jostle for recognition as they navigate the spaces of the College. We have already heard from many of these people as they tell stories about how they made and unmade their worlds through education; they have often speculated on the worlds of others, who differ from themselves according to a host of complex and often competing social characteristics, including gender, skin colour, class, sexual preference, disability, age, generation, and religion.

When seeking to understand the lives of such diverse Others, the concept of 'intersectionality' is useful. Birkbeck scholar Avtar Brah, who has been active in Black, anti-racist, and feminist struggles for her entire career, borrows this term from the work of critical race theorist Kimberlé W. Crenshaw.[2] Along with Crenshaw, Brah contends that racism, sexism, and class prejudices are not discrete realms of experience but interrelated, structural forms of oppression. As Brah and psychologist Ann Phoenix explain in 'Ain't I a Woman?' (2004), intersectionality refers to complex effects that 'ensue when multiple axes of differentiation—economic, political, cultural, psychic, subjective, and experiential—intersect in historically specific contexts'.[3] In other words, racial bigotry, misogyny, class snobbery, homophobia, ageism, and all the other forms of prejudice are not independent phenomena. As Brah put it, the 'oppression of each is inscribed within the other'.[4]

But it is equally vital, Brah insists, to ensure that we don't fall into the trap of thinking in terms of marginal identities. This assumes a 'centre' to which other persons are 'peripheral'.[5] This chapter should not be seen, therefore, as

---

[1] Les Back and Avtar Brah, 'Activism, Imagination, and Writing: Avtar Brah Reflects on Her Life and Work with Les Back', *Feminist Review*, 100 (2012), 49.

[2] Kimberlé W. Crenshaw, 'Demarginalizing the Intersection of Race and Sex: A Black Feminist Critique of Antidiscrimination Doctrine, Feminist Theory, and Antiracist Politics', *University of Chicago Legal Forum*, 139 (1989), 138–67, and Kimberlé W. Crenshaw, 'Mapping the Margins: Intersectionality, Identity Politics, and Violence Against Women of Color', *Stanford Law Review*, 43.6 (1991), 1241–99.

[3] Avtar Brah and Ann Phoenix, 'Ain't I a Woman? Revisiting Intersectionality', *Journal of International Women's Studies*, 5.3 (May 2004), 76.

[4] Avtar Brah, *Cartographies of Diaspora* (London: Routledge, 1996), 109.

[5] Ibid., 189.

contributing to the marginalization process. Rather, it focuses on certain social groups who are required to navigate and protest against the injustices inflicted upon them due to skin colour, sexual preference, religion, and gender. Their worlds have been radically diminished by ignorance, prejudice, and hatred. But, throughout their lives, including those years spent within the College, they have been creative in constructing alliances and challenging prejudice.

* * *

The first oppressive structures are 'race' and ethnicity. Marcus Garvey exemplifies both racist strategies and anti-racist struggles. In 1912, 25-year-old Garvey stepped off the boat at Southampton docks.[6] He had just arrived from Jamaica. According to the 1911 Census, there were only 4,540 'Africans' (which included West Indians) living in the United Kingdom at the time. They were spread out in a large number of towns and cities. Garvey, who had just begun thinking seriously about issues of identity and race when he arrived, spent the next two years travelling about the UK. His base, however, was London where, between 1912 and 1914, he attended classes in law and philosophy at Birkbeck.[7] We do not know for certain who taught him, but they almost inevitably included Beaumont Morice, a Liberal Party candidate, barrister, and prosecutor at London's Central Criminal Court. From 1914, Morice was a magistrate in Bradford, and had a reputation for supporting women accusing their husbands of domestic violence.[8] Garvey might also have been taught constitutional law by G. H. J. [Gilbert Harrison John] Hurst; conveyancing, equity, commercial, and bankruptcy law by J. Samuel Green; and patent law by William Martin. There was no philosophy 'department' at Birkbeck when Garvey attended, but logic was being taught by G. C. Rankin, who had scholarly interests in ethics, democracy, Hobbes, and international law, before becoming active in legal reform in India during the 1920s and 1930s.[9]

Twenty years after leaving the College, Garvey recalled Birkbeck with fondness.[10] His time in London had been enriched by his friendship with Dusé

---

[6] Note that Garvey claimed he arrived in 1911, but since he had witnessed the Kingston Streetcar Riot of 26 February 1912, it must have been 1912: see Robert A. Hill, 'The First England Years and After, 1912–1916', in John Henrik Clarke with the assistance of Amy Jacques Garvey (eds), *Marcus Garvey and the Vision of Africa* (New York: Random House, 1974), 38.

[7] 'Birkbeck College', *New Jamaican* (19 November 1932).

[8] 'Exposed: Lawyer's Tie to the King of Fraud', *Telegraph and Argus* (24 August 1998), at https://www.thetelegraphandargus.co.uk/news/8074119.exposed-lawyers-tie-to-the-king-of-fraud/, viewed 1 June 2021, and 'I Remember the Women's Champ', *Telegraph and Argus* (3 September 1998), at https://www.thetelegraphandargus.co.uk/news/8073724.i-remember-the-womens-champ/, viewed 1 June 2021.

[9] For example, see G. C. Rankin, 'Hobbes by Lesley Stephen', *International Journal of Ethics*, 15.3 (April 1905), 391–4; G. C. Rankin, 'International Arbitration as a Substitute for War Between Nations by Russell Lowell Jones', *International Journal of Ethics*, 9.4 (July 1909), 516–18; G. C. Rankin, 'The Development of European Polity', *International Journal of Ethics*, 14.4 (July 1904), 500–4; George Claus Rankin, 'Democracy in Literature', MA dissertation (Edinburgh: University of Edinburgh, 1898); and G. C. Rankin, *Background to Indian Law* (Cambridge: Cambridge University Press, 1946).

[10] Cited in Hill, 'The First England Years and After, 1912–1916', 38.

Mohammed Ali, a Sudanese-Egyptian. Ali worked as a journalist and stage actor but also wrote *In the Land of the Pharaohs*, the first modern history of Egypt written by an Egyptian. It was Ali who vouched for Garvey's honesty when he applied for a reader's ticket admitting him into the rotunda of the British Library, which was then housed within the British Museum.[11] There, Garvey first read Booker T. Washington's *Up From Slavery*. As he later recalled, this book made him realize his 'doom—if I may so call it': it was then the possibility 'of being a race leader dawned on me'.[12]

Garvey was a keen and vocal Birkbeck student; he could occasionally be heard haranguing crowds at Hyde Park's 'Speakers' Corner' and supporters read his articles in the *African Times and Orient Review*. In the *Review*'s October 1913 edition, Garvey contended that the British West Indies was 'the Mirror of Civilization' and he saluted 'History Making by Colonial Negroes' as an achievement that should be celebrated.[13] His time at Birkbeck was revelatory. He asked himself,

> Where is the black man's Government? Where is his King and his kingdom? Where is his President, his country, and his ambassador, his army, his navy, his men of big affairs?

When he realized that he 'could not find them', he contended that he had a duty to 'help to make them'.[14] On 17 June 1914, he boarded the SS *Trent* steamship as one of only three third-class passengers and made his way back to Jamaica.[15] During the month-long voyage, he had time to reflect on what he had learnt at Birkbeck and in the UK. Five days after disembarking in Jamaica, Garvey and Pan-Africanist Amy Ashwood co-founded the Universal Negro Improvement and Conservation Association and African Communities League. The Jamaican revolutionary Marcus Garvey—sometimes called the 'Black Moses'—was born.

Throughout his life, Garvey spoke warmly about his time at Birkbeck. His affection was not dented even after he discovered that, in the early 1930s, the College had briefly employed Sir Fiennes Barrett-Lennard as a lecturer. In 1929, when Sir Fiennes had been Chief Justice of Jamaica, he had not only imprisoned Garvey for contempt of court but also confiscated the property of the Universal

---

[11] Colin Grant, *Negro with a Hat: The Rise and Fall of Marcus Garvey and His Dream of Mother Africa* (London: Jonathan Cape, 2008), 49.

[12] Cited in ibid., 49. Also see Rosalind Yarde, 'Tribute to a Black Hero', *Acton Gazette* (9 October 1984), in the Birkbeck Archive.

[13] Marcus Garvey, 'The British West Indies in the Mirror of Civilization: History Making by Colonial Negroes', *African Times and Orient Review* (October 1913), republished in Robert A. Jill (ed.), *The Marcus Garvey and Universal Negro Improvement Association Papers*, Volume XI: *The Caribbean Diaspora 1910–1920* (Durham, NC: Duke University Press, 2011), 49–57.

[14] Rosalind Yarde, 'Tribute to a Black Hero', *Acton Gazette* (9 October 1984), in the Birkbeck Archive.

[15] Grant, *Negro with a Hat*, 49.

Negro Improvement Association. Sir Fiennes' racism was also evident during his time at Birkbeck. While lecturing there, he published a paper in the *Transactions of the Grotius Society* on colonial law, in which he referred to colonies such as Jamaica as 'backward' and unable to 'exercise the privilege of limited self-government'. West Indians were a 'savage race', Sir Fiennes claimed, and were 'not fit to pass [legal judgment] upon serious questions'.[16] Garvey was later to sardonically observe that there seemed to be

> a kind of inseparable relationship between us and the ex-Chief [that is, Sir Fiennes, former Chief Justice of Jamaica]. By goodness, he is to be connected to our Alma Mater. Little did we believe twenty years ago that Sir Fiennes would have become a member of the faculty of the College where we spent a little time.

On one of his visits to Birkbeck, Garvey noted that 'we had the honour of listening to Lord Balfour of Burleigh, the Chancellor', but he worried that 'next time we may have to listen to Sir Fiennes'. He admitted that he would 'feel very much embarrassed' if, while attending a College function such as a graduation, he discovered that the former Chief Justice was 'the guest of the evening'. Despite his disappointment in Birkbeck's choice of lecturer, Garvey insisted that the 'tradition of Berbeck [*sic*] College is one that every student can be proud of'.[17]

* * *

Garvey need not have been anxious: Sir Fiennes was a very marginal figure in the College and was never invited to speak in any official capacity. However, this was not the first time that the College had been home to people who espoused racist views. In 1848, for example, the LMI had invited anatomist Robert Knox, to speak about 'The Races of Men'—lectures which were published under that title two years later.[18] The lectures and subsequent book argued that 'different races were created through the arrest of embryonic development at different stages, a process paralleling the differential development of humanity along the evolutionary ladder'. The 'Saxon race' was at the pinnacle of humanity.[19] Knox's ideas were to become the key text for scientific racists.

Garvey was also right to notice that racism in Britain was taking a turn for the worse. Garvey had first attended Birkbeck in 1912. At that time, he was surprised that visitors like him ('who are not coloured but black') nevertheless 'found no

---

[16] Fiennes Barrett Lennard, 'Some Aspects of Colonial Law', *Transactions of the Grotius Society*, 19 (1933), 44, 52, and 55.
[17] Hill, 'The First England Years and After, 1912–1916', 39.
[18] Leaflet entitled 'The London Mechanics' Institution' (London: LMI, 1848).
[19] Kenan Malik, *The Meaning of Race: Race, History, and Culture in Western Society* (Houndmills: Macmillan, 1996), 89. See Robert Knox, *The Races of Men: A Fragment* (London: Henry Renshaw, 1850).

difficulty in securing lodgings'.[20] In 1928, when he visited Britain for a third time, he was 'astounded to be confronted with a pronounced prejudice that shocked our concept of things English'.[21] Between 1912 and the late 1920s, something had changed. His observation was correct. While the first ultra-right, anti-Semitic, racist political party had been established in Britain in 1901, called the British Brothers' League, the economic depression that followed the First World War had seen the rise not only of the left in Britain but also of the extreme right. The British Union of Fascists (BUF) was not established until 1932, but in the 1920s disillusionment with the establishment parties—what Oswald Mosley (the future leader of the BUF) was to call 'united muttons'[22]—was causing a minority of Britons to turn to authoritarian, racist, right-wing forms of politics. One of Mosley's active followers in the 1920s was Birkbeck student William Joyce, who went on to become the traitor and Nazi supporter known as 'Lord Haw-Haw' (see Chapter 15).

The next fifty years were uncomfortable, and sometimes dangerous, ones for Black Britons as well as for immigrants and visitors. The Second World War had made Britain increasingly dependent on workers of colour from the colonies, especially the West Indies. The post-war British governments were worried about how to deal with critical shortages of labour, so they encouraged West Indians, many of whom had fought in British regiments and worked in essential war industries between 1939 and 1945, to return to Britain to work and make lives for themselves. Most famously, 1,027 West Indians arrived on the ship *Empire Windrush*, which docked in 1948.[23] Most of these 'dark strangers', as they were called at the time, were from Jamaica, like Garvey, but they also included people from Trinidad and Tobago, Barbados, Guyana, and most of the other islands in the region. Racial tensions peaked ten years later, with major riots in Notting Hill. The various governments began introducing legislation to limit the ability of Commonwealth citizens to enter Britain. This didn't only affect West Indians and other peoples from the Commonwealth, but also Ugandan Asians, who (like Jamaicans) held British passports as Citizens of United Kingdom and Colonies. This was a disaster for these British citizens because they were being persecuted and forcibly pushed out of Kenya by President Idi Amin. Brah, with whom I began this chapter, was one of 150,000 Ugandan Asians forced to flee to Britain. As she later recalled, 'I was made a stateless refugee'.

* * *

[20] Cited in Hill, 'The First England Years and After, 1912–1916', 38.   [21] Ibid., 39.
[22] Oswald Mosley, *The Greater Britain*, 2nd ed. (London: Jeff Coats, 1934), 179.
[23] Matthew Mead, 'Empire Windrush: Cultural Memory and Archival Disturbance', *Moveable Type*, 3 (2007), 118. Note that this is more than double the number of passengers usually recorded, which is 492.

Fig. 12.1 James Julian Ben ('Sammy') Samnadan-Pillai in 1952. The original caption reads: 'Jimmy Ben Sammy, Athletics Secretary, looks after Greenford and the Athletics Clubs'. 'Introducing Council, 1952', *The Lodestone*, 44.1 (autumn 1952), 29.

One vocal critic of Birkbeck's treatment of minoritized ethnic communities was Trinidad-born James Julian Ben Samnadan-Pillai (see Fig. 12.1), who came to Birkbeck in the autumn of 1951 to study for a BSc in physics. Known by the diminutive 'Sammy', Samnadan-Pillai became increasingly upset by his treatment in the College. In Trinidad, he had been a star pupil, winning a scholarship from his missionary school and working as a teacher and civil servant. When he arrived at Birkbeck, therefore, he was an accomplished man of 27 years.

At first, his time at Birkbeck went smoothly. He paid £13 15s. each session for his part-time tuition, which lasted from October 1951 to July 1957, during which time he passed lower-level examinations in French, German, and mathematics. His main pursuit, though, was an Honours degree in physics. For his fourth-year experimental project, he studied the response of a scintillation counter to radiation. His supervisor was experimentalist physicist David K. Butt, who contended that Samnadan-Pillai 'showed himself to be a keen, hard worker and he completed the project satisfactorily'.[24]

Samnadan-Pillai also involved himself in College sport. Soon after arriving, he became Athletics' Secretary for the Students' Union, a taxing position since it meant being responsible for the large sports ground at Greenford. However, something was clearly not right. He was described as becoming increasingly

[24] David K. Butt, 'Draft. To Whom It May Concern' (1965), in 'Ben Sammy', in Birkbeck Archive, Box 14. This was a draft letter in case Butt would be asked to write a reference.

disruptive; he was dropped from the College's Cricket XI for 'persistently abusing both his colleagues and opponents'.[25] He also failed to be awarded the first-class degree he thought he warranted. He contended that his 'pass' grade excluded him from future research, causing 'loss and injury to him in his professional career' and, indirectly, leading to health problems.[26] Samnadan-Pillai appealed to the College's President, Lord Denning, saying that he had been 'discriminated against on the grounds of race and colour'.[27] Samnadan-Pillai then sued the College for breach of contract, fraud, and professional negligence.

There is more to this story than simply a student disgruntled by his grade. On the surface, Samnadan-Pillai's primary complaint, which was about his 'pass' mark, was unexceptional. After all, it is not uncommon for a small number of students to believe they have not been granted the degree they deserve. Occasionally, they are right. Examination papers can be too hastily marked; and illegible handwriting can lead examiners to miss important arguments. But most universities have rigorous processes of oversight and internal review. Today, there are elaborate systems in place to ensure that papers are 'marked blind'—that is, not with the examiners' eyes shut, but without any name or other identifying characteristics on the examination paper. Papers are also marked by more than one lecturer. In addition, 'external examiners' from other universities oversee all essays and examination scripts, and are usually required to assess scripts where 'internal examiners' disagree, as well as all scripts that have failed, gained 'Firsts', or been awarded 'borderlines' (such as 59 or 69 per cent, which are borderline marks for a Merit or Distinction). Most of these procedures were in place when Samnadan-Pillai was examined, but with additional protections, as we shall see shortly.

Samnadan-Pillai's complaint exposed broader problems. Despite its seriousness, his complaint seems to have been taken lightly by some of the College's administrators. The College's archive contains a letter from Arnolfo John Caraffi, as College Secretary, to the College's lawyers stating that

> Some future historian of the College could probably do with one or two items to relieve the lack of lustre not uncommon in College histories. It might be a service to him [sic] if we preserve a file of the Ben Sammy case and if you could let me have an appropriate selection of papers in your keeping I should certainly be happy to add them to the archive. Please do ['not' was handwritten in the margin] regard this as an urgent job.[28]

---

[25] 'James Julian Ben Samnadam Pillai', in 'Ben Sammy', in Birkbeck Archive, Box 14.
[26] 'Ex-Student Sues College', *The Times* (27 October 1964), 4.
[27] Letter from Sammy to the President, Lord Denning, November 1961, in 'Ben Sammy', in Birkbeck Archive, Box 14.
[28] Letter from the Clerk of Birkbeck to David M. Robson (of Bull and Bull law firm), 28 October 1966, in 'Ben Sammy', in Birkbeck Archive, Box 14.

In other words, Caraffi believed that I—as the 'future historian of the College'—would enjoy 'spicing up' my history by reciting the anguish of Samnadan-Pillai.

What if Samnadan-Pillai's complaints had substance? We will never know. During the subsequent investigation into his examinations, it became clear that his accusation about unfair marking was unwarranted. After all, at that time, the College only *prepared* students for examination: it did not set or even grade papers, which was the function of the University of London.[29] The actual examiners were drawn from the numerous colleges of the University of London. Each paper was allocated to examiners by the Chair of the University of London Board of Examiners and was graded independently by at least two examiners. The examiners did not know the candidate's names since each had been allocated a number. Furthermore, examiners from outside the University of London *also* reviewed the papers, especially borderline fails and Firsts, and scripts where the other examiners significantly disagreed.[30]

However, Samnadan-Pillai's anger was not only about his degree result: it was about racism. To understand his protests, we need to go back to 1952, when he and another self-described 'colonial' student exchanged their views about race and racism in the pages of *The Lodestone*. The discussion started in the autumn term, the month Samnadan-Pillai began his studies at Birkbeck. It was sparked off by an article written by John J. Searchwell, a fellow West Indian. Searchwell came from the distinguished family of 'Ole Farmers' in Jamaica and was popularly known as 'Ole Farmer John' and, less formally, as 'Screech'.[31] In 1933, he had graduated with a diploma in agriculture from the Jamaica School of Agriculture and went on to teach in secondary schools and a teacher training college in Jamaica. Like many of his generation, he came to the UK in the early 1950s to do an undergraduate degree in Birkbeck's Department of Geography. He must have been popular since he was appointed Vice-President of the Students' Union.[32] Searchwell's career after Birkbeck was to be stellar. He went on to study geography at Syracuse University in 1961–2, after which he returned to his wife and two children in Jamaica. From 1972, he served as President of the Jamaica Teachers' Association and was known for his 'fiery campaigns for the rights of teachers'.[33] When he died at home in Highgate, Jamaica, in 2014, a month before his ninety-

---

[29] 'Mr Sammy Starts Final Speech', *The Times* (31 October 1964), 5.
[30] 'In the High Court of Justice. Queen's Bench Division. Royal Courts of Justice, Monday, 2nd November, 1964. Before: Mr Justice Marshall. James Julian Ben Sammy v. Birkbeck College (University of London)', in 'Ben Sammy', in Birkbeck Archive, Box 14.
[31] '"Ole Farmer" John Searchwell Being Buried Today', *Jamaica Observer* (12 April 2014), at https://www.jamaicaobserver.com/news/-Ole-Farmer--John-Searchwell-being-buried-today_16460742&template=MobileArticle, viewed 1 July 2021, and Derek Allen, 'Tribute to John Searchwell by a Friend', at http://www.reggaeboyzsc.com/forum1/showthread.php?t=63519, viewed 1 July 2021.
[32] 'Geography at Syracuse', 6, at https://www.maxwell.syr.edu/uploadedfiles/geo/history/gas1962.pdf, viewed 1 July 2021. In 1961–2, he was a student in the Department of Geography at Syracuse.
[33] Everard Owen, 'John Searchwell remembered as Great Educator, Social Activist, Trade Unionist, Family Man', *Jamaica Observer* (20 April 2014), at https://www.jamaicaobserver.com/news/

sixth birthday, a headline was entitled 'John Searchwell remembered as Great Educator, Social Activist, Trade Unionist, Family Man'.[34]

At Birkbeck, Searchwell must have known Samnadan-Pillai. At the very least, Searchwell's reputation as one of Jamaica's 'fastest quarter milers' meant that they would have coincided at the Greenford sports ground.[35] Searchwell also came to Samnadan-Pillai's attention through his articles in Birkbeck's student journal. In 1951, Searchwell published 'Conversation Piece' in *The Lodestone*, satirizing British speech and customs. Searchwell claimed to be bemused by the 'time-honoured English tradition' of speaking about the weather, the obsession with horse racing, and the loquacious character of the British working class. He ruminated on the fact that 'black cats, black dogs, [and] black clothes' were all fashionable, which confused him: why, then, did 'black people...find less favour than these among so many English people', he sardonically asked?[36]

Searchwell continued to mock the English in the spring and then summer of 1952. Under the title 'The Education of a Colonial', he registered surprise that British people did not seem to know that 'colonial' people spoke English. This reflected their 'abysmal ignorance of and the lack of desire for enlightenment in things colonial'.[37] He observed that an elementary schoolchild in the West Indies would have 'learned more about the British Isles, Europe and English history than about the land where he was born'.[38] He gently informed readers that

> At eleven I knew most of the countries of Europe with their capitals, bays, capes, etc., the main cities of England and Scotland. Our songs were of 'Hearts of Oak', 'For who are not free as the sons of the waves'—though ships we had none nor sons in the navy—and 'Where the bee sucks'. We learned beauty of language from 'A barking sound the shepherd hears' and 'A host of golden daffodils'—to this day I am not certain what a daffodil looks like.

With bitter humour, he noted that his younger self had

> sailed the seas with Drake and Raleigh, Nelson and Rodney; fought like the Danes with Alfred and harried France with the Black Prince—I was proud to feel that this latter was a Negro, though it did seem a bit strange that an English

---

john-searchwell-remembered-as-great-educator-social-activist-trade-unionist-family-man_16491452, viewed 1 July 2021, and '"Ole Farmer" John Searchwell Being Buried Today'.

[34] Owen, 'John Searchwell remembered as Great Educator, Social Activist, Trade Unionist, Family Man'.
[35] Allen, 'Tribute to John Searchwell by a Friend'.
[36] John J. Searchwell, 'Conversation Piece', *The Lodestone*, 43.1 (autumn 1951), 11–15.
[37] John J. Searchwell, 'The Education of a Colonial', *The Lodestone*, 43.2 (spring 1952), 22.
[38] Ibid., 22.

king should have a black son—and carried the standards of Cromwell and Wellington.[39]

Even their examinations were set by English examining boards. This only began to change in Jamaica from 1938, with the growth of a 'national consciousness and of Trade Unionism' in the various islands. Schools became aware of the need to 'educate West Indians as West Indians, and not as "black Englishmen".[40] There was a revolution in consciousness, even if (he admitted) the expense of a higher education meant that so many 'colonials', presumably like him and Samnadan-Pillai, left their native lands for university instruction in Britain.[41]

By the summer of 1952, Searchwell's critique of British racism became more pronounced; his tone in *The Lodestone*, less jocular. 'Emotionally the Colonial has first to accustom himself to being surrounded by white faces', he began one paragraph. He then added that 'I well remember how my feeling of "foreignness" was relieved on my seeing near the Bank, during the afternoon rush-hour of my second day in London, a lone African face across the street.'[42] There was also his 'dumb fury' when searching for a place to rent and being told that 'a room has just been taken; or that the landlord has decided not to let, after all; or that you have not got an English accent'. One of his Nigerian friends had been bluntly informed that 'we don't take Nigerians'.[43] Such experiences felt 'like a red hot knife in the heart'.[44] It also seemed that, for white Britons, there was 'no job for which he is "qualified"'.[45] 'Colonials' were being treated as scarcely 'human'. It was not surprising, Searchwell commented, that Black 'colonials' concluded that

> the Englishman who has given him so shameful a reception has no moral or other right to exercise dominion over him, and that he himself would lose all claim to human dignity if he allowed it to continue.[46]

He declared that 'the Colonial realises that it is to his own people that he must look for spiritual sustenance'.[47] It was a comment almost exactly echoing that of Marcus Garvey forty years earlier.

However, Samnadan-Pillai—who had only newly arrived from Trinidad—disagreed. He believed that Searchwell had gone too far. He admitted that the issue of 'race' (which he placed in inverted commas) was one that raised 'many bitter differences of opinion' but asked readers of *The Lodestone* to approach the topic with 'goodwill and level-headedness'. Samnadan-Pillai maintained that his aim was not to 'criticize or ostracise the British people and government, or the English weather' and contended that he was 'mindful of those many fine traditions and customs without which the greatness of Britain could not have been achieved'.

---

[39] Ibid., 22–3.   [40] Ibid., 24.   [41] Ibid., 25.   [42] Ibid., 5.   [43] Ibid., 6.
[44] Ibid., 6.   [45] Ibid., 6.   [46] Ibid., 7.   [47] Ibid., 7.

This was why, 'being myself a "colonial"', he felt that he should respond to Searchwell's increasingly angry articles.

Samnadan-Pillai went on to condemn Searchwell for his 'sweeping general condemnation' of the responses of white British people to colonial peoples, since it denied 'the individual kindnesses and generosities which some of us experience here and, I feel, we would be lacking in honour if we did not acknowledge our gratefulness for such decencies, however isolated'. Samnadan-Pillai acknowledged the 'reserve and suspicion' that 'colonials' experienced especially from keepers of lodging-houses and employers. But he wanted to put such racist responses in perspective: they had been caused by the 'impressions brought back by explorers from certain primitive parts' that had produced 'a sense of superiority and prompted the instinct of fear' in many white Britons. Samnadan-Pillai refused to concede that this comment was in any way an 'admission of inferiority', stating that 'every man, be he black, brown, yellow or white has within him the capacity for self-improvement and even of greatness'. Furthermore, there *was* a 'problem' with some 'colonials', he contended, especially the 'loud-laughing, lazy, hangers-around, zoot-suit type[s]' who 'have no respect for God or man' and made themselves 'objectionable to our sensitive hosts'. Even more provocatively, Samnadan-Pillai claimed that not only 'English landlad[ies]' but also 'African' ones often refused to rent their homes to Black 'colonials'. Anticipating criticism from fellow West Indians in the College, Samnadan-Pillai insisted he was neither a 'stooge' nor a 'convert' but was following in the tradition of Gandhi and Booker T. Washington who insisted on 'asserting the dignity of their races' while 'never stoop[ing] to revile the weakness of their masters'. Samnadan-Pillai concluded with the hope that, 'as the world shrinks before our eyes and men and women of different races are brought together, a better understanding and tolerance [will] guide us in our relations with each other'.[48]

But Samnadan-Pillai's hopes of 1952 quickly collapsed. Within only a few years, he had changed his mind and could be heard loudly condemning British racism, including within the College. He observed that many 'coloured students' left the College after their first year, presumably because they lacked support or had experienced discrimination.[49] He accused professors and lecturers—including crystallographer J. D. Bernal and neo-Hellenic historian Douglas Dakin—for being dismissive of his complaints about 'obstruction and unwilling co-operation'.[50] Samnadan-Pillai started to become aggressive, hitting a postgraduate student in the department, as well as physically lashing out at both Dakin and a visiting lecturer from Imperial College.[51] He even 'raised his stick to the Master in

[48] J. J. Ben Sammy, 'The Education of a Colonial', *The Lodestone*, 44.1 (autumn 1952), 45–7.
[49] 'Briefing Notes', undated, in 'Ben Sammy', in Birkbeck Archive, Box 14.
[50] Ibid., and 'Statement of Claim', 1962, in 'Ben Sammy', in Birkbeck Archive, Box 14.
[51] 'James Julian Ben Samnadam Pillai', in 'Ben Sammy', in Birkbeck Archive, Box 14.

Malet Street'[52] and, on one occasion, burst into the Council Room in the middle of a Professorial Committee, shouting abuse.[53] Fearing the escalation of violence, by February 1962, the College had barred him from entering the premises.[54]

Samnadan-Pillai appealed his examination results. When his appeal reached court, he maintained that there was 'no proper liaison between the staff and the students, who were in the habit of concocting and spreading false tales to which members of staff gave undue credence'.[55] He also claimed that 'his colour aroused resentment amongst the native students and some members of staff, and he was told from time to time that he was too ambitious'.[56] As a result of his treatment, his confidence had been undermined, he was suffering from 'nervous debility', and he felt 'lost and unwanted'.[57] Samnadan-Pillai also accused the court of racism, reproaching the judge for 'treating me as a child. I come from Trinidad where English is spoken. We have courts of law there'.[58] Ironically, years earlier Samnadan-Pillai had repudiated Searchwell for making a similar (although more mildly expressed) observation about the 'abysmal ignorance' of white Britons about all things 'colonial'.

Samnadan-Pillai had no chance of winning the case. It was a battle between an unknown Trinidadian student, on the one side, and, on the other side, the elite of the educational establishment (including one of the most famous physicists of the century) and a knighted Master of a college in the University of London.[59] At the judgment, the judge concluded that Samnadan-Pillai

> suffers from an actual *folie de grandeur*, is hypersensitive and now, alas, suffers under a sense of grievance, which has twisted his outlook, distorted his judgement, and brought him to attach to completely innocent and friendly conduct on the part of the staff at the Birkbeck College, an unjustified, fraudulent and sinister meaning.[60]

---

[52] Ibid.   [53] Ibid.
[54] Letter from the Clerk to Mr Levy, 7 February 1962, and Letter to Sammy from Bull and Bull Solicitors, 9 February 1962, in 'Ben Sammy', in Birkbeck Archive, Box 14.
[55] 'Ex-Student Sues College', *The Times* (27 October 1964), 4.   [56] Ibid., 4.
[57] 'The Master Gives Evidence', *The Times* (28 October 1964), 3.
[58] 'Examination Papers Discussed', *The Times* (29 October 1964), 9.
[59] 'Mr Sammy Loses', *The Times* (3 November 1964), 13.
[60] 'In the High Court of Justice. Queen's Bench Division. Royal Courts of Justice, Monday, 2nd November, 1964. Before: Mr Justice Marshall. James Julian Ben Sammy v. Birkbeck College (University of London)', in 'Ben Sammy', in Birkbeck Archive, Box 14. He appealed this decision, but also lost. See 'Mr Sammy Loses Appeal', *The Times* (20 May 1965), 6; 'In the Supreme Court Judicature. Court of Appeal. From Mr Justice Marshall, Middlesex. Royal Court of Justice. Wednesday, 19th May, 1965. Before: Lord Justice Sellers, Lord Justice Danckwerts, and Lord Justice Diplock. James Julian Ben Sammy (Samnadan-Pillai) v. Birkbeck College (University of London) (Under Charter of Incorporation)', in 'Ben Sammy', in Birkbeck Archive, Box 14; and Letter from David M. Robson to A. J. Caraffi, 20 May 1965, in 'Ben Sammy', in Birkbeck Archive, Box 14.

Samnadan-Pillai was crushed; his experiences of racism, dismissed as a personal pathology.

* * *

Within only a few years of arriving in Britain, Samnadan-Pillai's distressing experiences within Birkbeck and the wider community had turned him from an admirer of certain 'British values' to one of its most vigorous critics. Some of the lecturers that Samnadan-Pillai accused of racism (Bernal, for example) were active in anti-racist movements, but that cannot excuse what Samnadan-Pillai perceived to be glib responses to specific complaints. His anger was likely to have been exacerbated by his isolation within the student body. Although he must have known Searchwell personally, Black students were a tiny minority at Birkbeck and other universities at the time. It is telling that the College did not even begin collecting statistics on the ethnicity of students until mid-century.

Samnadan-Pillai and Searchwell also lacked role models. Even today, there are relatively few Black professors in the UK. While 15 per cent of white male academics in Britain hold the title of Professor, only 8 per cent of Black male academics, 6 per cent of white female academics, and 3 per cent of Black female academics hold the same rank.[61] It is a stark illustration of the extent to which intersectional identities (in this case, skin colour and gender) combine to create oppressive hierarchies.

* * *

The first Black professor at Birkbeck was Jamaican-born economist Albert Gregorio ('Bertie') Hines. It was in 1971, more than a decade after Samnadan-Pillai's appeal. Hines' journey from a job in the Jamaican Civil Service to a Chair in Economics at Birkbeck had been meteoric. In the 1950s, frustrated by the university system in Jamaica, which was dominated by the medical school, Hines 'just decided to pack up and come here on my own steam', as he put it.[62] Arriving in London in 1957, he initially got a job as a clerk on the railways, then, because 'I was a bit of a politico', took a course in trade union studies at the London School of Economics, thinking that it 'might have come in handy back home'.[63] Instead, after completing his degree in economics, he decided on an academic career. He was appointed assistant lecturer, then lecturer in political economy, at University College London. In 1968, at the incredibly young age of 32 years, he was appointed Professor of Economics at Durham University. Three years later, he was at Birkbeck and, with Richard D. Portes from Princeton University, established the

---

[61] AdvanceHE, 'Equality + Higher Education. Staff Statistical Report 2020', 258, at https://www.advance-he.ac.uk/media/5941, viewed 1 August 2021.
[62] 'Jamaica's Loss—Durham's Gain', *The Times* (29 May 1968), 10. [63] Ibid., 10.

Economics Department.[64] Teaching in economics at Birkbeck formally started in October 1973, after a half-century hiatus.

Hines was aware of Birkbeck's ties to Garvey and Pan-Africanism and, although he followed a less revolutionary road, he was equally passionate in defence of Black communities. Hines' politics had been painfully marked by conservative politician Enoch Powell's infamous 'rivers of blood' speech, delivered on 20 April 1968 at a meeting at the Conservative Political Centre in Birmingham. During that speech, Powell referred to a letter he had received from a white woman in his constituency in Wolverhampton. It described a respectable, 'white' neighbourhood being transformed by the arrival of non-white immigrants. Powell claimed that the woman

> is becoming afraid to go out. Windows are broken. She finds excreta pushed through her letter box. When she goes to the shops, she is followed by children, charming, wide-grinning, piccaninnies. They cannot speak English but one word they know. 'Racialist', they chant. When the new Race Relations Bill is passed, this woman is convinced she will go to prison. And is she wrong?

It was a vicious speech that conjured up multiple racist motifs: 'white womanhood' as a symbol of the nation, in contrast to 'dark' immigrants 'invading' respectable neighbourhoods and transforming them into grimy enclaves.

The College's response was swift. By an unfortunate coincidence, Powell had been booked to give the annual Haldane Lecture only a few weeks after his speech. The invitation had been issued by Kenneth Hare, climatologist and Master for two years from 1966, but it was the duty of the new Master, economist Ronald Tress (who was to appoint Hines) to host it. Within days of Powell's speech, Birkbeck's staff and lecturers had vowed to boycott the lecture. Tress set out to extricate the College from what had become an odious commitment.[65] Tress wrote to Powell explaining that the College's Haldane Lecture had been booked to take place in a lecture theatre at University College London, not on Birkbeck's premises. He admitted that the 'subject of your lecture "A Citizen Voluntary Reserve" is very far removed from the subject matter of the speech which you made this last weekend'. Nevertheless, he continued,

> such advice as I have taken has confirmed to me the fear that the occasion will be used as an opportunity for demonstration[s] against your views. In such cases, were the demonstration to assume substantial proportions, we could find ourselves in an embarrassing situation bearing in mind that we were the guests of another institution.

---

[64] Richard D. Portes left Birkbeck in 1995, to go to the London Business School.
[65] 'Mr Powell's Engagement at LSE Cancelled', *The Guardian* (25 April 1968).

Tress then cancelled the lecture, although he politely told Powell that if he wanted to be paid the fee anyway, the College would do so.[66]

Hines had been enraged by the blatant bigotry of prominent Conservative Party politicians such as Powell. Five years after the 'rivers of blood' speech, by which time Hines was at Birkbeck, he could be heard loudly objecting to Powell's contention that the repatriation of 'coloured people' was necessary if the UK was to avoid racial conflict.[67] Speaking in February 1973 on BBC 1's *The Sunday Debate*, Hines reminded listeners of the positive contributions Black communities were making to the nation.[68]

Although he was a Professor of Economics, Hines did not restrict his anti-racism activism to issues of economics and employment. Like Garvey, Hines was an active proponent of the Black arts and culture as important sites of resistance. From September 1974, he was Chair of the advisory group, Minority Group Arts, which aimed at encouraging the arts within minority communities, 'thereby enrich[ing] the cultural life of the entire community'.[69] Minority Group Arts was also responsible for conducting the 'first comprehensive and independent study of arts activities' amongst Bangladeshis, Chinese, Cypriots, East and Central Europeans, Indians, Pakistanis, West Indians, and Africans living in the UK.[70] Their final report not only celebrated Black achievements but also damned the arts' establishments by revealing that only ten out of the 675 students enrolled in schools of drama (1.5 per cent) were Black British.[71]

The prejudices that Hines and other influential Black leaders faced can be illustrated by turning to a discussion that took place when Hines was called to give evidence to the Select Committee on Race Relations and Immigration on 15 May 1975. Hines appeared as a representative of the Constituent Committee of the Proposed National Black People's Organization. This organization had been established in January 1975 following a London-based conference involving between 300 and 400 delegates from 120 organizations.[72] The Committee's purpose was to set up a permanent organization representing Black, Asian, and

---

[66] Letter from R. C. Tress to Enoch Powell, 23 April 1968, in 'Guard Book 2', the Birkbeck Archive.

[67] See 'Powell Calls for Migrant Cut-Down', *Express Wolverhampton* (19 February 1972), and Mary Crozier, 'Television', *The Tablet* (24 February 1973), both in the Birkbeck Archive.

[68] 'The Sunday Debate', BBC 1 (18 February 1973), at http://genome.ch.bbc.co.uk/fd08afff1d1b4156a1f56a6c8ce2f6b6, viewed 20 March 2018.

[69] Letter from Professor A. G. Hines to Miss Jean Goose, Secretary to the Annan Committee on the Future of Broadcasting, Home Office (5 February 1975), in The National Archives HO 245/1681.

[70] Kenneth Gosling, 'Study Aims at Development of Minority Group Arts', *The Times* (17 May 1975), 4.

[71] Ibid., 4.

[72] *Select Committee on Race Relations and Immigration. Session 1974–75. The Organization of Race Relations Administration. Volume II. Evidence* [448-II] (London: Her Majesty's Stationery Office, 1975), 228.

Afro-Caribbean communities. It claimed to be in touch with 700 organizations working on behalf of minority groups.[73]

Despite these impressive credentials, as well as the fact that Hines was a full professor in the university, he was given a tough grilling by the Select Committee. Its Chair (Labour MP Frederick Willey) pressed him on what he meant by using the word 'Black'. Observing that Asians, Indians, and Pakistanis were members of the proposed National Black People's Organization, the Chair repeatedly asked Hines whether 'Black' meant 'black and brown'? When Hines responded by saying 'Yes, it is inclusive. Black is black', the Chair asked for further clarification: would it be more accurate, Willey asked, to say 'non-white' or 'the immigrant community'? Hines was clearly irritated, informing the Select Committee that

> The question of whether there are Asians or, dare I say, West Indians, who do not wish to call themselves black and so wish to call themselves orange, is slightly off the centre of the problem.[74]

It was a witty riposte, challenging essentialist tropes often employed by racists, while simultaneously drawing attention to coalitions of solidarity between minoritized communities.

Hines also informed the Select Committee that there was 'considerable disillusionment' within minority communities due to the failures of the Race Relations Acts of 1965 and 1968 and the Commonwealth Immigrants Act of 1968, which had restricted migration from the former colonies.[75] He welcomed further proposals to address discrimination, but called for the establishment of 'a strong national body... We are thinking of a national commission on racial equality, as we call it.' This organization would have two main duties. The first would be to enforce the existing law, ensuring that anti-discrimination legislation was actually implemented. The second duty for Hines' proposed 'national commission on racial equality' would be educational, fostering community relationships at both national and local levels.[76] In order to be credible to minority communities, at least half of the members of this proposed commission should be members of minoritized communities.[77] Acknowledging that this insistence on the full participation of Black commissioners might be seen as problematic, Hines explained that

> We do not mean by this that a man is to be judged simply by the colour of his skin and that if you have the wrong skin you cannot do good work, or that if you have the right skin you are capable of doing satisfactory work, but we do believe

[73] Ibid., 228.   [74] Ibid., 228–9.   [75] Ibid., 229.   [76] Ibid., 229.   [77] Ibid., 229.

that in the interests of this mutual credibility this would be a significant step forward.[78]

Members of the largely white Select Committee might have squirmed in their seats to hear their skin colour being described as 'wrong'.

Hines was grilled about conflicts *within* minority communities. He remained calm. 'We could not deny that there are differences', he patiently explained: after all, 'We have come from our own parts of the globe originally'. However,

> since coming here...a generation of us has grown up in this country. We have learned that there are things that divide us and things that unite us, and on this particular issue we see the things that unite us as being more important than the things that divide us.[79]

Unfortunately, Hine's rebuttal was disingenuous. He was only too aware of major divisions within Black communities. These came to a head during the Black People in Britain Conference in January 1975, in which a leaflet was circulated criticizing the National Black People's Organization.[80] In it, Hines was portrayed as an Uncle Tom figure: his conformist views ('join the police'), his eagerness to involve white supporters, and his status as a professor at the predominantly white Birkbeck made him suspect amongst a younger generation of radical activists (see Fig. 12.2). The attack must have been extremely painful.

* * *

This chapter has focused on only one vector of identity: race. All the academics and students discussed so far have been male, and relatively privileged, such as Hines, who reached the top of the academic hierarchy in 1968 (University of Durham) and then 1971 (Birkbeck). Black women make up only 3 per cent of the professoriate in Higher Education in the country.[81] In the entire sector, only six institutions of Higher Education have five or more Black female professors.[82] At Birkbeck, the first Black woman to become a professor was Patricia Tuitt, specialist in refugee law, race, and resistance, as well as serving as Dean of the School of Law between 2009 and 2017.[83] In the Department of Psychosocial Studies, Gail Lewis is another notable example. She was a Reader at Birkbeck, being awarded professorial status only after she left the College in 2020 directly as a response to racism. Today, the only Black female professor is Avtar Brah, with whom I started

---

[78] Ibid., 229–30.   [79] Ibid., 232.
[80] The image can be found in the archive of Liberty (formerly the National Council for Civil Liberties), file 01/04/04/01/03.
[81] 'Black Female Professors Forum', at https://blackfemaleprofessorsforum.org/about/about/, viewed 1 July 2021.
[82] Ibid.   [83] Tuitt had been appointed in 1998.

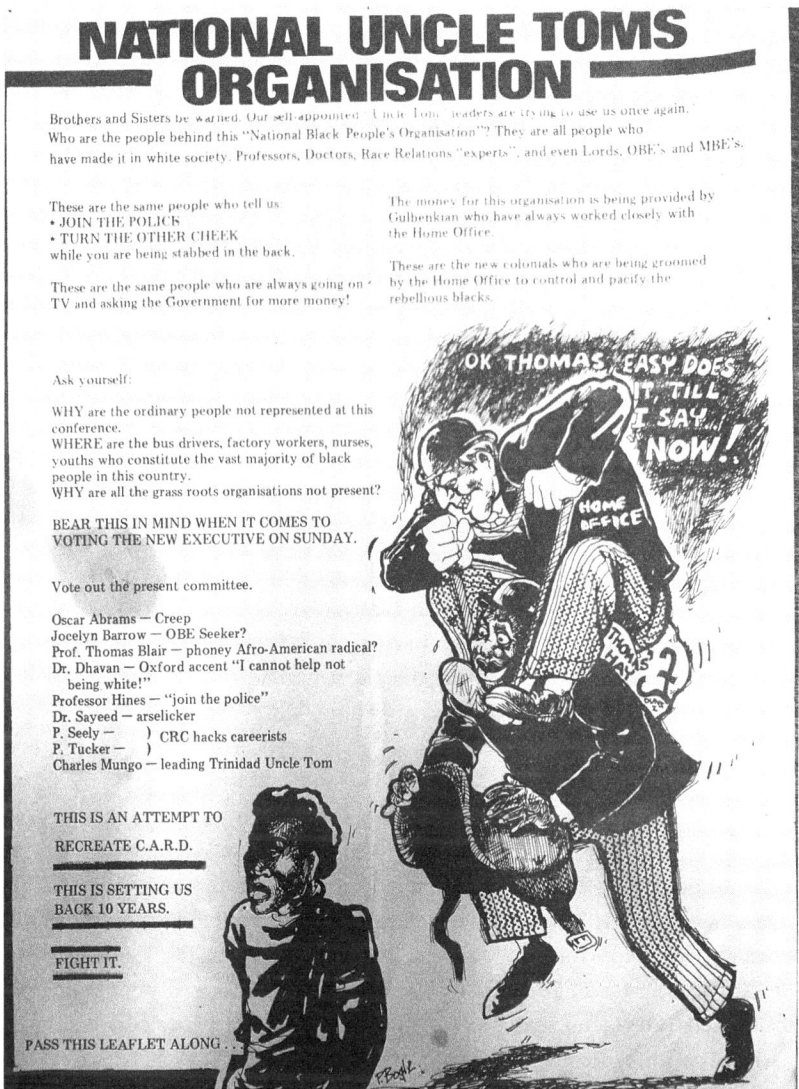

Fig. 12.2 'National Uncle Toms Organisation', a leaflet criticizing the Post-Conference Constituent Committee, 1975. From the archive of Liberty (formerly the National Council for Civil Liberties), file 01/04/04/01/03.

this chapter. She was a founding member of the Southall Black Sisters, a feminist collective of women of Asian and African-Caribbean descent who contested the masculinist ethos of the (Black) Southall Youth Movement. As an Asian Ugandan woman, Brah has often reflected on the tensions involved when siding with Black communities against racism and with white feminists against sexism. It may be disingenuous citing Brah as Birkbeck's (only) Black female professor at the time of writing this chapter (August 2021): after all, she is an Emerita (that is, retired) Professor. Women are a minoritized group within academic hierarchies; Black women, even more so.

Marginalized individuals and groups have often entered the academy via routes regarded as 'peripheral'. One of the most important of these was the 'university extension' movement, which has been known, in its various incarnations at Birkbeck, as the Centre for Extra-Mural Studies (CEMS), the Department of Extra-Mural Studies, the Faculty of Continuing Education (from 1999), and the Faculty of Lifelong Learning (from 2007). The incorporation of CEMS into Birkbeck is discussed in Chapter 28. For the purposes of this chapter, the CEMS was important in widening opportunities for marginalized communities.

As part of the federation of the University of London, the CEMS had an independent tradition of providing students with high-quality teaching based on syllabuses that were often negotiated between students and 'tutors' (they did not call themselves 'lecturers'). Unlike Birkbeck, it had historical links with organizations such as the Workers' Educational Association (established in 1903), trade unions, and community groups. Some critics have denigrated the movement as providing classes for allegedly idle white women ('housewives') seeking to absorb knowledge without committing themselves to rigorous essay writing and examinations. It is a critique that says more about the elitist and sexist assumptions of these critics than about the students actually attending CEMS classes.

Others, however, have pointed out that CEMS has been a hotbed of progressive politics. Since the 1960s, 'university extension' and 'extra-mural' movements have attracted radical academics, keen to use education to empower minoritized communities. Amongst other efforts, this has included plans to 'decolonize the curriculum' (although that term is a recent one), based on the awareness that the academic 'canon' has always reflected the economic, ideological, and cultural interests of elite, white men, followed by elite, white women. The 1960s generation sought to rewrite reading lists, actively encourage minoritized people (and specifically racial, class, and sexual minorities) to contribute to the curriculum, and experiment with radically democratic pedagogic practices. CEMS was a good place to start. As a leading member of CEMS, Brah contended that she and her colleagues were 'lucky' because 'there weren't that many bureaucratic obstacles to innovation' in CEMS: 'If you thought of an idea that was good, you could actually produce a course', she noted.[84]

Many of the innovations were explicitly feminist. They sought to make knowledge that that had conventionally been coded 'male' more accessible for women: this included courses on electronics, car maintenance, carpentry, computing,

---

[84] Back and Brah, 'Activism, Imagination, and Writing', 47.

mathematics, and navigation.⁸⁵ Similarly innovative courses included one on gerontology, which sought to draw attention to the harms caused by ageism, especially as experienced by women. Long before the main part of the College introduced classes in diaspora studies, it was being taught in CEMS. Brah remembered courses in

> Irish Studies, Jewish Studies, Palestinian Studies, Caribbean Studies, Asian Studies. We had a course in Black Theatre. We produced courses in Women's Studies and Lesbian Studies. And actually our Lesbian Studies programme was one of the first in London and Jane [Hoy] was very centrally involved in that.⁸⁶

Other classes could be taken in lesbian cinema and the psychology of sexual difference. Since such 'useful knowledge' might not be empowering for women lacking confidence., CEMS, tutors introduced classes on women's self-defence and 'Assertiveness for Women'. They were attempts to encourage women to 'communicate despite many imperatives to remain silent'.⁸⁷

As these courses suggest, many of the female tutors in CEMS were self-consciously feminist throughout the 1970s and 1980s. They not only emerged *from* but were also partly responsible *for* the development and flourishing of the Women's Liberation Movement. This was why Sally Alexander (one of the organizers of the first national Women's Liberation Movement in the UK) threw her energies into CEMS.⁸⁸ As tutor Rosemary Auchmuty pointed out to Tom Evans, the Deputy Director of CEMS, in 1983,

> We feel that it is time all part-time tutors realized that the study of women is part of the study of every subject and every discipline. However, simply including a mention of women is not enough; we have to consider *why* they've been left out, *why* (male) scholars have considered that certain topics (like domestic work and childcare) are unworthy of critical attention, and to start to ask the sorts of questions that are relevant to women's experience. This is what feminist scholarship is all about.⁸⁹

---

⁸⁵ Mary Kennedy, 'Women's Studies: Their Changing Role in Adult Education', notes for a paper she presented dated 22 March 1984, in the Mary Kennedy Papers at Bishopsgate Library, Kennedy/48.
⁸⁶ Back and Brah, 'Activism, Imagination, and Writing', 47.
⁸⁷ 'Speaking Out: Assertiveness for Women', in Mary Kennedy papers at Bishopsgate Library, Kennedy/46, and Mary Kennedy, conference notes entitled 'Women's Studies: Their Changing Role in Adult Education', dated 22 March 1984, in the Mary Kennedy Papers, Bishopsgate Library, Kennedy/48.
⁸⁸ See an interview with Sally Alexander on the Birkbeck Bicentenary website.
⁸⁹ Letter from Rosemary Auchmuty to Tom Evans, Deputy Director of the Extra-Mural Department at the University of London, dated 29 August 1983, and copied to Mary Kennedy and Nell Keddie, in the Mary Kennedy Papers, Bishopsgate Library, Kennedy/13.

Similarly, tutors such as Mary Hughes and Mary Kennedy passionately believed that 'Adult education is primarily a woman's service.' As a result, not only were a large majority of students female, so too were the teaching staff. This was intellectually invigorating but politically maddening. As Hughes and Kennedy admitted,

> Adult education can open windows into exciting ideas in a mind-extending, mind-blowing way, but also, sadly, it can be education for frustration. It gives women the desire for change[,] but the world remains the same.[90]

Women's studies in CEMS drew inspiration from new ways of teaching that were being introduced in Black studies. Both disciplines adopted 'a new approach to learning and knowledge, insisting upon equal student-tutor participation'.[91] This led to many challenges. For example, in 1986, Annabel Faraday (now, a distinguished ceramic artist) and Alison Oram (leading scholar of queer history) taught a course entitled 'Uncovering Lesbian History 1800–1970'. They acknowledged that there had been tensions about the style and content of the class, largely due to different expectations and desired outcomes. Students in their class made the 'obvious' observation that the two lecturers possessed 'a lot more information than most of the class'. This made it

> sometimes difficult for them to avoid being put in the position of 'experts'. In particular, this was an issue when we had wide ranging discussions about relating the history we were uncovering to our lives as lesbians today.[92]

In the words of one student, 'just because we all sat around in a circle did not mean that we were equally positioned in the power dynamic'.[93] Faraday admitted the point, adding that 'I was being *paid* to teach and the class was paying—a situation which hardly engenders a sense of equality and collective effort'.[94]

There were also heated discussions about what was meant by 'feminist'. After all, CEMS students had different personal histories, class backgrounds, and politics. As numerous minoritized women in the classes pointed out, most of the reading material had been produced by 'white, middle-class women'.[95]

What students and tutors agreed upon, however, was the need for consciousness raising. A fun poem about consciousness raising was written by Judy Alderson, a student in CEMS. Entitled 'Susie the Sex Symbol', the poem focused

---

[90] Mary Hughes and Mary Kennedy, 'Breaking Out: Women in Adult Education', *Women's Studies International*, 6.3 (1983), 261.
[91] Ibid., 261.
[92] Students on the course 'Uncovering Lesbian History 1800–1970', a 'work-in-progress no. 2', *For Those Who Would be Sisters: Uncovering Lesbian History* (London: Centre for Extramural Studies, 1986), 52.
[93] Ibid., 53. [94] Ibid., 54. [95] Ibid., 52.

on a young woman whom 'everybody fancied' because she had a 'big dumb smile' and 'sugar blond appeal'. One day, Susie picked up a book and began to read. Suddenly, 'her brain cells were stirring[,] aroused by the thoughts they were fed'. The next time her 'smarmy boss appeared' and murmured 'come and munch some creamy crepe suzette',

> susie swung round with her newly acquired self-respect
> and shot him an answer that had its desired effect
> then stronger than boadacea she lifted him clean off the ground
> and told him in earnest about the new life she had found
> little man on the make you make me sick
> today I learnt a lesson that's gonna stick
> yes, I can see you in my glasses now you'd rather have me thick
> now I know the pen...is mightier than the prick.[96]

It is easy to surmise that 'Susie' might have attended classes on 'Assertiveness Training'.

Although CEMS classes were empowering for female and other minoritized students, its tutors and administrators lacked power within the wider College.[97] Auchmuty complained about the 'blinkered thoughtlessness' of 'sexist and racist' weekend training sessions for CEMS tutors.[98] Women's studies was occasionally 'derided, dismissed, and semi-sabotaged'. It was charged with being a 'non-subject' as well as being 'middle-classed and irrelevant to ordinary women (whoever these might be)'. Some critics went so far to accuse the subject of being 'emotional "disturbers"' of the *natural order*'.[99] Feminist tutors and lecturers took that 'insult' as a compliment.

Anxieties about women's studies as part of a university curriculum were not confined to CEMS courses. Feminism was having an impact on the main part of the College as well—and conservative scholars took offence. Philosopher Roger Scruton, the nemesis of all things progressive, even publicly attacked a new professorial colleague for proposing to teach a course on 'Feminism and Social Relations', which sought to explore 'the complex relations of oppression with particular focus on the ways racism, class inequality, ableism and ageism shape and are shaped by gender inequality'. He justified his attack by telling the reporter that 'I thought readers would be interested to see the sort of feminist crap that's put

---

[96] Judy Alderson, 'Susie the Sex Symbol', in the Mary Kennedy Papers, Bishopsgate Library, Kennedy/22. I have been unable to trace the author of this poem.
[97] Hughes and Kennedy, 'Breaking Out: Women in Adult Education', 261.
[98] Letter from Rosemary Auchmuty to Tom Evans, Deputy Director of the Extra-Mural Department at the University of London, dated 29 August 1983, and copied to Mary Kennedy and Nell Keddie, in the Mary Kennedy Papers, Bishopsgate Library, Kennedy/13.
[99] Hughes and Kennedy, 'Breaking Out: Women in Adult Education', 261.

out.'[100] Perhaps encouraged by rants like those of Scruton, some male students joined the anti-feminist backlash. In November 1993, one 36-year-old male student argued that Birkbeck was engaged in gender discrimination: a CEMS course on 'Anglo-Saxon and French Feminist Philosophy' only admitted women. This, he claimed, infringed Section 47 of the Sex Discrimination Act. He argued that 'Feminists are being indoctrinated, men abase themselves, and there is tension and hostility between the sexes.' This student's view was that feminism was a 'revolutionary doctrine', which was 'galloping towards its logical extreme: the total exclusion of men'. Therefore, it was 'his duty to put his hand up when he feels that discrimination against men is going unnoticed'.[101] He won: the following year, he joined the class along with another male friend. The 'culture wars' of the 1990s never went away.

* * *

This chapter has briefly mentioned a few minoritized groups, primarily those of race and gender. There are a host of others that could have been discussed, and can only be mentioned briefly here. For example, in 2020, 12 per cent of Birkbeck's *staff* from cleaners to professors identified as LGBTQ. Overall, they were paid 6 per cent less than staff identifying as heterosexual.[102] Statistics about discrimination against LGBTQ *students* at Birkbeck does not exist, but we know that, throughout the UK, it remains shockingly high. In 2018, psychologist Diane Houston (who is Pro-Vice Chancellor for Education at Birkbeck) along with collaborators Dominic Abrams and Hannah Swift from the University of Kent, published the first, decade-long national survey of prejudice in the UK. The results were shocking, with nearly half of people from lesbian, gay, and bisexual communities reporting that they had experienced prejudices based on their sexual orientation.[103]

The report by Houston, Abrams, and Swift also revealed that, nation-wide, 61 per cent of people with mental health conditions reported that they had experienced impairment-based prejudices.[104] At Birkbeck, the evidence with regard to disability is surprising. In 2020, almost one quarter of Birkbeck students disclosed

---

[100] 'Turn the Corner', *The Standard* (n.d., September 1992), in the Birkbeck Library. This was an attack on Deborah Stein.
[101] 'Feminism, Opportunism, and the Equality of Mr [Ralph] Tager', *The Standard* (18 November 1993), in the Birkbeck Archive. Also see Matthew d'Ancona, 'Man Beats Feminist Course Ban', *The Times* (7 November 1993), in the Birkbeck Archive.
[102] Birkbeck, University of London, *Gender Pay Audit 2020* (London: Birkbeck, University of London, 2020), 29, at https://www.bbk.ac.uk/about-us/equality/equal-pay-audit, viewed 1 June 2021. This must be taken with caution since it omits those members of staff who either failed to disclose their gender identity or claimed no gender identity.
[103] Dominic Abrams, Hannah Swift, and Diane Houston, *Developing a National Barometer of Prejudice and Discrimination in Britain* (London: Equality and Human Rights Commission, October 2018), 10, at https://www.researchgate.net/publication/329751744_Developing_a_national_barometer_of_prejudice_and_discrimination_in_Britain, viewed 1 June 2021.
[104] Ibid.

a disability. This is considerably higher than the sector average of 13 per cent,[105] perhaps because evening classes are more suited to people with disabilities since they can avoid travelling during peak periods. Furthermore, disabled students at Birkbeck tend to perform *better* than students with no disabilities. While the retention of disabled students in universities throughout the UK is 6 per cent *worse* than for their non-disabled counterparts, at Birkbeck it is 9 per cent better.[106]

The well-being of students from economically deprived backgrounds is another area of concern. In the autumn of 2007, Birkbeck in partnership with the University of East London began teaching in a new, state-of-the-art building in Stratford, East London. This area has the lowest participation rate in Higher Education in London. Over 1,300 students enrolled. While 14 per cent of students in the Bloomsbury campus are under the age of 25, in Stratford this rose to one quarter. Similarly, while less than one quarter of the students in Bloomsbury were from Black and minority ethnic (BME) communities, this soared to 55 per cent in Stratford.[107] For his work in Stratford, Latchman was awarded the Times Higher Education Widening Participation of the Year Award in 2008.

In the main campus, encouraging lower-income students to enrol at Birkbeck remains a challenge. Today, according to the English Indices of Multiple Deprivation (IMD), 61 per cent of Birkbeck undergraduates come from the lowest two quintiles of IMD deprivation.[108] Crucially, the gap between those in the lowest quintiles and those in the higher quintiles gaining a 'good degree' (that is, a 'First' or '2.1') is smaller than it is both in the sector as a whole and in the Higher Education sector in London. There is still a long way to go, however, since the gap remains: more economically deprived students at Birkbeck are 7 per cent (full time) to 16 per cent (part time) less likely to be awarded a 'good degree'.[109] Providing opportunities for students from underprivileged backgrounds is a central goal. This is why the College introduced a Foundation Year in 2017–18, aimed at providing a pathway for students without traditional entry qualifications. At the same time, it greatly improved infrastructural support for such students.

In terms of absolute numbers of students from BME communities, Birkbeck looks relatively strong. In 2020, while 40 per cent of Londoners are BME, 56 per cent of the College's full-time students and 42 per cent of its part-time ones identified as BME.[110] However, in 2020, Black students were between 31 per cent (full time) and 39 per cent (part time) less likely to be awarded a 'good degree' (in

---

[105] Birkbeck College, 'Financial Statements for the Year Ending 31 July 2020', 43–4, at https://www.bbk.ac.uk/downloads/finance/financial-statements-2020.pdf, viewed 1 June 2021.
[106] Ibid.   [107] David Latchman, personal communication.
[108] Birkbeck College, 'Financial Statements for the Year Ending 31 July 2020', 42, at https://www.bbk.ac.uk/downloads/finance/financial-statements-2020.pdf, viewed 1 June 2021.
[109] Ibid.   [110] Ibid.

2014–15, this was worse at 50 per cent, so some improvements have occurred).[111] A lot more work is required to ensure that *all* Birkbeckians thrive.

Similar distortions are seen in terms of staff. In 2020, 27 per cent of Birkbeck's staff identified as BME, but they were concentrated in the more junior roles in the College. While 75 per cent of the cleaners and between 40 and 50 per cent of lecturers on the lowest pay grades (apprentices or on grades 2–4) were BME, only 10 per cent of those on the highest grade were BME. The pay gap overall for BME staff was nearly 20 per cent lower.[112]

Gender also makes a difference. Birkbeck first began reporting on its gender pay gap in 2003, revealing that female members of the academic staff were paid 17 per cent less than their male colleagues; in 2020, it was just under 7 per cent.[113] Admittedly, this gender pay gap is 7 per cent lower than in the sector as a whole, but the problem remains serious.[114]

* * *

The current Vice-Chancellor, David Latchman, and his senior team have made diversity and inclusion two of their top priorities. Proactive initiatives are important because not everyone treats other people fairly. Education can be transformative; as Birkbeck activists in the 1960s to the 1990s used to say, it can be 'mind blowing'. But it can also be a place where students, staff, and lecturers feel threatened based on skin colour, class, gender, sexual preference, disability, religion, and a host of other minoritized characteristics. Victim-survivors sometimes don't feel sufficiently empowered to report infractions to College authorities.[115]

In the past, we have seen how the activism of people like Garvey, Hines, and the feminists in both CEMS and the College has made a difference. These activists did this by using their intellectual expertise and social capital to publish robust research into the extent and effect of injustices, educate people about the harms of prejudice, and push through reforms. Individuals have also made a difference: take the international composition of the Departments of Physics and Crystallography under successive heads of departments or the dramatic increase of female scholars, including senior ones, during the period when distinguished German historian Richard Evans was head of the Department of History, Classics, and Archaeology between 1992 and 1998. At other times, they were impelled by union as well as student pressures and demands to see their communities represented fairly in the classroom. Today, the College is home to the Birkbeck Institute

---

[111] Ibid.
[112] Birkbeck, University of London, *Gender Pay Audit 2020* (London: Birkbeck, University of London, 2020), 16, at https://www.bbk.ac.uk/about-us/equality/equal-pay-audit, viewed 1 June 2021.
[113] Birkbeck College, 'Financial Statements for the Year Ending 31 July 2020', 19–20.
[114] Birkbeck College, *Gender Pay Gap Report 2020*, 2, at https://www.bbk.ac.uk/about-us/equality/gender-pay-gap, viewed 1 June 2021.
[115] For example, see Helen Bennett, 'No Protection from Harassment "Claim"', *Morning Star* (11 May 1984), in the Birkbeck Archive.

of Gender and Sexuality (founded in 2008 by scholars Matt Cook, Lynne Segal, Heike Bauer, Daniel Monk, and Rosie Cox) and, from 2015, the Birkbeck Institute for the Study of Antisemitism, supporting research into all forms of racism and intolerance. The College co-convenes (with Queen Mary University of London) the Raphael Samuel History Centre and the radical journal *History Workshop*.[116] Indeed, the first and second Directors of the Centre were Birkbeck historians Matt Cook and Julia Laite. Inclusivity is a much-lauded value. Nevertheless, the fact that harassment and abuse continue to take place is indicative of the deeply embedded prejudices within society.

[116] See Raphael Samuel History Centre: https://raphaelsamuelhistorycentre.com.

PART III
STUDENT LIFE

13
'Tea and Kippers'

> In our refectory, over tea and kippers,
> Lives the real Birkbeck, hair down, in its slippers!
> 'V', 'A Note on the Refectory', 1956

> If Birkbeck was a meal, it would be some kind of slightly tepid meat and two veg with roast potatoes and overdone vegetables, and some kind of gravy, maybe cold peas or something like that.
> Mike Berlin, Oral History Project, 2016

Emma 'Ma' Francis, née Steele (see Fig. 13.1), spent half a century cooking for and generally looking after Birkbeck staff and students.[1] She was their confidante, adviser, and mother-figure. 'Ma' Francis had long, silky, dark black hair; her eyes were 'a beautiful velvety brown'; and she was said to have a 'sweet & unselfish nature, ready to return good for evil'.[2] According to Arnolfo John Caraffi, the College Secretary between 1952 and 1979, 'Ma' Francis

> was demanding of respect—which she gained unquestionably—and was loved by all in so far as the boundaries of respect would allow. She was short, motherly in figure, and had jet-black hair piled in plaited ringlets on the top of her head with a precision which might have called for a template. She always wore a self-imposed jet-black, full-length dress, starched white cuffs and Eton collar, the latter secured at the throat by a large and beautiful cairngorm brooch, and a spotless white bib apron of ample Victorian cut. But beneath this impressive confection there beat a warm heart, most warmly for 'my' College and 'my' students who came jointly first in her loyalties and order of life.[3]

She was steeped in what it meant to be a Victorian woman. Although a woman of 'great character', she 'never departed from the behaviour or principles of her Victorian origin'.[4]

---

[1] L. B. Castello (solicitor at Bull and Bull), 'Gasson Correspondence', dated 13 September 1979, in 'Staff Correspondence 1929–1939', in Birkbeck Archive, Box 8.
[2] Letter from L. A. Wilson ('Ma' Francis' daughter) to Arnolfo John Caraffi, 17 December 1963, in the Birkbeck Archive.
[3] Arnolfo John Caraffi, 'Memories of Breams II', in Birkbeck Archive, Box 15.
[4] Ibid.

Fig. 13.1 'Ma' Francis in her youth (with her husband, Alfred) and in old age (with her daughter, L. A. Wilson, and dog). Birkbeck Archive.

'Ma' Francis joined the staff in the College's Fetter Lane refectory in 1896, when she was 30 years old. She left fifty years later when she was 80. When complaints about the refectory reached a fever-pitch, the catering company was dismissed but 'Ma' Francis remained. She pragmatically substituted cold ham for grilled steak and chops.[5] Admittedly, grumbles about College food never ceased, but she managed to 'hold her own' and became a popular fixture of the College. She was proclaimed a 'deity' who 'preside[d] over her food and the hungry children fighting over a sugar basin'.[6]

As was common in Britain prior to the First World War, employment tended to run in families. 'Ma' Francis' *mother* also worked at Birkbeck, probably in the kitchens alongside her daughter and, later, in the women's cloakroom. Indeed, 'Ma' Francis' mother was still being employed in the College in 1931 when she was 83 years old. She was described by the then College Secretary as 'a remarkably active old lady' who was 'allowed to do a turn of four hours each day in the women's cloak room'. In fact, he recalled, the job 'actually consists of little more than sitting in the room, as it is in the early part of the day when there are very few people about'.[7]

'Ma' Francis' husband, Alfred, also worked at Birkbeck. He was an attendant, working his way up to the position of Head Porter. Like his wife, Alfred was a 'striking example' of the 'Birkbeck spirit': he was a man 'in whom implicit reliance

---

[5] 'T.H.', 'Mrs Francis', *The Lodestone*, 39.1 (autumn 1946), 32.

[6] M. R., 'My Impressions of Birkbeck. By a Foreign Student', *The Lodestone*, 20.1 (Michaelmas 1924), 36.

[7] The mother's name was Emma Gasson, so she had probably married twice. Letter from Troup Horne to L. B. Castello (solicitor at Bull and Bull), dated 19 February 1931, in Birkbeck Archive, Box 8. The company was based at 238 Gray's Inn Road.

could always be placed' and who 'never failed in the fulfilment of his duty'.[8] Furthermore, he could 'turn his hand to most anything, cook, cobble or carpentry'.[9] The two Francises' value to the College is suggested by the fact that, in 1920, she was being paid 30s. and her husband earned 35s. a week. The wages of other attendants ranged from 15s. to 27s.[10]

The First World War bolstered 'Ma' Francis' already formidable reputation. She was known to 'express her opinion freely with regard to the Hun'.[11] Even when bombs dropped in Chancery Lane and the Strand, she was 'unruffled', calmly handing out mugs of coffee and 'sardines on toast, with fried tomatoes twopence extra'.[12] After all, as she put it, 'people still wanted to be fed'.[13]

Tragedy struck in close succession, however. In 1918, a son and a daughter died within nine months of each other, probably during the influenza epidemic that killed more Britons than had died during the war.[14] Five years later, in 1923, her beloved husband Alfred 'caught a chill and was dead in a few days'.[15] He was only 49 years old and had been Head Attendant for twenty-two years.[16] Then, on 18 February 1931, her elderly mother was knocked down in Theobald's Road by a delivery-boy on a bicycle who worked for the Anglo-French Drug Company. She was rushed to nearby Gray's Inn Hospital where she died. The solicitors for the College contended that the tragedy had been 'brought about by accident and not through any real negligence on the part of the boy'.[17] Faced with the death of the matriarch, 'Ma' Francis' family were plunged into 'poor circumstances'.[18] 'Ma' Francis was devastated, but told people 'Steele by name and steel by nature—that's me.'[19]

Although the interwar years were shrouded in mourning, 'Ma' Francis kept working, earning the respect and affection of everyone in the College. George Francis Troup Horne (the College's Secretary between 1919 and 1952) was one of her many friends. Indeed, he was 'Ma' Francis' clear favourite in the College. In

---

[8] 'G.F.T.H' [George Francis Troup Horne, the College Secretary], 'Alfred Francis (1901–1923)', *The Lodestone*, 19.2 (spring 1924), 90.
[9] 'T.H.', 'Mrs Francis', *The Lodestone*, 39.1 (autumn 1946), 33.
[10] These sums exclude the war bonuses: 'Minutes of Meeting of Governing Body. Monday 16th February, 1920', in the 'B.C. Minute Book. 22nd Sep., 1919 to 25th July 1922', in the Birkbeck Archive.
[11] 'T.H.', 'Mrs Francis', *The Lodestone*, 39.1 (autumn 1946), 32.   [12] Ibid., 32.
[13] Ibid., 32.
[14] L. A. Wilson (daughter) to Arnolfo John Caraffi, the College Secretary, 17 December 1963, in the Birkbeck Archive.
[15] 'T.H.', 'Mrs Francis', 33.
[16] *Birkbeck College (University of London). Report on the One Hundred-and-First Session 1923–1924* (London: Birkbeck College, 1924), 6.
[17] See the letter to Troup Horne from the solicitor's firm Bull and Bull, dated 20 March 1931 and the letter from Troup Horne to L. B. Castello (solicitor at Bull and Bull), dated 19 February 1931, in 'Staff Correspondence 1929–1939', Birkbeck Archive, Box 8.
[18] L. B. Castello (solicitor at Bull and Bull), 'Gasson Correspondence', dated 13 September 1979, in 'Staff Correspondence 1929–1939', Birkbeck Archive, Box 8.
[19] 'T.H.', 'Mrs Francis', 33.

1924, one student light-heartedly complained about 'Ma' Francis' soft spot for the College Secretary. The poem went:

> Of course, you know that everyone
> Who wishes to get tea,
> Must stand along the buffet bar,
> Thenceforth to wait and see.
> I saw a tray with rich fruit cake,
> I said, 'Is that for me?'
> The lady that took out the tray
> Looked up at me with scorn,
> And said the cake was not for sale,
> But kept for Mr. H—e.[20]

It is not too fanciful to imagine that their friendship was fuelled by their shared passion for cooking. The portly Troup Horne was an oenophile and gourmet, famous for his feasts, including ones featuring the pigeons he captured on the roof of the College.[21] He and 'Ma' Francis would don their chef's aprons and caps and, in a companionate fashion, prepare 'delicious titbits' for the various functions organized by the Students' Union.[22]

Their friendship was not only about matters culinary. Troup Horne was in awe of 'Ma' Francis' unwavering stoicism. He recalled hearing a deafening explosion one day and, rushing to the refectory, found 'Ma' Francis coolly serving scrambled eggs. 'That'll be 5d. the eggs, 2d. the coffee, cake 2d. and banana 2d. dear', he heard her telling 'a scared looking customer'. Horne asked: 'Anything wrong?', to which 'Ma' Francis replied: 'No, Sir.... The gas stove blew up and burned my eyebrows off, but I saved the eggs', before turning to the next customer with the words 'and what's for you?'[23]

'Ma' Francis did not only have to contend with technical mishaps and hungry students, staff, and scholars. Occasionally, she faced troubles with her own kitchen-helpers. One of these dramas involved a Mr Derbyshire from Poplar. On 2 January 1936, he wrote to Mrs Francis c/o 'The Canteen Staff, Birbeck [sic] College'. He advised her to ask the 'So Called Mrs Derbyshire' who worked in the canteen for her real name and address since 'she is no wife of mine'. She had left him eighteen months previously. This 'So Called Mrs Derbyshire' had told the College that she was living with her mother in Queens Building but, in reality, she was living in a 'Tap back room' (that is, in a room behind where brewers sell beer)

---

[20] 'Jake', 'To the Editor', *The Lodestone*, 20.1 (1924), 23–4.
[21] 'G. T.', 'A Word About G. F. Troup Horne', *The Lodestone*, 44.2 (spring/summer 1953), 4.
[22] W. R. Wooldridge, 'Birkbeck Reminiscences', *The Lodestone*, 53.2 (spring 1963), 11.
[23] 'T.H.', 'Mrs Francis', 33.

at 1 Dagmar Terrace, Essex Road. The 'So Called Mrs Derbyshire' was a grandmother with a 27-year-old son and a 30-year-old daughter but was living with a 'bit of a chap 2 years younger than her own son'. This 'chap' had formerly been a 'pal' of her son. The couple called themselves Mrs and Mrs Saunders even though they were not married. She 'as [sic] to come to work to help keep him', Mr Derbyshire informed 'Ma' Francis. He also accused the 'So Called Mrs Derbyshire' of stealing food from the College, including 'eggs bacon Tea Sugar bread and ham' as well as the popular brank of cigarettes called Churchman's. He said that his former wife used to be employed by her daughter's mother-in-law but had been 'put off' (that is, fired) for 'stealing £10 for this bit of a chap and Disgraced her own Daughter over him'.[24] Mr Derbyshire asked 'Ma' Francis to show his letter to 'Mr Troopon The (Secy)', by whom he meant Troup Horne, the Secretary. We do not know how 'Ma' Francis dealt with the 'So Called Mrs Derbyshire', but she clearly did pass the letter on to Troup Horne, who—efficient as always—filed it away.

If Troup Horne and Caraffi (the College Secretaries who, between then, served for an impressive sixty years from 1919) had been awestruck with 'Ma' Francis's sangfroid during the First World War, they were even more impressed by her mettle in the Second World War. In a letter to Miss Winsland, a refectory cook immediately before the war, Troup Horne wrote that

> Mrs Francis is really great. She clocks in at 10 a.m. Joints in the oven by 10.15, and ready to be carved by noon. Refectory luncheons commence at 12.30 and as the old lady insists on having half a dozen alternatives[,] the fun is fast and furious. However, she manages to get through this.[25]

As during the 1914–1918 war, 'Ma' Francis was not shy about expressing 'in a few concise phrases' about what she thought of 'Herr Hitler' and was unperturbed when 'bombs fell, fires started, mains burst'. Worse was to come, however. Early on the morning of Sunday, 11 May 1941, incendiary bombs started dropping on the College and surrounding buildings. Troup Horne recalled that, even though bombs destroyed the library and 'the whole district was a heap of rubble', 'Ma' Francis made her way to the College's kitchen. She told him that a 'Policeman in Fetter Lane tried to stop me', saying: 'Can't go down there, Ma.' She abruptly retorted, 'Impudence. Young man... I've got my work to do—you can't stop me.' And work, she did. Although the building next to Birkbeck was a 'a raging inferno'

---

[24] Letter from Mr Derbyshire to Mrs Francis, 2 January 1936, and letter from Mr Derbyshire to Mrs Francis, 21 January 1936, in Birkbeck Archive, Box 43–44. He claimed that a Mr Tutall knew about her 'going ons' before employing her.
[25] Letter from Troup Horne to Miss Winsland (refectory cook between 1936 and 1939), dated 22 January 1940, in Birkbeck Archive, 'Wartime Correspondence of the Clerk 1939–41' (p. 95 of file).

and the 'gas cut off, air full of smoke and the floors covered with ash and water', 'Ma' Francis made coffee for everyone on a primus and then set about serving 150 people for lunch. Troup Horne reported hearing her muttering, 'Lucky I cooked the joints yesterday'![26]

* * *

People like 'Ma' Francis are the often forgotten yet essential workers who sustain university life. Others in Birkbeck's history include Mary Bridget McNulty, telephonist, and Bikash Kusam Sarkar, General Office clerk, both of whom worked for Birkbeck for around twenty years each.[27] They also include 'porters' or 'attendants' like Alfred Francis, without whom the staff and students in the College would be—literally—lost.

For half a century, 'Ma' Francis made sure that Birkbeck's students, staff, and lecturers had a place within the College where they could purchase something to eat and drink before or after class. She exemplified the adage that food and drinks do more than merely sustain a community: they create communities.

The physical, emotional, and communal importance of food meant that its provision was always having to be negotiated and renegotiated. Indeed, one of the most contentious aspects of College life was its refectory, Staff Common Room, and other places of refreshment. The Staff Common Room was sometimes referred to as an 'obscure thieves' kitchen' whose 'gloom hastens the departure of any Staff member of sensibility & leaves others in the profundity of rank despair and cut-throat resolutions'.[28] This was not because these were badly managed spaces, although at times they probably were. Rather, preparing large quantities of cheap food for students who all planned to dine at around the same time (that is, immediately before their classes) was always going to be challenging. Student tastes also changed with lightning speed, catching menu-planners unaware. The symbolic power of specific 'tastes' and their visual 'staging' could baffle the most conscientious managers of student refectories.

Luckily for Birkbeck students and staff, however, the College was never a campus university, isolated on some green pastures on the outskirts of a town. Its central locations—whether in the Strand, Chancery Lane, Malet Street, Russell Square, Gordon Square, Gresse Street, or any of its other 'outposts'—meant that students could easily find sustenance outside its parameters. Small restaurants offering 'chop and steak' in the early evening before classes were plentiful,[29] as were coffee shops and bars selling cheap snacks. William Bull, who took art classes at the LMI during the 1880s, frequented Keenes Coffee Shop, close by in

---

[26] 'T.H.', 'Mrs Francis', 33.
[27] 'Mrs Mary Bridget McNulty' and 'Bikash Kusam Sarkar' both died in 1994, in Birkbeck Archive, Box 58.
[28] Letter from Arthur Jones to Troup Horne, dated 23 March 1943, in Birkbeck Archive, Box 43.
[29] Bull, 'Forty Years Back', 3. This restaurant was located 'where the Law Institution now stands'.

Holborn. Keenes had the added advantage of stocking the *Illustrated London News*: Bull delighted in the serial tales of James Payne while he gorged on 'tea, eggs, and bacon'.[30] Bull went on the establish 'Bull and Bull' solicitors, who were so important during the 'Sammy Crisis' of the 1960s, discussed in the previous chapter. By the 1920s, when Birkbeck was located in Bream's Building, 'multitudes of Birkbeck students' could be seen milling about 'in the restaurants and tea-shops in the neighbourhood of the College'.[31] When the College moved to its Malet Street accommodation, the indisputable favourite was Pizza Paradiso (now, Olivelli), a 'little piece of Sicily' that had been based in Store Street since 1934.[32] There was also the Alfred restaurant in Bloomsbury Street (a favourite of the Law Department) with its Formica tablecloths, abrupt waiters, and promises of a peculiarly 'English' menu. In those pre-Nigella days, that meant over-cooked meats and mushy peas.

College-based nutrition was less reliable. Complaints focused on two issues: quality and environment. First, there was the food itself. The 'stale cakes' and 'slack' service of 'The Refrec' (as it was called) were the focus of numerous jokes and complaints.[33] In 1924, a 'student from overseas' confessed that he always sat with his 'back turned to the buffet' since the 'sight of that food prevents me from feeling hungry'.[34] Wasn't it time, another student asked, that 'the Refectory was placed under the control of the representatives of these who use it most?' She wanted the Students' Union to take over control, preferably by appointing a 'Kitchen Committee, which would be a body approachable by students with suggestions'.[35]

The environment was also disagreeable. Musty green curtains and uncomfortable seats made dining an unpleasant experience, one student grumbled in the 1920s.[36] By the 1950s, severe over-crowding was reported, mainly because staff and students from other colleges in the University of London could use Birkbeck's canteen. Indeed, customers did not even need a connection with *any* college to purchase food and drinks there. Birkbeck students found themselves crowded out in the evenings, facing a choice between remaining hungry, arriving late for class, or even, in the sciences, slipping away during experiments to grab a quick bite to eat.[37] When the House Committee in 1955 proved slow in arranging a special

---

[30] Ibid.
[31] 'Editorial', *The Lodestone*, 22.1 (1926), 3; Sylverter Savigear, 'The Lost Wits', *The Lodestone*, 22.3 (1927), 123; 'Jake', 'To the Editor', *The Lodestone*, 20.1 (1924), 24.
[32] Melanis Pursey, '"Decadent" Food and Perfect Cappuccino', *Lamp and Owl*, 3 (February/March 2001), 10.
[33] 'Editorial', *The Lodestone*, 22.1 (1926), 3; Sylverter Savigear, 'The Lost Wits', *The Lodestone*, 22.3 (1927), 123; 'Jake', 'To the Editor', *The Lodestone*, 20.1 (1924), 24.
[34] 'By a Foreign Student' ['M.R.'], 'My Impressions of Birkbeck', *The Lodestone*, 20.1 (1924), 35.
[35] Miss E. P. Browne, 'Letter to the Editor', *The Lodestone*, 20.1 (1924), 23.   [36] Ibid., 23.
[37] Jean M. Clarke and E. Wasservogel, 'Report from the Union Representatives on the House Committee', in *Birkbeck College Students' Union Annual Report for the Session 1954-55* (London: BCSU, 1955), 4.

meeting to discuss what many students regarded as a crisis, student representatives went straight to the governors. There, it was decided that the refectory's priority should be the needs of Birkbeck students. Henceforth, only members of the College and the Institute of Education would be allowed to dine in the evenings. The unfortunate consequence was that prices had to be raised by 10 per cent. It was an acceptable compromise.[38]

* * *

Complaints continued, however, reaching a crescendo in 1970. There was talk of being served a 'grisley [sic] concoction' that was 'reminiscent' of the food meted out at cheap railway stations.[39] The President of the Students' Union claimed that the roast potatoes were over-cooked and usually cold; the 'state of the cabbage' was unspeakable.[40] To make matters worse, the food was served in a room that had opened twenty years earlier to cater for just over 1,500 students. By 1970, it was catering for 2,400. Crowding was inevitable.[41]

This time, however, the students had the active support of the academic staff—including the sociologist Sami Zubaida, who had recently been appointed to the new Department of Politics and Sociology. As a scholar who was to become a distinguished food sociologist and critic, he had more than a passing interest in the state of the College's stomachs. Although he had not published his important research on culinary cultures at that time, he already had an interest in the cultural and social meanings of food and the ritualistic value of 'breaking bread' together with other people. Zubaida was fascinated with the power structures underlying the consumption of food but also believed that 'those who eat together implicitly mark their common identity'.[42] In other words, he understood the importance of coffee shops, pubs, and restaurants for the advancement of educational, social, and political movements.

Along with Eila M. J. Campbell from the Geography Department, John Jennings from physics, and B. Plunkett of the House Committee, Zubaida decided the way to wield influence was through a systematic College-wide questionnaire. The results were not surprising. Nearly 60 per cent of the 109 respondents were dissatisfied with the quality of the food; over 70 per cent would be willing to pay more for higher-quality offerings.[43] Numerous respondents claimed that the food was over-cooked and cold. Prices were too high; portions, too small. Cleanliness was not satisfactory, either. Zubaida, Campbell, Jennings, and Plunkett loudly

---

[38] Ibid., 4.   [39] 'C.J.F.', 'New Refectory Boss', *Spectrum*, 3.7 (1970), 3.
[40] Tony Lake (President of the Student Union), 'Glorious Food?', *Spectrum*, 3.8 (1970), 2.
[41] Ibid., 2. Also see 'Action on Refectory', *Spectrum*, 3.8 (1970), 1.
[42] Richard Tapper and Sami Zudaida, 'Introduction', in Zubaida and Tapper (eds), *Culinary Cultures of the Middle East* (London: I. B. Tauris, 1994), 11.
[43] Eila M. J. Campbell, John Jennings, B. Plunkett, and S. D. Zubaida, 'S.C.R. Questionnaire on Refectory Facilities (December 1970)', in the 'House Committee Minutes Apl [sic] 1965 to Nov. 1983', in the Birkbeck Archive.

proclaimed that poor dining facilities in the College were having a 'disintegrative effect on our community', leading to a 'breakdown of the custom of meeting over meals'.[44]

Part of the problem was economic: the refectory staff were paid wages far below the minimum expected by the Employment Exchange. In fact, their wages were even lower than those paid to workers in the neighbouring Senate House canteen.[45] What could be expected from 'low-grade casual labour', especially when staff were often required to perform a large range of tasks due to unfilled vacancies in the kitchen?[46]

The pressure on the College was ramped up when, in 1973, other University refectories in the area (including SOAS, University College, School of Pharmacy, School of Hygiene, ULU, Senate House, and the Institute for Child Health) were surveyed. It revealed that Birkbeck was typically more expensive in every respect except for coffee.[47] Although the *quality* of the food in these different refectories were similar, the survey concluded that 'general cleanliness, quality of service and the whole environment were markedly inferior' at Birkbeck.[48] The problems were most pronounced in the newly opened refectory in Greese Street, which was where Zubaida and Campbell had their offices. To make matters worse, the Greese Street facility was making a 'crippling' £38.80 deficit for every £100 turnover.[49]

The problem could not be resolved quickly. After all, staff and students had 'lost the habit of eating at the Malet Street refectory and that habit will not be quickly restored', the House Committee reported.[50] The College's Working Party asked for an increase in the subsidy paid to the refectory, even though it would have to come from bar profits.[51] Even that would not be enough: the fundamental solution was only to be found in improving the way the refectory was managed.[52]

As a result of their report, a Senior Catering Adviser from the University Grants Committee was sent to investigate. He noted that there were two main causes of the deficit. The first was that Birkbeck, unlike many other colleges, did not have a 'fixed income to cover fixed costs' (as did colleges with a hall of residence, for example).[53] This meant that demand fluctuated widely over the course of the year, plummeting during the summer vacation. The fact that the Birkbeck refectory had to remain open until late in the evening exacerbated this problem,

---

[44] Ibid.
[45] G. B. Davenport (Chairman, Consumers' Group), 'House Committee—6th July 1972. Report of the Refectory Consumers' Group—June 1972', in the 'House Committee Minutes Apl [sic] 1965 to Nov. 1983', in the Birkbeck Archive.
[46] Ibid.
[47] J. Richardson (Chairman), 'House Committee—5th November 1973. Agenda Item 5. Interim Report of the Refectory Working Party', in the 'House Committee Minutes Apl [sic] 1965 to Nov. 1983', in the Birkbeck Archive.
[48] Ibid.   [49] Ibid.   [50] Ibid.
[51] Ibid.   [52] Ibid.
[53] F. M. Cowell (Senior Catering Adviser from the University Grants Committee), 'Catering Survey 1974', in the 'House Committee Minutes Apl [sic] 1965 to Nov. 1983', in the Birkbeck Archive.

as did the need to maintain a second refectory in Gresse Street and the fact that the profitable section of the catering—the bar—had been handed over to the Students' Union in April 1973.[54] The solution was dramatically to improve the management, training of staff, and facilities.[55]

* * *

The refectory was not the only place where Birkbeck's students, staff, and lecturers sought sustenance. For liquid sustenance, they also turned to local pubs and the College Bar. In the early decades of the LMI/Birkbeck, the management was hostile to the serving of alcohol on its premises. After all, as we saw in Chapter 2, the Institution was explicitly intended to provide working men with evening alternatives to the tavern. But by the early decades of the twentieth century, this puritanical approach to alcohol consumption was out of favour. By the 1930s, a student could be heard pleading with the College at least to allow students to purchase good-quality beer in the refectory. Beer was an indispensable 'aid to social intercourse, the loosener of tongues, the breaker down of barriers', he maintained. He believed that allowing staff and students to sip beer in the College refectory was better than requiring them to retire to the Blue Anchor pub, a favourite haunt for Londoners since 1749 and located next to Bream's Building, to discuss the most exciting ideas in their academic fields.[56] The importance of the Blue Anchor for Birkbeckian sociability can be seen in the words of a ditty composed around the time when plans were being made to move the College away from its Chancery Lane location and towards Bloomsbury. Students lamented what this would mean for sociability. They sang:

> Anchor, Blue Anchor, Oh what shall I do
> When I can hold fast no longer to you?[57]
> Henceforth only the prospect is blue—
> Bring back the Anchor to me.
> > Bring back, Oh bring back the Anchor to me!
> > Bring it to me! Bring it to me!
> > Bring back the Anchor, Blue Anchor to me!
> > Bring the Blue Anchor to me!
> Buildings, Breams Buildings are lost to the view.
> Gone are the Gas Lamps I oft have clung to.
> Lost, alas lost is my Anchor of Blue—
> Bring my Blue Anchor to me.
> > Never again the Blue Anchor shall see

---

[54] Ibid. [55] Ibid.
[56] 'Blue Anchorite', 'Letter to the Editor', *The Lodestone*, 31.3 (summer 1936), 137.
[57] 'Our "Kiddies" Corner', *The Lodestone*, 28.1 (Michaelmas 1932), 46.

> Me on the spree, Me on the spree.
> Never again shall it see
> Me up the Lane on the spree.
> Lanes—Fetter, Chancery—sights of the Strand,
> Buses and barrows and Bobbies all stand,
> But the old Cock and the Mitre are banned,
> With the Blue Anchor for me.[58]

A much more acerbic lament about the consequences of the move to Bloomsbury in terms of pub life could be heard in 1933. Like the author of the ditty 'Blue Anchor', this student lamented the absence of traditional pubs in that more 'refined' area of London. It went:

> Where are the Pubs in Bloomsbury
> Like those of Fetter Lane?—
> For Pubs, I'm told, in Bloomsbury
> Are looked on with disdain;
> And if no Pubs in Bloomsbury,
> Why, who can stand the strain?[59]

Who was to blame for the lack of pub life in Bloomsbury? The poet blamed the likes of writer Virginia Woolf and society hostess Lady Ottoline Morrell, whose homes in Gordon Square and Gower Street, respectively, are now owned by Birkbeck. He accused 'Bloomsbury folk' of being

> more *refaned*
> And terribly *polate*,
> *End et mai eccent* they'd be pained,
> *End* think me awful, *quate*,
> Till in the end you'd *faind mai maind*
> In *quate* a rotten state.
> The Bloomsbury *at* they "front" to *et*,
> Their *and* is "raised" to *end*,—
> End so Ai hev to reeze mai het—
> You see how diphthongs tend?
> Their [e] to [i] they have to get,
> Their sighs like saighs ascend.[60]

---

[58] Ibid., 46. There is one final verse, not included here.
[59] R. J. Mitchell, 'Bloomsbury', *The Lodestone*, xxviii.2 (spring 1933), 143.
[60] Ibid., 144.

Fig. 13.2 The Student Bar in 1970. Birkbeck Image Collections: Birkbeck History BH0237.

Bloomsbury 'folk' sip tea and expensive wines—their tastes are too rarefied for Beckbeckian students, more accustomed to the Blue Anchor.

Once the move to the Malet Street premise took place, tea, wine, and beer, as well as the occasional spirit, were imbibed in the Staff Common Rooms and Student Bar (see Fig. 13.2). For Amy Marjorie (A. M.) Dale, the first female Professor of Classics at Birkbeck, where she was based between 1959 until she retired in 1963, the Staff Common Room served as her 'own little salon' where she would sip tea with colleagues before lectures.[61] Something a lot stronger was introduced by Zubaida. One of the first things he organized when he arrived at Birkbeck was whisky tastings on Burns' night. Staff would gather in the Senior Common Room to taste malt whisky, after which they would switch to 'ordinary whisky' for the rest of the evening. Zubaida would bring home-prepared haggis and neeps; some members of the staff would wear kilts; others would recite poetry, chant, sing, and read aloud. On a couple of occasions, pipers accompanied the festivities. They all lamented the closing of the Senior Common Room by Master Tessa Blackstone who, Zubaida believes, thought that the very idea of a Senior Common Room was 'elitist'.[62] It was a food and drink tradition at Birkbeck that did not survive Zubaida's retirement in 2003, although he remains active within the school as Emeritus Professor.

---

[61] R. P. Winnington-Ingram, 'Amy Marjorie Dale, 1902–1967', *Proceedings of the British Academy*, 53 (1967), 434.
[62] Sami Zubaida, interviewed for the Birkbeck Oral History Project, 2017.

The bar, however, survived. As late as the early 2000s, it was routine (indeed, in some departments, *expected*) for lecturers to join their students after class for a beer or glass of wine after classes ended at 9 p.m. The more informal debates about academic issues that took place in the bar were believed to bolster student learning.

This practice was encouraged by the presence of 'legends' in bar management. One of these was Pat O'Shaughnessy, bar manager for twenty years from 1969.[63] Similar to 'Ma' Francis, he was a 'strong character' who added 'a bit of life and colour to what was once a dull place'.[64] He was also 'a shrewd judge of character.... Affectation, insincerity and pomposity got short shrift.' Crucially, he was a Birkbeckian, devoted to the students and determined to give them the 'best service at the least cost—as many [Students' Union] Presidents, with an eye on the bar profits, will testify!'[65] He never married and had no close family, but when he died on St Valentine's Day 1988 from an aggressive cancer more than a hundred Birkbeck staff and students attended Mass for him at St Dominic's Priory in Southampton Road, followed by a funeral in West Hampstead cemetery and a wake in the Junior Common Room. Like 'Ma' Francis, the College is sustained by people like O'Shaughnessy.

* * *

Unlike O'Shaughnessy, 'Ma' Francis aged slowly. By the mid-1940s, she began to suffer from aches and pains that could no longer be ignored. Her once-ample body gradually shrunk. Her dropsy required regular mercury injections.[66] She had heart problems. Her daughter reported that a growth at the back of her right eye 'causes a blob of light which she is so sure is a face where-ever she looks'.[67] When she was 95 years old, Caraffi as well as the wife of the Master (known as 'Mrs Gordon Jackson') would visit. Caraffi and the College remained loyal to 'Ma' Francis. When the owners of her home threatened to double the rent or evict her, Caraffi arranged for her mortgage to be paid and he ensured that her pension was generously supplemented.[68] After an operation, 'Ma' Francis' daughter taught her to crochet, embroider, and knit, hoping that it was be something to 'occupy her mind'. As she told Caraffi,

---

[63] Tony Lake, 'New Character', *Spectrum*, 3.2 (17 October 1970), 2.

[64] R. E. Swainson (Clerk to the Governors), in 'Pat O'Shaughnessy', *Spectrum*, 5 (April 1988), 2, and *Student Union. A Guide for the Session 1970–1971 and a Report for the Session 1969–70. Birkbeck College*, ed. Chris Milsome (London: BCSU, 1971), 39.

[65] Swainson in 'Pat O'Shaughnessy', 2.

[66] Letter from L. A. Wilson to Arnolfo John Caraffi, the College Secretary, dated 1 April 1959, 'Mrs Francis', in Birkbeck Archive, Box 33.

[67] L. A. Wilson of 120 Cranly Gardens to Arnolfo John Caraffi, the College Secretary, undated but 1959, 'Mrs Francis', in Birkbeck Archive, Box 33.

[68] Correspondence on 'Mrs Francis', in Birkbeck Archive, Box 33.

She was marvellous! I have a set of table mats she made when she was 85 years old which look machine made[,] they are so perfect. I have treasured them but I feel I would like you to have them, to show a little appreciation of your kindness.[69]

But 'Ma' Francis was also suffering from dementia. Her daughter informed Caraffi that 'Ma' Francis' 'poor mind' was confused. Her mind

> works in reverse, night is day and shaddows [sic] are people, sometimes friendly, sometimes malignant. We have most frightful nights even though she has sleeping pills. She is in and out of bed like a yo-yo.[70]

Other times, she went 'through the motions of picking flowers, talking to and fondling a cat or winding string'. That her decades at Birkbeck were formative for 'Ma' Francis was revealed in a comment made by her daughter in 1959, two years before 'Ma' died. 'She seems to think she is at College among ladies and gentlemen', her daughter reported, suggesting that despite her close friendship with the students, College Secretaries, and Masters of the College, this eminently Victorian woman always knew her 'place' after all.[71]

---

[69] Letter from L. A. Wilson of 120 Cranly Gardens to Arnolfo John Caraffi, the College Secretary, undated but 1959, 'Mrs Francis', in Birkbeck Archive, Box 33.
[70] Ibid.   [71] Ibid.

14
Hares versus Rabbits; Or, Social Lives

Are you a Hare or a Rabbit?

This question bounced off the walls of Birkbeck Students' Common Room in the 1920s. Hares were students who skipped with great speed between the various academic and social programmes offered by the College. In contrast, Rabbits dived into Birkbeck 'as a four-legged rabbit dives down its hole', taking no part in 'anything beyond its lectures, and then run[ning] out again'.[1] Rabbits used the College 'merely as a fountain of knowledge at which one may drink and pass on'.[2] They were 'shy, timid creatures' who could be seen 'scurrying to their homes on the strike of 9 p.m.' Indeed, one Hare scoffed, Rabbit-students were 'lethargic' and 'almost without volition'.[3] As a species, Rabbits never frequented Birkbeck's sports ground in Greenford (Middlesex) and, 'although an occasional stray has been known to wander in the Refectory, looking for food', they avoided the Common Room. In contrast, the library and lecture rooms were 'habitually swarming with them' because they 'live for the most part on dry lectures and the leaves of printed volumes'. As one student joked, unlike their animal-counterpart, student-Rabbits viewed 'wild oats…as poison' and they 'assiduously keep away from any one of human kind who they know, from instinct, sows them'.[4] Rabbits made 'those bold, dashing, young students' who were Hares look like frivolous, frolicsome beings who were always 'dash[ing] to the most comfortable chairs nearest the fire in the Common Room'.[5] It was time to change this misconception, was the Hares' rallying cry: 'Come and be a hare!' became the catchphrase for students involved in Birkbeck's clubs and societies.[6]

There was one obstacle to persuading everyone to be Hares: it was much less demanding to be a Rabbit. As one student lamented in 1925, dances might be well attended but even the most 'loudly trumpeted meeting' to discuss the National Union of Students was sparsely attended. The much-feted Union Dinner and the 'At Home' held in the theatre also only attracted between fifty and ninety people, many of whom were guests. Even worse, the events were organized and attended

---

[1] 'Cicerone', 'To the Editor', *The Lodestone*, 20.2 (1924), 30–1.
[2] 'Editorial', *The Lodestone*, 20.3 (1924), 106.
[3] 'Why the Student Union?', *The Lodestone*, 29.3 (summer 1934), 137.
[4] 'A Guide to Birkbeck', *The Lodestone*, 22.2 (1927), 68.
[5] Cuthbert, 'Rabbits and Elections', *The Lodestone*, 20.3 (1925), 4.
[6] 'Cicerone', 'To the Editor', 30–1.

by the same students. Hare-students often found that the person they sat alongside during the Union Dinner was 'our favourite dancing partner at the last "hop", our opponent in the last Parliamentary debate and our prayerful co-sojourner at the last Christian Union retreat'.[7]

For Hares, the 'morbibundency' [sic] of the Students' Union was frustrating.[8] Of the 1,100 students eligible to vote in the union elections in 1924, only 137 (or 12 per cent) bothered to return ballot papers.[9] Some blamed the low turnout on the fact that most students were 'exhaustively engaged during the day'. This general problem was exacerbated by the fact that students were also increasingly aware that they needed not only a degree but specifically an *honours* degree if they were to compete in commerce or business.[10] In the words of one Rabbit-wit called 'One of the Majority',

> I can't admire those students
> Who wallow in the mud
> With boots, and bats, and Bludgeons,
> To cool their youthful blood;
> Such rough and tumble pastimes
> Hold no appeal to me—
> *I* came to Birkbeck College
> To—get—a—degree...
> They say 'Do come to dances
> (And wear a pair of pumps,
> Because plus fours and plus hobnails
> Fetch up the floor in lumps)
> And meet your fellow-students'.
> Good heavens, can't they see,
> *I* came to Birkbeck College
> To—get—a—degree.[11]

But students were not the only ones divided between Hares and Rabbits. Staff, too, could be distinguished between those who dived into the College to teach their classes at 6 p.m. and left promptly at 9.05 p.m., and those who, in addition to their academic work, threw themselves into social and sporting events. Physicist Nettleton, for example, was a Hare: he was a passionate cricketer and chess player, as well as devoting incredible energy to promoting the women's suffrage movement.[12] So too was Douglas Dakin—known as much for his neo-Hellenic research

---

[7] 'Alpha', 'Are We Doing Too Much?', *The Lodestone*, 20.2 (1925), 20.
[8] 'H.G.', 'Letters to the Editor. The College Theatre—And a Policy', *The Lodestone*, 19.2 (1924), 88.
[9] Ibid., 85.   [10] Ibid., 85.
[11] 'One of the Majority', *The Lodestone*, 28.2 (spring 1933), 67. There are three other stanzas.
[12] W. Ehrenberg, 'Obituaries', *Nature*, 217 (20 January 1968), 296.

as for his work on modern Greece. Dakin and Nettleton were responsible for the successful Cricket Club in the College. In 1935, Dakin led the College's first of a series of cricket tours of Sussex, including matches against Littlehampton, Worthing, Bexhill, and Steyning. Similarly, classicist Frederick ('Freddy') A. Wright was not only a teacher of Latin (in which he was described as having an 'eager voice, now calling upon us to translate, now translating, now commenting, now questioning, kindly, humorous') but also active in Birkbeck athletics.[13] As we heard in the previous chapter, College Secretary Troup Horne threw himself into the kitchen, where he delighted in cooking up delicious food for student occasions. What is less well known is that he was also a committed bibliophile and a collector of over 700 English and American short stories, which are now housed, along with hundreds of other volumes from his collection, in the Senate House Library.[14]

In the English and Philosophy departments, too, Hares prevailed. Stephen Potter (lecturer in English literature at Birkbeck and author of books on Samuel Taylor Coleridge) and C. E. M. Joad (head of Philosophy and Psychology) were famed for skipping enthusiastically between academic and sporting activities. One of their tennis matches has become part of popular culture. On 8 June 1931, Potter and Joad were representing Birkbeck in a match against two much younger and more athletic men from King's College London. The Birkbeck team were 40–0 down when Joad volleyed the ball into the net. However, as

> the server was crossing to serve to Potter, Joad at exactly the right moment (when the server was *not less than one foot and not more than two feet* beyond the centre of the court) called across the net, in an even tone: 'Kindly say clearly, please, whether the ball was in or out.'[15]

Disconcerted and flustered, the Kings' men faltered: Joad and Potter won the match. There is another version of this story. In this version, Joad and Potter triumphed because Joad wore black socks under his immaculately white tennis clothes: the young men from King's could not keep their eyes off 'Joad's sinister black socks and lost the game'.[16]

Whichever version is correct, Potter was initially shocked by Joad's Machiavellian tactic—and then impressed. It was to result in what Potter called 'his sublimely anti-meritocratic theme': gamesmanship. Potter went on to develop this concept in four best-selling books called *Gamesmanship* (1947), *Lifemanship*

---

[13] 'H. G. R.', 'F. A. W.', 125.
[14] Karen Attar (ed.), *Directory of Rare Book and Special Collections in the UK and Republic of Ireland* (London: Facet Publishing, 2016), 239.
[15] Andrew Gimson, 'Boldly Meaningless Genius', *The Spectator* (6 December 1986).
[16] The second version is in George Mikes, '[Letter to the Editor] Origins of Gamesmanship', *The Times* (24 December 1977).

(1950), *One Upmanship* (1952), and *Supermanship* (1958). As Potter later explained, during his game with Joad, he learnt 'The Art of Winning Games Without Actually Cheating' and without 'being very good at them'.[17] Gamesmanship has been praised as an innocent way to 'get ahead' socially; but it has also been panned for epitomizing the vulgarity of capitalist competition.

* * *

There have been debates about the fluctuating vibrancy of social events at the LMI/Birkbeck. Many suspect that students and staff had been more active in the College's social lives in nineteenth-century and pre-war society. They are probably correct. The College can boast of a sporting tradition going back to the establishment of the LMI when physically active students made use of the field next to Southampton Buildings in Chancery Lane. At that time, sports were linked to exploration and empire. It was no coincidence that the main proponent of physical training in the early years of the Institution was John Borthwick Gilchrist, one of the LMI's first Vice-Presidents. He was a surgeon, philologist of Hindustani, and devotee of Carl Voelker's system of gymnastic exercises (see Fig. 14.1). After Voelker had been forced to emigrate from Germany in 1819, he became a passionate proponent of the German Turnen movement, which combined gymnastics with fencing, wrestling, swimming, weightlifting, jumping, and running. Voelker persuaded leading Utilitarians such as Lord Brougham and Jeremy Bentham to support this movement. Gilchrist quickly became a convert, extolling gymnastics as a form of 'national training for English youth with the view of rendering them more physically robust and healthy'.[18] Gilchrist, Voelker, and other enthusiasts set up a 'London Gymnasium' in a 2-acre field that they rented on the west side of Amwell Street, Clerkenwell. They fitted it up with parallel bars, horizontal and leaping poles, wooden horses, and ladders, as well as other gymnastic equipment which could be used by up to 300 people at any one time.[19] Members of the LMI were encouraged to participate in this outdoor 'London Gymnasium' and, when the Institution moved to the new building in Fetter Lane, James C. N. White (Treasurer to the Institution in the 1880s) ensured that the hall was set aside for one evening each week for physical exercise. He opened the classes to women at a time when, as the *Birkbeck Institution Magazine* noted in 1893, 'the attendance of ladies at gymnasia was not so ordinary an occurrence'.[20]

The popular craze for gymnastics was spurred by ideas about the relationship between education and sport, as well as what historians today called 'muscular masculinity'. Physical fitness literally 'maketh the man'. Individual 'character' was fashioned through physical exercise. It was not only a central component for the

---

[17] Andrew Gimson, 'Boldly Meaningless Genius', *The Spectator* (6 December 1986).
[18] Buss, *Eighty Years Experience of Life*, 22.   [19] Ibid., 22.
[20] 'Birkbeck Men. Mr James C. N. White', *Birkbeck Institution Magazine* (March 1893), 54.

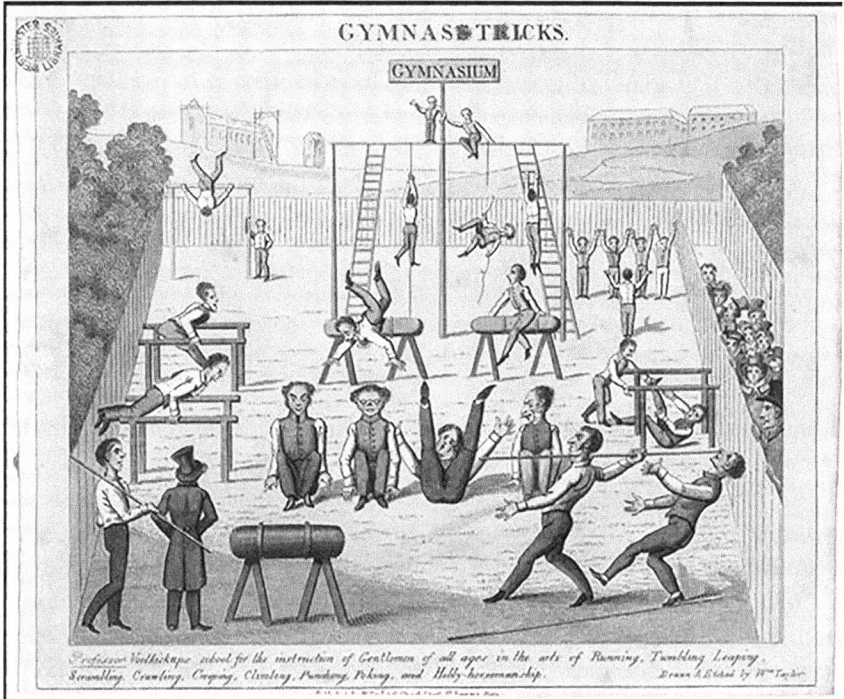

Fig. 14.1 A satirical cartoon captioned 'Professor Voelkickups school for the instruction of Gentlemen of all ages in the arts of Running, Tumbling, Leaping, Scrambling, Crawling, Creeping, Climbing, Pushing, Poking, and Hobby-horsemanship'. Westminster City Archives.

development of an upright personality but also preparation for the 'white man's civilizing mission' in the empire. Gilchrist epitomized this 'mission': he had joined the East India Company as a physician and later popularized Hindustani as the language of the British administration in India. According to all reports, Gilchrist was not a pleasant man—indeed, he was 'an obstreperous character', totally dedicated to 'harnessing the "national" language of "Hindustan" to the colonial yoke', according to historian Richard Steadman-Jones. Admittedly, Steadman-Jones conceded that Gilchrist regarded 'the adoption of an Indian "vernacular" as a liberatory act'. But this was 'only to the extent that it would allow the "benevolent" British regime to protect ordinary Indians from the predations of indigenous elites'.[21]

---

[21] Richard Steadman-Jones, *Colonialism and Grammatical Presentation: John Gilchrist and the Analysis of the 'Hindustani' Language in the Late Eighteenth and Early Nineteenth Centuries* (Oxford: Berg, 2007), 63 and 89–90.

Links between empire, physical prowess, and 'character' persisted throughout the century. At the fifty-eighth anniversary of the College in 1881, Robert Bulwer-Lytton (the 1st Earl of Lytton and Viceroy of India between 1876 and 1880) could be heard extolling the benefits of 'character' to the empire. Speaking in the College's lecture theatre, he told the assembled Birkbeckians that 'character was to knowledge just what interest was to money. It was the animating force that rendered it productive.' He reminded his listeners that

> when they considered the extent of this Empire, it was impossible for any of them to speculate, without occasional anxiety, as to the future career of a people invested by its destiny with a sway so vast and a responsibility so momentous.[22]

Team sports and athletics were crucial for developing and building self-control, courage, obedience, teamwork, 'pluck', and a sense of 'fair play'. The Earl failed to see the irony of his statement extolling the virtue of 'fair play' within the imperial mission.

Catchphrases such as self-control, courage, 'pluck', and 'fair play' took a battering with the 1914–18 and 1939–45 world wars. When Birkbeck students returned from each of these wars, sports at Birkbeck once again flourished. On both occasions, the revival was fuelled by the huge influx of ex-servicemen who not only were keen to resume their pre-war sporting lives but had also been exposed to a variety of sport while in the military services and developed a liking for it.[23]

Meeting the demand for sporting facilities in or near the College's main buildings in central London was logistically difficult, however. Before the First World War, Birkbeck's sporting clubs used simply to hire various playing fields in London, including Mill Hill Park and Paddington Green Athletic Ground, the first (from the 1880s) public athletic ground in London.[24] A photograph survives of the 1914 annual sports day held on the Green (see Fig. 14.2). Its finale was a tug-of-war between twelve female students and six male members of the staff and governing body. It was reported to have been 'a most successful innovation' although the 'handicap...was far too heavy', so the female students won 'too easy a victory'.[25]

Being dependent on outside managers for booking sports grounds did not please the enterprising College Secretary, Troup Horne. In 1920, he started looking to rent a specially dedicated College playing field. A subcommittee of the governors, chaired by Hume, persuaded the trustees of the City Parochial

---

[22] 'Lord Lytton on Culture', *The Standard* (10 December 1881), 3.
[23] C. W. Hume, 'How the Greenford Sports Ground was Acquired', *The Lodestone*, 55.3 (summer 1965), 18.
[24] It was first used for cricket in the 1860s but had operated as a public athletic ground since 1888.
[25] 'The College Diary', *The Lodestone*, 9.3 (summer 1914), 83–4. The photograph in *The Lodestone*, which shows the women just prior to starting, was taken by E. A. R. (Alec) Bousfield.

Fig. 14.2 Female students competing in tug-of-war at Paddington Green playing fields in 1914. Birkbeck Image Collections: Birkbeck History BH0212.

Foundation (CPF) to provide a grant enabling the College to purchase 8 acres of a former golf course at Greenford. The CPF then leased the land, along with its pavilion, to the College at 5 per cent interest.[26] Coincidentally, but fortuitously, the grounds were located on Birkbeck Lane, named after the Birkbeck Bank rather than George Birkbeck. Sportsmen and women were delighted.[27] In the 1920s, 17 per cent (or 200 of the College's 1,200 students) used the playing field at Greenford—a remarkably high proportion given that it took forty-five minutes to travel there from the College via the Central Line Tube.

Given such high demand, including from female students, it quickly became clear that the land as well as the pavilion were too small.[28] Six years after the initial purchase, the CPF extended the grounds by an additional 10 acres by annexing an adjoining Turner's Field.[29] By this stage, the site was over 17 acres and

---

[26] 'Application to the University Grants Committee for Non-Recurrent Grants (i) for a new Pavilion at the College Playing Fields (ii) for the Purchase of Back Numbers of Literary and Scientific Periodicals', n.d., 1, in 'UGC', Birkbeck Archive, Box 4; letter from the Clerk to the City Parochial Foundation, 18 October 1920, in 'Minute Book. Societies Finance Committee', in Birkbeck Archive BBK 11/2/1; 'B.C. Minute Book. 22nd Sep. [sic], 1919 to 25th July 1922', 'Minutes of Meeting of the Governing Body. Monday 16th February 1920', 5, in Birkbeck Archive.

[27] Letter from the Clerk to the City Parochial Foundation, 18 October 1920, in 'Minute Book. Societies Finance Committee', in Birkbeck Archive BBK 11/2/1.

[28] 'Application to the University Grants Committee for Non-Recurrent Grants (i) for a new Pavilion at the College Playing Fields (2) for the Purchase of Back Numbers of Literary and Scientific Periodicals', n.d., 2, in 'UGC', Birkbeck Archive, Box 4.

[29] Ibid.

contained facilities not only for cricket, hockey, rugby, and association football (whose motto, incidentally, was 'Ecce testiculos canem' or 'Behold the Dog's Testicles')[30] but also for tennis (grass as well as hard courts), athletics, and netball, and a 25- and 50-yard rifle range. If the size of grants allocated to *all* the societies belonging to the Students' Union is any indication of popularity, then cricket reigned supreme. In the late 1920s, it was allocated 28 per cent of all grants, followed by tennis at 15 per cent, the Law Society at 11 per cent, and fencing at 10 per cent. All other clubs received significantly less money.[31]

Birkbeck's sportsmen and women were also clamouring for an enlarged and more attractive pavilion. On a sunny Saturday in May 1928, it finally opened (see Fig. 14.3).[32] The pavilion cost £10,000—that is, two-and-a-half times the price of an average London house.[33] Scottish peer and banker, George Bruce (the 7th Lord Balfour of Burleigh) used the opportunity to make a speech in favour of female employment. He not only commended the College for giving its students a

Fig. 14.3 The opening of the new pavilion at Greenford in May 1928. Birkbeck Archive.

[30] John Porter, 'QPR, Giggling, Mind Games, and Greenford', 2014, at inbedwithmaradona.com/journal/2014/1/29/qpr-giggling-mind-games-and-greenford, viewed 1 June 2019.
[31] 'Student Union Estimates, 1928–29', 'Minute Book. Societies Finance Committee', 107, in the Birkbeck Archive.
[32] 'Birkbeck College's New Sports Pavilion at Greenford', *Acton Gazette* (1 June 1928), 5.
[33] The average house in London at the time cost £425.

'substantial share in the government of its affairs' but also praised Birkbeck's charter for insisting that 'no disability should be imposed on the ground of sex'. Lord Balfour stated that the 'great principle of partnership between men and women' was one that should be promoted both 'in the home or in general affairs'. He contended that

> The exclusive sphere of either men's work or women's work was a great deal smaller than many people supposed, and the great bulk of the world's work was capable of being done in partnership.[34]

It was a politically confrontational speech since the London County Council (LCC) had only recently decided to follow the Civil Service in banning married women from working as teachers or doctors. But, as Lord Balfour coolly informed the assembled crowds, 'marriage happens more or less equally to men and women alike'. And, contrary to the views of the LCC, the matrimonial state made women *more*, not less, suitable to professions such as teaching and medicine.[35] Lord Balfour then opened the pavilion door, which was decorated with the arms of the University and College; Lady Balfour unveiled a bronze tablet in the hall; and (after a cricket match and 'tea interval') the dancing began.[36] The enlarged grounds and new pavilion were a success. By the 1930s, Greenford was reported to be one of the 'largest sports grounds in London' and boasted about having 'one of the finest pavilions'.[37]

* * *

Sporting traditions were supplemented by other social events in the College's busy calendar, including dinners, the publication of journals and the establishment of clubs. The most notable was the annual dinner, which, in the late nineteenth century, saw between 200 and 300 students and their guests gathering for it. The Common Room and theatre were also crowded. During pre-war 'At Homes', hundreds of Birkbeckians would turn up in evening dress.[38] From the 1850s, students even organized summer excursions (see Fig. 14.4). A. Gavin Burns recalled daytrips to Buckhurst Hill, followed by 'tea at the "Roebuck"'. In the evening, 'the tea room was cleared and a pleasant afternoon concluded with a couple of hours' dancing before returning home'. On another summer jaunt, the 300 students went

---

[34] 'Greenford and Northolt College Sports', *West Middlesex Gazette* (2 June 1928), 10.
[35] 'Sex Equality', *Daily Herald* (28 May 1928), 7.
[36] 'Opening of the New Pavilion', *The Lodestone*, 24.1 (autumn 1928), 16.
[37] A. W. A. Rundle (Athletics Secretary), 'Student Unions, Report on Greenford. To the College Societies Committee, Wednesday, 27th Jan. 1939', 'Minute Book. Societies' Financial Committee', Birkbeck Archive, BBK 11/2/1.
[38] 'Alpha', 'Are We Doing Too Much?', 20.

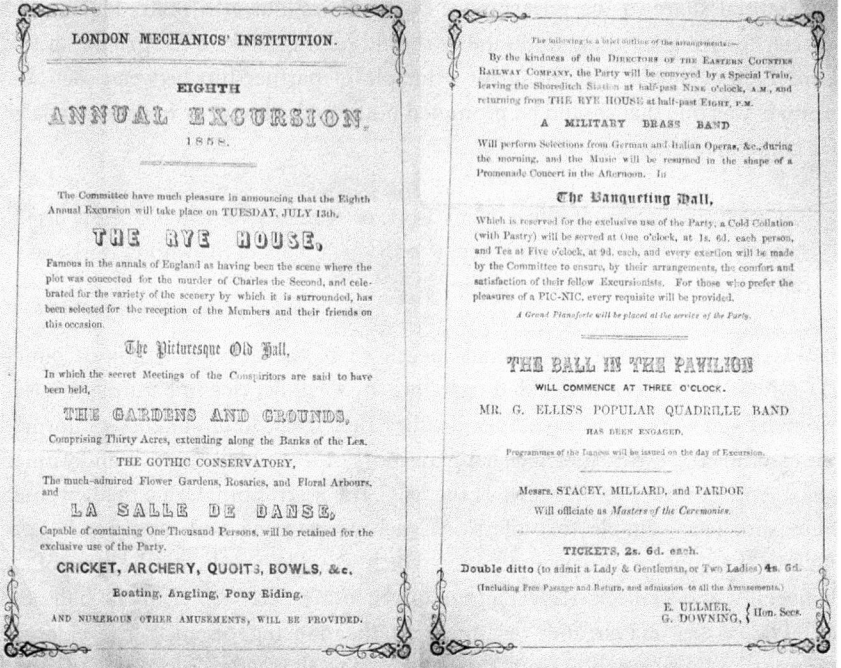

Fig. 14.4 The notice for the 8th Annual Excursion of the London Mechanics' Institution in 1858. Birkbeck Archive, 'A4 Black Ring Binder 1', 63–4.

for a 'moonlight trip' up the Thames, leaving 'the steamer at Richmond to have tea at the once famous hotel, the "Star and Garter"'.[39]

The students also published their own journals. In 1904, when the Students' Union was founded, one of its earliest actions was to inaugurate a student journal, which it called *The Lodestone* (see Fig. 14.5). Prior to this time, there had been a *Birkbeck Institution Magazine*, as well as a magazine published by the Science Society, a few volumes of *Converzational* and *Spectrum*, as well as *Minerva* from 1973. But *The Lodestone* trumped all others, running until the 1960s. Its aim was to provide a forum for communicating to students what was happening within the College, as well as to give students a place to display their creativity and publicize their opinions.[40]

In *The Lodestone*'s first edition, Principal George Armitage-Smith hoped the magazine would

> develop a feeling of *esprit de corps* towards the College, stimulate sentiments of good fellowship, and establish a new bond of sympathy and union among a

---

[39] Burns, 'Reminiscences of the Birkbeck Literary and Scientific Institution', 61.
[40] The Principal, 'Introductory', *The Lodestone*, 1.1 (July 1905), 2.

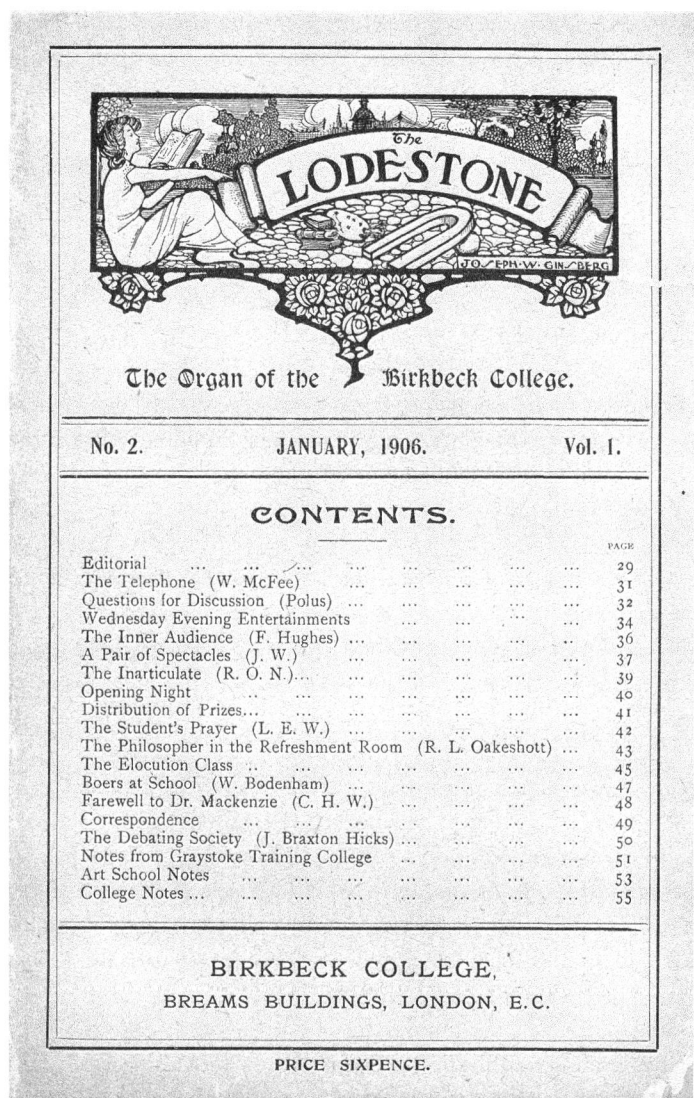

Fig. 14.5 *The Lodestone*'s cover for 1906. Birkbeck Image Collections: Birkbeck History BH0209.

body of students who have already much in common, seeing that they consist of busy and industrious workers, who are seeking earnestly to take advantage of the opportunities of higher education.[41]

[41] Ibid., 3.

In the same issue, and more in tune with the *creative* aims of the fledging magazine, William McFee (who went on to become a well-known author of nautical tales) set forth his views in poetry:

> This latest Bantling of the City's press
> Makes a bold claim for fame,
> Hoping to mould opinion, more or less,
> And justify its claim.
> 'T will prosper, for it bears, thro' storm and stress,
> A lucky name.[42]

That lucky name was *The Lodestone*, taken from Albertus Magnus' treatise on the lodestone. According to Magnus, when a lodestone is put into a fire, it releases its magnetic qualities. The thin blue vapour was the stone's 'disembodied magnetism' or 'soul'. As the Editor explained,

> Lying upon the embers of kindled enthusiasm, *The Lodestone* is giving off certain magnetic and attractive forces, which we may call the spirit of the College, a force that can stir hearts to vigorous and earnest work and awaken the dormant impulses of sympathy and helpfulness in all branches and classes of the College.[43]

Such optimism was almost immediately dashed. By its third issue, the magazine was already in financial crisis. It had 'not received as much support as was anticipated', the Editor conceded, adding that unless students rallied behind it, the magazine would have to be discontinued.[44] Birkbeck students heeded the call: within a couple of decades *The Lodestone* had a circulation of 500, which meant that it was read by at least half of all students.[45] It survived until the 1960s and has recently been revived as the *Lamp and Owl*.

These student journals are important not only because of the way they sought to create a community of Birkbeck students—they were also actively involved in creating communities of *former* as well as current Birkbeckians. The journal was an important resource for the Old Students' Association (OSA) which, when it was revived in December 1919, attracted over a hundred members.[46] The chief functions of the OSA were to arrange social events and reunions and suppers

---

[42] William McFee, 'A Preliminary Statement', *The Lodestone*, 1.1 (July 1905), 3. There is strong (but not definite) reason to believe that this 'William McFee' is the one who ran away to sea around this time and became a well-known author of sea tales: see James Norman Leatherby, 'William McFee: Writing Engineer', *Prairie Schooner*, 23.2 (summer 1949), 171–80.
[43] 'Editorial', *The Lodestone*, 2.2 (June 1907), 30.   [44] Ibid., 58.   [45] Ibid., 107.
[46] B. D. Watters (Hon. Sec.), 'Old Students' Association', *The Lodestone* 16.1 (Michaelmas 1920), 18.

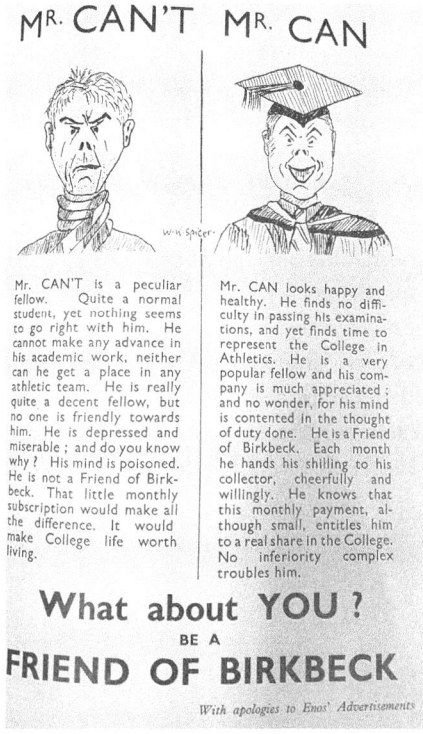

Fig. 14.6 'Mr Can't, Mr Can'. *The Lodestone*, 28.2 (spring 1933), 71.

while also raising funds for a new Common Room in the planned new building. In 1924, Ramsay MacDonald founded the Friends of Birkbeck (FOB). He had been a student in the College from 1885 to 1887 and governor from 1902 to 1907.[47] The FOB was open to 'all who may care to show their interest in the welfare of the College by subscribing to the funds of the Friends of Birkbeck'—in other words, its main function was to raise funds to help build and furnish the Malet Street building.[48] As Helen Gwynne-Vaughan boasted in 1934, the President of the FOB was the Prime Minister and members include former students of Birkbeck from Asia, Africa, Australasia, and America.[49] The main vehicle through which funds were appealed for was *The Lodestone* (see Fig. 14.6).

* * *

At the heart of the social life in Bream's Building (the main Birkbeck home until the opening of the Malet Street building in 1953) was the Common Room (see

---

[47] D. D., 'James Ramsay MacDonald', *The Lodestone*, 32.4 (autumn 1937), 2.
[48] 'Friends of Birkbeck', in Birkbeck Archive, Box 17, File 11.
[49] H. C. I. Gwynne-Vaughan, 'Forward, Birkbeck', *The Lodestone*, 29.2 (spring 1934), 64–6.

Fig. 14.7). To get to it, students needed to enter the main door and walk through the entrance hall to a stairwell on their right. After making their way to the first floor, they would have faced a large blackboard listing all the Students' Union activities for that week. They would then have turned left, pushed through students congregating outside classroom five, passed the Council Room on the left and the refectory on the right, before arriving at some double doors over which was a sign saying: 'Union Common Room'.

It was a bustling room, offering a large range of activities that, in the words of one Hare, were 'superficially a waste of time, yet gave us as much scope for individual development as many hours of lectures'.[50] Prior to the First World War, lecturers mingled with students in the Common Room, contributing to 'students' debates and entertainments as a matter of course', in a way that was thought to be 'agreeable for the students and a valuable education for the staff'.[51] From the 1920s, however, the Common Room became much more of

Fig. 14.7 The 'Old' Common Room, photographed by physicist B. D. H. Watters. Birkbeck Image Collections: Birkbeck History BH0298.

[50] 'Editorial', *The Lodestone*, 19.1 (1923), 3.   [51] Hume, 'Quorum Pars Parva Fui', 73.

an 'in' place for students only. By 1927, some students claimed that it was 'open only to those who can Charleston [a popular dance], play bridge and the gramophone, and who are sufficiently nimble to seize an armchair in front of the fire'.[52] The room was used as a 'dance hall, card-room, smoking lounge, writing room, concert hall, and football ground'—all in one space.[53] In other words, this was the lair of the Hares.

Students used to have to pay 7s. 6d. to use the Common Room, but, by the 1920s, this was not insisted upon: members were simply 'requested, merely as a matter of form, kindly to give a yearly subscription, though they need feel under no obligation to do so'.[54] Some students were said to use the room for 'athletic exercises with the furniture'.[55] It was not a large room but, as one student ruefully admitted, it had comfortable armchairs and it had to be admitted that 'Birkbeck has no spare space anywhere'.[56] This resulted in the over-use of the room, leading to situations in which students became frustrated to find it being occupied for meetings of 'no interest or which your labours have made you too tired to appreciate'.[57]

In 1924, someone signing himself 'a foreign student' described a typical scene in the Common Room. He recalled pushing its 'swing door' and entering a place where students lounged on couches listening to 'a sentimental tune played on an out-of-tune piano'. Amidst the confusion, students conducted numerous meetings. They could be heard

> discussing vital points. Will tenpence or a shilling be granted to the Dramatic Society? Has the Secretary of the Common Room a right to spend so much money on new curtains? Will sixpence be too much for the Christian Union? Will the French Society be granted any thing at all?[58]

This all took place within a 'thick atmosphere' of cigarette smoke. The

> mist [was] so thick with tobacco smoke that I can hardly distinguish the forms moving about the room or the corpses lying on armchairs in such a fashion that I wonder which are the heads, which are the feet.

This student's repeated mention of cigarette smoke was not coincidental: it was a Birkbeck obsession. In the early decades of the twentieth century, the rights of students and staff to smoke in the Common Room, as well as in classrooms and corridors, was hotly debated. Some of the debates harked back to earlier decades,

---

[52] 'A Guide to Birkbeck', *The Lodestone*, 22.2 (1927), 68.   [53] Ibid., 68.
[54] Ibid., 68.   [55] 'P. A.', 'The Common Room', *The Lodestone*, 22.1 (1926), 21–4.
[56] Ibid., 21–4.   [57] Ibid., 21–4.
[58] 'By a Foreign Student' ['M.R.'], 'My Impressions of Birkbeck', *The Lodestone*, 20.1 (1924), 36.

when leading members of the LMI sought to impose a strict moral code on its members, signalling to the outside world the respectability and social mobility of working men. This was why in 1906, when C. W. Hume joined the Institution, there were rules against smoking, swearing, drinking, and dancing in the college.[59] These had crumbled after the First World War but, by the 1930s, smoking was still not allowed in classrooms, corridors, and the entrance hall. However, it was actively *encouraged* in the refectory and Common Room. Indeed, the FOB even promoted its own brand of tobacco called the 'Birkbeck Rough Cut', which was 'blended from an old Naval formula by a leading City tobacconist'. It advised purchasers that the best way to smoke the 'Birkbeck Rough Cut' was in a 'Birkbeck Pipe'.[60] During the Foundation Day ceremony in 1933, the weed was commended by the Foundation Orator, Scottish novelist and Unionist politician John Buchan.[61] The Principal of the College also 'gave his blessing' to the 'Birkbeck Rough Cut' when he ceremoniously accepted 'the first Birkbeck hand-made cigarette'. The Secretary, Troup Horne, enthusiastically marketed the brand within the College.[62] It was for a good cause, after all. The FOB promised that all the profits from its sale of tobacco would be donated to the student's fund for building the proposed Malet Street premises.[63] Since the Malet Street building was entitled 'The College in the Stratosphere', some wit coined the rhyme:

> The College in the stratosphere
> On solid earth will soon appear,
> If 'FOBs'—let's cut all further parley—
> Discharge their debt to Walter Raleigh.[64]

This later mention of Raleigh was because he was the statesman and explorer who first brought tobacco to the UK. The enthusiastic promotion of 'the weed *Nicotiana*' did excite some protests, but it was generally recognized that 'to abstain from the briar can be construed only as hostility to the Friends of Birkbeck and rank treachery to the College'.[65]

To smoke or not to smoke was still a 'live issue' in the mid-1970s. By that stage, the College authorities were seeking to discourage, but not ban, it. 'No Smoking By Request' posters appeared in all teaching rooms, although 'those unable to refrain from smoking' were told simply to 'segregate themselves at the rear of the

---

[59] Hume, 'Quorum Pars Parva Fui', 73.
[60] 'We Give Ourselves a "Puff"', *The Lodestone*, 29.2 (spring 1934), 74. [61] Ibid., 74.
[62] 'Quixote', 'Letter to the Editor', *The Lodestone*, 29.2 (spring 1934), 104.
[63] 'We Give Ourselves a "Puff"', 74.   [64] Ibid., 75.
[65] 'Quixote', 'Letter to the Editor', 104.

rooms'.⁶⁶ The decisive death of the practice only happened in 2007, as a result of a government ban on smoking in all public buildings.

Second only to debates around smoking in the Common Room were those about whether religious discussions were allowed. When the LMI was established, George Birkbeck and the other founders were adamant that discussions about religion were to be prohibited, along with any mention of party politics. Although the LMI was never formally branded a 'Godless College', as was its neighbour, University College London, it was a religion-free site. As one student-poet jested in 1946,

> I dreamt that I died and to heaven did go,
> I rang the bell gaily, and bowed very low,
> I said, 'I'm from BIRKBECK',
> My! How they did stare,
> 'Come right in', said Peter,
> 'You're the first one from there'.⁶⁷

However, there were fervent Christians in the College who were increasingly demanding to be heard. The most prominent of these was Hume, who instigated a full-frontal attack on the ban in 1909. He founded the Christian Union and applied for permission for members to gather on College premises. When the governors indignantly refused, Birkbeck's Christian Union booked rooms in the offices of the Student Christian Movement in Chancery Lane and in the Baptist Missionary Society building. Although sincere in their beliefs, they were also motivated by 'the desire for trenchancy and dislike of half-measures', Hume admitted.⁶⁸ Despite the ban, members of the Christian Union participated in College life, including sporting events. They called themselves 'The Outlaws'.⁶⁹ The governors were obliged to give way only when the College's President, Lord Alverstone, supported their cause.⁷⁰

More controversial were debates about the establishment of the Jewish Society. This came to a head in 1985 when a group of Jewish students petitioned the Students' Union for the right to establish a society. The opposition they received was not unique. After all, throughout the UK, students' unions had been debating the issue, largely as a response to the 1975 resolution at the United Nations which declared that Zionism was 'a form of racism and racial discrimination'. By the mid-1980s, the issue was particularly heated, triggered by the Students' Union at Sunderland Polytechnic censoring the Jewish Society mention of Zionism in its

---

⁶⁶ 'House Committee Minutes Apl [sic] 1965 to Nov. 1983', in 'Minutes of the meetings of the House Committee. 26th May 1976', in the Birkbeck Archive.
⁶⁷ 'Just a Reminder', *The Lodestone*, 39.1 (autumn 1946), 5.
⁶⁸ Hume, 'Quorum Pars Parva Fui', 73.   ⁶⁹ Ibid., 73.   ⁷⁰ Ibid., 73.

constitution. The student left were divided.⁷¹ At Birkbeck, the minutes reported 'general concern amongst members of Council' about a similar initiative by Jewish students. They asked: 'Is the society to be religious or political, is it to be Zionist or not, will the acceptance of this Society lead to political controversy amongst students and set a dangerous precedent?' One member of Council drew attention to the phrase 'land of Israel' in the society's proposed constitution and there was debate whether the phrase 'had religious connotations' or 'political' ones. After a long discussion, the Jewish Society was given the go-ahead on the narrowest majority but on condition that the phrase 'land of Israel' was removed.⁷² Such divisions between Jewish students sympathetic to the state of Israel and those who identified Israel as a settler-colonial state and therefore racist were exacerbated in the late 1990s with the breakdown of the Oslo peace accords. In 2010, partly as a response to these divisions both within universities and nationwide, the Birkbeck (formerly, Pears') Institute for the Study of Antisemitism was created, headed by David Feldman.⁷³ It was an attempt to 'reconnect the study of antisemitism with academic and public-facing work on racialization, racism, and religious intolerance', as Feldman put it.

* * *

Only one topic excites more interested than religious engagement, and that is sexual intercourse. The early LMI had forbidden members from picking up their mail from the College, for fear this would be used for romantic assignations.⁷⁴ By the interwar years, the sexual politics of postage seemed archaic when compared with the carnal possibilities provided by the Common Room. Its reputation was risqué. In the words of an aspiring poet—albeit one possessing a lamentable sense of rhythm and rhyme—new students should be aware that

> C stands for Common Room, the place where the women
> Knit little nets, with an eye on Hymen.⁷⁵

Did that mean it was a room that Rabbits, who viewed students who sowed 'wild oats' with horror, ought to avoid?⁷⁶ 'T.H.T.' thought so. In some doggerel published in 1926, T.H.T. conjured up an image of the 'Bishop of Birkbeck' wandering into the Common Room. Some lines went:

---

⁷¹ I am grateful to David Feldman, Director of the Birkbeck Institute for the Study of Antisemitism, and to David Rich, whose Birkbeck PhD was on the history of the campus battles over anti-Zionism.
⁷² 'Birkbeck College Students' Union. Minutes of the Meeting of Council Held on Thursday, 7th November at 9.05 pm in Room E405', in 'Students' Union. Minutes. 1981–1985', in Birkbeck Archive, Box 3.
⁷³ Thanks to David Feldman and Dave Rich for this context.
⁷⁴ Hume, 'Quorum Pars Parva Fui', 73.
⁷⁵ Til, 'A Fresher's ABC', *The Lodestone*, 29.1 (Michaelmas 1933), 19.
⁷⁶ 'A Guide to Birkbeck', *The Lodestone*, 22.2 (1927), 68.

> The Bishop of Birkbeck looked out and about
> Around and about,
> Within and without;
> And he said, 'I feel much inclined to shout
> At the terrible state of affairs.
> The Common Room's now an unholy den
> Of Bridge-ites, loafers, and dancing men'...
> The piano was going, hammer and tongs,
> Whist threading between the clustered throngs
> Men danced to the tunes of raucous songs.[77]

This dancing simply had to stop. The Union Council stepped in, contending that the Common Room was not a dance hall. Despite the long tradition of dancing in the Common Room, it reminded people that it was a great inconvenience for students who came to the Common Room 'for a little quiet relaxation and conversation'. By 1927, dancing was no more.[78]

Of course, the edict forbidding dance was disheartening to Hares. Many resented the ban. A student signing herself 'Charleston Babe' claimed that banning 'the innocent pastime of dancing in the evening' was a 'deep injustice'.[79] Others accused the Union Council of double standards. Why didn't the Council recognize that the Common Room was 'also not a concert hall, or place for public meetings'. The author claimed to

> look forward to the time when I shall no longer be forced to seek refuge in the Refectory on Wednesday 'musical evenings' or go home when the various political societies choose to make a Hyde Park of the Common Room. I look forward to the time...when the piano shall be banished and the Common Room a fit place for me and my friends to sit and smoke and look at the ceiling or talk scandal in peace.[80]

The dancing ban was a response to Rabbit-anxieties about the 'sowing of wild oats' by Hares. It did not need much knowledge of Sigmund Freud to interpret jokes about sexual proclivities as concealing instinctual anxieties about bodies and aggression.[81] Interpersonal relationships in the Common Room were the subject of hundreds of wisecracks (see Fig. 14.8). For example, in 1923, a group

---

[77] 'T.H.T.', 'On a Conversation Accidentally Overheard in the Common Room', *The Lodestone*, 22.1 (1926), 26.
[78] 'P.M.', 'Letters to the Editor', *The Lodestone*, 22.3 (1927), 137–8. Also see 'P. A.', 'The Common Room', *The Lodestone*, 22.1 (1926), 21–4.
[79] Charleston Baby, 'Letters to the Editor', *The Lodestone*, 22.3 (1927), 137.
[80] 'P.M.', 'Letters to the Editor', 137–8.
[81] Sigmund Freud, *The Joke and its Relation to the Unconscious*, ed. James Strachey, 1st pub. 1905 (New York: Norton, 1963).

Fig. 14.8 The Students' Common Room 1943. Birkbeck Image Collections: Birkbeck History BH0055.

of students signing themselves 'The Unsaturated Carbon Compounds' (they were presumably members of the Chemistry Department) wrote a letter to the editors of *The Lodestone*. They professed to being anxious about the 'degradation, decimation, and devastation of the College', which was the inevitable result of 'the use, or, rather, the misuse of the Common Room by both sexes'. 'The Unsaturated Carbon Compounds' lamented the

> moral and intellectual degeneration, debilitation and debauchery of those unhappy victims, who, seduced by the aphrodisiacal atmosphere of that Room, have plunged into the depths of hymeneal gloom.

They warned that the 'sink of iniquity' into which the Common Room had descended was making them worried that the College was becoming nothing more than a 'matrimonial agency'. Professing to have a 'profound reverence' for the institution of marriage, these students argued that 'the ill-timed, hasty and oft-regretted' entry into the 'erotic orgies' of marriage amounted to a 'sacrilege'. They were not opposed to marriage *per se*, especially those in which one of the partners was 'free from the intoxication of academic spirit'. However, they were concerned about marriages between students belonging to the same college. Such unions represented 'a suicide of a student, a crime against his colleagues, and an insult to his inamorata'. If this wasn't bad enough, they fretted that these men and women were 'not content with consummating their own ruin', but could be seen 'casting proselytising glances on their yet untrapped companions and, claiming esoteric illumination, inciting these to imitate their own infamous escapes'. 'The Unsaturated Carbon Compounds' concluded by calling for a return to the ancient rule against the marriage of students. In their words:

> Alas, alas for Birkbeck! the voices of its deceived maidens and disappointed stalwarts cry aloud to the Governors, nay, to the Senate itself, for vengeance. Restore the primitive discipline of the University; purify the baccalaureate [undergraduate degree] by decreeing that aspirants to that degree vow themselves to celibacy in deed as well as in name.[82]

It was a witty exposition of the anxieties of some (presumably young male) students concerning love and sex. And these men were not alone. The following year, a particularly filthy story was told by 'Cicerone' (meaning 'guide'). After a lengthy article introducing new students to the various sports and games played in the College, the author referred to a different and very popular game. It was a 'sort of sport in which two play together' and which was a 'good enough game', if 'played slowly'. Innocent students might believe that the two were merely 'playing chess or talking mathematics' but could not have been more wrong. Admittedly, the two players seemed to have different goals:

> In some cases[,] one has to contrive to place a ring on third finger of opponent's left hand, and she becomes player's partner. I am not sure of the rules, really, but I believe it is the finger I name. If in any doubt, my child, ask your mother. Then another variation of the game appears to be to avoid placing the ring as aforesaid, and the one who avoids it, has won. The other, of course, has lost.[83]

It is not known whether George Senter, who was not only head of the Chemistry Department at Birkbeck from 1914 but also Principal of the College from 1918 to 1939, approved of what *The Lodestone* was publishing.

There was a more genteel way of facilitating courtships—and one that Senter might have assented to. This was exemplified by the physicist Harold Redmayne (H. R.) Nettleton, who arrived at Birkbeck as an assistant lecturer in 1906, was awarded his DSc there in 1922, and remained in the College his entire academic career, working on electrical resistance.[84] Nettleton was described as 'round-faced

---

[82] 'The Unsaturated Carbon Compounds', '[Letter to the Editor]', *The Lodestone*, 19.1 (1923), 21–2.
[83] Cicerone, 'To the Editor', 28.
[84] W. Ehrenberg, 'Obituaries', *Nature*, 217 (20 January 1968), 296.

and short-sighted' and, despite being deaf, had a 'soft and yet fluting voice'.[85] His obituarist noted that he was 'father confessor' to 'generations of Birkbeckians'.[86] Arnolfo John Caraffi, the College Secretary at the time, recalled that during one dance at the Physics Department's Christmas party, Nettleton boasted that

> I had a hand in most of these marriages: Jean and Bill there, Sheila and Joe...; got all their photos on my mantlepiece. Cost me an awful lot of money in wedding presents, but it was worth it![87]

* * *

Marriage was certainly not the aim of all students, even heterosexual ones (as 'Cicerone' joked), and certainly not gay ones. For much of Birkbeck's history, gay students (as well as students of nonbinary or other minoritized genders) had to be discrete about how they socialized. As one student quipped in 1956, 'The amorous student, underneath the table/ Feels for the hand of Jane, finds that of Abel.'[88] Homosexuality was illegal until 1967, and remained highly stigmatized well into the late twentieth century. As a result, talk about what were considered 'deviant' sexualities appeared in coded languages, which had the unfortunate effect of inhibiting knowledge amongst people who were not 'in the know' about the extent and normality of such desires. This was made worse by the fact that very little *openly published* scholarship about the gay community prior to the mid-twentieth century existed. Given increasingly vocal calls to decriminalize homosexuality, this was a problem. As Home Secretary R. A. Butler acknowledged in the House of Commons, serious attempts to debate the legal status of homosexuality immediately hit up against three difficulties: public opinion, the distinction between sin and crime, and the lack of research.[89] This third problem—the lack of research—was tackled by a postgraduate student at Birkbeck called Michael Schofield. Using the pseudonym 'Gordon Westwood', Schofield carried out the first social-scientific study into homosexuality in Britain. His research was supervised by Professor Alec Rodger,[90] who established Birkbeck's Department of Organizational Psychology in 1948, when he was only 31 years of age, and who is widely regarded as the UK's founding father of vocational guidance. From 1948 until his death thirty-four years later, this Birkbeck scholar, with his thick-rimmed glasses, bald pate and elongated forehead, and scruffy suit, was to pioneer many innovative projects, including Schofield's.

[85] Arnolfo John Caraffi, 'Memories of Breams II', *Court of Electors Newsletter* (spring 1981), 13, in Birkbeck Archive, Box 15.
[86] W. Ehrenberg, 'Obituaries', *Nature*, 217 (20 January 1968), 296.   [87] Ibid., 13.
[88] 'U', 'A Note on the Refectory', *The Lodestone*, 47.1 (1956), 15.
[89] 'Commons Sitting of Wednesday, 29th June, 1960', House of Commons Hansard, fifth series, vol. 625 (1959–60), n.p.
[90] 'Parliament', *New Society* (13 February 1964), 23.

Schofield's labours resulted in a book called *A Minority: A Report on the Life of the Male Homosexual in Great Britain* (1960).[91] It had a foreword by the educationalist John Wolfenden, whose 1957 Wolfenden Committee report recommended the decriminalization of homosexuality. In the frontispiece, Rodger was listed as an 'observer'. *A Minority* was an exploration of the family background, social behaviour, and sexual activities of 127 homosexual men. Schofield concluded that it was 'the attitude of the general public towards homosexuality', not their sexual orientation *per se*, that was a major factor in creating problems of adjustment for some homosexual men.[92]

Schofield's research was a risky project to pursue at Birkbeck. After all, Lord Denning, Birkbeck's President at the time, was virulently opposed to homosexuality. In the first sentence of the acknowledgements in *The Minority*, Schofield lamented the fact that research into homosexuality was almost impossible because of 'the repugnance with which homosexuality is regarded by many people'. When he applied to trusts and foundations for funds to support his research, he was 'promptly rejected... sometimes before an explanation of the aims and methods could be given'. The 'Medical Committees of some hospitals', he complained, even

> refused to allow doctors on their staff to help. Two excellent organizations which have done good work in the fields of broken marriages and human biology both agreed to the hire of one of their spare rooms for interviews; but when they realized that this would mean that homosexuals would have to enter their premises, the offers were withdrawn.

Schofield found 'all sorts of difficulties' placed in his way.[93]

Nevertheless, he persevered and, five years later, published a follow-up book, entitled *Sociological Aspects of Homosexuality: A Comparative Study of Three Types of Homosexuals*. This was also made possible by a 'considerable grant' from the Home Office and was, once again, supervised at Birkbeck under the direction of Rodger.[94] This research involved interviewing nearly twice the number of gay men as his previous book.[95] Furthermore, Schofield drew comparisons between homosexuals in prison, those undergoing 'treatment', and those who had been neither imprisoned nor 'treated'. He concluded that

---

[91] This was his second major study on the subject. The first was *Society and the Homosexual* (London: Victor Gollancz, 1952).
[92] Gordon Westwood [pseudo. Michael Schofield], *A Minority: A Report on the Life of the Male Homosexual in Great Britain* (London: Longmans, Green and Co., 1960), 4.
[93] Ibid., ix.
[94] Gordon Westwood [pseudo. Michael Schofield], *Sociological Aspects of Homosexuality: A Comparative Study of Three Types of Homosexuals* (London: Longmans, Green and Co., 1965), 1.
[95] He interviewed 300 men.

> Homosexuality is a condition which in itself has only minor effects upon the development of the personality. But the attitudes, not of the homosexual, but of other people towards this condition, create a stress situation which can have a profound effect upon personality development and can lead to character deterioration of a kind which prohibits effective integration with the community.[96]

This was why, Schofield reiterated time and again, legal reform was essential, as was public education. His main message was that 'homosexual conduct is variant behavior' but it 'need not be deviant'.[97]

In a debate in the House of Commons in 1960, the Home Secretary R. A. Butler admitted to having read *The Minority*. He had been impressed by its analyses of the 'psychological and other characteristics of homosexuals', including their 'family and social, educational and occupational background, and the personal characteristics', compared with non-homosexuals.[98] Butler argued that attempts to reform the law should 'freely acknowledge that homosexuality is, in general, an undesirable practice', but reform might nevertheless be appropriate.[99]

Butler was not the only politician who drew on Schofield's research. In the House of Lords in May 1965, for example, the Earl of Iddesleigh purported to be anxious that the Lords were not being given sufficient time to read Schofield's report, which would be published later that year. He confessed that he knew 'comparatively little of this subject'. This was not because he did not 'want to know': there was simply 'very little authoritative material' on the topic. The entire debate, the Earl complained, had been characterized by 'astonishing differences of view regarding the causation of homosexuality'. Some commentators were arguing that homosexuals are 'born, and not made' or that it was a 'matter of pre-natal influences'; others contended that it was a 'hangover from adolescent homosexuality'.[100] The Earl did not explain why causation should make a difference to a person's basic rights.

Although it would take until 1967 for homosexuality of adults in private to be decriminalized, this research at Birkbeck was important. By the 1970s, gay students in the College were confident enough to be fully 'out'. The *Students' Handbook* for 1974 even boasted that it was an 'exciting prospect' for a gay student to come to Birkbeck. 'Over the last four of five years', it observed,

---

[96] Ibid., 203.   [97] Ibid., 211.
[98] 'Commons Sitting of Wednesday, 29th June, 1960', House of Commons Hansard, 5th series, vol. 625 (1959–60), n.p.
[99] Ibid.
[100] The Earl of Iddesleigh speaking in 'Lords Sitting on Monday 24th May, 1965', *House of Lords Hansard. Sessional Papers*, 5th series, vol. 266 (1964–5), n.p.

the climate of opinion has changed radically. Gay people are now proud to be gay. Non-gays, especially at University, are ever more willing to accept gays without prejudice or condescension.

There was even a club devoted to gay students. This was the 'Gaysoc'. The handbook noted that the 'first concern for most Gay people is how to meet others' in 'ordinary casual surroundings'. Of course, gay students would meet 'nice people' in lectures and during other College events, but 'you have to remember NOT to fall in love'. In contrast, at the 'Gaysoc', students could be confident that they would know that the 'girls are interested in girls and the boys in the boys'. London had hundreds of gay bars, clubs, parks, and streets, but although these were 'good for sex or a night out', they were 'pretty hopeless for meeting people with common interests other than sex'. The report concluded with the words,

> It has never been easier to be gay, though the struggle is far from over. If you are gay, be proud. Take advantage of the new climate, join in with those who are campaigning, and enjoy yourself too. If you think you are not gay, then don't be left behind. Cast out old prejudice and help your friends to be glad to be gay.[101]

As such, the 'Gaysoc' was a political lobbying group as well as a social one.

* * *

As we have seen so far in this chapter, Birkbeck students, staff, and lecturers were profoundly concerned about the balance between their strictly 'academic' aspirations and non-scholarly spinoffs: that is, athletics, social and religious clubs, and romantic, marital, and recreational sexual activities. These tensions were most marked in the interwar years—and for a reason that has only been briefly alluded to so far: that is, international politics. Some of Birkbeck's most active Hares were being seduced by an ideology that would have world-shattering implications after 1933: fascism. Hume recalled that 'Some of the rugger people...used to parade around during the week wearing armbands with the initials "B. F.", which many onlookers considered to be very appropriate', perhaps believing it to mean Birkbeck Friend or Fellowship. In fact, he reported, 'they bore the less usual denotation "British Fascisti"'.[102]

One of the most disreputable of Birkbeck's Hares was William Joyce. He joined the College in the 1920s but, during the Second World War, refashioned himself as 'Lord Haw-Haw'. Adopting an affected British aristocratic accent, he used the

---

[101] David Dancer, 'Gay Students and ULU GaySoc', *Birkbeck Students' Handbook 1974–1975* (London: BCSU, 1975), 24.
[102] C. W. Hume, 'How the Greenford Sports Ground was Acquired', *The Lodestone*, 55.3 (summer 1965), 18.

radio broadcast 'Germany Calling' in an attempt to demoralize both British troops and civilians, hoping to encourage them to agree to Nazi peace terms.

Twenty years earlier, however, Joyce had been an academically and socially active Birkbeckian. In September 1923, he registered to take classes in English, French, Latin, and History. Academically, he thrived. One of his English teachers—Beatrice Marjorie Daunt—later recalled that, during his first class, he appeared dressed in military uniform, sat in the front row, and held a rifle across his knees. She thought, 'If he's as mad as he looks he may well stand up and shoot me.'[103] Joyce was also taught by John Hay (J. H.) Lobban, for whom a prize still exists at Birkbeck honouring students who 'have shown the greatest promise in English Literature'. Lobban inspired in Joyce a love of John Dryden and Thomas Carlyle. Rather bizarrely, Joyce was to claim that Carlyle was an early fascist. According to Joyce, Carlyle

> ranks first amongst British heralds of the Fascist revolution...in all the vast extent of Carlyle's writings there is nothing that could be regarded as other than the product of a National-Socialist mind. He himself had the spirit of National Socialism long before the name existed.[104]

Despite such dangerous beliefs, by June 1927, Joyce could boast a first-class honours degree in English. At that time, this was quite an achievement since only two students were awarded a First in English that year.[105] A popular biographer has rashly claimed that Joyce wrote 'the best paper on Shakespeare the university had seen in the twentieth century'.[106] Joyce then started research on a dissertation about medieval petitions, supervised by Daunt. Although he eventually abandoned his dissertation because of the lack of primary sources, he did publish a philological article on the 'long a' vowel sound in the prestigious *Review of English Studies*.[107]

Joyce's life at Birkbeck was politically tumultuous. On 6 December 1923, just a few months after starting in the College, he had joined the British Fascisti, a group formed by Rotha Lintorn-Orman. It was the first avowedly fascist movement in Britain. Its members were determined to resist internationalism, revolution, and Bolshevism of all kinds. Members could be identified by a black handkerchief they placed in their breast pocket.[108]

---

[103] J. A. Cole, *Lord Haw-Haw—and William Joyce: The Full Story* (London: Faber and Faber, 1964), 31.
[104] Cited by Mary Kenny, *Germany Calling: A Personal Biography of William Joyce, Lord Haw-Haw* (Dublin: New Island, 2003), n.p. (chapter 4).
[105] Ibid., n.p. (chapter 4). [106] Ibid., n.p. (chapter 4).
[107] William Joyce, 'A Note on the Mid Back Slack Unrounded Vowel [a] in the English of To-Day', *Review of English Studies*, 4.15 (1928), 337–40. Also see the response by A. H. Smith, 'Some Modern English Vowels', *Review of English Studies*, 5.7 (January 1929), 49–53.
[108] Cole, *Lord Haw-Haw—and William Joyce*, 29.

During Joyce's second year at Birkbeck, this membership got him into trouble. Joyce was in charge of 'I Squad' of the British Fascisti and, expecting trouble from 'the Reds' and Jewish communists, was acting as a steward for the Unionist parliamentarian candidate for Lambeth North, Jack Lazarus.[109] According to Joyce, during the scuffles, a communist slashed him from his ear to the corner of his mouth with a razor, requiring twenty-six stitches and leaving a permanent scar.[110] It should be noted that his wife, Hazel Kathleen Barr (who was also a student at Birkbeck), maintained that the scar had been inflicted by 'an Irish woman', not 'a Jewish Communist'.[111]

Whatever the case, Joyce identified strongly as a Hare at Birkbeck. He served as Chairman of the College's Conservative Student Society, enjoyed Birkbeck's fencing and chess clubs, became Assistant Secretary of the Birkbeck Boxing Club, and played the belligerent, duelling Kestrel in the Birkbeck Players' production of Ben Johnson's *The Alchemist*. He joined the University's Officer Training Corps (OTC) which, thanks to the enthusiasm of George Francis Troup Horne when he was still a student at Birkbeck (this was prior to him becoming College Secretary),[112] was to become a separate 'Birkbeck section' by 1928 and, within a decade, the 'largest combatant collegiate unit in the Corps'.[113] Joyce deprecated the 'ultra-democratic minds of to-day' who believe militarism was 'incompatible with the worship of the fetish known as Progress'. He claimed the OTC was not even militaristic but was intended 'to enable educated and intelligent men to discharge, in case of need, their military debts to the State'.[114] On joining, Joyce claimed to be of 'pure British descent', despite being Irish.[115] While he was disappointed with recruitment from Birkbeck to the OTC, he was proud that Birkbeck's Conservative Society was strong and growing. This was helped, he believed, by the fact that in Parliament, 'the upholders of Anglo-Saxon tradition and supremacy have been untiring, and often successful'.[116]

Joyce met his future wife, Hazel Kathleen Barr, while at Birkbeck (perhaps he met her in the notorious Common Room) and published at least two love poems to her in *The Lodestone*. In one of these, he claimed that

> The rich white fullness of those perfect limbs
> The cold chaste gaze with Passion's most bedims;
> They fill the icy veins with torrent fire

---

[109] Ibid., 29.
[110] This was on 22 October 1924.   [111] Cole, *Lord Haw-Haw—and William Joyce*, 30.
[112] G. F. Troup Horne, 'Correspondence. Country, College, and Corps', *The Lodestone*, 5.2 (Lent 1910), 56–9. Also see Cdt C.Q.M.S. Houchin, 'O.T.C', *The Lodestone*, 20.2 (1925), 55.
[113] 'Birkbeck', *The Lodestone*, 46.2 (spring/summer 1955), 30.
[114] William Joyce, 'The U. L. O. T. C', *The Lodestone* 21.2 (spring 1926), 101.
[115] Colin Holmes, *Searching for Lord Haw-Haw: The Political Lives of William Joyce* (London: Routledge, 2015), 28.
[116] William Joyce, 'The Conservative Society', *The Lodestone*, 21.2 (spring 1926), 102.

> And thrill the soul with strains from love's own lyre…
> Beloved Hazel…
> If Brynhild's soul lives on, then thou art she.[117]

The following year, 1928, he returned to the theme, writing that

> She who most deeply
> My spirit has moved,
> Never has hated me,
> Never has loved.
> Since love and hate are most
> Nearly related,
> 'Twere well for a little while,
> Dear if you hated.
> Since love and hate are so
> Neary akin,
> Lady, when hate was dead,
> Love might begin.[118]

Joyce was also friendly with Birkbeck's lecturers. He collaborated with Professor Helen Gwynne-Vaughan of the Botany Department in strengthening the College's Conservative Society[119] and, like Joad, was keen on Oswald Mosley's New Party, which was the predecessor of Mosley's British Union of Fascists (BUF). Unlike Joad, who quickly saw sense and repudiated the New Party, Joyce followed Mosley into the increasingly radicalized, violent, and anti-Semitic BUF, where he became Director of Propaganda and its leading orator.

Despite his extensive involvement in the social life of the College, Joyce was not popular amongst other Hares. Indeed, part of the reason that Joyce was so noticeable at Birkbeck was because he was a right-wing Hare, while most Hares at the time were politically liberal or left-leaning. These Hares didn't like the way Joyce sauntered around the College in plus-fours, wearing a black sweater emblazoned with the Union Jack.[120] When Joyce spoke at the students' mock parliament, fellow-students became irritated by his anti-Semitism.[121] During one English class, Joyce became over-excited while enacting a play, beating his fellow actors with a stick, knocking out a fellow student's tooth, and pushing another off the stage.[122]

---

[117] William Joyce, 'To Her', *The Lodestone*, 22.3 (summer 1927), 119. For another poem, see 'Lines', *The Lodestone*, 23.2 (spring 1928), 58, signed 'W.S.'.
[118] 'Verses', *The Lodestone*, 23.2 (spring 1928), 73.
[119] William Joyce, 'The Conservative Society', *The Lodestone*, 21.2 (1926), 102.
[120] Holmes, *Searching for Lord Haw-Haw*, 28.   [121] Kenny, *Germany Calling*, n.p. (chapter 4).
[122] Cole, *Lord Haw-Haw—and William Joyce*, 32.

He was also involved in a bad-tempered exchange about Bernard Shaw in *The Lodestone*. Admittedly, Joyce wasn't the only one to express frustration about the ubiquitous fawning over Shaw by Birkbeck's Dramatic Society.[123] As we saw in Chapter 10, other students were exasperated by the society's continuous staging of Shaw and other modern writers such as Michael Arlen and Noël Coward, who created psychologically 'complex' characters who preferred love and pleasure to fighting and martial masculinity.[124] However, Joyce's contribution to this debate was vitriolic. In a piece entitled 'Verses to an Impolite Reformer', Joyce wrote:

> Can we but love that impious reptile Shaw,
> And Arlen, Pandar, 'gainst all virtue soured,
> And sickly, putrid, maggot-eaten Coward.
> Away with livid plays of modern sex,
> Eradicate, destroy, efface 'complex'!
> In days when martial valour was appraised,
> They loved a duel or a standard raised;
> But now Hypocrisy and Humane Cant
> Transform the soldier's honest blows to rant.[125]

The poem's proto-fascist militarism annoyed fellow students. F. Oxley Read responded, rebuking Joyce for his 'turgid and incoherent tirade' and his 'rash and childish remarks'.[126] Student P. Loftus Ryan also criticized Joyce for his 'farrago of nonsense' and 'gratuitous rudeness' about Ireland, 'the shoes of whose lowliest peasant he is unworthy to lace'. With remarkable prescience, Loftus concluded that Joyce's rhetoric 'stinks strongly and most unpleasantly of the soapbox'.[127]

With the declaration of war, Joyce allied himself with Nazi Germany and began broadcasting pro-German propaganda. His notoriety was such that Ernst Gunther Michaelis, a Jewish refugee from Germany who joined Birkbeck as a student, then staff, after fleeing Germany (he is discussed in Chapter 18), dedicated a limerick to him in a 1944 edition of *The Lodestone*. It went:

> A radio announcer named Joyce—
> A German by personal choice—
> Will gladly acknowledge
> That he owes to the College
> The peculiar twang of his voice.[128]

---

[123] 'Cicerone', 'To the Editor', 29.
[124] Thanks to Anthony Bale and Tim Phillips for help in interpreting this poem.
[125] William Joyce, 'Verses to an Impolite Reformer', *The Lodestone*, 22.3 (summer 1927), 127.
[126] F. Oxley Read, 'Letters to the Editor', *The Lodestone*, 23.1 (1927), 44–5.
[127] P. Loftus Ryan, 'Letters to the Editor', *The Lodestone*, 23.1 (1927), 45, and P. Loftus Ryan, 'Correspondence', *The Lodestone*, 23.2 (spring 1928), 98.
[128] 'The Limerick Competition', *The Lodestone*, 36.2 (spring 1944), 25.

At the end of the war, Joyce was accused of high treason because of his radio broadcasts from Germany. He was convicted in 1945 and sentenced to death. When executioner Albert Pierrepoint arrived at Wandsworth Goal to hang him, Pierrepoint calmly told Joyce, 'Follow me, sir, it'll be all right' before efficiently 'dispatching' Birkbeck's most notorious Hare.

* * *

Unlike Joyce, most Hares were affable types, with a good-natured curiosity about other people. While Joyce espoused the most vicious form of racism, other student-Hares were using their abundant energy in aid of people less fortunate than themselves—people such as German-Jewish refugee Michaelis, who composed that limerick against Joyce. Refugees from the two world wars of the century, though, were not the only ones whom Birkbeck's students sought to help. In 1956, Birkbeck students watched in horror as the Soviet Union invaded Hungary and imposed draconian restrictions. Hungarian students had played a major role in the revolution against the Hungarian People's Republic and then in resisting the Soviet invasion. When the movement was crushed, 200,000 Hungarians fled the country. Most went to Austria, but around 21,000 came to Britain.[129] They were regarded by many Britons as 'deserving' refugees. In the words of a leaflet published by the Hungarian Relief Committee,

> Our Hungarian Friend, we greet you affectionately on English soil.... The British have paid admiring homage to the courage of the Hungarians and suffer with the Hungarians in the horrors of oppression and bloody repression. The refugees of the freedom fight are *welcome guests* in this country.[130]

There were pleas to help these refugees, as had happened during the First World War when Birkbeck offered free education to refugees fleeing Belgium. Most notably, University of Manchester microbiologist John D. Bu'Lock wrote a letter to the Editor of *The Times* in which he urged universities, whether 'acting individually or in concert', to

> provide places for Hungarian students and to ensure that they will be adequately supported.... Action of this kind, though limited in scope, would at least be an expression of our deep sympathy for the Hungarian people, and perhaps a more practical one than the composition of letters of protest and counter-protest

---

[129] Becky Taylor, 'Their Only Words in English were "Thank You": Rights, Gratitude and "Deserving" Hungarian Refugees to Britain in 1956', unpublished paper (2018), 1.
[130] Translation of a leaflet distributed by the Hungarian Relief Committee, n.d., London Metropolitan Archives MCC/CH/CO/1/81, cited in ibid., 1.

which seems to have been the main activity of Britain's intellectuals in the past week.[131]

Numerous organizations sprang up, including at Birkbeck. The fact that the College's Master, John Lockwood, was also the Vice-Chancellor of the University and therefore spearheading fund-raising activities on behalf of refugee students played an important role.[132] But Birkbeck students also took considerable initiative. *The Lodestone* paid homage to the 'deep emotion which the courage and endurance of the Hungarian people aroused', and students as well as staff joined protests against the Soviet invasion.[133]

Most important, though, was the attempt to house and lodge the refugees. At Birkbeck, the leading person taking on this role was John Berridge, President of the Birkbeck Student Union and later President of the London University Union and Vice-President of the National Union of University Students. Berridge was a former teacher who had enrolled in classes on Logic, English and Philosophy at Birkbeck. He was described as a 'character' who 'likes to think of himself as a countryman, and, if roused, will offer up very convincing arguments in favour of fox hunting'.[134] He possessed energy, formidable organizing skills, and a 'capacity for self-sacrifice to the job in hand'.[135] Through the estate agent Roy Brooks, a house—described as 'dangerous to enter'—was found in Kingston Hill (New Malden) in Surrey.[136] Thieves had stolen all the lead, so the entire plumbing system had to be replaced; there was dry rot in a number of floors; one main beam was in a dangerous condition, so had to be replaced.[137] There were also major repairs needed to the plasterwork, guttering, and brickwork, not to mention redecorating and furnishing every room.

Berridge organized a 'marathon campaign', appealing to major firms for money and equipment.[138] BBC broadcasts and even a Pathé newsreel publicized their cause.[139] In total, around seventy firms provided money as well as 'furniture, carpets, mats, gas stoves, dustbins, lead piping, sinks, cleaning equipment, china, curtaining, mattresses, cooking equipment, food, paint, wallpaper', and so on.[140]

---

[131] John D. Bu'Lock, 'Hungary', *The Times* (14 November 1956), 11.
[132] For example, see *Report of the Lord Mayor of London's National Hungarian and Central European Relief Fund Nov. 1956–Sept. 1958* (London: The Lord Mayor, 1958), 3, and Madga Czigánu, *'Just Like Other Students': Reception of the 1956 Hungarian Refugee Students in Britain* (Cambridge: Cambridge Scholars Publishing, 2009), 34.
[133] 'Birkbeck House', *The Lodestone*, 48.3 (spring 1957), 10.
[134] 'Berridge of Birkbeck. London's New President', *Sennet* (11 March 1958), 8.   [135] Ibid., 8.
[136] Ibid., 8.   [137] 'Birkbeck House', 10.   [138] 'Birkbeck House', 10.
[139] Ibid., 11. The Pathé newsreel can be seen here: https://www.britishpathe.com/video/students-prepare-home-for-hungarians/query/stolen+from+men. The people in the film include G. Hyland, schoolmaster Bernard Goodwin, Dermot McGovern, Sylvia Watts, Maxwell Lee, Margaret Baker, John Berridge (organizer), Margaret Dain, Valerie Colin-Russ, and Aileen Carpenter.
[140] 'Birkbeck House', 10.

In addition, 'householders in the home counties' donated everything from a mousetrap to a grand piano.[141] As one student recalled,

> We went into any empty, dirty, dilapidated house, without water, light or heating. The first scrubbing parties had to carry water from the house next door, and the food supplied by the Refectory had to be cooked on an improvised log fire. Electricity and gas supplies were connected almost at once and by the third weekend water supplies had been installed too. Plumbing and most other repairs were held up to a certain extent by delays in obtaining materials, for a time-lag is inevitable when supplies are entirely dependent upon the generosity of the manufacturers, but... slowly the house was transformed.[142]

Within three months, Birkbeck students had changed the decrepit house into a respectable hostel (see Fig. 14.9).

Fig. 14.9 Two Birkbeck students preparing the house for Hungarian refugees. Pathé newsreel 619.40.

---

[141] Ibid., 11.   [142] Ibid., 10.

It was finally opened in May 1957 by Boyd-Carpenter, Minister of Pensions and National Insurance. In attendance was the Master, Lockwood, and other Birkbeckians, along with the Mayor of Malden and representatives of the Red Cross, Women's Voluntary Service, the St John Ambulance Brigade, and the British Council for Aid to Refugees.[143] Fourteen Hungarian boys, aged 14 to 19, were its first residents.[144]

Revealingly, Pathé filmed a short newsreel about the Birkbeck refugees (see Fig. 14.10). In it, Birkbeck students are seen welcoming three young men to the house. The newsreel ends with one of the refugees, simply known as Joseph, with a wounded foot prominently displayed, drawing a picture of St Therese—written over the top is 'Budapest' and written underneath is 'St Therese of the Child Jesus'.[145]

Berridge went on to become a politics lecturer at Dundee University, as well as being active in the Scottish art and birdwatching community. He reached the

Fig. 14.10 Stills from the Pathé film, showing the railway sign telling refugees where to get off the train, the first young refugees arriving at the Birkbeck house, and a drawing of St Teresa. Pathé newsreel 619.40.

---

[143] 'Hungarian Refuge Hostel Opened', *The Times* (6 May 1957), 12.   [144] Ibid., 12.
[145] https://www.britishpathe.com/video/students-prepare-home-for-hungarians/query/birkbeck.

height of his political influence in the late 1960s when, while working as a politics lecturer at Dundee University, the then Prime Minister, Ted Heath, commissioned Berridge to create a policy for Scottish devolution. Although he was a Conservative Party activist all his life, he used to describe himself as a 'Tory Socialist'.[146]

* * *

Berridge described himself as a 'huntin', shootin', and fishin' type'.[147] Once the Birkbeck House was complete and the Hungarian students settled, he turned back to sport and other Hare-like activities. But sporting life at the College was experiencing difficulties (see, for example, Fig. 14.11). The College Secretary, Caraffi, complained that 'we never succeeded in squeezing out of [the College's Principal] the bawbees for a spiked roller for Greenford'. The Principal at the time was George Senter, a 'Scottish bachelor of somewhat dour and at times startled looks'. Although Senter regularly used to watch games at Greenford and could be heard 'mus[ing] wistfully how the "rrrollerr" might be got', he never seemed to find the cash.[148] The 1939–45 war had also created challenges. Although the College offered its fields to the government for the grazing of sheep,[149] the grounds were instead commandeered by the Home Guard who promptly installed a bar selling alcoholic drinks and cigarettes—all without a licence.[150] When a bar was finally licensed in the 1970s, the inexperienced staff led to a serious 'disparitory [sic: disparity] between expected profits and actual profits'.[151] Furthermore, overly aggressive players, especially those in the hockey team, generated complaints.[152] Drainage was another constant annoyance.[153] The pavilion required frequent repairs.[154] Illegal campers and non-Birkbeck players used the grounds without permission.[155] There were also the usual student 'high jinks'— fire extinguishers let off in the tea-room and cricket scoreboards mysteriously

---

[146] 'Obituary: John Berridge', *The Scotsman* (17 June 2010).
[147] 'Berridge of Birkbeck. London's New President', *Sennet* (11 March 1958), 8.
[148] Caraffi, 'Memories of Breams II', 11.
[149] Letter from Troup Horne to the Under Secretary for State, Ministry of Agriculture and Fisheries, dated 25 June 1940, in 'Wartime Correspondence of the Clerk 1939–41', in Birkbeck Archive (p. 52 of file).
[150] Memo dated 16 June 1942 from Troup Horne, in Birkbeck Archive, Box 43.
[151] 'Greenford Bar Committee Meeting—30th August, 1981', 1, 'Greenford Playing Fields and Pavilion. Use of Facilities 1977 to 1981', in Birkbeck Archive, Box 11.
[152] Letter from Peter Luck (General Secretary of the Harrow Hockey Club) to the Principal, 24 November 1981, and letter from W. E. Swainson (Secretary and Clerk to the Governors) to Mr P. Dobson, 26 June 1981, both in 'Greenford Playing Fields and Pavilion. Use of Facilities 1977 to 1981', in Birkbeck Archive, Box 11.
[153] A. W. A. Rundle (Athletics Secretary), 'Student Unions, Report on Greenford. To the College Societies Committee, Wednesday, 27th Jan. 1939', 'Minute Book. Societies' Financial Committee', Birkbeck Archive, BBK 11/2/1.
[154] Ibid.
[155] Letter from A. R. Drake, President of the Student Union, to Dr G. Senter, 21 September 1932, in Birkbeck Archive, and letter from the Clerk to the Master, 26 November 1979, in 'Greenford Playing Fields and Pavilion. Use of Facilities 1977 to 1981', in Birkbeck Archive, Box 11.

Fig. 14.11 Problems with the boilers at Greenford in 1969, resulting in months with very limited supply of hot water. 'Occasional Showers!', *Spectrum*, 2.9 (8 November 1969), 1.

appearing on the pavilion's roof, for example.[156] When the grounds were originally rented, the distance of Greenford from the main College buildings was not see as a major handicap. But eventually sports clubs complained about feeling 'isolated from the College'.[157]

There were also tensions between the College authorities and Greenford's permanent staff. From the 1920s until the mid-1980s (that is, for sixty years), the fields were maintained by the Oakley family.[158] Ron Oakley, then his two sons, were the groundsmen. But, since they were allowed to live in a cottage on the grounds, the groundsmen's wives were also expected to prepare, serve, clear away, and wash up the meals 'as shall be required during the time for which the opening of the Pavilion is authorised'.[159] This was no easy job. It involved catering for up to 200 players each Saturday. By 1934, Mrs Oakley had had enough. The crisis was spurred by the introduction of play on Sundays as well as Saturdays. Mrs Oakley tried to convey to the College what this meant in terms of her workload. She explained that

> The tables must be set early in the winter, as the Bread is to butter [sic] and get ready for approximately 150 people, the work is, say, from 1 o'clock till

---

[156] Letter from Drake to Senter, 21 September 1932, in Birkbeck Archive.
[157] *Birkbeck 1971–72. The Handbook of the Birkbeck College Students' Union* (London: BCSU, September 1972), 47.
[158] 'Obituary', *Spectrum*, 18.4 (January 1985), n.p.
[159] 'Minute Book. Societies' Finance Committee', 'Minutes of Meeting of the College Societies Committee. November 27th, 1934', 2.

7.30 o'clock. I cannot do it all by myself, I have to ask Mr. Oakley to help me out.... Well Sunday work is more now than I took on [14 years ago] I can't get a woman to take on the long hours we start at 11 o'clock in the morning till 6.30 p.m. at night. We begin by cleaning potatoes down in the garden as we can't have the Kitchen as the campers have use of that, but we are started [sic] if they don't see us, we don't get a lunch, then we begin to get the teas ready, number not known, when teas are over we wash and clear away, this takes us till 6.30 p.m.[160]

For this work, she was paid a miserly 10s., or 8d. an hour.[161] The College grudgingly agreed that Sunday work would count as overtime. Nevertheless, costs had to be reduced. In 1981, when Ron Oakley noted that in 'past years they worked [overtime] for nothing', an Assistant Bursar with an eagle eye for costs, blandly noted that 'I put it to them that all sections of the college are now "suffering" from some form of cost control.'[162] It was an incredibly unsympathetic response to a family who had laboured for the College at Greenford for nearly three quarters of a century.

Financial concerns were very pressing, however. By the late 1970s, fiscal cuts and an increasingly economizing University of London had pushed Birkbeck into sharing the playing fields with SOAS and Queens Park Rangers Football Club, whose lease of the Ruislip training ground had ended.[163] For surprising reasons, the latter agreement proved fractious. In what was wittily dubbed the 'Toddlers versus Queens Park Rangers' fracas, local mothers from a nearby estate noisily protested about being prevented from using the grounds to amuse their young children. Their children had nowhere else to play. Even Ron Jones, the chief executive of QPR, admitted that sharing the pavilion with mothers and young children was not 'an ideal situation', especially given the fact that 'players [were] charging around half naked'.[164]

The second major crisis came in 1981 when the University of London conducted a survey of sporting facilities throughout the University. When it suggested that Greenford was underused, Bob (R. E.) Swainson, then Birkbeck's Secretary and Clerk to the Governors, sent a stern response. He contended that many other colleges with comparable student numbers had larger grounds as well

---

[160] Letter from Mrs Oakley to the Principal, dated 12 October 1934, in 'Minute Book. Societies' Finance Committee', 'Minutes of Meeting of the College Societies Committee. November 27th, 1934', 4. Also see 'Minutes of Meeting of the Governors, November 15th, 1928', in 'B.C. Minute Book. 18th October 1928 to 18th July 1929', in the Birkbeck Archive.

[161] Ibid.

[162] 'Greenford', letter to R. E. Swainson (Secretary and Clerk to the Governors) from P. R. Woods, the Assistant Bursar, in Birkbeck Archive, Box 13, file 1.

[163] See 'Greenford Playing Fields and Pavilion. Use of Facilities Pre-1977', 22 December 1976 in Birkbeck Archive, Box 16; 'Student Union', 'Birkbeck College Students' Union. President's Report to Council for the Year 1977–78', in Birkbeck Archive, Box 4.

[164] 'Mums Protest as Soccer Stars Move In', unidentified newspaper cutting from August 1977, in 'Greenford Playing Fields and Pavilion. Use of Facilities 1977 to 1981', in Birkbeck Archive, Box 11.

as lower occupancy than Birkbeck. He rebuked the University for using Birkbeck's 'special nature' (that is, working men and women attending classes in the evenings) to argue that they did not need sports fields. 'On the contrary', Swainson contended, 'the fact that the College provides for mature students means...that sport is generally taken more seriously than elsewhere'. Turning to specifics, Swainson pointed out that

> Our hockey Club is affiliated to the Middlesex County Hockey Association, plays a winter programme of some 60 games, and participates in indoor competition and in summer games; the Cricket Club plays throughout the season, is a member of the Middlesex League, and frequently fields three XI's on the same day in term and vacation and the Football Club, in addition to its inter-collegiate commitments, is a member of the Middlesex League and has recently gained promotion.

Swainson also insisted that the grounds and pavilion at Greenford were in excellent condition, having been maintained by 'two long-serving groundsmen who have lived on the ground since birth—their father was Head Groundsman before them—and have always worked for the College'. These were the two sons of Ron and 'Mrs' Oakley. Swainson resolutely refused to accept any arguments for 'giving up our lease'. Greenford had been 'a valued and integral part of the College' for the past sixty years and its loss might 'kill participatory sport at Birkbeck'.[165]

Within a year, however, the game was almost over. Swainson and Paul Dobson (the Chairman of the Cricket Club) took matters in hand and formed the Birkbeck College Sports Association. Responsibility for costs (such as the lease) moved from the Birkbeck Students' Union and College to the individual sports clubs. Players were charged an annual subscription and they no longer needed to be current or former members of the College. In 2007, the lease was taken over by the London Marathon Playing Fields Foundation.

* * *

Student life at Birkbeck received a blow when the Greenford lease expired for the final time. Sporting life continued, but on a more ad hoc and fluctuating basis depending on the energies of individuals. Even the massive student 'revolution' of the 1960s, which resulted in social as well as political upheavals, failed to have as much impact on Birkbeck as it did in other universities throughout the country.

Over the past 200 years, the sociability of students, staff, and lecturers at Birkbeck has undergone major shifts. Many of the LMI's early members were so

---

[165] Letter from R. E. Swainson (Secretary and Clerk to the Governors) to Mr P. J. Griffiths (Secretary, Joint Planning Committee, Court Department, University of London), 2 June 1981, in 'Greenford Playing Fields and Pavilion. Use of Facilities 1977 to 1981', in Birkbeck Archive, Box 11.

eager to embody Samuel Smiles' single-minded work ethic that they were willing to forgo leisure in their pursuit of social advancement. In contrast, by the Victorian period, students were embracing games and athletics as next to godliness, with the added benefit of promoting Christian imperialism. A more secular version had taken hold of Birkbeck students by the interwar years when, as we have seen, sports flourished to such a degree that the acquisition of Greenford sports ground became imperative. After the Second World War, a more serious mood overtook the College, which, combined with the expansion of Higher Education generally and the need for students to acquire not only 'a degree' but 'a *good* degree', led to a curtailment of College recreations. These new students were more utilitarian in their approach to university education, seeing it as a path towards employment and promotions. This was cemented by the dramatic rise in fees (which were introduced in 1998 under Tony Blair's government but skyrocketed from 2012), which also dampened sporting activities and other forms of recreation.

Another era in College sociability ended in 2021, when Ricky King retired from Birkbeck after thirty years working as an attendant, attending supervisor, and finally, security team leader. King had been born down the road from Birkbeck. From 1993 to 2017, he was known as the 'Mystery DJ', performing sets at Students' Union events in which he would don costumes from well-known movies such as *Batman* and *Frankenstein*. Later, he adopted the stage name Ricky Martini and advertised club nights with his face superimposed on movie posters.

Today, the Students' Union spends significant time debating issues that are specific to the College's unique demographics: for example, twenty-four-hour opening of the library for people who work during the day and the provision of support services for students caring for children or aged relatives. Such issues preoccupy union officials at Birkbeck more than they do their peers at universities catering primarily for young school-leavers.[166] But Birkbeck's Students' Union is also aware that catering to this historically dominant demographic risks paying insufficient attention to the College's new but growing cohort of full-time and international students, who expect more expansive programmes of entertainment and sport.[167] Sports still flourish in the College, including a Cricket Club, which was established in 1832 and is still the largest of the clubs.[168] It remains to be seen whether the changing nature of Birkbeck's students, along with the development of a more 'campus-like' environment due to the acquisition of Student Central (discussed in Chapter 28), will see a return to a vibrant sport and social calendar.

---

[166] See the minutes and motions of the Students' Union at https://www.birkbeckunion.org/student-voice/student-council/previous-minutes-agenda-motions-and-officer-reports and https://www.birkbeckunion.org/student-voice/student-council/policies-passed-by-council.
[167] Ibid.
[168] The Birkbeck Students' Union, at https://www.birkbeckunion.org/groups/cricket-club--5, viewed 18 August 2021.

In the 1920s, students asked each other, 'Are you a Rabbit or a Hare?' They looked back to earlier decades, where they believed there was a richer sense of community belonging amongst students, staff, and lecturers. Of course, much of the nostalgia for the pre-war period when students were assumed to be extremely active in College was precisely that—nostalgia. The rhetoric of 'Hares versus Rabbits' was also largely instrumental: it was a rhetoric aimed at embarrassing Rabbits into engaging with other College activities. And it was fostered by students who wrote for *The Lodestone* and were not at all representative of average Birkbeck students. Nevertheless, the well-attended games at Greenford, the high jinks that took place during 'rags' (see Chapter 16), and the thriving theatrical performances do suggest that the period from the late nineteenth century to the 1930s was a high point in College sociability, during which education was a 'rounded' experience that addressed all aspects of life.

Perhaps some indication of the slow shift away from Hares and towards Rabbits can be traced in the fate of the 'Wright Love Feast'. Between 1947 and 1963, classics students banded together to raise money to pay for 'love feasts', with menus written in Latin. They were held in honour of classics professor Frederic ('Freddy') Adam (F. A.) Wright who had taught at Birkbeck from 1898 to 1935.[169] However, when the time for the Wright Love Feast arrived in 1968, head of department Robert Browning admitted that he 'did nothing about it, largely because I understood that the income available from the fund was insufficient to provide more than a glass of beer and a sandwich'.[170] The last 'love feast' seems to have been in 1981—and was subsidized by the College. A more utilitarian approach to education—that approach espoused by the Rabbits—prevailed.

---

[169] 'Wright Love Feast', in Birkbeck Archive, Box 27.
[170] Letter from Browning to the Master, 27 November 1970, in 'Wright Love Feast', in Birkbeck Archive, Box 27.

15
'Man versus Rabbits'

While I was writing this book, the main Birkbeck archive was housed in two places: a large, industrial storage facility just outside of Ely (Cambridgeshire) and a tiny, airless room in the basement of the Malet Street building. Before it became a store-room for part of the College's history, the Malet Street room had been an insectary, containing crickets, spiders, and snakes. To get to it, you had to walk down a dank corridor that used to be lined with cages containing mice and rabbits. One of the College's attendants swears that monkeys lived there at one time. Every time I sauntered down this passageway, I thought of these animals. What experiments did they take part in? What did they think? Were they thirsty, hungry, frightened? Or, having been bred in captivity, did they not know other worlds?

I was intrigued to find that, throughout the College's history, similar questions had been asked by Birkbeckians. A week after I had discovered that Birkbeck students used to be divided into 'Hares versus Rabbits' (see the previous chapter), I came across a pamphlet written at Birkbeck during that same period entitled 'Man versus Rabbits'. The authors were addressing a simple question: did people have a right to behave cruelly towards rabbits? They informed readers of the incredible suffering endured by hares and rabbits who were caught in 'gin traps'. The authors did not appeal to 'animal rights' but did have a lot to say about animal sentience and human responsibilities.

The pamphlet had been written on behalf of the University of London Animal Welfare Society (now, the Universities Federation for Animal Welfare). The original idea for this society emerged in 1926 during a discussion between two Birkbeck students in the Students' Common Room in Bream's Building. The students had been motivated to start the society while on a College trip to an unnamed 'foreign country' (probably Greece or Italy), where they witnessed a 'gross act of cruelty' against a nonhuman animal.[1] They resolved to do something about it.

The society was by no means the first of its kind. The first Society for the Prevention of Cruelty to Animals had been founded in 1823, the same year as the London Mechanics' Institution. Since then, the College had frequently hosted lectures opposing vivisection and advocating the protection of animals. However,

---

[1] 'Welfare of Animals. New University of London Society', *Shields Daily News* (8 February 1927), 5.

the University of London Animal Welfare Society (ULAWS) was the first *university-based* animal lobbying group.

The driving-force behind ULAWS was Captain Charles Wesley Hume, examiner in the Patent's Office and winner of the Military Cross during the First World War. He has already appeared in this book: from the early 1900s, Hume was a major figure in the fights for student representation in the College's governing bodies and the movement to become a full part of the University of London. Hume had joined Birkbeck as a physics student in 1907, graduated in 1910, and then joined the Mathematics Department.[2] If we adopted the terminology of the 'Hares versus Rabbits' debate, he was definitely a Hare, participating enthusiastically in the full variety of social as well as academic programmes offered by the College. Hume was President of the Student Union in 1913–14, Captain of the Hockey Club, winner of the University colours for hockey, and co-founder of Birkbeck's Christian Union (for which he had to lobby hard, since discussions of religion had been banned from the College since its founding, as discussed in Chapter 14).[3] For some years, Hume was also Chairman of the Court of Electors.[4]

At the inaugural meeting of ULAWS in February 1926, 1,200 people turned up in Birkbeck's lecture theatre, where the College's Principal, George Senter, took the Chair.[5] Other colleges and universities quickly affiliated themselves, starting with Wye College (the school for agricultural studies in the University of London), then King's, Bedford, Royal Holloway, and the Royal Veterinary College.[6] When, in 1938, the University of London blocked ULAWS's application to 'broadcast a Wireless Appeal' on behalf of animals (the University was anxious that such a transmission 'would damage the University's own appeal for funds'), the 'University of London' society simply became the Universities Federation for Animal Welfare.[7] The most immediate effect of this change of name was the affiliation of the University of Oxford, followed by other Higher Education institutions.[8]

ULAWS was inspired by the desire of Birkbeck's students, staff, and lecturers to contribute to solving problems in the wider world. As they insisted in the first few sentences of a 1931 pamphlet, a 'university ought not to restrict its interest to matters which fall within examination syllabuses and prescribed lines of research'. 'Centres of progressive thought', such as Birkbeck, had a duty to '*lead* public opinion to a proper understanding of the right relationship between man and the lower animals'.[9]

---

[2] Major C. W. Hume, 'An Egg that was Laid at Birkbeck', *The Lodestone*, 53.3 (spring 1963), 13.
[3] Ibid., 13.   [4] Ibid., 13.
[5] G. R. Dunstan, *Science and Sensibility. The Hume Memorial Lecture. 4th November 1982 at King's College, University of London* (London: UFAW, 1983), 2.
[6] Hume, 'An Egg that was Laid at Birkbeck', 14–15.   [7] Dunstan, *Science and Sensibility*, 3.
[8] Hume, 'An Egg that was Laid at Birkbeck', 15.
[9] *The University of London Animal Welfare Society* (20 January 1931), 1, in Birkbeck Archive, Box 21. Emphasis added.

Hume was an energetic propagandist. He explained that ULAWS was animated by two principles. The first was that 'the fair treatment of animals' was an

> important subject, which must interest everyone whose mind is not too small and narrow, too restricted in its outlook and sympathies, to care about creatures of any species except the one to which he himself happens to belong.[10]

The second principle was that the subject had to be 'dealt with objectively and not sentimentally'.[11] This second point was central to the society's entire ethos. They believed that animals required 'the help of minds trained in the discipline of accurate thinking, for all good causes are liable to be prejudiced by uncritical zeal'.[12] As Hume told Birkbeck's Principal in a letter dated November 1931, he hoped that the society would raise the debate 'above the level of passionate controversy'. 'In time', he anticipated, compassion towards animals would 'become a recognised department of scientific sociology'.[13]

This emphasis on detached objectivity set ULAWS apart from other animal welfare organizations of the time. Although the Royal Society for the Prevention of Cruelty to Animals (RSPCA) supported its activities,[14] ULAWS generated anxiety by actively courting the veterinary profession.[15] For the RSPCA, vets were part of the *problem* since they provided legitimacy for scientific experimentation. In contrast, ULAWS boasted that it 'sought to give the veterinary surgeon and the biologist their right places in the zoophile connection', acknowledging them as 'sane and progressive reformers'.[16] As the society was later to acknowledge, it had 'incurred bitter hostility and deliberately sacrificed much support' by allowing scientists who carried out animal experiments to become members. Nevertheless, ULAWS still believed that 'a good deal of common ground can be found if we patiently analyse it out'.[17]

---

[10] Hume, 'An Egg that was Laid at Birkbeck', 13.

[11] Ibid., 13. This dislike of sentimentality can be seen throughout ULAWS's publications: for example, see 'University of London Animal Welfare Society', *Illustrated London News* (11 May 1935), 17, and 'Thinking of Others', *Illustrated Sporting and Dramatic News* (3 May 1955), 10.

[12] *The University of London Animal Welfare Society* (20 January 1931), 1, in Birkbeck Archive, Box 21.

[13] Letter from Hume to the Principal, Dr George Senter, dated 26 November 1931, in Birkbeck Archive, Box 21.

[14] See the report on its inaugural meeting, which was opened by a lecture given by Captain Fergus MacCunn of the RSPCA: University of London Animal Welfare Society, *First Annual Report to September 30th, 1927* (London: ULAWS, 1927), 2.

[15] Ibid., 2. Also see *The University of London Animal Welfare Society* (30 January 1931), 3, in Birkbeck Archive, Box 21.

[16] E. M. Collins (Secretary of the Birkbeck College Branch of the ULAWS), 'University of London Animal Welfare Society', *The Lodestone*, 27.3 (summer 1932), 152. Also see C. W. Hume, 'Protection of Laboratory Animals', *British Medical Journal*, 2.4684 (14 October 1950), 888, and C. W. Hume, 'RSPCA Campaigning', *British Medical Journal*, 1.5280 (17 March 1962), 790 (where he distances the UFAW position from that of the RSPCA).

[17] C. W. Hume, 'Protection of Laboratory Animals', *British Medical Journal*, 2.4693 (16 December 1950), 389.

This meant that ULAWS had a very different stance to other animal lobbying groups about the legitimacy of using animals in scientific experiments. From its first meeting, ULAWS's stance on animal experimentation was neutral: 'individual members', it maintained, were 'free to express any views they may have formed on this subject, but collectively the Society abstains from entering the controversy on either side'.[18] Hume was heralded as the 'helmsman of the "middle course"'.[19]

ULAWS was extremely active. Hume was co-author of a series of widely reviewed animal 'year books', as well as dozens of pamphlets.[20] In 1956, he published a book on religious attitudes to animals.[21] At Birkbeck, ULAWS organized regular lectures, including a controversial one addressing the question of 'Humane Killing', in which the RSPCA appeared in conversation with representatives of the National Federation of Meat Traders Association.[22] The society set up drinking fountains for horses in Athens and invited the controversial author and renowned lesbian Radclyffe Hall to speak at Bedford College on 'Animals in Italy'.[23] It railed against cruel sports such as bull-fighting.[24] Castrating and spaying pigs and lambs without anaesthetic was denounced as cruel, as was releasing oil waste on the high seas.[25] ULAWS lobbied the Jewish community to adopt more humane ways of shechita.[26]

As might be expected from an organization that published 'Man versus Rabbits', one of its central concerns was the treatment of rabbits. ULAWS campaigned vigorously against women who wore furs[27] and took a leading role in the movement to outlaw 'gin traps'. While admitting that rabbits were a farm-pest, it argued that traps that crushed the limbs of rabbits in 'powerful steel jaws', resulting in a prolonged and agonizing death, were inhumane.[28] Surely, it pleaded, less cruel (as well as more effective) ways of killing rabbits could be introduced.

---

[18] University of London Animal Welfare Society, *First Annual Report to September 30th, 1927* (London: ULAWS, 1927), 2.
[19] Dunstan, *Science and Sensibility*, 1.
[20] University of London Animal Welfare Society, *Fifth Annual Report Year Ending June 30th, 1931* (London: ULAWS, 1931), 3. The first volume was edited by Dr G. Wright, assisted by C. W. Hume, *The Animal Year-Book*, Volume 1 (London: London University Press, 1931?).
[21] C. W. Hume, *The Status of Animals in the Christian Religion* (London: UFAW, 1956).
[22] University of London Animal Welfare Society, *Second Annual Report Year Ending September 30th, 1928* (London: ULAWS, 1928), 1.
[23] Ibid., 1, and University of London Animal Welfare Society, *Sixth Annual Report Year Ending June 30th, 1932* (London: ULAWS, 1932), 1.
[24] Dunstan, *Science and Sensibility*, 8.
[25] Captain C. W. Hume, 'Animal Welfare: Its Dependence on Accurate Information', in University of London Animal Welfare Society, *Animal Welfare: Its Dependence on Accurate Information. Report of a Meeting Held at the Seventh Annual Congress of the Association of Special Libraries and Information Bureaux, Oxford, September 20, 1930* (London: ULAWS, 1930), 6–7.
[26] University of London Animal Welfare Society, *Fifth Annual Report Year Ending June 30th, 1931* (London: ULAWS, 1931), 4.
[27] Hume, 'Animal Welfare: Its Dependence on Accurate Information', 5, and 'Women's Furs. Urged to Give them Up', *The Scotsman* (22 September 1930), 2.
[28] Hume, 'Animal Welfare: Its Dependence on Accurate Information', 5. Also see 'The Abolition of Steel Traps', *Wells Journal* (19 October 1934), 6; 'Should the Rabbit Trap Be Abolished?', *Illustrated*

Crucially, ULAWS worked closely with experimental scientists. For example, in 1957, 120 scientists met at Birkbeck to discuss 'Humane Technique in the Laboratory', a meeting that included lengthy discussions on how to replace sentient animals with non-sentient alternatives or 'biological systems of a lower order'.[29] Much time was devoted to considering ways to reduce the number of animals required for experiments while not compromising on the precision of results. They also debated ways to refine experimental techniques in order to reduce or eliminate animal suffering.[30]

Clearly, ULAWS was not advocating for absolute animal rights. Hume sought to distinguish between 'killing and hurting';[31] his society even published a pamphlet entitled 'Kind Killing'.[32] It believed that animals should be stunned first, *then* slaughtered.[33] Ironically, for a society committed to the protection of animals, it invested a great deal of thought developing more effective ways to kill. For example, while maintaining that it was wrong to kill rats and mice with cruel poisons, most of the organization's time was spent arguing with 'professional poisoners' about the *relative* cruelty of various poisons.[34]

Theirs was also a very 'muscular' creed, which abhorred 'fanatical propaganda' and (as Hume scoffed) the 'nightmares bred of a hypersensitive fancy'.[35] ULAWS lamented the fact that discussions about animal welfare were dominated either by apathy or by 'sentimental and even hysterical reactions'.[36] It avoided 'sensationalism and harrowing pictures of distress'.[37] Hume wanted the society to 'help to compensate [for] the harm done to the cause of animal welfare by animal lovers of an unbalanced kind'.[38] ULAWS disdained 'sentimental or controversial glamour'.[39] 'Steadying the hysterical' was loudly proclaimed as one of its aims.[40]

As this highly gendered language suggests, this was a self-consciously masculine approach to animal welfare. When asked why he did not think it was

---

Sporting and Dramatic News (9 November 1934), 30; 'Humane Rat Killing', *Yorkshire Post and Leeds Intelligencer* (25 July 1946), 2; Hume, 'An Egg that was Laid at Birkbeck', 14.

[29] Summarizing opening address by C. W. Hume, in 'Medical Research and Animal Welfare. Responsibility of the Experimental Worker', *British Medical Journal*, 1.5028 (18 May 1957), 1177.

[30] C. W. Hume (Secretary-General of the Universities Federation for Animal Welfare), 'Animals for Research', *The Times* (21 March 1958), 11.

[31] Hume, *The Status of Animals in the Christian Religion*, viii.

[32] Home Office, *Report of the Departmental Committee on Experiments on Animals*, Chairman, Sir Sydney Littlewood [Cmnd 2641] (HMSO, April 1965), 62.

[33] 'Humane Killing', *The Scotsman* (3 September 1927), 9, and 'Stunning of Pigs', *The Scotsman* (19 March 1938), 12.

[34] Hume, 'An Egg that was Laid at Birkbeck', 14.

[35] Hume, 'Animal Welfare: Its Dependence on Accurate Information', 4. Also see Dunstan, *Science and Sensibility*, 2.

[36] E. M. Collins (Secretary of the Birkbeck College Branch of ULAWS), 'University of London Animal Welfare Society', *The Lodestone*, 27.3 (summer 1932), 151.

[37] 'Notes on Books', *British Medical Journal*, 2.3790 (26 August 1933), 384. Also see A. St G. Huggett, 'Man's Debt to Animals', *British Medical Journal*, 1.5343 (1 June 1963), 1469–70.

[38] Dunstan, *Science and Sensibility*, 3.

[39] Collins, 'University of London Animal Welfare Society', 151.   [40] Ibid., 152.

anthropocentric to speak about animal-emotions, Hume made a revealing comment. 'I find it impossible to form a mental image of the feeling of a mother for a new-born baby', he contended, since 'to me [it] is a repulsive and even a disgusting object'. However, 'if I say that women love these creatures, I am not obliged to write the word "love" between quotes, and I am quite able to attach meaning to it'.[41] While female sentiments and animal emotions were both beyond Hume's comprehension, his feelings of 'disgust' for new-born babies were in stark contrast to his love for nonhuman animals. As one reporter observed, Hume's London flat was an '"Alice in Wonderland" den where animals and the lower orders of life are treated with as much care and interest as mere humans'[42] (see Fig. 15.1).

Despite their repudiation of 'hysteria' and 'sentiment', members of ULAWS were not always able to maintain an objective tone. They were bullishly 'British', for example, casting a superior eye on the habits of other peoples.[43] They also

Fig. 15.1 The zoology laboratory at Birkbeck College, c.1920s–1940s. Birkbeck Image Collections: Birkbeck History BH0124.

---

[41] C. W. Hume cited in Dunstan, *Science and Sensibility*, 8.
[42] 'Lobsters Do Mind Being Boiled', *Aberdeen Evening Express* (7 August 1961), 4.
[43] Hume, 'Animal Welfare: Its Dependence on Accurate Information', 4. Also see Dunstan, *Science and Sensibility*, 5.

employed highly emotive metaphors. Even Hume could be heard arguing that the pain of rabbits caught in traps was nothing short of a 'lesser Calvary', a 'long drawn out crucifixion', which was being carried out so that women could 'look a little handsomer in the eyes of their admirers'.[44] As a devout Christian, Hume's appeal to the language of Christ's crucifixion was significant.

The moralizing tone of ULAWS also led it to focus on 'less popular though equally sensitive species'. In other words, it was interested in animals who 'have no appeal to the uneducated and must look for sympathy to persons of more capacious mind, and especially to biological scientists'.[45] Hume maintained that 'sentimentalists care little what happens to rats and mice', scolding such people for having 'acquired in childhood a phobia' against these animals 'which only a psychiatrist, or alternatively a little common sense, could excise'.[46] Hume candidly maintained that students who joined ULAWS were 'usually out of the top drawer intellectually'. He contended that

> I hope we are not being too highbrow... but we have to throw our weight about a little in order to guard against the picture of sentimentality which the words 'animal welfare' conjure up in the minds of the normally unintelligent.[47]

As Hume caustically claimed in 1958, the 'only instances of antipathy which we have encountered have been on the part of a very few abnormal individuals', by which he meant the more 'sentimental' animal rights advocates.[48] This elitism was important to Hume and other members of ULAWS: only the highly educated could exercise truly civilized attitudes.

* * *

Despite its members' dogged elitism and insistence on a 'middle course', ULAWS thrived at Birkbeck and beyond. Students at the College signed up in large numbers and the society could count on the active support of George Senter (Principal of the College between 1918 and 1939), Professor H. G. Jackson (Professor of Zoology and Master from 1943 to 1950),[49] and Professor Helen Gwynne-Vaughan (head of the Botany Department and one of the first female professors in the field), all of whom agreed to serve as Vice-Presidents of ULAWS.[50] Professor

---

[44] 'Cruelty Cured by the Camera', *The Scotsman* (2 January 1931), 10.
[45] Hume, 'An Egg that was Laid at Birkbeck', 14.   [46] Ibid., 43.
[47] Ibid., 15.
[48] C. W. Hume (Secretary-General of the Universities Federation for Animal Welfare), 'Animals for Research', *The Times* (21 March 1958), 11.
[49] University of London Animal Welfare Society, *First Annual Report to September 30th, 1927* (London: ULAWS, 1927), 2.
[50] See University of London Animal Welfare Society, *Tenth Annual Report. 1st October, 1935. To 31st July 1936* (London: University Union, 1936), and *Annual Report. 1st August, 1936 to 30th September, 1937* (London: University Union, 1937), 8 and 34.

Eric H. Warmington (Professor of Classics and passionate birdwatcher) was an active member,[51] as was the legendary C. E. M. Joad from the Philosophy Department. Warmington was almost definitely present in 1936 when Joad chaired a packed theatre in which the distinguished ornithologist Professor Walter Garstang used 'his own vocal illustrations' in addition to recordings on 'gramophone records' to lecture on birdlife.[52]

Not surprisingly, the Second World War saw a slump in the society's activities, as Hume and many other members joined the armed forces. The society also experienced financial difficulties.[53] ULAWS's annual summer school, which used to be held in Brympton d'Evercy (an exquisite manor house in Somerset and home of Violet Clive, an eccentric sportswoman, obsessive gardener, and master carpenter), had to be cancelled since students and staff from Westcroft Preparatory School moved in after being evacuated from their north London residence.[54] To make things worse, ULAWS's offices in Gordon House were damaged by a bomb, so the entire operation was relocated to Hume's house.[55]

After the Second World War, however, a revival took place (see Fig. 15.2). The society (now known as the Universities Federation for Animal Welfare or UFAW) refocused its energies, concentrating on the welfare of laboratory animals. It established research units in the Royal Veterinary College and Birmingham Medical School and could boast the support of scientists who had won Nobel Prizes and Presidents of the Royal Academy.[56] Its influence soared from 1947 with the publication of the first edition of the *UFAW Handbook on the Care and Management of Laboratory Animals*, which set out in practical terms the way experimental animals should be treated. It rapidly became the standard textbook in the field, followed by new (often substantially revised) editions in 1949, 1957, 1959, 1972, 1976, 1987, 1995, 1999, and 2010.[57] As one zoologist commented in his review of the 1957 edition of the handbook,

---

[51] Hume, *The Status of Animals in the Christian Religion*, preface. Also see Eric H. Warmington, 'Ornithology Near Birkbeck College—I', *The Lodestone*, 37.1 (autumn 1944), 15; Eric M. Warmington, 'Ornithology at Birkbeck College (3)', *The Lodestone*, 45.1 (spring 1954), 11–12; Eric M. Warmington, 'Ornithology near Birkbeck College—II', *Lodestone*, 37.2 (spring 1945), 14–15; 'Singing', *The Sun* (15 August 1969), in 'Newscuttings 1968-71', in the Birkbeck Archive.

[52] See University of London Animal Welfare Society, *Tenth Annual Report. 1st October, 1935. To 31st July 1936* (London: University Union, 1936), and *Annual Report. 1st August, 1936 to 30th September, 1937* (London: University Union, 1937), 8 and 34.

[53] For example, see University of London Animal Welfare Society, *Sixth Annual Report Year Ending June 30, 1932* (London: ULAWS, 1932), 1; Universities Federation for Animal Welfare, *Fifteenth Annual Report. Year Ending September 30, 1941* (London: UFAW, 1941), 1; E. M. Collins (Secretary of the Birkbeck College Branch of ULAWS), 'University of London Animal Welfare Society', *The Lodestone*, 27.3 (summer 1932), 152.

[54] Universities Federation for Animal Welfare, *Fifteenth Annual Report. Year Ending September 30, 1941* (London: UFAW, 1941), 1.

[55] Ibid., 1.   [56] Hume, 'An Egg that was Laid at Birkbeck', 13.

[57] For favourable reviews, see 'C. E.', 'Alastair N. Worde (ed.), (1947). The UFAW Handbook on the Care and Management of Laboratory Animals', in *Journal of Animal Ecology*, 17.1 (May 1948), 87; J. O. I. 'The UFAW Handbook on the Care and Management of Laboratory Animals', *Journal of the*

Fig. 15.2 The Master Lockwood and his wife at the 'Chimpanzee Tea Party' in the London Zoological Gardens in 1956. It had been sponsored by Charles R. Clee, a former student of Birkbeck and generous donor to the Friends of Birkbeck fund. The main aim of the afternoon was social, but it was also the opportunity for a ceremony adopting an owl called 'George' (after George Birkbeck) as the College's Eagle Owl mascot. A 1970 article called the owl 'Twilight', an African Wood Owl, but by 1977, it was again 'George'. 'Mr. Charles Clee', in Birkbeck Archive, Box 5.

> It is fortunate that a movement which was started many years ago to protect the interests of animals has been guided away from the path that leads to inverted sadism and emotional anti-vivisection propaganda into more sensible channels, mainly by the devoted work of Major C. W. Hume.[58]

Hume was awarded the Albert Schweitzer Medal by the Animal Welfare Institute of America in 1956 and then an OBE for his services to animal welfare.[59]

Royal Statistical Society, 111.1 (1948), 81; A. L. Bacharach, 'Laboratory Animals', *British Medical Journal*, 2.4617 (2 July 1949), 21.

[58] L. Harrison Matthews, 'A. N. Warden and W. Lane-Petter (eds.) (1957). The UFAW Handbook on the Care and Management of Laboratory Animals', *Journal of Animal Ecology*, 27.2 (November 1958), 404.

[59] 'Albert Schweitzer Medal Award', *British Medical Journal*, 2.4998 (20 October 1956), 949, and G. R. Dunstan, *Science and Sensibility. The Hume Memorial Lecture. 4th November 1982 at King's College, University of London* (London: UFAW, 1983), 4.

The 1960s were an important decade for laboratory animals. As early as 1950, Hume had been concerned about the legislative inadequacies of the 1876 Cruelty to Animals Act. He had drafted a 'Model Act for the Protection of Laboratory Animals', which set standards that should be followed in Britain and abroad. However, it met with a mixed response, with some claiming that, if adopted, animal experiments 'would for all practical purposes be brought to an end'.[60]

* * *

By the 1960s, however, scientists and governmental officials had come to agree with Hume that the 1876 Act was obsolete. The older Act required all scientists carrying out animal experiments to be licensed, their laboratories registered and regularly inspected, and extensive records taken of procedures. However, the Act only applied to vertebrate animals involved in experiments 'calculated to cause pain'. In addition, there were five inspectors expected to deal with 520 laboratories and the 2.5 million experiments using animals undertaken every year.[61] The law was 'riddled with loopholes' and was thought to be 'a hollow sham to throw dust in the eyes of the critics and to salve the conscience of the apathetic'.[62] In 1963, Sir Sydney Littlewood was appointed to look into revising the Act and, when he reported in 1965, he made eighty-three recommendations, forty-nine of which would have required entirely new legislation.[63]

At Birkbeck, there was considerable hostility to the certification process. Professor William Sydney Bullough, head of the Zoology Department, was particularly antagonistic. Bullough depended on animal lives for his research. In his book, *Practical Invertebrate Anatomy*, he concluded each chapter with practical advice on how to kill animals most effectively. Suggestions included asphyxiating fish by placing them in bottles entirely full of water, adding alcohol to their tanks, and plunging them into boiling water.[64]

Although Bullough worked with mice and rats, some of his research involved rabbits. To see how germs spread, he would infect rabbits. Bullough and Dr Edna Laurence's research at Birkbeck also included studying what they called 'chalones', an internal secretion that seemed to stop cells growing and therefore might be used to inhibit cancer cells. In a review of their research in *British Science News*, Roger Lewin noted that, if their arguments were correct, they would need 'about 10,000 kg of blood to extract enough chalone to treat one patient with a form of leukemia'. However, Lewin observed, it was lucky that

---

[60] 'The Protection of Laboratory Animals', *British Medical Journal*, 2.4681 (23 August 1950), 725. Also see 'Protection of Laboratory Animals', *British Medical Journal*, 2.4688 (11 November 1950), 1114–16.
[61] Quoting Lord Dowding speaking in the House of Lords, in 'Medical Notes in Parliament', *British Medical Journal*, 2.5038 (27 July 1957), 241.
[62] Ibid., 241. Also see 'Medical Notes in Parliament', *British Medical Journal*, 2.4790 (25 October 1952), 946–7, and 'Medical Notes in Parliament', *British Medical Journal*, 1.5278 (3 March 1962), 650–1.
[63] W. Lane-Petter, 'The Ethics of Animal Experimentation', *Journal of Medical Ethics*, 2 (1976), 118.
[64] W. S. Bullough, *Practical Invertebrate Anatomy* (London: Macmillan and Co., 1950), v and 390–1.

although chalones are specific to tissues[,] they are not specific to a particular animal. In other words, skin-chalones from pigs, horses and even mice are effective... The job of getting enough raw material from which to isolate chalones for clinical purposes is therefore not as bad as it might be.[65]

In other words, chalones could be harvested from animals.

The 'harvesting' of such vast quantities of blood was out of the question. As head of the department, Bullough was frustrated by the interference of Home Office inspectors in scientific matters that, he believed, were outside their competency levels. In 1964, for example, Bullough complained to the College Secretary that a Professor of Zoology was 'better placed to judge the meaning of and the necessity for any particular piece of research work' than any outsider. He fumed at the assumption that scientists were cold-hearted: on the contrary, they were 'likely to be at least as responsible and humane as one of the Home Office Inspectors'.[66]

In 1962–3, the College was invited to respond to the Home Office's Departmental Committee on Experiments on Animals. Birkbeck's Department of Zoology contended that an Act of Parliament entitled 'Cruelty to Animals' was 'offensive to people who do experimental work with animals in an humane and responsible way'. They urged the government to rename the legislation something like 'The Experiments with Animals Act' or 'The Laboratory Animals Act'.[67] Given that the department's response was drafted by Bullough, it is not surprising that it insisted that responsibility for laboratory animals should lie with the head of department. Such a head would be 'at least as responsible and humane as an Inspector' and would most definitely be 'far better placed to judge the meaning of and the necessity for any particular piece of research work'.[68] In response to suggestions that all animals should be anaesthetized prior to any experiment, the Birkbeck response reminded the commissioners that psychologists in the College were often interested in investigating animal *behaviours*: therefore, 'the use of anaesthetics would make nonsense' of such experiments.[69] It concluded with a critique of Home Office inspectors. Whoever undertook such a job needed to 'understand the aims of modern biological research and the necessity or otherwise of the techniques employed'. Perhaps, the response pointedly asked, it would be advisable to employ 'younger men who are biologists' to the posts.[70] This was a reference to the fact that most of the inspectors were retired military medical

---

[65] Dr Roger Lewin, 'The Chalones and Cancer Therapy', *British Science News*, 114.1 (1974), in 'Newscuttings 1974–76', in the Birbeck Archive.
[66] Letter from Professor W. S. Bullough to Arnolfo John Caraffi, 9 April 1964, in Birkbeck Archive, Box 38.
[67] 'Departmental Committee of Inquiry into Experiments on Animals', 1962–3, in the 'Guard Book' in the Birkbeck Archive.
[68] Ibid.   [69] Ibid.   [70] Ibid.

officers who had sought the job to supplement their pensions.[71] Bullough and his department feared that such men would look askance at deliberately encouraging the growth of tumours in rats and rabbits.

Not surprisingly, Hume (representing UFAW) was also called to give evidence to the Committee.[72] Hume pressed the commissioners to employ properly trained veterinarians to supervise experiments on animals.[73] He insisted that 'further guidance' needed to be given to scientists on how to kill their animals when they were no longer of use. 'Manual methods' of killing rabbits, for example, included 'striking the back of the head smartly with the side of the hand or against the edge of a bench'. These methods might sometimes be 'quick...simple and painless', but they could be cruel in less 'experienced hands'.[74]

Hume and UFAW opposed arguments by the RSPCA, the Agricultural and Medical Research Councils, the Ministry of Agriculture, and the Imperial Cancer Research Fund that special protections should be given to cats and dogs. Along with the Research Defence Society, veterinary societies, and three anti-vivisection societies, UFAW argued that 'these species were not more sensitive to pain than others, and that it was a bad principle to provide special protection for them by diminishing the protection of others'. In other words, '*all* animals should receive the best possible treatment' within laboratories.[75]

The Departmental Committee on Experiments on Animals largely adopted UFAW's arguments. It proposed that the new Act should focus on the concept of preventing 'unnecessary suffering'. This required three regulations: licensees should be required to 'take effective precautions to prevent or reduce to a minimum, any pain or other distress or discomfort in the animals used'; 'every animal which [sic] is suffering discomfort' should be 'painlessly killed as soon as the experiment has been completed'; and 'in no case shall any animal be subjected to severe pain which endures or is likely to endure'.[76] By 1967, Hume and his society were being openly praised for 'getting on the right side of those who were in control of animal experimentation and getting practical results where the doctrinaire anti-vivisectionist has done nothing to improve things for laboratory animals'.[77]

* * *

It is difficult to know whether Hume had discussions with Birkbeck scientists during the hearings of the Departmental Committee on Experiments on Animals, although he had been invited to write an article in *The Lodestone* at the same time that Bullough and the College were responding to them.[78] Whether or not they

---

[71] Home Office, *Report of the Departmental Committee on Experiments on Animals*, Chairman, Sir Sydney Littlewood [Cmnd 2641] (HMSO, April 1965), 151.
[72] Ibid. [73] Ibid., 41–2. [74] Ibid., 62.
[75] Ibid., 106. Emphasis added. [76] Ibid., 100.
[77] 'Keith Brace on Animal Welfare', *Birmingham Daily Post* (11 March 1967), 9.
[78] Hume, 'An Egg that was Laid at Birkbeck', 14.

had conferred, Bullough was unconvinced that the compromise had been a good one. In 1974, he responded sarcastically to a Home Office questionnaire about the treatment of animals in laboratories. As head of the Zoology Department, he was ultimately responsible for the care of the experimental animals in the College, so the questionnaire asked him what procedures were in place if he needed to be contacted about any aspect of animal welfare. His response was terse: 'Means of communication with me: knock on my door'. Asked what would happen in the case of an emergency, Bullough contended that 'the technician would run rather than walk' to his door. Finally, to the question about how the animals were cared for at night, he responded: 'Outside normal working hours both the animals and their attendants sleep.'[79]

Bullough did admit that early-career scientists were being more thoroughly trained in the care of their experimental animals than had their predecessors. However, he remained adamant that the Home Office's inspectors were unhelpful. He wanted 'the present system whereby the Inspectors are older medical men' to be abolished. These men had 'little, if any, understanding of the aims of modern biological research, and their comments, often meant to be helpful, show only too frequently and too clearly their abysmal ignorance'. They should be replaced with 'younger men who are biologists in the widest sense of that term'.[80]

By the late 1980s, the care of laboratory animals in scientific establishments was largely based on UFAW's and the Royal Society's *Guidelines on the Care of Laboratory Animals and their Use for Scientific Purposes: I—Housing and Care* (1987).[81] These guidelines provided researchers with a detailed code of practice for the training of staff, the conduct of inspections, procedures in the event of any emergency, the environment in which the animals were to be kept (including the temperature, humidity, ventilation, lighting, noise, bedding and nesting materials, food, water, 'environmental enrichment', handling, and cleaning), and efficient methods of 'dispatch'. As the 'helmsman of the middle course', Hume had triumphed.

* * *

Nevertheless, the period from the 1970s to the 1990s was a difficult one for zoologists, biologists, and psychologists who used animals in their experiments. The specific species housed at Birkbeck varied according to the research

---

[79] Letter from Professor W. S. Bullough to Mr N. Gershan (Administrative Assistant at Birkbeck), 8 November 1974, in Birkbeck Archive, Box 38.
[80] Letter from Professor W. S. Bullough to Arnolfo John Caraffi, 9 April 1964, in Birkbeck Archive, Box 38.
[81] Home Office, 'Animals (Scientific Procedures) Act 1986. Code of Practice. For the Housing and Care of Animals in Designated Breeding and Supplying Establishments', House of Commons (24 January 1995), [125], 2. See the UFAW and the Royal Society's *Guidelines on the Care of Laboratory Animals and their Use for Scientific Purposes: I—Housing and Care* (London: Royal Society and Universities Federation for Animal Welfare, 1987).

interests of individual scientists. With Bullough's departure, the rabbits were 'dispatched'. By the 1980s and 1990s, the College was home to thousands of mice and rats, dozens of pigeons, and around 10,000 Japanese quails, which were bred for research on embryonic physiology.[82] These were the 'unlovely' animals championed by ULAWS.

In addition, the major changes that were being made to certification processes were having a significant impact on scientific research at Birkbeck, as elsewhere. In 1986, a new Act of Parliament was passed to regulate the use of animals for experimental purposes. Dr N. Burton from the Home Office's Animals Scientific Procedures Inspectorate informed Birkbeck that the new Act was not simply an updated version of its 1876 predecessor. 'Good intentions' on the part of the scientists were no longer good enough. Henceforth, licences to carry out experiments using animals would only be granted after weighing up 'the likely *adverse effect* on the animals used against the *benefit* likely to accrue from the work'. Scientists were also required to consider 'the feasibility of using alternative methods not involving live animals'—that is, the 'non-sentient alternatives' championed by ULAWS. Project design, facilities, and staff would all be inspected. Particular attention was paid to 'identifying pain, suffering, distress or lasting harm' that might arise before, during, and after the experiment. Scientists were henceforth required to describe the 'humane end-point' in detail.[83]

Tensions between the College and the veterinary surgeons appointed by the government flared up. The College was particularly wary of the Royal Veterinary College, believing that it was attempting to advance its own interests at the expense of universities.[84] Even Mike Chapman, the inspector assigned to oversee animal use at Birkbeck, admitted that the 1986 Act led to a 'forced' relationship between the College's scientists and the veterinary surgeons. This was 'probably not the best foundation for professional:client relations', he contended. After all, scientists resented interference from veterinary surgeons who, in turn, had been given 'statutory responsibility for a site' that they were only able to visit 'intermittently'. In a letter to the College's Secretary, Chapman noted conciliatorily that the arrangement 'relies on the named veterinary surgeon building good relations with the client. Something which I fear... I may have failed to do here.'[85]

---

[82] Letter from Professor W. G. Overend to Dr A. O. Betts (Principal and Dean of the Royal Veterinary College), 13 January 1984, in Birkbeck Archive, Box 38, which states that there were 1,110 mice, 300 rats, 110 quails, and 50 pigeons housed in the College; Letter from Helen Mortimer (Assistant Secretary, Resources) to Mr D. Anderson-Evans (Senior Administrative Officer, Committee of Vice-Chancellors and Principals), 12 September 1988, in Birkbeck Archive, Box 38, which states that there were 1,000 laboratory rats and 10,000 Japanese quails were being bred at Birkbeck every year; 'Review of the Fifth Floor Specialised Research Facility', 2000, 2, in Birkbeck Archive, Box 38.
[83] Dr N. Burton, 'Hints on Applying for a Project Licence', n.d., 1–4, in Birkbeck Archive, Box 38.
[84] Memo from Dr Christine Mabey to Eddie Hedgley, 'Questionnaire from Royal Veterinary College', 26 January 1989, in Birkbeck Archive, Box 38.
[85] Letter from Mike Chapman to Dr Mabey, 23 March 1989, in Birkbeck Archive, Box 38.

The situation was worsened by negative assessments of Birkbeck's animal facilities. There were reports about dirty quail houses and poor ventilation; silver fish and beetles scurried around under the linoleum. It was sometimes found that the pigeon and rat rooms were grubby and the pigeons had not been fed or given water. Day-to-day care was judged inadequate.[86]

Hostile inspectors were not the only headache for scientists employing animals in their research. A much more worrying development was the mobilization of animal rights militants who had been radicalized by anti-authoritarian struggles of the time. These radicals were disillusioned by the lack of progress made through lawful campaigning. For the first time since the anti-vivisectionist movements of the nineteenth century, animal rights activists were willing to use violence.

In the UK, the Band of Mercy (a name borrowed from the early nineteenth-century juvenile wing of the 'animals' guardian' movement) initiated a spate of violence, beginning on 10 November 1973 when they set fire to a laboratory for animal experimentation being built in Milton Keynes. In 1976, they changed their name to the Animal Liberation Front (ALF). In the words of its founder Ronnie Lee, 'Animal liberation is a fierce struggle that demands total commitment. There will be injuries and possibly deaths on both sides. That is sad, but certain.'[87] Even more radical groups included the Animal Rights Militia (established in 1982), the Hunt Retribution Squad (1984), the Justice Department (1993), and Stop Huntingdon Animal Cruelty (1999). High-explosive bombs were detonated at Bristol University and veterinary researchers working at Porton Down and Bristol in 1989 and 1990 were attacked.[88] Hume would have been appalled at the level of passion exhibited by what he would have called 'animal lovers of an unbalanced kind'.

In response, the Home Office sent all laboratories carrying out animal experiments, including ones at Birkbeck, detailed advice on how to protect themselves (see Fig. 15.3).[89] This advice emphasized the need to restrict access to laboratories and 'supporting facilities' (which meant, amongst other places, the animal cages on the fifth floor of the Malet Street building and those in the room that used to be the College's Archive). Offices inhabited by scientists should always be locked; recordkeeping and computer facilities had to be made secure. Prior to closing the College at night, all public areas (including 'coal chutes and air ducts') must be

---

[86] Letter to Dr Christine M. Mabey. From the inspector Dr N. Burton (Animals (Scientific Procedures) Inspectorate), 4 January 1989, in Birkbeck Archive, Box 47; letter from the College Secretary to Dr S. F. Walker, 2 April 1990, in Birkbeck Archive, Box 47; letter from the inspector Dr N. Burton, in a memo dated 30 March 1990, in Birkbeck Archive, Box 47; letter from Burton to Swainson, 30 September 1988, in Birkbeck Archive, Box 38.

[87] 'Animal Rights Terror Tactics', 30 August 2000, http://news.bbc.co.uk/2/hi/uk_news/902751.stm, viewed 1 January 2010.

[88] 'Home Office Notice on Human Rights Extremists', in Birkbeck Archive, Box 47.   [89] Ibid.

searched. Birkbeck staff were given instructions what to do if they observed anything suspicious or received a bomb threat. The Home Office warned that 'When a bomb threat is received police would not NORMALLY [sic] search the building. This is because your staff will be more familiar with the building than police and will be able to conduct a quicker and more thorough search.'[90] In other words, the attendants were made responsible for this potentially hazardous task.

The threats heated up in 1997. The Home Office's Constitutional and Community Policy Directorate sent our major warnings, spurred by the fact that dustman-turned-ALF-bomber Barry Horne was on hunger strike. 'There are indications', the Home Office warned the College in a letter to 'All Certificate Holders', that some of Horne's followers 'may start sending or planting incendiary devices'.[91] Birkbeck was a minor target (the main threats were made against the Huntingdon Life Sciences complex, where sixty activists set up a camp in support of Horne), but even Birkbeck staff were warned that 'Extra vigilance is advised'.[92]

* * *

By 2000, animal experimentation had fallen out of favour at Birkbeck. Although the Department of Psychology had been a hotbed for behaviourism—with its long history of studying nonhuman animals—this had been superseded by other intellectual approaches by the start of the twenty-first century; specifically, the neurosciences. Psychologist Simon Green was the only remaining member of the department engaged in animal research and even he admitted that he had little time for it, being preoccupied by serving as head of department.[93] The Zoology Department was dissolved and intellectual attention shifted to molecular biology. American physicist Evelyn Fox Keller explained the move towards molecular approaches as part of a shift away from the 'structures of the organism-niche complex, of the organism itself' and towards the 'physical-chemical structure of one particular component of the cell: namely, in the genetic material, or more exactly, in the gene'.[94] This fundamentally challenged and changed the discipline. In Keller's words, 'from the complex of living-organism characteristics that have historically been employed to define life (e.g., growth and development, reproduction, irritability), life came to be redefined by molecular biologists as... information... encoded in the genes'.[95] This revolution was driven by molecular

---

[90] Letter to R. E. Swainson (Secretary and Clerk to the Governors, Birkbeck) from Hugh Marriage, 21 April, c.1988, in Birkbeck Archive, Box 38.
[91] Letter to 'All Certificate Holders' from the Home Office Constitutional and Community Policy Directorate, 9 August 1997, in the Birkbeck Archive, Box 58.
[92] Ibid.
[93] Email from Simon Green to B. White, Julia Goodfellow, S. Walker (Dean of the Faculty), and David McGhie, 7 June 2000, in the Birkbeck Archive, Box 38.
[94] Evelyn Fox Keller, 'Fractured Images of Science, Language, and Power: A Postmodern Optic, or Just Bad Eyesight?', *Poetics Today*, 12.2 (summer 1991), 229.
[95] Ibid., 229.

Fig. 15.3 A Home Office pamphlet sent to Birkbeck College advising how to deal with the new threat from animal liberationist activists, c.1980s–1990s. Birkbeck Archive, 'A4 Black Ring Binder 1'.

biologists, biophysicists, biochemists, and geneticists. As J. D. Bernal had observed as long ago as 1967,

> Life is beginning to cease to be a mystery and becoming practically a cryptogram, a puzzle, a code that can be broken, a working model that sooner or later can be made.[96]

He called this 'the molecular immanence of life'.[97] By the new century, the older form of zoology/biology had fallen by the wayside.

More prosaic concerns were also driving this shift. As we have seen throughout the history of Birkbeck, space was a perennial source of crisis. The College had housed animals since the 1960s,[98] but by the twenty-first century providing facilities for animals was a luxury that a space-starved college could no longer afford.[99] In addition, staff began complaining about pungent smells in corridors.[100] When

---

[96] J. D. Bernal, 'Definitions of Life', *New Scientist*, 33.528 (5 January 1967), 13.
[97] Ibid., 14.
[98] Email from Simon Green to B. White, Julia Goodfellow, S. Walker (Dean of the Faculty), and David McGhie, 7 June 2000, in the Birkbeck Archive, Box 38.
[99] 'Review of the Fifth Floor Specialised Research Facility', 2000, 4, in Birkbeck Archive, Box 38.
[100] See the interview of Professor Michael Slater and the letter of complaint to the Master, in the Birkbeck Oral Interviews.

locusts escaped from their cages on the fifth floor of Malet Street, invading the offices of members of the English Department, it was agreed that 'enough was enough'.[101] The College decided to surrender its licences.

What happened to the remaining experimental animals at Birkbeck? The colony of quails was transferred to the animal house of the Royal Veterinary College and all the equipment was dismantled 'to demonstrate that the accommodation could not be used again for animal accommodation'.[102] The mice were also dispatched. Following the advice set out by Hume and ULAWS, seventy-three Hooded Lister mice were 'euthanised using CO_2 anaesthesia followed by immediate maceration' (the bodies were minced).[103] Hume's 'middle course' was at an end.

---

[101] See the interview of Professor Michael Slater, in the Birkbeck Oral Interviews.

[102] Letter to Dr Clive Wilkins, Home Office inspector, ASI, 6 December 2000, no author given, in Birkbeck Archive, Box 38.

[103] Letter from Simon Green, School of Psychology, to Dr Clive Wilkins, 15 November 2000, in Birkbeck Archive, Box 38.

16
The Students' 'Joy-Night'

> Fetter Lane: 'antiently [sic: anciently] a resort for idle and disorderly persons called Fewterers'.
>
> From David Hughson's 1807 history of London[1]

Once a year, students of the Birkbeck Literary and Scientific Institute went wild. They threw their energies into a boisterous ritual that saw hordes of fancifully dressed students waylaying the Foundation Day speaker prior to his lecture and ceremoniously carting him to the College's theatre, just off Fetter Lane. Once there, they sang silly songs, beat drums, released balloons or streamers, and mocked the authorities. To join in a 'rag', a student had to dress

> in old clothes that make you faintly resemble something or other. Then...behave like a boy of ten, or a girl of seventeen, with experience of twenty-five, [and] shout as though your lungs were those of an infant in arms, and generally go mad.[2]

This was a very public ritual: in Fleet Street and Fetter Lane, crowds of people stepped out of their offices and shops to watch this 'students' rag' or 'Joy-Night'.[3] Most witnesses to the 'ragging' cheered the high spirits of Birkbeck's students; a few 'tutted' disapprovingly about their childish antics.[4]

In 1925, it was the turn of Lord Eustace Percy, President of the Board of Education, to be 'ragged'. Nearly a hundred students of both sexes accosted his car near Ludgate Circus. The women were dressed like 'little girls, with pig-tails, socks, and short frocks'; the men had donned sailor suits. Some wore pyjamas and had blackened their faces. The noise was deafening: bells were rung, whistles blown, clappers thwacked, and rattles vigorously shaken.[5] The students dragged Lord Eustace's car along Fleet Street and then down Fetter Lane, before escorting

---

[1] 'Editorial', *The Lodestone*, 24.2 (spring 1929), 55. He is quoting from David Hughson, *London: Being an Accurate History and Description of the British Metropolis and Its Neighbourhood, to Thirty Miles Extent, from an Actual Perambulation*, vol. 4 (London: J. Stratford, 1807), 117.

[2] Cicerone, 'To the Editor', *The Lodestone*, 20.1 (Michaelmas 1924), 28.

[3] 'Lord E. Percy "Ragged". 14-Stone "Baby" Presented in Perambulator', *Daily Mail* (10 December 1925), 9. Also see 'Students' Joy-Night', *Birmingham Daily Gazette* (10 December 1925), 1.

[4] Letter to the Editor from A. W. Jackson, *The Lodestone*, 28.2 (spring 1933), 103.

[5] 'Students' "Rag" Lord Eustace Percy's Lively Experience', *Shield's Daily News* (10 December 1925), 5.

him to the College's theatre. There was a short period of calm while the President gave a lecture on 'The Adventure of Learning', before all hell broke loose again. Once the graduating students had been presented with their degrees, a 'perambulator' (that is, a pram) was solemnly pushed onto the stage. In it was a fat, male student, dressed in nappies and pyjamas, demanding to be 'presented' with a degree. Around the baby's neck was a card that bore the words 'The newest student'. After Lord Eustace solemnly shook the baby's hand, he was presented with a parchment-like scroll, tied in red ribbon and 'sealed' with a stale bun. On the scroll were the words 'The Freedom of the Refectory'. Mocking the head of the Board of Education's overly bureaucratic approach to College governance, the scroll degreed that, henceforth, whenever Lord Eustace entered Birkbeck's refectory he must 'conduct himself in the manner set forth on the "official order sheet, pink form A609T7684214Qp, par 922. Section (A) of Sub-section 99"'.[6]

Lord Eustace's 'ragging' was typical. Two years earlier, the victim had been the Earl of Balfour. During his Foundation Lecture, the Earl had also been subjected to 'college yells and the beating of biscuit tins'. Coloured paper streamers were thrown across the lecture room and 'a rope, like a line of family washing' had been suspended from one side of the theatre to the other, on which were attached 'a pair of trousers, shoes, empty bottles, sweaters, and boxing gloves' (see Fig. 16.1).[7]

In 1927, Sir Henry Hadow (Vice-Chancellor of the University of Sheffield and musicologist) was booked to speak. He was regaled by around 200 students while dining at the Falstaff restaurant. The students surrounded the restaurant, shouting 'We must have Hadow!'[8] A chef who had been looking out of the top window was 'vociferously requested' to throw down his white cap 'to decorate a student whose costume was lacking in this particular'.[9] A barrel organ (on which some joker had chalked the words: '4 wives, 400 kids') made a discordant racket.[10] Fifty students then dragged Sir Henry into a car drawn by men in brightly coloured costumes and took him down Fetter Lane and into Bream's Building.[11] Inside the theatre, there were trumpets, bugles, whistles, rattles, and a 'hurley gurdy', making a great deal of noise even during Sir Henry's speech on 'Landmarks in Education'.[12] When the students wanted to poke fun at what Sir Henry was saying, they would interrupt him with loud 'groans' and the 'occasional crash' of the barrel organ.[13]

---

[6] Ibid., 5.   [7] 'Lord Balfour. Noisy Welcome by Students'. *Daily Mail* (30 November 1923), 7.
[8] 'Fleet Street Rag', *Daily News* (8 December 1927); 'Sir H. Hadow "Ragged"', *Sheffield Daily Telegraph* (8 December 1927), 6; 'Students Drag a Car', *Westminster Gazette* (8 December 1927).
[9] 'Sir H. Hadow "Ragged"', *Sheffield Daily Telegraph* (8 December 1927), 6.
[10] 'Students Drag a Car', *Westminster Gazette* (8 December 1927).
[11] 'Sir H. Hadow "Ragged"', *Yorkshire Post* (8 December 1927). Also see 'Birkbeck Students "Rag"', *Daily Sketch* (7 December 1927).
[12] 'Students "Rag" Lord Haldane', *Morning Post* (1 December 1927).
[13] 'Sir H. Hadow "Ragged"', *Yorkshire Post* (8 December 1927).

Fig. 16.1 Ragging during the 1923 Centenary Celebrations. Birkbeck Archive.

Kidnapping Foundation Day speakers at the restaurant prior to their lecture seems to have been the norm. The Right Honourable Lord Macmillan had his meal interrupted in 1932 by a crowd of 'gaily dressed' ('and with a Scottish note predominating') Birkbeck students who took him on for a ride in a hansom cab, escorted by a 'barrel organ of ancient vintage' and a 'gallant steed' impersonated by two students.[14] When he arrived at the College, he was met by a crowd of students crying out 'We want Mac' and singing the College song. At least one newspaper observed that an 'amusing contrast was provided by a guard of honour of members of the college's O.T.C. who stood stiffly to attention in the entrance hall'.[15] Balloons were burst; streamers let fly.[16]

Two years later, the students ambushed the taxi of Walter Elliott (Minister of Agriculture) as it entered Fetter Lane. They forced the minister out of the taxi and made him ride up Fetter Lane on a pantomime-cow. Although Elliott was described as 'smiling' when he alighted from his taxi, he was much more hesitant when asked to climb on to the back of the 'cow'. After finding his balance, he was seen 'clinging with one hand' to the 'cow' and waving his hat with the other hand 'in the manner of a Wild West rider (but looking less sure of his seat)'.[17] The

---

[14] 'Law Lord in "Rag"', *Nottingham Evening Post* (8 December 1932). [15] Ibid.
[16] 'In Medias Res', *The Lodestone*, 28.2 (spring 1933), 77.
[17] 'Mr Elliott Turns "Cowboy"', *Daily Mail* (13 December 1934), 11.

minister (still on the back of the 'cow') was then led up the steps to the platform of the lecture theatre by two young men: one dressed as a yokel and the other as a fairy.[18] Once on the platform, the 'fairy' 'fell down and lay on his back kicking', then got up and, after curtsying, presented the Minister of Agriculture with 'a basket containing a pig's head and some kippers'.[19] The minister was then required to sign this declaration:

> I, Walter Elliott, alias Bo-Bo the Gadarene, whose father was Hi-To, begat of Circe, do hereby present all my estate in piggery to the students of Birkbeck College.
>
> And by these presents I do hereby engage the Pig Marketing Board, the dearest of my possessions, having regard to its especial qualifications in framing regulations for the guidance and administration of pigs, hogs, swine &c., to administer a prize fund under its peculiar regulations for those who do not bring home the bacon by not obtaining degrees.

Under Elliott's signature were the words 'Chief of the Pig Board, Chief of the Milk Board, Chief of the Hops Board, Chief of the Herring Board'.[20] The fairy then reappeared, giving everyone on the platform a bottle of milk, each with a straw stuck through the tab, to suck.[21]

* * *

Ridiculous? Well, yes, but that was the point. Foundation ceremonies could be very dreary occasions: 'ragging' certainly livened things up.[22] They were also an effective way for graduating students to 'let off steam', especially after years of academic study. Students who failed to join in rags were lampooned for being 'staid and respectable': they were said to be married and 'settled down'. If it was a female student, it was rumoured that she was 'a good deal older than she tries to look'.[23]

More importantly, College rags were a negotiated inversion of staff–student relations in an institution that was markedly hierarchical. 'Ragging' was a classic example of 'authorized transgression'. They were carnivalesque, temporarily inverting the rules as well as power structures while simultaneously blunting social criticism. In critic Umberto Eco's words, such carnivals are not 'instances of real transgressions: on the contrary, they represent paramount examples of law reinforcement'. They remind participants 'of the existence of the rule'.[24]

---

[18] 'Elliott "Ragged"', *The Scotsman* (13 December 1934), 13.
[19] Ibid., 13. Also see 'Peace and Liberty', *The Times* (13 December 1934), 9.
[20] 'Elliott "Ragged"', *The Scotsman* (13 December 1934), 13.   [21] Ibid., 13.
[22] Letter to the Editor from A. W. Jackson, *The Lodestone*, 28.2 (spring 1933), 103.
[23] Cicerone, 'To the Editor', 27–8.
[24] Umberto Eco, 'The Frames of Comic "Freedom"', in Thomas A. Sebeok, assisted by Marcia E. Erickson (eds), *Carnival!* (New York: Mouton Publishers, 1984), 6.

It must not be assumed that College authorities disapproved of 'rags'. Quite the contrary. In 1927, Lord Haldane (President of the College), Sir Henry Hadow (the Foundation Day speaker), and Dr George Senter (the College's Principal) entered fully 'into the spirit of the thing', rewarding each of the main 'raggers' with a 'hearty shake of the hand'.[25] The same phrase about 'entering into the spirit' of the ritual was used when Macmillan was ragged in 1932.[26] It was *de rigueur* for people who had been 'ragged' to declare that they had had a 'thoroughly enjoyable evening'.[27] Even the Minister for Agriculture, who had endured what must have been a fairly humiliating ride up Fetter Lane on a pantomime-cow, professed to have 'enjoyed the ride': he also signed away his possessions with 'a laugh and a flourish'.[28] On at least one occasion, the President of the College in 1932 (the newspaper proprietor and Liberal Unionist Harry Levy-Lawson, 1st Viscount Burnham) commended the President of the Students' Union for a successful 'rag', asking him to 'convey to those concerned' his 'appreciation of the behaviour of the students on the Founders' Day'. He praised them for 'their ceremony inside the building', which was 'both witty and well-carried through' and, although he admitted that he had not seen the 'rag' outside, noted that 'it appears to have been well done'. Of course, the College's President added, there was 'still room for improvement as regards giving the speakers a quiet hearing', but 'otherwise everything went very well. It was certainly a very successful function and the students played their part admirably.'[29] Such a tolerant attitude was predicated on the understanding that 'ragging' was a temporary, once-a-year flouting of the rules by educated youths. The whole point was to show 'how are the mighty fallen!'[30] Raggers were able to 'indulge their perverted instincts' but then 'came back to earth none the worse, even if none the better, for their "bit of a rag"'. They simply 'returned to the habits that they...usually pursue'.[31] It would be difficult to imagine a similarly indulgent attitude if the 'raggers' had been working-class youths ceremoniously defying their 'betters'.

Equally, 'rags' were not spontaneous outbursts. Rules had to be followed. In the words of one student writing in 1933, a rag 'does no harm and quite a lot of good' but 'only if the...rules are followed'.[32] 'Raggers' were required to keep it friendly, only involve people who want to take part, respect property, and ensure that any damage unintentionally inflicted was promptly compensated.[33]

---

[25] 'Students "Rag" Lord Haldane', *Morning Post* (1 December 1927).
[26] 'Law Lord in "Rag"', *Nottingham Evening Post* (8 December 1932).
[27] 'Sir H. Hadow "Ragged"', *Yorkshire Post* (8 December 1927).
[28] 'Elliott "Ragged"', *The Scotsman* (13 December 1934), 13.
[29] Letter from the President of the College to A. R. Drake (President of the Student Union), 1932, in the Birkbeck Archive, Box 21.
[30] Eustace, 'Letter to the Editor', *The Lodestone*, 21.2 (spring 1926), 96.
[31] 'Another Note on Ragging', *The Lodestone*, 24.3 (summer 1929), 118.
[32] A. W. Jackson, 'Letter to the Editor', *The Lodestone*, 28.2 (spring 1933), 103.
[33] Ibid., 103.

As this suggests, 'rags' were carefully choreographed. They were premeditated events that required considerable preparatory work. Take the Founders' Day 'rag' of 1925. The 'ragging' students were issued with a detailed script for the evening. They were told to assemble in a section of the Circle in the theatre that had been specifically reserved for them. They were to sing the songs in a specified order. First, 'Who killed cock robin (Harmony)'; second, 'Bangor (Unison)'; and, finally, 'John Brown's Body (Harmony)'. 'Raggers' were told that, while the graduates were being presented with their degrees, 'noises of most descriptions are permissible'. When Richard Haldane (1st Viscount Haldane), the President of the College, rose to speak to the question 'What is Truth?', however, they should recite the limerick:

> A philosophical peer so bright
> Who could travel much faster than light.
> He went out one day in a relative way
> And came back the previous night...
> ...quite knowledgably.

They pronounced the first syllable of 'knowledgeably' with a broad round 'o', as Haldane did.[34] The chant also shows that the students knew *in advance* of the ceremony that the President was going to speak about relativity.[35] Then, when George Senter (the Principal) delivered his annual report, he was to be greeted with:

> We know a bra' Scotsman named Sentor
> A regular hundred percenter
> Both at science and arts
> He's a man of SOME parts
> And a sportsman—is Dr George Senter.

A toast would then be sung. Immediately before Lord Eustace Percy delivered his oration, the 'raggers' would recite:

> Of Knuts we've met a number
> From Land's End to the Humber
> But the knutest of the knuts
> Is Eustace Percy.
> Of education you're the lead
> So just you drop your little seed
> While you've got us at your mercy—Eustace Percy.

---

[34] W. R. Wooldridge, 'Birkbeck Reminiscences', *The Lodestone*, 53.2 (spring 1963), 9.
[35] Lord Haldane, 'What is Truth? Lord Haldane Essays an Answer', in Birkbeck Archive, Box 9a.

The ragger's script noted that if the President of the Students' Union (whose surname was Moss) was asked to second a vote of thanks to the Chairman, he was required to say:

> Rolling stones do lots of things,
> But there's one, or so it seems,
> That they can't do—that is, gather any Moss.
> They may try what wiles they care to
> Gnash their teeth and tear their hair too
> But they'll ne'er disturb our little piece of Moss.

After Senter had finished giving his report and the applause had subsided, the raggers should sing:

> To the Head of the Coll. here is health and good luck,
> He's never found wanting in patience or pluck,
> While Birkbeck is sleeping, he faithfully, [sic] keeps watch,
> So again, here is health to the man (who is Scotch!).[36]

When Dean Inge (known as 'the gloomy Dean') came to speak, a green searchlight was trained on him from the gallery.[37] In this way, 'rags' were a highly controlled form of 'cocking the snook' against authority.

* * *

But uneasiness with the practice of 'ragging' was increasingly being heard. In 1927, for example, one critic described the 'choral singing of Aframerican spirituals and sea shanties by an misassortment of adolescents and young adults' as a 'fair indication of high spirits' but nonetheless 'not... particularly ear pleasant'. The student complained that

> The first part of the rag... was not particularly appropriate; but had the matter be left there, no great harm would have been done. As it was, the rag was proceeded with in a manner the thought of which brings a blush of shame to the cheeks of those present who, like myself, do not object to indecency as such but abhor vulgarity. For the finish of the rag was nastily vulgar.[38]

---

[36] 'Founders Day Rag 1925. Programme of Music Etc', 1925, in Birkbeck Archive, Box 9a. Note that this programme also gives the words and music to the songs. It gives the words to another song, not mentioned in the actual programme, called 'Grinding', which was about studying for Latin and Greek exams.

[37] Wooldridge, 'Birkbeck Reminiscences', 9.

[38] Halfish, 'Quis Custodiet Ipsoss Custodes?', *The Lodestone*, 22.2 (spring 1927), 139–40.

There were also rags that went horribly wrong. The informal contract between the authorities and the students taking part in 'rags' can be seen more clearly by looking at one 'rag' that was condemned. In 1928, Birkbeck students took part in a 'bad rag'.[39] The main part of the 1928 'ragging' involved the usual jocular harassment of the Foundation Day speaker. On 12 December 1928, fifty male and female students 'dressed and painted in jazz fashion' serenaded Lord Lurgan (Anglo-Irish aristocrat) from a 'motor-lorry' they had parked outside the restaurant where he was dining.[40]

The main difference with the 1928 rag was that, earlier that day, Birkbeck students had raided the refectory of King's College—their arch-rivals who were only 800 metres from Birkbeck's building off Fetter Lane. The reason for their raid was silly. Some students had created a mascot for Birkbeck. They had taken an advertising model of a young girl holding a large Swan pen and, with the aid of paint and a Birkbeck shield, transformed her into 'Egbert... A child of doubtful parentage but at once the darling of the college'.[41] These students then decided that Egbert should be introduced to 'Reggie', the wooden lion mascot that stood in the refectory of King's College.[42] They wanted to abduct Reggie, forcing him to 'pay homage' to their Egbert.[43]

Unfortunately, the Foundation Day raid on King's refectory did not go to plan. The King's men resisted and

> Chairs flew through the air, tables were overturned, cups, buns and chocolate cakes made handy missiles, and Reggie found himself on top of the railings outside, but thus far and no further.[44]

Believing the raid had been carried out by University College London (whose students had kidnapped Reggie in 1922), the King's students stormed that college, painting the statutes in front of UCL red and blue.[45] Meanwhile, Egbert was being 'shown the sights of London' in a 'motor-lorry'[46] before being returned to Birkbeck's refectory and everyone went home.

By the following day, King's students had realized their mistake. Birkbeck students nervously waited for a counter-raid. Suddenly, the lights throughout the College went out and Egbert disappeared. 'Ma' Francis, the titan in charge of Birkbeck's refectory (see Chapter 13), was immediately asked 'Where is Egbert,

---

[39] 'Another Note on Ragging', *The Lodestone*, 24.3 (summer 1929), 117.
[40] 'Students Injured in Raid', *Daily Herald* (14 December 1928).
[41] Mathdod, 'The Tale of Egbert', *The Lodestone*, 24.2 (spring 1929), 88.
[42] 'London Rag Between Two Colleges', *Daily Express* (14 December 1928). Also see Mathdod, 'The Tale of Egbert', *The Lodestone*, 24.2 (spring 1929), 88.
[43] Mathdod, 'The Tale of Egbert', 88.   [44] Ibid., 88.
[45] Ibid., 88. Also see 'Wild Scenes in a London College', *Daily Chronicle* (14 December 1928).
[46] Mathdod, 'The Tale of Egbert', 88.

Mrs. Francis?' to which 'Ma' Francis replied 'She's gone sir. When them lights went out she vanished.'⁴⁷

An hour later, the counter-raid began in earnest. A group of King's students ran into Birkbeck's Common Room; Birkbeck students responded by drenching them and the room with a fire extinguisher.⁴⁸ According to one witness, the King's students 'half wrecked the place...and tried to steal our mascot, Egbert'.⁴⁹ When the King's students retreated, they took with them 'the shield of Big Chief Hammer-Toe, and a small University shield'. The latter was recaptured after a struggle.⁵⁰

The following day, a counter-counter-raid was planned. The Birkbeck students had been 'piqued by the daring of the King's raiders' and were upset because they believed that Egbert had been stolen.⁵¹ Egged on by female students, between 60 and 200 (most commentators say 'over 100')⁵² students from Birkbeck 'marched from their headquarters, off Fetter Lane' to King's.⁵³ They were 'dressed in dungarees' (another report described their clothes as 'exotic raiment')⁵⁴ and made a lot of noise by singing and shouting.⁵⁵ Arriving at Kings at 6.30 p.m., they forced the entrance open with the help of an ornamental tree.⁵⁶ After throwing flour in a porter's face, they began a 'pitch battle', pelting King's students with bags of flour, dozens of eggs, and rotten fruit 'collected from the gutters of Covent Garden'.⁵⁷ The *Daily Chronicle* summarized the riot under the headline 'Wild Scenes in a London College'.

It was a 'fierce and unrehearsed battle'.⁵⁸ All west-bound traffic on the Strand came to a halt as hundreds of shoppers and local workers gathered to watch.⁵⁹ The Principal of King's College and his guests, who had been on their way to a Centenary Commemoration dinner, were trapped inside the college, and many students were forced to barricade themselves inside their rooms.⁶⁰ Birkbeck attackers sprayed the King's students with a fire hydrant from Somerset House.⁶¹ Some managed to enter the refectory where Reggie stood but were 'held prisoner'.⁶² Thirty window panes were broken and serious damage was done to

---

⁴⁷ Mathdod, 'The Tale of Egbert', 88.   ⁴⁸ Ibid., 88.
⁴⁹ 'London Rag Between Two Colleges', *Daily Express* (14 December 1928).
⁵⁰ Mathdod, 'The Tale of Egbert', 88.   ⁵¹ 'London Rag Between Two Colleges', *Daily Express*.
⁵² The lowest estimate is from 'Students' War of the Hoses', *Daily News* (14 December 1927), and the highest estimate is from 'Students Injured in Raid', *Daily Herald* (14 December 1928).
⁵³ 'Wild Scenes in a London College', *Daily Chronicle* (14 December 1928). The *Daily Sketch* article also reported that Birkbeck women 'inspired' the men.
⁵⁴ 'Students Injured in Raid', *Daily Herald* (14 December 1928).
⁵⁵ 'In Quest of Egbert', *Daily Sketch* (14 December 1927).
⁵⁶ 'Mascot Battle', *Daily Mail* (14 December 1927), and Mathdod, 'The Tale of Egbert', 88. The *Daily Mail* called it a 'log'!
⁵⁷ 'London Rag Between Two Colleges', *Daily Express*.   ⁵⁸ 'In Quest of Egbert', *Daily Sketch*.
⁵⁹ 'Students Injured in Raid', *Daily Herald* (14 December 1928), and 'In Quest of Egbert', *Daily Sketch* (14 December 1927).
⁶⁰ 'London Rag Between Two Colleges', *Daily Express*, and 'In Quest of Egbert', *Daily Sketch*.
⁶¹ 'Students' War of the Hoses', *Daily News* (14 December 1927).   ⁶² Ibid.

the Common Room. By the time the police arrived to disperse the rivals, the college looked like a 'battlefield'; bruises and dislocated fingers and thumbs were the main injuries.[63] As one participant boasted, 'We didn't kill anybody, but many of them had some nasty knocks.'[64]

Meanwhile, it was discovered that Egbert had not been abducted after all. When 'Ma' Francis had heard that King's students had invaded the College, she had locked Egbert 'in a cupboard with cakes, tomatoes, and a leg of ham'.[65] Not being able to identify 'who was friend and who was foe', she had 'simply told all and sundry that Egbert had gone'. The President personally rushed to King's to tell the Birkbeck students that Egbert was safe.[66] A bugle blew, and the Birkbeck raiders retreated to Chancery Lane. Some remained behind and, with a group of King's men, toasted the health of the two colleges in a local bar.[67] The Shield of the Big Chief Hammer-Toe was returned the following morning.[68]

* * *

This was not a 'good rag'. Writing in *The Lodestone*, 25-year-old Edward Moeran (who was to become a member of the socialist Common Wealth Party) was unimpressed. He regarded the whole event as 'degrading and somewhat disgusting', likening it to 'perverted instinctive action', such as a 'sexual perversion' or 'drug-taking'.[69] He observed that the 'popular conception of a rag is that of an outlet for exuberant youth, high spirits, and young virility'. This 'hero-worship of ragging and raggers' was what spurred on such displays of 'mass misconduct'. Moeran had

> sought in vain for any signs of such heroism in the spectacle of a body of young men, some few of them suffering from flat feet and many stricken with flatulence and cold in the head, self-consciously buying eggs at twopence a shot and then gravely flinging them at King's men.[70]

He was also appalled to see these 'young heroes preening themselves' afterwards in front of women students.[71] It was nothing less than a 'vainglorious' form of exhibitionism.[72] 'If our young man lived closer to Nature,' he continued, 'he would doubtless seek out his rivals, beat them about the head and return with their marrowbones as toothpicks for his Betsey.'[73] Perhaps, Moeran speculated, the 'strain of being a Bright Young Thing' was too much for these restless young

---

[63] 'Wild Scenes in a London College', *Daily Chronicle* (14 December 1928).
[64] 'London Rag Between Two Colleges', *Daily Express*. [65] Mathdod, 'The Tale of Egbert', 88.
[66] Ibid., 88. [67] Ibid., 89. [68] Ibid., 90.
[69] Edward Moeran, 'A Note on Ragging', *The Lodestone*, 24.2 (spring 1929), 91.
[70] Mathdod, 'The Tale of Egbert', 88. [71] Ibid., 88.
[72] Ibid., 88–9. [73] Ibid., 89.

men to bear.[74] It was a 'self-consciously organized display' of 'sanctified hooliganism'.[75]

The Editor of *The Lodestone* also condemned the 'rag', predicting that it would 'haunt us...afterwards'. For him, the 'rag' exhibited 'foolish manifestations of surplus student energy' and had marred the Founder's Day celebrations.[76] He concluded that

> In the rare circumstances where ingenuity, wit and spontaneity rule a rag., the spectacle is pleasing.... But of physical contests with other Colleges... [sic] 'these violent delights have violent ends'. We should prefer to see them confined to the sports field; for is not water sweeter from the hose of a shower-bath than from the nozzle of the enemy's chemical fire-extinguisher.[77]

Certainly, the embarrassing events of 1928 did not see the end of 'ragging' at Birkbeck, but it reminded students and staff of the risks.

* * *

Fetter Lane and its surroundings may have been known in 1807 as 'a resort for idle and disorderly persons called Fewterers', but the carnivalesque misconduct known as 'ragging' did not survive the Second World War.[78] 'Ragging' flourished in the interwar years because of specific contexts, including the violence of the 1914–18 war, economic depression, social upheaval, the rise of fascism (including in Birkbeck itself), and underlying tensions about another war-to-come. While universities presented themselves as places of reason and intellectual rigour, 'rags' provided an outlet for repressed violence, against an enemy that was other students and college authorities. From 1939, however, a more serious mood crept over university culture as well as British life more generally. Austerity was not conducive to the wild pelting of eggs and flour. Birkbeck students were also increasingly part time and older: they had less time for the high jinks of their predecessors. Although (unlike at other universities) women, as well as men, participated in rags at Birkbeck,[79] shifts in the gender of students also had an effect. Graduates of the post-war period were known for their solemnity: a degree meant a great deal to this post-war generation. Location also made a difference. In 1953, Birkbeck's main building moved to Malet Street, far from the 'disorderly persons called Fewterers'.

---

[74] Ibid., 89.   [75] Ibid., 89.
[76] 'Editorial', *The Lodestone*, 24.2 (spring 1929), 55.   [77] Ibid., 55.
[78] 'Editorial', *The Lodestone*, 24.2 (spring 1929), 55. He is quoting from Hughson, *London*, vol. 4, 117.
[79] John A. Murphy, *The College: A History of Queen's/University College Cork, 1845–1995* (Cork: Cork University Press, 1995), 240.

PART IV
WAR AND POLITICS

17
Worlds at War, 1914–1918

> England is to find her salvation in this war.
> Lord Mersey in a December 1914 address at Birkbeck College[1]
>
> We had no illusions of the immensity of the calamity that had befallen us.
> 'H. G. R.' reflecting on the 1914–18 war in *The Lodestone* in 1935[2]

On 13 December 1913, hundreds of Birkbeck students met for their annual dinner in the grand hall of Connaught Rooms in Great Queen Street. After feasting on 'croûte au pot crème Americaine', 'filets de sole ambassadeur', 'agneau roti bouquetière pommes rissolées', 'faisan en cocotté salade', 'poires melba wafers', and 'fromages', the students toasted the King and the College and sang the British national anthem. Then, before a long evening of recitations, speeches, and music began, they stood to sing the College's anthem:

> Some may vaunt their ancient name,
> Shining through the ages,
> Proudly on their record point,
> Writ on History's pages:
> But we glory in our youth,
> Vigour never dying,
> Fighting in the foremost rank,
> Father time defying.[3]

Eight months later, Britain was at war. Within four years, at least ninety-three Birkbeckians had been killed. Two decades later, another war slaughtered hundreds more students and staff of the College. They were killed by bullets, bombs, bayonets, gas, and gangrene. Some drowned after their ships were torpedoed or fell from fighter planes. Others froze or starved to death in prisoner-of-war camps. These were inglorious deaths. Lord Haldane—the Lord Chancellor who helped

---

[1] *Address Delivered by The Right Honourable Lord Mersey, 9th December, 1914* (London: Birkbeck College, 1914), 3.
[2] 'H. G. R.', 'F. A. W.' *The Lodestone*, 30.3 (summer 1935), 126.
[3] Birkbeck College Students' Union, 'Annual Dinner', 1914, in the Birkbeck Archive.

draft the declaration of war in 1914 – was the President of Birkbeck from 1919 to 1928. In the overblown rhetoric of *The Lodestone*, it was from Haldane's home that the 'fateful telegrams…in July and August, 1914, were composed' and 'in his room…this Empire drew up the formula which gave the English speaking peoples of the world that conscience which, in the long last, brought victory'.[4] The language of 'empire' and 'victory' would ring hollow in the years that followed. The two world wars of the twentieth century disrupted the lives of every student and member of staff at Birkbeck; the wars sometimes shattered those lives irredeemably. As an institution, the College survived the turmoil but the effects of both wars on the politics, class structure, and gender norms of British society were to have a lasting impact on student aspirations and expectations.

* * *

Death and destruction were the chief consequences of the world wars. Given the scale of the conflicts, it is not surprising that they also highlighted extreme ideological fissures in British society. This was especially the case with the 1914–18 war. The conflicting epigrams with which I began this chapter were indicative of a divided nation. For the testy 74-year-old Lord Mersey (the jurist John Charles Bigham, famous for heading the inquiry into the sinking of the *Titanic* in 1912), armed conflict would be a 'salvation'.[5] Shortly after the declaration of war in 1914, he told an assembly of Birkbeckians that military conflict would enable Englishmen and women to 'slough off the evil of luxury, of mean money-making, of idleness, of the love of paltry pleasures and of excessive wealth'. The war would not only 'purge and cleanse' but also 'awaken' the English people to

> the nobility of patriotism and of loyalty: to the value of obedience to authority which is often the real essence of freedom: to the beauty of manly strength and self-reliance: to the power of valour and of honour.

Lord Mersey believed that war would 'disperse the transient mists of delusions such as materialism, socialism, and syndicalism', enabling British 'manhood' to 'assert itself before the world'. Military conflict would be a regenerative, purifying force. As he put it, 'England is to be chastised and it will do her good'.[6] Fired up by such rhetoric, many of Birkbeck's male students immediately joined the College's Officer Training Corps or enlisted in the armed forces.[7]

---

[4] 'Centenary Speeches', *The Lodestone*, 19.2 (1924), 78.
[5] He was described as 'testy' in the *Oxford Dictionary of National Biography*.
[6] *Address Delivered by The Right Honourable Lord Mersey, 9th December, 1914* (London: Birkbeck College, 1914), 3.
[7] *Birkbeck College. Report. Ninety-Second Session, 1914–15* (London: Geo. Barber, 1915), 4.

In contrast, a Birkbeckian signing himself 'H. G. R.' recognized that the war was a 'calamity'. In 1935, he recalled that for him and the Professor of Classics, Frederick A. Wright, the war threatened

> all that we had stood for, all that gave meaning to life.... I do not think that the peril of England weighed with us so much as the threat to the common heritage of Europe, the things of the spirit we loved so passionately. But there was nothing for it except to return to the herd and fight with the herd to win.

The eventual victory, he later mused, was 'as disastrous to victors as vanquished' because 'the best, nearly all the best, were gone'.[8]

* * *

Reginald Francis Clements—a 22-year-old theological student at Birkbeck—was one of those swept away by the 'calamity' of war. It is likely that he was a guest at that dinner in the Connaught Rooms in Great Queen Street in 1913. We know that he intended to be ordained into the Church of England. He probably believed that 1914 would be little more than a temporary detour to this ambition.

On 4 September 1914, the day war was declared, a patriotic Clements presented himself to the recruiting office of the University and Public Schools Brigade. He was one of the first men to enlist in the brigade, which was later merged into the Royal Fusiliers. From that point, Clements fades from the historical record, only to reappear in November 1916. While on night patrol near Arras on the 14th of that month, Clements 'caught his legs in barbed wire entanglement & one of the spikes wounded the flesh of his left knee'.[9] The diagnosis: 'traumatic synovitis left knee'.[10] On his War Office form, the words 'wounded' had been crossed out and 'injured' substituted. It also stated that Clements was 'not entitled to gratuity'. In other words, although he was injured while patrolling a battlefield, he would not be entitled to compensation. This was the infamous hierarchy of war suffering, with 'battle wounds' ranking higher (and therefore being worthy of a gratuity) than 'war injuries' (with the suggestion that they were the result of carelessness, clumsiness, or, worse, malingering). 'Shell shock', of course, was ranked lowest of all.

If that seemed harsh, Clements nevertheless contended that he was treated kindly by the medical personnel. In 1917, to show his appreciation, he published a book of poems entitled *Salisbury Plain and Other Poems*. Many of these poems had originally been published in *The Gasper*, the unofficial trench magazine of the Royal Fusiliers. The book version, however, is dedicated to the Countess of

---

[8] 'H. G. R.', 'F. A. W.', 126.
[9] 'Proceedings of a Medical Board', 11 August 1917, in the National Archives WO339/60321.
[10] 'Proceedings of a Medical Board', 10 May 1917, and letter signed Charles A. Morris, Major in the Royal Army Medical Corps, 16 May 1917, in the National Archives WO339/60321.

Pembroke and Montgomery for her work on behalf of the British Red Cross Society. He wanted the Countess to see in his poems 'a soldier's expression of gratitude to one whose unceasing labours for the sick and wounded will not be forgotten while thankfulness exists in human hearts'. He was also grateful to his comrades-in-arms who had persuaded him to publish his poems. He claimed to be unable to 'forget that lofty example and cheery comradeship which have made those years in which I was privileged to serve in the ranks the proudest and happiest memory of my life'.[11]

Salisbury Plain and Other Poems contained poems that ranged from the poignant to the defiant. For example, the poem entitled 'Nec Aspera Terrent' ('Nor Do Hardships Terrify') effectively conjured up the 'shattering bomb and leaping murderous flame'.[12] In contrast, 'The Altar of England' concluded with the cloyingly patriotic lines:

> England! to thine altar now
> See thy manhood drawing nigh,
> This the sacrifice that pleads
> 'Motherland! for thee we die!'[13]

Similarly, the poem 'Salisbury Plain' alluded to the 'Glint of swords that never shall be still/While there be man to strike and foe to kill,/And all to sacrifice and all to gain!'[14] Although First World War poetry today is largely known through the works of men like Wilfred Owen and Siegfried Sassoon, with their bitter irony and impassioned denunciations of the 'sausage machine', in reality the 'high diction' of Clements (with its altars and swords, manly sacrifices and motherlands) more accurately reflected the poetry written and read at the time (see Fig. 17.1).

Clements was more than simply a theological student from Birkbeck with a penchant for poetry. He was also brave—or, at the very least, capable of behaving like the sacrificial warriors lauded in some of his poems. After his wounds healed, he was sent back to the front lines where he won a Military Cross for his actions during a raid at Fleurbaix in March 1918. The citation reads:

> For conspicuous gallantry and devotion to duty. In preparation for a raid on the enemy lines he carried out several patrols, and the accurate information which he obtained contributed very largely to the success of the operation. He led his men in the raid with great skill and determination, and rushed an enemy post which offered strong opposition, with the result that six of the enemy were killed and two prisoners were captured: He showed splendid initiative and coolness.

---

[11] Reginald Francis Clements, *Salisbury Plain and Other Poems* (Salisbury: Bennett Brothers, Military Printers, 1917), 4.
[12] Ibid., 8.   [13] Ibid., 16.   [14] Ibid., 5.

Fig. 17.1 Louis Raemaeker's cartoon 'The Spring Song', *The Studio*, vol. 65 (1918). An earlier version of this image inspired Clements' 'Death's Spring Song', which ended with the lines 'Sleep on! Sleep on!' It is the Voice of Death,/Though none but human eye shall e'er behold/His grim gaunt spectre standing scornful there/Beside the festal Queen, whose scented breath,/Alas! can never wake these corpses cold,/That pale and lifeless fill her kingdom fair!' 'R. F. C.', 'Death's Spring Song', *The Gasper: The Unofficial Organ of the 18th, 19th, 20th, and 21st Royal Fusiliers* (26 June 1916), 19.

Clements did not have time to enjoy the honour. Within five months (and only three months before the armistice), he was killed during the Battle of Amiens. The telegraph to his father simply reported 'Deeply regret Lt. R. F. Clements, MC, Royal Sussex Reg. killed in action August thirteenth, the Army Council express sympathy'. Clements was buried in the Morlancourt British cemetery, east of Amiens in northern France (see Fig. 17.2). On his headstone, his mother asked that the following words be engraved: 'The Righteous live forever, And in the Lord is their Reward'.[15]

This young theological student's story did not end with his death. Afterwards, there was an unseemly series of exchanges about Clements' estate, which, because he was unmarried and had not written a will, was managed by his father. The army owed Clements £140 12s. 11d. On 4 February 1919, his mother wrote a letter to the War Office. Referring to herself in the third person, her letter read:

> Mrs. Clements regrets troubling the Paymaster...but, in Mr. Clements['] absence from house, she would like to know when the money due to her late son will be forwarded. A very heavy expense is before them in getting the only surviving son into civilian clothing, and his own gratuity has not been sent. This is the only reason which induces Mrs. Clements to write this application.[16]

---

[15] This is according to the Commonwealth War Graves Commission.
[16] Letter from Mrs Clements to the War Office, 4 February 1919, The National Archives (UK).

Fig. 17.2 Photographs of Clements and his gravesite. The National Archives WO339/60321.

Clements' parents were sent his possessions through Messrs Cox and Co.'s Shipping Agency. His only remaining belongings were one diary, one MC ribbon, one flashlight, one safety razor, one prismatic compass in a case, one penknife with a silver handle, one pencil case, two badges, one pair of prescription glasses in a case, one service book, one pocket wallet, one cigarette case, one tobacco pouch, one cheque book, one advance book, and one key. Notably absent from his possessions was a Bible or prayer book.

* * *

Clements' life and death are only sketchily known, but they are a reminder of the distressing nature of war for many Birkbeck students: if they were not injured or killed themselves, they certainly had friends and family members who 'sacrificed' their limbs or lives. The College as an institution also underwent significant changes but, in comparison to lives destroyed, little long-term trauma. Compared to what was happening on the Continent, British students were lucky. They held out a hand to student refugees, who started to arrive in large numbers (an estimated 250,000 from Belgium) with the declaration of war in 1914. Principal Armitage-Smith offered these students a free education. A roll of those who were helped shows that many rapidly returned to Belgium to join the resistance (see Fig. 17.3).

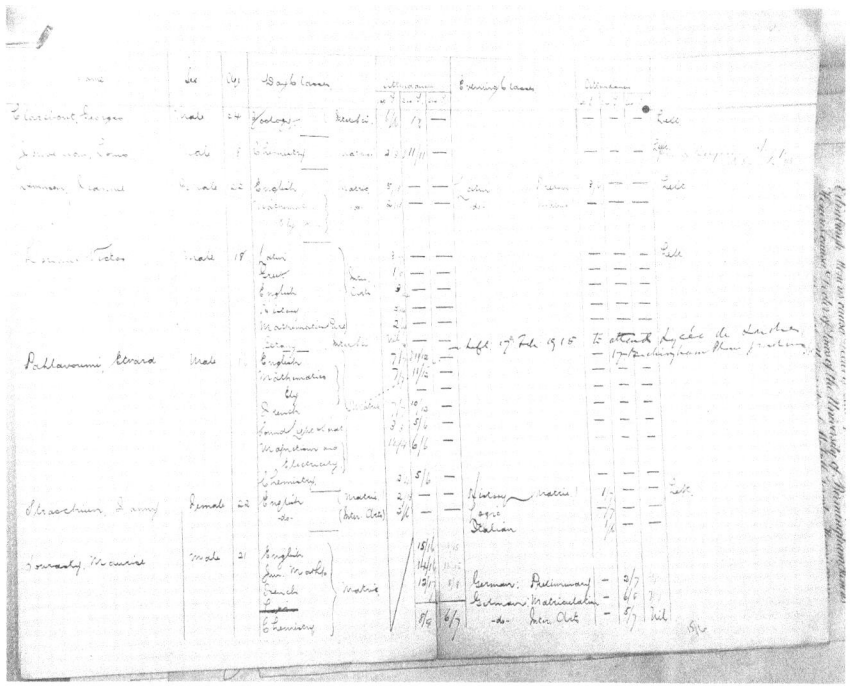

Fig. 17.3 A roll of some of the student refugees from Belgium to whom the College offered a free education. Birkbeck Archive, Box 9a.

But what should be done with 'enemy aliens'? The College had already enrolled several German-born students. In October 1914, these students were banished: the governing body stipulated that 'no alien enemy be allowed to attend the College classes during the continuance of the war'.[17]

Next, there was the question of British-born students and staff. In the early years of the First World War, the College had a moral obligation and patriotic duty to encourage male students to enlist and, after conscription was introduced, had no choice but to let staff go as well. This meant losing the College Secretary, Herbert Wells Eames, who joined The King's Shropshire Light Infantry, had a narrow escape in the trenches when his ear was pierced by a bullet, and subsequently won the Military Cross.[18] His job was temporarily taken over by the Master's Secretary, Miss Hilda Keet (see Chapter 7). By 1916, the governing body resolved that all male students applying for a place on a course had to sign a declaration swearing that they were not eligible for military service or had been given

---

[17] 'Minutes of Meeting of Governing Body, Monday, 19th October, 1914', in 'B. C. Minute Book. 16th Sep., 1912 to 29th July, 1919', in the Birkbeck Archive.

[18] 'Birkbeck College News Sheet', *The Lodestone*, 11.2 (lent 1916), 56.

an exemption.[19] A promise was made to all staff who left for war service that their positions would be given back to them on their return[20] (see Fig. 17.4).

College authorities were surprised that the number of students did not drop as much as they expected. Conscription reduced the number of male students by about one third, but men and women engaged in war-work on the home front (in armaments factories, for example) flocked to classes after finishing their shifts.[21] The decline in male students was also made up by an increase in the number of female ones, as women sought to reskill in response to the opening of jobs that had been vacated by men. These jobs included ones that had previously been totally or partially closed to them, such as medicine, dentistry, and pharmacy.[22] In Birkbeck's physics, botany, chemistry, and zoology laboratories, female demonstrators were, for the first time, appointed to replace their male counterparts.[23]

Fig. 17.4 Photograph of M. G. Varwell, President of Birkbeck Students' Union, in a trench, c.1914–18. Birkbeck Image Collections: Birkbeck History BH0261.

---

[19] 'Minutes of Meeting of Governing Body, Monday, 17th April, 1916', in 'B. C. Minute Book. 16th Sep., 1912 to 29th July, 1919', in the Birkbeck Archive.
[20] 'Minutes of Meeting of Governing Body, Monday, 21st September, 1914', in 'B. C. Minute Book. 16th Sep., 1912 to 29th July, 1919', in the Birkbeck Archive.
[21] *Birkbeck College. Report. 95th Session, 1917–18* (London: Geo. Barber, 1918), 3.
[22] *Birkbeck College. 94th Session, 1916–17* (London: Geo. Barber, 1917), 2.
[23] *Birkbeck College. Report. 93rd Session, 1915–16* (London: Geo. Barber, 1916), 4; 'Minutes of Meeting of Governing Body, Monday, 15th March, 1915', in 'B. C. Minute Book. 16th Sep., 1912 to 29th July, 1919', in the Birkbeck Archive; 'Minutes of Meeting of Governing Body, Monday, 17th March, 1915', in 'B. C. Minute Book. 16th Sep., 1912 to 29th July, 1919', in the Birkbeck Archive; 'Minutes of Meeting of Governing Body, Monday, 21st June, 1915', in 'B. C. Minute Book. 16th Sep., 1912 to 29th July, 1919', in the Birkbeck Archive.

As the war progressed, labour shortages meant that the College was reluctantly forced to keep increasing the wages of these female demonstrators and assistants.[24] Ex-servicemen who had been rendered disabled by war service were also hired to replace those on active service.[25] In 1917, a Birkbeck Active Service League was even established in an attempt to ensure that the College kept in touch with its colleagues in the front lines.[26]

One of these students was John Walsh, the first President of the Students' Union. This handsome young man, standing 6ft 2in tall, had been active in the College as Union President as well as a leading member of the London Irish Rugby XV, the University Athletic Sports, and the governing body. He was also active in Toynbee Hall, a radical social movement to help the poor in the East End of London. In November 1915, Walsh's battalion was sent to France and by March the following year he was gazetted Captain. In July he could be found in the Battle of the Somme, where he was gassed; in December, he was gazetted Major, but was killed a couple of months later, on 17 February 1917. Reports of his death—which were widely circulated within Birkbeck—described how he bore his 'fatal wound as gallantly as he has ever lived'. According to his commander, Walsh's company was charged with 'defending an exposed flank':

> The enemy was much on the alert, and began shelling heavily before we had even left our lines for the attack. Dawn had not broken—it was very late that morning—and our men had to go forward in the pitch darkness. Add to this heavy rifle and machine-gun fire, and you can imagine that there was grave danger of confusion and, thus, of disaster. John, of course, was equal to the situation and with G. H. Evans, his second in command, rallied the men, reorganised them and led them forward. He was shot in the diaphragm quite close to the enemy wire. The subsequent action was simply epic. The officers were all gone and the N.C.O.s all did splendidly and held up the enemy in his trenches. Unfortunately, towards midday they had to withdraw a bit and the result was that John could not be recovered till dawn.[27]

---

[24] For example, see 'Minutes of Meeting of Governing Body, 19th February, 1917', in 'B. C. Minute Book. 16th Sep., 1912 to 29th July, 1919', in the Birkbeck Archive, and 'Minutes of Meeting of Governing Body, Monday, 19th June, 1916', in 'B. C. Minute Book. 16th Sep., 1912 to 29th July, 1919', in the Birkbeck Archive.

[25] *Birkbeck College. Report. 93rd Session, 1915–16* (London: Geo. Barber, 1916), 4; 'Minutes of Meeting of Governing Body, Monday, 15th March, 1915', in 'B. C. Minute Book. 16th Sep., 1912 to 29th July, 1919', in the Birkbeck Archive; 'Minutes of Meeting of Governing Body, Monday, 17th March, 1915', in 'B. C. Minute Book. 16th Sep., 1912 to 29th July, 1919', in the Birkbeck Archive; 'Minutes of Meeting of Governing Body, Monday, 21st June, 1915', in 'B. C. Minute Book. 16th Sep., 1912 to 29th July, 1919', in the Birkbeck Archive.

[26] 'Circulars and Documents 1914–1918', in Birkbeck Archive, Box 1B, 'Early History of Birkbeck College'.

[27] Letter from R. Barrett-Barker, Lieut.-Col., 22nd Battalion, Royal Fusiliers, dated 4 February 1917, in the Birkbeck Archive, 'A3 Black Folder 3' (p. 100 of file).

A seriously wounded Walsh was eventually collected by the Medical Officer and taken to the Clearing Station, where he died in his sleep. He was buried near Harry Lauder's son, the comedian and war campaigner who famously contended that 'If these German savages want savagery, let them have it.'[28] In Walsh's company, fifty-two out of 120 men were wounded or killed during this battle and, of seventeen officers, only three returned.[29]

The sufferings of students who remained on the home front were minimal by comparison. Their main concern was coping with disruptions caused by air raids.[30] When the noise of German bombs or British guns became too deafening, students and teachers would retire to the basement where they drank coffee and sang songs.[31] Raids also led to emotional strain. At least one lecturer reported that he had 'completely broken down in health, owing to the raids at Southend', where he lived, so was unable to continue teaching.[32] In other colleges, classes were so unsettled by the war that they had to be closed or moved to other institutions. For example, the botany classes at the Northern Polytechnic Institute were transferred entirely to Birkbeck.[33]

Classrooms also had to be made available for military training. For example, the Marconi Company used rooms at Birkbeck to teach signalling to around 150 young men.[34] A series of lectures on 'Bacteria', 'Trench Making', 'Map Making and Map Reading', 'Range Finding', 'Explosives', 'The Field Telephone', and 'Hints on Hygiene' were initiated to prepare student members of the Officers' Training Corp (see Fig. 17.5).[35] Certain members of the College staff even threw themselves into testing munitions. On one occasion, Professor Arthur Griffith tested optical munitions (he was measuring the magnifying power of binoculars) in the middle of the road outside the College.[36]

The lives of female staff and students also changed. Anticipating invasion, they were taught to shoot at a rifle range near to the College. One sergeant was reported to have commented that 'you should see the ladies at Bisley [shooting range of the National Rifle Association], steadier than many of the men; but I should not like

---

[28] 'Impassioned Address by Harry', *Arbroath Herald and Advertiser for the Montrose Burghs* (11 June 1915).

[29] Letter from R. Barrett-Barker, Lieut.-Col., 22nd Battalion, Royal Fusiliers, dated 26 February 1917, in the Birkbeck Archive, 'A3 Black Folder 3' (p. 102 of file).

[30] *Birkbeck College. Report. 95th Session, 1917–18* (London: Geo. Barber, 1918), 3.

[31] Burns, *A Short History of Birkbeck College*, 146.

[32] Letter from Mr R. D. Monteverde, Professor of Spanish, in 'Minutes of Meeting of Governing Body. Monday, 21st June 1915', in 'B.C. Minute Book. 16th Sep. 1912 to 29th July, 1919'.

[33] *Birkbeck College. Report. 95th Session, 1917–18* (London: Geo. Barber, 1918), 7, and 'Minutes of Meeting of Governing Body, 18th June, 1917', in 'B. C. Minute Book. 16th Sep., 1912 to 29th July, 1919', in the Birkbeck Archive.

[34] *Birkbeck College. 94th Session, 1916–17* (London: Geo. Barber, 1917), 2.

[35] *Birkbeck College. Report. 92nd Session, 1914–15* (London: Geo. Barber, 1915), 4–5.

[36] H. G. B., 'A Fire-Watcher's Interview with his Own Memory', *The Lodestone*, 36.3 (summer 1944), 12.

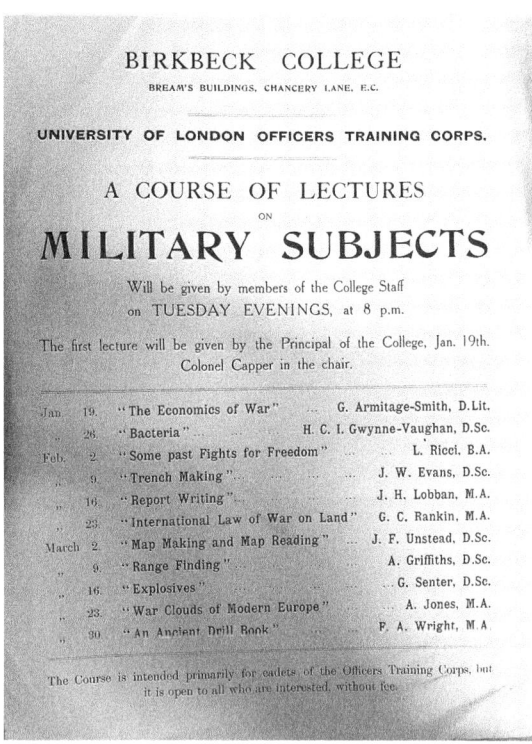

Fig. 17.5 Special classes taught at Birkbeck during the war. Birkbeck Archive, 'Wartime Correspondence of the Clerk 1939–41', p. 1.

one of them for my wife'. A Birkbeck retort would be to remind him that many of the College's female students at the range were already married.[37]

The Birkbeckian woman who made the biggest contribution to the war was Helen C. I. Fraser (better known as Helen Gwynne-Vaughan after her marriage to David Thomas Gwynne-Vaughan, former head of the Botany Department at Birkbeck). A mycologist or specialist on fungi, she was the first female professor at Birkbeck (see Fig. 17.6). In 1917, Gwynne-Vaughan was appointed the first Chief Controller of the Women's Army Auxiliary Corps (WAACs). One of her first tasks as Lieutenant Colonel was to create an appropriate uniform. —It was designed without a breast pocket, for fear of drawing attention to that part of a woman's anatomy, but its skirt was daringly short 12 inches off the ground—and the khaki cap (which featured a crêpe de Chine veil at the back) was considered sexy.

But the work of the WAACs was serious—deadly so. Gwynne-Vaughan led thousands of women to France to work behind the lines, thus freeing up men for

[37] 'Moke', 'Adventures in the Adelphi', *The Lodestone*, 10.2 (Lent 1915), 42.

Fig. 17.6 Portrait of Helen Gwynne-Vaughan, painted *c.*1910 by the Hungarian Philip de László for the price of 100 guineas. De László was later to become a leading society painter. Gwynne-Vaughan is clothed in scarlet and gold—the robes of a Doctor of Science—and she clasps a book on her knee. She is made to resemble one of Michelangelo's Sybils, reincarnated as a divinity of Scholarship and Science. Birkbeck Image Collections: Birkbeck History BH0016.

combat duty. When nine WAACs were killed during a raid on their army camp, Gwynne-Vaughan coolly informed the press that her 'girls' were in France as replacements for soldiers, so the enemy had every right to kill them.

As with many women in new and powerful positions, Gywnne-Vaughan's male colleagues were riled. Wasn't she too aggressive? Hadn't she ventured into what should have remained an all-male preserve? Her military mannerisms—including the way she would salute and cry 'sir!'—embarrassed then annoyed them. There was salacious gossip that hundreds of WAACs were falling pregnant. Although these rumours turned out to be totally unfounded, one tongue-in-cheek message from the General Headquarters to the War Office read, 'Hurry up with those reinforcements or you'll find we've provided our own. We already have one fine boy.'

Such disparaging tittle-tattle aside, the war transformed Gwynne-Vaughan's life. In 1919, she was made a Dame of the British Empire, in honour of her

Fig. 17.7 Helen Gwynne-Vaughan's election poster when she stood as a Unionist candidate in the 1922 general election. Birkbeck Archive.

war-work. During the 1922 general election, she stood as a Unionist candidate, led by Bonar Law, for North Camberwell (see Fig. 17.7). Her platform—education, child health, imperial defence, the claims of ex-servicemen and women, relief for the unemployed, 'freedom within the law', the ratification of the Irish treaty, and against prohibition of alcohol—failed to win her election.[38] However, she spent the interwar years juggling botany research with public service. By 1929, she had been made a Dame Grand Cross of the Order of the British Empire for 'civil and scientific services'.

* * *

The 1918 armistice came as a relief to everyone, even if it did not signal an abrupt end to war-work. At the request of the Ministry of Labour and the Council of Rubber Growers' Association, for example, special chemistry classes were established for ex-servicemen wanting to find employment on rubber and tea

---

[38] 'Election Address', 1922, in Birkbeck Archive, 'A3 Black Folder 1' (pp. 15–17 of file).

plantations.[39] The purpose was to 'provide a scientific foundation for plantation experience' rather than to offer a 'substitute for training which can only be given effectively on the spot'.[40]

In addition, former servicemen and women, including American ones, suddenly flooded classrooms, keen to make up for lost time and take advantage of opportunities to educate themselves.[41] This new cohort of students brought with them unfamiliar slang and other ways of expressing themselves. They spoke about taking 'a double bite' (having another chance) and 'spinning a dit' (telling a story with a funny ending). Former naval servicemen would 'masticate "jacky", a kind of tobaccy [sic], and scatter its juices abroad'. They would spin tall tales or 'fancies' to impress students who had not seen military service. When one of these 'innocents' (that is, someone who had not seen active service) admitted to an ex-service student that he had not been 'at Cairo in '17', he was regaled with 'all one would wish to know about Egypt'. When he then confessed that he had also not had 'the honour of being at Jutland', he was treated to an hour-long lecture on 'precisely how the action would have been fought had 2nd Class Stoker C. L. Bunker, of H.M.S. *Sealawyer*, been in command'. Non-service students described the experience as similar to being transported on a 'magic carpet' from the Common Room 'to the sands of the desert or the "bull-ring" at Etaples, to the cold North Sea or the back streets of Portsmouth; and still these stories grow in number and in wonder'. It was as if the Birkbeck Common Room in 1920 had turned into 'a miniature Valhalla—complete with Valkyries' of Norse mythology.[42]

The entry of ex-servicemen into the College was dramatic, but temporary. The resignation of the College's Principal, George Armitage-Smith, was more profound. As a political economist, Armitage-Smith had been a member of the College's staff for forty-two years. For twenty-two of these years, he had been its talented chief administrator.[43] By the age of 74, however, Armitage-Smith's eyesight was fading; his notoriously 'abundant stock of nervous energy' had also wilted.[44] Few leaders of Birkbeck had done more to ensure that the College flourished. Armitage-Smith had not only steered the transformation of the Birkbeck Literary and Scientific Institution into Birkbeck College but also laid the foundations for the College's acceptance into the University of London.

When Armitage-Smith died in 1923, his achievements as a 'shrewd and practical North Countryman' were lauded.[45] However, it was also recognized that

---

[39] *Birkbeck College (University of London). Report for 97th Session, 1919–20* (London: Geo. Barber, 1920), 6. Also see 'Education for Ex-Servicemen Including Special Course in Topic Agriculture', Birkbeck Archive, Box 17.

[40] Birkbeck College. Prospectus of Special Courses for Planters to be Held from May to December, 1920, in Birkbeck Archive, Box 17.

[41] *Birkbeck College. Report. 96th Session, 1918–19* (London: Geo. Barber, 1919), 3.

[42] Senex, 'The Ex-Service Student', *The Lodestone*, 16.2 (Lent 1921), 74–5.

[43] *Birkbeck College. Report. 95th Session, 1917–18* (London: Geo. Barber, 1918), 9.

[44] Mackenzie, 'The Birkbeck Institution', 376. [45] Ibid., 376.

Armitage-Smith had been 'a Victorian' in his view of the academic world. He might have been one of 'the best' in 'an age which was, after all, an age of great men', but many in the College believed that a newer, more 'Edwardian' or progressive leadership was needed. Armitage-Smith had been 'distrustful of the modern school of social teaching and not in touch perhaps with modern movements in the arts', observed one commentator. Nevertheless, he had been a humanist and sympathetic leader. According to one tribute in 1934, Armitage-Smith had been not only a 'distinguished economist' but also

> a greater teacher and a really great administrator, the creator of the College we know. *Requiescat a laboribus suis, opera enim eius sequuntur eum* ['They shall rest from their labour since their works follow them'].[46]

A memorial fund was established to honour his achievements and, in *The Times*, a letter asking for contributions was signed by many luminaries who had all spent time at Birkbeck, including Arthur Pinero (the famous playwright whose early career was nurtured in the Birkbeck theatre), William Bull (solicitor and Conservative politician), Frank Gossling (chemist), William Pett Ridge (popular novelist), and George Senter (the Principal who succeeded Armitage-Smith and served until 1939).[47] After much discussion, the words on Armitage-Smith's memorial stone read: 'Non mihi soli laboravi', or 'I laboured not for myself alone'.[48]

* * *

The deaths of ninety-three students and staff of Birkbeck between 1914 and 1918 required memorialization. College events and publications routinely included tributes to the dead. These often took poetical form, as in the following poem written by a bereaved student:

> 'What makes your eyes so strangely light,
> Your hair like sun-flecked gold?
> And why's your mouth all pale and still,
> That was so gay of old?'
>
> 'My Lover looked into these eyes,
> He kissed my long, red hair,
> He kissed my mouth... He's out in France:
> They left him buried there'.[49]

---

[46] 'Portrait of Dr. Armitage-Smith', *The Lodestone*, 29.3 (summer 1934), 137.
[47] William Bull, Rhondda, Frank Gossling, William Pett Ridge, George Senter, and Arthur Pinero, 'Dr. Armitage-Smith Memorial', *The Times* (2 November 1923), 10.
[48] 'Meeting of the Armitage-Smith Memorial Committee, Monday, 14th May 1923', in 'Birkbeck College Special Committee Minutes, 8th March to 25th May, 1939'.
[49] P. B. B., 'Initiation', *The Lodestone*, 16.3 (summer 1921), 135.

Fig. 17.8 The unveiling of the First World War memorial in Bream's Building on 11 December 1921. The photo shows Helen Gwynn-Vaughan, the President, Lord Haldane, and one unidentified man. Birkbeck Image Collections: Birkbeck History BH0213.

But something more institutionally dignified was demanded. A war memorial was commissioned, designed by the relatively obscure artist and designer Philip Harry Newman and costing £298 (approximately £12,000 today).[50] It took the form of a memorial tablet bearing the names of the ninety-three men who had died (see Fig. 17.8).[51] It was placed in a prominent position in the entrance hall of Bream's Building, facing the steps leading to the theatre.[52] The words 'Faithful Even Unto Death' were inscribed on it.[53] On 11 November 1920, Lord Haldane, President of the College but also the man who had effectively signed Clements' death warrant, unveiled the tablet.[54]

Unfortunately, the memorial was not to everyone's taste. Indeed, there was considerable hostility towards it. Someone signing himself 'B. D. W.' reminded people that works of commemoration were required to inspire

---

[50] 'War Memorial, 1914–18', in Birkbeck Archive, Box 11a, 'Buildings'. For the conversion of money, see https://www.measuringworth.com/calculators/ppoweruk/.
[51] *Birkbeck College. Report. Ninety-Sixth Session, 1918–19* (London: Geo. Barber, 1919), 7.
[52] 'Minutes of Meeting of Governing Body. Monday, 19th July 1920', in 'B. C. Minute Book. 22nd Sep., 1919 to 25th July, 1922', Birkbeck Archive. Also see 'From the Common Room', *The Lodestone*, 15.1 (Michaelmas 1919), 13.
[53] 'War Memorial, 1914–18', in Birkbeck Archive, Box 11a, 'Buildings'.
[54] 'Incidents of the Day', *The Times* (12 November 1920), iii.

reverence and honour for the dead, undistracted by any feelings of antipathy, contempt, or, still worse, mirth.... If we cannot give them dignity of speech the dumb walls are best left tongueless.

B. D. W. contended that the Birkbeck Memorial featured 'an extraordinary impressionistic aeroplane perched on the classic pediment'; its 'badly-modelled supports' conveyed 'a feeling of toppled insecurity'. He contended that the students 'strongly deprecate this commemoration of our fallen comrades by a pretentious, ugly and distressing Memorial'. Yet,

> The worst danger is not yet fully realised. In the passage of years, during which the personal memory must fade and pass, whilst the gilt and the carving stand unchanged, is it not inevitable that the record of the dead will become dimmed and distorted by the *grotesquerie* which enshrines their names.[55]

It seems that B. D. W.'s sentiments were widely shared. As early as 1927, the College Secretary, Troup Horne, had started discussions with the sculptor Allan G. Wyon (who was well regarded for his design of memorials) about whether anything could be rescued from the old memorial. In February 1927, Wyon reported that he had examined the College's war memorial and concluded that it required a 'dignified central figure'. He provided a 'rough sketch' of what he had in mind, reassuring them that

> I retain the conception of 'Fame' holding a torch in each hand. By employing the device of the two pairs of wings one is able satisfactorily to fill certain difficult spaces and at the same time to comply with the general principles of wing structure. The two inner pilasters are not necessary and this design involved their abolition.... The base as it now stands is too heavy for the superstructure. Side Figures of a simple architectural character are necessary for the complete balance of the Memorial. I suggest that these be added at some future date.[56]

Depending on what exactly was agreed, the cost would be anything between £37 and £150.[57] By July, though, it seems that the Finance and General Purposes Committee had decided to postpone deciding. Troup Horne informed Wyon that because the College might be moving to other premises, 'the feeling was in favour of leaving the present memorial untouched and spending the money which would be required to improve it, or rather to lessen its defects, on an entirely new memo-

---

[55] 'B. D. W.', 'An Ugly College', *The Lodestone*, 16.2 (Lent 1921), 62–3.
[56] Letter from the Secretary to Wyon, 14 July 1927, in 'War Memorial, 1914–18', in Birkbeck Archive, Box 11a, 'Buildings'.
[57] Ibid.

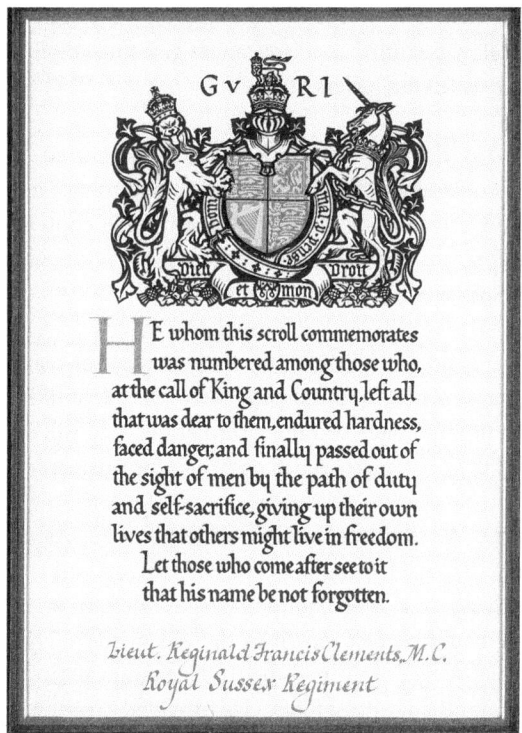

Fig. 17.9 Reginald Francis Clements' name on the scroll of honour. The National Archives WO339/60321.

rial'. He added as an aside that the Committee 'doubted if even your [Wyon's] magic touch could transform the exciting atrocity into a joy for ever'.[58] The memorial has disappeared, probably destroyed in the bombing of Bream's Building during the 1939–45 war, and is certainly not missed.

The most poignant sign that the war had made a difference to the College came in 1921, however, when Birkbeck students returned to the Connaught Rooms, where they had last dined eight years earlier. Unlike the pre-war dinner, this was a more sober occasion. In 1913, hundreds had attended; this time, there were only eighty. Instead of a long list of French delicacies, the highlight of the evening was 'tangerine ices'. The occasion was marked by a silent toast to 'Those who Fell' and to those who, like Clements (see Fig. 17.9), might have known 'these Union dinners in days gone by, but will now know them no more'.

---

[58] Letter from Allan G. Wyon, 7 February 1927, to Secretary Troup Horne, in 'War Memorial, 1914–18', in E Birkbeck Archive, Box 11a, 'Buildings'.

18
Worlds at War, 1939–1945

The devastation caused by the 1914–18 war encouraged anti-war sentiments. Between the late 1920s and the early 1930s, pacifism became a lively topic of debate in Birkbeck's Common Room, classrooms, and corridors. Prominent members of the College led the debate, nation-wide. On 9 February 1933, for example, Cyril Edwin Mitchinson Joad, the head of the Department of Philosophy and Psychology since 1930, was one of five speakers involved in the 'King and Country' debate in the Oxford Union. Joad argued in favour of the motion that 'this House will in no circumstances fight for its King and Country'. His oration was witty, passionate, and uncompromising. After telling the familiar joke about Lytton Strachey standing before the military service tribunal and saying that, if a German solider was about to rape his sister, he would 'try to come between them', Joad turned serious. He said that he had engaged in a similar debate prior to the First World War. A few months later, his best friend 'had hung on barbed wire for 24 hours with his entrails hanging out screaming in agony'. Joad insisted that the motion should read, 'that this House will never commit murder on a huge scale whenever the Government decided it should do so'. The motion was carried by 275 votes to 153.

It caused uproar. The *Daily Telegraph* attacked the debate for being 'an outrage upon the memory of those who gave their lives in the Great War'. In his memoirs, published in 1948, Winston Churchill lamented the 'foolish boys who passed the resolution' and who, only a few years later, were 'destined...to conquer or fall gloriously' during the 1939–45 war. At least these 'boys', Churchill continued, were able to 'prove themselves the finest generation ever bred in Britain', unlike their elders (like Joad, who had been 42 years old at the time of the 1933 debate), who had 'no chance of self-redemption in action'.[1]

The Second World War came as a shock to the pacifists. By 1939, Joad could be heard confessing that he used to believe

> that man was neither virtuous not wicked. Human nature, I have been taught, was infinitely malleable, and the qualities of the adult man were the outcome of the training and environment of the child, complicated perhaps by no more than a dash of heredity....I no longer hold this belief. I no longer hold...that a world

---

[1] Winston Spencer Churchill, *The Second World War*, Volume 1: *The Gathering Storm*, 1st pub. 1948 (New York: Rosetta Books, 2010), 77.

of adequately psycho-analyzed communists would be millennial. And I no longer hold this because I have come to believe in the reality of evil.[2]

Joad had not been alone in his pacifist beliefs. Philosopher C. Delisle Burns, a member of Joad's department, was another vocal pacifist prior to 1939. While Joad was debating the motion that 'this House will in no circumstances fight for its King and Country', Burns was busy writing *War and a Changing Civilisation*. In it, he attacked war as 'a disease.... A moral evil' that was 'partly a psychological abnormality and partly a cancer in political institutions'. He lamented the fact that 'flags and trumpets give some attractiveness to killing men'.[3] He did insist, however, that war was *statecraft*. He explained that war was

> an elaborate and complex institutional practice of States and their governments. It is not the result of passion and it has very little relation to street fights or to the impulsiveness due to a supposed instinct of pugnacity. War is an instrument of policy. In our days it requires great preparation in storage of material and readiness of manufacturing capacity. It cannot be carried on by a sudden seizing of sticks and stones. War leads good brains to the discovery of new poison-gas and more deadly guns.

In other words, Burns was reminding his readers that war was a deliberate policy of governments, rather than an inevitable consequence of human evolution or excitable emotions. As such, it could be avoided.[4] Unfortunately, when he wrote these words, he was in poor health so we do not know whether he, like Joad, would have responded to the rise of Nazism by recanting his pacifism.

The declaration of war in 1939, only two decades after the armistice of 1918, changed the College. This time, there was no Armitage-Smith at the helm to lead the College through those dark years. Rather, the Master was John Primatt Redcliffe Maud, 33-year-old politics lecturer from Oxford University, who was replaced in 1943 by Harold Gordon Jackson, expert on terrestrial and fresh-water crustaceans.

Preparations for the new war created discontent amongst Birkbeck students. In the spring of 1939, there was student-led opposition to the government's announcement that full-time students would be eligible for exemptions from conscription but not part-time ones. Chemistry student James Lovelock was livid. Lovelock had been born into a working-class family: his mother had worked in a pickeles factory from the age of 13 years and his illiterate father had served six months in prison (with hard labour) for poaching. Education provided a way for

---

[2] C. E. M. Joad, *Guide to Modern Wickedness* (London: Faber and Faber, 1939), 10.
[3] C. Delisle Burns, *War and a Changing Civilisation* (London: John Lane, 1934), 1.
[4] Ibid., 2–3.

Lovelock to escape his humble origins. To pay his way through Birkbeck, Lovelock took a job in the chemical photographic laboratory of Murray, Bull, and Spencer Ltd.[5] He was later to become a well-known independent scientist and proposer of the Gaia hypothesis, which maintained that the world functions as a well-regulated system. In 1939, however, he was a young chemistry student who believed that Birkbeck students were being discriminated against simply for studying part time. This was 'monstrously unfair', he raged. As Lovelock explained in his autobiography, entitled *Homage to Gaia* (2000),

> Here we were working both in the daytime and at night, the most diligent of students. How dare they penalize us. The political blood in my veins began to boil and I drew up a petition that the Student Union then circulated for signing. We addressed it to the vice-chancellor of London University.... The Student Union at Birkbeck was delighted with it.[6]

The President of the Students' Union at the time was Lena May Chivers, later known as the Labour peer, Lady Jeger (see Fig. 18.1). She completed a degree in English and French at Birkbeck and would go on to become an MP for the constituency of St Pancras in London. Chivers was a fervent socialist, feminist, and supporter of the Greek Cypriot community in the UK after Harold Macmillan's government refused the Cypriots' right to self-determination.[7] When Lovelock approached her with his petition, she actively solicited signatures from Birkbeck

Fig. 18.1 Lena May Chivers (more widely known as Lena May Jeger), President of Birkbeck Students' Union and later prominent Labour Party politician. This is a photograph from 10 November 1953 after her nomination to be the Labour Party candidate in the Holborn and St Pancras South by-election. Alamy.

---

[5] James Lovelock, *Homage to Gaia: The Life of an Independent Scientist* (Oxford: Oxford University Press, 2000), 40.
[6] Ibid., 42.   [7] Barbara Castle, 'Baroness Jeger', *The Guardian* (3 March 2007).

students as well as those engaged in evening teaching at other colleges. The petition was then passed to the Vice-Chancellor of the University of London, who invited Lovelock to his rooms for a chat over a glass of sherry. The Vice-Chancellor agreed to present the case to the government, but the plan stalled because Poland was invaded.[8] Lovelock noted that it was 'clear to me that my efforts for part-time students, although appropriate in peacetime, would not succeed now that we were at war'.[9] The entire protest was shelved, and Lovelock signed up as a conscientious objector, enrolling for full-time study at the University of Manchester.

Around 60,000 Britons joined Lovelock in registering as conscientious objectors during the 1939–45 war but many, like Joad, eventually recanted their pacifist principles as the threat of Nazism and German militarism edged ever closer to home. Compared to the 1914–18 war, civilians after 1939 were confronted with vastly more efficient killing machines. The statistics are revealing. In 1915, Zeppelins had dropped bombs on London; in 1917, Gotha-Giant bombers followed suit. In total, around 225 tons of bombs were released over the skies of Britain between 1914 and 1918, killing 1,300 people.[10] In comparison, a *single* raid during the Second World War could unleash many more tons of explosives over Britain than were dropped during the *entire* 1914–18 conflict.

The bombing assault on Britain began in earnest during September 1940 when the Luftwaffe added the terrorization of civilians to its mission of destroying aircraft, obliterating armaments factories, and disrupting communications and supply routes. From August to mid-November 1940, 200 raiders bombed London every night, except one. Thereafter, people in Birmingham, Bristol, Coventry, Southampton, Liverpool, Plymouth, Cardiff, Portsmouth, Avonmouth, Swansea, Merseyside, Belfast, Clydeside, Hull, Sunderland, Newcastle, and Nottingham were hit. In all, 43,000 people were killed and another 139,000 injured.

Even more devastating was the crisis in Europe, where the persecution of Jews and other groups (including political dissenters, religious minorities, homosexuals, and Roma peoples) was under way. Jean Floud (a member of a long-standing communist family and the aunt of Birkbeck economic historian Roderick Floud) was relief secretary for the International Student Service. She pleaded with Birkbeck to take more Polish, French, Belgian, and Czech refugees.[11] The fact that the College did accept many by offering either free places or the remission of fees is indicated by the fact that, in 1940, one quarter of Birkbeck students were refugees.[12]

---

[8] Lovelock, *Homage to Gaia*, 43.   [9] Ibid., 43.
[10] George H. Quester, 'The Psychological Effects of Bombing on Civilian Populations: Wars of the Past', in Betty Glad (ed.), *Psychological Dimensions of War* (Newbury Park: Sage, 1990), 203.
[11] Letter from Jean Floud, Relief Secretary of the International Student Service, to the Principal, dated 26 August 1940, in Birkbeck Archive, 'Birkbeck Students at War' (p. 84 of file).
[12] Letter from the College Secretary to Jean Floud, Relief Secretary of the International Student Service, dated 23 September 1940, in Birkbeck Archive, 'Birkbeck Students at War' (p. 88 of file).

One of these refugees was Ernst Gunther Michaelis, and his travails give an indication of what many refugee students must have faced. Michaelis was born to the physician Willy Michaelis and Marie (née Italiener). Before coming to Birkbeck, he grew up in Leipzig, Germany. For Polish Jewish families, these were dangerous times. Leipzig had a very high proportion of foreign-born Jews. According to one estimate, of the 11,564 members of *Gemeinde*, at least half were Polish Jews.[13] Even before the crisis of *Kristallnacht* in November 1938 (which led to the destruction of the 1855 Moorish Revival Leipzig synagogue, one of the city's architecturally significant buildings), all Polish Jews living in the city were expelled. The process of 'Aryanization' had begun. Michaelis was imprisoned in a concentration camp and, in November 1938, released on condition that he left Germany within a fortnight. Michaelis with three siblings fled with their parents to London; an older brother, to San Francisco.[14] In Britain, Michaelis was classified under Category C (Friendly Aliens) by the Military Tribunal.[15]

Within a few months of arriving in London, Michaelis was studying at Birkbeck and in June 1940 he was awarded a second-class honours in the General BSc Examinations. At that time, he was also reported to be 'well-versed in Radio Location', a course he attended in the College.[16] Despite his persecuted status, Michaelis was worried about being interned. He almost certainly knew Nikolaus Pevsner, the art historian who had been forced to resign his lectureship at the University of Göttingen in 1933 but was, nevertheless interned by the British government as No. 54829. Desperate, Michaelis wrote to the Master, informing him that

> During the last few days...a great number of Germans living in this country have been interred, and it is by no means unlikely, that all German subjects may be at least temporarily detained if it should be considered necessary.[17]

Michaelis was especially worried that he might be unable to take his Birkbeck examinations in the camp. Troup Horne reassured him, saying that it was unlikely that a Category C German would be interned and, if the worse did happen, he would personally ensure that Michaelis could sit his examinations.[18]

---

[13] Robert Allen Willingham II, 'Jews in Leipzig: Nationality and Community in the 20th Century', PhD thesis (Austin: University of Texas at Austin, 2005), 99.

[14] This is from an account of his brother's life: Rudy Michaels (Rudolf Hans Michaelis) in www.legacy.com/obituaries.

[15] Letter from Willy Michaelis to the Master, John P. R. Maud, dated 15 January 1941, 'Birkbeck Students at War', in Birkbeck Archive, Box 10, 'War 1939–45'.

[16] Letter from the Master, H. Gordon Jackson, to Dame Helen Gwynn-Vaughan, dated 9 January 1944, 'Birkbeck Students at War', in Birkbeck Archive, Box 10, 'War 1939–45'.

[17] Letter from Ernst G. Michaelis to the Master, dated 19 May 1940, in Birkbeck Archive, Box 10, 'War 1939–1945'.

[18] Letter from Troup Horne to Ernst G. Michaelis, dated 21 May 1940, in Birkbeck Archive, Box 10, 'War 1939–1945'.

Meanwhile, Michaelis volunteered for the army at least half a dozen times and, when rejected, applied to become a member of the Pioneer Corps, a combatant corps used for light engineering tasks. Despairing of being able to contribute to the war effort, he had taken a ship to Australia, with plans to enlist upon arrival. Unfortunately, while he was on the ship, his parents received the letter from the War Office informing him that his request had been accepted and he should go to a particular recruiting office to sign up. It was too late. So, when Ernst Michaelis arrived in Australia, he was immediately sent to an internment camp.

In 1941, Michaelis' father took up his case with the College. He pleaded with the Master, John Maud, to help his son get released in order to return to London to complete his studies in applied mathematics, physics, and chemistry at Birkbeck. This was possible under Article 21 of the White Paper, which set out the procedures to be followed in applying for the 'Release of a civilian internee of Enemy nationality (Cmd. 6233)'. In his father's words, Ernst had 'demonstrated his loyalty to England' and simply wanted to return home in order to help the war effort.[19] The Master and College Secretary (Troup Horne) agree to make an application on Ernst Michaelis' behalf. It obviously worked because, by 1943, Michaelis was back at Birkbeck. He was also working for the British Coal Utilisation Research Association, headed by the scientist and Gurdjieff-devotee John G. Bennett. There, he worked alongside Rosalind Franklin of Birkbeck (see Chapter 21) as well as fellow Jewish refugees Victor Goldschmidt and Marcelli Pirani.[20] Once again, though, Michaelis appealed for help to enlist in the Royal Air Force for air crew duties. The Master—who by this stage in the war was H. Gordon Jackson—appealed to Dame Helen Gwynne-Vaughan to use her contacts. 'He is of German nationality', Jackson admitted,

> but in spite, perhaps because, of that, he is all the more anxious to take part in the war against Hitler.... He is now reading for a Special Degree in Physics and is so highly thought of by the College authorities that he has been given a junior appointment on the Staff. He also takes an active and a very useful part in the social affairs of the students. Personally, I find him a very likeable fellow, but there is a certain diffidence in his manner which might tell against him in a preliminary interview.[21]

Strings were pulled. Dame Helen reported that someone very influential in the Air Ministry had approved Michaelis' appointment in the RAF.[22] There, Michaelis'

---

[19] Letter from Willy Michaelis to the Master, John P. R. Maud, dated 15 January 1941, 'Birkbeck Students at War', in Birkbeck Archive, Box 10, 'War 1939-45'.

[20] Letter from Ernst Michaelis to the Under-Secretary of State, Air Ministry, dated 26 November 1943, 'Birkbeck Students at War', in Birkbeck Archive, Box 10, 'War 1939-45'.

[21] Letter from Master H. Gordon Jackson to Dame Helen Gwynn-Vaughan, dated 9 January 1944, 'Birkbeck Students at War', in Birkbeck Archive, Box 10, 'War 1939-45'.

[22] Letter from the Air Ministry to Dame Helen Gwynn-Vaughan, dated 15 January 1944, 'Birkbeck Students at War', in Birkbeck Archive, Box 10, 'War 1939-45'.

trail runs cold, but we do know that he survived the war because, in 1947, he became a British citizen.[23] He also had a career as a physicist. In 1954, he was employed at Birkbeck supervising a research laboratory.[24] Two years later, he was the co-author (including with David Keith Butt of Birkbeck) of *The Elementary Particles of Nature*, which boasted a foreword by Nobel laureate C. F. Powell proclaiming the study of 'elementary particles' to be 'at the centre of interest in the development of physics'.[25] Michaelis proudly includes the letters BSc and PhD after his name.

The persecution of people like Michaelis enraged William Temple, Archbishop of Canterbury and President of Birkbeck during those terrifying years between 1942 and 1944. Temple responded to the crisis by co-founding the Council of Christians and Jews, dedicated both to helping the persecuted Jews in Nazi Germany and to fighting anti-Semitism in whatever guise. In one of his 1943 speeches in the House of Lords, Temple spoke about the 'extermination of the Jews' in Nazi Germany. He reminded listeners of the parable of the good Samaritan who came to the aid of a wounded traveller by the roadside. 'My chief protest', he began,

> is against procrastination of any kind.... The Jews are being slaughtered at the rate of tens of thousands a day.... We at this moment have upon us a tremendous responsibility. We stand at the bar of history, of humanity and of God.[26]

It was a statement that gives a lie to the view that Britons during the early 1940s did not know about what we now call the Holocaust (see Fig. 18.2).

While the College's President was fighting in the House of Lord for recognition of mass murder of the Jews and other persecuted communities, the College's administrators faced more prosaic questions. One of the first issues to be resolved was whether Birkbeck should follow the other colleges in London and close its doors or evacuate all personnel and equipment to the countryside. The decision was made to close but, with the raising of the minimum age for being called up for military duty, which meant that quite a few young men 'who [had] expected to be in the army found themselves with two years to spare and nothing to do', the College quickly decided to reopen. This decision made, the next immediate concern was to provide Air Raid Precautions (ARP) shelters for 300 people—these shelters had to be built in a fortnight and at a time when there was high demand

---

[23] The National Archives, HO 334/189/31822. In 1944, he wrote a (particularly bad) limerick about a 'Miss K' and 'Nina J-'. See 'The Limerick Competition', *The Lodestone*, 36.2 (spring 1944), 24.

[24] Reinhold Furth, *The Physics Department of Birkbeck College (University of London)* (London: Institute of Physics, July 1954), 7.

[25] David Keith Butt, Ernst G. Michaelis, Gabriel L. Miller, and P. L. Trent, *The Elementary Particles of Nature* (London: Science Information Service, 1956), 2.

[26] The Archbishop of Canterbury (William Temple), 'German Atrocities: Aid for Refugees', 'Lords Sitting of Tuesday, 23rd March, 1943', *Hansard*.

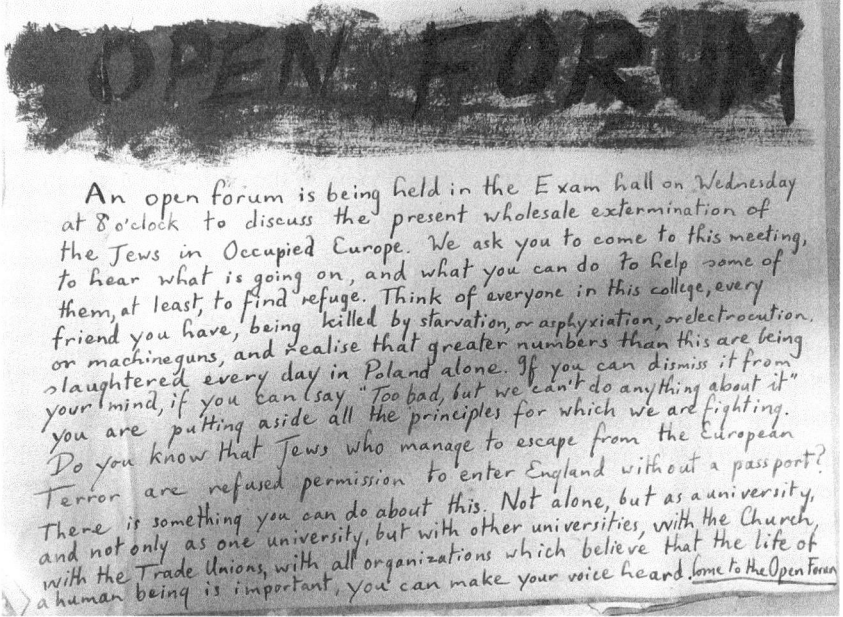

Fig. 18.2 Detail from a student poster near the end of the war, protesting the persecution of the Jews. Birkbeck Archive, Box 43–4.

for timber.[27] The attitude of the College authorities was summed up by College Secretary Troup Horne in a letter to botanist and conscientious objector Gerald A. Prowse: 'the College does not anticipate evacuation as everyone here prefers to stay in the front line'.[28] That front line was London as well as Flanders. Birkbeck was the only college of Higher Education remaining in London throughout the war.

The second question was: at what time of day should classes take place? The blackout, Blitz, and travel difficulties rendered evening classes virtually impossible, so the College switched its teaching to daylight hours and during the weekends.[29]

The third, and most important, question concerned the contributions of the College to the war effort. There were some unusual proposals. In July 1940, for example, Marjorie Daunt (a scholar of Old English) informed the Master, John Maud, that it would be a 'nice gesture' if Birkbeck 'offered General de Gaulle a

---

[27] Letter from Troup Horne to Dr Fletcher (representative of the London County Council on the College's Board of Governors), dated 10 October 1939, in 'Wartime Correspondence of the Clerk 1939-41', in Birkbeck Archive (p. 33 of file).

[28] Letter from Troup Horne to Gerald A. Prowse, dated 18 October 1940, in 'Wartime Correspondence of the Clerk 1939-41', in Birkbeck Archive (p. 83 of file).

[29] 'Birkbeck College 1939-41', 3, in 'Birkbeck Students at War', in Birkbeck Archive, Box 10, 'War 1939-45'.

class in English for say *ten* of his men'. She added that 'He must have officers who need it.'[30]

Staff in the sciences were of more practical use to the war effort. For example, William Wardlaw had been appointed Professor of Physical Chemistry in 1937, a position he held until he retired in 1957. However, he had only just started reorganizing the department when war was declared.[31] His expertise was quickly employed by the Chemical Defence Research Department at Woolwich,[32] and he was appointed a joint secretary of the War Cabinet Scientific Advisory Committee, followed by scientific adviser to the Committee of Appointments in the Ministry of Labour and National Service.[33]

The major contributions to the war made by crystallographer J. D. Bernal are discussed in the next chapter, but Bernal was also important in reversing what he called the 'intellectual blackout in London'.[34] He encouraged the College to introduce midday lectures aimed at the general public. These ending up drawing audiences of between 400 and 900 people each.[35] From the spring of 1940, Maud's wife inaugurated a series of lunch-time concerts, the first of which was given by the celebrated pianist Myra Hess.[36] There were other interesting visitors to the College, most notoriously 'a young woman graduate whose chief claim to fame' was the number of 'enemy [who] had fallen to her gun'.[37] This was, presumably, 25-year-old Lyudmila Pavlichenko, the Soviet sniper, commonly known as 'Lady Death'. Her boast of killing 309 'fascist oppressors' led folk legend Woody Guthrie to devote a song to her, with the bloody refrain, '300 Nazis fell by your gun'.[38]

Everyday routines were transformed. Rationing meant that food became a central topic of conversation. While the College's refectory had to 'make do', staff speculated about the food that men on active service were eating and how it might change their tastes post-war. Arthur Jones (the head of the History Department), for example, told Troup Horne that when classicist Douglas Dakin returned to the College he would have 'a lingering taste for olive oil, garlic, and maccaroni [sic] which you alone, as an expert *chef de cuisine*, will be able to satisfy'.[39] Troup Horne, who was known for his love of good food, was forced to

---

[30] Letter from Miss Marjorie Daunt to the Master, 8 July 1940, in Birkbeck Archive, Box 10, 'War 1939–45'.
[31] 'Prof. W. Wardlaw, C.B.E.', *Nature*, 4660 (21 February 1959), 505.
[32] Letter from the Director of Scientific Research at the Ministry of Supply, to Principal J. P. R. Maud, dated 7 January 1940, in the Birkbeck Archive, 'Birkbeck Staff During the War' (p. 352 of file).
[33] 'Prof. W. Wardlaw, C.B.E.', 505.
[34] 'Tradition of Pan-Germanism', *The Times* (15 November 1939), 4.
[35] 'Birkbeck College 1939–41', 6, in 'Birkbeck Students at War', Birkbeck Archive, Box 10, 'War 1939–45'. Also see 'Birkbeck', *The Lodestone*, 46.2 (spring/summer 1955), 30.
[36] 'Birkbeck College Concerts', *The Times* (21 December 1939), 6, and 'Miss Myra Hess's recital', *The Times* (13 January 1940), 4.
[37] 'Birkbeck', *The Lodestone*, 46.2 (spring/summer 1955), 30.
[38] Georgy Manaev, '5 Soviet Superheroes in World War Two who terrified the Nazis' (11 December 2017), at https://www.rbth.com/history/326983-5-soviet-superheroes-in-ww-2, viewed 10 August 2019.
[39] Letter from Arthur Jones to Troup Horne, dated 23 March 1943, in Birkbeck Archive, Box 43.

be inventive. He chastised 'Bussy' (A. Leslie Bostock, a former President of the Students' Union who was on active service in Abyssinia) for having the audacity to 'flaunt onions in my face when, at any time during the last six months, I would have bartered my soul for some'. He admitted, though, that he had considerable success in wooing shopkeepers to surreptitiously slip him scarce vegetables. In his words,

> By making shameless love to two separate purveyors of green grocery (one in Lamb's Conduit Street and the other in Chancery Lane), I am probably the only citizen in this village who has... been the proud possessor of that rare and exotic fruit [onions]. You must think from this that we are suffering from rationing. I am suffering, but not in the way you might imagine; I have put on two stone since the beastly thing started. If you know your catering way about Town, though, you can do quite well, but I must say that my wits are becoming sharpened.

He added that the 'Birkbeck spirit, you will be glad to hear, is unrationed and is stronger than ever'.[40]

Schedules underwent major changes. Dances took place in the afternoons, not evenings; dinners became lunches; instead of plays being held in the theatre (its roof had been bombed, so was 'somewhat draughty'),[41] films were watched in the Junior Common Room.[42] A 'spirit of reasonableness and adaptability' pervaded the College. One observer maintained that

> The Staff allowed the comforts of their Common Room to be sacrificed to make an air-raid shelter; the Student Union Council gave their Offices for a First-Aid Post without a murmur; crowded conditions in the Refectory were remedied by volunteer assistance organized by the Librarian; the attendant staff had faced up cheerfully to over 70% of their number being called back to the Navy.[43]

When the Battle of Britain heated up, windows had to be bricked up and 'baffle walls' erected as a protection against blast.[44] Students entering examination rooms were required to carry their gas masks.[45] An alarm, colloquially known as the DIVO (for 'Danger Imminent Vertically Overhead') was installed to warn of

---

[40] Letter to Bussy (A. Leslie Bostock, President of the Students' Union from September 1929 to September 1930) from Troup Horne, 17 July 1941, in Birkbeck Archive, Box 43.

[41] 'Draft. War-Time Diary', 3, in 'Birkbeck Students at War', in Birkbeck Archive, Box 10, 'War 1939–45'.

[42] 'Birkbeck College 1939–41', 4, in 'Birkbeck Students at War', in Birkbeck Archive, Box 10, 'War 1939–45'.

[43] Ibid., 2–3.   [44] Ibid., 4.

[45] 'Birkbeck College 1939–41', 2, in 'Birkbeck Students at War', in Birkbeck Archive, Box 10, 'War 1939–45'.

daytime raids.⁴⁶ The bomb shelter, which had originally been the Senior Common Room, was extended to include the basement and central landings on the ground floor, as well as staircases.⁴⁷

The first incendiary attack to affect the College occurred on 25 September 1940 when £25,000 worth of damage was done to four laboratories, the roof of the theatre, and other parts of the building.⁴⁸ When medieval scholar Louise W. Stone referred to the College's 'personal bouquet from Hitler', Troup Horne replied jocularly that 'the College accepted its bouquet (flaming June by Burnie Jones) with modesty'⁴⁹ (Troup Horne was probably mistaking Frederic Leighton's painting *Flaming June* for the art of fellow pre-Raphaelite artist Edward Burne-Jones, who was often exhibited alongside him). On 29 December 1940, incendiaries inflicted further damage. In 1944, flying bombs led to the collapse of a chimney stack which crashed through the roof of the main building.⁵⁰ There was a time when the theatre was so cold that architectural historian Nikolaus Pevsner wore an overcoat, a muffler, and a pair of thick woollen gloves when giving a lecture on French art.⁵¹ He later recalled that 'We are all freezing, and people walk about in the oddest garments.... Serious city men wear gum boots over their black trousers.' Joad even arrived at classes wearing 'a dark navy skiing costume', while another professor wore 'a balaclava'.⁵²

The most destructive attack occurred early in the morning of Sunday, 11 May 1941, when incendiary bombs started dropping on the College and surrounding buildings. The College's Fire Guard (which consisted of five students and one attendant), called for help and two fire squads did their best to put out the large fires.⁵³ By 3 a.m., everyone had to concede that it was an impossible task: a change in the wind, coupled with a shortage of water, led to the fires spreading. As Troup Horne noted in his 'War Diary',

> When daylight came the library of 40,000 volumes which, for its size, was one of the best in the University [of London], and was one of the few to remain open in London during the war, was little more than a smouldering mass of ashes [see Figs. 18.3 and 18.4].⁵⁴

---

⁴⁶ 'Draft. War-Time Diary', 4, in 'Birkbeck Students at War', in Birkbeck Archive, Box 10, 'War 1939–45'.
⁴⁷ Ibid., 4.
⁴⁸ Troup Horne, 'Fire at Greystone Place' (15 May 1941), in Birkbeck Archive, Box 10, 'War 1939–1945'. E. H. Warmington noted that repair of the damage cost £16,000: *A History of Birkbeck College University of London During the Second World War* (London: Birkbeck College, 1954), 65.
⁴⁹ Letters to and from Louise W. Stone and Troup Horne, dated 1 and 7 June 1940, in Birkbeck Archive, 'Wartime Correspondence of the Clerk 1939–41' (pp. 104 and 106).
⁵⁰ Troup Horne, 'Fire at Greystone Place' (15 May 1941), in Birkbeck Archive, Box 10, 'War 1939–1945'.
⁵¹ H. G. B., 'A Fire-Watcher's Interview with his Own Memory', *The Lodestone*, 36.3 (summer 1944), 12.
⁵² Cited in Harries, *Nikolaus Pevsner*, 325. ⁵³ Troup Horne, 'Fire at Greystone Place'.
⁵⁴ Ibid.

Fig. 18.3 Books drying outside the destroyed Birkbeck College library in Greystoke Place during the Blitz in May 1941. The books suffered water damage from the fire hoses used to fight the fire caused by bombing. Birkbeck Image Collections: Birkbeck History BH0056.

Despite the devastation, classes resumed at 10 a.m. that Sunday morning, with staff and students spending their time between lectures salvaging as much equipment and as many books as possible. The refectory also opened at 12.30 and, despite having neither gas nor water, 'Ma' Francis (see Chapter 13) served 150 lunches.[55] She was reported to have 'never done such a roaring trade'.[56] When members of the Fire Squad sat down to 'beef and beer' later that afternoon, they were heard saying that the Germans 'derived no advantage from the night's work'. They maintained that 'This sort of thing doesn't get him anywhere', adding that it 'only puts people's backs up'.[57] It was a classic statement of the myth of that war: 'British pluck'.

Humour and understatement were ways of coping with war's terrors. In a letter to Charles Fox, who had lectured in mathematics at Birkbeck since 1920, Troup Horne commented that a bomb had exploded just 75 yards from him the previous week. However, he joked, 'owing to a physical disability from which I have suffered for over thirty years' (that is, baldness), 'I didn't turn a hair, but the

---

[55] Troup Horne, 'War Diary', in 'Birkbeck Students at War', in Birkbeck Archive, Box 10, 'War 1939–45'.

[56] Troup Horne, 'Draft. War-Time Diary', 3, in 'Birkbeck Students at War', in Birkbeck Archive, Box 10, 'War 1939–45'.

[57] Troup Horne, 'Fire at Greystone Place'.

Fig. 18.4 Bomb damage to the College's library, May 1941. Birkbeck Image Collections: Birkbeck History BH0056.

building in front of which I was standing got a nasty shaking'.[58] In another letter, Troup Horne confessed to his 'boyish delight in swatting incendiaries'.[59] Ruth Suffield, former student and member of the Auxiliary Territorial Service (ATS), claimed to being nothing more than slightly 'disturbed by "Jerry" dropping things round about'.[60] Stoicism was a patriotic virtue.

The staff and students of Birkbeck threw themselves into war-work. In 1944, Chivers was employed by the Ministry of Information (responsible for propaganda as well as communicating factual information) to use her writing skills honed at Birkbeck to boost support for the war. *The Lodestone* published her (presumably fictionalized) account of working at a Casualty Clearing Station in the south of England. In that account, her job was to watch over the wounded patients

---

[58] Troup Horne in a letter to C. L. Fox, dated 26 April 1941, in 'Birkbeck Students at War', in Birkbeck Archive, Box 10, 'War 1939–45'.
[59] Letter to Bossy (A. Leslie Bostock, President of the Students' Union from September 1929 to September 1930) from Troup Horne, 17 July 1941, in Birkbeck Archive, Box 43.
[60] Letter from Ruth Suffield to Jackson on 29 January 1941, in 'Birkbeck Students at War', in Birkbeck Archive, Box 10, 'War 1939–45'.

during the nightshift. Chivers would put away the uniforms that had been dumped by the bedsides. She arranged the men's belongings, ensured that their talismans were carefully preserved for future good luck, changed pillows, provided cups of tea for the patients as well as their grieving wives, and checked that bandages had been correctly applied. She would also clean wounds stinking of the 'sweet and evil stench' of gas gangrene.[61] Most important, though, her job was to listen to patients who wanted to talk. At this point, Chivers' narrative took on a more obviously propagandist tone, as she recounted an atrocity story she had heard from a 'handsome parachutist'. He told her about coming across some 'French girls' next to a rustic cottage. When they waved at the British soldiers, 'a German sniper put a burst of rifle fire among them...he deliberately killed those girls, true as I'm here'.[62] She also recounted the shock of emptying ambulances packed with children and elderly civilians who had been wounded by German bombers: 'What kind of war do they call this?', a colleague asked. It was a war for morale as well as national survival.

And Allied victory was not inevitable. Arthur Jones, the head of the History Department, was dismayed by Churchill's rhetoric, comparing it to 'an empty bucket falling down two flights of stone stairs or a piece of resounding brass and a tinkling "thimble"'.[63] In 1942, Jones was equally dismissing of Liberal MP Herbert Samuel, who had earlier aligned himself with Neville Chamberlain's appeasement policy. Samuel had given the foundation lecture at Birkbeck on 24 June 1942. Entitled 'The World after the War', Samuel had conjured up Birkbeck's founders—George Birkbeck, Lord Brougham, and Francis Place—asking how they would

> find us at this moment tossed about in the great cataclysm in the modern history of mankind; at grips with enemies over half the globe; thousands of men and women being slaughtered by war, week by week, year by year; the great ideal with which France had inspired their generation and the century that followed; suddenly in our time, discarded and derided–Liberty, suppressed; Equality, condemned; and Fraternity...? 'Ah yes', as someone has said, 'we are all brothers now—all Cains and Abels!'

Samuel insisted, though, that Birkbeck's founders would have 'see[n] the higher spirit of man, calm and dauntless in the peril', and confident that 'victory would come, with sword in one hand and trowel in the other'.[64] Jones was unimpressed. He sneered that Samuel had no idea whether post-war Britain would be 'Nazi and so Nordic' or would be 'Churchillian and as sportingly Anglo-Saxon and Nasal'. He wanted Samuel to be asked 'when and if the British are going to win a battle

---

[61] Lena M. Chivers, 'Night Duty', *The Lodestone*, 37.1 (autumn 1944), 8.   [62] Ibid., 8.
[63] Letter from Arthur Jones to Troup Horne, dated 10 October 1941, in Birkbeck Archive, Box 43.
[64] Viscount Samuel, 'The World After the War', *Philosophy*, 18.62 (April 1943), 61.

before the next millennium. And how long, oh Lord, are we to be stuffed with glorious retreats?'⁶⁵

* * *

As with the 1914–18 war, the Second World War transformed the lives of Birkbeck staff and students. Paul Dienes was a member of the Department of Mathematics who, prior to the war, had made his name as an expert on the behaviour of Taylor series and their circle of convergence. This was published as *The Taylor Series: An Introduction to the Theory of Functions of a Complex Variety* (1931, 2nd edition 1957). In 1938, Dienes published *Logic of Algebra* and, a decade later, *Sign, Symbol, Expression*. A student recalled that when he gave his inter-faculty lecture on 'Signs, Symbols, and Expression', he

> provided a thrilling and most individual talk. The occasion was memorable for most of us—though not probably for mathematicians—because when his argument needed the addition of two or three units to a sum in three figures, he could only arrive at the answer by chalking the sum on the board; as it might be the subtraction sum in *Alice Through the Looking-Glass*: 365 − 1 = 364.

During the war, however, he would invite people to his flat in Cranley Gardens, North London, for 'seminars', which were described as 'very friendly' occasions.⁶⁶ Communist statistician George Alfred Barnard remembered leaving Dienes' flat 'a bit later than usual, so that the shrapnel from anti-aircraft fire was already falling rather thickly while we were walking rapidly (one didn't run) towards the underground station at High Gate'.⁶⁷ During this period, Dienes attracted and had a formidable influence on students including Ralph Henstock (known for the Henstock–Kurzweil integral), Abraham Robinson (famous for the development of non-standard analysis, whereby infinitesimal and infinite numbers are reincorporated into modern mathematics), and R. G. Cooke (described as 'the most active of the Birkbeck mathematicians', with a 'boundless enthusiasm for the Theory of Infinite Matrices and for Matrix methods for assigning limits to divergent series').⁶⁸ After the liberation of France in 1945, Dienes 'arranged seminars at Birkbeck College for his French colleagues, and was among the first to invite Mandelbrojt, Dieudonné, Laurent Schwarz, Cartan, and others to London'.⁶⁹

---

⁶⁵ Letter from Arthur Jones to Troup Horne, dated 19 June 1942, in Birkbeck Archive, Box 43.
⁶⁶ Joseph Warren Dauben, *Abraham Robinson: The Creation of Nonstandard Analysis, a Personal and Mathematical Odyssey* (Princeton: Princeton University Press, 1995), 155–6.
⁶⁷ Interview with George A. Barnard, in Dauben, *Abraham Robinson*, 155.
⁶⁸ The comments on Cook are from C. Ambrose Rogers, interviewed by Dauben, *Abraham Robinson*, 156.
⁶⁹ Dauben, *Abraham Robinson*, 155.

Women were also affected by the war. As the Director of the Auxiliary Territorial Service, Gwynne-Vaughan appeared in military garb once again (see Fig. 18.5). Dispiritingly, she had to fight the same gender-battles that she assumed she had won in 1914–18. When she heard people saying that women who joined the auxiliary services were doing a 'man's job', she rebuked them. 'Not a bit', she exclaimed, adding that women in the service were 'doing a human job'. She reminded them that 'many human jobs have hitherto been carried out almost exclusively by men. We must not be rushed thereby into supposing them unwomanly.'

However, by the early 1940s, Gwynne-Vaughan was two decades older than she had been in the previous war. She was less successful in leading 'her' women. Times had changed since 1917 and her austerity and strong sense of hierarchies and class privilege clashed with the young and more 'modern' women of 1941. She was seen as a hindrance to recruitment and abruptly ousted.

For Birkbeck men, joining the military exposed them to risk of mutilation and death. An unknown number were killed. The survivors had no option but to

Fig. 18.5 Dame Gwynne-Vaughan in the uniform of the Auxiliary Territorial Service with Queen Elizabeth, Queen Mother, in 1939. Birkbeck Image Collections: Birkbeck History BH0105.

'carry on'. This was what Troup Horne sought to remind Thomas Greenwood, lecturer in philosophy at Birkbeck, who spent most of the war in the USA engaged in propaganda to encourage the Americans to enter the war. In a letter to Greenwood dated 29 August 1941, Troup Horne maintained that 'we do not allow our activities to be unduly interfered with by the apostles of nazi [sic] culture. I trust that by the end of the Session the Hun will be well on their way to their inevitable destination', meaning hell.[70]

Troup Horne seems to have been a much loved figure. He elicited hundreds of letters from Birkbeck students and staff writing from bombed neighbourhoods in the UK as well as from the front lines (see Fig. 18.6). Many told stories about being exposed to different classes and types of people they would never have otherwise met. These encounters were not always welcomed. For example, Jethro Bithell, lecturer in German literature, lived in Penzance (Cornwall) during the war. He grumbled about war evacuees from the East End of London who were fleeing the Blitz. Prior to the war, the town had a population of around 20,000, so the sudden influx of 12,000 evacuees was a shock, especially since the hospital was over-crowded with 'diphtheria children'.[71] In one letter, Bithell complained

Fig. 18.6 Students sent hundreds of letters to the College Secretary, Troup Horne. Birkbeck Archive, 'Birkbeck Students at War', p. 37.

---

[70] Letter from Troup Horne to Thomas Greenwood, dated 29 August 1941, in Birkbeck Archive, 'Birkbeck Staff During the War' (p. 94 of file).
[71] Letter from Jethro Bithell to College Secretary, Troup Horne, dated 26 November 1940, in Birkbeck Archive, 'Wartime Correspondence with Clerk' (p. 132 of file).

that 'Jerry' had blown out all the front windows of his three-storey house and 'made "lefts" in the roof'. This meant that he would be forced to 'live till the end of the war with all the front boarded up'. There was a positive side to this catastrophe, however. 'It may save me from London evacuees', he gleefully exclaimed, claiming that the refugees were 'mostly burglars' wives with their children to judge by appearance...all Penzance agrees that they are worse than bombs and some people abandon house (storing furniture) when they get them'. Troup Horne commiserated, agreeing that 'town and country never will mix, but you seem to have got the dregs of Whitechapel–largely foreigners, I expect'. By 'foreigners', he meant the British-born families of Russian Jews who had fled previous pogroms.[72]

But others were intrigued in positive ways by the company in which they found themselves. Mathematician Charles Fox described his new comrades at great length. They were 'rough diamonds', he contended, and their 'ignorance and simplicity are sometimes unbelievable'. He was frustrated by their 'not too intelligent use of the radio'. By this he meant their obsession with 'hot' music and hourly news broadcasts. Fox claimed to find it 'disconcerting' to hear Bach's music responded to with the words, 'For Christ's sake turn that bloody row off, & let's have some –ing music!' He lamented that 'such [radio] items as the "Brains Trust" (starring your friend C. E. M. Joad) or J. B. Priestley's postscripts have to be fought for'. However, he conceded that

> they are on the whole a good-hearted and very genuine crew, & I have made some good friends amongst them. I have also acquired from them a good many English idioms that weren't in my vocabulary before.

He concluded that it was 'refreshing...to live with people entirely free from all humbug & affectation' and praised 'the tolerance & humility of the British working man'.[73]

Another member of the College's staff who was transformed by the war was classicist Douglas Dakin. He was only 32 years old when war was declared and had just published *Turgot and the Ancien Régime in France* (1939), which reviewers had hailed as an 'invaluable addition to our knowledge', 'scholarly, conscientious, and reliable', and 'one of the best studies of French eighteenth century history to come from England in many a moon'.[74] His research interests then

---

[72] Letter from College Secretary, Troup Horne, to Jethro Bithell, dated 1 December 1940, in Birkbeck Archive, 'Wartime Correspondence with Clerk' (p. 131 of file).

[73] C. L. Fox to Troup Horne, dated 24 April 1941, in 'Birkbeck Students at War', in Birkbeck Archive, Box 10, 'War 1939–45'.

[74] Frederick L. Nussbaum, 'Turgot and the Ancien Régime by Douglas Dakin', *American Historical Review*, 45.4 (July 1940), 865; A. Cobban, 'Turgot and the Ancien Régime by Douglas Dakin', *History*, new series, 25.97 (June 1940), 80; Shepard B. Clough, 'Turgot and the Ancien Régime by Douglas Dakin', *Journal of Modern History*, 12.2 (June 1940), 249.

moved to Greece, especially the revolution of 1821-9. When war was declared, Dakin had joined the Royal Air Force Volunteer Reserve and then served in Egypt and Greece as a liaison officer to the Royal Hellenic Air Force. In a letter to Troup Horne, Dakin admitted that he had been having

> an interesting time, since I left England. I have learnt a great deal in every way. I have improved my knowledge of topography: I have seen places & peoples and I am becoming polyglot.

Nevertheless, he still felt like he was 'missing much by being abroad', by which he meant that he regretted missing the Blitz and other home-front traumas. He was worried that

> when I return I shall be a 'colonial', well-pickled with outpost mentality & outdated. We just can't imagine what England is like... what are people thinking? In other words, what is Cyril [Joad] writing about?[75]

What Dakin failed to mention in his letters (which would have been censored) was that his wartime life was exciting, especially in 1944. During the 'Dekemvriana' or the 3 December Event, in which police fired into a crowd of ELAS (the Greek People's Liberation Army) demonstrators in Syntagma Square, Athens, Dakin was arrested. However, his love of English democracy and his persuasive argumentative style resulted in his converting an ELAS colonel to support the British.[76] His time in Greece, in which he was probably a British agent, although he was later described as a 'anarchist of the right', led him to shift much of his intellectual interests after the war to modern Hellenic studies. It was a field in which he subsequently became a world expert.

* * *

On 7 May 1945, General Alfred Jodl signed the unconditional surrender of the German forces. Three days later, the Master of Birkbeck, Harold Gordon Jackson, sent a message to King George VI, stating: 'Whilst rejoicing in the successful issue of all aspects of the War, it is a special honour for the College to have remained in London with Your Majesties throughout these recent years'. His Majesty responded (see Fig. 18.7).[77] The war in the Pacific continued until September. Six years and one day after Germany invaded Poland, the global war was over.

---

[75] Letter from Dakin to 'Trouper' [his preferred name amongst friends], dated 16 July 1941, in Birkbeck Archive, Box 43.
[76] Information from Yianis Yianoulopoulos, a friend of Dakin. Thanks to Professors Efi Avdela and Efi Gazi for tracking down this information.
[77] Copy of communication to King George VI, signed H. Gordon Jackson, dated 10 May 1945, in Birkbeck Archive, 'Birkbeck Staff During the War' (p. 1 of file).

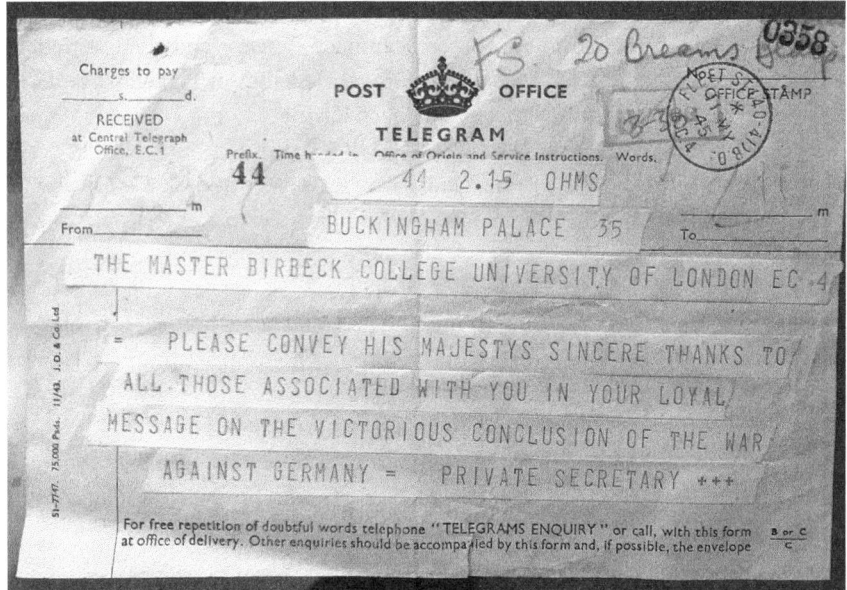

Fig. 18.7 Telegram from Buckingham Palace dated 10 May 1945. Birkbeck Archive.

The end of military conflict led to a reassessment of priorities. One of the most divisive was whether the College should continue teaching in the daytime and at weekends. Reverting to classes in the evening met with strong approval amongst the staff: after all, that had been the condition for Birkbeck becoming part of the University of London. However, 63 per cent of students expressed a preference for the continuation of weekend teaching.[78] This was not looked upon favourably by lecturers, particularly those teaching science subjects. They pointed out that weekend teaching did not give them enough time to set out the necessary apparatus; they reflected nostalgically about pre-war Sundays spent at home sipping tea.[79] They claimed that teaching on the weekends would compromise depth of learning and be an additional burden for lecturers.[80] A large minority of students agreed with them, resenting having to make trips into central London simply to attend weekend classes.[81] And what about the 'English week-end', one student complained: surely it was a 'national institution'? Admittedly, she continued, 'sacrifices… had to be made in war-time' but there was 'no reason why [weekends] should not be restored when peace-time conditions return.… May not the peace

---

[78] 'Correspondence', *The Lodestone*, 38.1 (autumn 1945), 16. Note that the Editor said there was a 69 per cent majority in favour of weekends: 'Editorial. Evenings or Week-Ends', *The Lodestone*, 37.3 (summer 1945), 1.

[79] H. R. Nettleton (lecturer in physics), 'Evenings or Week-Ends?', *The Lodestone*, 37.3 (summer 1945), 25–6.

[80] W. R. Woodridge (Governor), 'Evenings or Week-Ends?', *The Lodestone*, 37.3 (summer 1945), 26.

[81] Kitty Egan (student), 'Evenings or Week-Ends?', *The Lodestone*, 37.3 (summer 1945), 26.

Fig. 18.8 The steel frame of the Malet Street building under construction, 1947. Birkbeck Image Collections: Birkbeck History BH0041.

be won on the playing fields of Greenford!'[82] Another student mildly observed that it might be a good idea to attend church, not College, on the Holy Day.[83] In the end, Birkbeck's tradition of teaching in the evening during the working week was retained.

Accommodation continued to be a problem. The construction of the Malet Street building (which had been halted during the war) resumed but was progressing slowly due to the fuel crisis and 'appalling weather' (see Fig. 18.8).[84] The leading British industrialist William Lionel Hichens, who had been Chair of the governors for over twenty years and a leading figure in raising money for the building, had been killed in 1940 when a bomb 'burst practically in the room where he was sitting'.[85] In 1948, even the Master complained that the new building would be 'ludicrously inadequate' to meeting the College's needs and 'the only really sensible thing to do would be to scrap it at once and start on another'.[86]

In the meantime, the College had to deal with the 'badly blitzed' accommodation. It asked to be able to erect huts in front of the Greystone premises but was refused on the grounds that it was an old burial ground and it was not allowed to

[82] Ibid., 27.
[83] Rita Hancock (student), 'Evenings or Week-Ends?', *The Lodestone*, 37.3 (summer 1945), 27.
[84] The Master, 'The Foundation Day Oration of Birkbeck College. 25th March, 1947', in Birkbeck Archive, Box 64.
[85] 'Mr. Lionel Huchens', in Birkbeck Archive, 'Birkbeck Staff During the War' (p. 194 of file).
[86] 'Report 1947/48. The Master', 1, 'Foundation Oration. 4th May 1948', in Birkbeck Archive, Box 9B.

'interfere with the Resurrection'.[87] Although the College did manage to get permission to put huts on a nearby bomb site, it was a poor compromise while students and staff waited for the Malet Street building to be completed.[88]

As during the First World War, the memorial to the dead was also highly contested. A book listing the names of those killed was published, but the College recognized the need for something more monumental. This time, a better choice of artist was commissioned: Ralph Beyer, pupil of Eric Gill and friend of Henry Moore.[89] His memorial consisted of a statute which is similar to Moore's Northampton *Madonna and Child* (1944), minus the child (see Fig. 18.9). It was 4 feet high (excluding the plinth) and carved out of a single cube of brown Hornton Stone from Warwickshire. The memorial showed a woman sitting on a rectangular block on top of a pedestal. The woman's legs were close together, with her arms resting on her knees. While her hands and feet were large, her head was disproportionately small with very few discernible features or facial expressions. Her body was draped in a flowing garment. Her posture and heaviness suggested the grief or mourning of a mother. In a half-hearted attempt to remedy the problem with the First World War memorial, the years '1914–1918' joined those of '1939–1945', faintly engraved on two sides of the pedestal.

Once again, however, the artistic merits of the memorial were disputed. H. Eyles was unhappy that the memorial was 'at pains to conceal its identity' as a war memorial. 'Are we to suppose', he asked, 'that the artist' was 'more concerned with pleasing the living than honouring the dead?'[90] Admittedly, Eyles commended the artist for eschewing 'bad tradition'. Britain was 'cluttered up with Celtic crosses, cenotaphs, rolls of honour and other banalities, which pay tribute only to the bankruptcy of our national imagination', he grumbled. Nevertheless, the composition of the Birkbeck memorial was too simple, requiring onlookers to invest their own emotions in interpreting the figure since, by itself, it was difficult to know what story the artist was attempting to convey. Any 'artist who concludes complacently that his personal system of symbols is easily understood because it happens to be based on the straight line, the triangle, the cylinder and the cube, is making a sorry error', Eyles pompously contended.[91] In the end, he concluded, the memorial was both 'mediocre as a work of art [and] meaningless as a memorial'.[92]

Eyles was not alone in his critique. Frank Lissauer also complained that, unless viewers knew it was a war memorial, the figure might just as easily be a symbol of

---

[87] The Master, 'The Foundation Day Oration of Birkbeck College. 25th March, 1947', in Birkbeck Archive, Box 64.
[88] Ibid. [89] Personal email from John Neilson, 18 June 2020.
[90] H. Eyles, 'The Birkbeck War Memorial. 3 Options. Theme and Variations', *The Lodestone*, 47.2 (1956), 4.
[91] Ibid., 5. [92] Ibid., 7.

Fig. 18.9 The Second World War memorial. Birkbeck Archive.

'natural disasters, especially such as were concerned with agriculture: for instance, the evolution of a desert by careless husbandry'.[93] Lissauer recognized that Beyer had been influenced by Henry Moore, but why did he have to make 'the folds in her shift above the feet look like an afterthought' and weren't her face and hair 'a mere cipher'? The memorial, he observed, had 'so little to do with the college or with war or with memorials'.[94]

It was left to Pevsner to come to the memorial's defence. He reminded its critics that a utilitarian memorial had been ruled out as 'unsuitable to commemorate the sacrifice of so many young lives'.[95] The commissioning committee had also decided not to follow the example of the First World War memorial and simply inscribe the names of the dead on a tablet: too many men and women had 'given' too much and any list would inevitably be incomplete anyway. More practically,

---

[93] Frank Lissauer, 'The Birkbeck War Memorial. 3 Options. Gaea? The New War Memorial', *The Lodestone*, 47.2 (1956), 8.
[94] Ibid., 9.
[95] Nikolaus Pevsner, 'The Birkbeck War Memorial. 3 Options. The War Memorial', *The Lodestone*, 47.2 (1956), 9.

the College was 'devoid of acceptably monumental wall surfaces' for a painting.[96] The suggestion of creating a stained-glass window in the large staircase would not be pragmatic because, as a College in which teaching took place in the evening, the 'glow of colour and the composition would be lost'.[97] Pevsner also attempted to disabuse critics of the assumption that a war memorial 'ought to be a soldier with a gun or some such illustration'. After all, war of the scale seen between 1939 and 1945 depended on 'so many jobs of work, in different surroundings, and with different uniforms', all of which 'led to the same gateway of death'. A more abstract design risked not creating an appropriate 'mood' in onlookers, as well as being too 'impersonal'.[98]

The compromise, Pevsner noted, was a statute which they had intended to be placed on the lawn in front of the College. When it was discovered that the University of London, not Birkbeck, owned that space, the statute was relocated to the College's lobby. Pevsner argued that Beyer's design was 'both personal and universally valid'. The woman's face 'creates a sense of mystery and reverence', he contended. Her hands 'lie heavily on the thighs, as they do in archaic Greek statues of women, and that sense of weighing down is essential for the mood'. Pevsner concluded that the Birkbeck war memorial was 'a piece of sculpture which is of today and yet at the same time of an undated rightness'.[99] Unfortunately, like the 1914–18 memorial, this one, too, has disappeared. Where it is remains a mystery.

[96] Ibid., 10.   [97] Ibid., 9.   [98] Ibid., 11.   [99] Ibid., 13.

19
Reds in the Classroom

> HOBSBAWN (not HOBSBAUM as is stated in the above papers) is of Jewish parentage, his original surname being HOBSBAUM. He is a self avowed communist and is one of the intellectuals of the Communist Party. An accomplished linguist, speaking German and French fluently, he is a lecturer in history at Birkbeck College, E.C.4, and a confidant of Professor J. D. Bernal.
>
> Security Service memo, December 1952[1]

Historian Eric John Ernest Hobsbawm (not Hobsbawn, as was stated in the memo written by an undercover Security Service officer, above) and crystallographer John Desmond Bernal were two of the greatest intellectuals of the twentieth century and Britain's most famous communists. They both dedicated nearly all their careers to Birkbeck students.

Hobsbawm was appointed to the Department of History in 1947 and, when he died in 2012 at the age of 95, was the College's President. During his early decades in the College, the Security Service officers followed him around, opened his post, read telegrams, and tapped his phone. They also routinely commented on his appearance: he was slim and tall, with blue eyes, ginger hair, and a receding forehead. For a time, he wore large, horn-rimmed spectacles.

Bernal preceded Hobsbawm at Birkbeck by ten years. Hobsbawm described him as a 'short, bushy-haired man who looked like the essential scientist in a strip cartoon'. He claimed that Bernal 'walked like a sailor on shore or, as he said, [like] "the pobble who had no toes"'—a reference to Edward Lear's nonsense poetry—while at the same time 'entertain[ing] the staff room with well-honed anecdotes about his extraordinarily distinguished time as scientific adviser to Combined Operations during the war'.[2] Bernal remained at Birkbeck until he died in 1971: he was 70 years old.

* * *

From the 1940s to the early 1970s, these two scruffily dressed intellectuals would regularly meet for lunch in the Common Room of Birkbeck. Their conversations must have been remarkable.

---

[1] Security Service report, 5 December 1952, in The National Archives KV2/3981.
[2] Eric J. Hobsbawm, *Interesting Times: A Twentieth Century Life* (New York: Pantheon Books, 2002), 181.

It is important, however, to note that these two left-wing intellectuals, who will be the primary focus of this chapter, were not alone in their political beliefs. They would have been joined around the lunch or supper table by other communists and leftists who were attracted to jobs at Birkbeck during those heady years. The most important include mathematician Paul Dienes; classicists Geoffrey de Ste Croix and Robert Browning; and physicists/crystallographers J. W. Jeffrey, Alan Lindsey Mackay, and Patrick Maynard Stuart Blackett. Before turning to Bernal and Hobsbawm, then, it is worth visiting these other communists and fellow-travellers who made up the community of 'Reds' for which Birkbeck used to be famous.

Hungarian-born mathematician Dienes has already been mentioned in the previous chapter. He had been forced to flee Hungary after the fall of the Hungarian Soviet Republic. As a supporter of Béla Kun, leader of the Republic, Dienes had been responsible for reorganizing Hungarian universities with the aim of welcoming working-class students. This was not looked upon favourably during the 'white terror', when communist supporters were hunted down; large numbers, executed. Diene fled, bribing the captain of a river boat on the Danube to smuggle him out of the country, hiding in a wine barrel. He was unceremoniously decanted in Vienna, with nothing but the clothes on his back.[3] After time in Vienna, Paris, Aberystwyth, and Swansea, Dienes joined Birkbeck's Mathematics Department in 1929 and stayed until he retired in 1948, immersing himself in function theory, relativity, tensors, infinite matrices, axiomatics, and mathematical logic.[4] We don't know what Bernal and Hobsbawm thought of him, but Dienes was at the heart of mathematical sociability in the metropolis. He had as 'little liking for the starched and formal as anybody in Birkbeck', observed one Birkbeckian.[5] A former colleague recalled that, although Dienes laughed easily and loudly, his

> capacity for abstraction was formidable.... Sitting in the Common Room, he was often there only as matter. There were many occasions when the kind friend who sought to refill his teacup had to 'bring him to' by flourishing her hand before his eyes.[6]

More than the Department of Mathematics, the Classics Department was welcoming of leftist scholars. Ste Croix and Browning were the most prominent. Affectionately known as Croicks, Ste Croix taught part time at Birkbeck from

---

[3] Zoltan Paul Dienes, *Memoirs of a Maverick Mathematician* (Leicester: Upfront, 2003); online, chapter 2.

[4] Graham Sutton, 'The Centenary of the Birth of W. H. Young (20th October 1863)', *Mathematical Gazette*, 49.367 (February 1965), 19.

[5] 'G. T.', 'Paul Dienes', *The Lodestone*, 44.1 (autumn 1952), 48.

[6] Ibid., 48–9.

1950 to 1953, before moving to New College, Oxford. He was a member of the Communist Party of Great Britain and was to remain a committed Marxist and atheist all his life. During his time at Birkbeck, Ste Croix composed one of his classic articles, 'The Character of the Athenian Empire' (1954), which was to dwell on themes that continued throughout his career, including slavery, persecution, democracy, the poor, and the baneful impact of Christianity.[7] In this article, he contrasts two very different meanings of the Greek word δημοκρατία. According to one meaning, the whole people are sovereign; in the other, sovereignty resided with the mass of poor people. Government by all citizens was the definition employed by democrats. Government by the poor was the way oligarchs defined it; in Marxist terms, the 'dictatorship of the proletariat'. As Ste Croix explained,

> Greek oligarchs... naturally put first the interests of the propertied class (and if they were extreme oligarchs, only a section of that); it is hardly surprising, therefore, that they should have insisted on representing democracy as a form of government under which the poor necessarily exploited the rich for their own benefit.[8]

He was, according to his own reckoning, 'politely militant'.[9]

One of Ste Croix's successors was Browning, Professor of Classics and Ancient History from 1965 to 1981. Like Hobsbawm, Browning was a member of the Communist Party Historians Group and a famous Hellenist who campaigned against the dictatorship of the Greek Colonels (1947–74) and later served as the Chairman of the British Committee for the Restitution of the Parthenon Marbles.[10] Like Ste Croix, Browning applied a Marxist theory of history to the ancient world. But his approach was different to that of Ste Croix, as was revealed in a review he published in 1983 of Ste Croix's classic *The Class Struggle in the Ancient Greek Work* (1981). Browning observed that Ste Croix's book avoided the 'kind of sectarian infighting in which some Marxists indulge', and, as such, was 'a very English and pragmatic book, which may well infuriate some Marxist readers'.[11] In other words, Browning favoured a more unequivocal Marxist account of historical change, while still contending that 'I say *a* Marxist approach and not *the* Marxist approach'.[12] Browning was also loyal to the Soviet Union, not only publishing a couple of articles in Russian but also maintaining a 'close relationship... with the leading members of the national committees in the eastern bloc,

---

[7] Geoffrey E. M. de Ste Croix, 'The Character of the Athenian Empire', *Historia: Zeitschrift für Alte Geschichte*, 3 (1954), 1–41.
[8] Ibid., 22.   [9] David Harvey, 'Geoffrey de Ste Croix', *The Guardian* (10 February 2000).
[10] Judith Herrin, 'Robert Browning', *Past and Present*, 156 (August 1997), 3.
[11] Robert Browning, '[Review of] *The Class Struggle in the Ancient Greek Work: From the Archaic to the Arab Conquests* by G. E. M. de Ste. Croix', *Past and Present*, 100 (August 1983), 149.
[12] Ibid., 149.

accepting the structure of the academic community in the USSR as he did in politics'.[13]

Finally, it was not surprising to see a very large number of leftists or communists in the Departments of Physics and Crystallography. Bernal was a magnet for distinguished scholars. These included, amongst many others, David Bohm (who will be discussed in Chapter 21), communist physicist J. W. Jeffrey (keen trade unionist, tireless advocate for the College's technical staff, and anti-nuclear power campaigner), and fellow-traveller Alan Mackay (who in his youth had been one of the idealistic, international workers who helped build the 'Highway of Brotherhood and Unity' between Zagreb and Belgrade, Yugoslavia).

However, the most distinguished of these physicists was Blackett, who was made a Noble laureate in 1948. He was a great admirer of Birkbeck's educational mission and Fabian history.[14] Although he was only at Birkbeck between 1933 and 1937 (when he left for a Chair at the University of Manchester), these were important years for him as a scientist and a leftist commentator. Unlike many other leftist academics at Birkbeck, a high proportion of whom were Europeans (and many refugees), Blackett was the epitome of Englishness. Having served as a decorated naval officer during the 1914–18 war, he also carried a certain popular moral authority.

Blackett was described by the *News Review* as a 'tall, dark, handsome scientist with a taste for natty grey suitings'.[15] He arrived at Birkbeck in 1933 from the Cavendish Laboratory in Cambridge, where he had become increasingly disgruntled because an onerous teaching load was affecting his research capabilities.[16] He also longed to escape the heavy hand of its conservative director, Ernest Rutherford, who not only was dictatorial in manner and not expanding research in nuclear physics at the Cavendish but also disliked the vaguest waft of leftist politics.[17] This was a problem for Blackett who, like Bernal, had been convinced of the rightness of socialism by editor Kingsley Martin. Although never a member of the Communist Party, Blackett admired aspects of the Soviet Union, which he visited in 1935 and 1937. He was particularly fond of reminding people that the USSR spent a higher proportion of its gross domestic product on research and development than other European countries and the USA[18]

For the College, Blackett's appointment would have been a major coup, especially since he brought with him a sizable grant from the Royal Society. Blackett used it to design an electromagnet and construct a cloud chamber, a device used

---

[13] Judith Herrin, 'Robert Browning', *Past and Present*, 156 (August 1997), 4.
[14] Mary Jo Nye, *Blackett: Physics, War, and Politics in the Twentieth Century* (Cambridge, MA: Harvard University Press, 1935), 29.
[15] 'Newton, Einstein—and Now Blackett', *News Review* (29 May 1947), 14.
[16] Bernard Lovell, 'Patrick Maynard Stuart Blackett, Baron Blackett of Chelsea, 18 November 1897–13 July 1974', *Biographical Memoirs of Fellows of the Royal Society*, 21 (November 1975), 22.
[17] Nye, *Blackett*, 54.   [18] Ibid., 30.

to detect ionizing particles and to determine their trajectories. The magnet (named 'Josephine')[19] weighed 11,000 kilos and was originally used to 'study the energy spectrum of the cosmic rays'.[20] As the largest magnet in the UK, it was so unwieldy that Blackett had to persuade the Master to construct a wooden hut— the 'Magnet House'—on the land set aside for the new College building in Malet Street.[21] While at Birkbeck, Blackett also conducted research on the stratosphere and had 'special facilities for boring and excavation work into the London subsoil', which took place on an 'unused platform at Holborn Tube Station, 100 feet below London's pavements'.[22] Journalists liked to quip that Blackett was the 'Sherlock Holmes of Baker Street'.[23]

Clearly, Blackett was an intellectual of immense sophistication, but his political activism was equally attractive to Bernal, Hobsbawm, and the other left-wing lecturers in the College. Along with Bernal, Snow, Aldous Huxley, and Leonard Wolf, husband of Virginia Woolf, Blackett organized the 'For Intellectual Liberty' group, a popular front movement aiming to publicize the difficulties experienced by German Jews. His political energies also went into establishing with Bernal the Academic Assistance Council, which was renamed the Society for the Protection of Science and Learning (SPSL) three years later. It aimed at assisting academics fleeing Nazism and other tyrannical regimes. Today, Birkbeck scholars remain involved with it, under its new name of the Council for At-Risk Academics. Blackett was on its Executive from early 1936.

Blackett's involvement in these movements was driven by his anxieties about the way science in Nazi Germany was being used against working men and women. Science was being distorted to support hateful ideologies.[24] His fears about the threat that National Socialism posed for the world meant that he was no pacifist, believing as early as the mid-1930s in the necessity to prepare for war. Indeed, the year he arrived in Birkbeck also saw him advising Henry T. Tizard's Committee for the Scientific Survey of Air Defence on national defence. In March 1934, he turned to the radio waves to argue that

> There are only two ways to go, and the way we now seem to be starting leads to Fascism; with it comes restriction of output, a lowering of the standard of life of the working classes, and a renunciation of scientific progress. I believe that the

---

[19] Ibid., 54.
[20] Ian Butterworth, 'Sir Clifford Charles Butler, 20 May 1922–30 June 1999', *Biographical Memoirs of Fellows of the Royal Society*, 47 (November 2001), 43.
[21] Lovell, 'Patrick Maynard Stuart Blackett', 22.
[22] The first half of this sentence was from 'A Huge Magnet', *The Star* (7 November 1935), while the second half was from 'Obituary. Lord Blackett', *Daily Telegraph* (15 July 1974), in 'Newscuttings', in the Birkbeck Archive.
[23] Nye, *Blackett*, 29.
[24] William McGucken, *Scientists, Society, and State: The Social Relations of Science Movement in Great Britain, 1931–1947* (Columbus: Ohio University State University Press, 1984), 101–2.

only other way is complete Socialism. Socialism will want all the science it can get to produce the greatest possible wealth. Scientists have not perhaps very long to make up their minds on which side they stand.[25]

Some commentators believe that this radio speech was the '"reddest" talk ever transmitted from... Broadcasting House'.[26] It did mean, however, that his politics came to the attention of the American Federal Bureau of Investigation (FBI). George Orwell included his name in the list of thirty-eight 'crypto-Communists, fellow-travellers or inclined that way' that found its way to the Information Research Department of the British Foreign Office.[27] Blackett's politics were believed to be a threat to national security.

* * *

It is extraordinary that Dienes, Ste Croix, Browning, Jeffrey, Mackay, and Blackett overlapped with Bernal and Hobsbawm at Birkbeck during these decades. The atmosphere in Birkbeck's Common Room must have been astonishing. Is it any wonder that New Scotland Yard regarded Birkbeck as a hotbed of communism and kept a close watch over the Departments of History, Classics, Physics, and Crystallography in particular?

Of the formidable intellects seated around the Common Room tables, Hobsbawm and Bernal were unrivalled in terms of intelligence, wit, hard work, and conviviality. Both were cosmopolitan in background and taste. Academic research was never enough. They were intrepid travellers. Bernal got to know Chairman Mao; Hobsbawm interpreted for Che Guevara. Hobsbawm even hosted members of the Columbian revolutionary group FARC in Birkbeck's cafeteria.[28]

Who were these extraordinary men? Hobsbawm had been born in Alexandria and came to London as a schoolboy via Vienna and Berlin. He spoke seven languages, his knowledge was encyclopedic, and his memory for people, events, and ideas immense. As an historian, he was as comfortable writing about society in the Middle Ages as he was talking about twenty-first-century culture. Although he pioneered 'history from below', he was a master of the 'grand narrative'. The range of topics that interested him included the crisis of the seventeenth century, the industrial revolution, social protest, crime, nationalism, the uses and misuses of history, and jazz. In all these fields, Hobsbawm sought to bring the voices of marginalized people to life. In *Uncommon People* (1998), for example, he informed readers that 'the sort of people whose names are usually unknown to anyone except their family and neighbours' were nevertheless 'major historical

---

[25] Lovell, 'Patrick Maynard Stuart Blackett', 95. Also see P. M. S. Blackett, 'The Frustration of Science', in Frederick Soddy et al., *The Frustration of Science* (London: Allen and Unwin, 1935), 144.
[26] Nye, *Blackett*, 1–2.   [27] Ibid., 3.   [28] Hobsbawm, *Interesting Times*, 381–2.

actors' when considered collectively. 'What they do and think makes a difference. It can and has changed culture and the shape of history', he insisted.[29] Of course, these historical actors could only be understood within their specific material, ideological, and political contexts. 'It is an elementary observation of Marxism', Hobsbawm contended in *How to Change the World*, that 'thinkers do not invent their ideas in the abstract'. Karl Marx 'always stressed that men made their own history...he also insisted that they do so only under conditions in which they find themselves'.[30] Through his writings, the lives of working people, including bandits, factory workers, and trade unionists, were brought into historical focus.

Bernal was similarly encyclopedic in his knowledge. Sixteen years older than Hobsbawm, Bernal was born in Ireland in 1901 to a Sephardic Jewish father who had become a Catholic. His mother was an American Presbyterian who also converted to Catholicism. She only spoke to him in French. He was educated by the Jesuits and then went to Emmanuel College, Cambridge, in 1919. As an undergraduate, he worked out a proof of the 230 space groups in crystallography, thus bringing himself to the attention of his supervisors. By 1922, at the age of only 22, he was working with Sir William Bragg at the Royal Institution in London. In 1927, he returned to Cambridge as a member of Rutherford's Cavendish Laboratory, despite being loathed by Rutherford for being a communist, an antipathy that was later experienced by Blackett. At the Cavendish, Bernal was able to show that the Windaus–Wieland formula for the steroid ring system was incorrect, which led to the correct solution.[31] He then moved to working on the crystals of proteins and viruses. As Sir Laurence Bragg observed in 1948,

> no one has done more than he has as an explorer and pioneer. Time and again, when reviewing any branch of X-ray analysis which is now very active, we have to acknowledge that the first critical experiment was due to his inspiration.[32]

Bernal is now widely regarded as the founding father of molecular biology.

There was good reason why, when only an undergraduate, Bernal earned the nickname 'The Sage'. He was not only a brilliant crystallographer. He also published tales and treatises, poems and polemics, as well as articles in a vast array of journals, including those of physics, earth sciences, chemistry, engineering,

---

[29] Eric J. Hobsbawm, *Uncommon People: Resistance, Rebellion, and Jazz* (London: Weidenfeld and Nicolson, 1998), vii.
[30] Eric J. Hobsbawm, *How to Change the World: Marx and Marxism, 1840–2011* (London: Little, Brown, 2011), 316.
[31] See John D. Roberts and Marjorie C. Caserio, 'Steroids', 31 July 2021, at https://chem.libretexts.org/Bookshelves/Organic_Chemistry/Book%3A_Basic_Principles_of_Organic_Chemistry_(Roberts_and_Caserio)/30%3A_Natural_Products_and_Biosynthesis/30.04%3A_Steroids, viewed 1 August 2021.
[32] Laurence Bragg, address to the British Association for the Advancement of Science.

interplanetary science, cattle breeding, philosophy, politics, architecture, social science, and history.[33]

Two years after his arrival at Birkbeck, the Second World War broke out. Bernal took a break from theoretical science. Like many others, including Blackett, he had been aware that war was inevitable. In 1938, South African-born, University of Oxford zoologist Solly Zuckerman and Bernal had spoken about the possible uses of science in the forthcoming war. Both men were members of the dining club 'Tots and Quots' (an abbreviation and inversion from Terence's 161 BC play *Phormio*: 'Quot homines, tot sententiae' or 'However many men, as many opinions'), which had been established in 1931 to discuss politics and science. Together, they composed a memorandum which was sent to military theorist Basil Henry Liddell-Hart and then Leslie Hore-Belisha, Secretary of State for War.[34] A subsequent lunch with Parliamentary Secretary Arthur Salter and Home Secretary John Anderson enabled Bernal to convince them that he could contribute to air-raid defence. Anderson was particularly impressed, noting that he wanted Bernal as a scientific adviser even though Bernal was 'as red as the flames of hell'.[35] When war was declared, Bernal joined the Research and Experimental Department of the Ministry of Home Security at Princes Risborough in Buckinghamshire where he 'galvanized the Department'.[36] In 1941, Bernal was seconded to Bomber Command and then to Combined Operations. Two years later, he and Zuckerman could be found in Libya studying the effects of bombing. From there, Bernal was given the job of advising Lord Mountbatten, Chief of Combined Operations, with whom he helped plan the D-Day landings. After the war, Bernal was involved for some time as Chairman of the Scientific Committee of the Ministry of Works in rebuilding and rehousing bombed-out people, and helped establish the Architectural Science Board. As an acknowledgment of the importance of his war-work, Bernal was awarded the US Medal of Freedom—but ironically, from 1949 onwards, he would be denied entry into the USA because of his political beliefs. He was also awarded the Lenin Prize for Peace in 1953.

Bernal's wartime experiences contributed to his thinking about the misuse of science. This led directly to the establishment of a branch of the Association of Scientific Workers at Birkbeck. The Master of Birkbeck dryly reported that membership of the Association 'included a large proportion of the Science Staff, as well as postgraduates and undergraduates'.[37] After the war, Bernal and other scientists established the World Federation of Scientific Workers to work for 'science for the welfare of mankind'.

---

[33] John Meurig Thomas, *J. D. Bernal and the World of Catalysis* (London: Birkbeck College, 1997), 8.
[34] Dorothy M. C. Hodgkin, 'John Desmond Bernal, 10 May 1901–15 September 1971', *Biographical Memoirs of Fellows of the Royal Society*, 26 (November 1980), 53.
[35] Ibid., 53.   [36] Ibid., 54.
[37] Letter from the Master to W. R. Halliday (King's College), dated 17 May 1945, in Birkbeck Archive, 'Wartime Correspondence with the Master 1943–45' (p. 76 of file).

The war also encouraged Bernal's conviction of the need to put in place safeguards for world peace. In 1951, he founded Scientists for Peace, and he was, for a time, Chairman of the World Peace Council. Like Hobsbawm, he was also active in the Campaign for Nuclear Disarmament, an organization that cut across political affiliations. He would have agreed with Hobsbawm's sentiments, published in *Tribune* in 1962, that

> The case for nuclear disarmament is that a world war would wreck everybody, capitalist or Socialist.... Some peace-lovers may personally feel that the basic trouble lies with world capitalism, others that it lies with Soviet Government policies. But if we act as though nothing could be done unless Martin Luther King becomes president of the United States, or unless 'the working people of Russia' go 'over the heads of their rulers', we are *in practice* merely declaring that we have no hope.[38]

Bernal's passion for peace activism brought him and the College into contact with one of the greatest artists of his century, Pablo Picasso. In November 1950, the British Peace Committee had organized a World Peace Congress in Sheffield, inviting luminaries like Picasso, Nobel Prize winner, French war hero Frédéric Joliot-Curie, and Russian composer Dmitri Shostakovich. Believing that the conference was pro-Soviet, the Labour Prime Minister Clement Attlee made sure that many of the international delegates were refused visas. Picasso, however, had arrived earlier, via a visa arranged by the Arts Council who were sponsoring an exhibition, and found himself stranded in London. Bernal invited him and other friends to a party in his flat, which was above Birkbeck's crystallography laboratory. After consuming vast quantities of wine, Picasso was persuaded to use a multi-coloured grease pencil to draw a souvenir of the occasion on a wall above some bookshelves. Crystallographer C. Harry Carlisle, originally from Burma but employed at Birkbeck from 1942 until 1978 (and as professor from 1968), was present. He described the way Picasso 'jumped onto an armchair with the agility of a teenager and started drawing with a thick pencil, scarcely taking it off the wall until the first figure was complete'.[39] Lena May Chivers (best known as Baroness Jeger, as discussed in the previous chapter) observed the way Picasso

> began with a swish of line that immediately became a real face, but had devil's horns, closed blind eyes and a shut little mouth. Then he stepped back and shook his head, pounced on the wall and touched the horns into a laurel wreath, opened the devil's eyes, and widened his mouth till he looked like an anxious

---

[38] Eric J. Hobsbawm, '[Letter to the Editor] Leaflets in Moscow', *Tribune* (20 July 1962), in TNA KV2/3986.
[39] Roger Highfield, 'Sold for £250,000: A Doodle by Picasso', *Daily Telegraph* (2 April 2007).

god. Picasso stood back and said 'Il a l'air solitaire'—he began to draw a girl, who arrived on the wall firmly and suddenly. Someone then asked what this had to do with peace and Picasso gave them wings.[40]

Picasso's peace mural was later removed from Birkbeck premises and eventually sold to the Wellcome Trust in Euston Square, where it can still be seen.

* * *

Obviously, the intellectual, political, and social lives of Bernal and Hobsbawm were indelibly marked by their communist convictions. Bernal had converted to Marxism while an undergraduate at Emmanuel College. On 7 November 1919, he had attended a public lecture on socialism given by the economist Henry Douglas Dickinson. Later, Bernal recalled that Dickinson

> explained it all simply in a few hours, the theory of Marxism, the great Russian experiment, what we could do here and now. It was all so clear, so compelling, so universal. How narrow my Irish patriotism seemed, how absurdly reactionary my military schemes. It was the people themselves that would sweep away the things I hated. It would bring the Scientific World State.... My universe was broken to bits.[41]

In contrast, Hobsbawm's political epiphany was much more the result of witnessing the rise of fascism in Europe and the terrifying rise to power of Hitler when he was a young man in Weimar Germany. As he recalled in his autobiography, he came to communism 'as a central European in the collapsing Weimar republic.... And I came to it when being a communist meant not simply fighting fascism but the world revolution.'[42]

For the rest of their lives, both were devoted communists. The Communist Party of Great Britain (CPGB) was never a large movement (indeed, its membership never exceeded 60,000), but it attracted a disproportionate number of prominent intellectuals. Hobsbawm became a leading member of the Historians Group of the CPGB while Bernal belonged to the party's Engels Society. Nevertheless, neither were dogmatic ideologues; they believed that Marxism gave them a tool that could be used creatively to move science, history, and, indeed, the world revolution forward.

The primary attraction of communism for these two men was political: it would herald in a New Jerusalem. The rise of fascism, the pernicious effect of capitalism, and the multiplication of injustices were destroying not only people's

---

[40] Maurice Goldsmith, *Sage: Life of J. D. Bernal* (London: Hutchinson, 1980).
[41] J. D. Bernal, 'Microcosm', J. D. Bernal Archive, Cambridge University Library, B4.1.
[42] Hobsbawm, *Interesting Times*, 217–18.

freedoms but also their lives. Dialectic and historical materialism provided Bernal and Hobsbawm with an objective way to interrogate the biggest questions in science and history. This knowledge, they believed, would play a role in bringing about world socialism. As Bernal put it in his 1963 pamphlet entitled *Need There be Need?*,

> Our duty...nowadays includes first the understanding and then the changing of the world we live in. I would prefer however to look at it as a purely human consideration: I see in these nearly three thousand million people there are in the world enormous potentialities; I see the enormous possibilities for human development, for thought, for science, for poetry, which is stifled at the moment by sheer poverty. And I want to see mankind realise its full potentialities.[43]

They also viewed communism as a positive force for their academic disciplines. Before disillusionment set in, both men believed that the Soviet regime had productive influence in universities. Exciting new ideas were flourishing behind the Iron Curtain.

For Bernal, the decisive intellectual wakening occurred in 1931, when the Second International Congress of the History of Science and Technology met at the Science Museum in London. There, he listened to Soviet scientists, philosophers, and historians expound on dialectic and historical materialism.[44] Boris Hessen's paper on the 'Social and Economic Roots of Newton's *Principia*' was especially important because it argued that science in the seventeenth century was not a product of individual genius but arose from the economic and social conditions of the time, especially the rise of the bourgeoisie.[45] The Soviet delegates spoke eloquently about the relation of science to the mass public, to government, and to intellectuals more generally. In his review of the conference in *The Spectator* in July 1931, Bernal compared Soviet with British universities, contending that the British system exemplified the 'appalling inefficiency of science at the present time, tied to academic and impoverished universities and to secretive and competitive industries and national governments'. While a miserly 0.1 per cent of gross national product in the UK was being allocated to science, in the Soviet Union 850 linked research institutes and 40,000 research workers were being funded.[46] Bernal wondered whether it was better 'to be intellectually free but socially totally ineffective or to become a component part of a system where

---

[43] J. D. Bernal, *Need There be Need?* (London: Science for Peace Pamphlets, 1963), 16.
[44] Hodgkin, 'John Desmond Bernal', 64. He met Bukharin, Vavilov, Boris Hessen, and Joffé.
[45] Edwin A. Roberts, 'From the History of Science to the Science of History: Scientists and Historians in the Shaping of British Marxist Theory', *Science and Society*, 69.4 (October 2005), 533. Also see Edwin A. Roberts, *The Anglo-Marxists: A Study in Ideology and Culture* (Oxford: Rowman and Littlefield, 1997).
[46] Hilary Rose and Steven Rose, 'The Two Bernals', *Fundamental Scientia*, 1.2 (1981), 267–86.

knowledge and action are joined for one common social purpose?'[47] As this implies, Bernal was aware of the risks. In *The Social Function of Science* (1939), he warned that 'any measures aimed at giving greater assistance and scope to research must be balanced against the possible risks of restricting its freedom or limiting its imaginative possibilities'.[48] But, he maintained in *The Freedom of Necessity*, it was clear that the Soviet delegates in 1931 were fired up: 'the history of science was plainly vitally important to them; it was not only an academic study but a guide to action', he noted.[49]

Bernal and Hobsbawm also believed that academics had a role in bringing the revolution closer. Science and history had a duty to contribute to social betterment. Both men marched against nuclear weapons; both participated in anti-militarist sit-ins. But, fundamentally, they recognized that their most important roles were to spread ideas and contribute to knowledge. Ideas and knowledge had to be accessible to wider publics. This was Hobsbawm's main argument in a talk he gave to the National Cultural Committee of the CPGB on 25 September 1949. An undercover agent attending the meeting reported that Hobsbawm argued that the 'least educated Balkan peasant who today is helping to construct an ordered society is freer than are the university professors in this country'. Hobsbawm reminded his fellow Marxists that during times when

> the intellectuals have attached themselves to the people, they have performed their finest tasks. In the periods in which the intellectuals have retreated into their 'ivory tower' they have produced nothing of value due to their disassociation from the people.

He urged his fellow academics to have the courage to be 'free, to be real communist intellectuals'.[50] It was a position he repeated throughout his career. Thirty years after this speech, at the Tenth Communist University, Hobsbawm could be heard launching a 'vigorous attack' on 'abstract Marxist theorising'. He told his audience that 'intellectuals were prone to become too inward-looking if they were divorced from political activities.... Many of them were becoming lost in doctrinal disputes of a purely theoretical character.'[51] They needed to step away from their studies and into public squares.

Bernal, too, was committed to the betterment of society—something he believed could only happen if people were truly free. Marxism would create the

---

[47] Originally published in *The Spectator*, July 1931, and reprinted in J. D. Bernal, *The Freedom of Necessity* (London: Routledge and Kegan Paul, 1949), 339.
[48] J. D. Bernal, *The Social Function of Science* (London: George Routledge and Sons Ltd, 1939), 261.
[49] J. D. Bernal, *The Freedom of Necessity* (London: Routledge and Kegan Paul, 1949), 336.
[50] 'Extract from S.B. Report re. a Battle of Ideas Conference, on 25.9.49, on the Subject of "Communism and Liberty", Convened by the National Cultural Cttee, of the C.P. and Meeting Hobsbawm', in TNA KV2/3981.
[51] 'Vigorous Start at Communist University', *Morning Star* (17 July 1978).

context for the emergence of a 'society in which harmonious relations exist between human beings'.⁵² The alienation that dominated the lives of people in capitalist societies would be overcome and each person would have the capacity to develop their lives according to their talents, predispositions, and desires.⁵³ Bernal lamented the fact that the world seemed to be divided between a scientific elite and a scientifically illiterate public.⁵⁴ His greatest book—*The Social Function of Science* (1939)—was a call to action. He encouraged scientists to reflect on 'how the work they are doing is connected with the social and economic developments which are occurring around them'.⁵⁵ They had to recognize the immense burden of social responsibility placed on them, ensuring that they worked both intellectually and politically for the betterment of society. As he wrote, 'Science as Communism' was the 'prototype for all human common action'.⁵⁶ This was to be echoed by Hobsbawm who believed that history, like physics, followed scientific laws.

It was an interdisciplinary project. Neither man had any time for intellectual silos that pitted, for example, the arts against the sciences. As Bernal wrote in the first issue of the *Modern Quarterly*, a major journal of Marxist thought,

> The present situation, where a highly developed science stands almost isolated from the traditional literary culture, is altogether anomalous and cannot last. No culture can stand indefinitely apart from the dominating practical ideas of the time, without degenerating into pedantic futility.⁵⁷

Marxism provided the vital connections between the different branches of knowledge.

Finally, they lived in left-wing circles. Hobsbawm and Bernal were the most convivial of men. Bernal counted many artists as personal friends, including Henry Moore, Ben Nicholson, Barbara Hepworth, and Pablo Picasso. Although Hobsbawm's austere, even gaunt, visage could give the impression that he was a remote intellectual, nothing could be further from the truth. On Bastille Day in 1936, with the Popular Front in power, he drove through Paris in a trance, drinking and dancing till dawn. For ten years, he wrote a monthly jazz column for the *New Statesman*, signing himself Francis Newton in honour of Frankie Newton, the communist trumpetist who accompanied Billy Holliday in her original 1939 recording of 'Strange Fruit'. Jazz was his passion, since it was 'one of the few

---

⁵² Hodgkin, 'John Desmond Bernal', 66.   ⁵³ Ibid., 66.
⁵⁴ J. D. Bernal, *The World, the Flesh, and the Devil* (Bloomington: Indiana University Press, 1929), 79–80.
⁵⁵ J. D. Bernal, *The Social Function of Science* (London: George Routledge and Sons Ltd, 1939), xiii.
⁵⁶ Ibid., 415.
⁵⁷ J. D. Bernal, 'The Social Function of Science', *Modern Quarterly*, 1 (1938), 18.

developments in the major arts entirely rooted in the lives of poor people'.⁵⁸ He wrote that

> If I had to sum up the evolution of jazz in a single sentence, I should say: It is what happens when a folk-music does not go under, but maintains itself in the environment of modern urban and industrial civilization.⁵⁹

Finally (and this is a theme I will return to in Chapter 21 in relation to Bernal), both men had a gift for mentoring other scholars. In Hobsbawm's memorable words, 'the enormous advantage of communism, especially when reinforced by friendship, [was] that one could simply not treat a comrade other than an equal'.⁶⁰ At Birkbeck, there was an almost constant stream of scholars from all over the world seeking to share ideas with both Bernal and Hobsbawm.

* * *

Their communist convictions were the source both of incredible creativity and conviviality, but also of criticism and condemnation. Both had to deal with enemies from within the College. For Hobsbawm, this was the reactionary medievalist R. R. Darlington who, as head of the department, ensured that his promotion to professorial status stalled for some years. For Bernal, it was the reactionary Master (classicist John F. Lockwood) and the Dean of the Science Faculty (chemist W. G. Overend).

More broadly, their enemies attacked from two perspectives: academic and political. Bernal was accused of breaching academic freedom when, in 1949, he publicly defended the Soviet agronomist Trofim Denisovich Lysenko. From the 1930s, Lysenko had waged a campaign against more orthodox geneticists, especially Gregor Johann Mendel, Thomas Hunt Morgan, and August Weisman, whom he viewed as idealist, reactionary, and racialist. Lysenko claimed to have proven that environment was more important than heredity. After he converted Stalin to his cause, modern genetics were characterized as a 'bourgeois science'. Elsewhere, this might have been just another internal feud over scientific interpretation. In the Soviet Union, however, it came at the height of a series of political and social purges. Orthodox geneticists found themselves in the firing line—literally. Indeed, nearly all the Soviet delegates to the 1931 Congress mentioned earlier were purged, including Boris Hessen and Nikolai Bukharin.⁶¹ By 1948, Lysenko had succeeded in becoming the leading Soviet biologist, but at a bloody cost.

---

⁵⁸ Hobsbawm, *Uncommon People*, preface.
⁵⁹ Eric J. Hobsbawm, *The Jazz Scene*, 1st pub. 1959 (New York: Pantheon Books, 1993), xlix.
⁶⁰ Hobsbawm, *Interesting Times*, 366.
⁶¹ Diane B. Paul, 'A War on Two Fronts: J. B. S. Haldane and the Response to Lysentoism in Britain', *Journal of the History of Biology*, 161 (spring 1983), 6.

This led to a crisis for communist scientists, who were accused of prioritizing political affiliation over scientific integrity. Admittedly, Bernal's admiration for Lysenko was due less to the genetic controversy than to Lysenko's claim that he had produced grains that were superior in terms of their yield. In the famine-plagued USSR, this could have improved the lives of millions. However, Bernal's defence of Lysenko's theories, including the right of the state to decide on matters of science, appalled many fellow-scientists.[62]

Bernal defended the Soviet Union during the Cold War that sought to destroy it. In a conference on the Lysenko affair, Bernal pointed out that the 'first and most important thing for us to remember is that this controversy is already part of politics and is used today in this country as an auxiliary in the attack on the U.S.S.R. and in the drive to war'.[63] In other words, the Lysenko controversy had been harnessed to Cold War rhetoric: it was a time to stand up to defend the Soviets, despite the risk to academic freedom.

The Security Service reported that the scientists in Bernal's laboratory knew about the 'disappearances' taking place during the purges. For example, Bernal's close assistant was Hovhannes Francis ('Appie') Aprahamian. The Security Service had long been interested in this rather 'spivish'[64] scientist, describing him as Bernal's 'literary hack' and claiming that 'a book by BERNAL entitled "History of Science"... was almost entirely the work of APRAHAMIAN'.[65] With a casual anti-Semitism typical of its reports, the Security Service regularly drew attention to his 'Jewish appearance', 'swarthy complexion', and a 'prominent hooked nose'.[66] In January 1949, MI5 intercepted a telephone conversation between an unnamed person at the library of the *Daily Worker* and Aprahamian during which they discussed 'various inquiries'. The unnamed person informed Aprahamian that the *Soviet Monitor* had reported that the distinguished Soviet botanist and geneticist Nikolai Ivanovich Vasiloff had been

> exiled from 1939 to 40, and died in 41 or 42. Exiled presumably to the north of U.S.S.R. FRANCIS was rather surprised and said that this would confirm more or less the stories which were being passed by the reactionaries.[67]

---

[62] Edwin A. Roberts, 'From the History of Science to the Science of History: Scientists and Historians in the Shaping of British Marxist Theory', *Science and Society*, 69.4 (October 2005), 543. See 'The Biological Controversy in the Soviet Union and Its Implications', *Modern Quarterly*, 4 (1949), 203–17. Also see *The Guardian* (4 February 1949), 2.
[63] J. D. Bernal quoted in 'The Situation and the Science of Biology: Report of a Conference Called to Discuss the Issues Raised by T. D. Lysenko's Address on Soviet Biology', *Transactions of the Engels Society* (April 1949), 11.
[64] Security Service report, 'Lascar' (23 June 1960), in TNA KV2/3953.
[65] Security Service report (12 May 1962), in TNA KV2/3953.
[66] Lots of examples can be found in Security Service reports, in TNA KV2/3948.
[67] Security Service memo, 'Prof. Bernal' (1 November 1949), TNA KV2/3948. He was called 'Appie' according to Security Service files, 'Telephone Check on Clerkenwell 7404. London District Office C.P.' (14 May 1945), in TNA KV2/3948.

That same year, during a conference in Moscow of the Soviet Partisans for Peace, Bernal was heard praising Stalin as 'the great leader and protector of science'.[68] He was reported as saying that

> In capitalist countries the direction of science is in the hands of those whose only aim is to destroy and torture people so that their own profits may be secured for some years longer.

In the Soviet Union, he contended, the opposite was the case: 'science was at the service of the people'.[69] Bernal later denied the first part of this comment, but the damage had been done.[70] Not only did it result in the postponement of his election to the Council of the British Association,[71] but it also hurt his department since he found it increasingly difficult to win grants.

The need to defend the Soviet Union against Cold War intrigues was a problem that did not go away. As late as 1973, crystallographer J. W. Jeffrey advised fellow-scientists not to participate in an organized campaign against the Soviet Union's restrictions on the academic freedom of scientists. Jeffrey admitted that he had been a communist since 1932, and he passionately believed that the Soviet Union needed to 'open up the ways in which dissent can be expressed'. Indeed, he insisted, allowing academics to pursue their research unhindered was imperative if socialism, society, and science were to advance. However, Jeffrey warned, there were 'powerful anti-Soviet propaganda machines waiting for any material which can be used to stir up the cold war'. It would be 'counter-productive' to give them 'ammunition for their campaigns', he insisted.[72]

For both Bernal and Hobsbawm, a catastrophic assault on their long-held beliefs came in 1956. At the Twentieth Congress of the Communist Party of the Society Union in February, Soviet leader Nikita Khrushchev (pictured later, alongside Bernal, in Fig. 19.1) denounced Stalin for his crimes and for developing the 'cult of the personality', which had harmed the party and country. Then, on 4 November, the Soviet army invaded Hungary, brutally suppressing a popular uprising. When news of the attack reached Britain, crystallographer Rosalind Franklin was amazed and also 'amused' by the responses of the communists in her department to 'Hungarian things'. As she put it, 'really all the Party members were quite shaken, though I don't know of any who left the Party'. Bernal, she noted, was 'only temporarily' upset, adding that 'on the rare occasion when I heard

---

[68] 'Prof. Bernal Praises Mr. Stalin', *The Times* (29 August 1949), 3.   [69] Ibid., 3.
[70] 'Prof. Bernal's Moscow Speech', *The Times* (10 September 1949), 2.   [71] Ibid., 2.
[72] J. W. Jeffery, 'Soviet Science', *Nature* (28 December 1973), in the Birkbeck Archive. He said this was his response to the 'BBC Controversy programme' on 'Soviet Scientists'. Also see Andrew A. Zwarun (Johnston Laboratories, Maryland), 'Persecution of Soviet Scientists', *Science*, 182.4112 (9 November 1973), 535, and 'Five Soviet Scientists End Hunger Strike', *New York Times* (25 June 1973), etc.

Fig. 19.1 Nikita Khrushchev, General Secretary of the Communist Party of the Soviet Union, addressing the World Conference for General Disarmament and Peace, Moscow, July 1962. J. D. Bernal is immediately to the right of Khrushchev. Yuri Zhukov, head of the Soviet Peace Committee, is fourth from the right. Bernal had invited delegates from West Germany, Austria, Denmark, France, Italy, Spain, Norway, Sweden, the UK, and Canada, as well as individual leaders from the USA and elsewhere. The conference was attended by 2,200 people from 120 countries. Birkbeck Image Collections: Birkbeck History BH0029.

him speak about it, he got emotional and confused' but 'a few months later he was again talking in the old Party clichés'.[73]

Neither Bernal nor Hobsbawm had been wholly ignorant of the problems of Soviet life and politics prior to 1956. They were well aware that the Soviets had negotiated a pact with Nazi Germany between 1939 and 1941. They had heard rumours of intellectuals being sent into exile or simply 'disappearing'. Both men had visited the country and, although they were carefully chaperoned, could not have been totally blind to the sufferings of the common people. Indeed, in 1954, when Hobsbawm and other members of the Historians Group of the CPGB had been guests of the Soviet Academy of Sciences, they admitted that they had been dismayed by the dogmatism of the Academy and the depressing environment.

---

[73] Cited in Anne Sayre, *Rosalind Franklin and DNA*, 1st pub. 1975 (New York: W. W. Norton and Co., 2000), 168.

But news about Stalin's atrocious crimes and the invasion of Hungary were in a different league. We don't have extensive responses from Bernal, but Hobsbawm addressed the crisis head-on. In a letter to the *Daily Worker* on 12 November 1956, he referred to József Mindszenty, the leader of the Catholic Church in Hungary and fervent anti-communist. A 'Mindszenty Hungary', he claimed, would 'probably have become a base for counterrevolution and intervention'. This would have been 'a grave and acute danger' for the USSR, Yugoslavia, Czechoslovakia, and Romania. Hobsbawm admitted that, if the British 'had been in the position of the Soviet Government', they too 'should have intervened'. Nevertheless, he continued, the 'movement against the old Hungarian Government and the Russian occupation was a wide *popular* movement, however misguided'. The Hungarian Workers' Party had become 'isolated from, and partly hated by, the people'. He confessed that

> While approving, with a heavy heart, of what is now happening in Hungary, we should therefore also say frankly that we think the U.S.S.R. should withdraw its troops from the country as soon as this is possible. This should be said by the British Communist Party publicly if the British people is to have any confidence in our sincerity and judgment.[74]

One week later, a Security Service tap on a telephone in the CPGB's Headquarters revealed that Hobsbawm, along with Birkbeck classicist Browning as well as luminaries like writer Doris Lessing and historians E. P. Thompson and Christopher Hill, had signed a protest about the way the CPGB had responded to the crisis. The letter admitted that the signatories had 'for many years advocated Marxist ideas, both in our own special fields and in political discussions in the Labour Movement'. This meant that they had a particular 'responsibility to express our views as Marxists'. They were dismayed by the 'uncritical support' by the Executive Committee of the CPGB to the Soviet invasion of Hungary. They reminded the Executive that the revelations made at the Twentieth Congress in 1956 should have alerted them to the fact that

> Marxist ideas will only be acceptable to the British Labour Movement if they arise from the truth about the world we live in. The exposure of the grave crimes and abuses in the U.S.S.R. and the recent revolt of workers and intellectuals against the pseudo Communist bureaucracies and police systems in Poland and Hungary have shown that for the past twelve years we have made a political analysis on a false presentation of facts.

The signatories claimed that, although they were not unanimous in their critiques, they continued to be committed to Marxism. However, they called for 'the

---

[74] Eric J. Hobsbawm, '(Letter to the Editor] Suppressing Facts', *Daily Worker* (12 November 1956), in TNA KV2/3983.

immediate repudiation of the latest outcome of this evil past, the E.C.'s [Executive Committee's] underwriting of the current errors of Soviet Policy'.[75]

Two years later, a Security Service spy reported that, while the entire CPGB had experienced the 'greatest difficulties over the 20th Congress', its Cultural Committee was affected the most. In a secretly taped conversation with Aprahamian, John Gollan (the General Secretary of the CPGB) admitted that this committee had suffered 'the greatest number of casualties'. However, Gollan continued,

> a number of comrades remained on in spite of their moods or disagreements, because their loyalty to the Party was greater than any feelings they had about any particular questions. For a time it was a — [sic] committee and it was one of despondency; but the situation had now greatly improved, and he thought it was a question of 'time the healer and people realising that the bottom hasn't dropped out of their world after all'.

Gollan wanted Aprahamian to become the Secretary of the Cultural Committee. He argued that it was important that they resumed active work. After all, he warned, 'if they didn't then other folk would, and particularly the people associated with Universities Left Review'. This was the group of 'New Left' academics who sought a leftist alternative to communism, focusing on remaking socialism through an emphasis on moral values.[76]

Bernal and Hobsbawm were not only attacked by comrades who deserted the CPGB. They also came under fire from those who remained. Hobsbawm in particular was criticized for 'maintaining fraternal relations with both the New Left and the CP', which was a sign of his 'political dishonesty'.[77]

Both men attempted to act according to their conscience. They responded to the Hungarian crisis by seeking to help scientists and historians in that country. But they also moved significantly away from active Communist Party involvement. Bernal reorientated his energies towards the peace movement and his writings took on a much more historical character, as he investigated the dynamic relations between science and society. Hobsbawm, too, diverted his interests to Eurocommunism and the approach taken by the Italian Communist Party, with its Gramscian traditions, pluralist orientation, and strong intellectual focus. In his books, particularly the *Age of Extremes*, Hobsbawm included criticisms of the human costs of Soviet communism and Maoism.

---

[75] 'Copy of Telecheck on Temple Bar 2151, Communist Party H.Q.; Conversation Between John CAMPBELL and George MATTHEWS, Mentioning HOBSBAWM' (20 November 1956), in TNA KV2/3983.
[76] Security Service report, 'Lascar Extract' (3 October 1958), in TNA TV2/3951.
[77] Peter Sedgwick, '[Letter to the Editor] Committee of 100 in Moscow', *Tribune* (24 August 1962), in TNA KV2/3986.

In his autobiography, *Interesting Times*, Hobsbawm attempted to explain his refusal to resign from the CPGB before it was formally dissolved in 1991. 'We did not, and could not, envisage the sheer scale of what was being imposed on the Soviet people under Stalin', he mused, adding that Communist Party members were 'reluctant to believe the few who told us what they knew or suspected'.[78] He confessed that avid CPGB members, like himself, 'clearly underestimated the horrors of what had gone on'.[79]

As a party member since his youth in the Weimar Republic, Hobsbawm had believed that communism was the only responsible response to fascism.[80] But he admitted that his refusal to hand in his party card might also have been due in part to another, more private, emotion: that is, pride. In his words,

> Losing the handicap of Party membership would improve my career prospects, not least in the USA. It would have been easy to slip out quietly. But I could prove myself to myself by succeeding as a known communist—whatever 'success' meant—in spite of that handicap, and in the middle of the Cold War.[81]

Both Hobsbawm and Bernal remained loyal to their communist beliefs, if not directly to the CPGB, until the end of their lives, even though most other intellectuals left it.

* * *

The 1956 crisis led to a long period of reflection and self-doubt, which, for Bernal and Hobsbawm, lasted their entire lives. By the late 1960s, Bernal's health was in decline. He suffered a series of strokes, brought on in part by overwork and the stress of fighting for the survival of his highly respected Departments of Physics and Crystallography (this story is told in Chapter 26). The CPGB had been worried about his health for a decade, anxiously seeking ways to reduce his commitments, but Bernal found it impossible to refuse any request for a meeting, lecture, or campaign. As Aprahamian noted, 'A communist or near-communist academic can afford *less* to fall down on the academic job than if they weren't'.[82] He died in 1971, aged just 70. In contrast, Hobsbawm remained relatively healthy until his death, aged 95, in 2012. This chapter has only touched on the lives of these two remarkable men, who are the subject of a couple of outstanding biographies: Andrew Brown's *J. D. Bernal: The Sage of Science* (2005) and Richard Evans' *Eric Hobsbawm: A Life in History* (2019).[83]

---

[78] Hobsbawm, *Interesting Times*, 139.   [79] Ibid., 194.   [80] Ibid., 217–18.
[81] Ibid., 217–18.   [82] Social Branch report, 'Lascar' (20 September 1962), in TNA KV2/3953.
[83] Andrew Brown, *J. D. Bernal: The Sage of Science* (Oxford: Oxford University Press, 2005), and Richard Evans, *Eric Hobsbawm: A Life in History* (New York: Oxford University Press, 2019).

Their long Birkbeck careers had been a unique period in the College's history. There are numerous reasons why Birkbeck attracted 'red' scholars such as Bernal, Hobsbawm, Aprahamian, Dienes, Ste Croix, Browning, Jeffrey, Mackay, Blackett, and Bohm, to name just a few. In some cases, they came to Birkbeck because they were cast out of other universities or made to feel unwelcome because of their leftist politics. Fascism, the Cold War, McCarthyism, and conservative prejudices led them to seek a more congenial intellectual home. The cosmopolitan nature of the College made it an exciting and revealing place to work. In physics alone there was Werner Ehrenberg, a German refugee; crystallographer Käthe Schiff, who had fled Vienna; and Harry Carlisle from Burma. Having been attracted to Birkbeck, they created an active political and intellectual tradition which then drew in other radical intellectuals. A selective reading of the history of the LMI and its founders enabled them to invent a tradition of radicalism attached to the College—a 'brand' as a radical teaching and research university. The fact that classes were taught in the evenings was another allure: it meant that they could devote daytime hours to their research. Equally important, though, they were committed to the unique nature of Birkbeck's student body. Birkbeck gave them the opportunity to engage in serious debate with working men and women, thus linking their theory with practice.

Bernal, Hobsbawm, and the other leftists mentioned in this chapter were Birkbeckians, speaking often and warmly about Birkbeck as a place that possessed a 'built-in, unforced protection against the pressures of the Cold War outside', as Hobsbawm recalled. They had great admiration for Birkbeck students. Hobsbawm maintained that

> One of the reasons why I spent my entire British career [at Birkbeck], was the pleasure of teaching extraordinarily motivated men and women.... They faced their teachers weekly with the acid test of the profession: how to keep a bunch of people interested in what is being said to them between eight and nine p.m.... Birkbeck was a good school, not least of learning how to communicate.[84]

Many of his books 'either grew out of student lectures' or 'were tested in student lectures'.[85]

The era of Bernal and Hobsbawm (in addition to all the other 'Reds' of the post-war period) was a unique era in the history of Birkbeck and, indeed, the history of the left in Britain. From the 1970s, a different generation of left-wing intellectuals occupied the Common Room, before it was closed by Master Tessa Blackstone. This new group of leftists *started* with the premise that Stalinism had

---

[84] Hobsbawm, *Interesting Times*, 299. [85] Ibid., 300.

been responsible for serious crimes against humanity. While Hobsbawm criticized the 1968 generation of socialists for walking into revolution 'as into a political Club Med'[86] and never reconciled himself fully to 'identity politics', particularly feminism, the 'new lefties' sought to reconcile different approaches, often throwing themselves wholeheartedly into anti-racist, feminist, and other minoritized political movements. These intellectuals are the focus of the next chapter.

[86] Ibid., 129.

20
Radical Intellectuals

> If seven maids with seven mops
> Swept it [sea-sand] for half a year.
> Do you suppose', the Walrus said,
> 'That they could get it clear?'
> 'I doubt it', said the Carpenter,
> And shed a bitter tear.
> Lewis Carroll, *Through the Looking-Glass and
> What Alice Found There*, 1872[1]

Lewis Carroll's 'The Walrus and the Carpenter' was a clever meditation on powerful but uncompassionate rulers who were compulsively attempting to create order in impossible circumstances. One century after Carroll published *Through the Looking-Glass and What Alice Found There*, journalist and broadcaster Bernard Levin used the words of the Walrus and the Carpenter to highlight the 'gut-rotting fear that grips millions of our fellow-countrymen'. The year 1973 was a time of crisis in Britain: IRA bombs had been detonated in London and Manchester; government pay restrictions had forced millions of workers onto the streets in protest. 'Day by day', Levin contended, 'the currency rots' and 'day by day cost-pull and wage-push combine in their dreadful work'. Like the Walrus and the Carpenter, the Conservative government was simply shedding crocodile tears for those devoured by their ruthless policies. And there was nothing anyone could do about it. Levin entitled his article, 'Up Goes the Price of Shoddy and All that Poor Folk Can Do is Look On'.[2]

Two professors in the newly established Department of Economics at Birkbeck immediately wrote a rebuff. They refused to accept Levin's dispiriting message that no effective action could be taken. In a letter to *The Times*, Albert Gregorio (Bertie) Hines and Richard Portes agreed with Levin that 'the distribution of income should become the number one public issue'. Furthermore, this was a job for 'hard-headed scientific economists'. But Levin had assumed that the refusal of professional economists to 'dabble in value judgments' rendered them impotent

---

[1] Lewis Carroll, *Alice in Wonderland*, 1st pub 1872, ed. Donald J. Gray (New York: Norton, 1971), 141.
[2] Bernard Levin, 'Up Goes the Price of Shoddy and All that Poor Folk Can Do is Look On', *The Times* (30 October 1973), 16.

in the face of economic crisis. This assumption was a red flag to the two new professors. 'We, too, were sold this piece of theology', they exclaimed, adding: 'But it is wrong!' Hines and Portes contended that the dominant form of economics under the Conservative government was based on liberal, neoclassical formulations. The idea that it was value-free was unsustainable. It was ideologically committed to the belief that 'resources should be allocated through markets', for example, and that 'rewards to individuals should reflect the relative scarcity of resources which they happen to possess and can sell on the market'. They argued that neoclassical economics also 'wrongly supposes that it is possible to separate questions of ownership, production and efficiency from questions of distribution'. Instead, Hines and Portes reminded readers, it was 'no longer inconsistent with technical competence or professional respectability' to insist that economists should begin with the 'the general proposition that income and wealth ought to be equally distributed' and that '*exceptions* to this rule' were what 'need justification'.[3] They insisted that there was an alternative to neoclassical economics. That 'hard-headed' alternative could be found in Birkbeck's newly established Department of Economics—the main centre for neo-Keynesian economic thought in Britain.

But new ways of thinking about the world were not only flourishing in economics. The College also became an innovative hub for radical politics and sociology, activist social theory, critical legal studies, and innovative approaches to the past. Academics in these disciplines saw themselves as 'value-orientated intellectuals', to adopt Noam Chomsky's phrase, dedicated to critique and telling truth to power.[4] They emphasized political engagement and open, fierce debate across schools of thought and political positions. They were engaged with theory as well as the archives. They were fundamentally *serious* about ideas. It was a heady mix.

* * *

When Hines and Portes wrote to *The Times* in 1973, they sounded confident. Their department had only been in existence for two years, but they were reflecting a tradition that could be traced back to the very early days of Birkbeck. Economics had been taught at the LMI from its establishment in 1823, as 'Political Economy'. One of the original founders of the Institution, Thomas Hodgskin, was a radical political economist. As mentioned in Chapter 1, his 1827 book entitled *Popular Political Economy: Four Lectures Delivered at the London Mechanics' Institution* led Karl Marx to declare that Hodgskin was 'one of the most important modern English economists'[5] and Hodgskin's

---

[3] A. G. Hines and R. D. Portes, '[Letter to the Editor] Basic Value Judgments', *The Times* (7 November 1973), 19. Emphasis added.

[4] Noam Chomsky, *Language and Politics*, ed. Carlos P. Otero (Montréal: Black Rose Books, 1988), 173.

[5] Karl Marx, *Capital: A Critique of Political Economy*, vol. 1, trans. Ben Fowkes (Harmondsworth: Penguin, 1976), 1000, at https://www.surplusvalue.org.au/Marxism/Capital%20-%20Vol.%201%20

lectures had been central for Marx when he developed his labour theory of value in the third volume of *Capital*.

Since Hodgskin's famous lectures, however, the fortunes of economics in the College had been mixed. By the late nineteenth century, 'Political Economy' averaged around fifty students a year. In 1896, it was merged (along with 'Logic' and 'Psychology and Ethics') into a group of classes grouped under the heading 'Mental and Moral Science' which, until 1906, averaged about 112 students a year. This made it one of the most popular *academic* subjects in the College. By 1908, 'Political Economy' had been renamed 'Economics' and was included in the list of classes in the arts. It averaged sixty-eight students annually until numbers plummeted during the First World War.[6] Then, in 1921, it disappeared altogether. As a condition of Birkbeck becoming part of the University of London, the College had to give up teaching economics to avoid competition with the London School of Economics (LSE).[7] Ironically, (as mentioned in Chapter 8) one of Birkbeck's most famous former students and advocates—Sidney Webb—had been keen to ensure that Birkbeck gave up its economics teaching since he was one of the co-founders of the LSE in 1895. Birkbeck's annual report for 1920–1 claimed that the decision had been made with a 'natural regret in view of the prominent position which Economics occupied in the curriculum of the College'.[8] The College resumed teaching economics briefly during the 1939–45 war, to enable students from the London School of Economics to complete their degree, since the LSE had been evacuated to the countryside.[9] But economics did not finally return to Birkbeck until 1971.

The 1921 decision was only reversed after the appointment of a new Master, Ronald (Ronnie) Tress in 1968. Not only was Tress an applied economist himself—and therefore had a strong stake in promoting the discipline—but social scientific disciplines more generally were flourishing throughout the UK at this time. Indeed, economics was not the only innovation introduced by Tress in 1971. He also established a School of Politics and Sociology. A decade earlier, during a speech at the College's 138th anniversary, C. P. Snow claimed that the 'dangerous' growth of the 'two cultures' could be reduced by the introduction of sociology to university courses. He lamented that the discipline was 'not fashionable in this country', but argued that because sociology spoke the language of both science and the arts it was a 'very fragile and partial' but important bridge and, if it were

---

Penguin.pdf, viewed 1 June 2021. In the same footnote, Marx criticizes Brougham's work as characterized by a 'superficiality that marks all the economic productions of that windbag'.

[6] From the annual reports.

[7] *Birkbeck College (University of London). Report for 98th Session 1920–21* (London: Birkbeck College, 1921), 7.

[8] Ibid., 7.

[9] Letter from the Master to the Vice-Chancellor of the University of London, undated, in Birkbeck Archive, 'Wartime Correspondence with the Master 1943–45' (pp. 110–11 of file).

taught at Birkbeck, it would convey 'advantages to our entire intellectual world'.[10] It took the appointment of Tress for Snow's vision to be realized.

One of Tress' first decisions was to appoint Jamaican-born Hines to establish a Department of Economics. He was appointed in 1971 and set out to promulgate a radical economic theory that would 'include the best of Ricardo, Marx, Keynes, and the Neo-Classics'. His *On Reappraisal of Keynesian Economics* (1971) was a rousing call for a synthesis of economic theories that would 're-establish the claim of economics' to be the fundamental theory of society'.[11] Hines sought to put Keynes back 'on the agenda'. He sardonically admitted that 'there still existed in various corners of England some followers of Keynes', adding that 'But then the English are well known for their love and reverence for ancient monuments and relics'.[12] On the wall of a lift in the Gresse Street building, where the new social scientific departments had been housed, a student had scrawled graffiti that read: 'Keynes Means Hines', a play on the advertising slogan 'Beans Means Heinz', after the food-processing company that cans baked beans.[13]

One of Hines' first acts as head of the new department was to appoint Portes, his co-author in the letter to *The Times*, from Princeton University. These two men then began hiring other radical economists. One of these was Ben Fine, who confessed to being 'bewitched' by Marx, not only because Marx's analysis was 'in sharp contrast to the nonsense of mainstream economics' that dominated the early 1970s but also because 'stagflation had discredited orthodoxy, the social sciences were more radical than ever before, and heterodox economics prospered'.[14] Formal teaching in the department started in October 1973, after a half-century hiatus (see Fig. 20.1).

* * *

The radical economists attracted to the early Department of Economics were part of a wider upheaval in intellectual life at Birkbeck. It was a progressive revolution that was broadly 'leftist' but much more pluralistic than the earlier generation of post-war Marxists represented by Bernal and Hobsbawm. These economists, political scientists, sociologists, historians, and critical thinkers were engaged primarily with questions of politics and power, agency and vulnerability, identity and ideology. Except for a brief flirtation in the 1970s with Althusserian or 'structuralist' social theory by members in the Department of Politics and Sociology, none of the radicals discussed in this chapter attempted to create a unified or unifying

---

[10] C. P. Snow, *Recent Thoughts on the Two Cultures* (London: Birkbeck College, 1962), 6.
[11] A. G. Hines, *On the Reappraisal of Keynesian Economics: A Revised and Extended Version of a University Special Lecture Delivered at Queen Mary College in the University of London on 7th December 1970* (London: Martin Robertson and Co. Ltd, 1971), 62.
[12] Ibid., 8.   [13] Email from Ron Smith to the author, 29 March 2018.
[14] 'Ben Fine', in Philip Arestis and Malcolm C. Sawyer (eds), *A Biographical Dictionary of Dissenting Economists* (Cheltenham: E. Elgar, 2000), 173. Richard D. Portes left Birkbeck in 1995 to go to the London Business School.

Fig. 20.1 Heads of department in the Council Room, 1972–3. From left to right (as you look at the picture), regardless of which row or whether sitting or standing: Prof. Peter Murray (History of Art), Prof. David Ross (French), Prof. Douglas Dakin, Vice-Master (History), Dr Ronald Tress, Master, Prof. David Hamlyn (Philosophy), Mr A. J. (George) Caraffi, Clerk to the Governors, Dr Andrew Seager (Geology), Prof. Ronald Tiffen (Maths), Prof. Harry Carlisle (Crystallography), Prof. Alec Rodger (Occupational Psychology), Prof. Robert Browning, Sir Bernard Crick, Prof. Connor Fahy (Italian), Prof. Eila Campbell (Geography), Prof Philip Holgate (Statistics), Prof. A. G. (Bertie) Hines (Economics), Prof. Peter King (Computer Science), Prof. W. G. (Bill) Chaloner (Botany), Prof. Barbara Hardy (English), Prof Arthur Summerfield (Psychology), Prof. Charlotte Jolles (German), Dr Michel Blanc (Applied Linguistics). The heads of chemistry, physics, Spanish and zoology are absent. Birkbeck Image Collections: Birkbeck History BH0069.

theory, let alone a universalist one. Instead, they insisted on the dynamic interaction of values and institutions. If there was one unifying principle, it was summarized by distinguished historian of Germany, Richard J. Evans, in his book *In Defence of History* (1997) when he contended that 'I remain confident that objective historical knowledge is both desirable and attainable.'[15] This was echoed by sociologist and political theorist Paul Quentin Hirst in 'The Future of Political Studies' (2003): 'being engaged and maintaining objectivity is tough', he admitted, adding 'but it is the only serious approach'.[16] Both Evans and Hirst maintained

---

[15] Richard Evans, *In Defence of History* (London: Granta Books, 1997), 252.
[16] Paul Hirst, 'The Future of Political Studies', *European Political Science*, 3.1 (2003), 48. Based on a talk he gave at the Annual Conference of the Danish Political Science Association in October 2002.

this principle while nurturing a remarkably diverse array of approaches, ideas, and practices within their respective departments. This chapter will explore the complexity of such radical intellectuals within the context of three themes: pluralism, politics, and ethics.

* * *

Of the four departments explored in this chapter (Economics; History; Politics and Sociology; and Law), the History Department had the longest, continuous presence in the LMI/Birkbeck. As with economics, history was taught in several different administrative and disciplinary locations. In the early years of the LMI, it was taught in a sporadic manner, based on the personal interests of lecturers, 'members', and students. 'English History', as it was called, was usually listed alongside classes in 'English Grammar', 'Composition and Advanced Grammar', 'Anglo-Saxon', 'Literature', and 'Elocution'. 'Commercial History' was taught elsewhere, primarily linked with 'Political Economy' as a 'Mental and Moral Science'.[17] It was not until 1908 that 'History' appeared as a separate entity to 'English'. At that time, it was taught by Thomas Seccombe (MA, Oxon). His course was described as 'English History, from the earliest times to 1832, including constitutional, economic, ecclesiastical, and colonial history'.[18] There was also a history course entitled 'General Foreign History from 1452 to 1815'. By 1920, Arthur Jones (MA, Manchester) had become head of department for history, but the syllabus remained focused on politics, diplomacy, and the constitution. This syllabus was supplemented by the introduction of a more progressive course called 'Advanced Teaching in Local History', meaning the history of London.[19] Throughout this period, archaeology had a minor presence and, from the 1940s, was taught within the Department of English, except for four years from 1979 when it was a separate department. Archaeology only joined the Department of History at the end of the 1980s. 'Classics' was also listed separately from 'History'; it was closely allied to language departments. Classics only became part of the History Department in 1992, under the guise of 'ancient history'. The fortunes of archaeology and classics are told elsewhere in this book.

As late as the early 1960s, the two departments of History and Classics/Ancient History were tiny, consisting of nine and four people, respectively, including administrative staff. Their curricula mirrored those of the discipline more broadly in Britain. Leaving aside the innovative, social-historical, Marxist research of people like Hobsbawm, Ste Croix, and Browning, as discussed in the previous chapter, there was a strong emphasis on political and constitutional history. Editing primary texts was awarded a high status. R. R. (Reginald Ralph) Darlington, who was at Birkbeck for nearly a quarter of a century after 1945 and

---

[17] For example, see the leaflet 'Birkbeck Literary and Scientific Institution' (London: BLSI, 1896), 2.
[18] Prospectus for 1908, p. 32.   [19] Ibid., p. 41.

was a long-standing head of department, is a good example. His main works comprised editions of medieval documents including William of Malmesbury's *Vita Wulfstani*, *The Cartulary of Darley Abbey*, *The Glapwell Charters*, *The Winchcombe Annals*, and *The Chronicle of John of Worcester*. He never published a research monograph, the 'gold standard' for academic historians today.

The History Department changed dramatically from the 1960s. There was a rapid expansion in staff numbers and MA/PhD students, alongside a dramatic diversification in historical themes and methodologies. As Evans explains in his ground-breaking book *In Defence of History* (1997), the 1960s saw a shift away from more Rankean approaches to the past (that is, historical scholarship that followed the lead of German historian Leopold von Ranke in emphasizing source-based criticism). Politics, diplomacy, and conventional military history declined in popularity as historians turned towards more social-scientific, quantitative history (represented at Birkbeck by scholars such as Roderick Floud, whose work complemented approaches being espoused within the newly established Department of Economics), the study of societies (Jane Rowlandson, David Blackbourn, Vanessa Harding, and Catharine Edwards), mentalité (R. F. Foster), oral history (Hilary Sapire), grand narrative (Orlando Figes), and social history (Evans). When the 'social historical' approaches of the 1970s and 1980s waned, 'cultural history' came to the fore. This shift from social to cultural history can also be seen in my own work, particularly in my shift from the early 1990s *Working-Class Cultures* (which, despite the 'culture' in the title, was mainstream 'social and economic' history) to the history of emotions in *Fear: A Cultural History* (2005), to the Derridean-inspired, deconstructionist *What It Means to be Human* (2011) and the activist-academic book *Disgrace: Global Reflections on Sexual Violence* (2022). Even historians who produced voluminous volumes of primary sources did so in ways that their historical predecessors such as Darlington would not have recognized. For example, Michael Hunter published multiple editions of the works and correspondence of early modern scientist Robert Boyle, while also intervening in academic debates about magic, promoting the use of visual sources (including creating a digital library of British printed images from 1700), and experimenting with psychoanalytical approaches to the seventeenth century.

In addition, although every generation of scholars 'revises' the work of its predecessors, some historians began wearing the label 'Revisionist' (capital 'R') with pride. The department became Britain's leading research hub for the social, cultural, and political history of Ireland, exemplified by the work of Roy Foster and Marianne Elliott. Foster's best-selling *Modern Ireland 1600–1972* (1988), written and published while he was at Birkbeck, was an influential example of historical scholarship whose sensitivities to the different but interwoven cultures of Northern Ireland opened up dialogues between communities. It was his emphasis on complexity or, as Foster put it, on the 'varieties of Irishness', that changed the way Irish history was understood.[20] The same is true of Elliott's biography of Wolfe Tone and her intellectual interventions into questions of religion and sectarianism in Ireland. As we will see, these shifts were not only disciplinary but also tied to questions of pluralism, politics, and ethics.

* * *

Unlike history, politics/sociology and law were new arrivals at Birkbeck. Politics and sociology were introduced to Birkbeck in 1972 by Tress, who recognized the links between his own discipline of economics and that of politics. The first professor in the Politics and Sociology Department was political scientist Bernard Crick from the University of Sheffield, along with Hirst and Sami Zubaida, an expert in the complex historical and political interactions between the Middle East and the 'West'. Zubaida and Hirst had both studied under Norbert Elias at Leicester University. Elias is credited with renewing British sociology, especially with his influential yet controversial work on the 'civilizing process'. It was no coincidence that Elias was a German-Jewish refugee. In continental Europe, sociology was a powerful academic force. Prior to the influx of European refugees after 1933, this was not the case in England, despite the importance of Herbert Spencer and L. T. Hobhouse. Perry Anderson's assessment in 1968 was harsh but relevant. He maintained that English sociology was characterized by a 'listless mediocrity and wizened provincialism'. It was the 'poor cousin to "social work" and "social administration", the dispirited descendants of Victorian charity' (by which he meant Victorian empiricism).[21] Scholars in the new Department of Politics and Sociology were to bring the sociological rigour of Elias, as well as a 1968 anti-authoritarian fervour, to Birkbeck.

The department was housed in the newly acquired Gresse Street building (see Fig. 20.2), a converted warehouse just off Tottenham Court Road, and it focused on postgraduate teaching. The team was small but dedicated to advancing the College's central mission. Indeed, they believed that sociology and politics were suited to adult students, *par excellence*. One of Crick's first statements when arriving in the College was to admit that 'I've had a large bee in my bonnet about the social dangers of university education at eighteen, first job at twenty-one, and no real experience' before university. He maintained that 'sociologists brought up in this way can get very arrogant—very apt to generalise about the workers and so on, with no first-hand experience'.[22] This was why the fledging department sent out a strong message in statements to the press, explicitly welcoming teachers in Further or Secondary Education. They even stated that 'candidates from a first

---

[20] R. F. Foster, *Modern Ireland, 1600–1972* (London: Allen Lane, 1988).
[21] Perry Anderson, 'Components of the National Culture', 1st pub. 1968, in his *English Questions* (London: Verso, 1992), 53.
[22] 'Bernard Crick is New Birkbeck Professor', *Spectrum*, 4.13 (1 June 1971), 1.

Fig. 20.2 The library at Gresse Street in the 1970s. Birkbeck Image Collections: Birkbeck History BH0067.

degree into which they came straight from school will not usually be considered'![23] They wanted students with experience in the 'real world' of employment and politics, who could therefore make connections between theory and practice. It was a tradition that the department continues to emphasize. Prominent Labour Party MPs John McDonnell and Lisa Nandy, for example, studied for Masters' degrees in the department while working full-time.[24]

While the disciplines of economics, politics, and sociology were established by Tress, the Department of Law had to wait another twenty years. This does not mean that the teaching of law was absent entirely. From the foundation of the LMI, law was an important subject of study. Advertisements for Birkbeck courses at the beginning of the nineteenth century, for example, note that 'the courses of study provide for degrees in the faculties of arts, science, laws, and economics'. By the beginning of the twentieth century, the Master, George Armitage-Smith, was boasting that the College's 'proximity to the Law Courts and a legal community

---

[23] 'Crick to Head New Course in Politics', *Times Higher Educational Supplement* (29 October 1971).
[24] 'In Conversation with John McDonnell', 2016, at https://soundcloud.com/british-politics-centre/birkbeck-politics-in-conversation-with-john-mcdonnell.

Fig. 20.3 Portrait of Baroness Blackstone by Peter Douglas Edwards. Birkbeck Image Collections: Birkbeck History BH0122.

gave rise to lectures on Mercantile and Common Law, Equity and Conveyancing'.[25] In 1908, the law courses 'comprise mercantile and common law, equity, conveyancing, and patent law', as well as 'classes in English and Roman law, and constitutional law and history'.[26] Students doing these law courses sat the University of London examinations.[27]

The College ceased teaching law in 1937.[28] Its absence in the College's curriculum surprised Tessa Blackstone (see Fig. 20.3) when she was appointed Master exactly forty years later. It seemed a remarkable omission given the fact that mature students were particularly likely to be attracted to such a degree, with its

---

[25] G. Armitage-Smith, *Inaugural Address by the Principal G. Armitage-Smith on the Opening of the Seventieth-Nineth Session. Monday, 30th September, 1901* (London: Birkbeck College, 1901).
[26] Many locations, but see, for example, 'Birkbeck College', *Shoreditch Observer* (28 September 1908), 8.
[27] 'Extracts from Minutes of Governing Body, 19th December 1922', in 'Academic Board Minutes, 25th March 1908 to 8th June 1923', in the Birkbeck Archive.
[28] Eric H. W. Warmington, 'Confidential. Birkbeck College. Future Policy (Long-Term). Memorandum by the Acting Master', 14, in the file 'Future Development of the College 1963–68', in Birkbeck Archive, Box 43.

potential for employment. Blackstone won the support of Birkbeck's governors to establish a Law Department, and set about persuading the *other* colleges in the University of London to allow this initiative to go forward. After all, they saw the possibility of a Birkbeck Law School as competition. Blackstone promised to offer an undergraduate, *part-time* law degree with a small number of research students studying for PhDs. The department would not introduce a new Masters' degree (LLM), which was already offered as an intercollegiate degree by the existing five London Law Schools. These concessions eventually gained the approval of the other colleges. The financial arrangements were secured by judicious lobbying of the City of London Guild Hall by Judith Mayhew, leader of the Corporation of London and a governor of the College (she went on to become the first female Chair of the governors in 1999). The Guild Hall offered to fund a Chair—and the department was founded in 1992. The Department (now, School) of Law has thrived. It is amongst the top ten research institutions in the UK and in the top three in London. The legal subjects taught cover the entire range, but the department's uniqueness rests on being a centre for critical legal theory and socio-legal approaches to law and criminology. Crucially, in 2016, the Department of Criminology, along with the Institute for Crime and Justice Policy Research, was established to expand and intensify the original remit.

When the Department of Law was first established, it started admitting students before obtaining professional accreditation. The first year was anxious, as the small staff put together the relevant and very lengthy documents that would get the professions to recognize the degree, while teaching at the same time to the highest standards. In the early 1990s, the political environment was not conducive to progressive ideas. Conservative neoliberalism was at its peak; its mantra was 'get rich quick', which was anathema to critical theorists. Conservative lawyers were not inclined to welcome a radical, critically focused law school. The Society of Conservative Lawyers, which describes itself as the 'home of the legal profession within the Conservative Party', complained that two of the founders—Peter Goodrich and Costas Douzinas—were 'immersed' in poststructuralism: that is, they were teaching law as 'texts to which to apply methods of literary criticism'. It accused the department of representing 'English [sic] judges as inflexible dogmatists, habitual crushers of liberty'. The Conservative lawyers' chief objection, though, was that 'the course teaches law politically'.[29] They asked the Law Society and Bar Council to reject the degree's accreditation, claiming that the Birkbeck academics were too radical in their approach to be allowed to teach law. Without such accreditation, the department's graduates would not be able to join the profession. Blackstone sent a detailed response to the allegations, detailing the

---

[29] Clive Blackwood, Secretary of the Society of Conservative Lawyers, undated letter, in the School of Law archives and on the Society of Conservative Lawyers' website at https://www.conservativelawyers.com, viewed 1 October 2021.

academic credentials of the staff. The Law Society and Bar Council, after reviewing the documentation put together by the law academics, awarded the department 'Law Qualifying Degree status'. The senior law professors who acted as external examiners in the first years of the department judged the teaching and examination results to be excellent. Four years after being established, the Department of Law was awarded the highest ranking in the Research Assessment Exercise (RAE).

* * *

These four departments—Economics; History; Politics and Sociology; and Law—were crucial in introducing and promulgating radical and critical approaches to their disciplines. The last three, in particular, emphasized theoretical pluralism. The History Department from the 1990s saw an interest in social theories of agency and inequality, subjectivity and experience, atrocity and power, the body and sexuality. The Wellcome Trust provided financial and intellectual support for major, innovative projects on state medicine, brainwashing, humanitarianism and refugees, pain, and sexual violence. Rather than Freud (who, as we shall see, was important in law), many of these historians turned to Foucault and feminism. Although social-scientific Marxist approaches were promulgated by historian of science Dorothy Porter, it was more common for scholars to turn to postcolonial and poststructuralist approaches to the past.

However, concerted debates about the place of theory in the historical discipline were driven by Evans, who not only was a member of the department from 1989 to 1998 but also led the radical expansion of the department when he was its head between 1991 and 1993. In 1997, Evans published *In Defence of History*, a book that originated from his core lectures for the pioneering PPH (Politics, Philosophy, and History) Masters' programme. His book was a powerful argument for the importance of historical modes of thinking in helping people understand the world. In its many editions, it continues to excite debate in part because of its attacks on relativistic approaches to the past. Nevertheless, although Evans is fiercely critical of relativistic methodologies—which he loosely lumps together under the term 'postmodernist'—*In Defence of History* was also a progressive acknowledgement of some of the benefits of new historiographical and methodological approaches. He observed that, while hard-line relativism was dangerous, 'postmodernism in its more constructive modes' has had a positive impact.

> [It] has encouraged historians to look more closely at documents, to take their surface patina more seriously, and to think about texts and narratives in new ways. It has helped open up many new subjects and areas for research, while putting back on the agenda many topics which had previously seemed to be exhausted. It has forced historians to interrogate their own methods and procedures as never before, and in the process has made them more self-critical.... It has

led to greater emphasis on open acknowledgement of the historian's own subjectivity, which can only help the reader engaged in a critical assessment of historical work.[30]

This was by no means an endorsement! Evans noted that when historians analyse a diplomatic dispatch, they 'cannot recover a single, unalterably "true" meaning' from it 'simply by reading it'. But they also 'cannot impose any meaning we wish to on such a text either'.[31] He insists that

> The real question at issue here is *what enables us* to read a source 'against the grain', and here theory does indeed come in. Theory of whatever kind, whether it is a general set of theses about how human societies are structured and human beings behave, or whether it is a limited proposition about, say, the carnivalesque in history, or the nature of human communication within a pre-industrial city, derives from the historian's present, not from the historian's sources.[32]

For Evans, historians working within a postmodernist approach must ensure that they show how their arguments about the past actually engage intellectually with that 'past' as opposed to being reflections of current anxieties and interests. Evans' tenure as the head of the Department of History, Classics, and Archaeology was characterized by both intellectual dynamism and methodological heterogeneity.

In the Department of Politics and Sociology, theoretical pluralism came more slowly. In the 1970s, when Hirst joined the fledging department, he was an 'uncompromising Althusserian', a label named after French philosopher Louis Althusser who had attempted to build a universal, structuralist Marxist theory that could be used to understand all societies and histories.[33] Indeed, Hirst used to be known for his 'unbending theoretical rigour'.[34] He co-founded the Althusserian journal *Theoretical Practice*, which attacked empiricism and positivism, while defending the scientific study of Marxism. It was this anti-historical, anti-humanist, and structuralist approach that generated a furious backlash, most notably by Edward Thompson in *The Poverty of Theory*. Thompson accused Hirst and other Althusserians of 'theoreticism', or creating a 'self-generating conceptual universe' that 'imposes its own identity upon the phenomenon of material and social existence, rather than engaging in a continual dialogue with them'.[35]

By the early 1990s, however, Hirst had recanted dogmatism, choosing a more heterodox position.[36] Indeed, he was later to denounce the 'ideologisation of

---

[30] Evans, *In Defence of History*, 248.   [31] Ibid., 105–6.   [32] Ibid., 83.
[33] Andrew Gamble, 'Paul Hirst: An Appreciation', *Renewal*, 11.4 (2003), 1–2.   [34] Ibid., 1.
[35] Edward Thompson, *The Poverty of Theory, and Other Essays* (London: Merlin Press, 1978), 205. Thompson was especially critical of Barry Hindess and Paul Q. Hirst's *Pre-Capitalist Modes of Production* (London: Routledge and Kegan Paul, 1975).
[36] Paul Hirst, *Marxism and Historical Writing* (London: Routledge, 1985), 7.

political studies' in the 1970s, which led to 'so much energy' being 'consumed in infighting between Marxist sects'.[37] He argued against the 'if you are not for us, you are against us' mentality, maintaining that it was 'lethal to the scepticism and objectivity needed both for scientific work *and* credible political action'.[38] In this he was able to attack dogmatic 'left' and 'right' ideologies. Who could dispute, he suggested, that 'cosmopolitan idealism, neo imperialism and revived revolutionary leftism' were all failed forms of twentieth-century politics?[39] Twenty-first-century crises needed *real* solutions, grounded in a deep scrutiny of politics, publics, and economic patterns.

Hirst's position was that *both* the rigidly Marxian focus on structures *and* economic analyses that positioned individuals as 'rational interest-maximising' agents were flawed. Since, in the 1980s and early 1990s, the latter were ostensibly 'the winner' in this bruising battle, Hirst focused his critique on them. He accused them of

> treating all social action as if it were strategic, in the pursuit of interest, rather than as deriving from affect, from belief, or from morality. The latter motivations are treated as irrational residuals, to be explained away. It has dissolved institutions into the actions of individuals, not only because of its commitment to methodological individualism, but because it has no extended account of such things as institutions except as necessary to the pursuit of utility. It ignores solidarity, community, loyalty, and belief.[40]

It was a point succinctly expressed by Crick: 'a "university" should be a creative sharing, not a departmentalisation of learning'.[41]

The willingness—indeed, enthusiasm for—a plurality of approaches was also fostered by the Department of Law. Its specifically 'British' brand of critical legal studies (CLS), which was inspired *by* but different *from* the school of the same name in North American universities, revolutionized mainstream legal scholarship. CLS links theory and practice, drawing inspiration from deconstruction, postmodernism, postcolonialism, feminism, critical race theory, queer theory, art history, literature, aesthetics, and ethics. Goodrich, the ponytailed first head of school, introduced the study of rhetoric, semiotics, and psychoanalysis to legal scholarship. The journal *Law and Critique*, the best-known forum for critical legal theory, is based in the Law School and pioneered this new theoretical pluralism. In the 1980s, Douzinas, one of the inaugural members of the department, recalled that he and Ronnie Warrington had an article rejected by a leading law journal on

---

[37] Paul Hirst, 'The Future of Political Studies', *European Political Science*, 3.1 (2003), 47.
[38] Ibid., 47.   [39] Ibid., 48.   [40] Ibid., 49.
[41] Bernard Crick, *Political Thoughts and Polemics* (Edinburgh: Edinburgh University Press, 1990), vii.

the grounds that it included ten words that could not be found in the *Oxford English Dictionary*. These included 'deconstruction', a concept now familiar in many disciplines. The diversity of intellectual positions, along with the often-contradictory mesh of theoretical approaches, flourished because it was consciously self-reflective and critical. They were relentless in turning a critical eye on their own practices.

Adopting a plurality of approaches served the legal scholars at Birkbeck well. It distinguished the fledging department both from larger and wealthier London schools and from the vocational orientation of law units in polytechnics and new universities. The division between legal scholarship and vocational training had been entrenched in English history. Indeed, law did not even have a significant role in universities until the early twentieth century.[42] This relative isolation from university systems meant that 'the law curriculum and the model of legal academic within the traditional law school' remained 'a product of professional influence and vocational criteria' rather than 'independent scholarly concern'.[43] Undermining this convention was a key goal for the early scholars. They turned their attention to international (specifically continental) theoretical approaches, which had a much stronger focus on theoretical explorations and interdisciplinarity.[44] Perhaps the flagship event in meeting this ambition was the establishment of the first intercollegiate London Legal Theory seminar, aimed at introducing some of the most advanced, international social theorists to scholars in Britain. These included intellectuals as varied as Walter Benjamin, Maurice Blanchot, Gilles Deleuze, Jacques Derrida, Jürgen Habermas, Duncan Kennedy, Jacques Lacan, Ernesto Laclau, Pierre Legendre, Emmanuel Levinas, Niklas Luhmann, Jean-François Lyotard, Gillian Rose, Jacqueline Rose, and Slavoj Žižek (see Fig. 20.4). A few members of the College were scandalized; many more, exhilarated.

* * *

If the first key principle is theoretical pluralism, the second is politics. The previous chapter featured the historian Hobsbawm along with classicists Ste Croix and Browning, all of whom were members of the Communist Party. But Hobsbawm was not a dogmatist. His 'The Forward March of Labour Halted?', originally published in *Marxism Today* in 1978, became influential for decrying trade unionist sectarianism, which was damaging electoral chances. His intervention encouraged the Labour Party and its supporters on the left to adopt more realist policies, which led to the rise of 'New Labour'. Of course, despite Hobsbawm's support for Neil Kinnock, he was a member of the CPGB, not the Labour Party. The

---

[42] 'Department of Law. Birkbeck College. Academic Plan. 15.5.1995', 3, in 'School Correspondence. Law, 1991–2005', in Birkbeck Archive, Box 66.
[43] Ibid.   [44] Ibid.

Fig. 20.4 Costas Douzinas, critical legal theorist and co-founder of the Birkbeck Law Department and the Birkbeck Institute for the Humanities. Photo: The Author.

Department of History, Classics, and Archaeology was home to many non-communist historians who were Labourite in political persuasion while not inclined to wear their politics 'on their sleeves', let alone allow it to drive their scholarship. These historians were profoundly sensitive to the uses of history as a tool of political propaganda, whether in Germany, the Soviet Union, Japan, the UK, or the USA. They rallied against racism, misogyny, and anti-Semitism. In more recent years, they looked on with despair and anger as classical tropes were appropriated by right-wing extremists, as during the storming of the US Capitol on 6 January 2021 when Spartans and other classical models were referenced.

Political critique also departed from the cloistered university to engage in heated debates in public squares, halls, and courtrooms. This was the experience of Marianne Elliott, an historian of Ireland in the 1790s. In 1993, she became one of seven commissioners in the Opsahl Commission, an independent inquiry into the views of ordinary people in Northern Ireland about peace and reconciliation. The Commission's fundamental premise was that the resolution of the conflict had to involve everyone in Northern Ireland: they had to take 'ownership' of the process.[45] The commissioners invited submissions from any group or persons and held confidential focus groups and private sessions in eleven different venues throughout Northern Ireland, as well as in school assemblies.[46] Elliott recalled that

---

[45] Marianne Elliott, 'The Role of Civil Society in Conflict Resolution: The Opsahl Commission in Northern Ireland, 1992–93', *New Hibernia Review/Iris Éireannach Nua*, 17.2 (summer 2013), 86.

[46] Ibid., 87.

Many of those whom we had persuaded to go public were vulnerable and nervous. It takes courage to speak in public before television cameras or a hall full of strangers if you are a housewife from a republican or loyalist estate, or if you are a member of a Catholic religious community prepared to criticise your church.[47]

The Commission became an essential, early stage in the peace process that led to the Good Friday Agreement. The experience allowed Elliott to reflect on lack of public understanding about democracy and political accountability, the embeddedness of a 'dependency culture', and the importance of historical memory. These were insights that she reflected upon in her aptly named book, *When God Took Sides: Religion and Identity in Ireland—Unfinished Business* (2009).[48]

The political *ethics* of historical scholarship has also moved to the fore, with scholars increasingly willing to cast judgement by openly employing moral concepts, as in the use of the word 'perpetrator' when addressing past accounts of 'atrocity' or sexual 'harms'. As Evans maintains, while the historical discipline 'cannot bind itself wholly to any political ideology and survive unscathed', this 'does not mean it cannot be driven by a moral or political purpose and still retain its integrity'.[49] Evans was speaking through experience. In 2000, he was asked to write an expert report in the libel action brought by the pseudo-historian David Irving against Deborah Lipstadt and her publisher Penguin Books UK. In *Denying the Holocaust: The Growing Assault on Truth and Memory* (1994), Lipstadt had claimed that Irving had deliberately falsified historical sources to promote an extreme right-wing agenda. In terms of history, there was a great deal at stake, most notably Irving's invention of Jewish conspiracies, his belittling of Jewish suffering, and his minimization of Hitler's responsibility for the Holocaust. Evans spent twenty-eight hours giving evidence at the trial. That, along with his 740-page report, proved decisive in Irving losing his libel action. The case also led to reflections on the role of historians—is it moral judgement or explanation and interpretation, for example? Was there a risk of historical argumentation being 'instrumentalized by political imperatives'?[50] Crucially, as Evans points out, the trial was not about the Holocaust itself but about how Irving represented the past in the present.[51] The case highlighted threats to the free speech of historians, such as Lipstadt, to challenge Holocaust deniers. As Evans noted, 'Had Irving won,

---

[47] Ibid., 88.
[48] Marianne Elliott, *When God Took Sides: Religion and Identity in Ireland—Unfinished Business* (New York: Oxford University Press, 2009).
[49] Richard J. Evans, 'Introduction: Redesigning the Past: History in Political Transitions', *Journal of Contemporary History*, 38.1 (2003), 12.
[50] Richard J. Evans, 'History, Memory, and the Law: The Historian as Expert Witness', *History and Theory*, 41.3 (October 2002), 330–1.
[51] Ibid., 340.

such criticism would no longer have been possible in Britain.'⁵² It was a victory for the discipline and for truth.

Scholars of politics were understandably even more active than historians in intervening in political debate. In the Department of Politics and Sociology, Crick is prototypical. He refused to identify with doctrinaire partisans of either the left or the right but contended that political scientists should 'argue only for relevance', retaining an 'independent-minded critical engagement' rather than an 'uncritical commitment or loyalty to party'.⁵³ Tellingly, Crick was delighted when one interviewer called him an 'extremist at the centre'.⁵⁴

For Crick, politics was 'ethics done in public', the third theme of this chapter. His aphorism was another way of saying that he was an enthusiastic advocate of the unity of theory and practice. The entire *raison d'être* of academic politics was to forge an engaged citizenry. Indeed, the fate of democracy lay with people's civic literacy, which is why Crick was dismayed by the profound political ignorance of most Britons. This helps explain why the early Department of Politics and Sociology actively marketed its courses to teachers, as frontline workers in citizen-education.

Crick was also a pragmatist. 'Real' politics was messy. It had to deal with a vast diversity of competing and conflicting interests, as well as being unpredictable, which is one reason why Crick argued against the 'scientistic' behaviourism of many North American schools of political thought. His emphasis was on politics-*and-society*, rather than political *science*, with its emphasis on abstracted data rather than social values and meaning. Effective politics involved negotiating, compromising, and seeking consensus. In other words, the world of politics was about reconciling differences. As Crick wrote in 1971, political science had to be 'aware of the inextricable relationship of theory to practice and hence the need for political relevance'. He quipped that 'the world may not need political science...but political science needs to be relevant to the world to be profound as a discipline.'⁵⁵

This meant taking seriously both parts of the concept 'public intellectual'. Ben Pimlott's work is a good example. Pimlott joined the Department of Politics and Sociology in 1981 and, during his two decades at Birkbeck, published distinguished biographies of Hugh Dalton, Harold Wilson, and the Queen. Like Crick, who wrote a biography of George Orwell, Pimlott's aim was to communicate the importance of politics beyond the academy. For Pimlott, writing was a

---

⁵² Ibid., 341.
⁵³ Bernard Crick, *In Defence of Politics*, 5th ed. (London: Continuum, 2005), 242.
⁵⁴ Peter Hennessy, 'Bernard Crick: "A Pretty Potent Piece of Artillery" Letting Fly in All Directions', *Times Higher Educational Supplement* (29 November 1974), in 'Newscuttings 1974–76', in the Birkbeck Archive.
⁵⁵ Bernard Crick, *Political Theory and Practice* (London: Penguin, 1971), xi–xii.

'mechanism for revolution', argued Jean Seaton.⁵⁶ His sensitivities towards the political sensibilities of the wider British public were revealed in the immediate aftermath of the death of Princess Diana. When Number Ten telephoned him in panic, asking 'What can we do? What is the mood?', Pimlott is reported to have responded ' "we could call her the People's Princess", which was...what he had called Princess Elizabeth in *The Queen*'.⁵⁷ When Tony Blair used those words in his address to the nation, they became the touchstone for a nation in mourning.

Making a political difference outside of the academic world was also Crick's aim. In his second edition of *In Defence of Politics* (a title that predated Evans' *In Defence of History* by thirty-five years), Crick added a 'Rallying Cry to the University Professors of Politics'.⁵⁸ Social relevance, social responsibility, and civil duty were crucial. The 'public intellectual' had to be 'an explainer, generaliser, specific critic of other theories and...a continual critic of the concepts used in doctrines'.⁵⁹ This required scholars to 'meddle' in governmental affairs, which for Crick meant reforming parliamentary procedures, adjudicating on the Scottish Constitution, introducing citizenship education, and promoting reforms in Northern Ireland. For all members of the Department of Politics and Sociology, then and today, Orwell's famous aphorism is key: 'What I have most wanted to do...is to make political writing into an art.'⁶⁰

* * *

Crick's political vision emphasized prudence, adaptability, and the reconciliation of differences. It was a response to left-wing weariness and Thatcherism. It was a modernist vision that acknowledged the role of emotions in politics but nevertheless believed in the power of education to encourage the development of a participatory democracy. The limits of this approach were exposed in the twenty-first century—specifically by 9/11, the financial crisis of 2008, and global struggles against neoliberal capitalism. These new challenges elicited different responses from those Birkbeck's radical intellectuals who emphasized fractures and radical discontinuities in social theory and political practice. The distrust of politicians and pluralist politics that Crick had lamented deepened. Shifts of power within the UK, including devolution and the emergence of the European Union, drew attention to the move from government to governance. They decried the unaccountability of government executive and sought, through a Bill of Rights

---

⁵⁶ Dermot Hodson, 'Ben Pimlott, Political Writing and the Orwell Prize: An Interview with Prof. Jean Seaton' (19 May 2014), at http://10-gower-street.com/2014/05/19/ben-pimlott-political-writing-and-the-orwell-prize-an-interview-with-jean-seaton/, viewed 16 June 2021. Seaton is Professor of Media History at the University of Westminster and was married to Pimlott.
⁵⁷ Ibid.
⁵⁸ Bernard Crick, *In Defence of Politics*, 1st ed. 1962, 2nd ed. (Chicago: University of Chicago Press, 1972).
⁵⁹ Crick, *Political Theory and Practice*, 32–3.
⁶⁰ Hodson, 'Ben Pimlott, Political Writing and the Orwell Prize'.

(as argued by the cross-party reform group Charter '88, which many Birkbeck intellectuals such as Hirst supported), to put power back in the hands of citizens. To further their goal of incisive yet inclusive debates, scholars turned to empirical studies focusing on European Union policy and law, environmentalism, empire, and gender.

Dramatic shifts in the practice of democratic politics, including those spurred by social media, changed the ways citizens engaged in the world. Gradual reform of political institutions and law was no longer sufficient. What was needed was radical change: deconstruction replaced empiricism; the emphasis on pluralism was exchanged for attention to contingency and uncertainty.[61] Unlike the Marxist-inspired intellectuals of the earlier generation who saw legal and political institutions as expressions of class interests, these intellectuals focused on *form* as much as *content*. Discourse (words and images) was seen to construct the political and legal subject. It was the means by which the individual was 'constituted and defined, captured, circulated, and judged'.[62] Radical intellectuals turned their emphasis to political struggle. These thinkers aligned themselves with post-Marxists, influenced by critical theory, psychoanalysis, and postcolonial theories.

Their lens was ethics. Key concepts were justice, human rights, and resistance. Some (such as Sami Zubaida in the Department of Politics and Sociology) turned their focus to the Middle East; others, such as myself in books like *An Intimate History of Killing: Face to Face Killing in Twentieth Century Warfare* and *Wounding the World*, to militarist atrocities committed by the 'West'.[63] A revived form of domination was also explored—this was biopolitical governance, or the regulation of every part of human life, from bioinformation to the state regulation of torture. Attention was paid to 'otherness' and to the law's relation to violence. The impacts of imperialism, colonialism, and postcolonialism both in the UK and globally were spotlighted. Globalized capitalism, with its elaborate systems of domination and exploitation, led to a turn towards human rights. On the one hand, human rights were acknowledged to be a liberationist language for the dispossessed. On the other hand, 'rights' only operate within societal contexts: 'they do not belong to abstract men but to particular people in concrete societies', as Costas Douzinas insisted.[64] In other words, rights lack any inherent or permanent link to justice. They tie ethics to *law*, rather than *justice*.[65] And this simply wasn't good enough. As Douzinas expressed it in *The End of Human Rights* (2000),

---

[61] Peter Goodrich, Costas Douzinas, and Yifat Hachamovitch, 'Introduction: Politics, Ethics, and the Legality of the Contingent', in Goodrich, Douzinas, and Hachamovitch (eds), *Politics, Postmodernity, and Critical Legal Studies: The Legality of the Contingent* (London: Routledge, 1994), 8–9.

[62] Ibid., 15.

[63] Joanna Bourke, *An Intimate History of Killing: Face-to-Face Killing in Twentieth Century Warfare* (London: Granta, 1999), and Joanna Bourke, *Wounding the World* (London: Virago, 2014).

[64] Costas Douzinas, *The End of Human Rights* (Oxford: Hart, 2000), 99.

[65] Joanna Bourke, *What It Means To Be Human* (London: Virago, 2011), 163.

'a law without justice is a body without a soul and a legal education that teaches rules without spirit is intellectually barren and morally bankrupt'.[66]

It was also about feminism. In the words of Joni Lovenduski, in her inaugural address on becoming Professor of Politics at Birkbeck in 2002, 'feminizing politics...raises fundamental questions about democracy and representation'.[67] It raised questions about whether 'what is said is ever separable from who is speaking' and how minoritized groups within society can be represented.[68]

This turn to ethics by post-Marxist and poststructuralist intellectuals found expression in aesthetics. These thinkers exhibited a keen curiosity about the relationship between image and text. The politics of images—including the 'all-seeing eye' of military technologies, photography, and political iconography—came to the fore. They also encouraged explorations of underlying exclusions based on race, gender, sexual orientation, class, and, fundamental to it all, power. A conference at the Tate Gallery co-organized by the Departments of Law and Art History, on 'Law and the Image', brought to London some of the best-known art historians, lawyers, and critical theorists.[69] It was considered the beginning of a school of thought that brings together the aesthetics of law with the normativity of art. Similar collaborations between different disciplines have become one of the research innovations at Birkbeck.

For legal scholars, this meant repudiating the idea that law is exclusively a codification of norms, or the way particular societies assemble moral principles. Instead, they read legal texts through the lens of literary and aesthetic theory. As a form of discourse, attention had to be paid to rhetoric and to semiotics, or the relationship between the sign, object, and meaning. What had been omitted, repressed, and distorted? What were the underlying power structures and, once these had been identified, where could trauma be pinpointed? These questions were particularly astute in identifying oppressions based on racism, misogyny, and classism.

* * *

There was considerable resistance to many of these approaches. None was more bullishly expressed than by Roger Scruton in the Department of Philosophy. Scruton's 'knuckleduster'-type rhetoric was neatly summarized by David Selbourne in his review of *Thinkers of the New Left*, a compendium of Scruton's articles from the conservative *Salisbury Review*, which he edited between 1982 and 2001. Selbourne contended that Scruton lived in

---

[66] Douzinas, *The End of Human Rights*, vii.
[67] Joni Lovenduski, 'Feminizing Politics', *Women: A Cultural Review*, 13.2 (2002), 208.
[68] Ibid., 208.
[69] Costas Douzinas and Lynda Nead (eds), *Law and the Image: The Authority of Art and the Aesthetics of Law* (Chicago: University of Chicago Press, 1999).

a Dantesque world inhabited by 'implacable' or 'terrifying' socialist wraiths, and 'sinister' left tricksters; a world reverberating with 'dirge-like incarnation', and even (at one point) Schoenberg's 'vampiric screaming'. Among its accursed denizens are Marxist 'Fraud' and 'Fury', 'Tumult' and 'Bathos', writhing together in coils of socialist 'myth' and 'mumbo-jumbo', 'meta-dogma', 'mendacity' and 'mental contortion'; and racked by sundry left 'fixations', 'paranoias' and 'pathological obsession'.

For Scruton, a special place in hell was reserved for the heroes of Birkbeck's radical intellectuals, including 'Galbraith the "parasite"', Foucault the "cheat", and Lukacs the "monster"; Althusser the "charlatan", Thompson the "dupe".[70] He eventually relinquished his Chair at Birkbeck in response to the severe hostility of his colleagues to his criticisms of multicultural education.

Meanwhile, in the Department of Economics, a different ideological fight was under way. Two antagonistic 'tribes' had developed of Marxists and neoclassical economists. As the authors of an article entitled 'Division and Difference in the "Discipline" of Economics' (1990) explained, 'Marxian economic thought and neoclassical economic thought' had little in common, with the former making stronger alliances with the 'concepts, approaches, and methods' of Marxian literary theory.[71] While Marxian economics paid attention to historical conditions, modes of production and reproduction, class, distribution and consumption, and political power, the latter was fixated on modelling, equilibrium, the individual, and rationality. The two approaches are fundamentally incompatible. Clash was inevitable. John Broome, an early appointment to the Economics Department, remembered the department for being 'fraught'.[72] The 'conflict between the Marxists and the others' in the department, he recalled, meant that departmental meetings dragged on for many hours.[73] Tensions peaked in the 1980s when a new professor was chosen from outside the department. This was Robin Marris, who was to serve as head of the department from 1981 to 1987. Marris had developed a theory of 'managerial capitalism' and, although he had been associated with the Labour Party, became disillusioned in the 1970s with its connections with the trade unions. Marris' headship was described as a 'stormy' due to his 'intolerance of Marxists'.[74] He even sought to get a proposed programme of courses from his own department rejected by the University of London Board of Studies on the

---

[70] David Selbourne, 'The Right's Revenge', *New Society* (10 January 1986), 68.

[71] Jack Amariglio, Stephen Resnick, and Richard Wolff, 'Division and Difference in the "Discipline" of Economics', *Critical Inquiry*, 17.1 (autumn 1990), 109.

[72] John Broome, 'My Long Road to Philosophy', in Iwao Hirose and Andrew Reisner (eds), *Weighing and Reasoning: Themes from the Philosophy of John Broome* (Oxford: Oxford University Press, 2015), 2–3.

[73] Ibid., 2–3.

[74] Adrian Wood, 'Robin Marris Obituary', *The Guardian* (25 October 2012), at https://www.theguardian.com/business/2012/oct/25/robin-marris, viewed 2 May 2021.

grounds that it included Marxist approaches.[75] Marris also supported a directive from the Master, Overend, requesting that staff do not use College stationary or institutional affiliation when writing letters to the press. When Crick protested, realizing that the prohibition was directed against him and colleagues in the Department of Politics and Sociology, Marris sent an equally sharp response. Marris claimed that he had 'profound respect for Professor Crick as a scholar, colleague, and friend', but since he 'profoundly disagree[s] politically, [and] personally' with Crick's articles, added his weight to the prohibition.[76] It was a nasty ideological tiff, which was one factor in Crick taking early retirement.

In more recent years, the tension between pluralism and radicalism has come even more to the fore in university culture more generally. While both coexisted in the departments discussed in this chapter (and, indeed, at Birkbeck more generally) and even flourished in exchange with each other, post-Brexit Britain has seen a polarization of political discourse.

* * *

For these radicals, the role of intellectuals in forging more just, democratic, and fulfilling worlds was both a foundational belief and an animating principle. It was a response not only to the crises of the twentieth and twenty-first centuries but also to what they saw as the de-politicization of their disciplines or, more accurately, a de-radicalization of knowledge. They saw their role as not simply producing knowledge but contributing to the common good. Crucially, they saw this mission as that of the intellectual. Again, there was no agreement about the definition of the intellectual, but many would have been comfortable with the one popularized by Edward Said in *Representations of the Intellectual* (1994). Said maintained that

> The Intellectual is an individual endowed with a faculty for representing, embodying, articulating a message, a view, an attitude, a philosophy or opinion to, as well as for, a public. And this role has an edge to it. And cannot be played without a sense of being someone whose place it is publically [*sic*] to raise embarrassing questions, to confront orthodoxy and dogma (rather than to produce them), to be someone whose *raison d'être* is to represent all those people and issues that are routinely swept under the rug.[77]

The role of intellectuals was to speak the truth while correcting lies, to provide historical context, to remind people of who (and what) has been left out, and to expose underlying ideologies, as that other theorist of 'the intellectual', Noam

---

[75] Email from Ron Smith, 29 March 2018.
[76] Letter from Robin Marris to all Heads of Departments, the Chair of the Governors, and the Master, dated 3 February 1984, in Papers of Sir Bernard Crick, CRCK1/1/13.
[77] Edward Said, *Representations of the Intellectual: The Reith Lectures* (London: Vintage, 1996), 9.

Chomsky, expressed it.[78] During periods of history which are characterized by deliberate political disinformation and 'fake news'—sometimes disseminated by the most powerful people in the world—they believed that the role of the intellectual was needed more than ever. Although many of these radical intellectuals distanced themselves from the older, Marxist tradition in the College, they would have agreed with the sentiments with which Eric Hobsbawm concluded his autobiography. Hobsbawm hoped that reading his histories would help people

> to face the darkening prospects of the twenty-first century, not only with the requisite pessimism, but with a clearer eye, a sense of historical memory and a capacity to stand away from current passions and sales pitches.... Still, let us not disarm, even in unsatisfactory times. Social injustice still needs to be denounced and fought. The world will not get better on its own.[79]

---

[78] Noam Chomsky, 'The Responsibility of Intellectuals', in Chomsky, *American Power and the New Mandarins* (London: Penguin, 1969).

[79] Hobsbawm, *Interesting Times*, 418.

PART V
CLASSROOMS

21
Science in the World

> Terrible are the books,
> the mountains,
> the caverns of knowledge:
> matter made number,
> the exactness
> of the infinite...
>
> 'A Poem to J. D. Bernal', by Pablo Neruda[1]

The exploration of nature's foundational secrets has captivated students and scholars at the LMI/Birkbeck since 1823. The beauty of scientific data and images is undeniable: the patterns, symmetries, colours, and shapes of animate and inanimate matter unify science and aesthetics. Scientists not only uncover or reveal elemental mysteries but also are involved in mathematical and geometrical practices that *create* images of incredible splendour. From the study of nanoparticles to proteins, scientists at Birkbeck have transformed the way the world is perceived. Although this chapter takes as its staring point the achievements of specific individuals, its fundamental premise is drawn from the thinking of crystallographer J. D. Bernal: science is a social activity. The organic chemist Fred Barrow, who taught in the College for thirty-seven years from 1910, was fond of saying that 'theories change but the facts remain'.[2] He was only partially correct. The 'facts' also change through creative, collaborative, and egalitarian laboratory practices. This is why this chapter begins with the scientific revelations of Rosalind Franklin.

* * *

Franklin was a shy yet tenacious scientist. Since her death in 1958, however, she has been caricatured as 'the Sylvia Plath of molecular biology...a genius whose gifts were sacrificed to the greater glory of the male'.[3] The usual accounts of her life are reductive: they have become fused with stories about male scientists appropriating the work of their female colleagues; of prize committees

---

[1] Pablo Neruda, 'A Poem to J. D. Bernal', 1971, in *Tribute to John Desmond Bernal in his Seventieth Year, by Artists and Scientists* (Watford: Farleigh Press, 1971), n.p.
[2] D. J. G. Ives, 'Fred Barrow. 1882–1964', *Proceedings of the Chemical Society* (November 1964), 380.
[3] Brenda Maddox, 'The Double-Helix and the "Wronged Heroine"', *Nature*, 421 (23 January 2003), 407. Maddox argues against such caricatures.

overlooking the contributions of women scientists; of misogynistic men castigating their female counterparts for being 'bluestockings' and insufficiently deferential. Franklin's scientific life and achievements puncture assumptions about women in scientific disciplines. While not denying that female scientists are a minoritized group within the academy, this chapter also suggests that intelligence, hard work, and an inclusive laboratory culture mean that their marginalization is not inevitable.

Franklin was one of Birkbeck's most distinguished scientists. Physics and chemistry were life-long passions. She was born in Notting Hill in 1920, the daughter of a politically liberal, affluent British-Jewish family. At Newnham College, Cambridge, she read natural sciences, but, solely on account of her gender, was denied a degree. No matter what their grades, female students were refused degrees in Cambridge until 1948. With the declaration of war in 1939, Franklin threw her energies into the British Coal Utilization Research Association, a crucial job since the wartime economy was dependent upon this fuel. While based there, she studied why some carbons form graphite when heated. This research became the topic of her 1945 doctorate from the University of Cambridge. By the age of 26, Franklin had made her name as one of the most important coal chemists in the world.[4] She then spent four happy years working in the laboratory of crystallographer Jacques Mering in Paris, carrying out X-ray diffraction studies of the graphitization process.[5] This positive experience within the French scientific community gave her the confidence that enabled her to flourish in her later career.

This idyllic period ended in January 1951. John Randall, the Director of the Biophysics Laboratory at King's College London, invited Franklin to join his department to work on the structure of DNA. Unfortunately, another scientist—Maurice Wilkins—was also working in the department and, believing that Franklin was trampling on *his* territory, made life very uncomfortable for her. It was an unfortunate example of intellectual rivalry and truculence.

Despite Wilkins' opposition, Franklin single-mindedly dedicated herself to the job. By making radical changes to the systems used for taking high-resolution photographs of single fibres of DNA—she experimented with varying humidities—Franklin was able to show that there are two very different forms of DNA. She produced some of the most detailed images of DNA in both their 'A' and 'B' patterns. Without telling Franklin, Wilkins showed the X-ray pattern of the 'B' form to James Watson of Cambridge. In *The Double Helix*, Watson admitted that 'the instant I saw the picture my mouth fell open and my pulse began to

---

[4] Julie des Jardins, *The Marie Curie Complex: The Hidden World of Women in Science* (New York: Feminist Press, 2010), 182.

[5] Peter J. F. Harris, 'Rosalind Franklin's Work on Coal, Carbon, and Graphite', *Interdisciplinary Science Reviews*, 26.3 (autumn 2001), 205.

race'.⁶ Using her data, Watson and Francis Crick built the double-helix model of DNA. The world of science was transformed.

Meanwhile, things were getting more tense for Franklin in the laboratories at King's College London: when Birkbeck offered her a job running a research team, she was thrilled to accept. As soon as she arrived, she set about installing a more up-to-date diffraction apparatus and camera, then began researching the structure of the RNA virus Tobacco mosaic virus (TMV), so named because of the 'curling brittleness and mottled patches of light and dark green…that it caused on tobacco leaves'.⁷ She was delighted to be intellectually freed from the constraints of King's. Her work was valued, and not only by the rest of the department but increasingly internationally as well.

Admittedly, there were some disadvantages in moving to Birkbeck: its laboratories were inferior to those at King's, for example. In a letter to her friends, crystallographer David Sayre and author Anne Sayre, Franklin noted that 'Birkbeck is an improvement on King's, as it couldn't fail to be', adding that 'It's been very slow starting up there, but I still think it might work out all right in the end.'⁸ Her office was an attic-like, former maid's room on the fifth floor of an old house in Torrington Square. It had been bombed during the Second World War, so the roof leaked. When it rained, Franklin would scurry around arranging pots and beakers in strategic places. Furthermore, the X-ray equipment that was central to her research could only be accessed by walking down five floors, via a narrow staircase, to the basement. It was the opposite of her elegant apartment in Drayton Gardens, Chelsea.

Personality played a role: Franklin could be socially timid and abrupt. She was never a great conversationalist. According to one anecdote, when having lunch in Birkbeck's staff dining room one day, she 'plucked up the courage to comment, "It's a fine year for mushrooms", and lapsed into silence again'.⁹ Franklin was also critical of some aspects of the department, grumbling about the 'narrow-mindedness and obstruction directed especially at those who are not [Communist] Party members'.¹⁰ More annoying, to get funding for her group, she had to negotiate with Sir William Kershaw Slater, the Secretary of the Agricultural Research Council, who was not only misogynistic but anti-Semitic as well.¹¹

However, these challenges paled beside the immense intellectual freedoms and College support she received. For a young Jewish woman, Birkbeck was an agreeable contrast to King's College whose student body was dominated by its 400 male

---

⁶ James D. Watson and Gunther Siegmund Stent, *The Double Helix: A Personal Account of the Discovery of the Structure of DNA* (New York: Scribner, 1998), 167.
⁷ Brenda Maddox, *Rosalind Franklin: The Dark Lady of DNA* (London: HarperCollins, 2002), 229.
⁸ Letter to Anne and David Sayre, cited in Maddox, *Rosalind Franklin*, 231.
⁹ Maddox, *Rosalind Franklin*, 257.
¹⁰ Letter to Anne and David Sayre, cited in Maddox, *Rosalind Franklin*, 231.
¹¹ Carolyn Cohen, 'Restoring a Reputation', *Woman's Review of Books*, 20.2 (November 2020), 9.

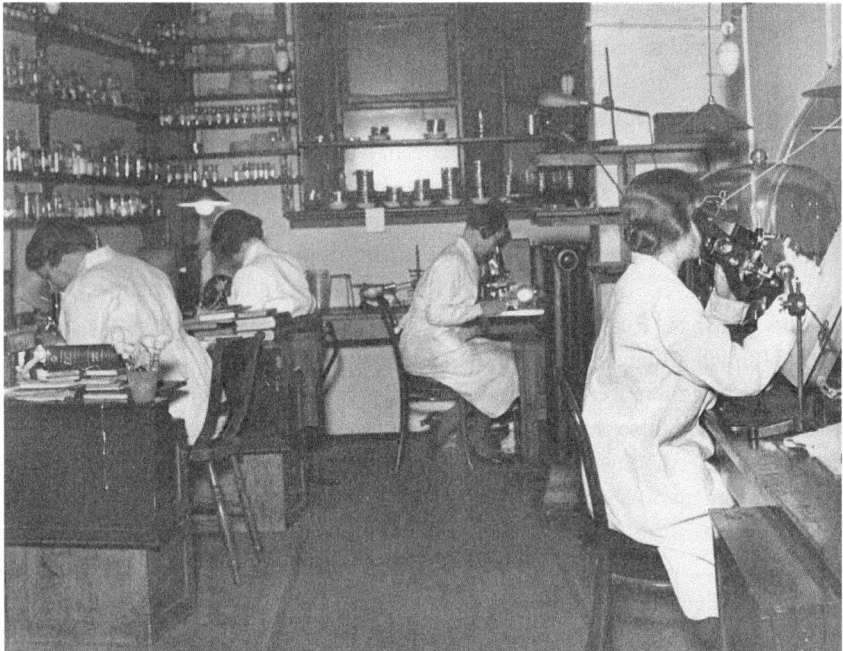

Fig. 21.1 Female students working in one of Birkbeck's laboratories. Birkbeck Image Collections: Birkbeck History BH0129.

Anglican ordinands, as well as a large number of male students who had served in the army. Worse: King's Senior Common Room was male-only.[12] In contrast, Birkbeck's Common Room was always 'mixed'.[13] The laboratories at Birkbeck were diverse, collaborative, and friendly (see Fig. 21.1). Bernal not only believed passionately in the intellectual equality of women but also was proactive in providing female scientists with the support they needed to flourish.

In such an environment, Franklin was able to build excellent working relationships with Birkbeck scientists such as electron microscopist John Thomas Finch and biophysicist Kenneth C. Holmes, as well as the Lithuanian-born, Jewish chemist and biophysicist Aaron Klug, who had joined her at Birkbeck in 1953, planning to work with Henry Carlisle. Klug later recalled his first meeting with Franklin. It was on the stairs of the laboratory in Torrington Square.[14] He was impressed by her attention to detail: 'she *noticed* everything', he later recalled. Klug contended that

---

[12] Sara Delamont, 'Rosalind Franklin and Lucky Jim: Misogyny in Two Cultures', *Social Studies of Science*, 33.2 (April 2003), 317.
[13] Marjorie Daunt, 'Marjorie on Birkbeck. Birkbeck 1915–1945', *The Lodestone*, 47.1 (1956), 7.
[14] Angela N. H. Creager and Gregory J. Morgan, 'After the Double Helix: Rosalind Franklin's Research on *Tobacco mosaic virus*', *Isis* (2008), 248.

The fact that she produced the best specimens of TMV wasn't due to chance, or simple mechanical skills. It's an art, doing this, it's a matter of the pains she takes, the way she nursed it, the keeping track of things, the *noticing*. That's how discoveries are made. And this was one of Rosalind's greatest gifts.[15]

Klug was becoming disillusioned with his work on Carlisle's project on the structure of ribonuclease and, being 'excited' by Franklin's 'beautiful diffraction patterns of TMV', he switched his research to viruses.[16] It was a decision that led to his winning the Nobel Prize twenty-nine years later.

Although Franklin has subsequently become known for her X-ray diffraction patterns of DNA, her intellectual energies at Birkbeck were channelled into understanding the three-dimensional structure of viruses. She established diffractional patterns of the TMV. She discovered that the RNA in that virus 'was embedded in its protein rather than in the central cavity and that TMV RNA was a single strand helix rather than the double helix found in the DNA of bacterial viruses and higher organisms'.[17] It was a momentous discovery. After all, DNA was 'not the only helix of significance' in the 1950s. Franklin's reputation soared: her model of the TMV was displayed at the international exhibition in Brussels, she lectured in the Royal Academy, and, in only four years, she produced seventeen scholarly papers.[18] By shifting attention to Franklin's virus research, we can appreciate fully her contributions to scientific knowledge.

Today, however, this influential work has been overshadowed by debates about her contribution to DNA discovery. Historians of science Angela N. H. Creager and Gregory J. Morgan explored *why* her 'work on RNA, TMV, and spherical viruses' had been 'so completely overshadowed in historical memory by the earlier DNA episode?', especially 'given the importance of these structural studies to molecular biology in the 1950s'.[19] There were four reasons. First, the 'pertinence of structural studies of viruses (as well as microsomes) to the genetic code ended in the 1960s; thereafter TMV and other well-studied viruses began to be viewed as models of self-assembly instead'. Second, scientists discovered that there was more than one type of RNA, including 'messenger RNA, transfer RNA, ribosomal RNA', all of which 'played distinct roles in protein synthesis, making viral RNA a less useful model for understanding the transcription and translation of genes'.[20] Third, Watson's popular *The Double Helix* shocked readers by its bitter misogyny. In it, Watson maintained that 'Rosy' (a name no one ever called her) would have

---

[15] Anne Sayre, *Rosalind Franklin and DNA*, 1st pub. 1975 (New York: W. W. Norton and Co., 2000), 177.
[16] Creager and Morgan, 'After the Double Helix', 248.
[17] Peter J. F. Harris, 'Rosalind Franklin's Work on Coal, Carbon, and Graphite', *Interdisciplinary Science Reviews*, 26.3 (autumn 2001), 205.
[18] 'Light on a Dark Lady', *Trends in Biochemical Sciences*, 23.4 (April 1998), 154.
[19] Creager and Morgan, 'After the Double Helix', 271.   [20] Ibid., 272.

'to go or be put in her place'. He caricatured her as 'unwomanly': he claimed she was a frump, sexually frustrated, and ugly. In fact, Franklin was an elegant, attractive sportswoman, mountain climber, and adventurer, who cultivated deep friendships. However, Watson's shocking allegations skewed discussions about female scientists towards questions of misogyny, and away from their actual achievements.

Finally, and perhaps most importantly, 'the double helix itself became a potent icon for molecular biology'.[21] As Creager and Morgan explained,

> This did not occur immediately in response to the appearance of Watson's and Crick's structural model for DNA but, rather, developed gradually...and the subsequent advent of both recombinant DNA techniques in the 1970s and the biotechnological industry in the 1980s gave the structure a wider circulation and cultural valence.[22]

Franklin's achievements, then, were side-lined for social, cultural, and symbolic reasons, rather than strictly scientific ones. Franklin died of ovarian cancer on 16 April 1958 before her contributions could be fully recognized. She was only 37 years old.

In his obituary, Bernal gave her credit for creating some of 'the most beautiful X-ray photographs of any substance ever taken'. Her scientific work was characterized by 'extreme clarity and perfection'.[23] Bernal also acknowledged something equally important: as with all forms of knowledge, scientific ideas don't emerge in a vacuum. Intellectual exchanges, teamwork, and international cooperation are key factors. Bernal praised Franklin for being 'an admirable director of a research team', who 'inspired those who worked with her to reach the same high standard'.[24] This had tangible outcomes. On 8 December 1982, a quarter of a century after Franklin died, Aaron Klug gave Franklin her due. During his lecture on being awarded the Nobel Prize in Chemistry, Klug explained to the distinguished assembly that

> In seeking to understand how proteins and nucleic acids interact, one has to begin with a particular problem, and I can claim no credit for the choice of my first subject, tobacco mosaic virus. It was the late Rosalind Franklin who introduced me to the study of viruses and whom I was lucky to meet when I joined J. D. Bernal's department in London in 1954.

---

[21] Ibid., 272.   [22] Ibid., 271–2.

[23] J. D. Bernal, 'Dr Rosalind E. Franklin', *Nature*, 182 (19 July 1958), at https://www.nature.com/articles/182154a0, viewed 2 May 2021 and reproduced in 'Dr. Rosalind Franklin', *London Times* (19 April 1958), 3.

[24] Ibid., 3.

It was Franklin, he maintained, who 'set me the example of tackling large and difficult problems. Had her life not been cut tragically short, she might well have stood in this place on an earlier occasion'.[25]

Today, Franklin's photograph hangs alongside those of Watson, Crick, and Wilkins in the National Portrait Gallery. Despite the disgraceful way she felt she had been treated at King's College London, it has subsequently seen fit to commemorate her by naming a building after her. Unfortunately, the Franklin–Wilkins Building ties Franklin to one of her persecutors. More happily, the Institute of Physics has a 'Rosalind Franklin Room' and awards a Rosalind Franklin Medal for distinguished contributions to physics applied to the life sciences, as does the Royal Society.

Franklin is interred in the family plot at Willesden United Synagogue Cemetery. On her tombstone are the words,

HER RESEARCH AND DISCOVERIES ON IRUSES REMAIN OF LASTING BENEFIT TO MANKIND

These words are followed by the Hebrew initials for 'her soul shall be bound in the bundle of life'.

* * *

Rosalind Franklin's scientific career flourished thanks to the fact that J. D. Bernal (see Fig. 21.2) recognized her talents and, from 1953, mentored her career. Bernal had been appointed Professor of Physics at Birkbeck in 1937 and, in 1965, founded the Department of Crystallography (see Fig. 21.3). For many years, he was head of both departments, an arduous and ultimately impossible task.

In Chapter 19, Bernal's politics and activism in leftist and peace movements were discussed. These parts of his life are pivotal to any understanding of his academic career, as we will see, but there is a risk that by focusing on Bernal's *politics*, his contributions to scientific *scholarship* become side-lined. His leadership in the Crystallography and Physics Departments was responsible for some of the most important scientific advances of the mid-twentieth century. Its contribution was decisive in the development of molecular science.

Bernal took up the post of Professor of Physics at Birkbeck on 1 January 1938. At that time, it was a tiny department, consisting of only one Reader and three lecturers.[26] It was housed in a small, poorly equipped space in Bream's Building. Physicist Otto Robert Frisch, who had fled Germany in 1933 and worked with Patrick Maynard Stuart Blackett at Birkbeck on cloud chamber technology and

---

[25] Aaron Klug, 'From Micromolecules to Biological Assemblies. Nobel Lecture, 8 December 1982', at https://www.nobelprize.org/nobel_prizes/chemistry/laureates/1982/klug-lecture.pdf, viewed 1 May 2021.
[26] Hodgkin, 'John Desmond Bernal', 52.

Fig. 21.2 J. D. Bernal, Irene Joliot-Curie, Frederic Joliot-Curie, and C. V. Ramon. Birkbeck Image Collections: Birkbeck History BH0028.

artificial radioactivity (as discussed in Chapter 19), recalled the financial strictures. He maintained that the laboratory

> had very little provision for instrumentation and none of the sort of rather pedantic tidiness that was the usual thing in Germany. I found after a while that my imagination to think up experiments was cramped when I felt that any experiment that required a rubber tube three feet long was impossible, because the only rubber tube we had in the lab was one foot and two inches.... I had to go to the lab steward who considered it an extravagance to buy an extra piece of rubber tube. If there were things one could buy at Woolworth's, I just bought them myself out of my own pocket.... Pencil caps for counters... I made my geiger counters out of pencil caps.[27]

Indeed, Bernal's room was nothing more than a 'small cupboard on the top floor in the corner of a large laboratory for his students'.[28] This was where he continued the research on proteins and viruses that he had started at the University of Cambridge.[29] He was assisted by Isidor Fankuchen (known to friends as 'Fan'),

---

[27] Cited in Nye, *Blackett*, 55.   [28] Hodgkin, 'John Desmond Bernal', 52.
[29] J. D. Bernal, 'Teaching and Research at Birkbeck College Crystallography Laboratory' (October 1962), 1, in 'Guard Book. Ib', in the Birkbeck Archive.

Fig. 21.3 J. D. Bernal and the Crystallography Department at the Royal Institution Faraday Laboratory where they were temporarily housed after the Second World War, 1946. Front row from left: Anita Rimmell, Werner Ehrenberg, J. D. Bernal, Helen Megaw, Harry C. Carlisle. Back row from left: Sam Levene, Jim Jeffery, Stefan Peiser, Geoffrey Pitt, and Helen Scoulaudi (who was the first foreign research student, from Greece). Birkbeck Image Collections: Birkbeck History BH0179.

who worked on the X-ray structure of chymotrypsin and haemoglobin, and Carlisle, whose favourite mantra was 'all vectors to a common origin'.[30]

Their work was interrupted by the war: bombs destroyed their laboratory, although most of their equipment was saved. When they returned from war-work, their research recommenced with support from the Nuffield Foundation. They devoted themselves to studying 'the application of physical methods to the understanding and reactions of molecules in biological systems'.[31] This 'organics' or biomolecular section was directed by Carlisle. The 'inorganic section', which was largely concerned with the structure and properties of cement and concrete, was financially supported by the Department of Scientific and Industrial Research (DSIR).[32] Although cement might seem an unusual focus for a biomolecular

---

[30] Anthony Michael Glazer, *Crystallography: A Very Short Introduction* (Oxford: Oxford University Press, 2016), 101.
[31] Bernal, 'Teaching and Research at Birkbeck College Crystallography Laboratory'.
[32] Ibid.

laboratory, it reflected Bernal's interests in 'matter as a whole', as well as his view that 'the properties of hydrated cements are closely related to those of many biological gels and are strongly influenced by the same long range forces'.[33] Initially, this inorganic research was directed by Helen Megaw, who studied ferroelectricity and whose work on the structure of ice led to the Antarctic island of Megaw being named after her, then Herbert Steffan Peiser, followed by Jim Jeffery.[34] The 'pure physics section' was run by Werner Ehrenberg, who worked on the development of X-ray tubes.[35] Finally, Bernal quickly recognized the incredible usefulness of early computing, so enlisted the talents of Andrew Booth to set up a small computing section. This was to become crucial for crystallography and, in 1957, the computer section under Booth became an independent sub-department of the College (see Chapter 23).[36]

Initially, this relatively small team worked in the laboratories of the Royal Institution and then in labs provided by the Medical Research Council. In 1948, when 21-2 Torrington Square became available, they moved in and built an annexe in an old static water tank. As Bernal described it, when they moved into Torrington Square, the builders were still working on the upper floors, there was no water or gas, and they had to deal with a 'very precarious supply of electricity'.[37] On 1 July 1948, the building was opened by Lawrence Bragg, who was then Director of the Cavendish Laboratory in Cambridge and is still the world's youngest ever Nobel Prize laureate in Physics.[38] It was part of Bernal's dream of establishing an 'Institute for the Study of Things'![39]

From 1948, this small department introduced an MSc in crystallography, an intercollegiate course that was taught at Birkbeck in the evenings.[40] It was one of only two advanced teaching departments in the field in Britain (the other was in Cambridge).[41] Between 1949 and 1962, fifty-sixth students were awarded the MSc in crystallography—that is, an average of four every year.[42] To these students, Bernal always emphasized the importance of crystallography to science as well as the modern world. As he put it, the 'elucidation of the structure and function of the nucleic acids' was a 'major breakthrough in the mechanisms of reproduction in biology'. In fact, it was 'one of the most important discoveries of the twentieth century'.[43]

Crucially, Bernal was a generous facilitator of other people's ideas. Indeed, he had trained both Watson and Crick, who went on to win the Nobel Prize. When

---

[33] Christopher Surridge, '50 Years of Biomolecular Structure at Birkbeck: Bernal's Legacy', *Nature Structural Biology*, 6.1 (January 1999), 13.
[34] Bernal, 'Teaching and Research at Birkbeck College Crystallography Laboratory'.
[35] Ibid.   [36] Ibid.   [37] Ibid.
[38] For details, see Sir Lawrence Bragg, *Opening of Biomolecular Research Laboratory, 21-2 Torrington Square, London, W. C. 1* (London: Birkbeck College, 1948).
[39] Hodgkin, 'John Desmond Bernal', 59.
[40] Bernal, 'Teaching and Research at Birkbeck College Crystallography Laboratory'.
[41] Ibid.   [42] Ibid.   [43] Ibid.

SCIENCE IN THE WORLD   417

Fig. 21.4   J. D. Bernal and Dorothy Hodgkin. Birkbeck Image Collections: Birkbeck History BH0024.

Dorothy Crowfoot Hodgkin of Oxford University won the Nobel Prize in 1964 for solving the chemical structure of vitamin B, the antidote to pernicious anaemia, she publicly announced that she should have shared it with Bernal (see Fig. 21.4).[44] Bernal was also a dedicated teacher. Birkbeck's 'mission' was crucial for him. As he noted in 1962, the 'rapid pace of modern life' was creating a situation in which 'a man [sic] would have to change his profession several times in his lifetime'. This was why 'education must continue throughout life', a factor that 'must be considered in organizing education'.[45] His lectures were renowned for their intellectual depth and witty breadth. According to Jeffery, he sprinkled his talks with anecdotes about

> the Emperor of China who had to get up at four o'clock every morning to enable the sun to rise; Galileo managing to get a large reward for his telescope, before a supply of cheap ones arrived from Amsterdam; the reason why it was twitching frogs' legs which led Galvani to the discovery of animal electricity.[46]

When he died in 1971, he left his income from copyright and royalties jointly to Anita Rimel (his secretary and one of his many lovers) and his laboratory assistant, Francis Aprahamian (whom we met in the Chapter 19). The remainder of his property was left to relatives.[47]

* * *

If Bernal was the 'Sage' who mentored the intellects of some of the brightest scientific stars in the world, then David (Dave) Bohm was the Pistol Star in the

---

[44] Lynn Margulis, '[Review of] J. D. Bernal: A Life in Science and Politics by Brenda Swann and Francis Aprahamian', *Science, Technology and Human Values*, 25.2 (spring 2000), 252.
[45] 'Russian Prediction of Power from the Moon', *The Times* (10 September 1962), 10.
[46] Prof. J. W. Jeffrey, 'Bernal's Lectures', *Morning Star* (1 March 1972) in the Birkbeck Archive.
[47] '£47,758 Will', *Camden Journal* (28 January 1972), in the Birkbeck Archive.

physicists' galaxy. He had been a graduate student of J. Robert Oppenheimer at Berkeley and a protégé of Albert Einstein at Princeton.[48] During his lifetime, Bohm was a serious contender for the Nobel Prize and is still widely thought to be one of the greatest physicists of the twentieth century for his pioneering work in the theoretical aspects of quantum mechanics. He remains the chief proponent of quantum mechanics, offering an alternative interpretation which is still being explored today.[49]

As with Bernal, the Communist Party changed his life—although for very different reasons. Bohm had been member for nine months in 1942–3 but left because he found party meetings 'interminable' and was disillusioned by the infighting.[50] However, Cold War politics meant he was tainted by even such a short membership. He was denied security clearance to work at Los Alamos on the atomic bomb project and refused to give evidence before the House Un-American Activities Committee. The President of Princeton, where Bohm was working in the 1940s, was Harold W. Dodds, a fervent anti-communist. In March 1949, Dodds gave a speech in which he argued that communists surrendered 'the rights as persons, made in the image of God', since they had 'submit[ted] to such slavery of bodies, minds and souls'.[51] Believing that they were unfit to teach, Dodds ensured that Bohm was stripped of all his responsibilities and barred from the campus, despite the fact that the Supreme Court eventually cleared him of contempt. In 1951, Bohm fled the USA. In 1961, after many unsatisfactory years working in physics departments in São Paulo, Haifa, and Bristol, Bohm was appointed Professor of Theoretical Physics at Birkbeck, where he remained until he retired in 1987.

Bohm's ideas were theoretically complex. It is impossible to do justice to his ideas in so few paragraphs but they can be summarized under three main headings: plasma physics, the Aharonov–Bohm effect, and 'quantum entanglement'. He laid the foundations for the modern understanding of plasma, the gas of ions and electrons, and developed a mathematical formula to explain how, as free particles, electrons could coordinate their movements. The Aharonov–Bohm effect was particularly important because it showed that the 'interference pattern of electrons in a multiply connected region can be influenced by magnetic fields outside that region'.[52] 'Quantum entanglement' was equally a fundamental challenge to classical physics. Bohm argued that quantum theory predicted 'entanglement': two entangled particles appear to have a 'direct interaction between them'

---

[48] Olival Freire, 'Science and Exile: David Bohm, the Cold War, and a New Interpretation of Quantum Mechanics', *Historical Studies in the Physical and Biological Sciences*, 36.1 (2005), 2.

[49] Basil J. Hiley, 'The Early History of the Aharonov–Bohm Effect', *History and Philosophy of Physics* (7 April 2013), 13.

[50] Alexei Kojevnikov, 'David Bohm and Collective Movement', *Historical Studies in the Physical and Biological Sciences*, 33.1 (2002), 164.

[51] Cited in Russell Olwell, 'Physical Isolation and Marginalization in Physics: David Bohm's Cold War Exile', *Isis*, 90.4 (December 1999), 744.

[52] Joseph Samuel, 'The Aharonov–Bohm Effect', *Current Science*, 66.10 (25 May 1994), 781.

irrespective of their distance apart.[53] Bohm's quantum potential contained 'within it information on the physical situation over a wide region of space. In principle it encodes information on the whole universe.' This meant that 'as the system changes', so too the 'relation between two particulars in the system change'.[54] The crucial difference was that, while classical physics paid attention to the 'microscopic world of the atom and smaller', Bohm and his long-term collaborator Basil Hiley suggested that quantum laws applied equally to the macroscopic world.[55]

Bohm's worldview, then, was fundamentally a critique of Cartesian dualism, in which consciousness or thought was distinct from matter. Descartes had postulated that God was the force that facilitated relationships between mind and matter. For Bohm, however, there was no dichotomy between consciousness and the physical world: the two could not be distinguished because they were 'enfolded' into each other in one single movement. In Bohm's words, 'we do not say that mind and body causally affect each other, but rather that the movements of both are the outcome of related projections of a common higher-dimensional ground'.[56] Because of this fundamental entanglement, it was wrong to speak of the world in terms of 'the' or 'it'. According to Bohm's quantum physics, the only correct way to speak about the world was to avoid all nouns and to use only verbs, connoting temporality, movement, and processes over time. Bohm called this verb-based language 'rheomode', from the Greek *rheo-*, to flow. In his words,

> the notion of a permanent object with well defined properties can no longer be taken as basic in physics.... Rather, it is necessary to begin with the event as a basic concept, and later to arrive at the object as a continuing structure of related and ordered events.[57]

Bohm was also deeply engaged with science *in the world*. During a conversation with physicist F. David Peat, Bohm insisted that intellectuals needed to reconsider what they meant by 'science': he called for a 'creative surge along new lines'. Like Bernal, who lamented that one of the most damaging aspects of the modern world was the 'rigid separation of human functions into different spheres'[58]—that is, radical specialization—Bohm blamed fragmented thinking about the problems of the environment (to take one example) for the 'destruction of forests and agricultural lands', deserts, and 'the melting of the ice caps'. He lamented the fact that too many scientists believed that the solution could be found in the study of

---

[53] Kevin J. Sharpe, *David Bohm's World: New Physics and New Religion* (Lewisburg: Bucknell University Press, 1993), 24.
[54] Ibid., 24. [55] Ibid., 24.
[56] Bohm, quoted in Ted Peters, *Science, Theology, and Ethics* (Aldershot: Ashgate, 2003), 108.
[57] David J. Bohm, *Problems in the Basic Concepts of Physics: An Inaugural Lecture Delivered at Birkbeck College 1963* (London: J. W. Ruddock and Sons, 1963), 6.
[58] J. D. Bernal, 'Art and the Scientist', in J. L. Martin, Ben Nicholson, and N. Gabo (eds), *Circle: International Survey of Constructive Art* (London: Faber and Faber Ltd, 1937), 119.

ecology. While not denying the contributions of that discipline, Bohm maintained that 'the problem is as much one of politics, and of the structure of society and the nature of human beings in general'. What was required to solve global problems was 'goodwill and friendliness', which was 'lacking today, among scientists as much as in the general public'.[59] It was a statement that could have come directly from the mouth of Bernal.

Although Bohm retired in 1987, he continued to work in the College, finishing the writing of a co-authored book with Hiley.[60] When *The Undivided Universe: An Ontological Interpretation of Quantum Theory* was published in 1993, however, Bohm was already dead.[61] In this book, Bohm and Hiley made a case for the '*undivided wholeness* of the measuring instrument and the observed object'. What this meant was that

> it is no longer appropriate, in measurements to a quantum level of accuracy, to say that we are simply 'measuring' an intrinsic property of the observed system. Rather what actually happens is that the process of interaction reveals a property involving the whole context in an inseparable way. Indeed it may be said that the measuring apparatus and that which is observed *participate irreducibly* in each other, so that the ordinary classical and common sense idea of measurement is no longer relevant.[62]

The book generated an excited debate that continues to this day.[63] In 1992, the year of his death, Bohm was being considered as a candidate for the Nobel Prize in honour of his work on 'the connectedness of apparently unrelated phenomena'.[64] Indeed, many scholars contend that it is 'a matter of acute embarrassment for the international community' that Bohm was not awarded the Nobel Prize since the 'groundbreaking significance' of his work had been recognized before he died.[65] Like Franklin, he died too soon.

* * *

Similar to Bernal, Bohm was a collaborative scientist, revelling in exchanging ideas with people from physics, crystallography, mathematics, politics, literature,

---

[59] 'From Science, Order, and Creativity', conversation with F. David Peat, undated, in the Bohm Archive, Box A43.
[60] B. J. Hiley, 'Professor David Bohm', *The Independent* (30 October 1992).
[61] David Bohm and Basil J. Hiley, *The Undivided Universe: An Ontological Interpretation of Quantum Theory* (London: Routledge, 1993).
[62] Ibid., 6.
[63] For just two examples, see Sheldon Goldstein, 'Review: Bohmian Mechanics and the Quantum Revolution', *Synthese*, 107.1 (April 1996), 145–65; Daniel M. Greenberger, '[Review] The Undivided Universe', *Science*, 266.5182 (7 October 1994), 147–8.
[64] 'David Bohm', *Daily Telegraph* (3 November 1992), in the Bohm Archive, Box 1A.
[65] Kent A. Peacock, '[Review] From Physics to Metaphysics by Michael Redhead', *Canadian Journal of Philosophy*, 28.2 (June 1998), 300.

and art. Roger Penrose was one of the College's scholars with whom Bohm and Hiley discussed such issues on an almost weekly basis.[66] Only 33 years old when he was appointed as a Reader (and then Professor) of Mathematics in 1964, Penrose was a leading person in the College's community until he left nine years later. He later recalled the incredible impression that Bohm made upon him. He maintained that

> Bohm always struck me as a bit like a wave function. You'd ask a question and he would zero right on that and give you a very profound, perceptive answer, and then he would begin to spread out and cover more and more of the universe, and then I would lose track of where he was going.[67]

A few years before being appointed at Birkbeck, Penrose had devised the Penrose Triangle (Tribar) and, along with his father Lionel Penrose (who was the Galton Chair of Human Genetics at UCL), the Penrose Staircase. Penrose Tiling is 'a non-periodic tiling whereby any given surface may be tiled to infinity using only two interlocking elements (shapes known as the dart and the kite) yet never precisely repeating the pattern'. These were 'impossible objects' because they represented three-dimensional structures that could not actually exist. In Penrose's words, they were 'impossibility in its purest form'. Such structures were to become important in the research of Alan MacKay, another influential crystallographer at Birkbeck. In 1977, they enabled Mackay to frame his theory that 'there could exist crystals displaying a comparable non-periodicity to Penrose tiling' which, four years later, led to his theoretical (mathematical-structural) discovery of 'quasicrystals'. In MacKay's words,

> The recognition of hierarchical structures in quasicrystals has broadened the horizons of what is possible. Many questions arise from the origin of life and the evolution of the genetic code, the operation of the brain, etc. but all these are to be answered by the methods of science rather than from the ruminations of academic philosophers. Serious philosophical questions arise at the level of chemistry.[68]

He loved to quote Einstein's statement that 'The human mind has first to construct forms, independently, before we can find them in things'.[69] It wasn't until

---

[66] Roger Penrose, 'Space-Time Quantum Non Locality: Does Palatial Tristor Theory Suggest an Objective Mathematical Framework?', Fetzer Franklin Fund, at https://www.fetzer-franklin-fund.org/media/space-time-quantum-non-locality-roger-penrose-video/, viewed 22 April 2021.
[67] Ibid.
[68] A. L. MacKay, 'Lucretius or the Philosophy of Chemistry', *Colloids and Surfaces A: Physicochemical and Engineering Aspects* (1997), 310.
[69] Ibid., 307.

1982 that Dan Shechtman became the first scientist to discover an *actual* quasi-crystal, for which he won the Nobel Prize in Chemistry in 2011.

Penrose had overlapping intellectual interests with Bohm, Hiley, and MacKay. As Hiley explained, Penrose's dissatisfaction with quantum field theory 'fitted in well with our own proposals of building spacetime from a discrete structure-process'. For Bohm and Hiley, 'the basic element was the "relationship" or "connection", which we represented by the one-simplex of an abstract simplicial complex, whereas for Penrose it was the light ray'.[70] They were curious about the paradox or puzzle of space-time. They rejected the Copenhagen Interpretation of quantum mechanics and sought to develop non-mechanistic consciousness-related processes. Penrose maintained that standard, non-relativistic quantum mechanics could be defended on two grounds. First, experimental results support it and, second, ('and it seems to me almost as important') 'it is a theory of astonishing and profound mathematical beauty'.[71] Penrose combined quantum mechanics with consciousness and gravity. For Bohm and Hiley, the emphasis was on the implicate order while Penrose focused on space. For Penrose in particular, non-computability was crucial to his thinking. Very early during his time at Birkbeck, he was influenced by Bohm's version of the Einstein–Podolsky–Rosen paradox, arguing that it showed that 'you did need something non-local to describe how nature behaved'.[72] As a result, Penrose developed his 'twistors' theory or a non-local description of massless quantum particles, which was also what Bohm and Hiley had been working on. As Penrose argued in *The Road to Reality: A Complete Guide to the Laws of the Universe* (2004), one

> guiding principle behind twistor theory is quantum *non-locality*. We recall from the strange EPR effects... and more specifically from the role of 'quanglement' [quantum entanglement], as manifest particularly in the phenomenon of quantum teleportation... that physical behavior cannot be fully understood in terms of entirely local influences of the normal 'causal' character. This suggests that some theory is needed in which such non-local features are incorporated.[73]

His 'twistors' theory was to become influential. As Hiley laughingly noted, 'my contribution to twistors was how to spell it!' Penrose had been explaining to Bohm and Hiley his 'twistor's' theory but admitted that he did not know whether

---

[70] Basil J. Hiley, 'David Joseph Bohm, 20 December 1917–27 October 1992', *Biographical Memoirs of Fellows of the Royal Society*, 43 (November 1997), 118.
[71] Roger Penrose, 'Gravity and State Vector Reduction', in Roger Penrose and C. J. Isham (eds), *Quantum Concepts in Space and Time* (Oxford: Clarendon Press, 1986), 129.
[72] Penrose, 'Space-Time Quantum Non Locality'.
[73] Roger Penrose, *The Road to Reality: A Complete Guide to the Laws of the Universe* (London: Jonathan Cape, 2004), 963.

it should be spelt 'E-R or O-R'. Hiley was definite: 'O-R', because 'Twist*ers*' was a party game!⁷⁴

Penrose's collaboration with Stephen Hawking also began while he was at Birkbeck. In 1970, they demonstrated that a singularity applied to the origin of the whole universe in the Big Bang. This work with Hawking continued when he left for the University of Oxford in 1973. In 1988, Penrose and Hawking were awarded the Wolf Foundation Prize in Physics, the most prestigious award in physics after the Nobel Prize.

During his time in Birkbeck's Department of Mathematics, however, the most significant research that Penrose completed was the publication of 'Gravitational Collapse and Space-Time Singularities' (1965). This world-shattering article proved that a singularity in space-time will occur in a gravitational collapse of a massive star.⁷⁵ It 'revolutionized the mathematical tools that we use to analyze the properties of spacetime'.⁷⁶

In later years, Penrose recalled how the idea came to him. As he explained in *The Emperor's New Mind*, a colleague

> was engaging me in voluble conversation on a quite different topic as we walked down the street approaching my office in Birkbeck College in London. The conversation stopped momentarily as we crossed a side road, and resumed again at the other side. Evidently during those few moments, an idea occurred to me, but in the ensuing conversation blotted it from my mind!

Later that day he remembered

> having an odd feeling of elation that I could not account for. I began going through in my mind all the various things that had happened to me... in an attempt to find what it was that had caused this elation. After eliminating numerous inadequate possibilities, I finally brought to mind the thought I had while crossing the street—a thought that had momentarily elated me by providing the solution to the problem that had been milling around at the back of my head! Apparently, it was the needed criterion—that I subsequently called a trapped surface—and then it did not take me long to form the outline of a proof of the theorem that I had been looking for.⁷⁷

---

⁷⁴ Basil Hiley interviewed by George Musser, 'The Wholeness of Quantum Reality: An Interview with Physicist Basil Hiley', *Scientific American* (4 November 2013), at https://blogs.scientificamerican.com/critical-opalescence/the-wholeness-of-quantum-reality-an-interview-with-physicist-basil-hiley/, viewed 22 April 2021. Penrose denies that this discussion took place, but Hiley insists it did: personal communication from Hiley.
⁷⁵ Roger Penrose, 'Gravitational Collapse and Space-Time Singularities', *Physical Review Letters*, 14.3 (18 January 1965), 57-9.
⁷⁶ Kip Thorne (Caltech) in 'Roger Penrose, 1931-', Jewish Virtual Library, at https://www.jewishvirtuallibrary.org/roger-penrose, viewed 1 March 2021.
⁷⁷ Roger Penrose, *The Emperor's New Mind: Concerning Computers, Minds, and the Laws of Physics* (Oxford: Oxford University Press, 1989), 543-4.

This was the work for which he was awarded the Nobel Prize in Physics in 2020. The Nobel Prize Committee noted that Penrose's article is 'regarded as the most important contribution to the general theory of relativity since Einstein'. They noted that 'black holes hide a singularity in which all the known laws of nature cease'. They were an inevitable consequence of Einstein's General Theory of Relativity.

* * *

How can we explain the incredible scientific and mathematical research carried out at Birkbeck? Obviously, it was due to the intellectual genius of the scholars. But scientific advances do not emerge in a vacuum. Other crucial factors can be summarized under four headings: the nature of the student body; the culture of internationalism; a belief in the power of science to change the world; and an engrained culture of collaboration, curiosity, and egalitarianism.

First, it is important not to underestimate the productive interplay between research and teaching. This was what attracted physicist Reinhold Furth, who specialized in theoretical problems of cosmic physics and the philosophy of Niels Bohr, to the Department of Physics at Birkbeck in 1947. In 1954, Furth praised the fact that a large proportion of the physics students who chose to attend evening classes at graduate level in the College were working either in technical firms or as science teachers. This meant that 'they know rather more about certain aspects of their subject than the average student of physics, and it is therefore possible to restrict the courses more or less to the systematic teaching of the fundamental principles of experimental and theoretical physics'.[78] For a Professor of Theoretical Physics, there could be no better environment.

Second, the internationalism of Birkbeck's science community was also crucial in advancing intellectual ideas. The three departments of Crystallography, Physics, and Mathematics are rightly celebrated for their cosmopolitan cultures. They were not alone, however. The Department of Chemistry was similarly internationalist in its outlook and composition. For example, Robert A. Shaw is one of the world's leading experts on phosphazenes, a group of cyclic and acyclic phosphorus–nitrogen compounds that he was responsible for naming. He forged international research collaborations with scholars in Bangladesh, Canada, France, Germany, India, Italy, the Netherlands, Poland, Turkey, the UK, and the USA. By the late 1960s and early 1970s, the Department of Chemistry's links were especially deep with the University Institute of Chemistry at the University of Punjab.[79] The research was not only theoretical but applied as well, since 'highly

---

[78] Reinhold Furth, *The Physics Department of Birkbeck College (University of London)* (London: Institute of Physics, July 1954), 4.

[79] Letter from the Clerk to Lord Blackett, 14 July 1971, in 'Departmental Correspondence Pre-1986. Chemistry', in Birkbeck Archive, Box 8, and 'Proposal for a Joint Research Project between the

concentrated fertilizers' could increase crops by up to 40 per cent.[80] The Department of Chemistry could also boast about its intellectual pedigree, having been home to organic chemist Derek Barton, who arrived at Birkbeck in 1950 and left five years later. In his first year in the College, he published 'The Conformation of the Steroid Nucleus' in *Experientia*, which showed how the reactivity of functional groups in steroids depends on their axial or equatorial positions in a given conformation. This work (which was only four pages long because, he confessed, he had to type it himself) earned him the Nobel Prize in Chemistry in 1969.[81]

Third, much of the research being carried out in the science disciplines at Birkbeck was the result of the incredible energy generated by a realization that intellectual passions could have meaningful and positive effects on the world. Science has been responsible for much of the atrocious violence that has plagued the modern world. But scientists at Birkbeck have been acutely aware of its potential for good. Bernal made the case most starkly, maintaining that

> the scientist is very directly affected by the social organization of which he is a part, and that he *must* therefore be directly concerned with the great political struggles of the present day.[82]

The 'immunity' of the so-called 'pure sciences' from politics was 'very superficial', he contended, which was why engagement with the problems of the world was essential.[83]

Finally, knowledge flourishes in egalitarian, collaborative environments. The most successful laboratories were headed by senior scholars who actively mentored their colleagues. This was recognized at Birkbeck from the beginning of the twentieth century. Fred Barrow, known affectionately as a 'walking Beilstein', taught in the Chemistry Department for thirty-seven years from 1910 (see Fig. 21.5).[84] He maintained that the growth in student numbers as well as the department's reputation was largely due to the mentoring of both staff and students. In a speech celebrating a quarter of a century in the department, he proudly proclaimed that his job entailed getting 'to know his students very well', including advising them 'on a variety of subjects, varying from where to find digs to the solution of domestic troubles!'[85] It was a practice endorsed when Shaw took over as the head of the Chemistry Department. In his words,

---

Department of Chemistry, Birkbeck College (University of London), and the University Institute of Chemistry, University of Punjab, Lahore', 1, c.1969/70, in Birkbeck Archive, Box 8.

[80] Ibid. [81] 'Professor Sir Derek Barton', an oration by Michael Slater, personal papers.
[82] J. D. Bernal, 'The Frustration of Science', in Bernal, *The Frustration of Science* (London: George Allen and Unwin, 1935), 130.
[83] Ibid., 131.
[84] D. J. G. Ives, 'Fred Barrow, 1882–1964', *Proceedings of the Chemical Society* (November 1964), 379.
[85] 'F. J. B.', 'Dr Barrow's Jubilee', *The Lodestone*, 31.2 (spring 1936), 74.

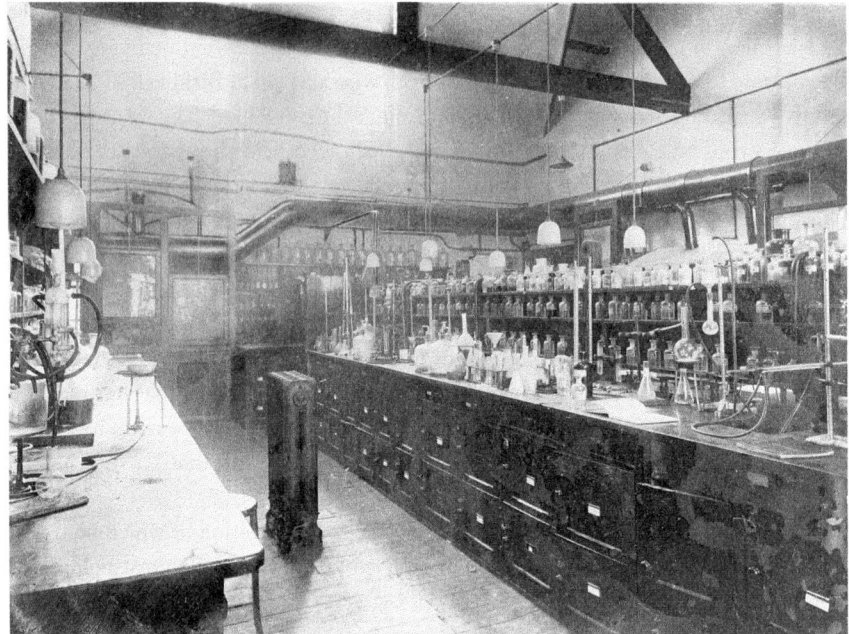

Fig. 21.5 Chemistry laboratory in Bream's Building, 1923. Birkbeck Image Collections: Birkbeck History BH0006.

If a member of my team had worries, be they financial, health, accommodation, emotional or a whole host of others, his performance will inevitably suffer.... What has been my response to these stress problems?... It was pastoral care in the widest sense.... I expected hard and dedicated work from my team. But, in turn, I felt responsible not only for their scientific education and training, but also for their wider cultural and educational nourishment, as well as their health, financial and emotional welfare.[86]

Similarly, the distinguished biological physicist Tom Blundell, Professor of Crystallography between 1976 and 1995 when he accepted the Sir William Dunn Professorship of Biochemistry at the University of Cambridge, was as committed to teamwork, multidisciplinary research, and racial and gender equality as was Bernal, his predecessor. It was, Blundell insisted, the only way that some of the most important issues in protein structure would be uncovered. It was this frame

---

[86] Robert A. Shaw, 'The Bangalore–Birkbeck Phosphazene Project, 1971–1981: A Retrospective on This and Other International and Interdisciplinary Scientific Research Collaborations', *Current Science*, 107.11 (10 December 2014), 1906.

of mind that led Blundell to encourage colleagues to bring their children into the laboratories and, if they chose, to work part time, both of which were very uncommon at the time—a fact that was responsible for considerable discrimination against female scientists. Blundell's policy enabled gifted scientists like Janet Thornton to flourish. Thornton joined Blundell's laboratory in 1979, where she stayed for eleven years. Thornton not only became expert at 'balancing the chaos of proteins with the chaos of children' but also became one of the founders of structural bioinformatics or on how structure affects the function of proteins.[87] Other female scientists—such as biomolecular scientist Julia Goodfellow, who was a professor at Birkbeck between 1995 and 2002, and went on to become the first woman to lead a UK Research Council (the Biotechnology and Biological Sciences Research Council)—also benefited by being allowed to combine motherhood with a career.

This ethos helps explain why Birkbeck has been the home of so many influential female scientists, such as Franklin. It is important to recognize that these academic disciplines were not generally supportive of women elsewhere. A majority of male professors in science were hostile or unwelcoming to female scientists. After all, it took forty years of activism by female scientists and their allies between 1880 and 1920 before the Chemical Society would even admit women as full members.[88] Many learned societies and laboratories created a subtly 'chilly climate' for female scientists, often through 'microinequities' that, when piled one on top of the other, formed barriers to scientific advancement.

The discrimination that Franklin experienced from her male colleagues in King's was not unusual for the time. Take June Sutor, who worked in the laboratories of Bernal, Franklin, and Klug from 1959 and became one of the first scientists to show that hydrogen bonds could form to hydrogen atoms bonded to carbon atoms. Her article proving this was published in *Nature* in 1962, with an expanded follow-up the following year in the *Journal of the Chemistry Society*.[89] However, her work was wrongly attacked by Jerry Donohue, who had shared an office with James Watson and Francis Crick and was considered the hydrogen-bond expert.[90] Although with much less justification when compared with

---

[87] Nick Zagorski, 'Profile of Janet Thornton', *Proceedings of the National Academy of Sciences of the United States*, 102.35 (30 August 2005), 12,297.

[88] Mary R. S. Creese, 'British Women of the Nineteenth and Early Twentieth Centuries Who Contributed to Research in the Chemical Sciences', *British Journal for the History of Science*, 24.3 (September 1991), 297–8.

[89] D. J. [Dorothy June] Sutor, 'The C-H⋯O Hydrogen Bond in Crystals', *Nature*, 195 (1962), 68–9, and D. J. Sutor, 'Evidence for the Existence of C-H⋯O Hydrogen Bonds in Crystals', *Journal of the Chemistry Society* (1963), 1105–10.

[90] Andy Extance, 'The Forgotten Female Crystallographer Who Discovered C-H⋯O Bonds', *Chemistry World* (8 July 2019), at https://www.chemistryworld.com/features/the-forgotten-female-crystallographer-who-discovered-c-ho-bonds/3010324.article#/, viewed 2 May 2021.

Franklin, Donohue was considered by some scientists to be the 'unsung hero of the DNA double helix' on the grounds that his 'advice to Watson and Crick on the appropriate tautomeric form to use for the bases was essential for the development of their model'.[91] His forceful dismissal of Sutor's research went unchallenged for decades. It only changed in 2012, when a study by Carl H. Schwalbe, which was published in the *Crystallography Review*, asked why Sutor's innovative research had been dismissed. He observed that, as a New Zealander, she had 'restricted networking opportunities'. More important, however, was her gender. In an understated way, Schwalbe observed that Sutor was

> a woman at a time when the acceptance of women in science, particularly the physical sciences, was by no means complete. A few exceptional women like Kathleen Lonsdale and Dorothy Hodgkin had achieved positions of eminence, and Lonsdale's laboratory provided a favourable environment for a gifted female crystallographer like Sutor. Nevertheless, there is anecdotal evidence that women in science were not welcome everywhere, e.g., 'Many old male organic chemists don't want a woman in the lab because they can't urinate in the sinks'. Perhaps at the time, some crystallographers would have paid less regard to a publication if its author was female.[92]

The arduous and extremely time-consuming process of crystal structure determination at the time was such that male crystallographers 'would put their wives to work doing a lot of this', Schwalbe admitted.[93] There might also have been considerable resentment that a young female crystallographer was able to publish her findings in the prestigious *Nature* journal, drawing largely on the research of other scientists (perhaps those who asked their wives to do the manual calculations).[94] Sutor's key research under the mentorship of Birkbeckian scientists was followed by a successful collaboration with crystallographer Kathleen Lonsdale, the most famous female scientist in twentieth-century Britain, at University College London on the constitution of kidney stones.

Lonsdale recognized the problems that female scientists such as Sutor faced. She noted that the crystallographer Lawrence Bragg, who was supportive of female scientists, 'once described the life of a university professor as similar to that of a queen bee, nurtured, tended and cared for because she only has one function in life'. But, Lonsdale added, 'nothing could be farther from the life of the

---

[91] Carl H. Schwalbe, 'June Sutor and the C-H⋯O Hydrogen Bonding Controversy', *Crystallography Review*, 18.3 (July 2012), 198.
[92] Ibid., 201–2.
[93] Carl H. Schwalbe, interviewed by Extance, 'The Forgotten Female Crystallographer Who Discovered C-H⋯O Bonds'.
[94] Schwalbe, 'June Sutor and the C-H⋯O Hydrogen Bonding Controversy', 202.

average professional woman'.[95] Those 'microinequities' faced by female scientists could be countered by 'micro-equities', as Lonsdale's actions suggest. It only required small attempts made to encourage communication throughout the group, to respect and engage with the ideas of all members, and to encourage critical yet friendly intellectual exchanges. This is why the presence of individual powerful male professors was crucial: crystallographers W. H. Bragg and W. L. Bragg at the University of Cambridge, and Bernal, Hiley, Blackett, Bundell, and Shaw at Birkbeck welcomed the expertise of women and minoritized groups in their laboratories. It is also no coincidence that all these male professors were politically progressive or leftists.[96]

This is not to exaggerate the progressive nature of the laboratory culture at Birkbeck. After all, Marianne Ehrenberg was a crystallography lecturer at Birkbeck who gave up her position after having a child. Her career was also rescued by Lonsdale, who employed her part time as a crystallographer technician at UCL. As Lonsdale admitted at the time, 'We hardly hoped to find anyone so well qualified who was ready to come in a relatively junior capacity.'[97] It is significant that Ehrenberg's *husband* did not relinquish his job at Birkbeck after the birth of their daughter. Instead, he became a distinguished X-ray physicist who co-discovered a quantum mechanical effect called the Ehrenberg–Siday effect (renamed the Ehrenberg–Siday–Aharonov–Bohm effect when rediscovered in 1959). Werner Ehrenberg went on to become Professor of Experimental Physics in the department, while Marianne Ehrenberg did not return to full-time employment until her daughter was 10 years of age.

* * *

The scientists explored in this chapter were extraordinary in their range of knowledge and the way they strove not only to advance science but also to change the worlds. They were courageous in their willingness to re-examine accepted 'truths'. Indeed, gender and political persecution might also be directly responsible for scientific resilience and openness to non-mainstream ideas and practices. As Hiley explained in his memoir of Bohm,

> The general discussions that went on in our group were probably very different from what is usually experienced in a physics department. Of course we kept our eyes on the significant developments that were taking place in physics, but our discussions involved a wide range of topics normally excluded from physics.

---

[95] Melinda Baldwin, '"Where are Your Intelligent Mothers to Come From?": Marriage and Family in the Scientific Career of Dame Kathleen Lonsdale FRS (1903–71)', *Notes and Records of the Royal Society of London*, 63.1 (20 March 2009), 87.
[96] Margaret W. Rossiter, 'Which Science? Which Women?', *Osiris*, 12 (1997), 177.
[97] A letter from Kathleen Lonsdale to F. B. Tours, 21 May 1958, cited in Baldwin, '"Where are Your Intelligent Mothers to Come From?"', 87.

> For example, our original investigations had as their focus the need to develop a new conceptual order in which to accommodate both quantum mechanics and relativity in a more coherent way.... This involved excursions into other disciplines like philosophy, biology, language and even art.[98]

It was this expansive, intellectual vision combined with a deep-seated egalitarianism and acceptance of all and any questions ('nothing was off-limits') that attracted people like Penrose, Franklin, Sutor, and Thornton to the College.

---

[98] Hiley, 'David Joseph Bohm', 116.

22
Disciplines

> Is there a discipline in the department?
> James C. Raymond in 1996[1]

Why do categories of knowledge appear and recede in university prospectuses? How does academic knowledge come to be 'bunched' into seemingly coherent entities called 'disciplines'? As we saw in Chapter 8, until the late nineteenth century, classes at Birkbeck were listed in an arbitrary fashion. Individual lecturers decided what they want to teach and offered their preferences to students. It was only when Birkbeck sought admission into the University of London that it began paying attention to academic disciplines and started listing classes under broad categories such as the Sciences, Arts, and Law. This chapter explores some of the ways academic disciplines have been constructed, demarcated, maintained, deconstructed, and reconstructed. The focus will be on four types of knowledge: mathematics, geography, occupational (later, organizational) psychology, and psycho-social studies. These epistemic fields and academic departments have not been chosen because of their contested histories—*all* disciplines are constructed and contested entities. Rather, they have been selected because they illustrate some of the ways academics have apportioned different 'ways of knowing' into ostensibly distinctive disciplines. They also show just how 'fuzzy' are the boundaries between different disciplines. Policing these indistinct borders requires a considerable expenditure of political, ideological, and social labour.

Why are 'disciplines' so important to academic life? Since the nineteenth century, universities have grouped forms of intellectual expertise into 'disciplines', often housed within 'departments' or 'schools'. The question is why, how, and which 'regimes of knowledge' become gathered into university units. They are historical artefacts. Disciplines are repositories of knowledge; they claim to possess rational, recognized, and ritualized sets of rules, processes, practices, methods, objects, and habits. As Higher Education scholar Paul Trowler observes, disciplines are 'reservoirs of ways of knowing' that 'condition behavioural practices, sets of discourses, ways of thinking, procedures, emotional responses and motivations'. Disciplines, he adds, 'have internal hierarchies and bestow power differentially,

---

[1] James C. Raymond, *English as a Discipline: Or, Is there a Plot in this Play?* (Tuscaloosa: University of Alabama Press, 1996).

conferring advantage and disadvantage'.[2] Indeed, this insistence on regimes of authority is present in the etymology of the word 'discipline' itself. As Keith W. Hoskin and Richard H. Macve point out, the term is derived

> from an Indo-European root '-da-', which is the root for both the Greek pedagogic term *didasko* (teach) and the Latin *(di)disco* (learn); and *disciplina* itself already has in classical Latin the double sense of knowledge (knowledge-system) and power (discipline of the child, military discipline).[3]

Philosopher Michel Foucault deftly encapsulated this duality in the concept 'savoir-pouvoir' or power-knowledge. Power creates knowledge and knowledge generates power.

This chapter addresses the historical specificity of academic disciplines. It shows how they change. They break apart; they merge. Entirely new 'ways of knowing' come into being. This may be the result of sudden upheavals (often sparked by external factors, such as war); other times, distinctive disciplines emerge through incremental adjustments in intellectual cultures. Less admirably, they may emerge through administrative and financial priorities, or even through scholarly rivalry and pique.

It would be misleading to assume that disciplinary shifts represent 'progress', although scholars initiating the changes always believe they do. Nevertheless, innovation is integral to the vibrancy of any field of intellectual pursuit. Foucault expressed this succinctly in 'The Order of Discourse', where he observed that 'to be a discipline, there must be the possibility of formulating new propositions, ad infinitum'.[4] As a result of this dynamic process, knowledge producers end up engaging in recurring practices of 'boundary work', as they struggle to define and delimit who (and what) is 'in' and 'out'. This process is aptly captured in the title of Tony Becher's influential book *Academic Tribes and Territories* (1989).[5] What can a survey of mathematics, geography, occupational psychology, and psycho-social studies at Birkbeck reveal about the ways academic tribes and territories are formed and fortified?

* * *

---

[2] Paul Trowler, 'Academic Tribes and Territories: The Theoretical Trajectory', *Österreichische Zeitschrift für Geschichtswissenschaften*, 25.3 (January 2014), 6–7.

[3] Keith W. Hoskin and Richard H. Macve, 'Accounting and the Examination: A Genealogy of Disciplinary Power', *Accounting, Organizations and Society*, 11.2 (1986), 107.

[4] Michel Foucault, 'The Order of Discourse', 1st pub. 1970, in Robert Young (ed.), *Untying the Text: A Post-Structuralist Reader* (London: Routledge, 1981), 59. For a good introduction to disciplinarity, see David R. Shumway and Ellen Messer-Davidow, 'Disciplinarity: An Introduction', *Poetics Today*, 12.2 (summer 1991), 201–25.

[5] Tony Becker, *Academic Tribes and Territories: Intellectual Enquiry and the Cultures of Disciplines* (Milton Keynes: Open University Press, 1989), 37–8.

Mathematics is crucial knowledge for mechanics, which is why it was taught at the LMI from its foundation. Not surprisingly, then, the LMI/Birkbeck has been the home to numerous distinguished mathematicians. This includes the celebrated number theorist Louis Joel Mordell, who was at Birkbeck between 1913 and 1920.[6] The Department of Mathematics and Statistics at Birkbeck was originally headed by David Roxbee Cox, who arrived as a Reader in 1956 and served as its Professor of Statistics between 1961 and 1966. He was succeeded by Harold Ruben (1966–9), then Philip Holgate, from 1970 (although he had been in the department since 1967). When Holgate died in 1993, the College attempted to close the Department of Mathematics and Statistics or rename it simply the Department of Statistics (1995) with Nicholas Hugh (N. H.) Bingham as Professor of Statistics. It wasn't until 1998 that it was re-established as the Department of Mathematics and Statistics.[7]

It is a good example, however, of the 'fuzzy boundaries' of disciplines that appear to outsiders to be internally coherent with clear parameters. In 1982, Chandra Shekhar Sharma reflected on this paradox. He had been appointed to the Department of Mathematics at Birkbeck twenty years earlier, served as professor between 1979 and 1998, and researched the role of mathematics in modelling (especially under uncertainty), as well as the mathematical foundations of Einstein's theory of relativity. Previously, Sharma had been taught chemistry at Patna University (India), then Wadham College, Oxford. However, despite working in mathematics at Birkbeck for thirty-six years, Sharma was forced to admit that he did not know what mathematics *was*. Sharma observed in the *British Journal for the Philosophy of Science* that, for some mathematicians and physicists, mathematics is simply whatever is taught in mathematics classrooms! Is mathematics 'a body of knowledge' that 'contains no truths', he asked? Is it 'a mere manipulation of symbols according to a set of rules'? Or perhaps 'nothing else but certain intuitive constructions with the help of symbols'? Still other philosophers of mathematics, the logicians Gottlob Frege and Bertrand Russell, contended that mathematics is

> that self-contained branch of knowledge which contains certain truths, the arguments which establish the truths, the constructions which underlie these arguments and the formal manipulations of symbols that express these arguments and truths.

---

[6] Ben Fairbairn, 'Louis Joel Mordell's Time in London', *BSHM Bulletin: Journal of the British Society for the History of Mathematics*, 32.2 (2017), 160–9.

[7] N. H. Bingham, 'Obituary. Philip Holgate (1934–1993)', *Bulletin of the London Mathematical Society*, 32 (2000), 489.

Basic questions, such as whether mathematics is 'the study of the nature of reality' (the Newtonian position) or, in contrast, 'has nothing to do with the reality of the world as perceived by our senses', divided the discipline.[8]

For Sharma, who originally trained in a Department of *Chemistry* and who worked on aspects of *physics*, this fluidity created conflict. He illustrated this by referring to a scientific paper that he and a colleague submitted to the *Journal of Physics A. Mathematical and Theoretical* in 1975. In it, they claimed to have established a modern differential calculus that could be applied to the space of non-holomorphic functions on a complex Banach space. Sharma (who had a reputation for being cantankerous) complained that their paper was rejected by the journal 'on the grounds that it contained nothing new and was merely a piece of propaganda for modern mathematics'. However, the journal later accepted the article once the authors stripped away the 'foundations of the new calculus' and simply provided '*applications* of the new calculus'.[9] The journal was engaged in boundary-work.

Sharma's anecdote illustrates the difficulties that even leading figures within a discipline can experience when they attempt to define their field of knowledge, let alone how adjacent disciplines such as mathematics, chemistry, and physics differ from each other. It reveals the function of academic journals in acting as powerful arbiters in the demarcation of fields and the policing of boundaries. It may also be an example of a factor that is almost never mentioned in debates about disciplinarity: the role of emotion—in this case, Sharma's lack of collegiality—in defining who or what is 'in' and who is 'out'.

* * *

Sharma's inability to answer the question 'what is mathematics?' was echoed by geographers with regards the boundaries of their 'discipline'. In UK universities,[10] geography was established from the late 1880s when the Royal Geographical Society, their learned society, persuaded Oxford and Cambridge to establish the first university positions in the field.[11] The problem they faced was distinguishing geography from already-existing spheres of knowledge. As with mathematics, opponents disparaged the fledging discipline by claiming that 'geography is what geographers write about'.[12] It was accused of being 'ill defined, borrowing (perhaps even stealing) material from other disciplines, lacking any clear content distinctive to itself, basing specious theories on inadequate foundations'.[13]

---

[8] C. S. Sharma, 'The Role of Mathematics in Physics', *British Journal for the Philosophy of Science*, 33 (1982), 275–6.

[9] Ibid., 285. My emphasis. The co-author of the original article was I. Rebelo.

[10] It has a longer history in continental Europe.

[11] H. C. Darby, 'Academic Geography in Britain: 1918–1946', *Transactions of the Institute of British Geographers*, 8.1 (1983), 14.

[12] Ibid., 15.

[13] T. W. Freeman, 'Geography Then and Now', *L'Espace géographique*, 14.1 (January/March 1985), 18.

This annoyed Harry Cyril Knapp (H. C. K.) Henderson, an early appointment to the Geography Department at Birkbeck in the 1920s. In his 1966 address on becoming President of the Institute of British Geographers, Henderson recalled that, in the early years of the discipline, many scientists believed that geographers were simply 'a group of people who skimmed the cream off other subjects and curdled it'. Birkbeck's geographers 'devoted a considerable amount of energy… trying to persuade scholars in other disciplines that geography was a distinct discipline'.[14] This often meant emphasizing the discipline's 'scientific side'. Such a status claim allied the discipline with the perception of science as arbiters of 'objective truth', unlike the interpretive focus of the arts.

In this fight for recognition, Henderson (called 'Doc' by his colleagues)[15] was joined by John Frederick Unstead (known affectionately as 'J. F. U.') who had originally been educated in politics and economics[16] and Eva Germaine Rimington Taylor, who had been trained in Oxford by the first academic geographers in the UK. Unstead had started at Birkbeck as a part-time lecturer in 1908; his position became full time in 1914. When Birkbeck became part of the University of London, he was given a professorship.[17]

During his twenty-two years in the College, Unstead devoted himself to ensuring that geography became a separate discipline at Birkbeck, as opposed to an adjunct to other disciplines. It was no easy matter. The problem was not student demand; rather, the Faculty of Science questioned whether geography was really a 'science' at all. This disciplinary 'boundary work' can be seen in a document entitled 'Geography in the B.Sc. Course'. Although it is neither dated nor signed, the document was most probably written by Unstead in the early 1920s. In it, Unstead complained that, in 1915, the Faculty of Science at the University of London had refused to accept geography as a subject for a degree in science. The chief opposition came from geologists, one of whom was extremely hostile. Another geologist (who, unfortunately for Birkbeck's geographers, happened to be both the Chairman of the Board of Studies for the University of London and one of two representatives of the Board of Studies in the Faculty of Science) was said to be 'luke-warm in the matter'. A third (who was the second representative of the Board of Studies in the Faculty of Science) 'practically never attends meetings of the Board'.[18] Unstead pleaded to be given reasons *why* they were so hostile

---

[14] H. C. K. Henderson, 'Geography's Balance Sheet', *Transactions of the Institute of British Geographers*, 45 (September 1968), 1.

[15] Robert W. Steel, 'Harry Cyril Knapp Henderson 1903–1983', *Transactions of the Institute of British Geographers*, 9.2 (1984), 256.

[16] Olive Garnett, 'John Frederick Unstead', *Geography*, 51.2 (April 1966), 151, and Edmund W. Gilbert, 'Professor J. F. Unstead', *Geographical Journal*, 132.2 (June 1966), 335. Note that he was a lecturer in geography at the newly established Goldsmiths College from 1905 until 1919, even though he started part time at Birkbeck from 1908.

[17] 'John Frederick Unstead', *Transactions of the Institute of British Geographers*, 38 (June 1966), 199.

[18] 'Geography in the B.Sc. Course', undated (c.1920s) and unsigned handwritten memo in Departmental Papers, Birkbeck Archive, Box 6. Hostility came from Miss Raisen, Professor Edmund Johnston Garwood, and Professor Watts.

to Geography as a discipline, especially since there was a 'strong & wide-spread ~~feeling~~ movement in this direction (the Royal Geographical Society and the Geographical Association are both taking up the matter)'.[19] The crossing out of the more feminine 'feeling' for the more masculinist 'movement' is not coincidental in such power struggles, as is the important role of learned societies in the creation of academic disciplines.

Much of the hostility to recognizing geography as a discrete discipline rested on the fact that its objects of study, methodologies, and ritualized practices overlapped with other disciplines. As a result, Unstead sought to show that such commonalities were not unique to geography. He went further, arguing that the fact that geography 'draws its subject matter from other branches of knowledge & shows certain interrelations between these' was an argument *in favour* of allowing geography to take its place in the sciences. The discipline's focus on 'the Earth's surface & its inhabitants' intersected with 'branches of knowledge' such as 'History, Economics, Geology, Physics (*via* Meteorology), Biology, & Astronomy', as well as mathematics. This meant that

> Geography is closely connected with several sciences, & in a University course it would seem to be grouped quite as naturally among the science subjects as among the Arts subjects. (Mathematics is similarly placed in both groups).[20]

Unstead reminded university officials that geography students were much more likely to take additional *science* subjects, including geology and physics, than arts ones.[21] As Eva Germaine Rimington—Unstead's successor as Professor of Geography—elsewhere there are no spaces on either side complained, scientists were acting unfairly when they rejected geography as a science on the grounds that it was 'not susceptible of study by the method of controlled experiment in the laboratory'.[22] There were many ways of 'doing' science, she argued.

As with many borderland disciplines, prestige depended on its description as a 'hard' science rather than a 'soft' or 'social' science. The latter was regarded as more 'feminine' and, therefore, of lesser intellectual rigour. The disciplines sought to 'harden' their field by emphasizing theoretical aspects, use of intricate technologies, and experimental design.[23]

Geologists, who as we have seen were the fledgling discipline's chief opponents, had a distinguished history at the LMI/Birkbeck. The growth of geology was encouraged not only by imperial expansionism but also by the related needs of industry. As the Master, Armitage-Smith, boasted in 1901, a 'growing demand for

---

[19] Ibid.   [20] Ibid.   [21] Ibid.
[22] E. G. R. Taylor, 'Geography in War and Peace', *Geographical Review*, 38.1 (1948), 132–3.
[23] Margaret W. Rossiter, 'Which Science? Which Women?', *Osiris*, 12 (1997), 179.

instruction in subjects which relate to Mining' meant that the metallurgical laboratory had to be enlarged and more lecturers appointed in geology.[24]

But by the twentieth century, geologists were fighting their own corner for disciplinary eminence, with pure scientists diminishing their scholarly standing by claiming that geologists were mainly travellers and explorers rather than 'true' scientists. Geologists were understandably not willing to cede yet more ground to geographers. The geographers were equally keen to differentiate themselves from geologists. One way they did this was by emphasizing the 'human factors' in environmental interactions.[25] They focused on 'the study of the physical & human characteristics of particular regions', insisting that it was not intellectually helpful to 'isolate physical phenomena'.[26] In the words of an unnamed geographer writing in the 1920s, 'a broad syllabus in Geography would not overlap with Geology [any] more than Chemistry does with Physics or Physics with Mathematics'.[27] Indeed, the author made the radical suggestion that

> the present Arts syllabuses should be transferred to the Sciences side. (so [sic] that, as in Physics, Chemistry, Botany, Psychology, Anthropology, and Military Science, the syllabus for Arts and Sciences would be identical. The present Arts syllabus... is broad, and reads as much like a Science syllabus.[28]

The tensions between the two different repositories of 'ways of knowing' were particularly stark at Birkbeck due to historical reasons. Geology had been a recognized subject in the College from its early origin as the London Mechanics' Institution. In the 1880s, geology became a separate *discipline* in the College. John Walter Gregory, after which the Gregory Rift was named (it is also known under the less imperialist name of the Eastern Rift Valley) matriculated with a first-class BSc in geology from Birkbeck in 1886.[29] This would mean that Birkbeck had one of the oldest geology departments in the UK. We don't know who taught it then but, from 1888, geology was taught by palaeontologist and co-founder of the Malacological Society of London, George Frederick Harris (who had previously studied geology in the College), and then, from 1906, by the distinguished mineralogist and traveller (in India, Bolivia, Brazil, the Amazon basin, and Egypt, to name a few locations)[30] John William Evans, who remained in the department until 1920.[31] The department's historical pedigree made it a formidable foe to the geographers.

---

[24] George Armitage-Smith, *Inaugural Address by the Principal G. Armitage-Smith on the Opening of the Seventy-Ninth Session. Monday, 30th September 1901* (London: Birkbeck, 1901), 4.
[25] 'Geography in the Faculty of Science', undated (c.1920s) and unsigned handwritten memo in Departmental Papers, Birkbeck Archive, Box 6.
[26] Ibid. [27] Ibid. [28] Ibid.
[29] Bernard Elgey Leake, 'The Life and Work of Professor J. W. Gregory FRS (1864–1932): Geologist, Writer and Explorer' (London: Geological Society Memoir No. 34, Geological Society, 2011), viii–ix.
[30] A. Brammall, 'John William Evans, C.B.E., D.Sc., LL.B., F.R.S', *Geological Magazine*, 68.1 (1931), 47–8.
[31] Letter from A. T. J. (John) Dollar to the Master, 'Future Development of College, 1963–68', 20 January 1964, in Birkbeck Archive, Box 43.

There was another problem. Many scholars were unclear what geography actually *was*. It may be a circular argument ('being a geographer means being educated in geography'), but one of the factors that help define a 'discipline' is training in that specialized field. However, as Henderson was forced to acknowledge, in the early years of the Geography Department at Birkbeck, 'all the senior and many of the junior academics had graduated in another discipline'.[32] Eva Taylor was one of the few geographers who had actually been trained in the history of geography and cartography, as well as in the application of mathematics to survey and navigation.[33] She was well recognized in the College, always wearing a hat when lecturing. One former pupil recalled that

> Her marking was severe—my first effort, written with some pride, came back slashed to ribbons and copiously annotated—and was rightly meant to set the high standards which she expected and applied strictly in her own lifetime of scholarship.[34]

When Unstead retired in 1930, Taylor replaced him, making her the first female Professor of Geography in the UK. As she noted in 1933, there was

> doubt in some people's minds as to whether academic geography has any contribution to make to knowledge. In respect to that I should like to remind people that, even at the present day, we are still only beginning to turn out fully trained academic geographers; and when I say 'fully trained' I mean those trained by teachers who have themselves been trained.[35]

Taylor was an exception (and, incidentally, not only intellectually but also as a collector of William Etty's nudes). Most early Birkbeck geographers had been trained in history or geology. W. Gordon East, who held the Chair in Geography at Birkbeck from 1947 to 1970, served as President of the Institute of British Geographers from 1959, and was crowned the 'doyen of British Geographers' after his death, had studied history at Peterhouse, Cambridge.[36] Sidney William Wooldridge (who succeeded Taylor as Professor of Geography at the College and was known as the 'doyen of British geomorphologists') trained as a geologist.[37]

---

[32] Henderson, 'Geography's Balance Sheet', 1.
[33] R. A. S., 'Obituary', *Imago Mundi*, 22 (1968), 114. Also see 'Professor Taylor', *The Lodestone*, 36.3 (summer 1944), 16. She was lecturer 1922–31 and, on the retirement of Prof. Unstead, professor 1931–44, when she retired. Also see *The Lodestone*, 36.3 (summer 1944), 11.
[34] 'Memories of Breams II', *Court of Electors Newsletter* (spring 1981), 11.
[35] 'The Urbanization of the Shetland Islands: Discussion', *Geographical Journal*, 81.6 (June 1933), 514.
[36] W. R. Mead, 'Obituary. William Gordon East, 1902–1998', *Journal of Historical Geography*, 24.3 (1998), 352.
[37] H. C. Darby, 'Academic Geography in Britain: 1918–1946', *Transactions of the Institute of British Geographers*, 8.1 (1983), 21, and 'Sidney William Wooldridge, 1900–1963', *Biographical Memoirs of Fellows of the Royal Society*, 10 (November 1964), 370.

He had attended Evans' geology lectures at Birkbeck when a schoolboy and the experience inspired him to follow in his hero's footsteps—which, for him, meant geography.[38] It is not surprising, then, that Wooldridge's inaugural lecture was entitled 'The Geographer as Scientist'. He was aligning himself with geology, which was accepted as a science, while also believing that geography's strength lay in its interdisciplinary nature or *range of* scientific frames.[39]

Despite these early difficulties, by the 1920s, geography was established as an academic discipline distinctive from geology. At the national level, changes in the British Association for the Advancement of Science's 'Section E' (Geography) illustrates this process. In the first fifty years of existence, Section E was chaired by 42 'gentlemen', 16 soldiers, 5 sailors, 2 geologists, and only 1 academic.[40] By the interwar period, 17 of the 21 presidents (81 per cent) were academics.[41] Furthermore, from the 1850s to 1870s, around two thirds of papers given in Section E were classed as those typical of geology at the time: that is, they were concerned with 'exploration' or general 'description'. This dropped to just over half by the 1880s and only 12 per cent by the First World War. Virtually none of the papers given were of that nature from the mid-1920s.[42] Geography was not only defining itself as separate from geology and other disciplines; it was also professionalizing.

The timing of these development was heavily influenced by historical events. For geographers, this was war. Both world wars revealed just how important the discipline could be militarily.[43] Demand for the skills and knowledge of academic geographers climbed sharply: they could interpret aerial photographs, make judgements about the weather, and advise on the impact of landscape on troop and mechanized movement.[44] The popularity of the discipline amongst students rose dramatically too. As Taylor observed in her presidential address to the Geography Section of the British Association for the Advancement of Science in Dundee in 1947, 'the older among us have twice experienced the sudden rise of geographical prestige which occurs in war time' where 'geographical intelligence of every kind then becomes vital'.[45] The discipline's prestige continued after the war, with the urgent demand for town planners to rebuild bombed cities and facilitate suburban expansion. Prior to the Second World War, there were only about eighty professional geographers teaching in British universities or university

---

[38] 'Sidney William Wooldridge, 1900–1963', *Biographical Memoirs of Fellows of the Royal Society*, 10 (November 1964), 370.

[39] From 'The Geographer as Scientist', in 'Sidney William Wooldridge: Biographical Memoirs' (London: Royal Society, 1944), 372, at https://royalsocietypublishing.org/doi/pdf/10.1098/rsbm.1964.0021. He stayed at Birkbeck until 1947.

[40] S. H. Beaver, 'Geography in the British Association for the Advancement of Science', *Geographical Journal*, 148.2 (July 1982), 177.

[41] Ibid., 178.   [42] Ibid., 177–8.

[43] H. C. Darby, 'Academic Geography in Britain: 1918–1946', *Transactions of the Institute of British Geographers*, 8.1 (1983), 14.

[44] Beaver, 'Geography in the British Association for the Advancement of Science', 179.

[45] E. G. R. Taylor, 'Geography in War and Peace', *Geographical Review*, 38.1 (1948), 137.

colleges; within fifty years, this had climbed to 600.[46] The status of the discipline can also be gauged by the number of professors appointed in universities. Although Geography Chairs had been established at Birkbeck and the LSE in 1922, this did not spread to other universities until 1930 and saw a dramatic increase after the Second World War.[47] The discipline had proved itself.

Taylor's career can be used to illustrate the burgeoning status of geography in Higher Education. The war catapulted her into important political posts. She was appointed, in 1940, to Lord Reith's Panel of Reconstruction and, the following year, to the Consultative Panel of the Ministry of Works and Buildings.[48] She later recalled that

> Many of our number [geographers] were seconded to various ministries during the war.... Others have honourable records of organizing and supplying geographical intelligence to the various Commands, and in many cases of adapting, interpreting, and applying such intelligence to the novel and intricate needs of commandos, bomber pilots and others engaged in particular operations.[49]

Geography's position as an *academic* discipline was crucial: after all, Taylor noted, there could 'be no *applied* geography', useful to wartime needs and post-war reconstruction, 'unless there has first of all been an adequate *pure* geography'.[50]

This is not to deny that war put incredible pressure on the young department. Demand for geography classes was huge; large cohorts of military cadets had to be taught how to read and interpret topographical maps. The department quickly became overwhelmed because of serious understaffing.[51] With so many men away on active military duty, the bulk of the teaching had to be done by female geographers, resulting in a feminization of the discipline. They were not always rewarded for their labour, as Eila Campbell discovered. Campbell began her training as a geographer by signing up for a part-time degree at Birkbeck (her main job was as a teacher in Southall). During the war, she worked on her MA while also acting as a part-time lecturer in the department.[52] Her mentor was Taylor, who, until she retired in 1944, turned out to be rather severe, insisting on reading each of Campbell's lectures prior to their delivery.[53] After the war, Wooldridge (Taylor's successor as professor) praised Campbell in the highest terms. 'Despite her youth and relative inexperience', he contended, Campbell was

---

[46] T. W. Freeman, 'Geography Then and Now', *L'Espace géographique*, 14.1 (January/March 1985), 16.
[47] S. H. Beaver, 'The Le Play Society and Field Work', *Geography*, 47.3 (July 1962), 233.
[48] 'Eva Germaine Rimington Taylor', *Transactions of the Institute of British Geographers*, 45 (September 1968), 181.
[49] Taylor, 'Geography in War and Peace', 137.   [50] Ibid., 137. Emphasis added.
[51] Avril Maddrell, 'The "Map Girls": British Women Geographers' War Work, Shifting Gender Boundaries and Reflections on the History of Geography', *Transactions of the Institute of British Geographers*, 33.1 (January 2008), 132.
[52] W. R. Mead, 'Eila as Geographer', *Imago Mundi*, 47 (1995), 6.   [53] Ibid., 6.

'the essential mainspring of the department in the routine of administration'. He also admitted that she taught more hours than any of her colleagues.[54] But, after heaping praise on Campbell for keeping the department afloat, Wooldridge argued *against* promoting her. In a confidential memo, he reminded the governors of Harry Henderson's 'years of effective and hard-working war service' in the Royal Air Force and the Inter-Service Topographical Department and stated that he was 'confident the Governors will agree that [Henderson] is entitled to an opportunity to repair the ravages of the years which the locust has eaten between 1940–5'.[55] Of course, Wooldridge's productivity had also been severely curtailed as a result of the war, perhaps making him especially sensitive to Henderson's predicament.[56] Campbell was only promoted from assistant lecturer to lecturer in 1948, then to Reader in 1963, and to professor and head of department in 1970.[57]

Despite winning a place at the disciplinary table, defining the boundaries of 'geography' as an academic discipline remained (and remains) an issue. In the mid-1940s, for example, when the head of the Geography Department made a plea for an expansion of staff, he explicitly stated that he was *not* proposing that the Department of Geology contribute to geography teaching. This was even though geology *did* contribute to geography teaching in the four other geography schools in the University of London.[58] This insistence on disciplinary coherence and specialization was reiterated in 1980, when there was a threat that staff in the department would be transferred to other disciplines—including geology, history, and economics. At that time, Birkbeck's geographers based their argument not only on disciplinary grounds but also on the College's financial crisis. They contended that disbanding the Geography Department would result in a loss of students.[59] At the same time, they rejected the idea of being amalgamated with the Department of Geology to form a Department of the Earth Sciences on the grounds that, in order to be credible, such a department would require an additional six new appointments.[60] Today, this division between geology and geography is represented in Birkbeck's schools: the Department of Geography is located within the School of Social Sciences, History, and Philosophy, while the Department of Earth and Planetary Sciences is within the School of Sciences.

* * *

---

[54] S. W. Wooldridge, 'Memorandum on the Staffing of the Geography Department', undated (c.1944–1945), in Departmental Papers, Birkbeck Archive, Box 6.
[55] Ibid.
[56] 'Sidney William Wooldridge, 1900–1963', *Biographical Memoirs of Fellows of the Royal Society*, 10 (November 1964), 372.
[57] 'Emeritus Professor Eila Campbell', in Birkbeck Archive, Box 58. She retired in 1981 and died in 1994.
[58] Wooldridge, 'Memorandum on the Staffing of the Geography Department'.
[59] 'Meeting of the Professorial Committee—27 May, 1980. Report of the Sub-Committee of the Review of the Department of Geography', 6, in Birkbeck Archive, Box 20.
[60] Ibid., 6–7.

Compared with geology and geography, languages and linguistics had a more recent and insecure position in Higher Education. Did they even have a place within the university? In the LMI, language classes had been considered essential. In the 1880s, for example, although around 45 per cent of students doing languages chose French, the requirement that students studying for a degree in the University of London passed examinations in ancient languages meant that around one fifth studied Latin and 12 per cent did Greek. However, other languages taught were German (10–15 per cent of all language students), Italian, Spanish, Portuguese, modern Greek, Dutch, Russian, Hebrew, Arabic, Hindustani, and Sanskrit.[61] Clearly, these classes were driven as much by the needs of the empire as by business concerns.

The Second World War, followed by the Cold War, were to be a major boost for language teaching. As with geography, war was important in the growth of language disciplines. In 1941, the College Secretary informed one student that 'Your knowledge of German will undoubtedly be wanted later on owing to the regrettable ignorance of many of the people in Berlin of the English language.'[62]

An example of military needs influencing academic disciplines can be seen in the appointment of French lecturer Ormond Uren to Birkbeck's Language Research Centre. What his colleagues did not realize was that Uren's exquisite linguistic skills had been honed after he was recruited by the Special Operations Executive (SOE) to work in its Hungarian section during the war. The SOE was not aware that Uren had become a fervent communist in 1940 when he was a 20-year-old officer in the Highland Light Infantry. Uren later explained that

> I was extremely depressed about the state of the world and, reading some communist literature while in this state of mind, I 'saw' with the force of a blinding illumination that communism was the only solution to the word's problems.

In 1943, at the height of his political fervour, Uren passed on information about his work in the SOE to Douglas Springhall, who was the National Organiser of the Communist Party of Great Britain and a Soviet agent. Shortly afterwards, Springhall was arrested: Uren was quickly identified and imprisoned until 1947, after which he escaped to France. But he remained a believer. When he refused to denounce Communist Party members of the World Federation of Trade Unions in Paris (where he worked as an interpreter), he was deported back to England in 1952. Four years later, Uren left the CPGB in protest over the Soviet invasion of Hungary in 1956. From 1962, however, he was a valued member of Birkbeck's Linguistics Department until he retired in 1983. None of his colleagues knew

---

[61] From the annual reports for 1883 to 1887.
[62] Letter from the College Secretary to Eric F. Northcott, dated 2 February 1941, in Birkbeck Archive, 'Birkbeck Students at War' (p. 135 of file).

about his spying past until 1981, when Nigel West went public with the claim that Uren had been a member of the Soviet spy ring that included Anthony Blunt, Kim Philby, Guy Burgess, and Donald McClean.[63] In response, Uren published an article entitled 'I Went to Prison for Espionage... If Only I'd Gone to Cambridge!' In it, he claimed that

> If I had been [in Cambridge] I might now be in possession of immunity for prosecution or be drinking vodka and Georgian wine in a luxury KGB ghetto in Moscow.

Instead, he had been stuck in England where he had been 'tried by court martial, cashiered, and sentenced to seven years penal servitude'.[64] He reflected that

> Having spent the best part of 40 years thinking that most of the people around me did not know about 'my past', the likelihood is that now most people will know. It is reassuring to realize that most of them don't give a damn.[65]

While Uren's career in linguistics arose out of wartime international disharmony, the growth of linguistics after the war was impelled by the opposite—that is, political moves towards greater European cooperation. This resulted in a dramatic increase in the demand for language teaching, including the teaching of English as a foreign language. Uren's department had been established in 1965, after Michel Blanc (a lecturer in the French Department at Birkbeck since 1959) along with Brian Dutton in Spanish and Brian Foss in Psychology applied to the Nuffield Foundation for a grant to establish the Birkbeck Language Research Centre. It became the Department of Applied Linguistics, headed by Blanc, in 1972. That same year, the first meeting of what was to become the British Association of Applied Linguistics was convened at Birkbeck.[66] This involved breaking away from the long-established Linguistics Association of Great Britain (LAGB), whose language teaching section was deemed to be 'an inadequate forum for the development of a new interdisciplinary area'.[67] In contrast to the 'established' LAGB, Birkbeck's applied linguistics scholars were interested in theoretical concerns, bilingualism, and the teaching of English as a mother tongue as well as a foreign language.[68] While the first academic department in the

---

[63] Frances Williams, 'Ormond Uren Obituary', *The Guardian* (23 July 2015).
[64] Ormond Uren, 'I Went to Prison for Espionage... If Only I'd Gone to Cambridge!', *The Times* (10 November 1981), 10.
[65] Ibid., 10.
[66] BAAL, 'Notes on the History of the British Association for Applied Linguistics, 1967–2017' (Leeds: BAAL, 2017), 5.
[67] Richard Hudson, 'A History of the LAGB: The First Fifty Years', *Journal of Linguistics*, 45.1 (March 2009), 14.
[68] Ibid., 14.

UK was the School of Applied Linguistics at the University of Edinburgh, established in 1957, Birkbeck's department was the first in England. It is still the only Department of Applied Linguistics in the University of London.

As with the other disciplines discussed in this chapter, there was considerable uncertainty about defining applied linguistics. When Blanc was asked by the Academic Board at Birkbeck to explain what was meant by 'applied linguistics', he wittily snapped that it was 'linguistics plus the application of money'. Delineating the precise boundaries of an imprecise discipline led to difficulties when the interdisciplinary team needed to be assigned to Research Assessment Exercise (RAE)/Research Excellence Framework (REF) categories. They tended to be distributed amongst Modern Languages, English, and Education sub-panels.[69] In recent years, they have even moved to psychology, in the form of psycholinguistics and neurological aspects of language.

* * *

As an academic discipline, psychology only came to Birkbeck in the 1940s. Like geography, it was an extremely interdisciplinary group, which often struggled to forge a discrete identity. Early scholars had been trained in disciplines such as philosophy, anthropology, and sociology; later ones have been influenced by educational psychology, industrial psychology, psycholinguistics, psychoanalysis, psychopharmacology, psychiatry, and neuropsychology. Identifying broad trends is always risky, but the department at Birkbeck tended to follow the trajectory of the discipline as a whole—that is, it was dominated by behaviourism from the 1950s and then the neurosciences from the 1990s. However, this trend not only masks the diversity of approaches within the discipline at Birkbeck but also ignores two major schisms, involving occupational (now, organizational) psychology and psychosocial studies. To understand these 'breakaway' disciplines, it is necessary to explore the origins of the Psychology Department in the College.

At its inception in Birkbeck, the discipline of psychology was embedded within the Department of Philosophy. Prior to 1940, students taking the degree in philosophy in the various colleges of the University of London were required to sit two papers in psychology.[70] Birkbeck's philosophy students went to King's College to do these classes. During the Second World War, however, most staff at King's College fled to Bristol, leaving behind Francis Arthur Powell Aveling, who was the head of King's Psychology Department. Birkbeck was the only college in the University of London to remain in London during the Blitz and Joad (who was the head of philosophy) seized the opportunity to invite Aveling to teach psychology on Birkbeck's premises. Aveling did more than this: he moved the entire

---

[69] BAAL, 'Notes on the History of the British Association for Applied Linguistics, 1967–2017', 19.
[70] C. A. Mace, 'Psychology Comes to Birkbeck (A Fragment for the Autobiography of its First Professor of Psychology)', *The Lodestone*, 52.1 (autumn 1961), 3.

Department of Psychology to Birkbeck. He brought to the department a strong philosophical focus—after all, his work revolved around that great question 'What is the ultimate nature of Reality?'[71] Aveling died the following year, so the lectures were taken over by Cecil Alec Mace, who was also teaching at Bedford College and the University of Cambridge during the week, and at Birkbeck (initially on behalf of King's College) at the weekends. Mace later recalled that he was surprised to be told by the University of London that King's Psychology Department was going to be transferred to Birkbeck. He had not been impressed with the College, admitting that

> on my first acquaintance with the College in its slum dwelling off Fetter lane (when I was quite a young lecturer at Nottingham) I had publicly said: 'If there is an academic institution with which I should never wish to be associated it is Birkbeck College'.

He was to change his mind. He later recalled that

> I was led to understand that among the reasons for this was the fact that the King's Department had so grown that there was no longer room for it in the Strand, whereas Birkbeck was about to complete its new building in Malet Street and all that was needed for the accommodation of Psychology was to add a Fourth Floor. By this time too I had come to know the Spirit of Birkbeck and the invitation to become the first Professor of Psychology [at Birkbeck] was most attractive to me.[72]

Like Aveling, Mace was as much a philosopher as a psychologist—indeed, he had been voted President of both the British Psychological Society as well as the Aristotelian Society, and worked both on the philosophy of mind and industrial psychology.[73] He was reported to have described his philosophy of teaching as 'All one can do is think aloud, and hope that some of it will brush off.'[74]

By 1944, the Philosophy and Psychology Departments had become separate disciplines with Mace professor for seventeen years until he retired in 1961. The granting of professorships is an often-unspoken contributor to the creation of disciplines. Until the dramatic expansion in Higher Education in the 1960s, academic departments were led by a sole professor (a 'Chair'), who would act as head of the department. In the early 1960s, 80 per cent of professors were departmental heads. In effect, the only exceptions to the rule that professors would be heads of

---

[71] C. Spearman, 'Obituary Notice. Francis Aveling, 1875–1941', *British Journal of Psychology. General Section*, 32.1 (1 July 1941), 1.
[72] Mace, 'Psychology Comes to Birkbeck', 4.
[73] 'Professor Alec Mace', *The Times* (9 June 1971), 16.
[74] 'S. G. L.', 'Prof. Alec Mace', *The Times* (15 June 1971), 17.

department occurred in very small or new disciplines.[75] One result was that for a distinguished academic to become a professor, with the accompanying status and pay implications, a separate department was required. Thus, Mace was able to become a professor by breaking apart the Philosophy and Psychology Department. The increased number of professors ('Personal' as opposed to 'Established' Chairs) within a single department occurred with the expansion in Higher Education, greater specialization within disciplines (so the 'Chairs' could no longer claim expertise in all aspects of the discipline), and the need for universities to attract distinguished academics.[76]

Unfortunately for Mace, the promised move from the 'slum dwelling' off Fetter Lane to the new Malet Street building was delayed by the war. Overnight, building materials became precious commodities; construction workers, scarce. The steel structure had already been erected, but further work had to be put on hold. It was 1951 before the College moved into the unfinished Malet Street premises, which weren't officially opened until 1953. There was other bad news: when the Psychology Department eventually moved to the fourth floor of the Malet Street headquarters, shortage of accommodation for Philosophy and Classics meant that the three disciplines (all of which had been closely linked historically) had to share the space.[77] Despite setbacks, when Mace died in 1971, *The Times* reported that he had been responsible for creating 'the biggest and best known psychology department in the country'.[78]

Mace led the move of the discipline of psychology to its own disciplinary status, separate from philosophy. But Mace's department experienced its own schism, which came to the fore in 1961, the year of his retirement. For a few years previously, Birkbeck's Psychology Department had been developing a behaviourist focus, led by Harry Hurwitz, who had been awarded a PhD at Birkbeck in 1953 entitled on 'Studies in Operant Chaining'. Impressed by this PhD student, Mace had offered Hurwitz a lectureship in the department, a post he held until 1964. Hurwitz promptly established an operant psychology laboratory, inviting prominent behaviourists such as B. F. Skinner to visit. He also founded the British Experimental Analysis of Behaviour Group, which was fascinated by animal learning and perception. They experimented with octopuses, rats, and mynah birds. Indeed, Brian Malzard Foss, who lectured a Birkbeck between 1951 and 1964, kept mynahs in his office. The fact that they could mimic the sound of his telephone and of motorcycles outside convinced Foss that 'imitation was a form of learning not dependent on reward'.[79] The behaviourist flavour of the

---

[75] Graeme Moodie, 'The Disintegrating Chair: Professors in Britain Today', *European Journal of Education*, 21.1 (1986), 43.
[76] Ibid., 45. [77] Mace, 'Psychology Comes to Birkbeck', 4.
[78] 'Professor Alec Mace', *The Times* (9 June 1971), 16.
[79] Mary J. Pickersgill, 'Obituary: Professor Brian Foss', *The Independent* (1 January 1998), at https://www.independent.co.uk/news/obituaries/obituary-professor-brian-foss-1136115.html, viewed 1 March 2021.

department was neatly encapsulated in a poem by David Warburton, published in *The Lodestone* in 1962:

> A more intelligent student never
> Did in Birkbeck exist.
> Up on the fourth floor
> Behind a green door
> A real psychologist.
> A Skinner Box I use all the time
> To create a steady state.
> With measures exact
> We try to extract
> Our behavioural postulate…
> In introspection we never indulge
> Nor believe the mind exists.
> In our nerves we believe
> Our ideas we conceive
> As good psychologists.
> Our complex brains possess a bulge
> Which is never quite what it seems,
> When given a shock,
> Gives a double thought block
> And multiple coloured dreams.[80]

This behaviourist orientation was not shared by the entire department, though. Fractures—or what Mace euphemistically called 'structural differentiation' or 'endedness'—developed. One of these differentiations involved Mace's own research interest: industrial psychology. One day, Mace later recalled, he 'ran into' an energetic psychologist called Alec Rodger outside the 'Moo-Cow Milk Bar' in Baker Street. At that time, Rodger was Principal Psychologist at the Admiralty. Mace propositioned him to 'come and help me teach psychology at Birkbeck', to which Rodger replied, 'Well perhaps I might.'[81] And *that* was the way appointments were made in those days!

Rodger was to spearhead a major section within Birkbeck's Psychology Department; they called themselves 'occupational psychologists'. Rodger had a successful career prior to arriving in the College. He had read psychology at the University of Cambridge, after which he joined the National Institute for Industrial Psychology, where he was appointed head of its Vocational Guidance Department. The Second World War gave Rodger an opportunity to put his ideas

---

[80] David Warburton, 'A More Intelligent Student Never', *The Lodestone*, 52.3 (summer 1962), 4.
[81] Mace, 'Psychology Comes to Birkbeck', 5.

into practice. Conscripted into the War Office and then the Admiralty, he metaphorically donned his armour in a fight to make 'the Mandarins of Whitehall' recognize the value of psychology in decisions about manpower. They did not need much convincing, especially after the fall of France in 1940 forced a realization that this was going to be a prolonged war, so 'manpower' selection was imperative. Rodger tells one story (probably apocryphal) of one Navy volunteer who was rejected because he misspelt 'Egypt'.[82] By the end of the war, Rodger had become the first member of the Civil Services Psychologist Class and was Senior Principal Psychologist in the Admiralty.

In 1948, at the age of 31, however, Rodger was ready for a change. He was appointed to Birkbeck and promoted to professor a dozen years later. This was to be his base for thirty-four highly productive years.

It was a formative period for Rodger. At the beginning, industrial or occupational psychologists were a minority but powerful presence within the department. Mace recalled that they were affectionately called 'The Other End' (meaning, they had offices at the far end of the corridor) before attaining 'a sort of Dominion Status' in which they were referred to informally but more respectfully as 'The Division of Occupational Psychology'. By the time Mace retired, even he was forced to recognize that they had 'finally... achieved Independence with the conferment of a title of "Professor of Occupational Psychology" on Alec Rodger'.[83] By 1962, this group had formed themselves into a Department of Occupational Psychology, sharing the fourth floor with their parent discipline. It was a divorce that had been encouraged by internal debates in the mid-1960s about how to respond to the University Grants Committee recommendation (in the wake of the call in the Robbins Report to expand university education) to introduce more 'vocational courses at postgraduate level'. This was exactly what Rodger had been doing with his manpower studies and ties with industry.[84]

Much of the success of this new discipline was due to Rodger's personality. He proved to be an inspiring, charismatic teacher, introducing the 'Seven-Point Plan' for psychological assessments and coining terms such as 'fmj-fjm' or 'fitting the man to the job and fitting the job to the man'. Pat Shipley, who joined the department in 1967 and remained until she retired, recalled that Rodger 'saw himself as a missionary for occupational psychology, rather than an academic'.[85] By the mid-1960s, Birkbeck's department was producing half of all newly qualified occupational psychologists in Britain.[86] Rodger worked long hours. He was also a national inspiration in the field. For decades, he served as the General Secretary

---

[82] Alec Rodger, 'The Work of the Admiralty Psychologists', *Occupational Psychology*, 19 (1945), 132.
[83] Mace, 'Psychology Comes to Birkbeck', 6.
[84] Anne Corbett, 'Society at Work: Birkbeck Looks Ahead', *New Society* (2 February 1967), 165.
[85] Pat Shipley, cited by Sylvia Shimmin and Don Wallis, *Fifty Years of Occupational Psychology in Britain* (Leicester: British Psychological Society, 1994), 60.
[86] Ibid., 88. For a discussion of the crisis of the 1970s and 1980s, see pp. 88–90.

of the British Psychological Society and then, between 1957 and 1958, as its President. Given the importance of specialized journals in playing 'gate keeping' roles, it is no surprise that Rodger edited *Occupational Psychology* for twenty-two years, transforming it from a slight journal with a tiny readership to a journal with international reach. Psychologists began talking about the 'Birkbeckian' school of occupational psychology, by which they meant a form of psychology that studied 'difficulties and distastes' inherent to different employments. 'Birkbeckian' psychology, explained one proponent,

> tends to be pragmatic rather than theoretical, generalist rather than specialist, and more appreciated in industry and government than in academia. There have been arguments... about the advantages and disadvantages of this sort of applied psychology; but while jobs are so difficult to find there is much to be said for producing psychologists of whatever variety, who are all-rounders, and capable of contributing effectively in a wide range of situations.[87]

It was also a psychology that emphasized the need for enjoyment at work. Rodger warned that, employees who failed to like what they did would end up developing hobbies outside of work, such as 'horse-racing, football, gardening, physical culture, [and the] cinema'. They might even amuse themselves by engaging in 'revolutionary politics'.[88]

Rodger's department was the first Department of Occupational Psychology in the UK and quickly allied itself with the School of Management. It is currently part of the School of Business, Economics, and Informatics rather than the School of Science, where the Department of Psychology remains. This reflects a broader trend where occupational psychologists work and research in business schools. The department continues to offer the first professional doctorate in the discipline, producing 'all-rounders' very much in keeping with Rodger's stance of doing psychology.[89]

* * *

The breaking away of occupational psychology from the main Psychology Department led to considerable 'frostiness',[90] but nothing in comparison to the dismay caused by another schism: the separation of psychosocial studies from the Department of Psychology.

Like the occupational psychologists, psychosocial researchers had been an influential part of the Department of Psychology for a long period. This was

---

[87] 'Obituary: Professor Alec Rodger, 1907–1982', *Australian Psychologist*, 17.2 (July 1982), at https://www.bps.org.uk/sites/www.bps.org.uk/files/Historypercent20ofpercent20Psychology/Obituarypercent20-percent20Alecpercent20Rodger.pdf.
[88] Alec Rodger, *On Vocational Guidance* (Loughborough: The Author, 1936), 35.
[89] Email correspondence with Professor Almuth McDowell, 21 April 2021.   [90] Ibid.

unusual; elsewhere in the UK, nearly all psychosocial research was conducted with departments of sociology or social work.[91] However, like other pioneering psychosocial clusters in UK universities, including ones in the University of East London from the 1980s and the University of East Anglia from the 1990s, the Birkbeck cluster has strong links to clinical and social work. Stephen Frosh was appointed to the Department of Psychology in 1979, but he initially worked only part-time in the College, dividing his time with clinical jobs in the National Health Service and (for a decade) at the Tavistock Clinic as Consultant Clinical Psychologist in the family department. He only stopped his clinical work in 1998 when he was appointed professor.

From 2000, however, a majority of researchers within the Department of Psychology began moving towards the neurosciences, marginalizing psychosocial approaches to human psychology. In response, those conducting more psychoanalytical and critical research decided to form a separate centre *within* the Department of Psychology. They considered calling themselves an Institute for Social Research or a Centre for Critical Theory, but in the end decided on Centre for Psychosocial Studies (CPS) because, as Frosh explains, 'we were Psychologists and it was a way of doing it and it wasn't really a term that anyone was using then'.[92]

Members of the centre were extremely interdisciplinary, with interests in critical psychoanalysis as well as social psychology, critical theory, critical psychological theory, and qualitative research methods. As Mats Alvesson and Kaj Sköldberg observed in *Reflexive Methodology* (2009), researchers within critical studies sub-disciplines typically included

> hermeneuticians, critical theorists, poststructuralists, linguistic philosophers, discourse analysts, feminists, constructivists, reflectivists and other trouble makers who render life difficult for the supporters of either quantitative or mainstream qualitative methods.[93]

It was this 'troublemaking' component, or what Alvesson and Sköldberg called a propensity for a 'hermeneutics of suspicion',[94] that created tensions. The department's research strategy involved prioritizing work in cognitive psychology and cognitive neuroscience. In particular, this led to a major research project exploring the psychological processes in infants' brains. The Centre for Brain and Cognitive Development's 'Baby Lab' has conducted renowned research into early markers for autism in babies, the relationship between Down syndrome and

---

[91] Stephen Frosh, 'Psychosocial Studies and Psychology: Is a Critical Approach Emerging?', *Human Relations*, 56.12 (2003), 1647–50.
[92] Oral interview of Stephen Frosh, conducted by Lorraine Blakemore.
[93] Mats Alvesson and Kaj Sköldberg, *Reflexive Methodology: New Vistas for Qualitative Research*, 2nd ed. (London: Sage, 2009), 3.
[94] Ibid., 94–5.

Alzheimer's disease, and how the brains of babies respond when spending time in front of computer and television screens. In 2020, it extended the use of wireless technology tracking brain activity to toddlers. The 'Toddler Lab' monitors the brain activity of young children carrying out normal day-to-day activities. One of its most innovative projects involves the 'CAVE', which scrutinizes their brain activity within simulated 'real world' environments such as supermarkets or farms.

In contrast, the questions that psychosocial scholars address are informed by psychoanalysis, narrative theories, and philosophy. They deny the neutrality of science. They hold that 'knowing is not separable from the knower'. For psychosocial scholars, science itself is a social practice. They are therefore critical of the positivistic orientations of the rest of the department. Their critical approach to the sort of psychology conducted by the majority of scholars in the Department of Psychology is 'important for engaging with, and shifting, some of the more fixed and limited assumptions of the traditional psychological knowledge-enterprise', Frosh explains.[95] Rather than the accumulation of 'objective knowledge', psychosocial scholars concern themselves with *interpretation* as a way of understanding human behaviours and psyches. This interpretive work involves paying attention to the fundamentally political nature of knowledge, psychodynamic interrelationality, the unconscious, power, and emotion.

Tensions peaked in the lead-up to the RAE in 2008. The College was under financial pressure due to reductions in funding from the Higher Education Funding Council for England (HEFCE). Research in the Department of Psychology was increasingly orientating towards the neurosciences, which required expensive laboratories and imaging technologies. In 2007, the Psychology Department at Birkbeck and at UCL agreed to joint management of the Neuroimaging Centre in Bedford Way, to better collaborate in cognitive neuroscientific research.[96] They wanted to expand such research—which meant achieving a high RAE 'score' which would bode well for grant applications. As head of the department, Mike Oaksford argued that the academic assessors on the 2008 panel for the Psychology Unit of Assessment would be unsympathetic to the research endeavours of psychosocial scholars, although this was disputed. He maintained that including psychosocial scholars in Birkbeck's psychology assessment would lower their overall grade. He urged the CPS to be included in a different Unit of Assessment—that of Sociology.[97] With great reluctance, and with only one year to

---

[95] Frosh, 'Psychosocial Studies and Psychology', 1550.
[96] 'Agreement between Birkbeck College and University College London (UCL) for the Joint Management of the Neuroimaging Centre Located at the Department of Psychology, UCL, 26 Bedford Way, London WC1H 0AP', signed by Birkbeck College Secretary Keith Harrison and Professor Peter Mobbs (Dean, UCL Faculty of Life Sciences) in January and February 2007, Birkbeck Archive, Box 65.
[97] 'CPS Meeting with Mike Oatsford, Tuesday 14th March [2007], 1.30–2.45', in my possession, file 'PsychosocialStudies2007Crisis'.

go before the census date, Frosh was tasked with inventing a Sociology submission from within the College.[98] He later recalled that

> it turned out that apart from my group in Psychology, there were another 20 or so people across the College [many in the Faculty of Continuing Education] who had nowhere to go. So almost anyone who could spell Sociology was in the Sociology Unit of Assessment in 2008! And it was alright, we didn't do well but we did do respectably given that it was a ragbag of people, most of whom didn't even know each other.... I didn't even know who they were, let alone having any sense of a research environment in which we did things together! Suddenly, we were all Sociologists.[99]

This crisis cemented their fate: the Centre for Psychosocial Studies no longer felt welcome in the Department of Psychology. Although there was some talk of resisting change, by this stage most psychosocial researchers were forced to admit that remaining within the Department of Psychology would simply 'institutionalise[ ] divisions... with the possibility of a later split left unresolved and without addressing the core issue of marginalization'. It would also exacerbate the 'relative isolation of a small CPS group from others doing related work outside the School of Psychology'.[100] Becoming a separate department was therefore deemed to be 'the most exciting option'.[101] Realistically, it was their only option.

To help the process of forging an intellectual community, Frosh founded and co-directed with interdisciplinary scholar Sasha Roseneil the Birkbeck Institute for Social Research (BISR) as an umbrella centre for people working in the field. He and five of his colleagues from the Department of Psychology set up the Department of Psychosocial Studies. Their former disciplinary home was renamed the Department of Psychological Sciences, eventually becoming part of the School of Science, while the Department of Psychosocial Studies was incorporated into the School of Social Sciences, Philosophy, and History. It flourished, becoming one of the most influential departments of its type in the world. But the birthing process had been painful.

The creation of 'psychosocial studies' illustrates some recurring aspects of disciplinarity. The splitting of psychosocial studies from the mainstream department is an example of the role played by national politics in the production of disciplinary knowledge. The schism was driven by decisions made in response to the introduction of governmental guidelines on the funding of universities. Increased

---

[98] There was a Department of Politics and Sociology, but they were all returned in the Politics Unit of Assessment.

[99] Oral interview of Stephen Frosh, conducted by Lorraine Blakemore.

[100] Stephen Frosh, 'Plans for the Centre for Psychosocial Studies' (May 2007), 3, in Birkbeck Archive, Box 65.

[101] Ibid., 3.

state managerialism meant that College as well as departmental heads were required to respond to these external pressures—in this case, the league tables of disciplines and the academic and political preferences of academic and non-academic members of disciplinary 'Units of Assessment'.

There was something much more fundamental, however, driving the creation of a separate field of knowledge called 'psychosocial studies'. Psychosocial scholars are intrinsically interdisciplinary: ironically, a disciplinary umbrella was required to safeguard interdisciplinarity. There would always be tensions—including *from within* the field (for example, feminism, systems theory, and psychoanalysis were often incompatible approaches within psychosocial studies).[102] The position of psychoanalysis, which was dominant within the Department of Psychosocial Studies, also caused internal debate. Was psychoanalysis a science (as Freud believed) or part of the arts and humanities? The International Psychoanalytic Association had been founded in 1910 in response to being rejected by 'official science'. Freud himself made a case for psychoanalytic approaches in Higher Education institutions. In 1919, he published a short essay entitled 'On the Teaching of Psychoanalysis in Universities'. In it, he maintained that a 'general psychoanalytic course' in universities and medical schools was important not only to teach 'psychological disorders' but to contribute to all 'branches of learning which lie within the sphere of philosophy and the arts'.[103] He urged students to 'learn something *about* psychoanalysis and something *from* it'. In other words, it was not enough for students to learn the 'facts' and mechanisms of psychoanalysis: 'to learn something *from* psychoanalysis might constitute the basis for revolutionizing learning and institutions of learning in general'.[104] In this way, psychosocial studies were intrinsically transformational—that is, they sought not only the production of knowledge but also to change the way knowledge is produced. As such, psychosocial studies exemplifies Foucault's observation cited earlier that 'to be a discipline, there must be the possibility of formulating new propositions, ad infinitum'.[105]

* * *

In this chapter, I have focused on a small number of 'invented disciplines', while insisting that *all* academic disciplines are historical constructs. Many important 'reservoirs of ways of knowing' (as Trowler put it at the start of this chapter) move with relative ease between 'disciplines'; while other schools of knowledge never

---

[102] Frosh, 'Psychosocial Studies and Psychology', 1559.
[103] Sigmund Freud, 'On the Teaching of Psychoanalysis in Universities', in *Standard Edition of the Complete Psychological Works of Sigmund Freud*, Vol. 17, 1st pub. 1919 (London: Hogarth Press, 1953–74), 173.
[104] Nicholas Royle, *The Uncanny: An Introduction* (Manchester: Manchester University Press, 2002), 58.
[105] Michel Foucault, 'The Order of Discourse', 1981, 59.

Fig. 22.1 Vera Evison, who carried out the first excavations on the West Stow Anglo-Saxon village site from 1957 to 1961, before its archaeology was destroyed by quarrying for sand. She is pictured with a cup of beer on the trench edge. It is presumably the last day of the excavation since it was traditional to bury a bottle of beer or whisky when backfilling a site. (Thanks to Tim Reynolds and Lesley McFayden for information about the tradition.) http://www.stedmundsburychronicle.co.uk.

translate into 'disciplines'. An example of the first is archaeology. At various times in the College's history, it has lodged in the Department of English, the Centre for Extra-Mural Studies, and (from 2007) the Department of History, Classes, and Archaeology. Vera Evison was a distinguished archaeologist who taught at Birkbeck for forty-seven years between 1947 and 1983 (see Fig. 22.1). She was unusual in that she made a reputation in a field that was dominated by men educated in the elite universities. She worked on Anglo-Saxon archaeology and early medieval European migration while teaching Old English and Old Norse in the Department of *English*. This enabled her to quip that she was the 'imaginary head of a non-existent Archaeology department' at Birkbeck.[106] In fact, a Department of Anglo-Saxon Archaeology was established at Birkbeck in 1979, with links to the University of London's Institute of Archaeology, but it had been dissolved within four years. The subject was only revived with the transfer of the Centre for Extra-Mural Studies to Birkbeck, with the energetic archaeologist Anthony ('Tony') Legge at its helm.

An example of the second trend (that is, towards 'reservoirs of ways of knowing' that are not 'disciplines') is creative writing. As with psychoanalysis, scholars used to argue that it did not belong on university curriculums at all. In *The Elephants Teach: Creative Writing since 1880*, David Gershom Myers tells the story of when Vladimir Nabokov applied for a chair in literature at Harvard University.

---

[106] Letter from Vera Evison to Mr West, 5 May 1969, in the museum of the West Stow Anglo-Saxon Village. Thanks to Alan Forth for bringing this to my attention.

The linguist Roman Jakobson was not impressed, quipping: 'What's next? Shall we appoint elephants to teach zoology?'[107] But creative writing has a long history in Higher Education—it was taught at the London Mechanics Institution from its inception, for example, under the title 'English composition'. In its current form, though, it came late to Birkbeck. While the University of Lancaster and the University of East Anglia introduced creative writing courses in the 1970s (responding in part to the disappearance of fiction editors in many publishing houses),[108] Birkbeck did so only in 2003. Although it is more of a 'sub-discipline' than a 'discipline' in its own right, creative writing has flourished by providing more vibrant ways of understanding literature than those offered by more traditional, highly theoretical courses.

The construction and deconstruction of disciplines is important. It draws attention to factors that construct knowledge, careers, and institutions. Power relations are central throughout as 'boundary work' is a continuous process. It is affected by external events such as war, governmental ideologies, finances, managerialism, lobbying by learned societies, and clashes between intellectual cultures, as well as by more banal things such as strong personalities, career prospects, and friendships/enmities. Finally, contingent reasons and happenstance have their role in the making and unmaking of disciplines. A lot is at stake, including the hiring and firing of staff, the allocation of research funding, and the distribution of power both within and without the university. It is often decisive in deciding who become tenured professors and who are employed on short-term, minimum wage contracts. Governments and other governing bodies are more likely to seek expert advice from scholars they recognize to be members of high-status disciplines. This means the voices of some academics are heard more clearly than others. Most importantly, though, universities are charged with teaching: students have to learn discipline-based rules, processes, practices, methods, objects, and habits. They 'pass' examinations only if they 'learn disciplinarity', speaking like a geologist, geographer, linguist, or (type of) psychologist.

---

[107] David Gershom Myers, *The Elephants Teach: Creative Writing since 1880* (Englewood Cliffs: Prentice Hall, 1996), 1.
[108] Matthew Wright, 'Education: Higher: Novel Career Goals: Creative Writing Courses are Booming. But Will They Lead to Fame and Fortune? And Why do they Cost So Much?', *The Guardian* (18 December 2007), 10.

23
Numerical Automation; Or, Computing

In the 1940s, physicist and computer engineer Ralph Slutz composed a limerick, dedicated to the extraordinary research being done at Birkbeck in the field of what came to be known as computing. The limerick went:

> There was a computer named Booth,
> Who said by-gad and forsooth,
> To shorten the delay of the highest speed relay,
> Apply a spot of vermouth![1]

The 'Booth' in the limerick was Andrew Donald Booth, a member of the Mathematics Department at Birkbeck where he headed the Electronic Computation Research Laboratory. In the late 1940s, almost no one knew what a 'computer' even was; if asked, they might have surmised that it was a name for bank-clerks responsible for making calculations. By 1952, the Computer Section under Booth had become an independent sub-department of the College.[2] In 1957, Booth's Electronic Computation Research Laboratory was renamed the Department of Numerical Automation. This department was the first academic department in the UK (and possibly worldwide) devoted to teaching and research related to computing. The first graduate of the College's MSc in numerical automation was Nobert (later, Norman) Kitz, who went on to design ANITA, the first desktop calculator.[3] By 1963, the department had become one of Computer Science, and the Diploma of Numerical Analysis had been changed to the Diploma of Computer Science.[4]

But Booth's real claim to fame was not his tireless labour establishing computing as an academic discipline. Rather, it was his work in partnership with Kathleen Hylda Valerie Britten, a formidable mathematician and one of the first female computer pioneers, which resulted in the development of some of the earliest digital computers. These included the Automatic Relay Calculator (ARC) in 1947,

---

[1] Personal communication with Andrew Booth, in J. A. N. Lee, 'Computer Pioneers', *IEEE Computer Society* at http://history.computer.org/pioneers/booth-ad.html, viewed 1 June 2019.
[2] J. D. Bernal, 'Teaching and Research at Birkbeck College Crystallography Laboratory' (October 1962), 3, in 'Guard Book. Ib', in the Birkbeck Archive.
[3] Roger Johnson, oral interview conducted by Dr Lorraine Blakemore, in the Birkbeck Oral History Archives.
[4] 'Minutes of a Meeting of the Faculty of Arts Held on 22nd October 1963', in the 'Faculty of Arts. Minutes of Meetings. Apl. 25th 1940', in the Birkbeck archive.

the prototype Simple Electronic Computer (SEC) in 1949, and the All Purpose Electronic Computer (APEC) in 1951. Andrew Booth was also the British inventor of the world's first rotating storage device in the form of a magnetic drum store, a brass cylinder that was coated with nickel. At the time, the technology was used in the UK's best-selling range of computers; indeed, magnetic disks are employed in many computers used today. His binary multiplication procedure (also known as Booth's multiplier) was devised over egg and chips in the ABC tearoom in Southampton Row. Today, billions of the Booth multiplier are used each year on microchips which are used in everything from computers to phones to washing machines.

* * *

Who was Booth? He was a talented mathematician and physicist, who joined the Mathematics Department at Birkbeck in 1946. The public school he had attended as a child—Haberdashers' Aske's Boys' School in Elstree (Hertfordshire)—had taught him Latin, Greek, and French, but not mathematics. He had been awarded only 6 per cent in his Public School Entrance examination in the subject. He recalled that his father was so 'livid' with this result that he 'took my mathematical education in hand': three months later, the young Booth resat the examination and was awarded 100 per cent.[5] By the age of 10, he was an expert in differential and integral calculus—neither of which talent protected him from being regularly flogged at school for 'foot in mouth disease'.[6]

Nevertheless, Booth flourished. Although he dropped out of the University of Cambridge, he got a 'First' in the University of London's external degree. After this, he took several jobs, including working in an aero-engine factory in Coventry, an actuarial department, and industry. Tired of this, he did a PhD in X-ray crystallography at the University of Birmingham. At that time, the intensive computational work of crystallography was done with only the most basic aids to calculation, which, Booth observed, was 'no fit occupation for a gentleman'.[7] In his words, 'I therefore determined that, if I could get an academic job, I would attempt to use my engineering knowledge to produce a computer to do this kind of work.'[8] Unfortunately, the war intervened, so he immersed himself conducting research into the crystallographic structure of explosives.[9]

Arriving in the Mathematics Department at Birkbeck immediately after the war, Booth quickly forged links with the College's crystallographers. As we have seen, this was the 'golden age' of Birkbeck science, employing such luminaries as Bernal, Franklin, and Klug. Booth's PhD work in crystallography was to be invaluable. Bernal adopted Booth, seeing in him someone who not only

---

[5] Personal communication with Andrew Booth, in Lee, 'Computer Pioneers'. [6] Ibid.
[7] Ibid. [8] Ibid. [9] Ibid.

understood the needs of crystallographers but also could sort out their most pressing problem: the incredibly time-consuming process of conducting research into the chemical bonding in complex organic molecules. As Booth complained, 'calculations of x-ray structural crystallography' would typically take a 'group of human "slaves"' between three months and three years to complete.[10] Furthermore,

> the work is of an excessively routine and uninspired character and is the most severe bottleneck in the extension of x-ray methods either to simple substances of chemical interest, or the exceedingly complex problems of protein structure determination.[11]

Anything that would 'reduce the time required for routine calculations to manageable proportions' would be a boon to science.[12]

Booth was joined at Birkbeck by mathematician Kathleen Britten. She had been Junior Scientific Officer at the Royal Aircraft Establishment in Farnborough and then Research Scientist for the British Rubber Producer's Research Association. They became the smallest of the early British computer groups and formed a lifelong working and marital partnership. He built the machines; she developed the programming language.

Less than a year after arriving at Birkbeck, Andrew Booth had secured a Rockefeller Foundation grant, enabling him to survey research on computers taking place in the USA. It was an important period, followed by six months spent with John von Neumann's computer group at Princeton University.[13] Kathleen Britten (as she was known prior to their marriage) joined him on this second trip. Although excited by von Neumann's research, he later reflected that it was 'discouraging' because the 'only machines under development were so large and costly as to be beyond the bounds of realism for a College laboratory'.[14] Booth refused to be daunted, however, concluding that a small machine would be possible to develop. After gathering financial support from the University of London, the Rockefeller Foundation, ICI, and the British Rubber Producers' Research

---

[10] Andrew D. Booth, 'Computers in the University of London, 1945–1962', in N. Metropolis, J. Howlett, and Gian-Carlo Rota (eds), *A History of Computing in the Twentieth Century: A Collection of Essays* (New York: Academic Press, 1980), 551.

[11] A. D. Booth, 'Establishment of a Centre for the Construction and Use of an Electronic Computer', in Sir William Bragg, *Opening of Biomolecular Research Laboratory* (1948), 15.

[12] 'Birkbeck College Computational Laboratory—Its History and Activities', 1, in Birkbeck Archive, Box 10, 'Computers Pre-1965'.

[13] Booth, 'Computers in the University of London, 1945–1962', 553; Andrew D. Booth, L. Brandwood, and J. P. Cleave, *Mechanical Resolution of Linguistic Problems* (London: Butterworths Scientific Publications, 1958), 1; Simon Lavington, *Early British Computers: The Story of Vintage Computers and the People Who Built Them* (Manchester: Manchester University Press, 1980), 62.

[14] 'Birkbeck College Computational Laboratory—Its History and Activities', 1, in Birkbeck Archive, Box 10, 'Computers Pre-1965'.

Fig. 23.1 Kathleen Britten (later, Booth), Xenia Sweeting (Research Assistant), and Andrew Booth working on ARC, December 1946. In fact, Britten and Sweeting did most of the construction. www.historyofinformation.com.

Association, Booth and Britten started to develop such a machine.[15] In Andrew Booth's words,

> Miss Britten and I divided our efforts. I designed a 21-bit parallel binary arithmetic and control unit using Siemens high-speed relays while at the same time she developed programs for this device.[16]

Although ostensibly driven by the desire to construct a 'relay calculator for the automatic computation of all the elements required in X-ray crystal structure analysis', he admitted that he and Britten (by this stage, Kathleen Booth) regarded the project as 'an exercise of mathematical enjoyment rather than anything of a practical nature'.[17]

There were many difficulties, not least the perennial problem of accommodation. The Booths' laboratory was located in a wartime emergency water tank, which could only be accessed by climbing up unstable wooden stairs.[18] Their team was always very small, consisting of the two Booths, joined by a few research students and a secretary. It was during this period that they started on the design of the machine that was to be called the ARC (Automatic Relay Computer) (see Fig. 23.1). It was a computational device that employed paper input and output; it had no memory. The Booths quickly realized that the main problem in electronic technology was storage. Within two months, he had designed 'a von Neumann type, parallel, machine (ARC) using Siemens high-speed relays.... These devices

---

[15] Ibid.   [16] Booth, 'Computers in the University of London, 1945–1962', 553–4.
[17] Ibid., 552–3.
[18] Andrew Colin, 'Andrew Booth's Computers at Birkbeck College', in *Resurrection: The Bulletin of the Computer Conservation Society*, 5 (spring 1993), n.p., at http://www.computerconservationsociety.org/resurrection/res05.htm, viewed 1 June 2019.

had a switching time of less than 1 milli-second and, by devising an anticipatory carry mechanism', he was able to produce a device that was even faster. The prototype machine could 'carry out a complete set of three dimensional Fourier syntheses for the substance Oxalic Acid' in only thirty-six hours. This would have taken an entire year using 'the old-fashioned hand methods'.[19] By 1948, the Booths had established a Centre for the Construction and Use of an Electronic Computer at Birkbeck.

It was in this centre that Andrew Booth developed a machine which possessed 'a memory of a new type'. This was 'a drum coated with ferromagnetic material rotating at a speed of between 30,000 and 50,000 r.p.m. and having a capacity of about 4,000 numbers each of forty digits'.[20] It would prove a godsend in solving 'problems of crystallographic interest'.[21] As Roger Johnson, long-term member of Birkbeck's Computer Department and historian of computing, noted, this was 'the first time anyone successfully creating a rotating storage device—a memory— and connected it to a computer. A world first'.[22]

Booth's ambition, though, was to build smaller computers—indeed, he exclaimed, his plan was to build a computer that was so small that every university would possess one! In 1954, Booth told the *Banbury Guardian* that computers were 'primarily invented to help scientists in their work, but there is no reason why it should not be used commercially'. After this remarkable insight, however, he less optimistically noted that he did not 'think the machine will become a commercial proposition' until a computer could be designed that was the size of a suitcase.[23] In 1954, that idea was regarded as wholly fanciful.

What he did do, however, was reduce the number of electronic valves in the computer to fewer than 500. This compared with between 1,000 and 18,000 in other machines at that time.[24] Further innovations included the ferro-magnetic rectangular hysteresis loop digit store and the magnetostrictive nickel line store.[25] Crucially, his computer needed a floor area of only 4 square feet and its power consumption was similar to that of a large electric fire.[26] Compared to the Ferranti computer, which had 3,500 valves and cost £85,000, Booth's machine had 415 values and cost less than £5,000.[27]

The contributions of Kathleen Booth were equally distinguished, although she has been largely forgotten or relegated to the position of 'research assistant'

---

[19] 'Birkbeck College Computational Laboratory—Its History and Activities', 1, in Birkbeck Archive, Box 10, 'Computers Pre-1965'.
[20] Booth, 'Establishment of a Centre for the Construction and Use of an Electronic Computer', 15.
[21] Ibid., 15.
[22] Roger Johnson, oral interview conducted by Dr Lorraine Blakemore, in the Birkbeck Oral History Archives.
[23] 'Robot Translator is Developed at Fenny Compton', *Banbury Guardian* (19 August 1954), 5.
[24] 'Birkbeck College Computational Laboratory—Its History and Activities', 2, in Birkbeck Archive, Box 10, 'Computers Pre-1965'.
[25] Ibid.   [26] Ibid.   [27] Ibid.

to Andrew Booth. Indeed, in a book written by Andrew Booth with linguist William Nash Locke of the Massachusetts Institute of Technology, they even get the first initial of her name wrong.[28] But Kathleen Booth was a formidable mathematician in her own right, writing an important book on programming for automatic digital computers as well as articles on machine-aided translations.[29] As she noted in the first sentence of *Programming for an Automatic Digital Calculator* (1958),

> In spite of the considerable growth in the electronic computer population during the last decade very little published literature exists on programming and even less on programming for a two address machine; it is hoped that this account of some of the routines used on APEXC, the machine at Birkbeck College, will be of interest to those who have to make use of automatic digital calculators.[30]

She admitted that a detailed knowledge of mathematics was an important skill for programmers but boasted that she could train anyone 'with a capacity for accurate detailed thinking and a talent for solving puzzles' in the techniques within a fortnight.[31] Kathleen Booth also developed a programme to simulate a neural network investigating the ways animals recognize patterns.[32] The computer revolution was under way.

* * *

Funding these projects was always a challenge. The Booths faced fierce competition from American computer scientists. Very early on, they recognized that potential donors would want a machine that did more than 'mere calculation'.[33] Could computers be used to diagnose disease, Andrew Booth asked in the 1950s? He believed that 'it would effect great reductions in the sufferings of patients if the diagnostic process were turned over to a machine'.[34] He divided the process of diagnosis into three tasks: physical observation, association of symptoms, and conducting tests to confirm or otherwise any provisional diagnosis. The first and third of these tasks, the Booths decided, were currently not feasible tasks for computers, 'although such things as the analysis of electrocardiograms and

---

[28] A. Donald Booth and William Nash Locke, 'Historical Introduction', in Locke and Booth (eds), *Machine Translation of Languages: Fourteen Essays* (London: Chapman and Hall, 1955), 3.
[29] Kathleen H. V. Booth, *Programming for an Automatic Digital Calculator* (London: Butterworths Scientific Publications, 1958); Kathleen H. V. Booth, 'Machine Aided Translation with a Post-Editor', in A. D. Booth (ed.), *Machine Translation* (Amsterdam: North-Holland Publishing Co., 1967).
[30] Booth, *Programming for an Automatic Digital Calculator*, preface.   [31] Ibid., 1.
[32] *Annual Report of Birkbeck College 1958–9* (London: Birkbeck College, 1959).
[33] Personal communication with Andrew Booth, in Lee, 'Computer Pioneers'.
[34] Letter from Booth to the Master, Lockwood, dated 30 October 1954, in Birkbeck Archive, Box 10, 'Computers Pre-1965'.

electroencephalograms' were 'properly functions of mathematics rather than medicine'.[35] In contrast, symptom association could easily become part of computing since it was 'used in the normal operation of a computer under the title of "Collation"'.[36] Rather caustically, Andrew Booth observed that 'precision is often sadly lacking in the lower grades of the medical fraternity', but since 'modern mathematical machines have large and extremely reliable storage organs ("Memories") they are inherently capable of great precision in the associative process'.[37] The fact that Andrew Booth put 'memories' in inverted commas suggests just how new this neologism was at the time. Indeed, in their textbook, *Automatic Digital Calculators* (1953), the two Booths even apologized to readers for their 'use of such an anthropomorphic term as "memory"'.[38]

More important than their ideas about the clinical potentialities of computers was their work on 'machine translation' or 'translation by purely automatic means'.[39] After all, Andrew Booth reasoned, translation was 'simply a form of code'.[40] The Booths were active presences at the First International Conference on Machine Translation, which was held at the Massachusetts Institute of Technology in June 1952, and Andrew Booth was even assigned the task of editing its proceedings.[41] It was a field that was to be galvanized in 1957 with the publication of Noam Chomsky's *Syntactic Structures*.[42]

At that time, no machine had the storage capacity capable of translating a book or even a shorter scientific text. The advantages of having a computer that could translate texts would be immense: for example, being able to translate texts rapidly from behind 'the Iron Curtain' was of huge political importance during the Cold War.[43] Translating *from* English *to* other languages was equally crucial. The Booths succeeded in translating short paragraphs of around forty words from English into Albanian, Arabic, Danish, Finnish, French, German, Hungarian, Indonesian, Italian, Japanese, Latin, Latvian, Norwegian, Polish, Portuguese, Rumanian, Russian, Spanish, Swedish, and Turkish.[44] They also created a computer that translated English into Braille[45] and, in collaboration with the University of Glasgow, placed the entire New Testament on computer for the first time.[46]

---

[35] Ibid. [36] Ibid. [37] Ibid.
[38] Andrew D. Booth and Kathleen H. V. Booth, *Automatic Digital Calculators* (London: Butterworths Scientific Publications, 1953), v.
[39] 'Birkbeck College Computational Laboratory—Its History and Activities', 4.
[40] Personal communication with Andrew Booth, in Lee, 'Computer Pioneers'.
[41] 'Birkbeck College Computational Laboratory—Its History and Activities', 4. It incorrectly states that the conference was held at Harvard. See John Hutchins, 'Milestones in Machine Translation', *Language Today* (13 October 1998), 12.
[42] Noam Chomsky, *Syntactic Structures*, 1st pub. 1957 (Berlin: Mouton de Gruyter, 2000).
[43] 'Translations Limited. Experiments with Computers', *The Times* (21 October 1955), 5.
[44] Ibid., 5. [45] Ibid., 5. [46] 'The Computer Composes?', *The Times* (24 April 1963), 7.

Although Birkbeck was at the forefront of 'mechanized linguistics', there were many complex problems to solve. First, the 'absence of statistical data on real languages' delayed progress.[47] Second, while the length of any text was not decisive, the 'size of the dictionary which can be stored in the computing machine' was. In the 1950s, scientists were 'limited to a vocabulary of about 1000 words'. This was made more complex by the fact that grammar was crucial. As Booth and Locke explained in their 1955 history of machine translation,

> The grammatical structure of a language is the heart of its individuality, much more than its words, paradoxical as this may seem. Of course, each language used different words for concepts such as tree, foot, love, justice, but it is not possible to define a language in terms of its words alone. Its grammar must be taken into account. In fact, it may not be going too far to state that only in terms of its grammar can a language be defined.[48]

Third, some texts presented more problems than others. Scientific tomes—such as articles on nuclear physics or X-ray crystallography—were relatively easy to translate 'word for word': these translations could be 'read without difficulty' by any 'person who is skilled in the subject'. It was quite another thing to translate works of art such as 'a book by Shakespeare into German or by Goethe into English'. Such a task 'cannot be done because, although the stuff which comes out is intelligible, it is not by any means a work of art'.[49] This did not dent the enthusiasm of Arnolfo John Caraffi, the College Secretary, who informed the Editor of the *Manchester Guardian* that one of the most exciting aspects of 'machine translation' was 'the collaboration of scientists with Arts men [sic]'. Michael Levison was a member of the Computational Laboratory at Birkbeck, where he completed his PhD in 1962 on 'The Application of a Computer to Linguistic Problems'. Both he and Booth quickly realized that the Ferranti Mercury computer, despite being 'primarily designed for the solution of mathematical problems', could be incredibly useful for linguistic work, such as creating glossaries and concordances, adjudicating on authorship and relative chronology, as well as machine translation.[50] He was involved with building up 'a nucleus of a library of Greek prose...including tapes of the whole of the New Testament, parts of the Septuagint, substantial

---

[47] Letter from the Master, Lockwood, to Leslie Farrer-Brown, Director of the Nuffield Foundation, dated 11 July 1961, 2, in Birkbeck Archive, Box 10, 'Computers Pre-1965'.
[48] Booth and Locke, 'Historical Introduction', 5.
[49] 'Translations Limited. Experiments with Computers', 5.
[50] Michael Levison, 'The Application of the Ferranti Mercury Computer to Linguistic Problems', *Information and Control*, 3 (1960), 231 and 245, and Michael Levison, 'The Computer in Literary Studies', *IFIP Congress '68*, 1 (1968), 175–94.

excepts from Xenophon and Thucydides'.[51] Homer's *Iliad* and *Odyssey* were later added. Caraffi contended that

> We hear so much nowadays of the incompatibility of an education in the humanities with the technological structure of society that it is refreshing to find at least one field in which scientist and classic [sic] may breathe the same air.[52]

In other words, the computing team and academic administrators at Birkbeck believed that computers were essential in bridging the 'two cultures' of the arts and sciences.

* * *

The most intransigent problem faced by the Booths in their mission to revolutionize computing systems concerned hardware. This was not unique to Birkbeck. In 1954, the colleges of the University of London recognized that computing was going to be indispensable to the future of scholarship. The University's Ferranti Mercury computer was 'completely unsuitable, both because of its limited storage and because of its exclusively arithmetical design'.[53] Storage capacity was also inadequate. Even worse, 'Mercury' was 'in such demand for arithmetical work in the sciences that 6–8 weeks elapse between a request for machine time and its availability'.[54] The system was over-loaded.[55] Larger storage facilities and the ability to deal with more complex data processing not only were essential for academic research but also could be a part of what Birkbeck academics hoped would be an 'Institute for Computer Sciences' in the University of London.[56]

With this in mind, on 18 January 1954, a meeting was called at Senate House, the administrative heart of the University of London. In attendance were the Vice-Chancellor of the University of London (Air Chief Marshal Sir Roderic Maxwell Hill), the Clerk of the Court (Mr Stewart), and senior professors from King's College London, Imperial College, and University College London.[57]

---

[51] Michael Levison, 'The Computer in Literary Studies', in A. D. Booth (ed.), *Machine Translation* (New York: John Wiley, 1967), 177.

[52] Letter presumably from Caraffi to the Editor of the *Manchester Guardian*, dated 1 September 1955, in Birkbeck Archive, Box 10, 'Computers Pre-1965'.

[53] Letter from the Master, Lockwood, to L. Farrer-Brown, Director of the Nuffield Foundation, dated 11 July 1961, 2, in Birkbeck Archive, Box 10, 'Computers Pre-1965'.

[54] Ibid.

[55] Memo from H. Bondi (Chairman) and R. A. Buckingham (Director), 'University of London Computer Unit. Memorandum to Boards of Studies' (February 1960), in Birkbeck Archive, Box 10, 'Computers Pre-1965'.

[56] Ibid.

[57] Arnolfo John Caraffi, 'Personal Notes on Informal Meeting Concerning Computers Held at the Senate House—18th January 1954', in Birkbeck Archive, Box 10, 'Computers Pre-1965'. The members were the Vice-Chancellor of the University of London (Air Chief Marshal Sir Roderic Maxwell Hill), the Principal, John Semple (Professor of Pure Mathematics at King's College London and Dean of the University Faculty of Science), the Clerk of the Court (Mr Stewart), Sir David Brunt (Professor of Meteorology at Imperial College and Vice-President of the Royal Society), Ifor Evans (Provost of

Birkbeck sent John Lockwood (the Master), Arnolfo John Caraffi (College Secretary), J. D. Bernal (Physics Department), and Andrew Booth. This distinguished group began a discussion about applying to the University of London for a substantial capital grant in order to 'purchase or build a computing machine', which was considered essential particularly for research in physics.[58] Lockwood, Caraffi, Bernal, and Booth, however, had other interests in mind: they were keen to 'protect the interests of the computer research unit' at Birkbeck.[59] While the estimates provided for the purchase of a University of London computer ranged from £14,500 (for the Hollerith model, which had been based on Booth's Model No. 1) and £85,000 (for Ferranti's model), Booth offered to design and build a computer for the University of London at a cost of £8,500.[60] It was a bargain. The project would take two years and, in addition, would require salaries for people responsible for what 'the Americans describe as "getting the bugs out of the machine"', as the Provost of University College London put it.[61] Within five months, the University had agreed to offer a capital grant of £9,000 to Andrew Booth to design and construct a computer for the colleges of the University of London. It was to be installed in the new Physics Building at University College London.[62] The Clerk of the Court made it clear that

> The acquisition by the University of an electronic calculating machine for installation in the new Physics Building of the College [UCL] is conditional upon a fair proportion of the working time of the machine being reserved for University work from outside the College and upon the transfer of the machine in due course to the proposed central University Computational Unit when it proves possible to establish such a unit.[63]

There was also the question of staff. In 1954, the post of an electronic engineer or physicist was advertised to 'assist in installation and operation of electronic digital calculator', with a salary of between £600 and £900 annually.[64] At the same time, a post was advertised for a secretary to help Andrew Booth. Her salary—which was advertised at the substantially lower fee of £325—would include not

---

University College London), Harrie Massey (the Quain Professor of Physics at UCL), John Lockwood (Birkbeck's Master), J. D. Bernal, A. D. Booth, and Arnolfo John Caraffi (Birkbeck's College Secretary).

[58] Caraffi, 'Personal Notes on Informal Meeting Concerning Computers Held at the Senate House'.
[59] Ibid.   [60] Ibid.
[61] Letter from B. Ifor Evans (Provost of UCL) to the Master, Lockwood, dated 8 February 1954, in Birkbeck Archive, Box 10, 'Computers Pre-1965'.
[62] Letter from Mr Steward (Clerk of the Court) to John Lockwood, dated 20 June 1954, in Birkbeck Archive, Box 10, 'Computers Pre-1965'.
[63] Letter from Mr Stewart to B. Ifor Evans (Provost of UCL), dated 11 June 1954, in Birkbeck Archive, Box 10, 'Computers Pre-1965'.
[64] Letter presumably from Caraffi to Mr P. C. Bartlett, dated 3 September 1954, in Birkbeck Archive, Box 10, 'Computers Pre-1965'.

only basic secretarial tasks but also feeding 'punch cards' into the computer. Caraffi noted that

> Previous experience of punched card operation is not expected, but I feel that a girl [sic] would get much more fun out of the job if she had a mathematical bent or some experience of physics.[65]

In 1957, the University of London Computer Unit was finally established, providing computing services to all colleges. By 1961, International Computers and Tabulators Ltd (ICT) made its first customer sale of the 1301 model to the University of London. This computer did not require programmers to learn binary or octal arithmetic and, unusually, used British not American currency. Pounds, shillings, and pence were to win the day.

This was not the end of the story, however. Even with these greatly improved facilities, the Chairman and Director of the University of London Computer Unit conceded that it would not be able to 'meet all the computing needs of the University'. Individual colleges needed to introduce their own computing facilities which would be 'complementary to those in the central organization'.[66] Birkbeck was thrilled, therefore, when ICT offered the College its '1400' computer, at a nominal annual rent of £100. This 'data processing machine' had been specifically designed to advance research on 'machine languages and machine translation'.[67] Caraffi reported that it was a 'very attractive' offer and was 'without question a great compliment to Dr. Booth's efforts in promoting the analysis of language'.[68]

Its acquisition in 1961 caused a flurry of activity: where was it to be housed? The '1400' required 2,000 square feet of floor area.[69] The money was found, partly through a grant from the Nuffield Foundation but also, and to the College's surprise, from money hoarded within Booth's department. It turned out that the Booths and their tiny team had amassed a handsome 'nest egg' by manufacturing computers for other colleges and universities.[70] In the end, the '1400' computer

---

[65] Letter presumably from Caraffi to Mrs Skemp, dated 24 September 1954, in Birkbeck Archive, Box 10, 'Computers Pre-1965'.

[66] Memo from H. Bondi (Chairman) and R. A. Buckingham (Director), 'University of London Computer Unit. Memorandum to Boards of Studies' (February 1960), in Birkbeck Archive, Box 10, 'Computers Pre-1965'.

[67] Letter from the Master, Lockwood, to L. Farrer-Brown, Director of the Nuffield Foundation, dated 11 July 1961, 2, in Birkbeck Archive, Box 10, 'Computers Pre-1965'.

[68] Letter presumably by Caraffi to H. D. G. Trew, dated 2 June 1961, in Birkbeck Archive, Box 10, 'Computers Pre-1965'.

[69] 'Some Notes on the ICT 1400 and Its Use in Linguistic Analysis', dated 29 May 1961, in Birkbeck Archive, Box 10, 'Computers Pre-1965'.

[70] Letter presumably from Caraffi to Dr Walter Reginald Wooldridge, dated 27 July 1961, in Birkbeck Archive, Box 10, 'Computers Pre-1965'.

was shared between Birkbeck and the London School of Hygiene and Tropical Medicine, with Booth appointed Director.[71] In a 1961 document entitled 'Some Notes on the ICT 1400 and Its Use in Linguistic Analysis', Andrew Booth suggested that, in order to 'exploit the machine to its full capacity', he wanted to convert the Department of Numerical Automation into a 'Department of Linguistic Analysis' or a 'Department of Analysis of Language'. It would consist of academic staff divided equally between linguists and mathematicians; in addition, it would serve as 'an auxiliary to all language departments'. The 'equipment of the new department would include, not only the machine, but also the necessary equipment for phonetic analysis and for the teaching of spoken language in general'. The cost? £10,000 in the first five years. The advantages? It would 'make the department the best equipped of its kind in the world and would give this Country a facility which was the same as those enjoyed in the USA and the USSR'.[72]

Unfortunately, the Booths never got to establish their department. Offended at not being awarded a full professorship, Andrew Booth along with Kathleen Booth left Birkbeck for the University of Saskatchewan (Canada) in 1962. The department did have a later incarnation, however, with the establishment of the Birkbeck Language Research Centre in 1965 and then, in 1972, the Department of Applied Linguistics (see Fig. 23.2).

* * *

The Booths never regretted accepting posts at the University of Saskatchewan. Not only Andrew Booth, but Kathleen Booth too rapidly gained the promotions they both deserved. Kathleen Booth became Director of a National Research Council of Canada project on machine translation and, within a decade of moving to Canada, Professor of Mathematics at Lakehead University, where Andrew Booth was President. Both Booths found the energy and freedoms of scientists in Canada to be in stark contrast to the continued austerity of British society at that time. As Andrew Booth once explained, nothing in British life could compete with a stateroom in America which had three taps: one for drinking water and the other two for red and white wine. He was also exasperated by what he called the 'hive of socialist mediocrity which England had become'.[73] For the rest of his life, Andrew Booth called himself a philosophical anarchist and he railed against the 'Cancer of Socialism which seeks to make all men equal—of course to the

---

[71] 'Agreement Concerning the ICT 1400 Computer Laboratory', 1961, in Birkbeck Archive, Box 10, 'Computers Pre-1965'.
[72] 'Some Notes on the ICT 1400 and Its Use in Linguistic Analysis', dated 29 May 1961, in Birkbeck Archive, Box 10, 'Computers Pre-1965'.
[73] Personal communication with Andrew Booth, in Lee, 'Computer Pioneers'.

Fig. 23.2 A demonstration of the Computer Science Department during the 1973 Open Day, Birkbeck's 150th anniversary. Birkbeck Image Collections: Birkbeck History BH0240.

lowest'.[74] It was a harsh judgement, especially since it was the fervent communist Bernal who first recognized and then fostered his talent at Birkbeck.[75] The Booths' pioneering work in computing made possible the computer revolution that has transformed human history.

[74] Ibid.
[75] For a more complete history of computer science at Birkbeck, see Roger Johnson, 'School of Computer Science and Information Systems' (London: Birkbeck College, 2008), at www.dcs.bbk.ac.uk/site/assets/files/1029/50yearsofcomputing.pdf, viewed 1 June 2019.

24
Paranormal Sciences

October 1974.¹ Uri Geller—celebrated for his demonstrations of clairvoyance, telepathy, and teleportation, and his ability to bend spoons and keys through the power of thought alone—was holding a press conference at the Savoy Hotel in London. The room was buzzing with energy: it was like 'a revivalist meeting', observed one journalist.² Although Geller had summoned the press to the hotel to launch his new music record, those who turned up were more interested in his paranormal proclivities. Sensing scepticism, Geller was bullish, promising journalists that one day he would host a 'big television spectacular in front of all the top sceptics and scientists in the world'. This event would 'settle once and for all the validity of his powers'. Unfortunately, Geller contended, 'the presence of conjurors, professional tricksters, and other 'negative' doubting Thomases' was having an inhibiting impact on his psychic energies but 'in the long run[,] criticism does not hurt, because scientific tests will eventually justify me. If you do not believe in what I do, that is your problem.'³ At this point in the press conference, there was an unexpected interruption. John Barrett Hasted of Birkbeck College and John Taylor of King's College London—both respected professors of physics—spontaneously rose from their seats to 'give testimony to the genuineness of Mr. Geller'. Hasted admitted that 'scientists should not do this sort of thing' but, undeterred, announced that 'the time has come to stand up and be counted'. He told the assembled journalists that he had personally tested Geller's extraordinary talents in his laboratory at Birkbeck College and swore that Geller had not been 'a phoney'. Hasted maintained that he had no explanation for 'what causes the phenomenon, but I believe in what Uri Geller does. Science will discover how he softens metal, though science may be changed in the process.'⁴

For a respected scientist to make such a pronouncement in 1974 was brave but not particularly foolhardy. Paranormal shows were popular at the time. Numerous academic conferences showcased the phenomenon.⁵ On stage in France, Jean-Pierre Girard was wowing audiences by demonstrating his ability to lift objects

---

¹ A version of this chapter was published as 'Radical Physics: Science, Socialism, and the Paranormal at Birkbeck College in the 1970s', *Journal of the British Academy*, 7 (2019).
² 'Unpoetic Uri Geller has a Musical Bent', *The Times* (31 October 1974), in 'Newscuttings 1974–76', and 'Scientists Stand by Geller's Claims', *Yorkshire Post* (31 October 1974), in 'Newscuttings 1974–76', in the Birkbeck Archive.
³ 'Unpoetic Uri Geller has a Musical Bent'.   ⁴ Ibid. and 'Scientists Stand by Geller's Claims'.
⁵ Dennis Hackett, 'To Bend, or Not to Bend', *The Times* (10 March 1983), 9.

without touching them; in Germany, the aptly named Professor Hans Bender was championing poltergeists and clairvoyants.[6] Israel-born Geller was himself a global phenomenon, appearing on television in the USA, Japan, South Africa, and most European countries.[7] He had arrived in London in October 1972, two years before the press conference in the Savoy Hotel where he had attempted to launch his record. With the encouragement of his main champion, Andrija Puharich, Geller had demonstrated his psychic powers at the Royal Garden Hotel. Witnesses, including quantum physicist Edward 'Ted' Bastin from Cambridge, were smitten. On 23 November 1973, people throughout the UK echoed Bastin's amazement when Geller appeared with Taylor on David Dimbleby's *Talk-In* show. Geller bent spoons and engaged in other paranormal tricks on live television, encouraging children, adolescents, and adults watching from their living-room sofas to discover suddenly their own hitherto unnoticed paranormal capacities to bend spoons.

Almost overnight, metal bending, telepathy, clairvoyance, and remote viewing became popular pastimes at parties throughout the UK. Admittedly, there were some farcical incidents (in Sweden, for example, a woman who had watched Geller perform his metal-bending exploits on television accused him of causing the metal birth-control device in her uterus to straighten, resulting in pregnancy),[8] but the paranormal also attracted the attention of the CIA, the Pentagon, the Soviet secret intelligence service, and defence laboratories throughout a world that was deeply embroiled in Cold War intrigue.[9] In 1969, eminent anthropologist Margaret Mead convinced the American Association for the Advancement of Science to bestow 'Associate status' on parapsychology.[10] In other words, there were many believers in para-physics and psychokinetics, which involve phenomena as diverse as telepathy, clairvoyance, precognition, and telekinesis, the ability to move physical objects by mental power alone.

This was the context in which highly respected physicists based at Birkbeck (and in other universities) decided that the 'Geller phenomenon' was worth exploring. At Birkbeck, the chief proponent was Hasted. He was born into a distinguished, albeit tragic, family. His mother, who died when he was 3 weeks old, was the daughter of Field-Marshal Arthur Barrett. His father was in the army but committed suicide early in the Second World War.[11] Hasted must have been a

[6] Ibid., 9.
[7] John Hasted, *The Metal-Benders* (London: Routledge and Kegan Paul, 1981), 14.
[8] Stuart Holroyd, *PSI and the Consciousness Explosion* (London: The Bodley Head, 1977), 105.
[9] For example, see David Kaiser, *How the Hippies Saved Physics: Science, Counterculture, and the Quantum Revival* (New York: W. W. Norton and Company, 2011); J. W. Grove, 'Rationality at Risk: Science Against Pseudoscience', *Minerva*, 23.2 (June 1985); Sheila Ostrander and Lynn Schroeder, *PSI: Psychic Discoveries behind the Iron Curtain*, 1st pub. 1973 (London: Abacus, 1977).
[10] Margaret Mead, 'Introduction', in Russell Targ and Harold E. Puthoff, *Mind-Reach: Scientists Look at Psychic Ability* (London: Jonathan Cape, 1977), xv–xvi. Also see Martin Gardner, *Science: Good, Bad and Bogus* (Buffalo: Prometheus Books, 1989), 185, and Grove, 'Rationality at Risk', 226.
[11] 'Lives in Brief', *The Times* (6 June 2002), 35.

lonely child. He boarded at Winchester College and then studied at New College, Oxford. He specialized in experimental physics, particularly atomic physics and the dielectric and electromagnetic properties of water. His intellectual reputation took off in 1964, when he published *The Physics of Atomic Collisions*. It quickly became a major textbook in the field. Four years later, in 1968, he was appointed Professor of Experimental Physics at Birkbeck and, in 1971, was elected a Fellow of the Institute of Physics. He remained in Birkbeck's Physics Department until he retired in 1986.

Hasted was more than just a distinguished physicist. He was also a fervent communist, active peace campaigner, and prominent folk musician who was widely credited for having brought Skiffle music to Britain. As we shall see, these four passions—physics, communism, peace, and folk music—are important elements to this story.

The other distinguished para-physicist at Birkbeck was David Bohm. His exceptional theoretical research has been discussed in Chapter 21, where it was pointed out that he was a serious contender for a Nobel Prize. He was also an intrepid scientist, believing that nothing—absolutely nothing—was 'off limits' for scientific investigation. Hasted and Bohm set out to see if psychic phenomena were 'real' and, if so, what this meant for science. In this, they were following their revolutionary and paradigm-changing approach in more established physics research. Although their quest would result in public ridicule and humiliation, Hasted and Bohm were intellectually committed to unravelling this scientific mystery. Of the two, Hasted was unquestionably the most committed. He insisted that 'I don't care if the world believes me or not.... I only want to get to the bottom of it.'[12] He contended that he wanted 'to find out and test the accepted laws [of physics] and see whether they need changing'.[13] For him, the issue was simple: 'I encountered a physical phenomenon which I could not explain', and so he set out to make sense of it.[14] As Hasted wrote in his *Alternative Memoirs* (1992),

> If we accept what has always seemed more likely, namely that the universe behaves as a closed system, then we must be continually watchful for unexpected phenomena, that is to say, for miracles. It is such discrepancies which offer clues to any deficiencies in existing theory.

He observed that, in the past, unexplained phenomena were typically 'attributed to the action of God', but that would no longer suffice. Instead, psychic phenomena offered 'a possible channel for enlargement' of knowledge through the

---

[12] Mary Owen, 'Britain's Key-Bending Kids Baffle Top Scientist', *Weekend* (16 August 1978), in 'Newscuttings 1976–80', in the Birkbeck Archive.
[13] Joyce Robins, 'The Young Mindbenders', *Woman* (8 September 1979), in 'Newscuttings 1976–80', in the Birkbeck Archive.
[14] John Hasted, *Alternative Memoirs* (Itchenor, West Sussex: Greengates Press, 1992), 181.

construction of hypotheses, rigorous testing, and careful observation.[15] Hasted admitted to being a 'Baffled Boffin',[16] but he was confident that through scientific experimentation and observation he would find the answer.

Their investigations into the paranormal began in earnest in 1974. On 21 June that year, Geller walked into their rooms at Birkbeck. Also present were Bastin and Brendan O'Regan from the parapsychological research institute called the Institute of Noetic Science, author Arthur Koestler, science fiction writer Arthur C. Clarke, physicist Keith Birkinshaw,[17] and theoretical physicist Jack Sarfatti,[18] who had been a research fellow at Birkbeck but was also a member of the American counterculture Fundamental Fysiks Group. Under their close scrutiny, Geller bent four keys and a molybdenum disc. He caused half a disc of vanadium carbide, a substance as hard and brittle as thin glass, to disappear.[19] He also triggered a Geiger counter to jump dramatically and deflected a compass needle while at the same time producing a pulse on a magnetometer.[20] Hasted found in these experiments 'strong evidence that the energy bursts were electrical in origin'. Geller, he believed,

> was not producing radio-activity but electrical pulses. In fact, Uri himself seemed to suffer some kind of electric shock. I'm convinced the effects were genuine. We have gone well beyond bending keys.[21]

Hasted announced that 'these observations are consistent with the hypothesis that Mr Geller could by concentration produce occasional and rather unpredictable pulses of electromotive force'.[22]

Bohm was impressed, but significantly more cautious. 'Unfortunately, there were a lot of people in the room', he conceded, adding that 'as far as the key bending is concerned, we had much better conditions in his hotel room [in February 1974] where it was much quieter'. He acknowledged that he could not be certain that 'there were no tricks' because Geller 'works in a very high state of excitement which communicates to the experimenter, and that makes it hard to keep your mind on what is happening'.[23] In a statement that was to be echoed repeatedly by proponents of paranormal activity, Bohm reminded sceptics that paranormal effects required a particular state of mind. Subjecting Geller to a body-search

---

[15] Ibid., 181.   [16] Ibid., 181.
[17] He was present according to Jack Sarfatt, 'Off the Beat: Geller Performs for Physicists', *Science News*, 106.3 (20 July 1974), 46.
[18] His name is sometimes spelt Sarfatt. He was a research fellow at Birkbeck between 1971 and 1972.
[19] Holroyd, *PSI and the Consciousness Explosion*, 107.
[20] 'Geller Performs at Birkbeck'. *New Scientist* (17 October 1974), in 'Newscuttings 1974–76', in the Birkbeck Archive.
[21] Roy Stockdill, 'Uri's No Phoney Say the Experts', *News of the World* (6 October 1974), in 'Newscuttings 1974–76', in the Birkbeck Archive.
[22] 'Geller Performs at Birkbeck'.   [23] Ibid.

prior to the experiments would be counterproductive, Bohm believed, because 'it would put him off'.[24] Geller also 'tends to get discouraged by complicated set-ups', he noted, adding that 'We had some set-ups that would have given stronger proof, but he was never in the right state of mind.'[25] All in all, Bohm concluded, 'My attitude is that whatever he requires, we must accept.'[26]

The following day, Geller was subjected to yet more tests. Once again, the room was crowded. Not only were Hasted, Bohm, Clarke, Sarfatti, and Koestler present, but also distinguished rocket engineer Arthur Valentine Cleaver, engineer and President of the Society of Psychical Research Arthur Ellison, and American concert pianist Byron Janis with his wife, the artist Maria Cooper Janis. Once again, Geller elicited a 'very strong burst from a Geiger counter tube that he held in his hand'.[27] Koestler was reported to be visibly shaken after the burst because he had felt a 'strong sensation simultaneous with the Geiger tube burst'.[28] Sarfatti concluded that

> My personal professional judgment as a Ph.D. physicist is that Geller demonstrated genuine psycho-energetic ability at Birkbeck, which is beyond the doubt of any reasonable man, under relatively well controlled and repeatable experimental conditions. While the experimental conditions were not perfect, the events at Birkbeck do represent a major step forward in the new field of experimental psycho-energies.[29]

Clarke belligerently 'challenged any magician to 'put up or shut up' in regard to duplicating Geller's feat under identical conditions'.[30]

Hasted also conducted experiments with Geller in the stately home of Langley in Wiltshire, where Geller's powers were so great that one of Hasted's cuff-links broke.[31] In another experiment, a 'crystal of vanadium carbide, a rare and very hard metal, was placed inside a cellulose capsule and laid on a piece of metal in front of witnesses'. Hasted swore that

> Geller never went nearer than eight inches to it, and I put my hand between his hand and the crystal. As Geller moved his hand above mine, I felt a tingling sensation in my hand. Suddenly the capsule gave a little jump. We looked at the capsule—and only half of the crystal was there.[32]

---

[24] Ibid.   [25] Ibid.   [26] Ibid.   [27] Sarfatt, 'Off the Beat', 46.
[28] Ibid., 46.   [29] Ibid., 46.   [30] Ibid., 46.
[31] 'Uri Geller Polishes Off the Langley Silver', *Birmingham Post* (3 October 1975), in 'Newscuttings 1974–76', in the Birkbeck Archive.
[32] Frederic Rolph, 'Does Uri's Power Come from Outer Space?', no source given, in 'Newscuttings 1976–80', in the Birkbeck Archive.

Hasted confessed that domestic tensions arose when Geller visited his home. In the presence of Hasted and his wife, objects moved between rooms and a clock that had been silent for thirty years suddenly chimed. Hasted's wife (who had been 'deeply dismissive' of the paranormal prior to Geller's visit) became 'increasingly frightened' when poltergeist-type phenomena took place.[33] Hasted admitted that it was 'a hard time for my wife and myself—we nearly fell out. We really had quite serious emotional troubles about it.'[34]

Domestic tensions aside, Hasted and Bohm announced that the 'human mind' was capable of 'distorting matter on the atomic and molecular level through activity patterns of the brain'. They were confident that the data they and other physicists were collecting would eventually be so extensive that there would be 'no room for reasonable doubt that some new process is involved here, which cannot be accounted for or explained in terms of present known laws of physics.'[35] Bohm's earlier caution was also thrown to the wind. When he was finally allowed to return to the USA in 1977, he told a packed Berkeley physics audience of the results of these Birkbeck experiments with the 'psychic wunderkind, Uri Geller'. As one commentator noted, the 'much-revered quantum physicist held up several pieces of bent metal for his audience of fellow physicists to eagerly peruse' and 'For a moment the unthinkable seemed thinkable—that the paradoxes of quantum mechanics might be connected to the field of parapsychology.'[36]

Unfortunately for the two Birkbeck scientists, Geller was more interested in his lucrative career as a media personality than in serving as an unpaid experimental subject for university physicists. Luckily for them, others proved willing. Hasted and Bohm turned their keen intellects to 'mini-Gellers' (in Italian, known as 'Gellerini')[37]—that is, young people who claimed to be able to replicate Geller's paranormal feats. These 'mini-Gellers' were able to bend metal, scrunch paperclips, levitate, move objects, view objects in remote places, take 'thought-photographs' (that is, produce photographic images on light-sensitive film by paranormal means), communicate with people in other countries as well as in UFO spaceships, read minds, predict future events, and summon poltergeists.[38] Hasted and Taylor eventually identified forty-six people with metal-bending powers in Britain,[39] and Hasted was able to document psychic capabilities in at least eighteen children.[40]

---

[33] Jonathan Margolis, *Uri Geller: Magician or Mystic?* (London: Orion, 1998), 213.
[34] Ibid., 213.
[35] 'Science Bends its Mind to Uri Geller', Binton [?] *Daily Mail* (26 September 1975), in 'Newscuttings 1974–76', in the Birkbeck Archive.
[36] Trevor Pinch, 'Review: Karen Barad, Quantum Mechanics and the Paradox of Mutual Exclusivity', *Social Studies in Science*, 41.3 (June 2011), 435.
[37] Hasted, *The Metal-Benders*, 29. [38] For details, see ibid., throughout.
[39] Holroyd, *PSI and the Consciousness Explosion*, 108. [40] Hasted, *The Metal-Benders*, 30.

Fifteen-year-old Julie Knowles and 10-year-old Stephen North were two of these extraordinary children. Julie was a pupil at St Augustine's Roman Catholic School in Trowbridge. Like nearly all 'mini-Gellers', she had discovered her psychic powers while watching Geller on television.[41] Initially, she caught the attention of researchers at the nearby University of Bath. However, under experimental conditions, Julie failed to bend any spoons despite her mother swearing that Julie had bent two spoons just prior to entering the laboratory. Her mother explained the discrepancy by maintaining that her daughter 'didn't like the conditions in the laboratory. She can't bend things on demand, she has to feel in the mood.'[42]

This was where Hasted stepped in. He contended that a 'genuine spontaneous physical phenomenon' was 'being killed off by the continued insistence by psychologists and others on "performance" under video tests with complicated protocol'. He believed this was unnecessary since 'all that is really needed is to record instrumental data' in the relaxed environment of a home.[43] He invited Julie into his home to meet Geller: in that relaxed environment, she was easily able to complete a psychic test, which was 'witnessed carefully by a number of scientists'.[44]

Under Hasted's casual experimental conditions, Julie flourished. After all, she explained, 'I have to be in the mood to do it and it holds me back if I sense there is someone present who does not believe it.'[45] In one experiment, a 'T-shaped strip made of drinking straws was placed on a plastic base floating in a glass of water' and the whole 'apparatus was covered by a sealed glass dome'. In front of six witnesses, Julie 'concentrated from a distance' and 'slowly, she swivelled the strip through 85 degrees'.[46] A few minutes after picking up a teaspoon, Julie

> said she had a 'feeling'... she had a pain at the top of her right arm and then felt water and wax as she was rubbing the spoon. The moment she said wax, the bowl of the spoon bent downwards sharply.[47]

Julie's powers extended beyond revolving drinking straws and bending spoons. She claimed to be able to 'listen in to the conversations extra-terrestrial beings have in their flying saucers', although she confessed that 'it didn't make any sense'.[48] On one occasion, she 'even met *herself* in the street' and, looking down, observed that 'it was all misty round my feet'.[49] Julie also had premonitions.

---

[41] 'Julie's a Mini Mind-Bender', *Reveille* (5 November 1976), in 'Newscuttings 1976–80', in the Birkbeck Archive.

[42] Joyce Greenwood, 'Why Life is Tough for Spoon-Bender Julie', *British Evening Post* (24 June 1976), in 'Newscuttings 1974–76', in the Birkbeck Archive. Note there is a photograph of Julie.

[43] J. B. Hasted, 'Letter to the Editor', *New Scientist* (28 July 1977), in 'Newscuttings 1976–80', in the Birkbeck Archive.

[44] Greenwood, 'Why Life is Tough for Spoon-Bender Julie'.

[45] Ibid. A minor typo has been silently corrected. [46] 'Julie's a Mini Mind-Bender'.

[47] Greenwood, 'Why Life is Tough for Spoon-Bender Julie'.

[48] 'Julie's a Mini Mind-Bender'. [49] Ibid.

She predicted 'major world events', specifically the Chinese earthquake in the summer of 1976 and the Moroccan invasion of the Spanish Sahara.[50] After such feats, she would be ravenously hungry.[51] Hasted maintained that he was 'absolutely convinced [that] she is absolutely genuine', although he admitted that he was struggling to find any scientific explanations for her powers. He did speculate, however, that 'it involves the dematerialisation of matter—rather like the transporter system on science fiction films'.[52]

Stephen North, from Cranley Gardens, Highgate, north London, was another talented youngster.[53] Stephen was 10 years old when, while eating dinner, he saw Geller performing on television. Suddenly, he later recalled, his spoon snapped in his hand. Imitating Geller, Stephen began stroking his fork, which also promptly cracked into two pieces. His father, Arthur, a university senior lecturer in architecture, initially believed that Stephen was 'playing a joke on us.... But when we stood him in the middle of the room, watching him every minute, he still bent every piece of cutlery we gave him.'[54] While writing a school essay on the Queen's Silver Jubilee, Stephen used thought alone to bend a piece of metal to resemble a crown; he also used his mind to bend three strips of metal into a bracelet for his mother.[55] Stephen professed to be bewildered about his newly found powers. He bragged that

> In the first year everything around me seemed to bend, whether I wanted it to or not.... We didn't have a straight door key in the house. My mother wasn't a bit pleased when her egg-whisk twisted up and when all the pins in her sewing box curled around one another.

Gradually, Stephen gained some control over his powers, but 'even so, if I have a row with my mother, a few things in the kitchen tend to curl up!'[56]

Stephen worked with Hasted for around five years. It was found that he could remove money from sealed boxes, making it reappear in his back pocket, although 'neither of them saw it vanish or re-appear'.[57] Stephen could also 'create electrical interference in television sets'. He was telepathic, communicating with a young German girl living in Russia.[58] Even Geller conceded that Stephen might have 'stronger teleportation powers than I have.... I think the younger you are, the less

---

[50] Ibid.
[51] Greenwood, 'Why Life is Tough for Spoon-Bender Julie'. [52] Ibid.
[53] A clip of Stephen North can be seen in 'Psychokinetic Metal Bending', on the Discovery Channel: a section is available on YouTube at https://www.youtube.com/watch?v=QPrJ1pSP2UI.
[54] Robins, 'The Young Mindbenders'. [55] Ibid. [56] Ibid. [57] Ibid.
[58] John McShane, 'Vanishing Tricks of a New Wonder Boy', *Sunday Mirror* (10 June 1979), in 'Newscuttings 1976–80' in the Birkbeck Archive, and Robins, 'The Young Mindbenders'.

sceptical you are. If you believe you can do these things, then it makes the power you have stronger.'[59]

* * *

But what could be the explanation of such strange powers? Here, Bohm and Hasted turned to quantum mechanics. They believed the clue lay in the famous paradox elucidated by Albert Einstein, Boris Podolsky, and Nathan Rosen in 1935. Known as the EPR paradox (after the first initial of their surnames), it postulated that, theoretically at least, quantum information could 'be transferred instantaneously from one part of the universe to another part, no matter how remote: in brief, an action at a distance is in principle possible'.[60] In his book *Mind-Benders*, Hasted explained how this might work. He began by making a distinction between mind and brain. 'Unlike the rest of matter', Hasted believed, mind has 'characteristics which are apparently trans-spatial and trans-temporal'.[61] He alluded to Bohm's theory of 'hidden variables', which 'determine the indeterminate quantities but at the same time conform to the probability distribution'.[62] Although no one had found these 'hidden variables', Hasted believed that 'we are now coming increasingly to believe that the mind is the only remaining undiscovered hidden variable'.[63] Quantum theory allowed for 'the reality of simultaneous universes' which 'cannot communicate physically with each other, because the vectors are mutually orthogonal'.[64] These simultaneous universes were constantly 'splitting...into an infinite (or very large) number [of other universes] each time an observed quantum transition occurs'.[65] This was Bryce de Witt's proposition. For de Witt,

> The universe is constantly splitting into a stupendous number of branches, all resulting from the measurement-like interactions between its myriads of components. Moreover, every quantum transition taking place on every star, in every galaxy, in every remote corner of the universe is splitting our local world on earth into myriads of copies of itself.[66]

These two ideas were 'uncomfortable' for physics. As Hasted admitted, 'We do not like the idea of countless...doppelgängers of ourselves, increasing in number all the time, even if they can never communicate physically', although he held open the possibility of telepathic communication.[67] This 'many-universes theory'

---

[59] McShane, 'Vanishing Tricks of a New Wonder Boy'.
[60] Grove, 'Rationality at Risk: Science Against Pseudoscience', 227.
[61] Hasted, *The Metal-Benders*, 2.   [62] Ibid., 240.   [63] Ibid., 240.
[64] Ibid., 241.   [65] Ibid., 241.   [66] Ibid., 241.
[67] Ibid., 241. For a largely positive review of this idea of 'many selves', see Derek Parker, 'The Metal-Benders by John Hasted', *The Times* (17 June 1981), 13.

suggested that 'each atomic transition in our own insignificant bodies causes the remotest galaxies to split into an infinite number'.[68]

In attempting to understand psychic phenomena, our scientists believed that 'non-material, or at least trans-spatial minds' were productive.[69] Hasted speculated that the 'unconscious mind' possesses the faculty of receiving 'trans-spatial' information from the corresponding minds in other 'universes'. Because, in Euclidean space, two vectors are orthogonal (their dot product is zero), 'physical signals cannot pass from one universe to another', so the 'unconscious mind' must be assumed to possess 'trans-spatial properties' and be 'able to communicate with physical reality in other universes only through other unconscious minds'. He asked scientists to consider the possibility of 'parallel universes', in which there are 'millions of copies of each individual', all conducting 'parallel existences, but ... entirely isolated physically from each other by orthogonality, which prevents the passage of physical signals between universes'. Concretely, what would this mean? Hasted provided an example:

> Let us propose that each one of these individuals possesses his own mind, and that communication between these corresponding minds is sometimes possible. No individual knows of the existence of his many *alter egos*. But if he were able to adopt the mind of one of these *alter egos*, he would then take the other universe to be his reality, without knowing that any change had occurred. Moreover, at the moment he successfully does this, one might suppose that his neighbours' minds (the observers' minds) could also come to be dominated by those of their own *alter egos*, so that they could also take the other universe to be their reality. All observers could now notice whatever physical differences there might be between the two universes. The differences could be that psychic phenomenon, metal-bending, psychokinesis or teleportations have taken place.[70]

This was the simplified model. After all, there was no need to assume that there were only two universes. It was also possible to 'propose that we all pass through life in a continual state of subtending many universes at the same moment of time', and 'since these universes are in nearly all respects identical, we have hitherto imagined them to be a single universe'. On extremely rare occasions, this illusion could be breached when, for example, 'a unique universe forces us to notice it, and it is then that we say that an atomic physical phenomenon has occurred'.[71]

Accordingly, teleportation could be understood by 'using the hyperdimensional character of the many-universes model'.[72] The 'reorganizational forces

---

[68] Hasted, *The Metal-Benders*, 244.   [69] Ibid., 244.
[70] Ibid., 244.   [71] Ibid., 245.   [72] Ibid., 245.

which must occur in the creation or annihilation of atoms at the inter-universe boundaries' could explain metal bending.[73] Other 'quasi-forces' could be interpreted

> in terms of a rapid series of local transformations into universes, each one with its own individual momentum, each slightly greater than the last. The rate of change of momentum would then have the appearance of a force acting on the transformed subject.[74]

It was a complex model that also helped explain phenomena like teleportation. As Hasted explained,

> when metal bends, atoms move about in the metal, and if enough atoms move around, then the whole object could jump, and this would be teleportation—which I now believe to be merely another branch of metal-bending. In fact, teleportation is probably the more fundamental event.

In other words, teleportation was 'another demonstration of quantum non-locality' or 'being in two places at once, things not moving, but just appearing, going through walls'. Even if the science was not fully understood yet, he insisted that teleportation was possible: it has 'been my experience. I have seen it happen.'[75]

* * *

Neither the experiments nor the theory convinced sceptics. In 1977, a Committee for the Scientific Investigation of Claims of the Paranormal was established. The Committee was criticized for 'gnat-killing by sledgehammer'.[76] However, the scientists, science reporters, and magicians who joined deemed it necessary, given the number of respected physicists who were publicly endorsing paranormal phenomena.

Journalists also began registering their doubts. In 1974, the *New Scientist* published an attack by journalist Joseph Hanlon, who had a doctorate in physics. How could John Taylor seriously inform the audience watching Dimbleby's *Talk-In* that there was no scientific explanation for Geller's ability to bend the forks, he asked? After all, Geller had unguarded access to the forks prior to the programme.[77] Hanlon maintained that 'so long as a good magician could do what Geller does, then the Geller effect is not scientifically validated'.[78] Fraud 'permeates psychic research', Hanlon insisted. Hasted's comment that 'I have no personal interest in proving that the phenomena produced by Uri Geller are genuine….

---

[73] Ibid., 245.   [74] Ibid., 245–6.   [75] Margolis, *Uri Geller: Magician or Mystic?*, 214.
[76] 'Science, the Media, and the Paranormal', *Science News*, 112.8 (20 August 1977), 118.
[77] Joseph Hanlon, 'Uri Geller and Science', *New Scientist* (31 October 1974), 314.
[78] Ibid., 314.

My only intention is to inquire and see whether or not we can learn something' was, at best, naïve and, at worst, duplicitous.[79]

Hasted was unrepentant. He chided Hanlon for basing his article on a preliminary report which had not been intended for publication. If Hanlon had talked to him, he would have been informed that the room in which the experiments had taken place was not always crowded. A 'sleight of hand' on Geller's part would 'not have been possible' on every occasion.[80] Hasted reminded Hanlon that he was a highly trained physicist, with well-honed observatory skills: how dare Hanlon attempt to 'bring into disrepute the whole process of laboratory training'. 'Unlike Dr Hanlon,' Hasted dryly commented, 'I am prepared to comment only on events I have personally witnessed.' He was 'confident of the abilities of scientists to make observations [and] to avoid writing [Geller] off as a subject because some of his performances are suspect'.[81]

If Hasted thought that this would end the matter, he was wrong. Worse was to come. Popular science magazines smelled blood. *Scientific America* called Hasted a 'self-deceiver', who was starring in a 'Mathematical Circus'. The author of the article mocked Hasted for experimenting with

> young people who can, if they are not watched, somehow pass distorted paper clips into a sealed glass globe. Well, not quite sealed; you do need to leave a small hole, or curiously the parapsychological effect does not work![82]

It was a point picked up by Martin Gardner in *Science: Good, Bad and Bogus* (1989). He ridiculed Hasted for claiming that one of his 'mini-Gellers' could 'scrunch up' paper clips that were inside a glass globe. The problem, Gardner scoffed, was that the globe had a hole in the top. He asked whether 'anyone [has] actually *seen* paper clips in the act of bending, or recorded it on a videotape?' The answer was clearly 'No'. A 'mini-Geller' was allowed to take the globe home 'and comes back with the scrunch'. 'Mysteriously,' Gardner noted, 'clips never scrunch in globes without holes or when someone other than the child is watching.'[83] Gardner accused Hasted of 'boundless gullibility and bumbling experiments'. He was 'embarrassing...his Birkbeck colleagues'.[84] Unfortunately, the latter comment seems to have been true.[85]

---

[79] Ibid., 314.
[80] J. B. Hasted, 'The Geller Correspondence', *New Scientist* (31 October 1974), in 'Newscuttings 1974–76' in the Birkbeck Archive.
[81] Ibid.
[82] Philip Morrison, 'Mathematical Circus', *Scientific American*, 245.4 (October 1981), 41.
[83] Gardner, *Science: Good, Bad and Bogus*, 205.   [84] Ibid., 205.
[85] John Hasted, 'Letters', *Spectrum* (15 May 1975), 4, and personal interview with Professor Basil Hiley, 29 June 2018.

When a group of physicists defended the experiments in the *New York Review of Books*, claiming that these physicists' research demonstrated 'a possible connection between quantum mechanics and parapsychology',[86] Gardner responded with yet more ridicule. Hasted's research was 'hilarious', he contended. At the very basic level, Hasted had 'failed to take into account amplification by his sensitive strain gauges of slight static charges produced by body movements'. Gardner asked readers to 'judge for themselves whether Hasted is a competent psychic investigator'.[87]

Magicians joined in the debunking. After all, they were perfectly capable of replicating the 'tricks' of Geller and co.[88] The fact that Geller was never able to perform if he knew that a magician would be present was widely considered to be suspect.[89] This reticence on Geller's part led magician Michael Nass to call for a 'battle of the psychics', confident that magicians would 'easily win'.[90]

Illusionist James Randi was a particularly dogged opponent. He promised a substantial sum of money to anyone who could demonstrate verifiable paranormal capabilities.[91] Randi also set up a simple spoon-bending experiment with 'mini-Geller' Julie Knowles: she failed dismally. To Randi's astonishment, he then discovered that no one had actually *seen* Julie execute her psychic powers despite her feats being widely publicized for more than three years.[92]

In 1975, Randi was responsible for Sarfatti's very public retraction of his endorsement of Geller's 'psychoenergetic authenticity', which he had made at Birkbeck just the previous year. Randi had shown Sarfatti how conjurors were able to 'fracture metal and move the hands of a watch in a way that is indistinguishable from my observation of Geller's "psychokinetic" demonstrations'.[93] Sarfatti remained convinced that 'the ambiguity in the interpretation of quantum mechanics leaves ample room for the possibility of psychokinetic and telepathic effects'. However, he maintained that the psychic effects he had witnessed at Birkbeck had not occurred 'under controlled and reproducible conditions'.[94]

---

[86] Olivier Costa de Beauregard, Richard D. Mattuck, Brian D. Josephson, and Evan Harris Walker, 'Parapsychology: An Exchange', *New York Review of Books* (26 June 1980), at http://www.nybooks.com/articles/1980/06/26/parapsychology-an-exchange/.

[87] Martin Gardner, 'Parapsychology: An Exchange', *New York Review of Books* (26 June 1980), at http://www.nybooks.com/articles/1980/06/26/parapsychology-an-exchange/.

[88] T. V. Wolansky, 'Geller and Magicians', *Science News*, 106.5 (3 August 1974), 78.

[89] Jim Gerrish and Steven Okulewicz, 'Geller and Magicians', *Science News*, 106.5 (3 August 1974), 78.

[90] Michael Nass, 'Geller and Magicians', *Science News*, 106.5 (3 August 1974), 79.

[91] Dennis Hackett, 'To Bend, or Not to Bend', *The Times* (10 March 1983), 9.

[92] James Randi, 'Paranormal Powers in the U.K. and France', *The Humanist*, xxxvii.5 (September/October 1977), 44–5.

[93] Jack Sarfatti, 'Retraction on Geller', *Science News*, 108.23 (6 December 1975), 355. The endorsement had been published in *Science News* and 'Geller Performs for Physicists', *Off the Beat* (20 July 1974), 46.

[94] Sarfatti, 'Retraction on Geller', 355.

Most damningly, evidence of fraud began to emerge. The paranormal experiments at the University of Bath (where Julie had *failed* to bend a spoon) were axed when a one-way mirror (which was introduced without the knowledge of the 'mini-Gellers') showed all of them, except Julie, cheating. The 'mini-Gellers' were bending metal with the help of table tops and chair legs.[95]

Hasted and Bohm remained defiant, but the relentless tsunami of ridicule must have been painful. As early as April 1975, Hasted, Bohm, Bastin, and O'Regan hit back in the pages of *Nature*. They implored scientists to maintain an open mind as to whether there was some 'force, energy or mode of connection' that was 'at present unknown'.[96] After all, they reminded critics, 'when magnetic and electrostatic effects were first observed', it had also been 'impossible to account for them in terms of the known forces'.[97]

While admitting that their experiments with Geller and the 'mini-Gellers' were not 'loop-hole-free', they nevertheless insisted that 'the experiences we have gained may be of value to other physicists interested, like ourselves, in the interactions between mind and physical systems'.[98] They repeatedly stated that paranormal research could not be conducted along conventional lines because 'the phenomenon under investigation' had to 'be produced from the minds of one or more of those who participate'.[99] Therefore, the relationship between *all* participants was crucial if anything extraordinary was to be observed.[100] This did not mean that everyone in the laboratory had to be believers, but they *did* have to ensure that their minds remained 'open to all possibilities'.[101] Rigour was crucial but, equally, any 'preconceived pattern of tough-mindedness' could 'destroy the very possibility of the phenomenon that we wish to study'.[102] The 'entire process' was more likely to succeed 'when all those present actively want things to work well' and when the 'experimental arrangement is aesthetically or imaginatively appealing to the person with apparent psychokinetic powers'.[103]

Hasted, Bohm, Bastin, and O'Regan pleaded with fellow-scientists to remember that negative energies, such as 'tension, fear, hostility', had no place in the laboratory. They observed that any

> attempt to concentrate strongly in order to obtain a desired result (the bending of a piece of metal, for example) tends to interfere with the relaxed state of mind needed to produce such phenomena. It appears that what is actually done is mainly a function of the unconscious mind, and that once the intention to do something has been firmly established, the conscious functions of the

---

[95] Philip Morrison, 'The Magic of Uri Geller', *Scientific American*, 234.2 (February 1976), 134. For Hasted's view of this, see Hasted, *The Metal-Benders*, 28. He used it as an argument against testing the 'mini-Gellers' in a laboratory because it might make them too anxious to 'achieve success'.
[96] J. B. Hasted, D. J. Bohm, E. W. Bastin, and B. O'Regan, 'News', *Nature*, 254 (10 April 1975), 471.
[97] Ibid., 471.   [98] Ibid., 470.   [99] Ibid., 470.   [100] Ibid., 470.
[101] Ibid., 470.   [102] Ibid., 470.   [103] Ibid., 470.

mind...tend to become more of a hindrance than a help. Indeed, we have sometimes found it useful at this stage to talk of or think about something not closely related to what is happening.[104]

They pointed out that this was akin to what happens when people tried too hard to get to sleep. Concentrating on falling asleep was similarly guaranteed to inhibit it.

Of course, they conceded, there was no point denying that fraudsters existed. And it may have been easier for cheats to fool physicists rather than trained magicians. However, in answer to the criticism that they should therefore allow professional magicians into the laboratory, they gave two responses. First, magicians were generally hostile to psychics, so they created tension in the laboratory that would inhibit unusual energies.[105] Second, the 'corpus of tricks' available to a skilled magician was always evolving, so inviting comments by magicians would never remove the possibility that the person claiming paranormal abilities had simply invented a trick to which other magicians were not yet privy.[106] They insisted that it was more rational to trust the vigilance of scientists who had extensive training in close observation.

Meanwhile, Hasted braced himself for being 'cold shouldered by the academic top dogs'.[107] He claimed that his treatment amounted to a 'witch-hunt'.[108] Bohm eventually dropped away, persuaded by fellow-physicists at Birkbeck that paranormal research was damaging his reputation. Hiley engaged Hasted personally, pointing out the obvious flaws in his reasoning and weakness in his 'experiments', but it was to no avail. Other members of the department were very concerned and there were protracted meetings at Birkbeck in which colleagues debated how or whether Hasted should be persuaded to drop this line of research. Hiley was not the only member of the staff worried by the 'sloppy' nature of his experiments and the lack of academic rigour. Hiley was also 'very worried about the potential damage to the well-being of the children involved in the experiments particularly with the surrounding publicity'. In the end, however, the department concluded that academic freedom should be defended even in the face of the most uncomfortable mockery.[109]

It was patently obvious that Hasted's views could never be reconciled with those of most other scientists. As Collins and Pinch put it in their Kuhnian-informed analysis in *Frames of Meaning* (1982), the scientific paradigm emerging from research on paranormal metal bending was incommensurate with that of

---

[104] Ibid., 470.   [105] Ibid., 472.   [106] Ibid., 471.
[107] Herbert Kretzmer, 'The City that Beat the Bomb', *Daily Mail* (27 January 1981), 19, and Elizabeth Cowley, 'Horizon', *Daily Mail* (26 January 1981), 199. The quotation is from the *Horizon* programme.
[108] John Hasted, 'Letters', *Spectrum* (15 May 1975), 4.
[109] Personal interview and email exchange with Professor Basil Hiley, 29 June 2018 and 8 October 2018.

orthodox science.[110] Hasted accepted his outsider status. With dogged chutzpa, he accepted invitations to speak at seminars about 'Scientific Controversies',[111] defended the proposition that 'parapsychology is a proper subject for scientific investigation' on *You the Jury* (BBC Radio 4),[112] and even appeared on *Horizon*'s 'No One Will Take Me Seriously' (BBC 2).[113]

Hasted was not the only one who felt that his 'star was waning'. He observed that the number of people with psychic powers was also in a steep decline. Metal bending, Hasted was later to reflect, was becoming 'an endangered talent, at risk of dying out in the world'.[114] How could this be explained? Obviously, the relentless sneers were powerful disincentives to 'coming out'. Absurd claims by enthusiasts such as Andrija Puharich that Geller had been transported to earth by extra-terrestrials also didn't help.[115]

In addition, and much to Hasted's dismay, the 'mini-Gellers' seemed to be 'growing out' of it. Bending spoons and keys was not a glamorous adolescence pastime. When Julie Knowles entered her teenage years, she became increasingly uncomfortable about being stopped in the street by strangers asking her to bend their keys. She was indignant about accusations that she was making money from her notoriety.[116] Julie had been 'a real Top of the Pops girl before it all happened', recalled her mother, adding that, since she had revealed her paranormal talents, people were looking at her as though she was 'not quite normal'. There was 'tremendous pressure on her to prove herself', her mother noted. Was it really surprising that she 'gets really cross when people disbelieve her and sometimes she has got so fed up that she doesn't want to do it any more'?[117] Stephen North underwent a similar transformation. At the age of 15, five years after discovering his powers, Stephen became weary of attempting to prove this authenticity to his disbelieving school friends. Strumming his guitar was a much more agreeable pastime.[118]

The political context was also changing. After Mikhail Gorbachev came to power in 1985 and the Cold War started to wind down, there was less need to cultivate paranormal energies capable of stopping 'the Bomb' in its tracks. The McCarthyite witch-hunts that had brought men like Bohm to Birkbeck were over. Hasted remained a believer until the end of his days, but Bohm moved the focus

---

[110] Harry M. Collins and Trevor J. Pinch, *Frames of Meaning: The Social Construction of Extraordinary Science* (London: Routledge and Kegan Paul, 1982), 5 and 11.
[111] 'Scientific Controversies', part of the Oxford Science Studies Summer Seminar, advertised in *Review*, 2.4 (winter 1984), 36.
[112] 'Today's Television and Radio Programmes', *The Times* (20 June 1984), 31. *You the Jury* was chaired by Geoffrey Robertson. Professor Eric Ash opposed the motion.
[113] *Horizon*'s 'No One Will Take Me Seriously' (BBC 2), reported in 'Personal Choice', *The Times* (26 January 1981), 23.
[114] Hasted, *The Metal-Benders*, 255.   [115] Parker, 'The Metal Benders by John Hasted', 13.
[116] Greenwood, 'Why Life is Tough for Spoon-Bender Julie'.
[117] Ibid.   [118] Robins, 'The Young Mindbenders'.

of his attention to the ideas of Krishnamurti, which provided a parallel way of making sense of multiple universes, non-locality, and the enfoldment of all life.

* * *

Why did para-physics become prominent in the first place—and especially in institutions like Birkbeck? To answer this question, we might mention three things: the proponents' outsider status, their ambition, and the institutional milieu. Although each has some validity, arguably it is more convincing to see para-physics as providing these scientists with a radical, dialectical solution to the three crises of politics emerging out of capitalism, the Cold War, and the Stalinist international.

Hasted and Bohm were professional, social, and political outsiders. Both physicists struggled with a tension between identity and power. They were the embodiment of powerful, highly educated, white male elites. But by immersing themselves in scientific, cultural, and political subcultures not endorsed by dominant paradigms, they also epitomized subaltern (or subordinate) identities.[119] Their *orthodox* scientific research at the frontiers of existing knowledge familiarized them to incredulous responses from fellow-scientists. They believed passionately that nothing in the world should be 'off limits': they sought to move the boundaries of what it was possible to think. This was why Bohm never censored Hasted, even after he became embarrassed by his obsessiveness. In this sense, they represented the modernist belief not to leave anything unexamined and to test all theories, conjectures, and refutations.

Their politics followed their scientific radicalism. Hasted's communist involvement cost him a job in Oxford: the politically conservative physicist Frederick Alexander Lindemann was happy to support him in junior roles, but would never promote him.[120] Bohm was literally a political refugee. Despite strong support from Oppenheimer, Bohm's left-wing views meant that he was refused security clearance to work on the Manhattan Project. At Princeton University, Bohm worked closely with Albert Einstein but the university failed to renew his contract after he refused to give evidence before the House Un-American Activities Committee. He had been forced to leave America, for São Paulo, Heifa, Bristol, and then Birkbeck.

Socially, too, Bohm and Hasted were often on the 'wrong side' of fashionable trends. Hasted was a leading promoter of skittles at a time when 'pop' was on the rise. Similarly, Bohm's infatuation with Krishnamurti raised eyebrows.

Their radicalism was fuelled by ambition. On the first page of *The Metal-Benders* (1981), Hasted puts himself in the same company as scientific luminaries

---

[119] Dipesh Chakrabarty, *Provincializing Europe: Postcolonial Thought and Historical Difference* (Princeton: Princeton University Press, 2000), 101.
[120] Hasted, *Alternative Memoirs*, 84.

like the founder of modern chemistry Robert Boyle, Michael Faraday (the greatest experimental physicist of the nineteenth century), the influential Victorian naturalist Alfred Russel Wallace, German physicist Heinrich Friedrich Weber, chemist and physicist Sir William Crookes, Lord Rayleigh (Nobel Prize in Physics, 1904), and French physicist Paul Langevin.[121] Cynics gossiped that Bohm and Hasted were hopeful of becoming Nobel laureates. Indeed, Hasted openly admitted to this ambition, and many believed that Bohm would have been a worthy recipient.[122]

More important was the institutional milieu they worked in. Birkbeck's intellectual tradition cultivated radical thought. Only three years after the establishment of the London Mechanics' Institution in 1823, 'alternative' scientific teachings such as phrenology had a prominent place in the college. Johann Caspar Spurzheim's 1826 lectures were intensely popular and, despite being denounced for being 'atheistic' and 'dangerous',[123] phrenological science continued to be taught at the Institution well after it had been dismissed as 'quackery' elsewhere.

Spiritualism also had a long tradition at Birkbeck. Hasted, as well as many others, acknowledged that para-physics was the late-twentieth-century successor to spiritualism.[124] Both 'sciences' believed that remote viewing, levitation, poltergeists, and communication across time and space were plausible. The nineteenth- and early twentieth-century spiritualists had attracted the interest of major scientists of the time, including William Ramsay (who won a Nobel Prize in Chemistry, 1904) and Sir J. J. Thomson (Nobel Prize in Physics, 1906), as well as three of the scientists whom Hasted viewed as his precursors (Wallace, Crookes, and Rayleigh).[125] Like Hasted and Bohm, these scientists were all obsessed with the 'laws of nature' that science had yet to discover. Indeed, the Society for Psychical Research, which had been established in 1882 by spiritualists in Cambridge,[126] published and promoted the paranormal research of both Hasted and Bohm.[127]

From the mid-twentieth century, Birkbeck had also been the home to Samuel George Soal, mathematician and then Honorary Fellow in Birkbeck's Psychology Department from 1954 to 1958. Soal and Kathleen M. ('Mollie') Goldney (a midwife who became the President of the Society for Psychical Research) carried out

---

[121] Hasted, *The Metal-Benders*, 1.
[122] Hasted, *Alternative Memoirs*, 182–3. He makes an identical statement in an interview with Margolis, *Uri Geller: Magician or Mystic?*, 213.
[123] 'George Combe and the Philosophy of Phrenology', *Fraser's Magazine for Town and Country*, 131.21 (November 1840), 511–13.
[124] Hasted, *The Metal-Benders*, 25–6.
[125] Grove, 'Rationality at Risk: Science Against Pseudoscience', 225.
[126] Ibid., 226. [127] Ibid., 226.

experiments claiming to prove the existence of extra-sensory perception (ESP).[128] Unfortunately, what subsequently became known as the Soal/Goldney controversy was a reference to the fraudulent nature of their evidence. At Birkbeck, Soul continued to conduct paranormal experiments, desperate to prove that the phenomenon existed. When spiritualism was bolstered by tsunamis of grief arising out of the First World War, prominent Birkbeck academics (such as Helen Gwynne-Vaughan, first female Professor of Botany, and Cyril Joad, first head of the Department of Philosophy and Psychology) were keen followers.[129] Joad had been a close friend of Harry Price, most famous for his psychic research associated with the Borley Rectory and the experiment Blocksberg Tryst. This Tryst was:

> On the top of the Brocken, in the Harz Mountains, an 'un spotted maid' would be introduced to a white goat which, after magic ceremony, would be transformed into 'a youth of surpassing beauty'. Before the gathered press of all Europe precisely nothing happened.[130]

* * *

Hasted's and Bohm's outsider status, personal ambition, and institutional location are relevant to an understanding of their paranormal enthusiasms but are insufficient in themselves. To understand their interest in para-physics, we need to take seriously their ideas and philosophies of life.

Two factors are paramount: first, para-physics challenged the dominant practice of science and of scientific evidence; second, it opened up new possibilities for a radical, dialectical solution to the crises of the modern world. These two explanations overlap, but can be examined in turn.

Paranormal scientists held beliefs about the status of science and scientific evidence that were incompatible with those of mainstream physics. They emphasized the importance of emotions, insisted on the effect of the observer on the observed, recognized the co-production of knowledge, and extolled the power of the people or ordinary 'folk'.

For Hasted and Bohm, emotions did *and should* play a pivotal role in physics research. Hasted upbraided sceptics for accusing paranormal scientists of being 'emotionally committed to the phenomenon'. Surely they were forgetting their own emotional desire 'to finding... *no* phenomenon', he asked?[131] He urged everyone with a sincere interest in the natural world to develop a 'sense of

---

[128] Nigel Hawkes, 'Doubts Cast on Classic ESP Test', *The Observer* (29 December 1954), in 'Newspaper Cuttings 1974–76' in the Birkbeck Archive.

[129] For example, see '"Spectre" Weds and Runs Away', *Daily Mail* (15 December 1937), 9; F. G. Prince-White, 'Bond of Sympathy Among Twins', *Daily Mail* (6 October 1933), 7.

[130] Alan Jenkins, *Stephen Potter: Inventor of Gamesmanship* (London: Weidenfeld and Nicolson, 1980), 9.

[131] Margolis, *Uri Geller: Magician or Mystic?*, 212. Hasted makes this comment in Hasted, *The Metal-Benders*, 4.

wonder'.[132] The awesomeness of unexplained phenomenon should excite curiosity, which must be allowed free rein. As Taylor rhetorically asked his readers in *Nature* (before his cynicism for para-physics set in): 'Do we necessarily have to doff the garb of scientist when satisfying our curiosity about such events?' If this was required, then science would be 'circumscribed in a very peculiar way'.[133]

Para-physics also held to the fundamental tenet of relativity theory that the 'observer' changes the 'observed'. Bernal's *The Social Function of Science* (1939), which had proven so influential in both Hasted's and Bohm's life-philosophy,[134] proposed wide themes about the social '*construction*' of science: science *itself*—that is, the way humans strive to make sense of and give meaning to the world—was implicated in the creation of these worlds. This approach to science and evidence was influenced by Marxist historical materialism. Scientific laws explain society and its progressive historical movements, but the intervention of the political subject (that is, the proletariat and its representatives in the Communist Party) accelerates the movement towards socialism and eventually changes the laws of society. The political subject observing the process is participating at the same time in its change.

Hasted and Bohm were also drawing on a new philosophy of physics—one that challenged classical physics by insisting on the 'entanglement' of the entire universe. This was discussed in detail in Chapter 21. In the context of the paranormal, however, it meant that 'quantum objects that had once interacted would retain some strange link or connection, even after they had moved arbitrarily far apart from each other', as physicist John S. Bell (who had been inspired by Bohm) famously argued.[135] Both Bohm and Bell developed concepts such as 'nonlocality' and 'entanglement'. As David Kaiser explained,

> Bell's theorem and quantum entanglement seemed to suggest that one could use quantum theory to act at a distance, instantly. Nudge a particle here and its partner would instantaneously dance over there, regardless of whether it was nanometers or light-years away.[136]

This, combined with the thought that it might (contrary to Einstein) be possible to travel faster than the speed of light, encouraged the question: 'Was acting at a distance really so different from clairvoyance, psychokinesis, or the Eastern mystics' emphasis on holism?'[137]

Another inference from such ideas was that the 'mini-Gellers' were not isolated, docile, or disciplined bodies. They drew upon unconscious forces within

---

[132] Hasted, *Alternative Memoirs*, 182.
[133] John Taylor, 'Letter to the Editor', *Nature*, 254 (10 April 1975), 470.
[134] Hasted, *Alternative Memoirs*, 17.
[135] Kaiser, *How the Hippies Saved Physics*, xxiv. This was 'Bell's theorem'.
[136] Ibid., xxiv.   [137] Ibid., xxiv.

their *entire* environment to harness their psychic powers. There was nothing 'supernatural' about the process. Rather, the 'Geller kids' seemed to be 'drawing their strange power from another dimension in a reservoir of energy that is all around us but inaccessible to all but a few'.[138] In an attempt to simplify these arguments, Hasted, Bohm, Bastin, and O'Regan drew analogies to the relationship between a partially paralysed man and his physiotherapist. In order to

> regain the use of his hand, he must somehow activate new nervous pathways. How he is to do this, he does not know. All he can do, with all his energy, is to feel out the possibilities of movement and to observe with great attention and alertness what movements actually take place. He cannot describe or even think about just what it is that he does in getting his hand to move.... The contact between brain and hand is brought about almost entirely by unconscious functions of the mind, which tend to be erratic and fortuitous.[139]

Crucially, too, for the hand to move, the physiotherapist *also* had to profess faith in the patient's capabilities. The 'necessity of open-ness to the possibility of an ultimate result must be maintained in the minds of *all* concerned', they contended.[140]

This meant that knowledge was co-produced. Unlike most scientific experiments, the distinction between 'scientist' and 'subject' was blurred, even eradicated altogether. Para-physicists pleaded with their fellow scientists to remember that the 'person who produces these [psychic] phenomenon is not an instrument or a machine', and even less is he or she an '"object" to be observed with suspicion'. Indeed, 'cold and impersonal' interactions as well as 'any attempt to treat him [sic] as such will almost certainly lead to failure'.[141] Hasted lashed out at people who criticised para-physicists on the grounds that such researchers 'wanted the events to happen'. Of course, Hasted scolded, this was 'in some degree true, *and it may be that this is why they did happen*'.[142] Hasted's argument was critical of the dominant scientific regime and its conception of truth, particularly 'objectivity'.

The breach of the 'detached objectivity' norm of scientific experimentation is movingly depicted in a short film-clip of Hasted's interactions with Stephen North. In the film, the older scientist and the young Stephen are depicted sitting companionably together in a laboratory in front of a vast array of complex recording devices. Hasted is being interviewed, but, as he speaks, he repeatedly nods and gestures towards Stephen, making reassuring grunts and friendly interjections, while seeking Stephen's consent and inviting his involvement. His fatherly demeanour is most evident when he jests that sometimes 'we' can't make the

---

[138] Owen, 'Britain's Key-Bending Kids Baffle Top Scientist'.
[139] Hasted, Bohm, Bastin, and O'Regan, 'News', 470–1.   [140] Ibid., 471. Emphasis added.
[141] Ibid., 470–1.   [142] Hasted, *The Metal-Benders*, 4. Emphasis in the original.

experiment work and have to break for a cup of tea—whereupon, they both chuckle. Tea in hand (and, cynics might add, suitably distracted), Stephen *and* Hasted succeed in harnessing Stephen's paranormal energies. What is clear in this film-clip is that the distinguished physicist is *enjoying himself*, proudly acknowledging the inter-personal nature of science. He is also gesturing towards the leftist commitment to collective work which, in theory, values all participants equally. It was an unorthodox model of science in which experimental practices and intellectual reasoning are fundamentally shared.

The final challenge to the status of science and scientific evidence was the para-physicists' unshakable belief in the 'folk'—people like Julie from Trowbridge and Stephen from Highgate. Power resided in the people—literally. Any person capable of tuning into Geller on television or simply being receptive to paranormal energies could harness these abilities within themselves. Admittedly, Hasted did privilege youth, maintaining that he 'preferred to deal with child metal-benders' because he believed that they were 'less likely to cheat than adults', as well as being more accepting and therefore receptive.[143] Of course, this was yet another target for ridicule, with opponents sneering about Hasted and Bohm's experiments with 'innocent young girls' and '11-year-old innocents'.[144] Nevertheless, Hasted repeatedly insisted that psychic abilities had nothing to do with intelligence, social background, or gender (although girls outnumbered boys in a ratio of three to two).[145] All that was required was the will to believe in their own power.

For both Hasted and Bohm, science had meaning; and that meaning was political. For Hasted, in particular, all his passions—physics, communism, peace, and folk music—were about forging better worlds. As he expressed it in his *Alternative Memoirs* (1992), his principle was

> Sing me a song of significance,
> No other song will do.[146]

The 'armies of Kings and Emperors' could be overthrown by 'folk' loudly singing 'The Marseillaise' and 'The Carmagnole';[147] the Cold War could be halted if other ordinary 'folk' sang peace songs. Even the atom bomb (whether American or Soviet) could not be detonated if a significant number of psychically sensitive

---

[143] Owen, 'Britain's Key-Bending Kids Baffle Top Scientist'.
[144] Morrison, 'The Magic of Uri Geller', 134.
[145] Owen, 'Britain's Key-Bending Kids Baffle Top Scientist'. The ratio between girls and boys is from Holroyd, *PSI and the Consciousness Explosion*, 108.
[146] Hasted, *Alternative Memoirs*, 1.   [147] Ibid., 37.

people 'concentrate[ed] on the trigger mechanism'.[148] The psychic energies of ordinary 'folk' could change the world.

* * *

The attraction of para-physics was not only in the way it challenged the dominant paradigm of science; it also opened up new possibilities for radical, dialectical responses to three crises: capitalism, the Cold War, and Stalinism.

Capitalism's failure was self-evident to these para-physicists. Hasted had turned to leftist politics because of witnessing the hunger marches of the 1930s and reflecting on the ineffective remedies ('Buy British!') proposed by Prime Minister Stanley Baldwin.[149] During his time at Oxford, he began

> to understand just how isolated from the real world scientific research had become. This was surely a political problem. Scientists did not seem to have any contact with the social and economic problems of the world.... They just persevered with own academic tasks, having apparently despaired of the rest of mankind, particularly the politicians, ever taking them seriously. This syndrome had become known as 'the frustration of science'.[150]

Both he and Bohm had also been profoundly shocked by the financial crash of 1973–4. Radical solutions seemed to be both necessary and possible.

The second crisis was the Cold War. Nuclear war was a real possibility, which Hasted addressed directly in a book he wrote with physicist E. H. S. Burhop, entitled *The Challenge of Atomic Energy* (1951).[151] In it, they argued that Britain would become a 'smoking, radioactive ruin' if there was a nuclear war.[152] Much of Hasted's early life was devoted to anti-war activism.[153] As a musician, he used to perform 'Talking Atomic Blues'.[154] He led the singing on CND marches.[155] His second wife was Lynn Wynn-Harris,[156] the secret 'Voice of Nuclear Disarmament', a radio station which broadcast on BBC and ITV channels after they signed off at midnight.[157] The fact that the western powers (particularly the USA) were engaged in psychic research worried him. In 1975, he explained that 'one reason for our staying in the parafield is in order that it does not become a military monopoly'.[158]

---

[148] This was a statement on a Discovery Channel programme, uploaded onto YouTube under the title 'Psychokinetic Metal Bending': https://www.youtube.com/watch?v=QPrJ1pSP2UI, viewed 15 May 2018.
[149] Hasted, *Alternative Memoirs*, 17.   [150] Ibid., 17.   [151] Ibid., 11.
[152] E. H. S. Burhop with John Hasted, *The Challenge of Atomic Energy* (London: Lawrence and Wishart, 1951).
[153] Stanley Bonnett, 'A Man's Wife is a Private Radio Girl', *Daily Mail* (8 December 1961), 13. He noted that neither of them was a member of the Committee of 100.
[154] Hasted, *Alternative Memoirs*, 111.   [155] Ibid., 155–7.   [156] He married her in 1958.
[157] Bonnett, 'A Man's Wife is a Private Radio Girl', 13.   [158] Hasted, 'Letters', 4.

The third crisis was Stalinism. Bohm's left-wing beliefs were rapidly subsumed by eastern mysticism, but a substantial part of Hasted's life was spent in the Communist Party. In 1949, he had been elected 'Commandant' of the Third Brigade, consisting of around a hundred young British leftists who volunteered to help build a road from Belgrade to Zagreb.[159] Thanks to his prodigious energy and charisma, his unit was dubbed the 'Shock Brigade'.[160] He had been Secretary of the Oxford University Communist Party and, while at Birkbeck, was active (along with Bernal, Hobsbawm, and Browning) in the London University branch of the Communist Party of Great Britain (CPGB). At the same time that fellow nuclear physicist Eric Burhop was being hounded for his communist and internationalist beliefs, Hasted and his wife Elizabeth were energetic members of the Notting Hill branch of the CPGB, selling copies of the *Daily Worker* door-to-door. They scrawled 'OUT WITH THE TORIES' on public walls, a crime that could have seen them sent to prison for three months.[161] It was Hasted who used his physics training to reveal that the CPGB headquarters in King Street was being bugged by the security services.[162] Later in life, he admitted to having been pro-Stalin. He had boasted about 'our adored Uncle Joe'. He had loudly sung 'Joe Stalin was a Mighty Man'[163] and

> Your Uncle Joe's a worker
> And a very decent chap.
> Because he smokes a pipe
> And wears a taxi-driver's cap.[164]

Like many British communists, he discounted rumours of oppression and murder 'right up to the time when Kruschev [sic] lifted the lid off the whole can of worms'.[165] At the end of his life, he recalled with poignancy the 'shock of the revelations'.[166]

The exposure of Stalin's purges shattered the communist hopes of party members like Hasted. This did not mean, though, that they had to forsake all hope in the power of the 'folk', the physical force of 'spectars' (Latin for 'that which is not seen'), and the inexorable march of history (although given their repudiation of time-as-forward-movement, they would have preferred 'the irresistible laws of a new physics'). In the opening lines of *The Communist Manifesto* (1848), Marx and Engels contended that 'A spectre is haunting Europe—the spectre of communism. All the powers of old Europe have entered into a holy alliance to exorcise this spectre.' For Hasted and many of his comrades, the spectre of communism had

---

[159] Hasted, *Alternative Memoirs*, 103. [160] Ibid., 106.
[161] Ibid., 96–7.   [162] Ibid., 102.
[163] Hylda Sims, 'On that Train and Gone', *English Dance and Song*, 62.4 (winter 2000), 2.
[164] Hasted, *Alternative Memoirs*, 103.   [165] Ibid., 103.   [166] Ibid., 80.

been tarnished by Stalinism, but they had an idea of another spectre—one that was equally invisible but had incredible power. Para-physics provided a way to think about an invisible, invincible spectre that haunted both the past-in-the-present and the future-in-the-past.

The impact of these three crises should not lead us to assume that para-physics was simply 'something to believe in'.[167] That is far too simplistic. Hasted and Bohm did not simply repudiate capitalism, the Cold War, and Stalinism. They embraced a praxis that took economics, war, and Marxism/Hegelianism to a new level. The three crises encouraged them to embrace para-physics as a form of radical, dialectical, and scientific utopianism. Marxism (for Hasted) and Hegelianism (for Bohm) provided them with the assurance that they would be at the vanguard of a revolution in physics; it also provided them with an ideological 'frame of meaning' which demystified science as bourgeois.

However—and crucially—Hasted and Bohm went far beyond dialectical or historical materialism, as well as other processual ways of thinking (such as the belief in progress or evolutionary mechanics). For them, *process* itself was the wrong way to frame the world because it was based on a notion of time-as-linear, forward movement and place-as-location. Instead, their revolutionary, new interpretation of quantum mechanics taught them that the historical present was effectively to be transcended, folded into the future. The future was also always folding into the past. What this meant was that the future could be reclaimed (for the Marxist); it could also be forestalled through the unconscious energies of ordinary people. The 'folk' could literally stop the Cold War from heating up. There was no need to counter bourgeois economics or the liberal marketplace, because power *resided with the people*—literally. As Hasted insisted time and again, the 'social consequences of such an understanding [of physics] could be very great'.[168]

As should now be obvious, utopian para-physics was concerned with much more than identifying and explaining a set of scientifically inexplicable phenomena: it was centrally about political change. Although Hasted believed that 'a practical application is a long way off', he was equally confident that 'one day these kind of powers could be used for healing'.[169] Hasted did admit to feeling anxious about whether there might be 'social dangers' associated with possessing extraordinary abilities such as metal bending. Although he could find no 'experimental evidence', he did speculate that there might be a 'built-in safety-catch on psychokinetic phenomena, ensuring that we cannot bring about anything which will harm ourselves or our friends'.[170] Admittedly, there was room for 'playful

---

[167] This was a common interpretation. For example, see Morrison, 'The Magic of Uri Geller', 134.
[168] Hasted, *The Metal-Benders*, 1.   [169] Robins, 'The Young Mindbenders'.
[170] Hasted, *The Metal-Benders*, 249.

misdemeanours' (for example, one of his 'mini-Gellers' bent his grandmother's knitting-needles 'when she was at a critical stage of purl and plain'), but it was rare for his subjects to suffer even a 'skin abrasion by metal-bending'.[171]

* * *

Para-physics appealed to physicists like Hasted and (for a much shorter period) Bohm because it provided a way to develop the idea of a radical break with time and space—that is, the realization of a new form of human subjectivity that was cooperative, shared, and universal. Theirs was a philosophy that literally transcended geopolitical space, opening the possibility for unity across the globe. True solidarity with other peoples, whose space and locality were far away and unknown, was a possibility after all. Knowledge of physics could be mobilized for political ends; science itself was political praxis.

Neither scientist was afraid of radical disruption, exceptionality, the unexplained, and spectacle. They defied orthodox physics, challenging theories of time (linearity), space (effects are weaker at a distance), and energy. They showed little interest in what Slavoj Žižek called a 'performative reconfiguration' of their discipline. They were subversive, but in a way that stepped outside the 'hegemonic field' of mainstream physics. They sought nothing less than a 'thorough reconfiguration of the entire field which redefines the very conditions of socially sustained performativity', such as conventional ideas of time and space, observed and observer.[172]

Para-physics has become a footnote in the history of physics. It is usually mentioned as a warning to other intrepid souls or as a way of introducing a little humour to an otherwise wholly earnest science. But this should not blind us to its perceived radical potential.

Hasted remained a believer to his dying day. In his old age, speaking from his bungalow in St Ives, Cornwall (a home, incidentally, that overlooked Virginia Woolf's lighthouse), he mused poignantly about his collaborations with 'his' mini-Gellers. 'Are we supposed [to believe] that it was just a one-off?', he asked. He admitted that his para-physics experiments

> may not be a significant part of knowledge, but that is not to say it didn't happen. I stand by what I reported, although I don't know whether it will ever happen again or not. What is left of those metalbending days is a collection of specimens, chart-records and literature reports; things of the past.

---

[171] Ibid., 249.
[172] Slavoj Zizek, *The Ticklish Subject: The Absent Centre of Political Ontology* (London: Verso, 1999), 264.

As Hasted repeated: 'nothing beside remains....I could not even weep. I was reminded of my bent spoons. Did it all really happen?'[173] He concluded his book on *The Mind-Benders* with the verse:

> Now, reader, that our tale is told,
> Canst thou the riddle guess?
> Such things in simpler days of old
> Were heard with faithfulness.
> But we, it seems, are wiser grown
> Less willing to believe.
> And till we see the causes shown
> Can scarce effects believe.
> But if these pages serve to show
> A truth, their moral brings
> How much imperfectly we know
> Even in trivial things;
> If you our sense of wonder call
> From where it's idle lain,
> Why, then, good METALBENDERS all,
> You'll not have bent in vain.[174]

---

[173] Hasted, *Alternative Memoirs*, 182.
[174] Ibid., 182. This is also cited (with some minor differences) at the end of Hasted, *The Metal-Benders*, 257.

25
Teaching

A word of advice to anyone applying for a lectureship at Birkbeck: be entertaining as well as scholarly. At nearly every interview for a lectureship at the College in recent decades, the same question is asked: 'What would you do if you walked into a seminar room on a bleak winter evening and were faced with a dozen weary civil servants, teachers, clerks, homemakers, taxi-drivers, and accountants?' When, in 1991, Tessa Blackstone—the first and, so far, only female Master (never Mistress) of Birkbeck—asked me this question at my interview, I quipped: 'Sex and violence should get them going!' I meant, of course, the history of gender and war—topics I was researching at the time. A stony silence descended on the room. They still appointed me.

Despite my failure to impress, it is an extremely germane question to ask anyone wanting to teach at an evening college for working Londoners. The unique challenges of providing the highest level of university education to men and women who have already put in a full day's work were recognized from the foundation of the College. As one member of the LMI's management committee ruefully admitted in 1853, 'I have myself seen working men attending a lecture and going to sleep, from mere exhaustion.' It was hardly surprising, he acknowledged. After all, anyone who had been working from six o'clock in the morning until seven in the evening might struggle to pay attention, especially 'to lectures on the more abstruse sciences'.[1] But if too many students dropped off and out of the classes, Birkbeck would be no more.

This chapter explores some of the pedagogic challenges facing students and teachers attending classes in the evening. Effective and intellectually rigorous teaching are at the heart of the College. Lecturers need to be at the forefront of their field, but they also need to be able to inspire themselves and their students to strive for greater knowledge. When chemistry lecturer George Chaloner informed his class of 1870 that the person 'who eliminates phosphorous by means of the Bessemer converter will make his fortune', he was not to know that an ambitious student called Sidney Gilchrist Thomas was listening keenly. Thomas set his mind to discover the process of dephosphorization, effectively transforming the industrial revolution.[2] Thomas' discovery was momentous, but even more

---

[1] Evidence from Samuel Vallentine, member of the management committee of the LMI, in *Report from the Select Committee on Parliamentary Papers; Together with the Proceedings of the Committee, Minutes of Evidence, Appendix, and Index* [720] (London: HMSO, 1853), 115–16.

[2] Burns, *A Short History of Birkbeck College*, 86.

typical students often find their worlds changed by inspired teaching. What do we know about Birkbeck's lecturers—their pedagogic styles, peculiarities, and passions? What about Birkbeck's students? What were their occupations, ages, and living arrangements? These are big questions, which can only be addressed in a 'snapshot' version here. Consequently, this chapter will begin by looking at one lecturer: philosopher Cyril Edwin Mitchinson Joad. He was a consummate performer, writer, and public intellectual. While not typical of lecturers at Birkbeck, Joad's highly masculine academic persona provides a lens through which to explore issues of teaching 'styles', including the ways academics perform their roles as intellectuals, teachers, and administrators. The chapter then directly addresses a question that appears sporadically throughout this book: who are our students?

* * *

Philosopher Cyril Edwin Mitchinson Joad was a flamboyant personality. He smoked a pipe, sported a bristly goatee, spoke in a squeaky voice, and took male-academic shabbiness to new depths. Nevertheless, he was a mesmerizing lecturer and, wherever he went, he courted controversy. At the height of his fame, he was a household name and the UK's best-known public intellectual.

Throughout his life, Joad was active in progressive causes. He was a keen speaker in the Oxford Union Debating Society, an energetic Fabian (that is, democratic socialist), a member of the Independent Labour Party, and supported the countryside movement. He championed women's rights, so long as they didn't hamper his sexual appetites. He firmly believed in the power of rational arguments to change minds. During the First World War, Joad joined the pacifist 'No Conscription Fellowship'. In 1933, as discussed in Chapter 18, Joad took part in 'King and Country' debate in the Oxford Union, convincing listeners to vote that 'this House will in no circumstances fight for its King and Country'. But from the mid-1930s, Joad became anxious about the rise of fascism and militarism. At the 1936 annual congress of the National Union of Students, he warned that science had given humanity 'powers fit for the gods and they brought to their use the mentality of public schoolboys or savages'.[3] He extolled students to use all their powers—intellectual and moral—to rid the world of war.[4] Human cruelty in the form of Nazism led him to repent of his pacifist principles; and the Blitz confirmed his change of mind, catapulting Joad to the front of Birkbeck's mission during the war. Indeed, his lunch-time lectures were so popular that they continued even after bombs fell directly on the College.

Joad's first major job was not at Birkbeck, however: he was originally a civil servant, but quickly became bored. In his spare time, therefore, he began teaching

---

[3] 'The Perils of Modern Civilization', *The Times* (17 April 1936), 14.   [4] Ibid., 14.

for the Workers' Educational Association and the University of London's extension classes. Joad proved extremely popular. Students loved him. His writing career was also taking off. Despite being technically employed at the Ministry of Labour, Joad was briskly writing books, including philosophical texts, critical essays, biographies, satires, and novels. Indeed, for much of his career, he wrote two books a year, championing what he called 'common-sense philosophy'.[5] If all these activities were not enough, at the same time, Joad was developing a huge radio presence. Radio had been introduced to Britain in 1922 and, under its energetic and paternalistic director John Reith, the BBC was doggedly devoted to enlightening the *hoi polloi*. Joad's easy style of philosophy—as well as his wit and humour—was perfectly suited to the medium.

But what Joad really wanted was a permanent academic job. Birkbeck was to become his scholastic home for his entire adult life. He was appointed the head of the Department of Philosophy and Psychology at Birkbeck in 1930. It was a tiny department, consisting of three (sometimes fewer) members of staff, but the students were more than happy to be taught by Joad on multiple courses. Indeed, it was so difficult to get him to stop talking that, well after the lights of the College were switched off at night, Joad and his students could be found continuing their debates in Lyons Corner House tea shop, which was open twenty-four hours a day.[6]

Not surprisingly, Joad was a great defender of the kind of education offered by Birkbeck. His educational philosophy was simple: he believed in 'the unity of learning', or a broad humanities education. As he argued in an inter-faculty talk at Birkbeck on 12 March 1947, students who pursued 'humane studies, literature and languages, history and philosophy' would always retain a 'richer and wider mind than that of the specialist'. In a 1933 article entitled 'Praise of Birkbeck', Joad argued that education was 'essential in a democracy': indeed, democracy could only flourish if people were 'able and anxious to pronounce a free and independent judgment upon the affairs of the community'.[7] Without an expansive education, citizens were nothing more than 'sheep, ready to flock into the appropriate pen at the voice of the first dictator who can catch their ear with the latest political scare or stunt'.[8]

Joad took this educational mission outside the classroom. From January 1941, he joined evolutionary biologist Julian Huxley and retired naval officer A. B. (Archibald Bruce) Campbell on *The Brains' Trust*, which was broadcast during the 'best Sunday-afternoon spot'.[9] This BBC radio programme took the format

[5] C. E. M. Joad, *Essays in Common-Sense Philosophy* (London: The Swarthmore Press, 1919).
[6] Tony Judge, *Radio Philosopher: The Radical Life of Cyril Joad* (Charleston: Alpha House, 2012), 98.
[7] C. E. M. Joad, 'Praise of Birkbeck', *The Lodestone*, 29.1 (Michaelmas 1933), 11.   [8] Ibid., 11.
[9] Ernest O. Hauser, 'The Englishman Who Loves to Insult Us', *Sunday Evening Post* (29 November 1952), in 'Newscuttings 1975–76'; 'The Brain, the Tongue, and the Heart of the Brains' Trust', *The Listener* (18 May 1978), in 'Newscuttings 1976–80', in the Birkbeck Archive.

Fig. 25.1   Cover of C. E. M. Joad's *More Opinions by Joad* (1946).

of a question-and-answer panel that (uniquely for the time, especially under Reith's directorship) never talked down to the audience. The three presenters were also incredibly funny and pithy. At its height, 29 per cent of people in the UK, including the royal family, tuned in to hear these men answer questions such as 'How does a fly land on the ceiling?', 'Why is music beautiful?', and 'Why don't you laugh when you tickle yourself?'[10] When Joad quoted Confucius' question— 'What economy is it to go to bed in order to save candlelight, if the results be twins?'—it was even discussed in Parliament.[11] Joad's slogan—'Well, it depends what you mean...'—became the catchphrase in every debating club and pub in the country. Joad was unquestionably the star of the show. Fans followed him wherever he went; mounted police had to be called to control the crowds gathering to hear his lectures. During the 1939–45 war, the Ministry of Food even named a recipe after him: Joad in the Hole.

At least in the early years of his academic career, Joad was known to be 'a typical left-wing intellectual; skeptical, anti-Christian, socialist; an up-to-the-minute "progressive" on all matters concerned with the state'. From the 1940s, however, he began defending the 'objective reality of goodness, truth, and beauty'.[12] His philosophical work was varied, but included *A Critique of Logical Positivism* (1950), which attacked the view that ethics and aesthetics were simply a matter of personal preference.[13] By promoting a 'complete skepticism about all ethical, aesthetic, and religious beliefs', he argued that positivists 'cannot but have a paralysing effect on young and generous people who would otherwise be protesting passionately against cruelty, injustice, and other evils'.[14]

Joad's publishing output was prodigious (see Fig. 25.1). He wrote around fifty books, including *Guide to Philosophy* (1936), which sold 45,000 copies, and

---

[10] Hauser, 'The Englishman Who Loves to Insult Us'.   [11] Ibid.
[12] Robert Hamilton, 'Dr Joad and the Angels', *Irish Ecclesiastical Review* (December 1955), 509.
[13] Ibid., 509.   [14] Ibid., 509.

Guide to the Philosophy of Morals and Politics (1938), which sold over 30,000 copies.[15] These were enormous sales for the time. He wrote on education, free will, genius, the nature of mind and matter, democracy, culture, the philosophy of pleasure, vitalism versus idealism, biology, evolution, sex, art, music, the countryside, and nature. He was famous for his provocative statements and was a virulent critic of American culture. For example, in *The Pleasure of Being Oneself* (1951) he quipped that

> One bit of sea is so very like another bit. Why then, one wonders, [is there] so much of it? I often have the same thought in regards to Americans. Why did God make so many?[16]

More frivolously, he judged beauty contests. Baby boys were christened 'Cyril' in his honour.[17] Virginia Woolf even quoted him in *Three Guineas*.[18]

Public recognition, an aptitude for teaching, and an ability to churn out books and journalistic articles do not bring scholarly distinction, however. Academically, Joad remained an outsider. Although he was head of the Department of Philosophy and Psychology, he was never promoted to professor. That honour was given to Ruth Saw, an expert on the fourteenth-century metaphysical nominalist William of Ockham and enlightenment philosophers Baruch Spinoza and Gottfried Wilhelm Leibniz. 'Weighty' topics, indeed.

It did not help Joad's reputation that he was frequently accused of plagiarism— and by the great philosopher Bertrand Russell, no less. This must have been a painful blow because Joad revered Russell, although critics sniped that he had probably never actually read *Principia Mathematica*. Joad also failed to produce any lasting philosophical works. Ludwig Wittgenstein famously remarked that Joad should be 'put out of business' as the philosophical equivalent of a 'slum landlord'. Reviewers quipped that Joad was 'not a great original thinker'.[19] Joad responded to such jibes in his usual fashion: mockery. In 1942, he published an obituary for himself, claiming that Joad 'might have been taken seriously as a philosopher if it had not been that his feet' refused 'to rest content with the floors of the philosophy lecture rooms' and 'insisted...on sticking themselves in the mire of politics'.

Joad's professional reputation was also stymied by the fact that he was a sensualist—unapologetically so. He wrote eloquently about

---

[15] Hauser, 'The Englishman Who Loves to Insult Us'.
[16] C. E. M. Joad, *The Pleasure of Being Oneself* (London: George Weidenfeld and Nicolson, 1951), at https://archive.org/stream/pleasureofbeingo029119mbp/pleasureofbeingo029119mbp_djvu.txt, viewed 1 June 2021.
[17] Ibid. [18] Virginia Woolf, *Three Guineas* (London: Harcourt, Brace, and Co., 1938), 43.
[19] Hamilton, 'Dr. Joad and the Angels', 510. Also see 'Obituary. Dr. C. E. M. Joad', *The Times* (10 April 1953), 8.

the pleasures of strawberries and cream, or burgundy and brie, of roast lamb (English) and green peas (untinned), of walking over moors and mountains, of winning the fifth set at tennis or hitting a tour at cricket, of a fine spring morning or of a fine winter morning with hoar-frost sparkling in the sun...or of making love.[20]

This caused problems. After divorcing his first wife, he lived—indiscreetly—with many lovers, all of whom he introduced as 'Mrs Joad'. His frequent dalliances were probably the reason he was unable to forge a career in politics, something he would have relished. His sensualism coincided with an underlying misogyny. In 1948, when he was in his mid-fifties, he admitted that one of the best things about growing old was his 'emancipation from dependence upon women arising out of my servitude to my senses'. He confessed that when he was young, 'sex was like a mosquito buzzing in a room in which one was trying to write': it was impossible to get any work done until that mosquito was 'swatted'. Women, he insisted, were 'capricious, self-important, touchy, egotistical, and, above all, boring'.[21] And he simultaneously proclaimed an ardent feminism!

Nevertheless, Joad, whose portrait is shown in Fig. 25.2, inspired an entire generation of students to read philosophy; his radio programmes and performances contributed to the 'common good' by encouraging millions of Britons to think seriously about some of the most pressing problems of their times. However, in 1948, he spectacularly fell from grace. Over the years, Joad had often been heard discussing that popular philosophical question: 'how far' should a person 'try and obey the rules of the laws of one's community when one disapproves of them...and how far one ought to break them?' On 5 January 1948, he learnt the answer. Joad was caught on the train from London Waterloo to Exeter without a ticket, which would have cost only 17s. 1d. He was hauled before the Police Court at Tower Bridge, fined the maximum penalty of £2, and ordered to pay costs of 25 guineas. His celebrity status meant that his court appearance hit the headlines. Priding themselves on high moral conduct, the BBC banned him from the airwaves. Admittedly, the listening figures for *The Brains' Trust* were already falling rapidly, largely due to competition from Light programmes, especially the *Carroll Lewis Show*.[22] After the scandal, Birkbeck stood by him, but he was blackballed by the media. His star had fallen.

* * *

The personal and professional life of Joad provides an interesting lens through which to reflect on the role of academics as teachers and public intellectuals. He

---

[20] Joad, *The Pleasure of Being Oneself*, 7.
[21] C. E. M. Joad, *A Year More or Less* (London: Victor Gollancz, 1948), 218.
[22] 'The Brain, the Tongue, and the Heart of the Brains' Trust'.

Fig. 25.2 Oil painting of C. E. M. Joad by artist J. M. Clark, 1947 © The Artist's Estate.

was easy to caricature—his appearance, sensual abandonment, and penchant for glib aphorisms set him apart from many of his peers. Even his opponents had to admit that he was a consummate communicator. In the classic text, *The Elements of Style* (1918), William Strunk contended that 'vigorous writing is concise',[23] which precisely describes Joad's prose: punchy, precise, and rhythmic. Of course, not all academic prose can avoid using complex concepts and dense argumentation. Many university texts are only intelligible to people who have spent years immersing themselves in a particular body of knowledge. Complex ideas often require specialist language. Calls for academics to make everything they say and write comprehensible to everyone fail to appreciate the complexity of our worlds. And, it must be noted, accusations of 'jargon' and 'linguistic elitism' are levelled primarily at scholars in the arts and humanities: who would dare accuse a molecular biologist or mathematician of using specialist languages?

---

[23] William Strunk, *The Elements of Style* (New York: Macmillan, 1979), 23.

Nevertheless, *caricatures* of academic prose typically complain about a penchant for the 'passive voice', textual diversions, bulging footnotes, and flabby sentences containing multiple clauses. Even friendly critics enjoy parodying 'academic-speak'. As one reviewer complained about geology scholar George MacDonald Davies' *A Student's Introduction to Geology (Mainly Physical)* (1949), the text required students to 'wade through turgid or nebulous writing'.[24] It was a criticism that Davies himself employed against his predecessor George F. Harris, a specialist on granites. Harris had a 'rotund style of lecturing', Davies teased Harris for his pompous lecturing style, which involved the repetition of phrases such as 'You will ask me...My reply to you is...'. Harris' lectures were said to drive students to drink beer 'as an antidote'.[25]

It is one thing to criticize a lecturer's prose; quite another, personal traits and appearance. Unfortunately, academics are easy to mock. In 1926, for example, students ridiculed an unnamed lecturer for having 'discovered the delightful function of a necktie as a means of removing dust from his spectacles'.[26] British intellectuals were often satirized as corduroy-clad geeks, which is why so many academics today avoid the fabric. Historian Eric Hobsbawm was accused of exuding the 'studied inelegance of the British Old Left'. A Special Branch spy put it more brutally: Hobsbawm dressed 'in a slovenly way'.[27] Some academics went to the opposite extreme. Frederic John Cheshire, who was famous for his design of optical instruments, was educated at Birkbeck before being appointed a physics lecturer there from 1895. He appeared in lectures dressed in tails and a top hat, cigar clenched between his teeth.[28] In contrast, others earned reputations for ascetic ardour. Reginald Ralph Darlington, Professor of Medieval History from 1945 until his retirement in 1969, was an example. His obituarist conceded that he possessed 'a somewhat formidable reputation for austere behaviour', projecting an 'almost monastic devotion' to Old English studies.[29] Darlington 'did not favour Christian-name familiarity', demanding to be known as 'Darlington' even during informal discussions.[30] He was a man who 'concealed, if he did not suppress, sentiment and emotion'.[31] He was celibate throughout his life.[32] Indeed, Darlington

---

[24] Lou Williams Page, 'A Student's Introduction to Geology (Mainly Physical) by George MacDonald Davies', *Journal of Geology*, 59.4 (July 1951), 412–13.
[25] 'G.M.D.' (George MacDonald Davies), 'Forty Years On', *The Lodestone*, 35.2 (Easter 1943), 8.
[26] 'P.A.', 'The Common Room', *The Lodestone*, 22.1 (1926), 21.
[27] 'Sartorial Socialism', *Times Higher Education Supplement* (13 April 1973), and 'Secret Report', date unknown, *c.* early 1950s, in TNA KV2/3981.
[28] H. G. B., 'A Fire-Watcher's Interview with his Own Memory', *The Lodestone*, 36.3 (summer 1944), 12. Also see 'Prof. F. J. Cheshire, C.B.E.', *Nature*, 143 (13 May 1939), 792, and Stephen Curtis Sambrook, 'The Optical Munitions Industry in Great Britain, 1888–1923', PhD thesis (Glasgow: University of Glasgow, 2005), 156.
[29] 'Obituary. Professor R. R. Darlington. Saxon and Medieval Studies', *The Times* (6 June 1977), 10.
[30] R. Allen Brown, 'Reginald Ralph Darlington, 1903–1977', *Proceedings of the British Academy* (1981), 427.
[31] Ibid., 430.   [32] Ibid., 435.

advised male scholars to avoid marriage (at least before reaching the age of 40) because it would interfere with their careers.³³ He informed one young colleague that

> there are two kinds of scholars. There are those who work late into the night and those who get up early in the morning. Myself, I am seldom in bed before one, but then, I never get up before seven.³⁴

It is not surprising, therefore, that Darlington was accused of severity. He had 'no mercy for his intellectual peers', being willing to prolong staff meetings in order to lecture his colleagues 'on the foolhardiness of a proposal which everyone else had assumed was already agreed to'. He devoted much of his time as head of department to blocking Hobsbawm's promotion to Reader and professor.³⁵ Only his closest friends knew that he had a sensitive side, revealed by his devotion to ornithology, cats, gardening, fine china, and horses with 'a bit of "go" '.³⁶

Female lecturers find themselves parodied in different ways. In part, this is due to the belief (which is still largely, and unfortunately, correct) that, in order to be taken at least half as seriously as their male equals, they must adopt performance norms grounded in gender- and class-based conceptions of 'the intellectual'. For example, geographer Eva Germaine Rimington Taylor had the term 'redoubtable' thrown at her numerous times. In the words of Arnolfo John Caraffi (a Birkbeck student before serving as College Secretary between 1952 and 1979), Taylor's

> marking was severe—my first effort, written with some pride, came back slashed to ribbons and copiously annotated—and was rightly meant to set the high standards which she expected and applied strictly to her own lifetime of scholarship.

Whether he did so at the time is unclear but, later, Caraffi was able to put her academic strictness in perspective. He noted that 'the number of women Professors throughout the land was pitifully small', when he was a student, which meant that 'each would have felt moved, by whatever means, to be seen to justify her position in the eyes of her male colleagues'.³⁷ Female lecturers also had a novel way 'into' the academic profession—via jobs as 'secretary'. This was the case with medieval historian Edith ('Emma') Mason, who joined the Department of History in the early 1960s as secretary to Professor R. R. Darlington but by the end of that

---

[33] Ibid., 435. [34] Ibid., 436.
[35] Evans, *Eric Hobsbawm*, 213.
[36] 'Obituary. Professor R. R. Darlington. Saxon and Medieval Studies', 10, and Brown, 'Reginald Ralph Darlington, 1903–1977', 437.
[37] Caraffi, 'Memories of Breams II'.

decade had been appointed lecturer. When she retired, she had been employed in the department for nearly four decades.[38]

Such representations of academics took place in the context of numerous shifts in College practices. Take, for example, punctuality. Accurate timekeeping was essential if lecturers and students were to move from one class to another in an orderly fashion. When the LMI first opened its doors, wristwatches and pocket watches (women wore the former; men, the later) were owned by the middle classes, as well as many working-class people. But members of the Institution were often still dependent on church bells and public clocks in town halls, banks, and railway stations to judge the time. As Paul Glennie and Nigel Thrift argued in *Shaping the Day: A History of Time Keeping in England and Wales, 1300–1800* (2009), well into the nineteenth century, clock-time was a heterogeneous and relativist notion; even people with watches would check and adjust them against public timing devices.[39] These clocks had to be manually wound.[40] Clock-time was not standardized until 1847 (nearly a quarter of a century after the establishment of the LMI), driven primarily by the scheduling needs of railways. It took another eight years for most of Britain's public clocks to be standardized to Greenwich Mean Time. It is impossible to know for certain, but members of the LMI had perhaps a keener sense of time than many working people. After all, watches were not only about punctuality: they also connoted frugality, sobriety, and respectability—traits that were central to the self-image of members of the Institution.

In this context, the College needed a system to denote time. Although wearing wristwatches dramatically increased because of the 1914–18 war (in part because precise synchronization was required by modern artillery), the College continued to ring bells at regular intervals to mark the passing of time. Immediately prior to the war, this was one of the tasks for 'porters', who would ring the College's fire-alarm on the hour to tell lecturers that they needed to conclude their classes within twenty minutes. It was 'a soul-destroying, nerve-shattering ritual', recalled one lecturer.[41] In the 1920s, students began complaining about the ringing of the fire-alarms every hour, claiming it was having 'serious effects upon our physical and mental well-being', perhaps due to the very frightening resonance of fire-alarms being sounded during the war.[42] The porters substituted small bells, similar to ones on bicycles, rung on the landing of each floor.[43]

---

[38] Emma Mason, interviewed by Jonny Matfin, 10 October 2019.
[39] Paul Glennie and Nigel Thrift, *Shaping the Day: A History of Time Keeping in England and Wales, 1300–1800* (Oxford: Oxford University Press, 2009).
[40] For a witty discussion on time and the length of lectures, see Lector Emeritus, 'The Lecturette', *The Lodestone*, 18.1 (autumn 1922), 37.
[41] 'The Power of the Press', *The Lodestone*, 20.2 (1925), 12.
[42] Pro Bono Publico, 'To the Editor', *The Lodestone*, 20.1 (Michaelmas 1924), 32.
[43] 'The Power of the Press', 12.

The ringing of bells was not the only ritual that can shed a light on changes in the conduct of the College. Prior to 1845, lecturers were paid a proportion of the student fees. This made sense to classicist Frederick A. Wright. He recalled that if a teacher at Birkbeck

> did not want to teach[,] he merely called in some one else and then went off to some more desirable engagement. It was an excellent system, for teaching is an art and it is just as unreasonable for a teacher to teach if he does not feel like teaching as it would be for a painter to paint if he does not feel like painting.[44]

Wright argued that this system encouraged the teacher to be 'capable and energetic', otherwise 'his classes dwindled and so did his pay'.[45] When George M. Norris became Principal in 1885, this was one of his first reforms. Henceforth, lecturers were to be given fixed salaries. Luckily, Wright's fears of a lowering of standards did not materialize. As Wright himself would have admitted, the new system of fixed salaries attracted more competent and committed lecturers, including ones like himself.

The way wages were paid had also changed. At the beginning of the twentieth century, wages were not paid directly into the bank accounts of staff but handed out by the administrative staff. In 1915, when literary scholar Marjorie Daunt arrived at Bream's Building (where she remained for thirty years), she recalled that a 'kind old Secretary' would suddenly appear in the Senior Common Room, which, incidentally, was housed in a 'converted coal-cellar', and place a notice on the mantelpiece reading 'Cheques ready in the office'. Later, when 'the seed of academic propriety began to sprout' (presumably as the College began the process of becoming part of the University of London), lecturers feigned to ignore the notice. In retaliation, the Secretary resorted to visiting each lecture room personally, 'fluttering a sheaf of cheques'. To Daunt's mortification, when he presented her with the cheque in front of the students, he would purr, 'There, my dear, is something nice for you.'[46] The automatic payment of salaries into bank accounts was not common until the 1970s.

It was the move to becoming a member college of the University of London that led to changes in the relationship of students to their lecturers. In short, they became less deferential. They demanded certain rights. In 1919, even the student-editor of *The Lodestone* was prepared to attack College authorities publicly. After accusing the governors of sitting in 'senile decay' over the College, he turned his criticism to lecturers. He claimed that students who were 'eager for living food' often found themselves 'fed with the dead bones of arid facts and the too often

---

[44] 'F. A. W.' [Frederick A. Wright], 'Birkbeck in the Past', *The Lodestone*, 30.3 (summer 1935), 123.
[45] Ibid., 123.   [46] 'Marjorie on Birkbeck. Birkbeck 1915–1945', *The Lodestone*, 47.1 (1956), 5.

repeated lecture, marked by its age-worn jokes'. He pleaded with the staff 'to produce original work, to discover new theories and assail again the walls of ignorance', otherwise the College would continue to 'plod on as we have done for so long...through the wilderness'.[47] Surely, Birkbeck was 'not a mere cramming shop' but had the potential to become distinguished part of the University.[48]

This student-editor's attack on the governors and lecturers met with furious rebuttals, but it was not the only question mark hovering over the College in the lead-up to joining the University of London. There were also demands for increased formality, specifically whether (and when) students and lecturers should wear academic gowns. On ceremonial occasions, wearing academic dress was (and continues to be) *de rigueur* but, in the past, Birkbeck students and lecturers debated whether they should be expected to wear their gowns when attending classes as well. After all, students at King's College did so until the 1970s.

Discussions about the wearing of gowns were especially prominent once students and staff sought to move towards becoming part of the University of London. This was why the Principal in 1908 was keen to encourage the practice, as were student representatives.[49] This issue was satirized in a 1920 yarn entitled 'Naked and Unashamed'. The unnamed author reported that, when a 'high authority' from the University of London made an impromptu inspection of Birkbeck, he was outraged to discover that everyone, except the librarian, was 'unclad'. Immediately inside the College, he saw

> two girls talking together, one of them holding an armful of books and the other carrying an attaché case, but both stark naked. He rubbed his eyes, coughed, and rubbed his eyes again....As he stood there[,] embarrassed[,] he was equally bowled over by a youth leaving the library equally unclad....He sat down for a short time to get his breath. 'Strange', he murmured to himself. 'Very strange'.

The inspector was aghast because, up until 1921, academic dress at Birkbeck was only donned on special occasions, such as Opening Night and Founders' Day. He insisted on meeting with the President of the Students' Union who, similarly 'naked', was found in the Refreshment Room consulting 'Mrs. Francis about the pastries'. The inspector remonstrated to the President, stating that 'surely you know that all Undergraduates are expected to wear their gowns. Academic dress is not exactly compulsory: but it is very important that it should be worn'. The President was persuaded. Quick to realize the symbolic importance of routine

---

[47] Editor, 'Editorial', *The Lodestone*, 15.1 (Michaelmas 1919), 3. This was probably H. Broadley, listed as the Editor that year. There was a response by C. W. Hume, 'Letter to the Editor', *The Lodestone*, 15.2 (Easter and summer 1920), 19–20. Another response came from H. G. Richardson, 'Letter to the Editor', *The Lodestone*, 15.2 (Easter and summer 1920), 21–2.
[48] Editor, 'Letter to the Editor', *The Lodestone*, 15.2 (Easter and summer 1920), 26.
[49] 'From the Common Room', *The Lodestone*, 4.1 (December 1908), 20.

wearing of academic gowns as a soon-to-be member of the University of London, as well as a marker of scholarly privilege and identity, the Council amended the College's constitution. It decreed that, henceforth,

> All members of the [Students'] Union are expected to wear academic dress and those appearing at Union functions or attending College without them will be deemed to be guilty of conduct unworthy of the Union.

The Council hoped that 'if all members of the Union set a good example by purchasing and wearing academic dress forthwith, other members of the College and members of the Staff may be encouraged to follow suit' and the 'unfortunate occurrence' of 'Naked and Unashamed' students would 'soon be forgotten'.[50] It was, according to the pompous 'Cantus Planus', an affirmation of

> the glorious principle that 'the dignity that doth hedge' a member of the Union can only be enhanced by the apparel pertaining to academic position; nay, more, that vestiture in this raiment is the strict duty of those who assume collegiate functions.[51]

That lecturers *did* 'follow suit' for nearly forty years is indicated in 1959 when, only after a lengthy discussion, the Faculty of Arts decided that wearing academic gowns would henceforth be left to the 'taste' of individual lecturers.[52]

* * *

So far, this chapter has explored general College procedures. However, pedagogic 'styles' at Birkbeck could be discipline-specific, often influenced by the personal inclinations of individual professors, heads of department, or charismatic lecturers. For example, in 1920, the Geology Department was described as

> one of the happiest and most friendly in college, and there is the greatest good feeling between students and staff. I remember a fellow geologist's remark in praise of the department: 'When you go in there they ask you, "What would you *like* to do this evening?"'.[53]

---

[50] 'Naked and Unashamed', *The Lodestone*, 15.2 (Easter and summer 1920), 34–6.

[51] Cantus Planus, 'Neo-Confucianism: Review of the report of the Committee of the "Brighter Birkbeck" Society', *The Lodestone*, 18.1 (autumn 1922), 13.

[52] 'Minutes of the Meeting of the Faculty of Arts, 27th January, 1959', in 'Faculty of Arts. Minutes of Meetings. Apl. 25th 1940', in the Birkbeck Archive.

[53] 'Pastor', 'From the Geology Department', *The Lodestone*, 16.1 (Michaelmas 1920), 20. The author could be George MacDonald Davies who was an instructor in 1920 but went on to become head of department.

Fig. 25.3 J. D. Bernal with his students on a field trip to Stonehenge, Wiltshire, to study mineral crystallography. Birkbeck Image Collections: Birkbeck History BH0128.

The most enjoyable of these lecturers was John William Evans, whose 'enthusiasm for the subject' was 'only tempered by regret that the students did not take to crystal optics like ducks to water'.[54]

Similarly, the Department of Physics and Crystallography has long been known for its informal ethos. Albert Griffiths, Professor of Physics, 'made it a habit to invite students to tea with him in groups of four in the tiny glazed box in a corner of the laboratory which was his private office'. There, he would feed them on 'brown bread and butter, cheese and apples'.[55] J. D. Bernal (see Fig. 25.3) was renowned for fostering a non-hierarchical atmosphere in his laboratories. As Dorothy M. C. Hodgkin noted, Bernal ensured that technicians were able to 'continue their studies and take part in college social life' while working in his labs. He also introduced monthly meetings when staff would meet with undergraduates to 'discuss difficulties' and make 'suggestions for improvement'.[56]

In many other departments, there was a high degree of intimacy between staff and students. As Daunt observed, Birkbeck students would 'come to a lecturer's house to do an evening's work', after which they 'clear and wash up as a matter of course and not as a favour, which is very charming'.[57] Similarly, the architectural historian Nikolaus Pevsner would invite his graduate students to his home for dinner parties. He also often accompanied his undergraduate students to the

[54] Ibid., 20.   [55] Caraffi, 'Memories of Breams II', 12.
[56] Hodgkin, 'John Desmond Bernal', 61.
[57] Daunt, 'Marjorie on Birkbeck. Birkbeck 1915–1945', 9.

Fig. 25.4 Oil painting of C. A. Mace, unknown artist. Birkbeck Image Collections: Birkbeck History BH0119.

refectory for a hasty dinner or, after class, to the Bonnington Hotel bar in Southampton Row.[58] From the 1990s, such intimacy was rare due to neoliberal moralism and feminist sensibilities, although cautious forays to the Norfolk Arms in Leigh Street are not unknown.[59]

Communications between lecturers and students are often mediated through administrative staff. Office personnel are especially indispensable. Nothing would happen without their expertise. They are also important in narrowing hierarchies between lecturers and students. Cecil Alec A. Mace, the College's first Professor of Psychology (see Fig. 25.4), was one of the few who publicly admitted this fact. In establishing and developing the department, Mace acknowledged that he had been 'greatly helped by the secretaries of the Department—first by Phyllis Taylor and then by Mrs. Carver (better known as Vida)'. He believed that 'a piece of equipment essential in a department of psychology' was 'a *shoulder* to weep on', which, he quipped, was 'much more essential than a psychoanalytic couch'.[60] Although referring to a human being as a 'piece of equipment' betrayed his chauvinism, Mace went on to contend that, for twelve years, 'Vida's shoulder must have been one of the most wept on in the academic world'. She was not only the personal secretary to the head of department, but also 'an editorial assistant, a

---

[58] Harries, *Nikolaus Pevsner: The Life*, 431.

[59] Thanks to Sasha Dovzhyk, fact-checker for this book, for informing me that this tradition is not dead!

[60] Mace, 'Psychology Comes to Birkbeck', 4.

research officer, and adviser to research students who cannot write English'. Mace joked that 'Vida' was the 'Lady Troglodite', who 'occupied the Outer Cave protecting the Professor in the Inner Cave'. Her trick was designated the 'two-minute rule', whereby students

> filed into the Outer Cave. 'Can I see the Professor?' they asked. Vida replied: 'The Professor is very busy, but I will see if he can spare you just two minutes'. *Tinkle-tinkle* on the phone. 'Could you possibly see Miss A or Mr. B. for a "moment"?'.[61]

This female 'Troglodite' controlled the borders between the professor and his students. What Mace must have known at the time, but failed to mention, is that Vida Carver was editing a book in his honour.[62] She later became an academic in her own right, specializing in disability and ageing.

At the time, Mace was not only the most senior manager in psychology. He was also an accomplished lecturer, revelling in giving his students highly stylized performances on subjects as diverse as the psychology of study, scientific management, the structure of the mind, mental deficiency, and logic. His performative approach to teaching was not unusual, as we saw with Joad. Individual lecturers often fostered quirky ways of delivering their classes. Take the philosophers Roger Scruton and Ian McFetridge. Scruton was at Birkbeck from 1971 to 1992. Although he specialized in the philosophy of aesthetics, he clearly took as much pleasure in 'Red-baiting' as in serious philosophy. His defence of hunting and embrace of right-wing causes set him apart from most lecturers at Birkbeck and scandalized Birkbeck students.

McFetridge was an equally complex professor of philosophy, whose intellectual passion was symbolic logic. Even though his classroom was hardly ideal (both he and his students complained about the 'numbing glow of neon lights'), everyone agreed that he was a mesmerizing teacher. During class, McFetridge would take out a package of tobacco, roll a pinch in thin paper, lick the side to seal, and then smoke it as part of 'the expression of an idea'. Philosopher John Haldane, who wrote his Birkbeck PhD on 'Intentionality and Epistemological Realism', recalled that 'striking a match, inhaling and so on, were elements in the extended syntax of [McFetridge's] speech'. Haldane had

> a very vivid image of a type of situation when someone would have been reading a philosophical paper. At some point in the proceedings, not having yet spoken, Ian would light a cigarette, or put one out, with a deliberation that indicated an objection had become clarified in his mind. When he then went on to present

---

[61] Ibid., 6.   [62] Vida Carver (ed.), *C. A. Mace: A Symposium* (London: Penguin, 1962).

it—again with draughtsmanlike precision—he would as often proceed to suggest how the objection might be replied to.

Lighting his cigarette, inhaling and exhaling the tar and smoke, were all part of McFetridge's pedagogy, not only communicating 'the structure of a problem,' but also revealing 'what possibilities were available on various ideas of the issue'.[63] McFetridge's possibilities ended in 1988 when, aged just 40 years, he committed suicide.[64]

Styles of pedagogy were influenced by intellectual fashions. This can be illustrated by turning to the Department of English. Under Geoffrey Tillotson (head of the English Department between 1944 and 1969 and known for his work on Alexander Pope), Marjorie Daunt (Anglo-Saxon scholar), Harold Fletcher Brooks (general editor of the Arden Shakespeare), and Barbara Hardy (expert on the Victorian novel), students were encouraged to indulge directly in the 'raw material of literature itself'. This went against the usual pedagogic approach in undergraduate English at the time, which focused on 'secondary commentary'.[65] Members of the department also experimented with teaching students in 'bursts', with one lecturer focusing on a particular author for three weeks of concentrated lectures and seminars, after which students were required to write an essay.[66]

Derek Oldfield was a graduate and then postgraduate student in this department for ten years from 1951. He went on to become a prominent adult education teacher but, at Birkbeck, he studied George Eliot's prose style in *Middlemarch*. Later in his life, he quipped that 'the shared faith' of the department

> was radically Protestant; we were to address our God without a priestly intermediary. And since our tutors and we ourselves believed that all our writers were Gods, the only appropriate way to meet them was down on our knees. The text judged us, not we the text.[67]

This meant that the lecturers were both inspirational and ferocious. As a tall, lean, ascetic-looking Yorkshireman, Geoffrey Tillotson was a master of irony, bordering on sarcasm. 'Do not omit to be literate', he wrote in his immaculate italic handwriting when a student left out an apostrophe.[68] One of Tillotson's favourite aphorisms was 'Criticism, trembling with sympathy, cannot but be ruthless!'[69] In contrast, Oldfield remembered Barbara Hardy for her leftist feminism. One minute, she could be heard laughing with students in the refectory; the next,

---

[63] John Haldane, 'A Memorial Address', in I. G. McFetridge, *Logical Necessity and Other Essays*, ed. John Haldane and Roger Scruton (London: Aristotelian Society, 1990), 2.
[64] John Haldane and Roger Scruton, 'Preface', in McFetridge, *Logical Necessity and Other Essays*, vii.
[65] Derek Oldfield, *Slow to Begin With: A Memoir* (London: Privately Printed, 2004), 315.
[66] Ibid., 321.   [67] Ibid., 315.   [68] Ibid., 322.
[69] Mr G. Singh, 'Prof. G. Tillotson', *The Times* (25 October 1969).

Fig. 25.5 Marjorie Daunt. *The Lodestone*, 47.1 (1956), 31.

indignantly railing against gender inequalities.[70] Marjorie Daunt (see Fig. 25.5) was equally daunting. She was not averse to placing her fingers in students' mouths as they struggled to correctly pronounce Old English, a 'tough Germanic dialect' spoken prior to 1066, which all students in the University of London were required to learn.[71] In contrast, the diminutive, frail Harold Fletcher Brooks was often observed 'dash[ing] the tears from his cheeks at the merest hint of pathos' in Shakespeare and Chaucer. He was also indignant if any student exhibited 'crudity of interpretation or careless mis-reading'. Brooks 'loved us', Oldfield recalled, adding 'but he loved Chaucer more'.[72]

Intellectual fashion was also dictated by the 'rock stars' of the profession. Joad was clearly one of these stars. On a more academic level, there were people like Barry Coward, profoundly scholarly historian of the English Civil War, whose work was so keenly appreciated by students doing their A-levels that they would perform a 'Mexican wave' when he entered the lecture theatre.[73] Perhaps no one fitted this description better than Slavoj Žižek, international Director of the Birkbeck Institute for the Humanities, who is the subject of the *International Journal of Žižek Studies*.

* * *

Passionate engagement with a particular academic specialism could lead to friction. After all, academics are a highly competitive tribe. Academic research and

---

[70] Oldfield, *Slow to Begin With*, 347.   [71] Ibid., 318–19.   [72] Ibid., 317 and 319–20.
[73] Interview of author with Richard Evans, 17 September 2021.

writing are intimately intertwined to a person's self-image and identity. This is hardly surprising given than it is not unusual for researchers to devote decades of their lives to investigating one specific topic. As Stephen Frosh, Professor of Psychosocial Studies at Birkbeck, explains, academics are

> deeply invested in their subject matter and in their own intellectual work; it is, after all, their livelihood and also the way in which their worth is measured. Within its individualistic promotion and recognition structures and its consequently competitive social ethos, academic life is rife with rivalries and suspicions.... Differences of status and power in the group create ripples which are difficult to control; people have their legitimate ambitions; resources are scarce, there is a lot of work of the kind that does not necessarily bring advancement.[74]

In the past couple of decades, these pressures have soared, as academic 'performance' has been scrutinized and assessed in increasingly draconian ways. Frosh observes that it is too often the case that 'bruising others' in intellectual debates is 'taken as a sign of virility, a kind of intellectual machismo'.[75] As we have seen, this is not inevitable—after all, great intellectuals like Bernal combined intellectual generosity with the most rigorous scholarship. But 'intellectual machismo' is unfortunately too common.

Tensions could also arise between colleagues who had radically different ideas for the future of their discipline. What began as friendly banter could quickly turn bitter, especially over questions about new members of staff. For example, should a newly vacated Chair in the History of Art be an art-historian or an art-theorist?[76] Was it advisable to hire a lecturer in Iberian languages, where there is high student demand, or should the College diversify into Arabic languages? Was banking finance less essential than sports management?

Struggles for recognition could be acrimonious. In 1982, relationships in one department broke down entirely, with colleagues accused either of 'making denigratory remarks about colleagues' research' or of doing 'very little work'. One lecturer complained that 'the handling of promotions had led to unhappiness'. His proposal that 'all files on promotions in the Department should be destroyed, so that we could start again' was welcomed and 'implemented'. As one professor in the department admitted, 'University dons throughout the world have a reputation for their cliquishness, their petty intrigues and for being generally unprincipled'.[77] His department took this to an extreme.

---

[74] Frosh, 'Psychosocial Studies and Psychology', 1562–3.   [75] Ibid., 1564.
[76] See the heated correspondence in 'Review of the History of Art Department', 1978, in Ely Archive, Box 48.
[77] 'Personal Relations in the Department of Mathematics', in Ely Archive, Box 25.

Some staff, usually senior ones, are known to 'dig in their heels' and refuse to shoulder administrative or teaching duties. In the mid-1980s, one distinguished professor responded to having his request to take unpaid leave denied by refusing to teach.[78] When the Master of the College attempted to dismiss him on the grounds of 'serious misconduct in refusing to carry out teaching duties', the case went to court.[79] It caused an outcry because academics on permanent contracts had assumed that they had tenure, and were therefore safe from being fired unless they could be shown to be 'grossly incompetent' or guilty of 'gross moral turpitude'. This professor lost his case, but the case was instrumental in leading to the insertion of a new clause in the Education Reform Act of 1988 making it possible to 'dismiss any member of the academic staff for good cause'.[80]

An equally indignant, although less publicly vindictive, dispute occurred in the Classics Department from the late 1970s. It was triggered by the imminent retirement of A. G. Way, a translator of Julius Caesar's works, but precipitated by the personality of the department's Professor of Classics and Ancient History, Giuseppe Giangrande. He was a Byzantinist who worked at Birkbeck for twenty-one years from 1966. Tensions arose because Giangrande saw his role as a *research* professor; this was not the College's understanding. This led to frequent clashes with the head of department, fellow Byzantinist Robert Browning. In one letter, Giangrande informed his boss that it was a 'physiological as well as a legal impossibility' to transform himself into a 'complete department of Greek'. In a witty letter, which must nevertheless have annoyed Browning, Giangrande noted that 'every mental asylum is full of people who proclaim themselves to be Napoleon, but their proclamations, no matter how shrill, cannot suffice to make any of these unfortunates into a real Napoleon'. Similarly,

> even if I were demented to the point of proclaiming myself a complete Department of Greek—and I am still sane enough not to make such a proclamation—I could not become one such Department, i.e. I could not, insofar as I am one isolated individual, offer to our undergraduates any amount of tuition even remotely aspiring to cover the whole Greek syllabus of our B.A. Honours degree.[81]

Giangrande's solution was unhelpful. He announced that 'in fairness to our undergraduates whose interests I have at heart as warmly as anybody else, and in

---

[78] 'Visitor's Jurisdiction and That of the Courts', *The Times* (23 July 1985), 4, and 'Repeat Action Valid', *The Times* (17 June 1991), 24. For the duties of a professor in the University of London, see Regulation 4.5.2, in Chad Long, 'Hines v. Birkbeck College', 3 November 2014, no page, in www.docsford.com/document/1387923, viewed 20 March 2018.
[79] Chad Long, 'Hines v. Birkbeck College'.
[80] 'Education Reform Act 1988', para. 203, at https://www.legislation.gov.uk/ukpga/1988/40/section/203, viewed 1 June 2021.
[81] Letter from Giuseppe Giangrande to Robert Browning, 9 November 1977, in Ely Archive, Box 23.

consideration of my professional dignity as a teacher who strives not to be a charlatan', he would cease undergraduate teaching altogether![82]

If Giangrande's first grudge was having to teach undergraduates, his second was about workloads. He claimed that the four members of classics' teaching staff were shouldering a workload more appropriate for fifteen.[83] In 1979, he sent a letter to 'Bob' (that is, College Secretary Robert E. Swainson) asking whether Swainson would 'agree that Dr White and I are by far [in red ink] the hardest [red ink] working members of the academic staff? I should very much like to have your reply to this very simple question.'[84] Hearing about potential College-wide cuts in staffing, he wrote to the Master (who was climate geographer Tony Chandler) in October 1976 arguing that he would accept cuts to Classics only after all other departments in the College shed two thirds of their staff. Giangrande provided concrete examples. He would countenance reductions in Classics once the English Department had reduced its number of lecturers from twelve to four. Anticipating objections, he contended that the much large 'number of undergraduates' taught in English was 'irrelevant' since 'the complexity of the BA Honours Degree in Classics is the same whether our undergraduates are 10 or 100'.[85] This attack on English was followed by an assault on the Department of German, which, he observed, taught 'only one language and literature, and in particular a literature which has a rather short history'. In contrast,

> we in Classics are teaching a syllabus (BA Honours) which is *unanimously* regarded as the more vast and complex in the whole of the Faculty of Arts, involving as it does *two* languages and literatures, each of which has the largest history in literary terms in Western Europe: in addition to this, we also teach Ancient History.[86]

These were not arguments likely to endear him to colleagues in either English or German. The Professoriate Committee dryly responded by noting that the Classics Department had a low staff student ratio of 8.6, compared with a ratio of 12.8 in other arts departments; their 'unit cost' per student was also 35 per cent higher.[87]

Giangrande may have been overruled but he stubbornly refused to give up the fight. When Browning retired, Giangrande wrote to the Master (by that stage,

---

[82] Ibid.
[83] Letter from Giangrande to the Master, dated 14 November 1977, in Ely Archive, Box 23.
[84] Letter from Giangrande to 'Bob' [Secretary Robert E. Swainson], dated 4 January 1979, in Ely Archive, Box 23.
[85] Letter from G. Giangrande to the Master, 6 October 1976, in Ely Archive, Box 23.
[86] Letter from Giuseppe Giangrande to Robert Browning, dated 1 October 1976.
[87] 'Report of the Sub-Committee on the Review of the Department of Classics', 1979, 2, in Ely Archive, Box 23.

chemist William George Overend) stating that he hoped that the Professoriate Committee would not even *consider* 'appointing as head a person other than me'.[88] When David W. Hamlyn, a Professor of Philosophy at Birkbeck but a trained classicist, was appointed to the post in 1981, Giangrande behaved as though the appointment was 'subject to appeal'. He 'is refusing to recognise my status', Hamlyn complained, and 'says that he will not attend departmental meetings etc.'[89] Four years later, Giangrande was still causing Hamlyn difficulties. Giangrande was refusing to teach either BA or MA students and, although he was 'asked annually to give a course of lectures...for one reason or another that is always a ritual act' so 'students will not now come to his lectures'.[90] It was an impossible situation and may help explain at least in part why Overend and others failed to strongly defend Classics when it was dismantled only two years later. Giangrande was unceremoniously shunted off to King's College London.

* * *

So far in this chapter, we have looked at only one half of the teaching framework: that is, the lecturers and professors. Equally important in understanding the pedagogic tone of the College is the nature of its students. This applies to every section of the College but can be illustrated by turning to two departments: psychology and law.

Degrees in psychology have always interested students from a wide range of backgrounds. This was what attracted Jon Shum to the College. He spent his youth in Hong Kong during the Japanese occupation of the Second World War, so his schooling had been disrupted. In 1951, however, Shum made his way to Britain, eventually working as a researcher processing telemetry data from the early British satellites for University College London's Space Research team. By his late twenties, however, he had decided he was more interested in becoming an academic so he took a part-time degree at Birkbeck in psychology.[91] In 1963, as he was about to start his final year, he mused that, in the first-year class on psychology, he sat alongside 'Ph.D.'s (in a non-psychological subject), B.A.'s (failed), special teachers for handicapped children, artificial satellite data analysts, [and] Chinese restaurant dish-washers'. He was impressed to discover that, after only one term of classes, he and his fellow students quickly learned to write 'lengthy essays for group discussions...on topics such as "Symbolism—Fact or Myth?" or "Dreams, are they better rationalized or rationed?"'[92] Shum went on to finish his

---

[88] Letter from Giuseppe Giangrande to the Master, Overend, 5 February 1980, in Ely Archive, Box 23.
[89] Letter from David W. Hamlyn to the Master, 9 October 1981, in Ely Archive, Box 23.
[90] Letter from David W. Hamlyn to the Master, 26 January 1984, in Ely Archive, Box 23.
[91] Information on his life was given by his son, Simon Shum, and can be found at simon.buckinghamshum.net/2011/12/jon-shum, viewed 1 March 2021.
[92] J. C. Shum, 'Last Year Birienbeck [sic]', *The Lodestone*, 53.2 (spring 1963), 12.

BA in psychology in 1965, followed by a Birkbeck M.Phil., after which he lectured at Glasgow Caledonian University.

Shum's enthusiasm about the range of students in Birkbeck classes was echoed by students within the Department (now School) of Law. Although law had been taught in the LMI/Birkbeck from the 1820s to the 1930s when its department closed, it was re-established in 1992 under Master Blackstone. Despite being the only part-time law degree in the University of London, it was by no means certain that the new department would be attractive to students. The intellectual vibrancy of its inaugurate staff was a good omen, however: these were the ponytailed, loquacious Peter Goodrich (Professor of Rhetoric); the cosmopolitan, ebullient Costas Douzinas (doyen of human rights); suave Matthew Weait (who went on to be a leading expert on AIDS); and, in contrast to these bullish male intellectuals, the reserved, but super-resourceful administrator Valerie Hoare. With such a team, the department's first year witnessed an explosion of interest. Over 850 people applied for a place on the new degree programme; 200 were interviewed, and places were awarded to 75.[93] Of these, 60 per cent were women and nearly 40 per cent were from ethnic minorities.[94]

This diversity was a deliberate policy: after all, the legal profession is predominantly white and male. From its inauguration, the department was dedicated to providing 'access to a high quality legal education for individuals who had not previously had the opportunity of studying law'. It admitted students from 'widely varying educational and cultural backgrounds...necessary to devise a distinctive degree programme sensitive to the needs of different ethnic groups'.[95] The founders were highly committed to social justice for people who had traditionally been denied it. Alongside their classes, they also offered legal advice to people from economically and ethnically marginalized communities.

In other ways, however, that first cohort of law students were typical of those at Birkbeck more broadly. They included cabbies, law clerks, PhDs in physics and mathematics, a musician (who went on to become one of the biggest names in the pop scene), an elderly Irish aristocrat, a shop steward from Harrods, and a libertarian bookseller, as well as a number of unemployed Londoners. In one of their first classes, a representative of the Palestine Liberation Organization sat next to a security officer from the Israeli embassy. Debate was never difficult to stimulate.

* * *

Recruitment to law had some unique components but was not exceptional. The LMI/Birkbeck had been founded by and for 'working Londoners', and its unique

---

[93] 'Department of Law. Birkbeck College. University of London. Continuing Vocational Education. Development Funds Application for a Law Centre at Birkbeck', 1, in 'School Correspondence. Law, 1991–2005', in Ely Archive, Box 66.
[94] Ibid.   [95] Ibid.

mission had always been committed to providing face-to-face Higher Education to adults who are employed in other fields. One unanticipated consequence was that lecturers were often of similar ages to many of their students. Given that students ranged in age from 20 to 80 years (with most falling between the ages of 25 and 35), lecturers might even be significantly younger than those they taught. Today, the mean age of Birkbeck students is 28 years;[96] 93 per cent of part-time students and 67 per cent of full-time ones at Birkbeck are over 21 years.[97]

This was not always the College's age profile. In the nineteenth century, classes were open to anyone over the age of 15 years. The lack of alternative places for working people to gain a post-elementary education meant that students could be teenagers, especially since young people typically began paid work at much earlier ages than they do today. It wasn't until 1880 that education became compulsory for all children up to the age of 10 years; the Fisher Act of 1918, raised this to 14. In 1893, for example, one mother could be heard pleading with the Principal, Norris, to allow her 12-year-old daughter to join the German class. This would mean that mother and daughter could study together and accompany each other home—something the mother regarded as important: 'the class hour is very late', she observed, so they could chaperone each other home. She also argued that her daughter 'can scarcely be called a school-girl in the usual sense, as at present she is a pupil in a Typewriting Office in Cornhill.... She also commenced French some time ago, and already writes 60 words a minute in Shorthand.'[98]

The other side to this was the longevity of students attending classes. Students in the early LMI/Birkbeck could take individual courses rather than focusing on a specific degree programme, which meant that many remained subscribers or members of the Institution for years, even decades. Henry Buss, for example, was a subscriber for twenty-five years and noted that, during that time, he had 'profited by taking copious notes of between two and three thousand lectures'.[99] In 1945, one student was reported to have joined the College in 1908 and was still taking courses thirty-seven years later.[100] In 1956, William Urry bragged that he had joined Birkbeck in 1930 and, except for the war years, was still a student twenty-six years later. He went on to use his history degree to become an archivist at Canterbury Cathedral.[101]

---

[96] 'Birkbeck, University of London. Access and Participation Plan 2020–21 to 2024–25' (London: Birkbeck, 2021), 6.
[97] Birkbeck College, 'Financial Statements for the Year Ending 31 July 2020', 42, at https://www.bbk.ac.uk/downloads/finance/financial-statements-2020.pdf, viewed 1 June 2021.
[98] Letter from Mrs E. McPhillop of 25 Lambeth Square, to G. M. Norris, 21 April 1893, in 'Of Some Historical Interest, pre-1914/18', in the Ely Archive, Box 43–4.
[99] Buss, *Eighty Years Experience of Life*, 24.
[100] Letter from Troup Horne to Flight Lieutenant Adrien L. Williams, dated 26 July 1945, in Ely Archive, folder 'Birkbeck Students at War' (p. 25 of file).
[101] William Urry, 'Letter to the Editor', *The Lodestone*, 47.1 (1956), 22.

The fact that students were working adults, with limited time and, in its early years at least, an unsystematic approach to courses, encouraged a move towards what is now called 'modularization'. Prior to 1970, all examinations were sat in the students' final year. If they failed, they had to take *all* their papers again. From 1970, they could sit course units. They allowed students to get practice in the technique of sitting exams, as well as receiving feedback which could improve their performance. However, it also meant that there was more regular pressure on students, which some critics believe was a further death-knell to social and Students' Union activities in the College.

The working status of Birkbeck students brought benefits as well as challenges. Many students came to classes with an already accumulated wealth of knowledge and skills. For most lecturers, this was exhilarating. As politics professor Bernard Crick admitted, he left Sheffield University because he was 'tired of undergraduates'. He admitted that 'One can be very lazy and rhetorical and a bad teacher with undergraduates', while students at Birkbeck 'keep me on my toes much more'.[102]

A significant challenge was the one admitted at the start of this chapter: students came to classes after a full day's work. This meant that they were tired, even if highly motivated. As C. Lewis Hind (who used his education at Birkbeck in the 1880s to catapult himself into journalism) put it, 'in Victorian days a youth who wishes to "get on" and who had been through *Self-Help*, by Samuel Smiles, willingly accepted such curtailment of pleasure' in order to get a higher education.[103] It did mean that students were often weary, however.

And not all students heeded Smiles' philosophy. Daunt was unhappy that 'any one could join any class by paying his fee'. She complained that 'Some paid a fee and never attended a class because the College was such a good club'. Daunt was particularly infuriated by 'a series of odd, elderly, peculiar and sometime tragic students' who struggled to keep up with the class. 'I remember a suburban headmistress of a private school who never used any of the texts prescribed', she recalled. When Daunt informed her that 'her work was not correct', the headmistress retorted, 'I'm older than you, I ought to know better!'[104] Other students were simply confused by the lack of clear age-based indicators of authority. As early as 1909, a lecturer attending a Students' Union 'At Home' event was bemused when a female student asked him what classes he had signed up for.[105] Even today, it is often difficult during social events to distinguish lecturers from students.

Age was not the only similarity between staff and students, at least in the post-1920s College. Their social and marital statuses tended to be comparable. Unlike students who came to university straight from A-levels, Birkbeck students

---

[102] Rhil Ryland, 'Professor Who Can't Stand Students', *Kensington Post* (21 July 1977), in 'Newscuttings 1976–80', in the Birkbeck Archive.
[103] Hind, *Naphtali*, 34.
[104] 'Marjorie on Birkbeck. Birkbeck 1915–1945', *The Lodestone*, 47.1 (1956), 6.
[105] 'Cases of Mistaken Identity', *The Lodestone*, 3.3 (summer 1908), 86.

TEACHING   521

Fig. 25.6   Thorndike's 'Back at Birkbeck Again!' *Spectrum*, 3.2 (17 October 1970), 7.

were much more likely to have familial responsibilities (see Fig. 25.6). In the mid-1970s, for example, half of the College's male students and 40 per cent of female students were married.[106] A survey in the early 2000s found that nearly half of Birkbeck students were living with a partner and nearly one quarter had dependent children. Some 67 per cent were employed *full time* when they started their studies; taking into consideration full-time, part-time, and self-employed status, three out of four Birkbeck students were employed. In the sciences, an even higher 84 per cent were economically active while studying.[107] This had serious ramifications for social activities in College. Although a great deal of kudos attaches to being a university lecturer or professor, the College's students arrived in class with specific work-related skills and accomplishments. Lecturers could not 'talk down' to students who possessed their own independent, working lives.

Furthermore, throughout Birkbeck's modern history, a large proportion of students were teachers themselves. In the early twentieth century, the number of teachers who signed up for Birkbeck classes was boosted after the London County Council (LCC) offered a bonus to teachers with university degrees.[108] The LCC's Greystoke[109] Place Training College for teachers was located opposite the College's Bream's Building. They were obvious recruits. Around eighty trainee teachers were taught at Birkbeck annually.[110] Indeed, of all the students taking

---

[106] In 'Guard Book 3' in the Birkbeck Archive.
[107] Leon Feinstein, Tashweka M. Anderson, Cathie Hammond, Anne Jamieson, and Alan Woodley, 'The Social and Economic Benefits of Part-Time, Mature Study at Birkbeck College and the Open University' (London: Open University and Birkbeck College, 2007), 22–4, at https://citeseerx.ist.psu.edu/viewdoc/download?doi=10.1.1.612.4686&rep=rep1&type=pdf, viewed 1 October 2021.
[108] *Birkbeck College. Report. 82nd Session 1904–1905* (London: Witherby and Co., 1905), 5.
[109] It is often spelt 'Graystoke'.
[110] Letter from the Clerk to Alexander M. Carr-Saunders (Director of the London School of Economics), dated 12 September 1939, in Ely Archive, 'Wartime Correspondence of the Clerk

evening classes in 1909–10, around 60 per cent were teachers.[111] In the dry language of a governmental committee on education, published in 1918, this meant that 'the actual and prospective salaries of such students' was 'frequently higher than those of the assistant lecturers' at Birkbeck.[112] When the training college was closed in the mid-1930s, its building was transferred to Birkbeck for use as classrooms until it was destroyed by bombs during the Blitz. Each year between 1918 and the 1970s, the proportion of teachers declined, but they still comprised around one third of Birkbeck's student population.[113] As a proportion of students, clerks were second only to teachers. They made up between one third (1910s) and 11 per cent (1970s) of students.[114]

Teachers and clerks are good examples of how *location* affects the student population. In the first decade of the twentieth century, most students lived close to the College's accommodation in Bream's Buildings, Chancery Lane. College authorities complained that their location 'lacks the advertisement of a public throughfare'. But it did mean that just over one fifth of students lived within 2 miles of the College and 60 per cent lived between 2 and 5 miles away. In contrast, only 18 per cent lived more than 5 miles from the main building.[115] By the mid-1960s, by which time the College had settled into its Malet Street address, the spatial distribution of students was very different. Fewer than 6 per cent of students lived within 2½ miles of the College while 30 per cent lived between 2½ and 5 miles. One quarter of the College's students lived between 5 and 10 miles always, while 40 per cent lived over 10 miles away.[116] In part, this reflected vastly improved public transport networks, especially the underground, in the first sixty years of the century. By the mid-1960s, over 53 per cent of people travelled to the College on public transport (see Fig. 25.7).[117] However, more interesting is the fact that 53 per cent of students *worked* less than 5 miles from the College.[118] In other words, Birkbeck benefited from the fact that many students could wander into the building after work and before trekking home.

However, it was not always the case that a large proportion of students travelled to the College after completing a day's work nearby. Although classes in the

---

1939–41' (p. 9 of file). For the number of student teachers, see H. R. N., 'Dr. B. W. Clack', *The Lodestone*, 32.4 (autumn 1937), 16.

[111] Report of 1910 and *Birkbeck College. Report 86th Session, 1908–1909* (London: Witherby and Co., 1909), 6.

[112] *Report of the Departmental Committee for Enquiring into the Principles Which Should Determine the Fixing of Salaries for Teachers in Secondary and Technical Schools, Schools of Art, Training Colleges and Other Institutions for Higher Education*, Vol. II: *Summaries of Evidence* [Cd 9168] (London: His Majesty's Stationery Office, 1918), 78.

[113] 'Guard Book 3'.   [114] Annual reports and 'Guard Book 3'.

[115] *Birkbeck College. Report 85th Session 1907–1908* (London: Witherby and Co., 1908), 7.

[116] 'Social Survey of Birkbeck Students', survey of 1966–7, 3, in Ely Archive, Box 21.

[117] Ibid.   [118] Ibid.

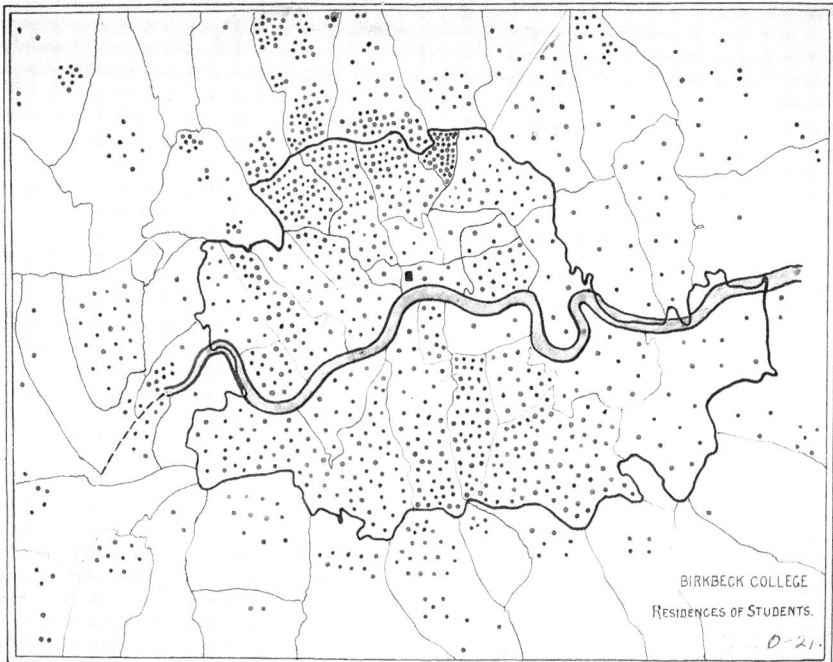

Fig. 25.7 Map of student residences, 1920–1. Birkbeck Image Collections: Birkbeck History BH0276.

nineteenth century typically took place between 7 p.m. and 10 p.m.,[119] around one fifth of students studied in the daytime.[120] This dropped dramatically when part-time teaching was made a condition of joining the University of London in 1921. But this also fluctuated significantly over time. For example, the proportion studying in the daytime dropped to only 12 per cent in 1913–14, probably because of the closure of the Art Department, while, in 1919–20, it reached a high of 25 per cent due to the influx of ex-service students. Today, only the Department of Psychosocial Studies teaches a significant number of classes in the daytime, while Biological Sciences, Philosophy, Computer Science, Law, and Management have a few daytime components.

For the majority of the College's students, however, part-time, evening classes have numerous advantages. When students in the mid-1960s were asked why they chose to take a *part-time* course, nearly half cited 'financial necessity' while another one fifth claimed it was because they were employed; 11 per cent cited domestic responsibilities.[121] The reasons for choosing *Birkbeck* were more evenly

---

[119] Letter from the Secretary to Delisle Burns, dated 25 September 1923, in 'Birkbeck College letters 1923.2', Ely Archive, Box 65.67.
[120] From the annual reports 1908–21.   [121] 'Social Survey of Birkbeck Students'.

spread, with between one fifth and one quarter citing the fact that they were attracted to the College because it offered internal degrees through part-time study, had a high reputation, and offered the required course.[122] While half gave professional advancement or 'to further knowledge' as reasons for taking a higher degree, one fifth simply said it was due to 'general interest, pleasure'.[123]

A similar survey was undertaken in 2020–1. When these students were asked why they chose to take a *part-time* course, 4 per cent said they could not afford to give up work, while another 34 per cent claimed it was because they wanted to combine study and work. Only 4 per cent cited domestic responsibilities. The reasons for choosing *Birkbeck* were more varied, with 34 per cent saying they wanted to work during the day, 24 per cent citing the attractiveness of the course content, 16 per cent the College's research reputation, and 6 per cent being part of the University of London.[124]

* * *

This chapter started with the story of philosopher Cyril Edwin Mitchinson Joad, who embodied a particular version of a university teacher—one that was focused on popular appeal, charismatic teaching, and a masculine style. It made him into one of the most prominent public intellectuals in the world but did not endear him to those academics striving for an in-depth understanding and interpretation of the world. His academic fame failed to survive his social disgrace. The other lecturers and professors discussed in this chapter have a more enduring legacy in terms of their scholarship, as well as the subsequent intellectual achievements of those they taught. This has always been Birkbeck's fundamental mission: to broaden and disseminate the highest-quality education, to instil academic rigour and curiosity, and to critique and expand the base of knowledge for future generations.

---

[122] Ibid. [123] Ibid.
[124] Email from Gretchen O'Neill, Planning Manager, Birkbeck, on 26 August 2021. See https://cis6.bbk.ac.uk/#/views/EnrolmentSurveyReport/EnrolmentSurveyReport?:iid=2.

PART VI
BATTLES FOR BIRKBECK

26
'Birkbeck's Unique Mission?'

'Who killed the night-owl?'
We, said the robbins,
With a bit of hob-nobbing,
We killed the night owl...
'Who'll dig his grave?'
We, said day-students,
Because we're imprudent,
We'll dig his grave...
'Who'll be the chief mourner?'
I, said G.B.'s ghost.
                Trevor Machin, 'Who Killed the Night-Owl?', 1964.[1]
                                    'G.B.' is George Birkbeck

At every graduation, David Latchman, Vice Chancellor of Birkbeck at the time of our bicentenary, congratulates the new graduates, welcomes their families and friends, and then makes a speech. It typically includes the claim that 'should George Birkbeck walk through that door today, he would be thrilled that we remain true to "Birkbeck's unique mission": that is, to provide evening education for working Londoners'.

Threats to that 'unique mission' have usually been the result of governmental policies biased against or, more commonly, woefully ignorant of, part-time, adult students. On one occasion, however, the threat came from within. In 1964, the Master—classicist John F. Lockwood—was preparing a revolution: he planned to overhaul the College, eradicating Birkbeck's four cornerstones: providing part-time, evening education for working men and women in the centre of London. What he had not anticipated was the strength of resistance from Birkbeck's staff and students.

* * *

Lockwood stepped into the post of Master in 1951, after H. Gordon Jackson died in a road accident. Although he had spent much of his career at University College London and was a keen scholar of Greek lexicography, particularly Greek criticism, educational innovation was his primary interest. From the late 1950s onwards, Lockwood was actively engaged in educational initiatives such as

---

[1] Trevor Machin, 'Who Killed the Night-Owl?', *The Lodestone*, 54.3 (summer 1964), 31.

establishing new university colleges in East Africa, Nairobi, Nigeria, and Zambia, as well as south-east Asia and Northern Ireland.[2]

His appointment as Master of Birkbeck came at a difficult time for the College. It was in the middle of yet another crisis of accommodation. Parts of the College, including its library, had been bombed in 1942. Construction of the new college on Malet Street had been halted 'for the duration' of the war. When building was resumed in 1947, the 1939 deficit of £40,000 had soared to over £300,000 and the cost of equipment, which had been estimated at under £200,000, had risen to over £500,000.[3] The College had also acquired a thriving Department of Psychology from King's College London, which needed office space.

The Faculty of Arts was in a particularly desperate state: staff and students had been forced to spend the early post-war years shuffling between different lecture and seminar rooms at the whim of 'several neighbouring institutions'.[4] Timetabling classes was practically impossible because 'the availability of specific rooms for longer than a term at a time can be uncertain'.[5] Some newly acquired accommodation in 29 Russell Square, together with a 'couple of huts on a bomb site in Fetter Lane' (see Fig. 26.1), were clearly inadequate for the College's needs.[6]

These accommodation problems had serious implications for students arriving at Birkbeck after a full day's work. Even the inventive College Secretary, Arnolfo John Caraffi, recognized that 'Long treks, whether by staff or students, between widely separated buildings at the change of lectures are wasteful of already severely restricted time and, in the depth of winter, unwelcome.'[7] Caraffi lamented that students 'committed to so itinerant a life' were being 'deprived of the benefits of a corporate community'.[8]

Lockwood acted decisively. Although the Malet Street building was far from being finished, he insisted on parts of the College occupying it. This immediately drew attention to the fact that Malet Street was already too small to solve Birkbeck's space crisis. There was barely enough room in the new building for the science departments, let alone the rapidly expanding Arts Faculty.[9]

For the next decade, then, this was to be Lockwood's challenge. He approached it with gusto. As we shall see, however, his responses were regarded by many students and staff to be a direct attack on 'Birkbeck's unique mission'. In the first Foundation Oration after moving into the new Malet Street building, George

---

[2] 'Sir John Lockwood. Education at Home and Abroad', *The Times* (12 July 1965), 12.
[3] G. F. Troup Horne's Foundation Oration of 2 December 1952, cited in 'Birkbeck', *The Lodestone*, 46.2 (spring/summer 1953), 31.
[4] Arnolfo John Caraffi (College Secretary), 'Memorandum on Accommodation' (April 1965), 3, in 'Guard Book 2', in the Birkbeck Archive.
[5] Ibid.
[6] G. F. Troup Horne's Foundation Oration of 2 December 1952, cited in 'Birkbeck', *The Lodestone*, 46.2 (spring/summer 1953), 31.
[7] Caraffi, 'Memorandum on Accommodation', 5.   [8] Ibid.   [9] Ibid.

Fig. 26.1 Temporary, prefabricated classrooms for geography and psychology classes on a bombed site beside Bream's Building. Birkbeck Image Collections: Birkbeck History BH0229.

Francis Troup Horne (a loyal Birkbeckian with half a century's association with the College as Secretary and Clerk to the Governors) praised Lockwood for managing the move of staff into the Bloomsbury premises during the 'Long Vacation of 1951'. 'Those of us who have had the privilege of serving on his Staff during the first Session', he contended, 'have every confidence that the traditions of Birkbeck are safe in his keeping'.[10] He could not have been more wrong.

* * *

> 'Who killed the night-owl?'
> We, said the robbins,
> With a bit of hob-nobbing,
> We killed the night owl.[11]

In the early 1960s, after a decade in post, Lockwood set out his radical plan for Birkbeck. There were two pretexts: significant increases in student numbers and

---

[10] G. F. Troup Horne's Foundation Oration of 2 December 1952, cited in 'Birkbeck', *The Lodestone*, 46.2 (spring/summer 1953), 32.
[11] Machin, 'Who Killed the Night-Owl?', 31.

the 1963 Robbins Report. First, the university sector in the UK was expanding rapidly. After the war, five provincial colleges (Nottingham, Southampton, Hull, Exeter, and Leicester) had been granted university status and, from 1961, new universities were established in Sussex, East Anglia, York, Essex, Kent, Warwick, Lancaster, and four in Scotland. In the decade from 1951 to 1961, student numbers in the UK grew from 83,000 to 113,000—that is, an increase of 36 per cent.[12]

Birkbeck mirrored this expansion. Between 1951 and 1963, student numbers at the College surged from 1,532 to 1,710 (a 10 per cent increase), including a massive increase of 37 per cent in the number of postgraduate students.[13] Full-time teaching staff rose from 77 to 140 (an increase of 45 per cent): the number of professors and Readers, by 38 per cent.[14] This growth was not accompanied by any significant increase in the provision of office or teaching accommodation.

Second, in 1963, Lionel Charles Robbins, an economics professor from the London School of Economics, published his influential parliamentary report on Higher Education. Lord Robbins' committee proposed to dramatically increase the number of full-time undergraduates throughout Britain. The plan was to double the percentage of 18-year-olds in Higher Education by 1980. Interestingly, the report had almost nothing to say about the type of students educated at Birkbeck. Indeed, the report explicitly noted that part-time students were outside its 'terms of reference'. Nevertheless, the report did genuflect towards the value of part-time provision for 'those who have missed it earlier in life, and...those wishing to qualify in many professions and vocations'.[15] While there was evidence put forward (most notably by the National Institute of Adult Education)[16] to the Robbins Committee in favour of increasing opportunities for evening degrees the Committee operated from the assumption that full-time participation was the way forward.

Birkbeck couldn't pretend that nothing was happening. Lockwood publicly declared himself in favour of expanding university provision. In order to 'play a part' in this expansion, Birkbeck needed to draw up plans to admit full-time students, he concluded. This was to be done on the understanding that part-time provision would not be harmed.[17] The College agreed to increase its numbers of full-time undergraduates by between 100 and 170, and of full-time postgraduates

---

[12] T. W. Heych, 'The Idea of a University in Britain, 1870–1970', *History of European Ideas*, 8.2 (1987), 213. Also see A. L. Halsey, 'The Decline of Donnish Domination?', *Oxford Review of Education*, 8.3 (1982), 215–29.

[13] Caraffi, 'Memorandum on Accommodation', 4.   [14] Ibid.

[15] Committee on Higher Education, *Higher Education. Report of the Committee Appointed by the Prime Minister Under the Chairmanship of Lord Robbins 1961–63* [Cmnd. 2154] (London: Her Majesty's Stationery Office, 1963), 313.

[16] Committee on Higher Education, *Higher Education Evidence—Part One. Volume A. Written and Oral Evidence Received by the Committee Appointed by the Prime Minister Under the Chairmanship of Lord Robbins 1961–63* [Cmd 2154—iv] (London: HMSO, 1963), 128.

[17] 'Minutes of the Meeting of the Faculty of Arts, Held on Tuesday, 14th January, 1964, at 2.15 p.m.', in 'Faculty of Arts, Minutes of Meetings. Apl. 25th 1940', in the Birkbeck Archive.

by 100. Although these students would be spread across departments, the sciences would admit two thirds of them.[18]

Indeed, the Departments of Mathematics and Chemistry led the way. This was not the first time they taught full-time students in the daytime. In 1897, for example, the Departments of Biology, Mathematics, and Physics were already teaching day students and there were plans for Chemistry to follow suit.[19] There were even day courses in Latin, Greek, and French.[20] But these had stopped after the war.

When day classes for full-time students were proposed in the 1960s, however, the institutional memory of these precedents had disappeared. Nevertheless, even before the official approval of the Robbins Report, the Mathematics and Chemistry Departments had decided to accept full-time students.[21] Tactically, however, it had been a mistake to announce this shift in student intake without consulting more widely in the College.[22] The Faculty of Arts was particularly furious, arguing that supporting the Robbins' agenda could have been done more effectively by introducing new academic disciplines (such as economics and sociology) to the College's provisions, rather than diverting resources into full-time teaching.[23] (These disciplines were introduced a decade later.) They unanimously urged the College to 'reconsider' its plans on the grounds that, first, other universities had already offered to increase their numbers substantially, so there was no urgency for Birkbeck to do so, and, secondly, admitting full-time undergraduates was 'a more radical step' for a college that specialized in part-time education than it would be for more traditional daytime universities.[24]

Attempting to calm tempers, the classicist and Vice-Master Eric Warmington called a joint meeting of the two faculties, at which he conceded that there had been insufficient consultation within the College.[25] But then he dropped another bombshell: why not transform Birkbeck into a wholly postgraduate college and move it outside of London?[26] Unkind references were made about building on a 'little used site readily available' at Greenford (a sly reference to the expensive but underused College's sports field), or taking over what was the 'Somers Town Potato Market' near King's Cross. But the Master had a move to somewhere in the Home Counties in mind.[27]

---

[18] Ibid.
[19] 'Report of the Birkbeck Literary and Science Institution (City Polytechnic) for the Seventy-Fourth Session 1896–97', 5, in the Birkbeck Archive.
[20] Ibid., 5.   [21] K. Wilson, 'The Birkbeck Dilemma', *The Lodestone*, 55.2 (spring 1965), 7.
[22] 'Proposal to Discontinue Certain Part-Time Courses in Favour of Full-Time Courses in Mathematics and Chemistry', in 'Minutes of a Meeting of the Faculty of Arts Held on 21st May, 1963', in 'Faculty of Arts. Minutes of Meetings. Apl. 25th 1940', in the Birkbeck Archive. Also see 'Minutes of Meetings of the Faculty of Arts Held on 22nd October 1963', in same location.
[23] Ibid.   [24] Ibid. This resolution was passed: twenty-six votes for and two abstentions.
[25] Ibid.   [26] Ibid.
[27] Keith Watts, 'Letter to the Editor', *The Lodestone*, 54.3 (summer 1964), 15.

A large proportion of the faculty and students issued a collective *cri de cœur*: Lockwood, the College Secretary, and the Vice-Master were threatening the College's identity of 140 years, they exclaimed. Protest was particularly strong from the arts departments, which were almost unanimously in favour of continuing the 'traditional Birkbeck pattern'.[28] In a memorandum to the Academic Advisory Committee on the Future of the College, they contended that remaining in central London was 'absolutely essential for a College concerned with part-time students, who, in view of the radial character of London's communication system, would not be readily able to attend courses otherwise'.[29] Being in the immediate vicinity of unparalleled library facilities (including the British Library, British Museum, Institute of Classical Studies, Warburg Institute, and University of London Library in Senate House) was also crucial.[30] The faculty made positive suggestions to welcome the proposal to introduce disciplines such as sociology and anthropology and, given that the London School of Economics was no longer going to offer part-time courses in economics, to take over teaching in that field too.[31] They were firm in their belief, however, that the faculty's 'future will consist in its following its traditional role—that is preparing part-time students for undergraduate degrees and both part-time and full-time students for postgraduate degrees'. 'Nothing', they insisted, 'should stand in the way of its performing that function'.[32] After all, they were recruiting well and flourishing.

Not everyone agreed. In Classics, G. Giangrande couldn't make up his mind. He believed that providing part-time classics training in central London was important. As he argued in a letter to Warmington in 1964, in

> a large area like London—whose population equals that of many a minor European state—it is likely to supply a continuous, if not enormous, stream of people who, for all sorts of personal reasons (early marriage, now fashionable; holding of a secure job as a guarantee for the future, which leaves one sufficient leisure for higher things etc.) are not able to be 'normal' (i.e. full-time students) and yet love Classics so much as to *want* to study the subject.... Since we are the only evening institution at University level in London, it would be a pity if this potentially good material were denied any opportunity of studying.[33]

---

[28] J. D. Bernal, 'Part-Time Students in Birkbeck and their Future', *The Lodestone*, 54.3 (summer 1964), 6.
[29] 'Memorandum Submitted by the Faculty of Arts of Birkbeck College to the Academic Advisory Committee on the Future of the College', in 'Faculty of Arts. Minutes of Meetings. Apl. 25th 1940', in the Birkbeck Archive.
[30] Ibid.   [31] Ibid.   [32] Ibid.
[33] Letter from G. Giangrande to Eric H. Warmington, c.1964, in 'Future Department of the College 1963–68', in 'Birkbeck College. Department of Classics. Future Development', in Birkbeck Archive, Box 43.

But, as far as undergraduate students were concerned, the Department of Classics should follow the sciences and become a day-college. In large part, this was because the post-war Education Act made it

> possible for every student of average ability (let alone above average) to attend the University…as a 'normal' full time student in a day-college by means of state grants. The pre-war type of self-supporting undergraduate, which formed the bulk of our evening clientele, is rapidly disappearing.[34]

To compete with other colleges in London, Giangrande believed that Birkbeck must become a day-college. But he also argued that classics was more like the sciences than to modern languages or English. He pointed to the 'inherent technical difficulties (lexicographical, material, syntactical, palaeographical, etc.)' in classics that made it 'less capable of part-time study'. In the end, Giangrande simply wanted the College to wait a few years before deciding either way, at least in terms of classics.[35]

From the perspective of the sciences, though, the scene looked very different. Except for the Physics Department (which only admitted postgraduate students anyway), student recruitment had plummeted. Only two years earlier, the Botany Department terminated teaching the Special Botany classes because student numbers no longer warranted it.[36] As a Birkbeck botanist lamented, 'to get a good Special Degree under evening part-time conditions demands a very high standard of academic ability and mental and physical toughness'. He was not surprised that 'the number of candidates who are likely to be able to do this has fallen' since 'five years' hard labour is a long sentence'.[37]

Why were the sciences struggling? In large part, their crisis was externally driven. The establishment of new universities (which were recruiting twice as many science students as arts ones) had hit them particularly hard.[38] Increased competition from full-time science departments was 'siphon[ing] off the "best" potential Birkbeck students'.[39] In addition, the disciplines of mathematics, chemistry, and botany had recently undergone dramatic changes, which were difficult to reconcile with part-time study. Laboratory work was becoming 'more diverse and time-demanding' than ever before.[40] As Bernal noted, 'science is undergoing a new revolution; its content is doubling about every six or seven years'.[41] Like a good Marxist, Bernal believed that the crisis had a 'material base': increasingly,

---

[34] Ibid.   [35] Ibid.   [36] Wilson, 'The Birkbeck Dilemma', 6.   [37] Ibid., 7.
[38] This is the statistic for 1953 to 1961: British Information Services, *Universities in Britain* (New York: British Information Services, 1963), 13.
[39] Wilson, 'The Birkbeck Dilemma', 7.
[40] Ibid., 7.   [41] Bernal, 'Part-Time Students in Birkbeck and their Future', 7.

any half-decent scientific education required access to expensive equipment and laboratory space.[42]

Chemistry was a case in point. David James Gibbs Ives lamented the dramatic dwindling of student numbers that had taken place since he arrived at Birkbeck over three decades earlier. The reasons were many. In the early 1950s, Birkbeck decided that it would no longer prepare students for the Intermediate Examination in the sciences. This was a pre-university degree, intended to get students ready for a full university course, but primarily serving as a funnel to prepare students for a full-degree course at Birkbeck. Ives also noted that chemistry admission had been cut due to

> The institution of the New Regulations for the B.Sc. (Special) Degree in Chemistry, the accelerating expansion of the subject...the increase in the number of places and grants for full-time students elsewhere, the development of alternative routes to professional qualification (Dip. Tech., G.R.I.C.), changes in industrial organisation which have largely dried up our previously steady source of supply of students from large firms, and a somewhat intangible advent of the Welfare State.[43]

Ives admitted that attempts to reverse the decline—by sending a glossy brochure lauding the achievements of the Chemistry Department to high schools and potential employers of chemistry students—had failed because potential students and employers did not believe that part-time evening study was better than full-time study.[44] In effect, Ives noted, they were asking

> Are you telling us that study under difficult conditions is *better* than study under favourable conditions?...Do you tell us that Birkbeck part-time graduates would not have seized the opportunity of full-time study for their degrees if it had been presented to them?[45]

Ives believed the only way forward was to introduce full-time study in chemistry at Birkbeck. In this way, they would be able to attract more honours students, which would also help improve morale.[46] If this step was not taken, he warned, 'the time may come quite shortly when there are no genuine, properly qualified applicants for part-time special Chemistry'.[47] He issued a conciliatory plea to other departments, particularly those in the Faculty of Arts, urging them not to succumb to the College policy of pitting departments against each other.

---

[42] Ibid., 7.
[43] David James Gibbs Ives, 'The Future of Birkbeck College', *The Lodestone*, 55.1 (autumn 1964), 9–10.
[44] Ibid., 10.   [45] Ibid., 10.   [46] Ibid., 10.   [47] Ibid., 11.

Departments should not 'condemn each other to death, nor force each other into straitjackets; they must each have what is necessary for continued healthy existence, co-operating together harmoniously'.[48]

Introducing full-time courses was only one plank in the changes proposed. The other was the move out of central London. For Ives and most of his colleagues in the Faculty of Science, this was just as important. As Ives put it, 'It is demonstrably impossible for Birkbeck to keep up' with the needs of students and scientific developments 'in a building of restrictive pre-war design'. The current accommodation was 'derisory' and, since it had to be 'multiplied, rather than added to', the most sensible solution was to 'move the whole College elsewhere'.[49] Birkbeck philosopher A. Phillips Griffiths was more succinct: in the sciences 'not to be able to expand, is to contract'.[50]

* * *

> 'Who'll toll the bell?'
> We, said the arts,
> He was dear to our hearts,
> We'll toll the bell.

The dispute was about a lot more than 'Birkbeck's unique mission'. It was also tied into the 'two cultures' debate. Less than five years before the publication of the Robbins Report, C. P. (Charles Percy) Snow, physicist and novelist from Christ's College, Cambridge, had given the Rede Lecture. On 7 May 1959, he had stood at the podium in the Senate House of Cambridge, magnificently attired in his robes, and informed the assembly that science and literature constituted 'two cultures'. By 'culture', Snow explained that he meant 'common attitudes, common standards and patterns of behaviour, common approaches and assumptions': it was what enabled people to 'respond alike...without thinking about it'.[51] Science and the arts, he contended, represented two different mental worlds which defined themselves in hostility to each other. Between these two cultures, he observed, stood 'a gulf of mutual incomprehension'.[52] It was a statement that entered common parlance after critic F. R. Leavis attacked it viciously in 1962.[53]

---

[48] Ibid., 12.   [49] Ibid., 12.
[50] A. Phillips Griffiths, 'The Future of Birkbeck', *The Lodestone*, 54.3 (summer 1964), 26.
[51] C. P. Snow, *The Two Cultures and the Scientific Revolution: The Rede Lecture 1959* (Cambridge: Cambridge University Press, 1959), 10–11. Also see C. P. Snow, 'The Two Cultures and the Scientific Revolution', *Encounter*, 12 (June 1959), 17–24, and C. P. Snow, 'The Two Cultures and the Scientific Revolution', *Encounter*, 13 (July 1959), 22–7. For the best analysis of the lecture, its context, and controversy, see Stefan Collini, 'Introduction', in Snow, *The Two Cultures and the Scientific Revolution*, vii–lxxi.
[52] Snow, *The Two Cultures and the Scientific Revolution*, 4.
[53] F. R. Leavis, 'Two Cultures? The Significance of C. P. Snow', *The Spectator* (9 March 1962).

This was not the first time the 'two cultures' debate had been aired. Nearly a century earlier, biologist T. H. Huxley and cultural critic Matthew Arnold battled it out.[54] In 1923, the University of Cambridge had debated the motion of whether 'the sciences are destroying the arts'.[55] In the late 1940s, the producer of twelve BBC radio broadcasts, *The Challenge of Our Time*, also claimed that most pressing problem of the post-war world was 'the wide gulf between the scientific and humanistic approach to life'.[56]

Snow returned to his 'two cultures' argument in 1962 in the Birkbeck lecture theatre. He was speaking on the 138th anniversary of the College. His remarks were prefaced by a confession: in his entire career, he had 'occupied a fairly large number of jobs, far too many', but had only once actually made a formal application for a job. That job was to be Master of Birkbeck: 'I did not get it', he ruefully admitted, so was thrilled to be able to 'have Birkbeck...at my mercy' during an hour-long lecture, albeit twenty-two years later.[57] Snow then rehearsed his famous arguments. He told the crowd assembled at Birkbeck that he had

> spent a lot of my life moving at very rapid intervals between scientists and literary persons. This was simply a chance, because I intended to be a writer and I happened to be trained professionally as a scientist.... Soon it struck me that I was moving between two bodies of persons who represented in every way in which one can use the phrase, two cultures. They were different in a whole range of intellectual attitudes, and often in a whole range of moral attitudes. They were ceasing to communicate in intellectual terms across the gulf... neither had any really serious intellectual understanding of the other.[58]

Scientists rarely read novels; their literary friends had no idea of the second law of thermodynamics.[59] Snow warned that if the world became 'split into groups which cannot communicate with each other', then it would 'become a hell'.[60] Literary culture

---

[54] Stanley Jaki, 'One Hundred Years of the Two Cultures', *University of Windsor Review*, 11 (fall–winter 1975), 55–79; Lionel Trilling, 'Science, Literature, and Culture: A Comment on the Snow–Leavis Controversy', *Commentary*, 33 (June 1962), 461–77; Collini, 'Introduction', vii–lxxi.

[55] John De la Mothe, *C. P. Snow and the Struggle of Modernity* (Austin: University of Texas Press, 1992), 65.

[56] Grace Wyndham-Goldie, 'The Story Behind the Challenge of our Time', in Arthur Koestler, E. L. Woodward, J. D. Bernal, et al., *The Challenge of our Time: A Series of Essays* (London: Percival Marshall, 1948), 12.

[57] C. P. Snow, *Recent Thoughts on the Two Cultures: An Oration Delivered at Birkbeck College, London, 12th December, 1961, in Celebration of the 138th Anniversary of the Foundation of the College* (London: Birkbeck College, 1961), 3. Note: there are two versions of this lecture, with slightly different materials in each.

[58] Ibid., 4.   [59] Ibid., 4–5.   [60] Ibid., 7.

needs some of the refreshment and the spring and the optimism and the confidence of science. And I believe too the scientific culture needs indirectly the human wisdom which still exists in parts of literary culture.[61]

But Snow's real passion was science; he loathed esoteric literary intellectuals. He was a friend of two of Birkbeck's most famous physicists: Bernal and Blackett. Indeed, a few years earlier Snow wrote in the *Atlantic Review* that 'Between Rutherford and Blackett on the one hand, and, say, Wyndham Lewis and Ezra Pound on the other, who are on the side of their fellow human beings?'[62] The true scientist had 'the future in his bones'.[63] The

> lack of communication between these cultures is going to be terribly dangerous for everyone. Most of the decisions of absolutely major importance all over the world in the next 20 years are going to have a large scientific content. If those decisions are taken by people without scientific insight, without scientific experience, then the likelihood is that they are going to be unwise and unimaginative decisions.[64]

The problem was that the English system of schooling was the 'worst in the world' because children specialized very early.[65] The solution was better education, such as was offered at Birkbeck.

Lockwood's radical plans in the early 1960s brought the 'two cultures' dispute to Birkbeck: the College's Arts and Sciences Faculties found themselves with fundamentally different conceptions of the idea of the university, as well as totally different models for growth. Should the less popular science departments simply accept their fate and be closed in order to free up space for the arts? Should the Faculty of Science be required to 'stand or fall within the general framework of the College', asked a Birkbeck botanist?[66] Or should the College embrace the 'two cultures', allowing the arts to remain in central London, teaching part-time students in the evenings, while the sciences (perhaps with the exception of first-year students or those doing a part-time General Degree) moved to some 'non-Metropolitan pastures lock, stock, and barrel'?[67] Practically, dragging the 'entire Arts staff' and the most successful science department (Physics) 'kicking and screaming, out into the bush' would be 'difficult', to say the least.[68] Equally, English professor Barbara Hardy warned her arts colleagues, scrawling 'Scientists, go home' on the walls of Malet Street was unhelpful.[69]

---

[61] Ibid., 3.   [62] C. P. Snow, 'The Age of Rutherford', *Atlantic Monthly*, 102 (1958), 79–80.
[63] Ibid., 79–80.   [64] Snow, *Recent Thoughts on the Two Cultures*, 10.
[65] Ibid., 8–9.   [66] Wilson, 'The Birkbeck Dilemma', 8.
[67] Griffiths, 'The Future of Birkbeck', 28.   [68] Ibid., 28.
[69] Barbara Hardy, 'The Disadvantages of Being a Birkbeck Teacher', *The Lodestone*, 54.3 (summer 1964), 18.

However, *something* had to be done. Hard choices had to be made. Bernal gave the most insightful response. The College faced a crisis, he observed, due to the 'great movement of expansion of higher education'. The decline in student numbers in certain science departments, specifically Chemistry and Mathematics, would not be solved by introducing daytime courses: that was merely a 'temporary make-shift solution'. Worse: it would constitute a 'breach in the whole principle of Birkbeck', leaving the College with no *raison d'être*.[70] As he saw it, there were three options: 'to shut down Birkbeck as a separate institution and merge it with other sectors of a reformed London University'; to move Birkbeck out of central London and begin teaching full-time students; or abandon undergraduate teaching altogether and convert Birkbeck into a postgraduate college.[71] True to his leftist credentials, he appealed to the 'democratic character' of Birkbeck: its students needed to decide what kind of college they wanted and 'campaign for it'.[72]

In the end, the battle was won by those who favoured retaining 'Birkbeck's unique mission' of teaching working Londoners doing part-time courses in the evenings. There were pragmatic reasons for this victory. The government seemed to be offering support for part-time teaching—at least in theory. Many politicians and civil servants as well as educators believed that there would continue to be a demand for part-time courses, especially from women rebuilding their careers after child-rearing and for those who had missed the chance of a university education at the age of 18 due to 'illness, slackness, or late development'.[73] Birkbeck, therefore, had a 'moral obligation' to continue supplying such education. Furthermore, this obligation could only be fulfilled if Birkbeck remained in its 'central site'.[74]

There was also a growing awareness of the longer-term implications of the change. If a dual system was introduced (that is, part-time students in the arts and full-time ones in the sciences), it was feared that part-time students would eventually lose out. Birkbeck would become 'two communities, a community of adults and a community of adolescents, with a widening age-gap between them'.[75] Introducing large numbers of full-time students, it was feared, would act as the 'cuckoo in the nest'.[76]

Fundamentally, though, the battle for retaining 'Birkbeck's unique mission' was won because a large number of lecturers and students fought for it. One of the most eloquent defences for continuing teaching part-time students was given by Hardy. Her statements were intended to be funny and conciliatory—uniting both

---

[70] Bernal, 'Part-Time Students in Birkbeck and their Future', 6. [71] Ibid., 8.
[72] Ibid., 8.
[73] Marcus Knight (Dean of the University of Exeter and Birkbeck student between 1920 and 1924), 'Letter to the Editor', *The Lodestone*, 54.3 (summer 1964), 9.
[74] R. L. Saw and D. W. Hamlyn, 'Birkbeck and Philosophy', *The Lodestone*, 54.3 (summer 1964), 14.
[75] H. G. Richardson, 'The Future of Birkbeck', *The Lodestone*, 54.3 (summer 1964), 12.
[76] D. S. Duncan, 'Letters to the Editor', *The Lodestone*, 55.1 (autumn 1964), 4.

science and arts factions. She began by joking that one of the advantages of working at Birkbeck included 'a perpetual and automatic alibi for declining unwanted invitations': lecturers simply had to say 'Sorry I lecture in the evenings'. This also gave lecturers a 'plausible excuse' for watching a film in the mid-afternoon or even simply 'lingering over coffee'. Turning more serious, she then admitted that the most significant advantages were intellectual. Because academic staff taught in the evenings, she maintained,

> there is still a goodish chunk of daylight time for research and writing, and the boon of having students who already know the facts of life. This is probably helpful in subjects like psychology...but in teaching English literature it is splendid never to encounter the kind of student who once asked me (in a full-time college) why Othello and Desdemona couldn't just have talked the whole thing over.[77]

Of course, she continued, there were some disadvantages as well. Birkbeck students could be 'maddeningly opinionated' and there was the perennial problem of getting adequate teaching rooms. But these 'crumples in the roseleaf' were 'mere fleabites'.[78]

The most moving tributes, however, came from former students of Birkbeck. *The Lodestone* published a series of articles entitled 'What Part-Time Study at Birkbeck Has Meant to Me'. One student (tactlessly signing himself 'Unrepentant Wastrel') reminded readers that 'Birkbeck gives a second chance to those who missed the first', which was why it must be 'preserved'.[79] The promise of a 'second chance' was applauded by a sexagenarian who testified that in her youth she had no option but to earn a living, and so had been unable to go to university. Part-time study had broadened her world: in her case, there was 'no *other* means' to attain this experience. She praised Birkbeck lecturers for exuding 'a sort of superhuman ability and kindness' towards anyone receptive to knowledge.[80] Another student feared that Birkbeck risked 'becoming the preserve of the comparatively privileged'. Birkbeck students, this student contended, already 'know all about mumps and snowbound mothers-in-law, teething and tax assessments, migraine and the vagaries of the outer London transport systems': what they required was an opportunity to expand their minds *intellectually*.[81] Ruth Smith was similarly enthusiastic. She explained that she had come to Birkbeck with a 'well-developed

---

[77] Hardy, 'The Disadvantages of Being a Birkbeck Teacher', 17.   [78] Ibid., 17.
[79] 'Unrepentant Wastrel', 'Letter to the Editor', *The Lodestone*, 54.3 (summer 1964), 26.
[80] E. M. Hodgson, 'What Part-Time Study at Birkbeck Has Meant to Me', *The Lodestone*, 54.3 (summer 1964), 20–1. She was a headmistress in the UK and Argentina: Hodgson, 'John—or Charles—Wesley?', *Proceedings of the Wesley Historical Society*, 7.41 (October 1977), 6 at https://biblicalstudies.org.uk/pdf/whs/41-3.pdf, viewed 14 July 2021.
[81] B. Wright, 'What Part-Time Study at Birkbeck Has Meant to Me', *The Lodestone*, 54.3 (summer 1964), 21. Note it is unclear whether this is a male or female student.

love of literature', despite not having 'understood it fully'. At Birkbeck, she could indulge this interest without being 'considered freakish'. The College, she continued, consisted of 'teachers, who by their scholarship and enthusiasm relate literature to life, making one realise with [E. M.] Forster that books are not the destination, but the signpost to the destination'. Plans to 'convert Birkbeck into a full-time college would be to deprive those with responsibilities of the opportunity of increasing their wisdom, knowledge, and joy in life'.[82] It was, in the words of another student, a college that prides itself on its 'tradition of concern' and whose staff do 'more than merely transfer factual knowledge': the Birkbeck graduate is 'a graduate "plus"' who carries 'the influence of Fetter Lane and Malet Street to every corner of the earth and into some of the highest positions of authority'.[83]

Perhaps the most pertinent response, though, came from Charles Wesley Hume, who had joined Birkbeck in 1906 and later served as President of the Birkbeck Students' Union. Hume had imbibed 'Birkbeck's unique mission'. In 1964, when he was well into his seventies, he remained a proud Birkbeckian. The College's students were a

> special breed. They had to be tough to stand the strain; they brought to their studies the advantage of adult minds; their intelligence was sharpened by experience of the world, and on the average they brought better powers of discrimination and judgement to bear on their reading than day students can do.[84]

They were, in short, unique.

* * *

The more radical innovations of Lockwood were quietly shelved. The College did admit school-leavers to some of its courses, but that plan also faded within a few years. In 1967, the Academic Advisory Committee, chaired by Sir Eric Ashby, concluded that the demand from mature students for university education was high and therefore Birkbeck should concentrate on educating them. The Ashby Report rejected the idea of a mixed intake of students to Birkbeck, anxious that if mature undergraduates joined with school-leavers, the 'education of both groups' was 'likely to suffer', but especially that of the part-timers.[85] Part-time adult students in the College agreed. In December 1966, BBC 2 broadcast a programme entitled *How to Start*, and one of the students it interviewed was Jim Greaves, President of the Birkbeck Students' Union and student governor between 1965

---

[82] Ruth Smith, 'What Part-Time Study at Birkbeck Has Meant to Me', *The Lodestone*, 54.3 (summer 1964), 22.
[83] R. K. Wood, 'Letter to the Editor', *The Lodestone*, 55.1 (autumn 1964), 7.
[84] C. W. Hume, 'Comments on Birkbeck Past and Future', *The Lodestone*, 54.3 (summer 1964), 24.
[85] 'Employed Students Only for Birkbeck College', *The Times* (26 January 1967), 12.

and 1967, who led the campaign against expanding full-time undergraduates. Greaves had left school aged 15 years to become an insurance clerk but, keen to educate himself, enrolled in an occupational psychology degree in 1961 at Birkbeck. He lauded the 'atmosphere in the college, where other people of the same age are studying'. He told listeners that

> I think having a part-time institution, solely part-time institution, is a very good thing for mature students. You don't have the distraction of people with long hair walking about and the whole thing becomes an entity in a community in itself.[86]

Also interviewed on the programme was Kathleen (Kathy) Greaves. She had met Jim at Birkbeck, fallen in love, and married. She had chosen a career in the dairy industry, including working in research laboratories, but, blocked from further promotions because of the lack of a university degree, had signed up for a part-time arts degree. She argued that the advantages of doing a degree in a college that was dedicated to mature, part-time students were 'enormous'. She observed that

> You are mixing with people of your own age, and a mature student has a totally different attitude towards taking a degree. You do get very much more interested in the subject matter, you approach it with a more mature viewpoint. And the company therefore is just right for you.[87]

Doing a degree while working full time did mean 'quite a hectic life' for both Greaveses, but they were passionate advocates.

Kenneth Hare, Lockwood's successor as Master from 1966 to 1968 (when he left to become President of the University of British Columbia), also welcomed the Ashby Report. The College immediately stopped full-time teaching of school-leavers at undergraduate level. Hare explained that the College had decided to 'concentrate its resources on the part-time undergraduate, for whom London makes no other internal provisions'.[88] The last full-time undergraduate graduated in 1970.[89]

---

[86] Jim Greaves, transcript of the BBC 2 programme *How to Start*, broadcast immediately after Christmas 1966, in 'Publicity General', Birkbeck Archive, Box 48.
[87] Kathy Greaves, transcript of *How to Start*.
[88] F. Kenneth Hare, 'Birkbeck and the Future: Address Given to the Court of Electors of Birkbeck College' (18 November 1967), in 'Future Development of College 1963–68', in Birkbeck Archive, Box 43.
[89] Peter Wilby, 'Ambition Drives the Part-Time Student', *The Observer* (22 June 1969), in 'Newscuttings 1968–71' in the Birkbeck Archive, and *Student Handbook: A Guide for the Session 1970–71 and a Report from the Session 1969–60. Birkbeck College* (London: BCSU, 1971), 36.

This decision was only reversed in 2010, when Birkbeck joined the Universities and Colleges Admissions Service (UCAS), through which all students wanting to study full-time in the UK must apply. Today, the ratio of full-time to part-time students in terms of full-time equivalents (FTE) is 55:45.[90] The radical nature of this shift can be seen in the fact that, in 2011–12, 38 per cent of undergraduates were part time, which dropped to 16 per cent in 2019–20; the College only had 3 per cent of undergraduates doing full-time degrees in 1911–12, but 30 per cent in 2019–20.[91]

* * *

> 'Who'll carry the coffin?'
> We, said future years,
> With our unstudied tears.
> We'll carry the coffin.

While the battle to retain 'Birkbeck's unique mission' was taking place, Lockwood was also locking horns with Bernal on a separate front. Despite difficulties with the media about its communist-leaning staff, crystallography at Birkbeck had become 'the principal centre' for this specialism in London, with a highly regarded MSc, state-of-the-art research facilities, and a prestigious international reputation.[92] Aware that his retirement was approaching, though, Bernal sought to ensure the long-term survival of the discipline in the College. This could be done, he believed, by making crystallography a department in its own right, as opposed to a sub-section of the Department of Physics, of which he was the Chair. All the College would need to do was to create a separate Chair in Crystallography.[93] In terms of research, teaching, and administration, the two halves of the Department of Physics had been operating separately for many years anyway.[94]

Bernal initially believed that this proposal would succeed. In the College's development plans for the years 1962 to 1967, several new departments were to be created, including separate Departments of Occupational Psychology and Statistics, as well as Crystallography.[95] However, Bernal had not taken into account the hostility of the Master. Lockwood had been frustrated by the leftist views held by Bernal and most of his team. He was furious that Bernal was

---

[90] Matt Innes, 'Academic Strategy', PowerPoint presented 2021, personal communication.
[91] Ibid.
[92] J. D. Bernal, 'Case for the Maintenance of College Policy for a Department of Crystallography' (October 1962), 1, in 'Guard Book. Ib', in the Birkbeck Archive. He is citing from a quinquennial report of plans for 1962–7.
[93] Ibid.
[94] 'The Continuation and Organisation of Crystallography in Birkbeck College (Some Notes Prepared and Agreed by the Academic Staff of the Physics Department in the Main Building)' (1962), 3–4, in 'Guard Book. Ib', in the Birkbeck Archive.
[95] Bernal, 'Case for the Maintenance of College Policy for a Department of Crystallography', 1.

Chairman of the World Peace Committee, a job that involved his entering negotiations with Nikita Khrushchev and Mao Zedong. The idea that Bernal would create what was effectively a living scientific memorial to himself was abhorrent to this right-leaning, Christian classicist.

Lockwood's initial attempt to thwart Bernal involved him claiming that the College lacked the financial means to support a new Chair in Crystallography. Bernal compromised: it would simply be a matter of transferring his professorship and headship to a newly created Department of Crystallography while conferring the title of Professor of Experimental Physics on Dr W. E. Ehrenberg, who would then take over the headship of the Department of Physics.[96] The cost to the College would be nil.

To Bernal's astonishment, on 13 June 1962, the Professorial Committee rebuffed this suggestion as well. Bernal compromised once again, proposing that crystallography simply became a sub-department of the Department of Physics. He would relinquish his title of Chair in Physics so it could be awarded to Ehrenberg and his own Chair would become one in crystallography.

However, another hurdle was thrown in his way. In October 1962, the Academic Board ruled that the future of crystallography should be decided by a select committee of science professors of the College and then by the Professorial Committee, which would pass it to the Academic Board and then the governors.[97] Bernal was both dazed and enraged. He could only surmise that the problems had arisen because the College did not want to 'bind itself in advance to continuing the teaching or research of Crystallography as a department or even as a sub-department'.[98] This implied that the College saw no value in either teaching or research being carried out in crystallography. This was absurd. After all, crystallography at Birkbeck was 'recognised not only in Britain but throughout the world'.[99]

Meanwhile, the Communist Party was anxious that Bernal was over-worked, leading to a deterioration of his health. Even the Special Branch began worrying. A spy within the department reported that Bernal's assistant, Aprahamian,

> spoke of BERNAL's University work, and said it had been arranged that his department should be split, and one half put in charge of two other professors, but now complications had arisen, it was just like C. P. Snow. If this arrangement had been carried out it would have rescued his academic commitments. As it was, BERNAL was waging a major academic battle with the college.[100]

Bernal realized that the College's arguments about 'administrative inconvenience or impropriety' were red herrings. The real purpose of all this manoeuvring was

---

[96] Ibid., 1.   [97] Ibid., 2.   [98] Ibid., 2–3.   [99] Ibid., 3.
[100] Special Branch report, 'Lascar' (23 June 1960), in TNA KV2/3953.

concerned with whether crystallography would continue to be taught at Birkbeck after Bernal retired.[101] But, Bernal asked, what would happen if crystallography was banished from Birkbeck? Since Birkbeck was the main institution where part-time PhD research in the field occurred, where would such teaching take place?[102] More fundamentally, what was the place of 'modern structural crystallography... in a modern university'?[103] Bernal agreed that there was a good argument for setting up a separate institute of crystallographic studies in the University of London, which would be independent of any college.[104] This had already happened with the Computing Centre.[105] Nevertheless, Bernal contended, it was surely 'undesirable to break up a going concern which has both its apparatus and its space, to build a new one'.[106]

Influential crystallographers, physicists, and chemists lent support to Bernal's cause. The most fulsome defence came in a letter from Kathleen Lonsdale. She had been the first woman appointed to a professorship at University College London and, in 1945, shared the honour of being one of the first two women elected as Fellows of the Royal Society. She went on to become the first female President of the International Union of Crystallography (she was Vice-President at the time of writing her letter) and the first female President of the British Association for the Advancement of Science. Lonsdale was adamant that, if crystallography at Birkbeck was wound up when Bernal retired, it would be 'an academic tragedy'.[107] She was also anxious to dispel any suggestion that crystallography was 'a useful technique rather than a subject in its own right'.[108] Today, she contended, X-ray techniques were 'only one among many techniques' employed in the 'investigation of the structure, dynamics and other properties of organised matter'.[109] Claims that crystallography was a 'specialization built around the technique of x-ray diffraction' were like 'describ[ing] chemistry as a subject built around the technique of cooking'.[110] The discipline was, however, at risk of dying out because of the reluctance of universities to establish Chairs *in Crystallography* as opposed to, for example, Chemistry.[111] She concluded by saying that Birkbeck

> has a real opportunity at this time to become a pioneer in Britain by putting on to a permanent footing the admirable Department of Crystallography that you have built up. If you had a *Chair* of Crystallography you and your successors would be in a very strong position to obtain considerable sums of money from

---

[101] Bernal, 'Case for the Maintenance of College Policy for a Department of Crystallography', 5.
[102] Ibid., 3.   [103] Ibid., 5.   [104] Ibid., 6.
[105] Ibid., 6.   [106] Ibid., 6.
[107] Letter from Kathleen Lonsdale to Bernal, dated 31 October 1962, 1, in 'Guard Book. Ib', in the Birkbeck Archive.
[108] Ibid., 1.   [109] Ibid., 2.
[110] Ibid., 2.   [111] Ibid., 3.

external sources for research work and also from the D.S.I.R. [Department of Scientific and Industrial Research] or any other body.[112]

It would make Birkbeck 'one of the more far-sighted of all the Schools in the University of London'.[113]

But Bernal's proposal had fierce critics—and not just in the Master. Within the Faculty of Science there had been long-standing jealousies about the attention and resources given to the Department of Physics. Not everyone warmed to the 'red Sage'. William Sydney Bullough (Professor of Zoology) and W. G. Overend (Professor of Chemistry and Dean of the Science Faculty) led the attack. Their opposition was fourfold. First, there were financial implications. Bullough and Overend believed that there were other priorities, such as improving financial support for the library, providing departmental maintenance grants, investing in expensive scientific apparatus, and increasing the number of technical and administrative staff.[114] They disputed Bernal's claim that making crystallography into a separate entity would not incur any additional expense. After all, they observed, crystallography was an 'experimental science requiring expensive apparatus and technical assistants'.[115] Secondly, Bullough and Overend pointed to the College's chronic shortage of accommodation. At the very least, they argued, since construction of an extension to the Malet Street building had been delayed, so too should the decision to house a new department there.[116] Establishing a separate Crystallography Department would also be a radical initiative. This was their third point of opposition. Most other universities included the study of crystallography within Physics or Chemistry Departments and most crystallographers indeed 'find stimulation in being associated in a department with other chemists, biochemists, etc., who are concerned with structure determinations by other methods'.[117] Why should crystallographers at Birkbeck be any different?

Their final opposition was the most significant: they were not convinced that crystallography should be privileged in this way. Without crystallography, the Department of Physics would be much smaller. Bernal's successor would be faced with a situation of having 'at his disposal only the rump of the present Physics Department'. This would be untenable, forcing any new head of the Physics

---

[112] Ibid., 3.   [113] Ibid., 3.

[114] William Sydney Bullough and W. G. Overend, 'Memorandum on the Proposal to Establish a Department of Crystallography in the College' (26 October 1962), 1, in 'Guard Book. Ib', in the Birkbeck Archive.

[115] Ibid., 1.   [116] Ibid., 1.

[117] Ibid., 1. For the statistics of where crystallography departments were housed in other universities, see 'The Continuation and Organisation of Crystallography in Birkbeck College (Some Notes Prepared and Agreed by the Academic Staff of the Physics Department in the Main Building)' (1962), 4, in 'Guard Book. Ib', in the Birkbeck Archive.

Department to expand and thus increase competition still further for accommodation.[118] Bullough and Overend concluded by stating that

> the fact that part of the effort of the Physics Department is devoted to crystallography is...a reflection of the research interests and inclination of Professor Bernal as Head of the Department....It does not follow that the specialism *must* be continued at the same level of activity when there is a change in the headship of the department.[119]

Despite some sweet-tongued caveats, this was an ugly fight. In general terms, it was resolved in Bernal's favour. In 1963, he was appointed to the first Chair of Crystallography in the UK and, a year later, a Department of Crystallography was established at Birkbeck, the first in Britain. Historian Eric Hobsbawm concluded that, while crystallography at Birkbeck 'thus survived Bernal',

> The whole miserable episode is an example of the tangled and trivial civil wars with which anyone with experience of colleges and universities will be familiar....It is difficult for anyone who was involved in these disputes at the time, or who surveys the record impartially, to look back on them with anything but a sense of shame. They forced a scientist of extraordinary gifts to pursue his and his colleagues' work under constant strain of strangulation, in constant uncertainty about its very survival.[120]

The two disputes—over 'Birkbeck's unique mission' and the fate of crystallography and physics—had taken their toll. Lockwood died in July 1965: the bitter feuding had worn him out. In September that year, while on holiday in Cornwall, Bernal had the first of several strokes that were to kill him in 1971.[121] According to Hobsbawm, the battles of the early 1960s had 'unquestionably shortened the lives' of Lockwood and Bernal.[122] But Birkbeck's unique model of allowing students to work while completing their degrees in the evening was saved.

---

[118] Bullough and Overend, 'Memorandum on the Proposal to Establish a Department of Crystallography in the College', 1.
[119] Ibid., 1.
[120] Eric Hobsbawm, 'Bernal at Birkbeck', in Brenda Swann and Francis Aprahamian (eds), *J. D. Bernal: A Life in Science and Politics* (London: Verso, 1999), 252.
[121] 'Prof. Bernal Has Stroke', *The Times* (15 September 1965), 10.
[122] Eric Hobsbawm, 'Birkbeck and the Left', *Times Change: Quarterly Political and Cultural Review*, 21 (spring/summer 2001), 17.

27
Containing the Crisis

> Here lies continuing education, killed off by an accounting error.
> Historian at Birkbeck, Ben Pimlott in 1986

The period between the late 1970s and 1980s, then after 2008, were not happy years for university educationalists. Shifting demographics resulted in a sharp decline in student numbers. Non-European students found themselves charged 'full economic costs' for their degrees; over the entire sector, there was an 8 per cent cut in financial support. From 1986, the old system of allocating funds to universities through the University Grants Committee was overhauled, academic tenure was abolished, and the Research Assessment Exercise (RAE; later Research Excellence Framework or REF) was instigated. The RAE/REF started a process that was to see increased research (and, eventually, teaching) evaluation, selective funding, tactical submission policies, and staff transfers. Civil servants in Conservative governments began a relentless scrutinizing of public spending, especially in education and science. For Birkbeck, the years 1986 and 2008 inaugurated battles for its survival. They were the worst crises faced by the College in the twentieth century.

* * *

The assault on Higher Education, and particularly provisions for part-time students, could not have been predicted in 1973 when Margaret Thatcher—then Secretary of State for Education and Science in the Conservative government—visited the College during its Open Day. She had been invited by the Master of Birkbeck, economist Ronald Tress, as part of the College's celebration of its 150 years in existence. The Birkbeck Students' Union were aghast when they heard of the invitation, reminding students that Thatcher was 'the Minister responsible for the cutback in higher education'.[1] They printed a pamphlet reminding students that '*YOU* are a member of Birkbeck College. What happens at Birkbeck concerns *YOU*'.[2] They contended that it was 'inappropriate' for the College to 'welcome with open arms the dignitaries of government', especially when that government's policies were aimed at providing 'less education at a cheaper price'. Whatever

---

[1] 'Open Day 1973. Publicity', in 'Thatcher's Visitation', in Birkbeck Archive, Box 27.   [2] Ibid.

happened to the College's promise of expanding opportunities for part-time, adult students, they asked?[3]

Nevertheless, in July 1973, Thatcher's visit went ahead. The Open Day was an 'orgy of self-congratulation', according to the *Times Higher Education Supplement*.[4] There were special exhibitions and colloquia as well as a buffet lunch for 1,200 people on the College's lawn.[5] Most of the celebrations, though, took place in the modest accommodations of Birkbeck's Malet Street building. When the press and staff gathered in the Council Room for speeches and cocktails, what was most notable was the imposing portrait of a *former* Master of the College, H. Gordon Jackson, hanging behind the main speakers (see Fig. 27.1). Jackson was a zoologist by training, although crustaceans came second to his passion for Mozart. He had also been the Master of Birkbeck during the Second World War. In his portrait, Jackson could be seen standing proudly in his Air Raid Precautions uniform complete with tin hat. The symbolic significance of this portrait of Master-as-Warrior was not lost on some of the guests in 1973: perhaps the Master in 1973 also had to be prepared to fight to the death against the raids that were going to be launched against British universities by the woman he had invited to the celebrations.

Tress, however, was a milder man than Jackson. He was also determinedly optimistic. Standing in front of Jackson's portrait, Tress reminded Thatcher that Birkbeck had been mentioned in a White Paper that had been written under her direction. Entitled *Education: A Framework for Expansion* (1972), the report had praised Birkbeck for being 'a long-standing example' of an institution that sought to help individuals who had missed out on 'earlier opportunities' of Higher Education. The White Paper had also claimed to want to 'encourage the renewal of knowledge and skills made obsolete by the explosion of knowledge and the impact of technology on a rapidly changing environment'.[6] This was exactly Birkbeck's mission, Tress exclaimed.

Thatcher's presence in his Council Room also inspired Tress to make the point that 'with continuing education now being an 'in' phrase, we're rather conscious of the fact that we've been doing it for rather a long time and we're as up-to-date as anybody'.[7] He then spoke passionately about the need for part-time, mature students to be allowed to apply for grants to enable them to pursue their studies: it was a right that full-time students possessed. The LSE had given up evening classes for part-time students five years earlier, Tress observed, which made Birkbeck the sole provider of university education for working men and women

---

[3] 'Open Day', *Spectrum* (27 April 1973), 1.

[4] 'Birkbeck's Open Day', *Times Higher Education Supplement* (20 July 1973), in the Birkbeck Archive.

[5] Ibid. and Janet Townsley, 'Tinker, Tailor, Soldier, Sailor', *Times Education Supplement* (13 July 1973), both in the Birkbeck Archive.

[6] Secretary of State for Education and Science, *Education: A Framework for Expansion* [Cmnd. 5174] (London: Her Majesty's Stationery Office, December 1972), 30.

[7] 'Birkbeck's Open Day', *Times Higher Education Supplement*.

Fig. 27.1 An oil portrait of H. Gordon Jackson, Master of Birkbeck during the Second World War, by Sam Morse-Born, c.1940. Birkbeck Image Collections: Birkbeck History BH0020.

in London. Surely, he quipped, it was time to recall the gospel that 'The Lord loveth a cheerful giver!'[8] Thatcher seemed bemused.

Thatcher's speech, which she gave in the College's library in front of 600 educationalists and staff, was less warmly received. In what was disparagingly described as her 'silkiest' voice, Thatcher eulogized Birkbeck's founder. She contended that George Birkbeck had required students at his institution to be 'respectable' but, she joked, that condition no longer applied in 1973 because 'only politicians have to be respectable these days'.[9] Showing a blatant disregard for the occasion being celebrated, Thatcher announced that she did *not* think that university education was the 'only avenue' for thousands of school-leavers. Instead of celebrating the College's status as a leading institute for research, she lauded 'adult education through university extra-mural work, voluntary bodies and local education authorities, and the further education system'.[10] Reporting on her speech in

---

[8] Ibid.   [9] Ibid.
[10] 'Six-Part Education Plan Unveiled', *Liverpool Daily Post* (14 July 1973), in the Birkbeck Archive. Also see 'Mrs Thatcher Seeking More Flexible Higher Education', *The Times* (16 July 1973), in the Birkbeck Archive.

The Guardian, John Hall sardonically observed that these were 'issues on which Birkbeck could take her and the Government sharply to task'.[11]

Although Thatcher's 'creamy delivery'[12] marked her out as a force to be reckoned with, not everyone was cowed. Speaking from his splendid office, with its oriental furniture and enormous mahogany bookcases, David Ross, Professor of French and (fittingly) expert on the iconography of Alexander the Great, admonished Thatcher. He observed that the 'pursuit of learning is the function of the university and many of our masters and mistresses, including Mrs. Thatcher, seem to have forgotten this'.[13]

Even more impressively, 26-year-old Jonathan Harris confronted Thatcher personally over a pre-lunch cocktail in the Master's rooms. The heavily bearded Harris was the dynamic President of the Birkbeck Students' Union. As an environmental psychologist who also happened to work in the Civil Service Department, which had been set up by Prime Minister Harold Wilson's Labour government in 1968, he attempted to persuade Thatcher of the need for adult education at university level. Even he was forced to acknowledge, though, that he didn't get very far. Thatcher was 'non-plussed', he admitted, adding that she was 'not prepared to commit herself to anything other than taking notes' and 'adopted a moral Samuel Smilesish self-help approach'.[14] Perhaps he should have reminded Thatcher of Smiles' contention that 'What Clarkson did for negro slavery, and Rowland King for cheap postage, and Cobden has done for free trade, Dr Birkbeck did for popular adult education.'[15]

Not all was grim. Thatcher was paraded around the College, where she was shown numerous exhibits (see Fig. 27.2).[16] Individual departments had gone to considerable trouble to spread word of their intellectual strengths, while wooing potential students with vast quantities of alcohol. Perhaps the star show, however, was organized by Phyllis Travis, chief operator of the computer unit. She had dressed her eight assistants in 'very striking yellow dolly-bird outfits', who then 'impressed their visitors enormously by printing out a facsimile of Snoopy'. Professor Anthony Watson, head of the Spanish Department, was unkind: they had 'turned the place into a Butlin holiday camp', he fumed.[17] What no one doubted was that the day's happenings had cultivated an atmosphere of 'fluid bonhomie'.[18]

* * *

---

[11] John Hall, 'Leisure Classes', *The Guardian* (10 July 1973), in the Birkbeck Archive.
[12] 'Birkbeck's Open Day', *Times Higher Education Supplement*.
[13] Quoting David John Athole Ross, in 'Birkbeck's Open Day', *Times Higher Education Supplement*.
[14] 'Birkbeck's Open Day', *Times Higher Education Supplement*.
[15] This was cited in http://www.mmtrust.org.uk/mausolea/view/251/Birkbeck_Mausoleum, viewed 1 July 2019, but is probably from Thomas Kelly, *George Birkbeck: Pioneer of Adult Education* (Liverpool: Liverpool University Press, 1957), epigraph.
[16] 'Birkbeck's Open Day', *Times Higher Education Supplement*.
[17] Ibid. [18] Ibid.

Fig. 27.2 The Master, Ronald Tress, showing Margaret Thatcher, Secretary of State for Education and Science, a set of rocks used for teaching in the Geology Department during her visit to Birkbeck during the 150th anniversary, 14 July 1973. Birkbeck Image Collections: Birkbeck History BH0046.

Five years later, Thatcher was no longer Secretary of State but Prime Minister. The election of Thatcher's governments in 1979, 1983, and 1987 heralded difficult times for education in Britain. There was unprecedented scrutiny of public sector spending. Hawk-eyed civil servants under the cost-cutting Thatcher governments were circling ever closer over science and education budgets. In 1980, the *Times Higher Educational Supplement* sported the scary headline: 'Birkbeck May Close Seven of 24 Departments'. The article was reporting on a confidential memorandum to the Court of the University of London in which Tress's successor as Master, the chemist Professor William George Overend, worried about a drop in the College's income of just over £500,000. There were freezes on staff recruitment.[19]

The College survived; but only six years later, it faced one of two of the greatest threats to Birkbeck in the twentieth century. In 1983, Sir Peter Swinnerton-Dyer

---

[19] Birkbeck Archive, Box 09, File 9-D, 002, p. 1.

had been appointed Chairman of the University Grants Committee (UGC), responsible for public funding of universities. Swinnerton-Dyer was Professor of Mathematics at Cambridge and, in his younger days, an international bridge player who had represented the British team twice in the European Open team championships. Working out how the UGC made its funding decisions, and then revising the rules, was to test his bridge-playing skills to their limits. The old system was 'shrouded in mystery', Swinnerton-Dyer later recalled, adding that 'we had to find a system for allocating money that was fair, but a system that was not egalitarian'.[20] The idea that 'fair' excluded 'egalitarian' allocations encapsulated Thatcherite politics.

For Birkbeck, the most monumental decision taken by the reforming UGC was to decree that a part-time student was equivalent to 0.5 of a full-time one: in the past, a part-time student had been deemed equivalent to 0.8 of a full-time one. Not only would this slash £2.5 million off Birkbeck's budget of £10 million, but it also made no accounting sense since an undergraduate degree at Birkbeck took four rather than three years (that is, 75 per cent of a full-time student, not half).

Ironically, the whole crisis had probably been the result of a 'regrettable accident', Birkbeck historian Ben Pimlott maintained. Only a few months earlier, the College had been 'assured that its uniqueness would continue to be acknowledged in the allocation of funds'. However, without any 'rumour, hint or warning', the 'thunderbolt' fell. As an astute historian of post-war British politics, Pimlott knew more than most people how political decisions came to be made. 'Stratospheric committees, composed of busy people,' Pimlott mused, 'do not always make perfectly considered choices. Conceivably, at the end of a long afternoon, the new method of assessment went through on the nod.'[21]

The College and its supporters went into battle (see Fig. 27.3). Roderick Floud, an economic historian who specialized in anthropometric history and was described by one reporter as a 'loose-limbed ginger-haired man, with a conspiratorial smile',[22] was appointed Chair of the campaigning committee. He observed that Birkbeck was unique. After all,

> For most colleges, part-time students are tagged on the end of the full-time provision. We have to maintain our building and staff on part-time student funding alone—that is why we have previously been given the more generous ratings.[23]

---

[20] Swinnerton-Dyer, cited in Lee Elliot Major, 'Living with RAEs', *The Guardian* (30 October 2001). Also see 'Evaluation of the REF', *Times Higher Education Supplement* (17 October 2013), *Culture, Education, and Society*, 38.2 (spring 1984); Swinnerton-Dyer, 'Prospects for Higher Education', *London Review of Books*, 3 (November 1981), 9–10.

[21] Ben Pimlott, 'Accidental Death of an Anachronism', *The Guardian* (9 June 1986).

[22] Adriana Caudrey, 'The Mature Student Boom', *New Society* (20 November 1987), 11.

[23] Roderick Floud, cited by Sarah Thompson, 'Birkbeck Hit by University Grant Cutback', *Daily Telegraph* (17 June 1986).

Fig. 27.3 'Government Threats + Government Cuts = Our Misery'. Cover of *Spectrum*, 18.4 (January 1985).

Floud launched an appeal 'calculated to appeal to the British sense of fair play'. He berated 'faceless bureaucrats' who acted in a way that, by 'bungling oversight rather than vindictiveness', threated to destroy a much loved institution.[24] After all, as historian Eric Hobsbawm lamented, 'Everyone's for adult education, like they're for happiness and marriage.... But they [politicians] don't do anything about it';[25] or, in the words of David Walker in *The Times*, it was as if the 'British government, alone in the western world, wants less higher education'.[26]

As early as 1980, the crisis had been anticipated, which was why the Friends of Birkbeck society had been revived to deal with 'the parlous financial situation facing universities in general and the College in particular'.[27] In the words of the Master, W. G. Overend,

> Never before has it been so difficult to see clearly the way forward, never before has it been more necessary for the field of part-time education to have its champion. The Friends of Birkbeck Trust are committed to ensuring that standards do not fall.[28]

When the crisis hit in 1986, the students were ready. Hundreds of students wrote to Kenneth Baker (the Secretary of State for Education and Science) as well as to Swinnerton-Dyer protesting the decision.[29] An article in the *Financial Times* concluded that, in a 'hamfisted attempt to restructure the funding of part-time

[24] Michael Prowse, 'The Birkbeck Controversy', *Financial Times* (13 June 1986).
[25] Eric Hobsbawm cited by Caroline St John-Brooks, 'Society at Work: The Grown-Ups' College', *New Society*, 61.1024 (1 July 1982), 15.
[26] David Walker, 'Writing off a Second Chance', *The Times* (20 June 1986).
[27] Letter from R. E. Swainson to A. Niekirk of Dawson and Co., dated 11 May 1981, in Birkbeck Archive, Box 17, File 11.
[28] Memo from the Master W. Overend, no date but 1981, in Birkbeck Archive, Box 17, File 11.
[29] '1986 Petitions', Birkbeck Archive, Box 42.

students', the UGC has 'qualified for the dunce's hat, with first class honours'.[30] Despite freezing conditions, in the week of 20 November 1986, Birkbeck staff conducted their classes outside in protest against the swingeing cuts.[31] It was said to be a 'David and Goliath' story, in which the academics at Birkbeck proved 'pretty adept with a sling'.[32]

Floud and other senior colleagues, including head of the Classics Department and ancient history philosopher David Hamlyn, economist Richard Portes, and political scientists Bernard Crick and Ben Pimlott formed the 'Zoo Group', named because they met in the café of London Zoo, to organize a concerted campaign. They felt that this was necessary because the Master, Overend, was a 'shy' person and

> very unwilling to be a spokesman for the college—very unwilling to do any kind of publicity or PR or anything, and one of these people who likes working behind the scenes, in the corridors of power, without actually putting his head above the parapet.[33]

The Zoo Group decided that, 'in default of the college leadership...taking any proactive action', it would mount a public campaign in defence of Birkbeck.[34]

Shrewdly, Floud and his team decided to invoke not only 'British fair play' but also that doyen of Victorian values: Samuel Smiles. In 1859, Smiles had published his classic *Self-Help; With Illustrations of Character and Conduct*. In it, he famously argued that all that was needed for social advancement was hard graft and perseverance. Although Smiles' analysis was actually much more subtle than this suggests, the *politically* popular version of his message was that poverty was the fault of the poor: if they only worked more and made frugal choices, they too could triumph like their 'betters'. Thatcher famously wanted to give a copy of *Self-Help* to every schoolchild in Britain.

It made strategic, although perhaps not ideological, sense for some Birkbeck defenders to conjure up this text. For example, Paul Meara, a founding member of Birkbeck's Department of Applied Linguistics, maintained that 'Birkbeck should be the blue-eyed baby of the government': after all, the College consisted of 'individual people pulling themselves up by their own bootstraps'.[35] Going even further, Tory defender and philosopher Roger Scruton argued that Birkbeck was 'a paradigm of Thatcherite principles—an expression of the principle of individual

---

[30] Prowse, 'The Birkbeck Controversy'.
[31] Steve Connor, 'SERS Set to Abandon Autumn Great Review', *New Scientist* (20 November 1986), in 'Newscuttings', in the Birkbeck Archive.
[32] Prowse, 'The Birkbeck Controversy'.
[33] Professor Roderick Floud, interviewed by Dr Lorraine Blakemore: Part I; 00:34:17.
[34] Floud, interviewed by Dr Lorraine Blakemore: Part II; 00:02:53.
[35] Paul Meara cited by St John-Brooks, 'Society at Work: The Grown-Ups' College', 14.

respectability'.[36] Not surprisingly, *The Times* agreed. It even contended that Birkbeck students were

> the very model of modern Thatcherites (devoutly though many of them would reject that description), the unconscious bearers of Victorian values, adherents (despite themselves) of Samuel Smiles' *Self-Help*. Mrs Thatcher's father would have been proud of them.... To close such an institution would be a plain contradiction of this government's rhetoric of self-improvement.[37]

The financial cuts were clearly political, Walker noted slyly in *The Times*. He alluded to four of Birkbeck's professors: Bernard Crick (political theorist and democratic socialist whose chief message was 'politics is ethics done in public'), Pimlott, Robin Marris (who in the 1970s had expressed dismay about the power of trade unions), and Scruton. According to Walker,

> If Birkbeck College were wall-to-wall Crick and Pimlott...the cut in its grant might just, in these political times, be understandable. The government, disliking both socialism and its putative cousin, social science, would applaud the decision of the University Grants Committee to cut Birkbeck's income.

However, Walker continued, 'that mould does not hold'. He reminded readers that

> Birkbeck is as much the home of conservatives such as the economist Professor Robin Marris and *The Times*' own Professor Roger Scruton.... As its staff point out, a latter-day Samuel Smiles would surely applaud.[38]

Many left-wing intellectuals at Birkbeck had to swallow their scruples to promote a Thatcherite, 'Victorian values' message.

The College proved very adept at eliciting support from politicians in both Houses. Furthermore, this support was not partisan: politicians from all parties rallied behind Birkbeck. In the House of Lords, there was strong support from the Conservative Lord Denning (the College's President and, Margaret Thatcher claimed, 'probably the greatest English judge of modern times')[39] and the Liberal Lord Scarman, as well as Jo Grimond (former Liberal Leader) and Desmond Plummer (Conservative).[40] In the House of Commons, Ivor Stanbrook

---

[36] Roger Scruton, cited by Sarah Thompson, 'Birkbeck Hit by University Grant Cutback', *Daily Telegraph* (17 June 1986).
[37] 'A Special Case', *The Times* (27 June 1986).   [38] Walker, 'Writing off a Second Chance'.
[39] Ian Burrell, 'Lord Denning, the Century's Greatest Judge, Dies at 100', *The Independent* (6 March 1999), viewed 7 July 2019. https://www.independent.co.uk/news/lord-denning-the-century-s-greatest-judge-dies-at-100-1078587.html
[40] Sarah Thompson, 'Funding for Birkbeck to be Reviewed', *Daily Telegraph* (14 June 1986).

(Conservative MP for Orpington) revealed that his studies at Birkbeck had changed his life.[41] Sir Geoffrey Finsberg (Conservative MP for Hampstead and Highgate) called the UGC's cuts 'one of the most inept and stupid decisions that it has ever taken'.[42] Many others put their names down for an 'early day motion calling for the direct intervention of the Government' to 'ensure a viable future for the only specialist university college in this country dedicated to face-to-face further adult evening education'.[43] Dr Keith Hampson, Conservative MP for Leeds North-West, presented a petition.[44] Six MPs, including Conservative MP Sydney Chapman (representative for Chipping Barnet) joined the campaign.[45]

Many of these politicians also appealed to Thatcherite 'Victorian values'. Frank Dobson, Labour MP for Holborn and St Pancras, which was Birkbeck's electoral district, wrote a strongly worded letter to Mrs Thatcher, reminding her that when she had attended the 150th anniversary celebrations at Birkbeck in 1973, she had been 'glowing in her praise' of the College. At that time, Thatcher had spoken of the need for 'second chance' education and had contended, as with her Victorian predecessors, that knowledge acquired 'by dint of self-denial and self-reliance' was superior to other kinds.[46] Dobson brusquely informed Thatcher that, 'on the assumption that you have not changed your views', she should take immediate steps to 'preserve some useful Victorian values for a change'.[47] Social Democratic Party co-founder Shirley Williams claimed that the Tories were 'Knocking the Best of Britain'. She caricatured the Thatcherite ideology as: 'Work hard, keep your head down, get your diploma or degree, and you're on your way. Good Thatcherite stuff'. The 'toughest way' to do this was by 'working all day and studying all night' at a place like Birkbeck. This was why the

> new rule is both unfair and crazy. It's unfair because Birkbeck's student[s] work from six till nine every evening. They take four hard slogging years to graduate. It's crazy because all Britain's employers say they need many more graduates.[48]

Most importantly, though, the 'Battle for Birkbeck' was led by its students and alumni. Only two weeks after the launch of the campaign to save Birkbeck, 15,000 people had signed a petition calling on the Education Secretary, Kenneth Baker,

---

[41] For example, see speeches by Ivor Stanbrook (MP for Orpington), in *House of Commons Debates*, 25 July 1986, vol. 2, pp. 887–94.
[42] Sir Geoffrey Finsberg (MP for Hampstead and Highgate), in *House of Commons Debates*, 25 July 1986, vol. 2, pp. 887–94.
[43] Peter Aspden, 'MPs Join Fight to Save Specialist College', *Times Higher Education Supplement* (4 July 1986).
[44] Ibid.   [45] 'Birkbeck Scheme "Devasting" [sic]', *Hendon Times* (17 July 1986).
[46] 'PM's Praise Bounces Back', *Hampstead and Highgate Express* (18 July 1986), in 'Newscuttings', in the Birkbeck Archive.
[47] Ibid.   [48] Shirley Williams, 'Knocking the Best of Britain', *Today* (20 June 1986).

to stop the cuts.⁴⁹ Students, too, appealed to Conservative values. For example, Ros Herman, who had completed an MA in the College, published a moving account of the way Birkbeck had transformed not only her life but her mother's as well. She told readers of the *New Scientist* that her mother had been forced to leave school aged 15 to earn a living. However,

> She was determined to go on and study her way out of menial jobs.... Birkbeck proved to be her salvation. It provided her with all the resources she needed to complete the English degree that cleared the way for her to become a teacher.⁵⁰

Although not a Tory, Herman concluded, both her and her mother's stories of transformation through evening education 'fit into the Conservative rhetoric of self-help and self-improvement'.⁵¹ Similarly, Brenda H. Taylor, writing in the *Daily Telegraph*, testified that, without Birkbeck, her 'own story would have been different'. She had left school aged 14 years, but Birkbeck gave her the opportunity eventually to obtain a BA (Hons), which catapulted her into a teaching job at the Central Foundation Girls' School in Mile End. Taylor reminded politicians that

> Destruction is easier than creation, and once destroyed, Birkbeck can never be re-created in its present form with its caring, dedicated staff who produce excellent academic results. The closure of Birkbeck would be a loss to the nation.⁵²

Still another student, who was taking a postgraduate degree in Politics and Administration, contended that the cuts were from 'a world gone mad'. She attested to the incredible 'loyalty' that Birkbeck inspired in its students, claiming that, like the suffragettes, she would be prepared to be 'bolted to the railings in support'.⁵³

The crisis highlighted other inequities as well. It enabled the College to draw attention to the fact that Birkbeck students paid fees while ordinary, full-time students had theirs paid for by the local authorities, as well as being eligible to apply for grants for living expenses.⁵⁴ In 1980, the College was educating 2,273 undergraduates and postgraduates, of whom 78 per cent were wholly self-supporting.⁵⁵ Floud announced that the College should be seen as

---

⁴⁹ 'Crucial Talks on Birkbeck', *Holborn Guardian* (16 July 1986), in 'Newscuttings', in the Birkbeck Archive.
⁵⁰ Ros Herman, 'Why Clobber Birkbeck?', *New Scientist* (17 July 1986), in 'Newscuttings', in the Birkbeck Archive.
⁵¹ Ibid.
⁵² Brenda H. Taylor, '[Letter to the Editor] The Future of Birkbeck College', *Daily Telegram* (15 July 1986).
⁵³ Gillian Darley, '[Letter to the Editor] The Birkbeck Controversy', *Financial Times* (20 June 1986).
⁵⁴ Prowse, 'The Birkbeck Controversy'.
⁵⁵ St John-Brooks, 'Society at Work: The Grown-Ups' College', 14.

a model for similar institutions elsewhere in Britain. The College was highly cost effective in producing graduates: the net costs against public funds for each graduate was £10K at Birkbeck against £19K elsewhere in the UGC sector, whilst the costs to society were respectively £12K and £35K. The economic return to a Birkbeck degree is calculated to be nearly three times that of a conventional degree: the latter is put at 8% whilst the Birkbeck figure is over 20%.

He concluded that it was 'manifestly unfair that full-time students had their fees met from public funds whilst part-time students did not'.[56] Indeed, Marris maintained that

> in terms of cost to public funds (either per student or per degree awarded) Birkbeck is the most economical university institution in Britain. It is a sad irony that... it is the most cost-effective part of the university sector that is expected to bear such very heavy costs. It is also fundamentally inequitable that mature part-time students should be expected to pay for their education from taxed income while full-time undergraduates are largely if not wholly maintained from public funds.[57]

Donald Bisset was Birkbeck's oldest student at the time. In 1982, he was 71 years old and a well-known children's book author and illustrator with books published in at least sixteen languages. He explained that 'It's not just the desire to get the exams—it's to gain more knowledge and wisdom as well. It's not just the vocational thing.'[58]

* * *

In the end, the UGC compromised. An impartial review of the College's finances, conducted by consultants Deloitte Haskins and Sells, provided evidence that the College was not responsible for its financial crisis.[59] This review was used to appeal to the UGC, which then allowed Birkbeck to recruit an additional 300 students[60] and offered a supplementary grant of £600,000 for 1986–7. These were only temporary measures: as Overend explained, this only 'deferred the financial consequences of the full-time equivalence factor'.[61] He warned that the College might still become bankrupt in 1987–8.[62]

---

[56] Roderick Floud in 'Note on the Meeting with the Secretary of State for Education on Thursday 2 October 1986', 13 October 1986, 2, in the Papers of Sir Bernard Crick, CRCK 1/1/13.
[57] Cited in Barney Hayhoe, 'Birkbeck College. A New Structure. The Report of the Committee on Restructuring the College. February 1987' (London: Birkbeck College, 1987), 6.
[58] Donald Bisset, cited by St John-Brooks, 'Society at Work: The Grown-Ups' College', 14.
[59] Katherine Webb, 'A Tribute to Tessa Blackstone. Master of Birkbeck College 1987–1997' (7 March 1998), 4, in Birkbeck Archive.
[60] Tessa Blackstone, 'From the Master', *Spectrum*, 5 (April 1988), 3.
[61] 'Note on the Meeting with the Secretary of State for Education on Thursday 2 October 1986', 13 October 1986, 1, in the Papers of Sir Bernard Crick, CRCK 1/1/13.
[62] Ibid.

Swinnerton-Dyer admitted that a mistake had been made but, despite this, insisted that a committee be established to 'decide what level of resourcing was needed' for Birkbeck to 'operate effectively'. He also argued that the College should explore 'opportunities for collaboration, particularly in the use of accommodation, with other institutions'.[63] In October 1986, the College appointed a committee to review the

> role of the College in terms of the needs of part-time higher education and to examine how the academic and administrative structures might be adjusted both in the context of the resources available and to facilitate further developments.[64]

Chaired by Conservative politician Sir Barney Hayhoe, the committee also included Tessa Blackstone (the College's Master-elect), David Hamlyn (Vice-Master and philosopher), Floud, and Barry W. Ife (Hispanic scholar and musician).

Serving as Master-elect on the Hayhoe Committee was a baptism of fire for Blackstone. Overend had retired in 1987 as Master, after teaching at Birkbeck since 1955 and serving as Master for eight years. Unlike Overend, Blackstone was a fighter. Her early career as an academic meant that she understood the demands upon lecturers but, crucially, she arrived at Birkbeck with a formidable record as a member of the think-tank 'Central Policy Review Staff'. This had been followed by stints as Deputy Education Officer, Clerk, and finally Director of Education to the Inner London Education Authority (ILEA). She was accustomed to battle. On her appointment as master, *Spectrum* (the students' magazine) called her a 'leftwing radical, dark-eyed evil genius, union champion, etc.'[65] She was definitely five of those six things.

Sitting on the Hayhoe Committee, Blackstone quickly realized that all members agreed that part-time education was 'an urgent national need', but they all also recognized that Birkbeck had to reform if it was to survive.[66] Increasing student numbers was paramount. This was not only because of the massive government cuts, but also because the post-war 'baby boom' would peak in 1992, after which the number of 28-year-olds (the median age of Birkbeck students) in the UK would inevitably decline.[67]

---

[63] Sir Peter Swinnerton-Dyer (Chairman of the UGC), in 'Note on the Meeting with the Secretary of State for Education on Thursday 2 October 1986'.

[64] Hayhoe, 'Birkbeck College. A New Structure. The Report of the Committee on Restructuring the College. February 1987', 1.

[65] 'Who Wants to Go to the Basement?', *Spectrum*, 1 (October 1988), 2. The term 'black-eyed evil geniuses' was applied to Blackstone and Kate Mortimer who recommended cutbacks of foreign office staff in their 1975–7 review.

[66] Hayhoe, 'Birkbeck College. A New Structure. The Report of the Committee on Restructuring the College. February 1987', 1.

[67] Ibid., 10.

The Committee introduced five major reforms. The first involved incorporating the University of London's Centre for Extra-Mural Studies (CEMS) into the College. This was an important merger. The history of the CEMS predated the establishment of the Workers' Educational Association (1903). It can be dated back to 1876 with the formation of the London Society for the Extension of University Education. In 1898, this became the London University Extension Board following the London University Act. By the 1944 Education Act, it became the London University Department of Extra-Mural Studies. However, the CEMS was informed by a different tradition to Birkbeck's. It taught in locations throughout London and the Home Counties, including at the City Lit, the Mary Ward Centre, the Highgate Institute, church halls, Workers' Education Associations, workingmen's colleges, adult education centres, and Further Education colleges in Barnet, Camden, South Kensington, West London, and so on. Its 'book boxes' contained reading materials that the lecturers thought relevant to their classes; they were transported to each teaching location, enabling students to borrow them. According to the Hayhoe Report, 'Extra-Mural work should be developed as one of the primary access routes to part-time higher education.'[68] The CEMS formally joined Birkbeck in August 1988. The chief purpose of the decision was fulfilled: the merger added an additional 18,000 extra-mural students to a cohort that had consisted of only 6,000.[69]

By 2003, however, the model that had been adopted in response to the 1986 crisis was clearly not working. Many students taking classes in the Faculty of Lifelong Learning (FLL) were doing so for interest, and therefore not sitting the examinations. This was devastating for Birkbeck since funding was dependent on student completions. The FLL had also started offering undergraduate *degree* courses, effectively creating competition for students *within* the College. Latchman's response was to fully merge it with the rest of the College, with each 'Super School' subsuming the appropriate subject areas from the FLL. It was not an easy transition. The staff of FLL often felt marginalized within the College and University more broadly. Many Birkbeck academics in the 'central' part of the university regarded the FLL as a 'kind of Cinderella service of the college.'[70] Even worse, some academics sneered about 'leisure learning.'[71] There were hurtful comments about the introduction of 'non-academic' subjects and less qualified lecturers. The fears were unwarranted. Henceforth, however, schools of the College would offer a single pathway in any particular discipline, ranging from certificates and diplomas, to doctorates.

---

[68] Ibid., 11.
[69] Ben Pimlott, 'Speech for the Presentation of Baroness Blackstone as a Fellow of Birkbeck College', in Katherine Webb, *Birkbeck under Tessa Blackstone: A Brief History* (London: Birkbeck College, 1997), 14.
[70] Interview of Mike Berlin for the Birkbeck Oral History Project, 21 June 2016.   [71] Ibid.

The second reform in the mid-1980s was a major restructuring of the entire administrative framework of the College. The Hayhoe Committee disapprovingly observed that the College was organized around academic departments, many of which were very small. This resulted in a considerable overlap in administration. Furthermore, departments had 'little control over the funding and little opportunity to show initiative in altering the pattern of their activities or seeking outside support'. In fact, many were not even 'aware of the full costs of their activities or of the competing demands for finance within the College'. Funds were distributed by informal mechanisms; incentives to balance budgets were weak.[72] The solution was to merge departments into seven large resources centres: Life Sciences; Chemistry and Geology; Crystallography and Physics; Computer Sciences; Social Science; Language and Literature; and the Humane Sciences.[73] At the same time, Blackstone co-located the Departments of Chemistry and Geology within University College London (UCL).[74]

Fourthly, staff was reduced. Given that salaries accounted for more than two thirds of the College's total costs, any reduction in costs would require staffing cuts. By the end of September 1988, twenty members of staff had taken early retirement and another dozen were planning to go in the following year (although some were re-employed on a part-time basis).[75] Finally, the College's administration 'was at last computerised', eradicating a time-consuming and inefficient manual process.[76]

Ironically, the College's finances were also helped by the legal judgement following libel proceedings. In July 1986, the *Mail on Sunday*, the *Sunday Times*, and the *News of the World* had erroneously reported that the Ministry of Defence had withdrawn defence research contracts from Birkbeck on the grounds that some members of staff were security risks (specifically: a member of staff had been associating with Sinn Féin leaders).[77] The College won £22,500 in damages and legal costs in an out-of-court settlement. The money could not have come at a better time.

* * *

There was one further decision, made in 1986 and implemented the following year, that was to have huge implications. Even though classics had been taught at Birkbeck from the 1820s, it was to be cut.[78] This was not the first time there had been questions about the teaching of classics at Birkbeck. In the early 1960s, a

---

[72] Hayhoe, 'Birkbeck College. A New Structure. The Report of the Committee on Restructuring the College. February 1987', 19.
[73] Ibid., 27.
[74] *Birkbeck College. University of London. Annual Report 1988–89* (London: Birkbeck College, 1989), 6.
[75] Ibid., 5. [76] Ibid., 6. [77] Webb, 'A Tribute to Tessa Blackstone', 5.
[78] Note that the Department of Italian had also been recently closed.

memorandum by the Acting Master, Eric H. Warmington (himself Professor of Classics at Birkbeck with a formidable reputation for his Latin translations), observed that the College planned to periodically review the existence of classics teaching, 'the value of which in British education is under criticism'.[79] But when the crisis came, it was an immense shock. After all, the Classics Department at Birkbeck had been home to classicists such as F. A. ('Freddie') Wright (1898 to 1935), who was passionate about Greek social life. More significantly, it was the intellectual base for Byzantinist Robert Browning (1965 to 1981), who was known for his zealous defence of Greek as a single language, as opposed to a series of distinct languages, as well as his succinct analysis of 'diglossia' (where two languages are used under different conditions often by the same speakers within a community, such as the demotic or popular and the 'katharevousa' or formal, modern Greek). Indeed, Browning was widely considered one of the most distinguished classicists of the twentieth century.[80]

Swinnerton-Dyer and the University Joint Planning Committee were responsible for this momentous change. As Chair of the UGC, Swinnerton-Dyer sent a questionnaire to all university vice-chancellors and principals asking for information about the size and balance of their classics departments and the range of work done. On 5 November 1987, he sent a copy of the Committee's report (known as the Barron Report after its author John Barron) to all vice-chancellors and principals of universities. Its impact was to be devastating for classics teaching at Birkbeck. The report noted that thirty-one universities in the UK had classics departments.[81] After deliberating, the Committee hit upon a formula for assessing whether a classics department was viable and offered a 'well-balanced and sufficiently wide degree'. It decided that there had to be a minimum of eight members of staff.[82] To 'cover a reasonable spectrum of Classical studies at specialist level', there had to be at least two teachers of Greek language, two of Latin, two historians, one philosopher, and one archaeologist or art specialist.[83] Birkbeck failed to meet this threshold: it employed only three classicists.[84] As a result, the Committee proposed that Birkbeck should discontinue its classics teaching and its staff be transferred to King's College London.[85]

[79] Eric H. W. Warmington, 'Confidential. Birkbeck College. Future Policy (Long-Term). Memorandum by the Acting Master', 9, in the file 'Future Development of the College 1963–68', in Birkbeck Archive, Box 43.
[80] Angeliki E. Laiou and Alice-Mary Talbot, 'Robert Browning, 1914–1997', *Dumbarton Oak Papers*, 51 (1997), ix.
[81] 'University Grants Committee. Review of Classics' (5 November 1987), 2, The National Archives (TNA) UGC 6/68/.
[82] John Connor, 'Classics Department—Going…Going…Gone!', *Spectrum*, 5 (April 1988), 1, and 'Letters', *Spectrum*, 5 (April 1988), 5.
[83] 'University Grants Committee. Review of Classics' (5 November 1987), 5, TNA UGC 6/68/.
[84] Connor, 'Classics Department—Going…Going…Gone!', 1.
[85] 'University Grants Committee. Review of Classics' (5 November 1987), 9, TNA UGC 6/68/.

There was widespread protest. Even the Editor of *The Times* was distressed. He observed that for two months previously the *New York Times*' best-sellers included *The Trial of Socrates* by I. F. Stone who had learnt Ancient Greek at the age of 70 years. He noted that

> Until now, anyone in Britain who late in life wanted to make a serious study of the classics but, for professional, family or other reasons needed to study at night, would have been able to apply to take a degree at Birkbeck College, London. But soon this opportunity, the only one of its kind, will have gone.[86]

The Editor noted that Stone's example showed that 'old-age beginners have much to offer others', but also that interest amongst adult students was increasing. Surely, he exclaimed, 'those with worldly experience have greatly more to contribute to discussions of Horace or Tacitus than those straight from school'. Such students had to be encouraged in part because the subject was less popular among the young.[87] Furthermore, he continued,

> Unlike others, these students mostly pay their own fees. Their studies are not capital-intensive. They cost the tax-payer little. They contribute to the preservation of a tradition. They may, indeed, help restore it—by bringing boldness into intellectual debates which have become becalmed.[88]

Used to fighting crises by this stage, the Birkbeck Students' Union made its voice heard, complaining that this closure was simply one of a 'series of body blows to our provision for adult part-time students'.[89] Floud, Roland Mayer (convenor of the Classics Department and specialist in Roman literature and culture), and Jane Rowlandson (who was a leading authority on Greek and Roman Egypt) hastened to reassure existing students that they would be able to complete their degree, with all the necessary resources.[90] Floud, who boasted of classicists in his family, admitted to feeling 'distressed and depressed', contending that the College had fought to keep the department going but 'we were overcome by superior force and by a national organisation over which we had no control'.[91]

In 1988, Birkbeck's remaining classicists were transferred to King's College London, with some evening teaching remaining at Birkbeck.[92] The discipline was only revived in 1992, with the appointment of Emma Dench, an authority on the

---

[86] 'Adult Literature', *The Times* (27 July 1988), 11. This was the leader article. [87] Ibid., 11.
[88] Ibid., 11.
[89] John Allen, President of the Birkbeck Students' Union, '[Letter to the Editor] Classical Values in Adult Studies', *The Times* (2 August 1988), 11.
[90] Connor, 'Classics Department—Going…Going…Gone!', 1. [91] Ibid., 1.
[92] See TNA UGC 7/1459.

Roman world. The post was designated one in 'ancient history' to avoid accusations that 'classics' was being stealthily reintroduced.

A decade later, the world-renowned Physics Department went through a similar traumatic cull. Concerned that the department had run at a financial loss for a few years, Blackstone transferred the majority of the department to UCL.[93] A fourth-year physics student echoed the complaint of classicists a decade earlier, stating that 'the closure will mean the loss of 50% of the part-time undergraduate physics places and hundreds of evening part-time physics places in the country'.[94] On 1 October 1997, the department was closed, with only a small group headed by Basil Hiley, Professor of Theoretical Physics, remaining at Birkbeck as the Theoretical Physics Research Unit. As with the classics fiasco, this cull was a response to a broader crisis in physics teaching in schools and universities. In 1997 alone, the universities of Coventry and East Anglia ended undergraduate teaching in physics and the Physics Department at De Montfort University merged with Chemistry.[95] The reasons were many, including declining teaching of the subject at A-level. In 1989, nearly 50,000 students took physics for their A-levels but this fell by one third (to around 32,000) within less than a decade.[96] It was also a relatively expensive subject to teach, leading to complaints from other departments that they were cross-subsidizing the small amount of physics teaching.[97] A College investigation into the department had exposed the fact that in 1994–5, it had a deficit of nearly £400,000 and only sixty-eight full-time equivalent students.[98] And the College had a £2.7 million deficit.[99] The assumption that physics was being sold off was not helped when the *Times Higher Education Supplement* reported the closure under the title 'Birkbeck Turns Physics Faculty into Gold'.[100]

The physicists did not go without a fight. The Association of University Teachers (AUT) launched a massive campaign, lobbying more than 400 leading physicists, MPs, and peers, making the case for its survival.[101] Hiley was furious that he had not even been asked to make cuts, which he could have achieved. The lack of consultation was insulting. He also worried that it was a 'slippery slope', a comment echoed by senior physics lecturer Malcolm Coupland who feared a 'rapid domino effect'.[102] Was it even possible 'to have a credible science representation in universities without physics', some asked?[103] One senior Birkbeck physicist

---

[93] Webb, *Birkbeck under Tessa Blackstone*, 9.
[94] Letter from Louise Dash, 'Your Views', *The Independent* (5 December 1996).
[95] Lucy Ward, 'Physics First Aid', *The Independent* (6 February 1997), E2.   [96] Ibid., E2.
[97] Ibid., E2.   [98] 'Birkbeck College', *Times Higher Education Supplement* (24 January 1997).
[99] 'Birkbeck Turns Physics Faculty into Gold', *Times Higher Education Supplement* (28 March 1997), and 'Birkbeck Board Backs Axe for Physics', *Times Higher Education Supplement* (28 February 1997).
[100] 'Birkbeck Turns Physics Faculty into Gold', *Times Higher Education Supplement*.
[101] 'Birkbeck College', *Times Higher Education Supplement* (24 January 1997).
[102] 'Science Fears for Birkbeck', *Times Higher Education Supplement* (13 December 1996).
[103] 'Birkbeck College', *Times Higher Education Supplement*.

(who did not want to be named) noted that the College had closed the Mathematics Department in 1995, and that colleagues teaching chemistry and biology at Birkbeck were afraid that they would be next.[104]

The downgrading of science at Birkbeck was to be reversed under the Mastership of David Latchman, who had been Professor of Molecular Pathology at UCL and head of the Institute of Child Health before he accepted the post in 2003. Within a week of arriving at Birkbeck, he could be heard promising that any further loss of science subjects would be a 'retrograde step' and that he was committed to maintaining a balanced science/arts profile in the College.[105] It is a promise that he has maintained, resulting in the College being home to distinguished scientists.

* * *

Despite the crises (which included the collapse of Barings Bank, where the College held its accounts), by the 1990s the College had grown immeasurably. At the height of the troubles at the end of the 1980s, Birkbeck had a deficit of £500,000 and net assets of £3.5 million. By 1996–7, the College recorded a surplus, and net assets were four times as high.[106] Blackstone was responsible for the opening of two new departments—Law as well as Management and Business Studies, which recruited high numbers of students. The latter was moved into a new building called the Clore Management Centre, which opened in July 1997. This was the College's largest building project since the extension to the main building in 1966[107] and was achieved with the help of more than £2 million given by the Clore Foundation, the largest single donation at that date to the College Appeal.[108]

Blackstone also worked to give Birkbeck greater autonomy within the University of London. In the first half of the 1990s, there were three initiatives. First, no longer was its UGC grant allocated *via* the University of London. Henceforth, the College could bid directly to the UGC. Second, Birkbeck could hold its own degree presentation ceremonies, as opposed to being part of the University's ceremonies in the Royal Albert Hall. Finally, the University of London delegated powers to colleges to confer degrees of the University as well as to appoint and confer titles (such as professor).[109] Having arrived during a crisis, Blackstone left the College in a stable position when in 1997 she became Minister for Education and Employment in the new Labour government.

* * *

---

[104] Ibid.
[105] 'Image Revamp for Birkbeck', *Times Higher Education Supplement* (10 January 2003).
[106] Ben Pimlott, 'Speech for the Presentation of Baroness Blackstone as a Fellow of Birkbeck College', in Webb, 'A Tribute to Tessa Blackstone', 11.
[107] Webb, *Birkbeck under Tessa Blackstone*, 10. [108] Ibid., 10.
[109] Webb, 'A Tribute to Tessa Blackstone', 8.

While Birkbeck struggled with the crisis of 1986 and its aftermaths, other major changes were under way in British Higher Education. Some of these changes were mentioned in Chapter 7, but the most important was the funding of universities being made dependent on the assessment of research and then teaching. In 1986, the first Research Assessment Exercise (RAE; later Research Excellence Framework or REF) was introduced. RAEs/REFs were subsequently held in 1989, 1992, 1996, 2001, 2008, 2014, and 2021. These audits were based primarily on the published 'outputs' of staff as well as the research environment of academic disciplines. From 2014, 'impact' was added, weighed at one fifth of the total. In 2021, the 'impact' variable was increased to one quarter. This masks the fact that 'impact' indicators are also found in the research environment statement, which is weighted at 15 per cent. Henceforth, the ranking of academic staff in disciplinary Units of Assessment (such as History, Law, Mathematics, and Molecular Biology) determined the amount of money each university was allocated in the 'research' element of the block grant.

At Birkbeck, as in universities throughout the country, these changes dramatically transformed the way the College was run. When the first RAE took place in 1989, no elaborate structures existed in the College to deal with its demands. For example, on the evening before the Department of History and Classics' submission was due, the distinguished European historian Richard Evans (who was head of department) and Marianne Elliott (historian of Ireland) sat up until midnight writing the report. The strategy worked. The department was ranked well above the University of Oxford's History Department. It prompted claims that this was proof that the process was fair and would encourage a redistribution of government funding to universities.

However, the casual approach of 1989 (at least in some sections of Birkbeck) did not last. Birkbeck, and other universities, rapidly discovered the formidable power of RAE/REF on budgets and reputations. The monetization of Higher Education, a side effect of wider neoliberal approaches to public services, had begun in earnest. The survival of entire disciplines often depended on achieving high RAE/REF rankings. Academic departments found themselves required to justify decisions based on projected RAE/REF assessments. Multiple committees were established to manage the process; hundreds of hours were spent preparing the 'returns'. Competition between (and within) universities soared. To 'win', academic staff were transferred from one discipline to another (this is what happened to psychosocial studies, for example, as discussed in Chapter 22). Smaller disciplines and interdisciplinary research were especially vulnerable. Realizing that large departments were significantly more likely to be awarded the higher grades, senior administrators established coalitions with departments elsewhere in the University of London (with UCL, for example), to present 'joint returns'. Many universities (although not Birkbeck) began 'cherry-picking' staff—that is, submitting only the research of academics they were certain would be awarded the highest scores and excluding others. For example, over one fifth of 'eligible' academics within the Russell Group (which represents twenty-four leading universities) were *not* included in their REF submission for 2014.[110] Some universities even began relegating less 'productive' researchers to 'teaching-only contracts'. This did not happen at Birkbeck, where a policy of 'entering' nearly all of its staff was established. But the monetization and bureaucratization of research led to demoralization and dismay, nevertheless.

From 1995, governmental funding was also distributed according to the quality of teaching provision. Teaching quality was assessed through regular inspections and audits conducted by the Quality Assurance Agency for Higher Education (QAA). Teaching was also assessed through the National Student Survey (NSS) of student satisfaction. In combination with the RAE/REF, the various teaching assessments proved to be extremely time consuming. Relentless auditing means that time is diverted from the central aim of the university—that is, teaching and research: universities risk becoming part of an education–business panopticon. The various audits are central components of the 'new public management', requiring universities such as Birkbeck to become increasingly sensitive to their position in league tables, especially those published by *The Times* and *The Guardian*. It fuelled Master David Latchman's decision in 2018 to withdraw from these league tables on the grounds that they did not take account of Birkbeck's unique student composition and actively discriminated against minoritized students. For instance, the metrics placed great weight on entry qualifications and money spent on student facilities, neither of which applied in the case of an institution providing University of London-standard education for people based on merit. For Birkbeck, what mattered was not *entry* qualifications but *exit* qualifications—and Birkbeck's high ratings in terms of research (RAE/REF) and teaching (Teaching Excellence Framework, or TEF) were proof of its high academic standards. The league tables also ignored the fact that spending on student facilities, in a college with part-time students taking classes in the evenings and living at home rather than on a campus, is obviously significantly lower. Rather than penalizing Birkbeck for these differences, Latchman argued, the College should be rewarded for spending proportionately more on *access*.[111]

For Latchman and the rest of the College, the stresses and anxieties of RAE/REF and TEF paled when compared to the second major crisis to hit the College in the twentieth century. In 2008, without warning, the government introduced the Equivalent and Lower Qualification (ELQ) policy. This meant that students taking an equivalent or lower degree to the one they already possessed were not

---

[110] Richard Watermeyer and Mark Olssen, '"Excellence" and Exclusion: The Individual Costs of Institutional Competitiveness', *Minerva*, 54.2 (2016), 208.

[111] David Latchman, 'Why Birkbeck is Leaving the UK Rankings Race', *Times Higher Education* (10 October 2018), at https://www.timeshighereducation.com/blog/why-birkbeck-leaving-uk-rankings-race, viewed 13 April 2021.

entitled to any financial support. Overnight, 30 per cent of Birkbeck's teaching funding disappeared. It was a devasting attack on Birkbeck's mission, part of which involved reskilling people for new careers. Latchman campaigned heavily against the policy and, when it became clear that it was not going to be reversed, engaged in a dramatic reorganization of the College. The sixteen schools of the College were reorganized into a smaller number of 'super schools'. Currently, these are: Arts; Business, Economics, and Informatics; Law; Social Sciences, History, and Philosophy; and Science. They are run by Executive Deans and assisted by Directors of Operations. Finance was devolved from the College to the schools. This would allow each school to make resource decisions against a strategic plan, approved annually by the College's management. In 2010, the College introduced three-year degree programmes, allowing students to study full time, albeit in classes held in the evenings (thus retaining its unique model). Although part-time undergraduates declined by over 60 per cent, this was compensated for by the growth in full-time evening degrees.[112] By 2020, the College could boast of 3,200 full-time undergraduates and 1,500 part-time undergraduates. (In 2011–12, full-time undergraduates were 3,800.)[113]

The scale of the changes can be illustrated by the School of Business, Economics, and Informatics, created in 2009 as a direct result of the withdrawal of ELQ funding. It contained Computer Science and Informational Systems, Management, Economics, Mathematics and Statistics, and Organizational Psychology. Within two years, the school had developed over thirty new courses and, within six years, had increased student numbers by 60 per cent.[114] Its mantra was 'do a lot more with a bit more'. Economist Ron Smith—who has worked at the College for forty-seven years—reflected that the School of Business, Economics, and Informatics, and indeed the College, only 'stayed afloat by transforming how it met its mission. Despite much unhappiness during the process, the transformations worked and Birkbeck emerged stronger, doing the same thing but in a different way'.[115]

Such shifts were taking place within a broader context which saw declining state funding of universities, accompanied by the introduction and escalation of student fees. Fees were introduced by the Labour government in 1998 as 'top-up fees' compensating for the reduction in state funding. In 2006, they became 'variable fees', which were nothing of the kind because practically all universities, including Birkbeck, charged the maximum amount of £3,000. Then, the Conservative/Liberal Democrat coalition government of 2010–15 tripled the

---

[112] Birkbeck College, 'Financial Statements for the year ended 31 July 2020', 9, at https://www.bbk.ac.uk/downloads/finance/financial-statements-2020.pdf, viewed 1 June 2021.
[113] Ibid., 9.
[114] Andi Schmidt, 'A Very Short History of BEI With Associated Tables and Figures 2009–2019', departmental file (2020), 1.
[115] Ron Smith, email to author, dated 13 September 2021.

ceiling of students' annual fees to £9,000 a year, thus cementing the image of students as 'customers', with colleges as 'service users'. The effect was a fall in part-time students by at least 40 per cent. As we will see in the next chapter, the College was emerging from this crisis through astute reorganization and retention policies when the COVID-19 pandemic struck.

The 1980s through to the early 1990s, then the 2008 funding bomb, involved years of crisis, in which staff and students found themselves under siege by a series of governmental measures that attacked the fundamental mission of Birkbeck. The College survived, but the cost was huge. The College had nevertheless shown a great ability to adapt and adjust to the politico-economic environments and wider social crisis. Ben Pimlott's gloomy prediction of 1986—'Here lies continuing education, killed off by an accounting error'—underestimated the resilience of the College and its preparedness to make significant changes to governance, institutional structures, and the student cohort.

PART VII
CONCLUSION

28
Into the Twenty-First Century

On 16 March 2020, Birkbeck closed its doors for only the second time in nearly 200 years. The last occasion was in September 1939, when war was declared on Germany. *That* decision had been quickly reversed: the College remained defiantly open throughout the war, even when its classrooms, laboratories, and library were directly hit by bombs.

In contrast, the closure in 2020–1 was to last over a year and a half. The cause was the global epidemic of the virus SARS-CoV-2 or COVID-19 (CO stands for corona, VI for virus, D for disease, and the virus was first identified in 2019). It causes severe acute respiratory symptoms and is extremely contagious and lethal. On 6 March 2020, the Conservative government reported the first death in the UK from COVID-19. Thereafter, infections and deaths began rising at an exponential rate.[1] Within days, it was clear that a deathly epidemic was raging throughout the country, and the government began to agonize about the ability of the NHS to cope. Drastic measures were necessary. The government issued a 'work from home' order for everyone except 'essential workers'. By 23 March, 364 people had died—although no one doubted that this was a vast underestimate since many of the most vulnerable people (such as those in care homes) were not being counted. Prime Minister Boris Johnson announced that, from 26 March, people were *required* to stay at home unless their job made this impossible. People in the UK, as in many parts of the world, were only allowed to leave their homes to seek medical help, shop for essential items such as food and medicine, or exercise, although this was allowed only once a day.

Birkbeck acted quickly, before most universities. For lecturers and students, the first official sign of the College's response to the crisis came in the form of an email from Keith Harrison, College Secretary, on 13 March. He advised staff that

> if you have a high temperature or a new, continuous cough, you should stay at home for seven days and we are asking members of the College community to follow this advice and to report their absence in line with the sickness absence policy. Over the coming weeks and months, it is inevitable that a number of staff and students will become unwell and will need to self-isolate because of the virus, and some will test positive for it.

---

[1] For monthly deaths in the UK, see https://www.statista.com/statistics/1109595/coronavirus-mortality-in-the-uk/, viewed 1 July 2021.

Harrison promised that the College would 'do all that we can to support colleagues during this difficult time and to mitigate the impact of the virus on the College Community'.[2] Although it was examination season, all forms of assessment were postponed. By 16 March, all teaching had been cancelled, with lecturers instructed to transfer their classes to the online learning platform Moodle. Computing facilities began working day and night to set up remote teaching in a way that could be used by staff and students, the vast majority of whom were unfamiliar with the practice. No one was surprised when, on the first evening of online classes, the whole system collapsed. But, as during the war of 1939–45, members of the College rallied together. Within a day, the system was working smoothly, at least for users: behind the scenes, frantic work was continuing.

By 20 March, restrictions in the College had to be scaled up. The Estates Department announced that entrances to College buildings would be locked from 5 p.m. until further notice. The eatery, bar, and cafés were closed; the cleaning services, reduced; portering services, stopped; the post-room, abandoned.[3] Heating was switched to a minimum. In the hours before this lockdown, lecturers and other staff dashed to their offices to retrieve essential notes, books, and equipment; they left behind unwashed coffee cups, used teabags, leftover snacks and fruit, and pot-plants.

The impact of COVID-19 on teaching was nothing short of revolutionary. For nearly 200 years, students at the LMI/Birkbeck had had face-to-face interactions with their teachers. Prior to the pandemic, only a tiny number of classes had any online components. For decades, College personnel had discussed the possibility of recording live lectures, enabling students to watch and rewatch their classes from their own homes. One of the few disciplines with experience in online teaching and learning was the Department of Organizational Psychology whose MSc had been online since the financial crisis of the mid-1980s. At that time, the move online was due to the need to recruit outside of London as well as to provide training for the psychologists of the Manpower Services Commission. But other than this MSc (probably the first MSc degree in the country to be conducted online),[4] most staff had no idea of how to teach in this way. It was extraordinary, then, that within thirteen days of the realities of the pandemic restrictions hitting home, everything had been transferred online. Behind the scenes, an army of computer programmers and technicians worked long into the night setting up complex systems. Birkbeck's Information Technology Services (ITS) were

---

[2] Email from Keith Harrison, to all staff, 13 March 2020.
[3] Email from Jeremy Tanner and Jossette Leigh, to all staff, 23 March 2020.
[4] Malcolm Ballantyne, 'Twenty Years of Network Learning', at http://blogs.bbk.ac.uk/bbkcomments/2020/10/14/twenty-years-of-network-learning/, viewed 26 May 2022.

expected virtually overnight to introduce a high-quality online learning environment for 500 lecturers teaching 4,700 students.[5]

The Vice-Chancellor, David Latchman, and the College's governors approved a major investment in student support services. The library's e-books collection was expanded by an additional 180,000 books.[6] A 'no-detriment assessment policy' was quickly introduced, meaning that stress and disruption would be taken into account without students having to submit a mitigating circumstances application. Birkbeck was one of the first UK universities to introduce such a policy, which was copied elsewhere.[7] Academics were encouraged to access advice via the 'My ASK' information platform, as they frantically worked to transform their modules into something that could be described as 'online friendly'. Alternative teaching and assessment models had to be instigated. Lecturers not only had to create pre-live learning materials, including lectures delivered via online platforms that most found confusing, but also to restructure their classes to encourage student participation. This proved difficult especially for those struggling with poor internet connections. Workloads soared.

Personnel in ITS faced formidable challenges, which demanded radically new ways of thinking and working. The Digital Education team had to ensure that around 1,400 modules were accessible online.[8] Support systems were imperative. They introduced a massive training programme for lecturers, teaching and scholarship staff, and part-time teachers.[9] Digital Education Partners and Associates were appointed in every school of the College. To help lecturers navigate the system, digital experts provided templates for Moodle courses, highlighting the need to upload pre-recorded lectures, establish live interactions with small groups, and organize post-class activities. Interactivity and diversity of pedagogic approaches were key. To the surprise of the management team, not only did the Birkbeck community adapt remarkably quickly and (largely) in good humour, but some sections of the community reported positive outcomes. For example, for years, students with disabilities had been pleading for lectures to be captioned and handouts presented in accessible ways: suddenly, these were not only *recommended* but *mandatory* practices. Surprisingly, student satisfaction surveys reported high levels of positive responses. While only 54 per cent of students nationally agreed with the statement 'I am satisfied with the academic experience so far', 80 per cent of Birkbeck students did so.[10]

---

[5] Birkbeck College, 'Financial Statements for the year ended 31 July 2020', 9–10, at https://www.bbk.ac.uk/downloads/finance/financial-statements-2020.pdf, viewed 1 June 2021.
[6] 'Our 2020/21 Student Fees and COVID-19', online document, at https://www.bbk.ac.uk/downloads/registry/policies-2020–21/student-fees-and-covid-19.pdf, November 2020, viewed 1 June 2021.
[7] Birkbeck College, 'Financial Statements for the year ended 31 July 2020', 9.
[8] Brett Lucas, personal email to me, dated 25 May 2021.
[9] Ibid.
[10] Birkbeck College, 'Student Satisfaction Surveys', EC 28 2020/21, 3.

The College weathered the restrictions much better than the rest of the Higher Education sector. In part, this was because Birkbeck was less exposed. For example, universities that had large numbers of residential students housed in student halls faced immense challenges in acting *in loco parentis*. Birkbeck was not reliant on campus income. It was also spared the tensions created by the enforcement of social distancing and lockdown amongst the young. Most Birkbeck students were adults employed in other sectors of the economy. This meant that they had alternative benchmarks with which to compare the College's policies and accomplishments. Furthermore, in the years prior to the pandemic, many UK universities had been strategically moving their provision towards international students, who paid significantly higher fees. This had never been a top priority for Birkbeck. Three quarters of Birkbeck's students were from the UK, while only 16 per cent came from the EU and 9 per cent from the rest of the world.[11] This meant that, at the peak of COVID-19, which coincided with Brexit, the College was less affected by the 30 per cent decline of international students in Higher Education.[12] Indeed, total enrolments actually *increased* by 8 per cent during the pandemic.[13] Matt Innes, historian and Deputy Vice-Chancellor, observed that this was probably due to women and young mothers, in particular, using the lockdown as an opportunity to retrain and change careers—for example, to teaching.[14]

But, overall, the experience was painful. The shift online exposed huge discrepancies in access to adequate computing facilities in people's homes. Indeed, one quarter of students had to use their mobile phones to study or attend classes; some attempted to sit their examinations on small mobile devices.[15] Many teachers and students were forced to conduct their activities from bedrooms or crowded kitchens. Reluctance to turn cameras 'on' was fuelled by embarrassment about having one's domestic chaos exposed to outside scrutiny. Lecturers had no choice in the matter, but students often opted to turn their cameras off, making it almost impossible for teachers to judge through their image whether students were even present, let alone understanding what was being said.

As the lockdown was extended, the full economic cost of COVID-19 sank in. Normally, Birkbeck would rent around eighty-five teaching rooms to other colleges and universities during the day; this dried up. The loss was partly offset by the fact that the College no longer had to rent 120 rooms from other institutions in the evenings. During brief respites from lockdowns, social distancing rules meant that lecture theatres, classrooms, and laboratories could only accommodate small numbers of people. For example, at the height of the social distancing

---

[11] Matt Innes, 'Academic Strategy', PowerPoint presented 2021, personal communication. These percentages refer to FTE numbers or full-time equivalent.
[12] Ibid.   [13] Ibid.   [14] Matt Innes, interview, 21 May 2021.
[15] Interview with Brett Lucas, Head of Digital Education, 24 May 2021.

measures it was calculated that the Clore lecture theatre, which normally holds 230 people, would only be allowed to admit seventeen.[16]

Some research projects and administrative services could not be halted. Many laboratories, for example, had to remain operational, albeit under very different and difficult circumstances. Fire and water systems still had to be maintained; statutory inspections on lifts and safety equipment continued. The Estates Department experienced raised work levels, while the main Malet Street building had to remain open, albeit to a select number of staff, who were masked and provided with elaborate protocols for handwashing. Sanitizers were liberally distributed.

The basic components of teaching and research were swept away as laboratories, libraries, and archives closed. In the Biology Department, lecturers quickly verified what they already knew; teaching students using pre-existing data was no substitute for hands-on experiments. Face-to-face practicals had to be introduced which, due to social distancing, were incredibly time consuming. In some departments, including the Earth Sciences, ingenious use was made of virtual resources, such as Google Earth. Psychology students abandoned face-to-face interviews for online surveys. 'Study abroad', which was crucial to many disciplines but especially the languages, was abruptly abandoned. Archaeologists cancelled site visits, field studies, and museum trips. Research projects had to be placed on hold. Conferences were abandoned, sometimes at high costs in terms of forfeited flight tickets and hotel bookings. Many were eventually rescheduled as online events. Numerous members of the core staff, such as caterers and cooks, were 'furloughed'.

Changes to the College's environment were equally dramatic. Overnight, Russell Square, Torrington Place, Gower Street, and Gordon Square were deserted. As the months passed, mail began to pile up in the entrance hall to the Malet Street building. Cleaning staff faced the demoralizing task of vacuuming miles of empty corridors. No one would appreciate their efforts, making their labour look pointless. Water in unflushed toilets stagnated. Spiders wove their webs, undisturbed. Mould grew in abandoned coffee cups. Office plants slowly shrivelled up and died.

In lockdown, each week resulted in mounting emotional challenges. After days sitting in online meetings and classes, staff and students were exhausted. Frustration with online technologies sometimes turned into anger. Everyone struggled with anxiety, loneliness, and fear. A lucky minority kept a positive outlook, either through temperament or through good luck: lecturers without heavy teaching and administrative responsibilities, for example, used the externally imposed isolation to concentrate on writing. But most found juggling much

---

[16] Thanks to Daniel Xuereb, Director of Estates.

higher workloads with other responsibilities, including caring for young, elderly, and vulnerable dependants, debilitating.

And, then, there was death and illness, including what came to be called 'long COVID' or chronic illness and distress. At the time of writing this book in late 2021, over 158,000 people were reported on their death certificates as having died of COVID-19—most certainly a significant underestimate.[17] Compared to other universities, it is likely that Birkbeck experienced elevated levels of illness and death compared to the average, since the College has a relatively high proportion of older students with families, as well as students from minoritized communities, all of whom were more vulnerable.[18] How they will be memorialized is as yet unknown.

* * *

The pandemic that swept the globe immediately before Birkbeck's bicentenary year disclosed varying degrees of individual, community, and institutional resilience. People and institutions everywhere reflected on values. *Who* and *what* mattered? Where does real power lie? Which structures could adapt in the turmoil, and which would snap? Many saw the pandemic as an opportunity for change, including wholesale transformation of the economy and society.

For Birkbeck, the pandemic foregrounded the importance of community. Ironically, quarantine, social distancing, and online communications brought people together, forging a renewed recognition of the complex elements that make up a successful academic community. Bonds of solidarity were forged between students, lecturers, administrators, and technical staff. There was increased recognition of the significance of staff such as attendants, cleaners, plumbers, builders, caterers, and security personnel to the life of the institution.

There was also renewed interest in the College's previous experiences of extreme strain, especially those crises of the 1820s, 1939–45, and the 1980s. These were the other times when Birkbeck could have closed its doors permanently. In the 1820s, when the LMI was established, the country was in turmoil. The aftershocks of the French Revolution still troubled British elites; the blood of the Peterloo Massacre stained the squares; pro-democracy chants rent the air, demanding the rights of 'man', including those of citizenship. The most basic premise of the Institution was considered revolutionary: educating working people threatened powerful men and their minions, who rallied against its launch.

Around 120 years later, the Second World War tested the resilience of every member of the College. Rather than decamp to the countryside, Birkbeck

---

[17] UK government, 'Coronavirus (COVID-19) in the UK', at https://coronavirus.data.gov.uk/details/deaths, viewed 30 September 2021.

[18] Birkbeck College, 'Financial Statements for the year ended 31 July 2020', 9.

expanded its activities within London, defying restrictions, blackouts, and bombs. A high cost was paid, but the College survived.

In the 1980s, the assault on Birkbeck and other institutions of Higher Education was not launched by foreign powers but from the seat of British government, pursing market-driven policies of privatization, deregulation, managerialism, and commodification. While not openly disparaging education, as the College's enemies in 1823 had done, the government's swingeing cuts in funding, particularly of part-time university education for working men and women, threatened Birkbeck's survival. Only a campaign by the staff, students, and alumni kept the College afloat. The lessons learnt during the 1820s, world war, and 1980s helped the College survive the COVID-19 crisis as well. They will serve us well into the future.

* * *

The dramatic changes to the College's life imposed by the pandemic were also a reminder that, despite the continued commitment to its original 'mission', Birkbeck has seen many dramatic shifts in the underlying structures and rituals of the academic profession. In 1830, when the LMI first opened its doors to women—a radical proposition in itself—female students wore hats and gloves; they had to be chaperoned to classes. Female lecturers wore gloves when teaching.[19] Demonstrators and lecturers in science labs experienced embarrassing difficulties because the corsets worn by female students distorted magnetic experiments.[20] The College even employed someone to guard the 'belongings' of its female members 'while they were "above stairs"'. In the 1920s and early 1930s, this was a Mrs Ray, a 'wonderful old lady who never failed to remember to whom a hat belonged'. It was said that 'in times of stress induced by ladders in stockings and forgotten umbrellas', Ray could be depended upon to come to the rescue. On her retirement from this 'arduous position' in 1933, Birkbeck's female students presented her with a 'substantial sum' of money as a token of their gratitude.[21] Women like Mrs Ray and 'Ma' Francis (see Chapter 13) were essential personages in the institution, as are the staff who oversee the reception desks inside the College's buildings today.

In the early decades of the College's existence, rooms had to be lit by candles or gas lights, which is why the LMI regularly invested in candlesticks and snuffers.[22] Electrical lighting finally replaced coal gas light in 1898, although the Art School

---

[19] Robert Greaves, 'Penson, Dame Lillian Margery', in H. C. G. Matthew and Brian Harrison (eds), *Oxford Dictionary of National Biography*, vol. 43 (Oxford: Oxford University Press, 2004), 620.

[20] H. G. B., 'A Fire-Watcher's Interview with his Own Memory', *The Lodestone*, 36.3 (summer 1944), 13.

[21] 'D.F.M.S.', 'J.M.S.', and 'J.M.S.', 'Letter to the Editor', *The Lodestone*, 29.1 (Michaelmas 1933), 53.

[22] Committee report for 6 August 1832, reported in 'This Time Last Century', *The Lodestone*, 28.1 (Michaelmas 1932), 15–7.

and the lecture theatre had to wait another year.²³ The Common Room was still dependent for light on a 'hideous brass candelabra' until 1920.²⁴ Whereas today, lecturers illustrate microscopic organisms or list French declensions on 'smart screens' using sleek presentation software, in the past they were scrawled in chalk on blackboards or with markers on whiteboards. Earlier lecturers also displayed text and images on 'lantern slides', until these were dumped for ungainly slide projectors. In 1952, the College proudly purchased its first microfilm reader.²⁵ For scholars performing complex statistical analyses, the use of punched or perforated cards gradually gave way to sophisticated data analysis programmes.²⁶ Similarly, the library's card catalogues (see Fig. 28.1) eventually capitulated to searchable, computerized ones.

In classes, students wrote with chalk, then pencils, then pens, until, finally, they stopped writing altogether, but simply typed lecture notes and experimental results directly into 'laptops'. The physical layout of classrooms has been transformed. Lecture 'theatres' which were semi-circular in shape gradually gave way to lecture 'halls' in which the seats were arranged in straight rows. Rooms with

Fig. 28.1 A member of staff uses the library card catalogue in the building at Gresse Street in the 1970s. Birkbeck Image Collections: Birkbeck History BH0067.

---

²³ *Birkbeck Literary and Scientific Institution. Report. Seventy-Fifth Session, 1897–98* (London: Witherby and Co., 1898), 6.
²⁴ 'Birkbeck College News Sheet', *The Lodestone*, 16.1 (Michaelmas 1920), 36.
²⁵ 'Annual Report of the Librarian for the Session 1952/53', in 'Birkbeck College Guard Book I', in Birkbeck Archive.
²⁶ N. E. Coe, K. J. Hedley, and L. H. Longley-Cook, 'Punched-Card Equipment', *Journal of the Institute of Actuaries*, 74.2 (1948), 247.

distinctive areas set aside for male and female students are now occupied by students with multiple or no sex/gender identity. Face-to-face instruction on uncomfortable benches in the College lecture theatre were replaced by online lectures that could be watched from the comfort of couches at home.

* * *

These shifts pale beside those activated by the internet. Well before the pandemic, digital technologies had transformed the ways knowledge is exchanged and communicated. Birkbeck has a long and extensive tradition of engaging with the media. Four factors have encouraged this practice: the College's location close to numerous central London broadcasting studios, Parliament, and governmental offices; evening teaching, which means that lecturers are free to be interviewed during peak daytime hours; an absence of the smug condescension towards 'mass media' expressed by many university dons in Oxbridge; and an institutional commitment to communicating with wider publics.

Forms of public engagement have greatly expanded in response to twentieth-century developments in new media, opening up an 'invisible college' of different and more diverse publics. This is a 'public good' that early career Birkbeck academics, in particular, have embraced with enthusiasm. The advantages are many: to gain access to these platforms, academics no longer need to court the attention of editors ruling from newspaper offices, let alone those managing major television and radio studios. They can address the 'public' directly. It is a development that has been encouraged by funders as well as auditors of the REF. Today, every grant proposal requires applicants to fill in sections concerning 'public engagement' and 'impact'; very large grants invariably employ a full-time Public Engagement Officer, a new specialism within academia. The importance of the College's relationship to the wider public was recognized when Tricia King, Director of External Relations who has first been appointed in 2004, was made the first non-academic Pro-Vice Master of Strategic Engagement and Recruitment. She recognized that student recruitment, business engagement, alumni relations, fundraising, media, and communication with governmental representatives were all interlinked—like the different segments of an orange, as she had explained during her first interview for the post at Birkbeck.

But perhaps the greatest shift in recent decades lies in the use of digital technologies for teaching and learning. The expansion of the internet led to the introduction of different modes of accessing knowledge and interpersonal communication. As mentioned, this accelerated exponentially during COVID-19 (primarily in the context of classes, which were rarely online prior to 2020) but had been central to the College's activities for decades earlier in the form of the dependency of staff, lecturers, and students on internet searches, email communications, and access to academic ejournals. It is also central to fundamental research. Researchers now routinely read 'primary material' online—for historians, for example, this means access to fully digitized medieval and early modern texts, nineteenth-century newspapers and periodicals, social surveys, and governmental reports. Today, Birkbeck's library provides access not only to 254,000 books and 133 print journals but also to 230,000 ebooks and more than 61,000 ejournals.[27]

With increased attention paid to the multiple ways people transmit, acquire, and create knowledge, learning spaces have dramatically expanded and diversified. Even the 'traditional lecture', with the professor pontificating from a podium at the front of a lecture theatre, has been transformed. The shift from a one-way model in which lecturers provide information which is then regurgitated by students in examinations and other assessment modes have been exchanged for learner-centred practices. Admittedly, the LMI/Birkbeck had long experimented with such ways of teaching. The mid-nineteenth century Birkbeck School (see Chapter 5) was innovative precisely because it shunned rote learning for a more participatory model, as did the LMI more generally during its early decades. Indeed, from its beginnings, 'mutual instruction' was central to the Institution's educational policy. The prospectus for 1839 advertised that classes in 'Chemistry', 'Experimental Philosophy', 'Natural History', and 'Phrenology' were 'conducted on the principle of mutual instruction, by the members delivering Lectures' and attendees being able to consult 'a collection of books which treat upon its particular topics of study'.[28] In 1853, a list of the 'Teachers, Messieurs' for the evening classes shows that four of the twenty-one classes (that is, one fifth) were taught via 'Mutual Instruction'. These were 'Composition, Literary', 'Philosophy, Natural and experimental', 'Musical Practice', and something described vaguely as 'Discussion'.[29] As early as the 1830s, one commentator approvingly observed that the LMI's students flourished because they were 'active searchers' rather than 'passive recipients' of knowledge.[30] But this insight was dropped when Birkbeck became part of the University of London and sought to emulate the teaching practices of other colleges.

A more participatory model was only reintroduced with the integration of the Centre for Extra-Mural Studies into the College, which had long employed a more open model of 'tutors', not 'lecturers', who engaged with students on a more equal basis. New pedagogic philosophies of the late twentieth century also saw the return of the idea that students thrived when they were encouraged to explore their own ideas, evaluate competing pieces of evidence, and discuss their conclusions with their peers as well as lecturers. This participatory model was part of the

---

[27] Email from librarian Emma Illingworth to author, 10 and 12 May 2021.
[28] Leaflet entitled 'London Mechanics' Institution' (London: London Mechanics' Institution, 1839), 2.
[29] Leaflet entitled 'London Mechanics' Institution…The Following Lectures Will Be Delivered During the Present Quarter' (London: London Mechanics' Institution, 1853), 4.
[30] *Phrenological Journal*, 7 (1831–2), 479.

move towards seeing students as producers of knowledge and not simply consumers, a trend that is in opposition to another that we will turn to shortly.

While such shifts in teaching and communicating practices have largely been welcomed by members of the College, there have also been major challenges. Most of these are related to government policies over the last thirty years, which have imposed new governance structures on universities. Most important has been the consequences of the increasingly regulatory framework that all institutions of Higher Education must comply with if they are to receive government funds. As argued in the previous chapter, the British educational system has been moving towards a culture dominated by recurrent auditing of research and teaching, the publication of performance league tables, bureaucratic accreditation of courses, the metricization of knowledge, and the imposition of ill-defined 'frameworks of excellence'. For senior researchers, the abolition of academic tenure was a blow to their sense of employment security and research continuity. Recent changes to the Universities' Superannuation Scheme (USS) which increased employer contributions and reduced pension outcomes for lecturers were also a shock, resulting in widespread strike action and 'working to contract' throughout the country, including at Birkbeck. The casualization of the labour of early career scholars represented an attack of more momentous proportions. Demoralization set in. And students as well as staff responded angrily. The exponential rise of fees (to £9,000 a year in 2012) created a private fee structure within what were meant to be public universities. Faced with rising levels of debt and shrinking labour markets, students refashioned themselves as consumers with an automatic right to a 'good' degree. There was dismay all round.

Lecturers and students were not the only ones feeling besieged. So too were some of Birkbeck's most essential workers: that is, cleaners, night security, and catering staff. As elsewhere in the University of London, these essential workers had been 'outsourced' to private companies, dragging down their wages and excluding them from basic employment rights. Between 2018 and 2021, Birkbeck workers, staff, students, and UNISON officers organized a 'Justice for Workers' campaign, fighting to have its cleaners, night security, and catering staff directly employed by Birkbeck. The campaigners were victorious, effectively improving conditions of labour in terms of pensions, job protection (such as access to Birkbeck's grievance and disciplinary procedures), and study assistance.

Finally, these challenges took place in the context of two external political events that sent shockwaves through the College. The first was the need to respond to the threat of terrorism on UK soil. On 7 July 2005 (known as 7/7), four suicide attacks were carried out against commuters on the London Underground and a double-decker bus in Tavistock Square, adjacent to the College. Over 700 people were wounded and fifty-four were killed, including citizens from eighteen countries. One of the dead was 30-year-old Benedetta Ciaccia, who was doing a Foundation Degree in Computer Science at Birkbeck. Another student—Jeff

Porter—was later hailed as a hero. Porter was doing an MA in Contemporary History and Politics at Birkbeck and went on to complete a PhD on post-war Germany. He had left school at 16 years old and worked in an engineering factory until deindustrialization led him to take a job on the London Underground as a ticket collector, guard, and train driver, while serving as a councillor in Dagenham's Goresbrook ward and studying in the evenings.[31] On 7/7, he was driving his underground train on the Circle Line when one of the bombs exploded close by. Porter made a mayday call, attempted to calm the passengers, and helped evacuate hundreds to safety. Meanwhile, on the surface, police and paramedics in Tavistock Square were tending to the dead and wounded there. People with no obvious injuries were directed to Birkbeck, where staff attempted to provide consolation.

The bombs radically changed life for British Muslims throughout the UK, including in the College. Although community leaders rapidly condemned the attacks, they were anxious. On the first anniversary of the bombings, a Populus Survey found that four out of five British Muslims felt that the rest of society had become increasingly hostile towards their values and presence.[32] They had good reason: there was a sharp rise in faith hate crimes[33] and the Blair government introduced a draconian Terrorism Act.[34] Successive government legislation had a long-term impact on Muslim students, largely because the government identified universities as one of the key sites for the radicalization of young men. Under the Conservative government's Counter-Terrorism and Security Act of 2015, all institutions of Higher Education were instructed that they must have 'due regard to the need to prevent people from being drawn into terrorism'. The law was predicated on a rejection of multiculturalism. Although not targeting Muslim students explicitly, this 'Prevent duty' has had a major impact on them and other minoritized students. They were increasingly subjected to surveillance by staff and, if various changes in their behaviour (for example, observing daily prayers), appearance (growing a beard), or views (support of Palestine) changed in ways deemed 'suspect', reported to the police of the Channel Programme.[35]

---

[31] 'Students Tell of Lives Transformed by Part-Time Study', at https://www.bbk.ac.uk/news/students-share-stories-of-lives-transformed-by-part-time-study-as-they-support-national-campaign, viewed 1 September 2021.

[32] Reported in '13 Percent of UK Muslims Believe July 7 Bombers are "Martyrs"', *Daily Mail* (4 July 2006).

[33] European Monitoring Centre on Racism and Xenophobia, 'The Impact of 7 July 2005 London Bomb Attacks on Muslim Communities in the EU' (November 2005), 5, at https://fra.europa.eu/sites/default/files/fra_uploads/197-london-bomb-attacks_en.pdf, viewed 1 September 2021.

[34] For a discussion, see Javaid Rehman, 'Islam, "War on Terror" and the Future of Muslim Minorities in the United Kingdom: Dilemmas of Multiculturalism in the Aftermath of the London Bombings', *Human Rights Quarterly*, 29.4 (November 2007), 831–78.

[35] See Mark McGovern, 'The University, Prevent, and Cultures of Compliance', *Prometheus*, 34.1 (March 2016), 49–62, and A. Kundnani, *Spooked! How Not to Prevent Violent Terrorism* (London: Institute of Race Relations, 2015).

Birkbeck attempted to adopt a less draconian approach by complying with the 'Prevent duty' in tandem with its Freedom of Speech, Safeguarding, Health and Safety, and Dignity at Work and Study policies and procedures. In 2019–20, only one incident was reported to the SO15 counter-terrorism police. It involved an online research seminar conducted on the Collaborate platform, which was hacked by people unknown who shouted and posted links to terrorist videos on the dark web platform 'Discord'. None of the legitimate participants opened the links,[36] but it was an example of the way terrorism and fear of terrorism have had an impact on life within universities.

The second shock was the June 2016 referendum on 'remaining' or 'leaving' the European Union. It produced a surprise result. Throughout the country, 52 per cent of the population voted 'leave'; 48 per cent, 'remain'. In the borough where Birkbeck is located, the result was 25 per cent 'leave' and 75 per cent 'remain'. The effect of the vote on the College was immediate. In 2017–18, the College recruited nearly 400 fewer students from the EU than it had done the previous year.[37] Post-Brexit uncertainty over residency and employment rights of EU people already living in London led to a sharp decline in enrolments from this group as well.[38] Overall, between 2016 and 2019, there was a 30 per cent decline in EU enrolments.[39] It was a crisis that threatened not only Birkbeck students but also the livelihoods of (continental) European citizens who were employed by the College. Their future rights in the UK were no longer assured.

* * *

In other areas of College life, however, growth was the catchphrase. For 200 years, the College's locations in central London meant that it never managed to secure adequate laboratories, classrooms, common rooms, or office accommodation. As early as the mid-1930s, more than half of all students were being taught outside the main premises.[40] Even when the much-anticipated Malet Street building opened in the early 1950s, it was already too small for the needs of students and lecturers. In 2019, around half of classes were taught in rooms that had been rented from other colleges (primarily UCL and Westminster Kingsway College) and institutions (such as the Friends House and British Medical Association). It has been a constant source of complaint by students.[41]

Solving this problem was a priority for David Latchman, for whom the bicentenary year will mark his twentieth year in office (see Fig. 28.2). A first step involved acquiring Cambridge House on Euston Road. This renovated 1920s building added 440 square metres of teaching space to the College and

---

[36] Birkbeck, University of London, 'Meetings of the Governors. 26 November 2020', Appendix B.
[37] Birkbeck College, 'Financial Statements for the year ended 31 July 2020', 11.   [38] Ibid., 11.
[39] Ibid., 12.   [40] 'A Worthy Home for Birkbeck', *The Times* (8 November 1935), 11.
[41] Jeremy Tanner, 'Student Experience Review Update and Start of Session Report', Estates Committee (23 October 2018).

Fig. 28.2 Professor David Latchman during the graduations, 2003. Birkbeck Image Collections: Birkbeck History OBC0022.

accommodated 600 students and staff.[42] The greatest coup, however, came in 2021 when Latchman, Sir Andrew Cahn (Chair of the Governors), Keith Harrison (College Secretary), and Matt Innes led a bid to purchase the large premises next door to Birkbeck's Malet Street campus. This seven-floor building, which is contiguous to Birkbeck's main Malet Street premises and was built at around the same time, so is of similar appearance, had been part of Student Central, the federal University of London's building for student events and leisure facilities. For years, however, students had been deserting Student Central—it was a long distance from many colleges and even students in premises nearby preferred using facilities on their own campuses. The acquisition of Student Central by Birkbeck increased the College's space by around 25 per cent. Crucially, it also helped to fulfil William Beveridge's original vision in 1927 when he purchased the site, stretching from Montague Place to Byng Place, for £525,000 as part of his plans for a more centralised University of London. As Innes explains, Beveridge's

> initial plans were for a single complex encompassing the entire site, with a series of wings and courtyards emanating from a central spine, a perimeter facade and two towers, with the current Senate House landmark echoed by a slightly smaller structure at the northern end of current Torrington Square.[43]

[42] Birkbeck, University of London, 'Financial Statements for the year ended 31 July 2019', 12, at https://www.bbk.ac.uk/downloads/finance/financial-statements-2019.pdf, viewed 1 August 2021.
[43] Matt Innes, 'A New Era for Birkbeck's Bloomsbury Campus', at http://blogs.bbk.ac.uk/bbkcomments/2021/07/26/a-new-era-for-birkbecks-bloomsbury-campus/, viewed 1 August 2021.

However, Beveridge's vision was progressively whittled down, with the more Oxbridge-like wings and courtyards cut. Birkbeck's purchase of Student Central in 2021 will change the College's environment in ways that even the promoters of Malet Street in the early 1950s could not have imagined, let alone the College's original founders. It effectively creates an integrated campus running along Torrington Square, bounded on the other side by the Clore building, Toddlerlab, and Babylab. It is a triumphant start to the College's next 200 years as a university with a unique mission to provide part-time Higher Education to working people in the evening.

* * *

Birkbeck, University of London, enters its 200th year with a confident stride, although trials will still lie ahead. In its two-century history, the LMI/Birkbeck has viewed itself as performing transformative work. Latchman is one of the keenest promoters of the College's distinctive mission. Members of the College have retained a passionate commitment to its foundational values, specifically the provision of the highest level of Higher Education to working people on a part-time basis in the evening. As with any dynamic institution, however, diversity of provision is important. Today, although the majority of students study part time, in terms of 'full-time equivalents' (FTE), 45 per cent study full time versus 55 per cent part time. However, most subjects continue to be taught in the evening, even for full-time students. The radical vision of George Birkbeck, Joseph Clinton Robertson, Thomas Hodgskin, Francis Place, and Henry Brougham to provide a place of learning for working men and women continues to make Birkbeck distinctive. Even the increase in fees and a pandemic have not dented the students' loyalty to and support of the College.

Today, as in the past, the College has benefited from the fact that the vast majority of its students bring with them the skills and knowledge developed at their employment. At the LMI, this included the knowledge and skills of engineers, clerks, printers, scientific instrument makers, cabinetmakers, teachers, and drawing and singing instructors. Today, they include, among others, those of educators, politicians, civil servants, homemakers, journalists, taxi drivers, designers, musicians, health professionals, and lab technicians. One of the central functions of the modern university is to prepare people like these for fulfilling working lives and careers. Although instrumentalist approaches to Higher Education fail to capture its full worth, it is nevertheless true that university learning is often a way for economies to grow and for individuals to improve their material, physical, and psychological well-being. Universities enable people to develop skills that will result in increased individual productivity, improved industrial innovation, and economic growth. A neoliberal version of this function maintains that students are responsible for their own employability, showcasing their ability to negotiate market competitiveness by making astute consumer choices. Such ways

> Privy Council,
> Whitehall, S.W.1.
> October 31st 1935.
>
> My dear Lord Mayor,
>
> It is a very great regret to me that I am unable to be present with you this afternoon on so auspicious and important an occasion in the history of Birkbeck College.
>
> Upwards of half a century has passed since I joined the College as a student, and it is nearly forty years on from the date of my appointment as a Governor. During that time Education has travelled a long and arduous journey and the road has been over steep and stony places, but Birkbeck has ever been in the van.
>
> I hear with satisfaction of its twelve hundred men and women who are pursuing in the evenings University studies of a standard as advanced as that of any more favoured Institution which opens its doors in the day-time. I have observed with the greatest admiration that two hundred of these students are engaged in post-graduate research charged in many instances with potential possibilities of the highest importance to our industrial centres, and it is encouraging to know that this branch of the work of the College is to be developed.
>
> I would urge upon all those whose sympathy is evoked by the spectacle of difficulties faced and conquered to aid to the utmost limit of their capacity the appeal with which Their Royal Highnesses The Duke and Duchess of York have so graciously allowed their names to be associated.
>
> Yours very truly,
>
> Ramsay MacDonald

Fig. 28.3 Letter from Ramsay MacDonald in 1935. From 1886–7, he studied science, botany, agriculture, mathematics, and physics at Birkbeck. He later became the British Prime Minister in the 1920s and 1930s and the first Labour Prime Minister. Birkbeck Image Collections: Birkbeck History BH0227.

of thinking about Higher Education emphasize the fact that technological changes, along with geopolitical and demographic developments, are creating entirely new types of jobs and occupations—all of which require different skills and knowledge. As the World Economic Forum (WEF) maintains, workers need to be engaged in constant processes of retraining and reskilling: individuals must 'take a proactive approach to their own lifelong learning' and governments have to be prepared to 'create the enabling environment, rapidly and creatively, to assist these efforts'.[44]

In the case of Birkbeck, the generic benefits conferred by all forms of high-quality university education are augmented by *specific* 'goods' related to the *type* of education offered at the College. The demand for people with new and renewed skills as they go through life has been widely acknowledged. This was the point made by former student and Prime Minister J. Ramsay MacDonald (see Fig. 28.3). He contended that people who found themselves 'walled in by the limits of their

---

[44] World Economic Forum, *The Future of Jobs* (Geneva: WEF, 2016), v and 8, at http://www3.weforum.org/docs/WEF_Future_of_Jobs.pdf, viewed 20 July 2021. Also see CBI and Birkbeck, *Skills for an Inclusive Economy: CBI/Birkbeck Education and Skills Survey 2021* (London: CBI/Birkbeck, 2021); Joop Schippers, 'On the Need for Universities to Engage in Lifelong Learning', in Armand Heijnen and Rob van der Vaart (eds), *Places of Engagement: Reflections on Higher Education in 2040—A Global Approach* (Amsterdam: Amsterdam University Press, 2018); Barbara Baarsma, 'Don't Be Scared; Be Prepared', in Heijnen and van der Vaart (eds), *Places of Engagement*; Simeon Djankov and Federica Saliola, 'The Changing Nature of Work', *Journal of International Affairs*, 72.1 (fall 2018/winter 2019).

own occupations' could use the College to 'adventure into the wide fields of Learning and Opportunity'.[45] The Master, Ronald C. Tress, echoed these sentiments in 1973. He reminded university students that 'If we are not to have out-of-date people as well as out-of-date machines, there must be re-training as well as training, re-education as well as education.' This was essential if everyone is to achieve a 'life-long participation in a democratic society'. Tress warned students that 'in our age the price of liberty is still eternal vigilance', adding that, nevertheless, 'watchfulness is not enough—we need a knowing eye'.[46] The same could be said for us today.

However, Birkbeck has always insisted that Higher Education is a process, not a product. Of course, students learn knowledge and skills that will be used professionally and productively: the convergence of education with the reproductive needs of society is therefore important. But just as work is not the whole of life, so professional knowledge does not exhaust the task of learning. The College has always contended that knowledge is intrinsically as well as instrumentally worthwhile, seeing its mission as transforming its members and students throughout their lives. In this way, the College understands that Higher Education does not set out to teach people simply to 'contribute' to the economy, but to learn to think, judge and develop a deeper understanding of themselves and the world. In short, the LMI/Birkbeck is a transformative university. In an era of fake news, rising authoritarianism, and global financial, environmental, and health crises, the need for the kinds of critical thinking that comes from Higher Education are more imperative than ever. It was a fact that H. G. Wells was referring to when he quipped that 'human history becomes more and more a race between education and catastrophe'.[47] Birkbeck offers that education.

The ways the LMI/Birkbeck has sought to transform the lives of its members and students have changed over its 200-year history. This is hardly surprising since the vitality of any institution depends on its responsiveness to the times, or its ability to be reimagined, reformed, and modified. When the LMI was first established, transformative education was about participatory democracy, civil rights, and Benthamite utilitarianism, in which knowledge was the road to rational, practical happiness for the greatest number. Today, transformative education is more likely to be seen as enabling people to critically understand their chosen cognitive or disciplinary field, pursue fulfilling careers, and contribute to the life of their communities both locally and globally. In this way, the university offers alternative ways of living full and good lives.

---

[45] 'The Court of Electors', *The Lodestone*, 20.3 (1924), 149.
[46] 'Students Must Keep "Re-Tooling"', London Educator Says', *Freemantle and Richmond S. Gazette* (25 April 1973), in 'Newscuttings 1971–73', in the Birkbeck Archive.
[47] H. G. Wells, *The Outline of History: Being a Plain History of Life and Mankind*, vol. 2 (New York: The Macmillan Company, 1920), 588, at https://www.gutenberg.org/files/45368/45368-h/45368-h.htm, viewed 1 August 2021.

In order to succeed in these goals, the College is committed to removing the personal, institutional, structural, economic, and ideological barriers that threaten to restrict the lives of its students, staff, and lecturers. The College has always stood against the cynical adage, 'If at first you don't succeed...you don't succeed.' Central to Birkbeck's ethos is the conviction that the world can be improved by the pursuit of truths, the application of thought, the commitment to knowledge, and hard work. In these ways, Birkbeck's students, lecturers, and staff assume responsibility for the world.

This book has explored some of the ways that, as a transformative university, the LMI/Birkbeck has harnessed the emotions of its members. In its foundational years, these could be animated—the enthusiasm of George Birkbeck and Francis Place, for example. They include the excitable hopes of young women seeking to expand their horizons, and older men and women keen to abandon dreary occupations for new spheres of labour and fulfilment.

Despite the rivalry inherent in much pathbreaking scholarship, lecturers at Birkbeck have attested to the presence of that elusive but recognizable concept of collegiality. In this, Birkbeck's relatively small size, its commitment to a unique mission, its distinctive student population who command respect, and an historical tradition of cooperation have meant that it has limited patience for infighting. It is worth recalling that the original LMI was nearly destroyed by the bitter jealousy of Robertson in the 1820s and 1830s.

The LMI/Birkbeck has also benefited from its foundational covenant: that of making knowledge accessible to people whose needs have been traditionally overlooked, even denied. Its initial focus was 'mechanics', or working men. Although governments in the late twentieth and twenty-first centuries have sometimes also believed that university education bred discontented citizens, it is difficult to grasp the vehemence with which some British elites from the 1820s to the late part of the nineteenth century argued against educating the 'lower orders'. Not only did they believe that working people were incapable of the sustained intellectual thought integral to Higher Education, but, perhaps more importantly, they believed that it was socially, politically, and economically threatening to the power of privileged people. Founding members of the LMI believed that education was an empowering force—which working people could use to further their own political ends. For many, this meant applying their new-found knowledge and skills to making modest modifications to their societies or to opening up opportunities based on merit rather than birth right; for others, it spurred efforts to make radical changes to inequitable social worlds.

Class privilege was not the only bastion that the LMI/Birkbeck sought to topple. So, too, was the stranglehold of established religion. From its conception, the LMI was resolutely non-sectarian. Unlike Cambridge and Oxford which, until 1871, required students to adhere to the Thirty-Nine Articles of the Church of

England as a condition of enrolment, the LMI/Birkbeck never attempted to dictate religious belief. Its founders were Quakers, nonconformists, Jews, and atheists, as well as members of the established Church. This has continued to this day, while also including a sizeable minority of Muslims, Hindus, Buddhists, Sikhs, and people from numerous other religious communities. This inclusive approach was neatly summarized by Armitage-Smith, the Master when Birkbeck's bid to become part of the University of London meant attacking King's College, whose student body was dominated by its 400 male Anglican ordinands. Birkbeck, he contended, had 'always been a people's college, democratic in the truest sense of the term'.[48]

Gender has been another unique component of the LMI/Birkbeck's history. As early as 1830, the Institution welcomed women as students, lecturers, and staff. This tradition has meant that the College has been an important force in contributing to movements to improve the position of women in the community. Admittedly, this tradition is frequently breached in practice—there is still a gender-based wage gap in the College, for example—but the College's commitment to equality for all genders (binary and non-binary) is resolute.

There are other disadvantaged groups within the Birkbeck community. For example, a large proportion of the College's students come from very deprived communities. Over 60 per cent of undergraduates come the lowest two quintiles of the Index of Multiple Deprivation (IMD).[49] These students succeed in entering graduate employment at the same rates as students from more advantaged backgrounds.[50] Birkbeck also admits onto its programmes a large proportion of people with disabilities. In 2016, 23 per cent of full-time students disclosed a disability compared with 13 per cent in the sector as a whole. Unlike in the overall Higher Education sector, they have even better continuation rates and a greater proportion achieve a good degree than their non-disabled counterparts, evidence of the higher levels of support they receive at Birkbeck.[51]

Under Latchman, the 'politics of presence' has moved to the forefront of the College's agenda, including an acknowledgement that there is still a great deal of work to do to improve racial and ethnic inclusion. Today, while 40 per cent of London's population are from Black and minority ethnic (BME) communities, 56 per cent of the College's full-time students and 42 per cent of its part-time students are BME.[52] However, racism continues to have a detrimental impact on levels of degree attainment. There are very few Black professors and senior

---

[48] Evidence by G. Armitage-Smith to the *Royal Commission on University Education in London. Appendix to Third Report of the Commissioners. Minutes of Evidence, November 1910–July 1911; with Appendices and Index* [Cd. 5911] (London: His Majesty's Stationery Office, 1911), 244.
[49] 'Birkbeck, University of London. Access and Participation Plan 2020–21 to 2024–25' (London: Birkbeck, 2021), 2.
[50] Ibid., 3.   [51] Ibid., 7–8.   [52] Ibid., 3.

managers, so BME students lack role models. Recently, the problem has been tackled by the establishment of a Decolonizing the Curriculum Working Group, committed to tackling the damaging legacies that have arisen from colonial encounters.[53]

Finally, Birkbeck has always been welcoming of refugees and asylum seekers. This was most evident around the times of the two world wars of the twentieth century, when the College supported refugees from continental Europe. In 2016, the College created the Compass Project to support asylum seekers, mainly from Syria, Iran, and the Democratic Republic of Congo. In 2017, the College explained that

> Asylum seekers often arrive in the UK without documentation, limiting their ability to find work or to enrol in courses of study. Unlike those classified as refugees, their immigration status means that they are treated as international students, with fees set at the higher international rate and with no access to loan support.[54]

The programme offered asylum seekers not only free workshops and events but also funds for undergraduate and postgraduate courses in the College.

In other areas, however, today's Birkbeck is significantly different from the one founded in 1823. Most notably, the original principles of the LMI did not emphasize academic *research*. This was typical of universities throughout the UK in the nineteenth century. Unlike their continental counterparts, the established British universities were primarily teaching institutions, rather than hubs for rigorous research. This only started changing from the early twentieth century, at Birkbeck, as well as other universities. Today, however, research and research-led teaching are the foundations upon which Birkbeck's claim to excellence rests. The College's administrators as well as all of its members are dedicated to ensuring that the College retains these commitments. It is worth reminding ourselves, therefore, that the value of Birkbeck as a repository of knowledge, and a space within which that knowledge can be relentlessly assessed, contested, and refreshed, was propelled by the College's *students*, as much as by its staff and lecturers. The incredible energy that went into late-nineteenth-century campaigns to transform the LMI into a full member of the University of London was driven by student ambition. It was the students who decided that the Birkbeck Scientific and Literary Institution would flourish only if it became Birkbeck, University of London. This is why students are at the heart of the College. Armitage Smith maintained that the fact that Birkbeck students were employed during the daylight hours meant

---

[53] Ibid., 21.
[54] Birkbeck College, 'Financial Statements for the year ended 31 July 2017', 27, at https://www.bbk.ac.uk/downloads/finance/financial-statements-2017.pdf, viewed 1 June 2021.

that they possessed 'more stamina and greater capability of work' than other students. Indeed, he bragged, Birkbeck students were nothing less than 'the *élite* of the day worker; they represent not the average nor the many, but are the chosen few'.[55]

This is why the chief reason for the transformative impact of Birkbeck has been the aspirations, needs, and desires of all its members. We have encountered many of them in this book. Most have been students and staff, but we have also met caterers, cooks, attendants, groundsmen, and inspectors of animal cages. Credit for the success of the College over 200 years must be given to Birkbeckians who have promoted intellectual curiosity and the cultivation of independent thinking. They have ensured that our premises provide forums for open debate where the public good can be served. Birkbeckians have taken care to produce, transform, enact, store, and disseminate knowledge in ways that are critical, ethical, politically aware, and responsive to the challenges of civil society. In order to do this, Birkbeck has provided spaces for thinking, testing hypotheses, and communicating truths—while always acknowledging that those 'truths' are partial and contested, waiting to be tweaked, sharpened, or spurned by future generations of scholars and students. As a result, the College celebrates its 200 years of history, and looks forward to a future that takes pride in being an engaged community, committed to understanding and transforming complex worlds through the sciences, social sciences, arts, and humanities. By creating free-thinking, independent, and culturally aware citizens of the globe, Birkbeck provides a basis for exploring the irreducible plurality of the human condition. This is the role that Birkbeck pursues as it moves into its third century of service to its members, students, communities, nation, and world.

---

[55] Evidence by G. Armitage-Smith to the *Royal Commission on University Education in London. Appendix to Third Report of the Commissioners. Minutes of Evidence, November 1910–July 1911; with Appendices and Index* [Cd. 5911], 245.

Bibliography

People curious to hear more about the history of the London Mechanics' Institution and Birkbeck can find articles, images, blogs, interviews, bibliography, and documents through Birkbeck's 200th Anniversary website. Please visit us.

1. Archives and Collections

Bernal, J. D., Papers, Cambridge University Library
Bohm, David, Papers (Birkbeck)
Birkbeck Archive
Birkbeck College, Annual Reports
Birkbeck College, Departmental Papers
Birkbeck College, Financial Statements
Birkbeck College, Prospectuses
Birkbeck College, Student Handbooks
Bishopsgate Library
British Library
Crick, Bernard, Papers (Birkbeck)
Hobhouse, John, papers, British Library
Howell Collection, Bishopsgate
Liberty (formerly National Council for Civil Liberties) Archive
London Mechanics' Institution leaflets
London Metropolitan Archives
The National Archives, UK
Pathé Archives
Place, Francis, Papers, British Library
Slater, Michael, Private Papers and Annual Reports
University of London Animal Welfare Society, Papers
West Stow Anglo-Saxon Village Museum

2. Newspapers and Periodicals

Aberdeen Evening Express
Aberdeen Press and Journal
The Academy
Acton Gazette
Animal Year-Books
Arbroath Herald and Advertiser for the Montrose Burghs
The Athenæum: Journal of Literature, Science, and the Fine Arts
Australian Psychologist
Banbury Guardian

Bath Chronicle and Weekly Gazette
Belfast News-Letter
Bell's Life in London and Sporting Chronicle
Bell's Weekly Messenger
Birkbeck's Institution Magazine
Birmingham Daily Gazette
Birmingham Daily Post
Birmingham Post
Blackwood's Edinburgh Magazine
British Evening Post
British Medical Journal
British Parliamentary Papers
British Science News
British Women's Temperance Magazine
Building Societies' Gazette and Companies Record
Burlington Magazine for Connoisseurs
Camden Journal
Cardiff Times
Century Guild Hobby Horse
Chambers's Papers for the People
Chester Chronicle
City Press
Court of Electors Newsletter
Coventry Standard
Daily Chronicle
Daily Gazette for Middlesbrough
Daily Herald
Daily Mail
Daily News
Daily Sketch
Daily Telegram
Daily Telegraph
Daily Worker
Dublin Evening Telegraph
Dumbarton Oak Papers
Dundee Evening Telegraph
East and South Devon Advertiser
Edinburgh Review
English Gentleman
The Examiner
Exmouth Journal
Express Wolverhampton
Faringdon Advertiser and Vale of the White Horse
Financial Times
Fraser's Magazine for Town and Country
Freemantle and Richmond S. Gazette
Friendly Companion and Illustrator Instructor
The Gasper: The Unofficial Organ of the 18th, 19th, 20th, and 21st Royal Fusiliers
Glasgow Evening Post
The Globe

BIBLIOGRAPHY 597

Gloucester Citizen
Grantham Journal
The Graphic
The Guardian
Hampstead and Highgate Express
Hansard
Hendon Times
Holborn Guardian
Household Words
Howitt's Journal of Literature and Popular Progress
Huddersfield Chronicle
Hull Daily Mail
The Humanist
Illustrated London News
Illustrated Sporting and Dramatic News
Imago Mundi
Imperial Magazine; or, Compendium of Religious, Moral, and Philosophical Knowledge
The Independent
Jamaica Observer
John Bull
Journal of the Royal Society of Arts
Journal of the Society of Arts
Justice
Kensington Post
Lady's Newspaper
Labour Leader
Lamp and Owl
Lancashire Evening Post
The Lancet
Leeds Times
Leigh Chronicle and Weekly District Advertiser
The Listener
Literary Chronicle and Weekly Review
Literary Gazette: A Weekly Journal of Literature, Science, and the Fine Arts
Liverpool Daily Post
Liverpool Mercury
Lloyd's Weekly Newspaper
The Lodestone
London Courier and Evening Gazette
London Evening Standard
London Mechanics' Register
London Review of Books
London Saturday Journal
Manchester Courier and Lancashire General Advertiser
Manchester Times
Mechanics' Magazine, Museum, Register, Journal, and Gazette
Middlesex and Surrey Express
Morning Adviser
Morning Post
Morning Star

Nature
Newcastle Courant
New Jamaican
New Scientist
New Society
New York Review of Books
New York Times
News of the World
News Review
Nottingham Evening Post
Nottingham Journal
Nottinghamshire Guardian
The Observer
Off the Beat
Penny Satirist
People's Magazine
Percival's Annual Guide to the Principal Exhibitions of London
Phrenological Journal
Preston Herald
Punch, or the London Charivari
Quarterly Review
Reading Mercury
The Republican
Resurrection: The Bulletin of the Computer Conservation Society
Reveille
Reynold's Newspaper
Saint James' Chronicle
The Satirist; or, The Censor of the Times
Saturday Review
Science
Science News
The Scotsman
Sennett
Sheffield Daily Telegraph
Sheffield Independent
Shield's Daily News
Shoreditch Observer
South London Press
South Wales Echo
The Spectator
Spectrum: Birkbeck College Student Magazine
The Sphere
Staffordshire Advertiser
The Standard
The Stage
The Star
Stroud News and Gloucestershire Advertiser
The Studio
The Sun
Sunday Evening Post

Sunday Mirror
Sunday Times
Telegraph and Argus
Tenbury Wells Advertiser
Theatrical Journal
The Times
Times Higher Education Supplement
Today
Torbay Express and South Devon Echo
Totnes Weekly Times
Tower Hamlet's Independent and Easy End Local Advertiser
Trends in Biochemical Sciences
Tribune
Weekend
Wells Journal
West Middlesex Gazette
Western Courier
Western Daily Mercury
Windsor Magazine: An Illustrated Monthly for Men and Women
Woman
Woman's Signal
Women's Herald
Women's Review of Books
Worchester Journal
Working Man's Friend
Yorkshire Gazette
Yorkshire Post and Leeds Intelligencer

3. Oral and Email Interviews

Alexander, Sally
Bale, Anthony
Berlin, Mike
Clarke, Richard
Crinson, Mark
Douzinas, Costas
Dovzhyk, Sasha
Evans, Richard
Feldman, David
Floud, Roderick
Frosh, Steven
Harrison, Keith
Hiley, Basil
Illingworth, Emma
Innes, Matt
Johnson, Roger
Latchman, David
Lucas, Brett
McDowell, Almuth

McFayden, Lesley
Mason, Emma
Phillips, Tim
Reynolds, Tim
Rich, David
Slater, Michael
Smith, Ron
Topolovec, Evana
Vaughan, William
Xuereb, Daniel
Zubaida, Sami

4. Books and Articles

Abrams, Dominic, Hannah Swift, and Diane Houston, *Developing a National Barometer of Prejudice and Discrimination in Britain* (London: Equality and Human Rights Commission, October 2018).
Address Delivered by The Right Honourable Lord Mersey, 9th December, 1914 (London: Birkbeck College, 1914).
Allen, Grant, *The Woman Who Did* (London: John Lane, 1895).
Alvesson, Mats and Kaj Sköldberg, *Reflexive Methodology: New Vistas for Qualitative Research*, 2nd ed. (London: Sage, 2009).
Amariglio, Jack, Stephen Resnick, and Richard Wolff, 'Division and Difference in the "Discipline" of Economics', *Critical Inquiry*, 17.1 (autumn 1990).
Anderson, Perry, *English Questions*, 1st pub. 1968 (London: Verso, 1992).
'Appeal from the Greek Committee to the British Public in General, and Especially to the Friends of Religion' (London: Greek Committee, 1823).
Arestis, Philip and Malcolm C. Sawyer (eds), *A Biographical Dictionary of Dissenting Economists* (Cheltenham: E. Elgar, 2000).
Armitage-Smith, George, *Inaugural Address by the Principal G. Armitage-Smith on the Opening of the Seventy-Ninth Session. Monday, 30th September 1901* (London: Birkbeck, 1901).
Attar, Karen (ed.), *Directory of Rare Book and Special Collections in the UK and Republic of Ireland* (London: Facet Publishing, 2016).
Aveling, Edward and Eleanor Marx Aveling, *The Woman Question* (London: Swan Sonnenschein, 1886), 6.
BAAL, 'Notes on the History of the British Association for Applied Linguistics, 1967–2017' (Leeds: BAAL, 2017).
Baarsma, Barbara, 'Don't Be Scared; Be Prepared', in Armand Heijnen and Rob van der Vaart (eds), *Places of Engagement: Reflections on Higher Education in 2040—A Global Approach* (Amsterdam: Amsterdam University Press, 2018).
Back, Les and Avtar Brah, 'Activism, Imagination, and Writing: Avtar Brah Reflects on Her Life and Work with Les Back', *Feminist Review*, 100 (2012).
Baldwin, Melinda, '"Where are Your Intelligent Mothers to Come From?": Marriage and Family in the Scientific Career of Dame Kathleen Lonsdale FRS (1903–71)', *Notes and Records of the Royal Society of London*, 63.1 (20 March 2009).
Balfour, Clara Lucas, *Working Women of the Last Half Century: The Lessons of Their Lives* (London: W & F. G. Cash, 1854).
Bamford, Samuel, *Passages in the Life of a Radical*, 1st pub. 1839–41 (Oxford: 1984).

Barrell, John (ed.), *Painting and the Politics of Culture* (Cambridge: Cambridge University Press, 1992).
Beaver, S. H., 'Geography in the British Association for the Advancement of Science', *Geographical Journal*, 148.2 (July 1982).
Becker, Bernard H., *Scientific London* (London: Henry S. King and Co., 1874).
Becker, Tony, *Academic Tribes and Territories: Intellectual Enquiry and the Cultures of Disciplines* (Milton Keynes: Open University Press, 1989).
'Benjamin Robert Haydon (1786-1846)', *Burlington Magazine for Connoisseurs*, 88.519 (June 1946).
Bernal, J. D., 'Art and the Scientist', in J. L. Martin, Ben Nicholson, and N. Gabo (eds), *Circle: International Survey of Constructive Art* (London: Faber and Faber Ltd, 1937).
Bernal, J. D., 'The Biological Controversy in the Soviet Union and Its Implications', *Modern Quarterly*, 4 (1949).
Bernal, J. D., *The Freedom of Necessity* (London: Routledge and Kegan Paul, 1949).
Bernal, J. D., 'The Frustration of Science', in Bernal, *The Frustration of Science* (London: George Allen and Unwin, 1935).
Bernal, J. D., *Need There be Need?* (London: Science for Peace Pamphlets, 1963).
Bernal, J. D., 'The Social Function of Science', *Modern Quarterly*, 1 (1938).
Bernal, J. D., *The Social Function of Science* (London: George Routledge and Sons Ltd, 1939).
Bernal, J. D., *The World, the Flesh, and the Devil* (Bloomington: Indiana University Press, 1929).
Besant, Annie, *The Gospel of Atheism: A Lecture* (London: Freethought Publishing Co., 1877).
Bingham, N. H., 'Obituary. Philip Holgate (1934-1993)', *Bulletin of the London Mathematics Society*, 32 (2000).
The Birkbeck Building and Freehold Land Societies Simplified and Explained in a Conversation between a Manager and a Person Desirous of Becoming a Member (London: London Mechanics' Institution, 1855).
Birkbeck College, 1823-1913. Reception at Grafton Galleries, Grafton Way, W., 27th October, 1913, in Celebration of the Ninetieth Anniversary of the College (London: Birkbeck College, 1913).
Birkbeck College (University of London) Centenary 1823-1923. Verse Book. Being an Anthology Compiled from Poems which have Appeared in the Pages of the 'Lodestone', the Magazine of the Students' Union (London: Birkbeck College, 1923).
'Birkbeck Literary and Scientific Institution' (London: BLSI, 1896), 2.
'Birkbeck, University of London. Access and Participation Plan 2020-21 to 2024-25', London: Birkbeck, 2021).
Birkbeck, University of London, *Gender Pay Audit 2020* (London: Birkbeck, University of London, 2020).
Blackett, P. M. S., 'The Frustration of Science', in Frederick Soddy et al., *The Frustration of Science* (London: Allen and Unwin, 1935).
Blyth, Edmund Kell, *Life of William Ellis (Founder of the Birkbeck Schools) with Some Account of his Writings and of his Labours for the Improvement and Extension of Education*, 2nd ed. (London: Kegan Paul, Trench, Trübner and Co. Ltd, 1892).
Bohm, David J., *Problems in the Basic Concepts of Physics: An Inaugural Lecture Delivered at Birkbeck College 1963* (London: J. W. Ruddock and Sons, 1963).
Bohm, David and Basil J. Hiley, *The Undivided Universe: An Ontological Interpretation of Quantum Theory* (London: Routledge, 1993).

Booth, Andrew D., 'Computers in the University of London, 1945–1962', in N. Metropolis, J. Howlett, and Gian-Carlo Rota (eds), *A History of Computing in the Twentieth Century: A Collection of Essays* (New York: Academic Press, 1980).

Booth, A. D., 'Establishment of a Centre for the Construction and Use of an Electronic Computer', in Sir William Bragg, *Opening of Biomolecular Research Laboratory* (London: Birkbeck College, 1948).

Booth, Andrew D. and Kathleen H. V. Booth, *Automatic Digital Calculators* (London: Butterworths Scientific Publications, 1953).

Booth, A. Donald and William Nash Locke, 'Historical Introduction', in Locke and Booth (eds), *Machine Translation of Languages: Fourteen Essays* (London: Chapman and Hall, 1955).

Booth, Andrew D., L. Brandwood, and J. P. Cleave, *Mechanical Resolution of Linguistic Problems* (London: Butterworths Scientific Publications, 1958).

Booth, Kathleen H. V., 'Machine Aided Translation with a Post-Editor', in A. D. Booth (ed.), *Machine Translation* (Amsterdam: North-Holland Publishing Co., 1967).

Booth, Kathleen, *Programming for an Automatic Digital Calculator* (London: Butterworths Scientific Publications, 1958).

Bourke, Joanna, *Disgrace: Global Reflections on Sexual Violence* (London: Reaktion Books, 2022).

Bourke, Joanna, *Fear: A Cultural History* (London: Virago, 2005).

Bourke, Joanna, *An Intimate History of Killing: Face-to-Face Killing in Twentieth Century Warfare* (London: Granta, 1999).

Bourke, Joanna, *Loving Animals: Bestiality, Zoophilia, and Post-Human Love* (London: Reaktion Books, 2019).

Bourke, Joanna, 'Radical Physics: Science, Socialism, and the Paranormal at Birkbeck College in the 1970s', *Journal of the British Academy*, 7 (2019).

Bourke, Joanna, *Rape: A History from 1860 to the Present* (London and New York: Virago and Shoemaker and Hoard, 2007).

Bourke, Joanna, *The Story of Pain: From Prayer to Painkillers* (Oxford and New York: Oxford University Press, 2014).

Bourke, Joanna (ed.), *War and Art: A Visual History of Modern Conflict* (London: Reaktion Books, 2017).

Bourke, Joanna, *What It Means To Be Human: Historical Reflections 1791 to the Present* (London: Virago, 2011).

Bourke, Joanna, *Wounding the World: How Military Violence and War-Play Are Invading Our Lives* (London: Virago, 2014).

Bragg, Lawrence, *Opening of Biomolecular Research Laboratory, 21–22 Torrington Square, London, W. C. 1* (London: Birkbeck College, 1948).

Brah, Avtar, *Cartographies of Diaspora* (London: Routledge, 1996).

Brah, Avtar and Ann Phoenix, 'Ain't I a Woman? Revisiting Intersectionality', *Journal of International Women's Studies*, 5.3 (May 2004).

Brammall, A., 'John William Evans, C.B.E., D.Sc., LL.B., F.R.S', *Geological Magazine*, 68.1 (1931).

Briggs, Asa, *Communications and Culture 1823–1973: A Tale of Two Centuries—An Oration Delivered at Birkbeck College, London, 4th December 1973 in Celebration of the 150th Anniversary of the Foundation of the College and the Commencement of the 151st Session* (London: Birkbeck College, 1974).

British Information Services, *Universities in Britain* (New York: British Information Services, 1963).

Broome, John, 'My Long Road to Philosophy', in Iwao Hirose and Andrew Reisner (eds), *Weighing and Reasoning: Themes from the Philosophy of John Broome* (Oxford: Oxford University Press, 2015).

Brougham, Henry, *Practical Observations Upon the Education of the People: Addressed to the Working Classes and their Employers*, 1st pub. 1825 (Manchester: E. J. Morten, 1971).

Brown, Andrew, *J. D. Bernal: The Sage of Science* (Oxford: Oxford University Press, 2005).

Brown, R. Allen, 'Reginald Ralph Darlington, 1903–1977', *Proceedings of the British Academy*, 66 (1981).

Browning, Robert, '[Review of] *The Class Struggle in the Ancient Greek Work: From the Archaic to the Arab Conquests* by G. E. M. de Ste. Croix', *Past and Present*, 100 (August 1983).

Bullough, W. S., *Practical Invertebrate Anatomy* (London: Macmillan and Co., 1950).

Burhop, E. H. S. with John Hasted, *The Challenge of Atomic Energy* (London: Lawrence and Wishart, 1951).

Burns, C. Delisle, *A Short History of Birkbeck College (University of London)* (London: University of London Press, 1924).

Burns, C. Delisle, *War and a Changing Civilisation* (London: John Lane, 1934).

Buss, Henry, *Eighty Years Experience of Life* (London: Thomas Danks and Sons, 1893).

Butt, David Keith, Ernst G. Michaelis, Gabriel L. Miller, and P. L. Trent, *The Elementary Particles of Nature* (London: Science Information Service, 1956).

Butterworth, Ian, 'Sir Clifford Charles Butler, 20 May 1922–30 June 1999', *Biographical Memoirs of Fellows of the Royal Society*, 47 (November 2001).

Cajori, Florian, *A History of the Logarithmic Slide Rule and Allied Instruments* (London: Archibald Constable and Co., 1909).

Carlile, Richard, *An Address to Men of Science; Calling Upon Them to Stand Forward and Vindicate the Truth from the Foul Grasp and Persecution of Superstition; and Obtain for the Island of Great Britain the Novel Appellation of the Focus of Truth; Whence Mankind Shall be Illuminated, and the Black and Pestiferous Clouds of Persecution and Superstition be Banished from the Face of the Earth; as the Only Sure Prelude to Universal Peace and Harmony Among the Human Race, in which a Sketch of a Proper System for the Education of Youth is Submitted to their Judgment* (London: R. Carlile, 1821).

Carroll, Lewis, *Alice in Wonderland*, 1st pub. 1872, ed. Donald J. Gray (New York: Norton, 1971).

Carver, Vida (ed.), *C. A. Mace: A Symposium* (London: Penguin, 1962).

CBI and Birkbeck, *Skills for an Inclusive Economy: CBI/Birkbeck Education and Skills Survey 2021* (London: CBI/Birkbeck, 2021).

Chakrabarty, Dipesh, *Provincializing Europe: Postcolonial Thought and Historical Difference* (Princeton: Princeton University Press, 2000).

Chapman, Don, *Wearing the Trousers: Fashion, Freedom, and the Rise of the Modern Woman* (Stroud: Amberley Publishing, 2017).

Chase, Malcolm, *Chartism: A New History* (Manchester: Manchester University Press, 2007).

Chomsky, Noam, *Language and Politics*, ed. Carlos P. Otero (Montréal: Black Rose Books, 1988).

Chomsky, Noam, 'The Responsibility of Intellectuals', in Chomsky, *American Power and the New Mandarins* (London: Penguin, 1969).

Chomsky, Noam, *Syntactic Structures*, 1st pub. 1957 (Berlin: Mouton de Gruyter, 2000).

Churchill, Winston Spencer, *The Second World War*, Volume 1: *The Gathering Storm*, 1st pub. 1948 (New York: Rosetta Books, 2010).

Clarke, John Henrik with the assistance of Amy Jaques Garvey (eds), *Marcus Garvey and the Vision of Africa* (New York: Random House, 1974).
Clarke, Richard, 'Really Useful Knowledge and 19th Century Adult Workers Education—What Lessons for Today?', unpublished (c.2016).
Clarke, Richard, 'Self-Help, Saving and Suburbanization: The Birkbeck Freehold Land and Building Societies, Their Bank, and the London Mechanics' Institute, 1851–1911', *London Journal*, 40.2 (2015).
Clements, Reginald Francis, *Salisbury Plain and Other Poems* (Salisbury: Bennett Brothers, Military Printers, 1917).
Clifton-Taylor, Alec, 'Address Given at the Memorial Service in the Church of Christ the King, Bloomsbury, for Nikolaus Pevsner: 6 December 1983', *Architectural History*, 28 (1985).
Clough, Shepard B., 'Turgot and the Ancien Régime by Douglas Dakin', *Journal of Modern History*, 12.2 (June 1940).
Cobban, A., 'Turgot and the Ancien Régime by Douglas Dakin', *History*, new series, 25.97 (June 1940).
Coe, N. E., K. J. Hedley, and L. H. Longley-Cook, 'Punched-Card Equipment', *Journal of the Institute of Actuaries*, 74.2 (1948).
Cole, J. A., *Lord Haw-Haw—and William Joyce: The Full Story* (London: Faber and Faber, 1964).
Collini, Stefan, 'Introduction', in C. P. Snow, *The Two Cultures and the Scientific Revolution* (Cambridge: Cambridge University Press, 1993).
Collini, Stefan, *Speaking of Universities* (London: Verso, 2018).
Collins, Harry M. and Trevor J. Pinch, *Frames of Meaning: The Social Construction of Extraordinary Science* (London: Routledge and Kegan Paul, 1982).
Combe, George, *The Constitution of Man Considered in Relation to External Objects*, 1st pub. 1828 (Edinburgh: John Anderson jun., 1835).
Cook, J. Mordaunt, *Bedford College University of London: Memories of 150 Years* (London: Royal Holloway and Bedford New College, 2001).
Creager, Angela N. H. and Gregory J. Morgan, 'After the Double Helix: Rosalind Franklin's Research on *Tobacco mosaic virus*', *Isis*, 99.2 (June 2008).
Creese, Mary R. S., 'British Women of the Nineteenth and Early Twentieth Centuries Who Contributed to Research in the Chemical Sciences', *British Journal for the History of Science*, 24.3 (September 1991).
Crenshaw, Kimberlé W., 'Demarginalizing the Intersection of Race and Sex: A Black Feminist Critique of Antidiscrimination Doctrine, Feminist Theory, and Antiracist Politics', *University of Chicago Legal Forum*, 139 (1989).
Crenshaw, Kimberlé W., 'Mapping the Margins: Intersectionality, Identity Politics, and Violence Against Women of Color', *Stanford Law Review*, 43.6 (1991).
Crick, Bernard, *In Defence of Politics*, 1st ed. 1962, 2nd ed. (Chicago: University of Chicago Press, 1972).
Crick, Bernard, *In Defence of Politics*, 5th ed. (London: Continuum, 2005).
Crick, Bernard, *Political Theory and Practice* (London: Penguin, 1971).
Crick, Bernard, *Political Thoughts and Polemics* (Edinburgh: Edinburgh University Press, 1990).
Czigánu, Madga, *'Just Like Other Students': Reception of the 1956 Hungarian Refugee Students in Britain* (Cambridge: Cambridge Scholars Publishing, 2009).
Dalrymple, Theodore, 'A Painter's Writings', *British Medical Journal*, 343.7830 (5 November 2011).
Darby, H. C., 'Academic Geography in Britain: 1918–1946', *Transactions of the Institute of British Geographers*, 8.1 (1983).

Dauben, Joseph Warren, *Abraham Robinson: The Creation of Nonstandard Analysis, a Personal and Mathematical Odyssey* (Princeton: Princeton University Press, 1995).
Dawick, John, *Pinero: A Theatrical Life* (Niwot: University Press of Colorado, 1993).
De la Mothe, John, *C. P. Snow and the Struggle of Modernity* (Austin: University of Texas Press, 1992).
De Mora, Joseph Joachin, 'Appeal to the People of Great Britain' (London: Richard Taylor, 1823).
de Ste Croix, Geoffrey E. M., 'The Character of the Athenian Empire', *Historia: Zeitschrift für Alte Geschichte*, 3 (1954).
Delamont, Sara, 'Rosalind Franklin and Lucky Jim: Misogyny in Two Cultures', *Social Studies of Science*, 33.2 (April 2003).
des Jardins, Julie, *The Marie Curie Complex: The Hidden World of Women in Science* (New York: Feminist Press, 2010).
Desmond, Adrian, 'Artisan Resistance and Evolution in Britain, 1819-1848', *Osiris*, 3 (1987).
Dickens, Charles, *Hard Times* (London: Chapman and Hall, 1905).
Dienes, Zoltan Paul, *Memoirs of a Maverick Mathematician* (Leicester: Upfront, 2003).
Disraeli, Benjamin, *Conningsby*, vol. 1 (London: Henry Coulburn, 1844).
Djankov, Simeon and Federica Saliola, 'The Changing Nature of Work', *Journal of International Affairs*, 72.1 (fall 2018/winter 2019).
Doern, Kristin G. 'Equal Question: The "Woman Question" and the "Drink Question" in the Writings of Clara Lucas Balfour, 1808-78', in Sue Morgan (ed.), *Women, Religion, and Feminism in Britain, 1750-1900* (Basingstoke: Palgrave Macmillan, 2002).
Douzinas, Costas, *The End of Human Rights* (Oxford: Hart, 2000).
Douzinas, Costas and Lynda Nead (eds), *Law and the Image: The Authority of Art and the Aesthetics of Law* (Chicago: University of Chicago Press, 1999).
Draper, Peter (ed.), *Reassessing Nikolaus Pevsner* (London: Ashgate, 2004).
Dunstan, G. R., *Science and Sensibility. The Hume Memorial Lecture. 4th November 1982 at King's College, University of London* (London: UFAW, 1983).
Elliott, Marianne, 'The Role of Civil Society in Conflict Resolution: The Opsahl Commission in Northern Ireland, 1992-93', *New Hibernia Review/Iris Éireannach Nua*, 17.2 (summer 2013).
Elliott, Marianne, *When God Took Sides: Religion and Identity in Ireland—Unfinished Business* (New York: Oxford University Press, 2009).
Ellis, William, *Conversations Upon Knowledge, Happiness, and Education Between a Mechanic and a Patron of the London Mechanics' Institution* (London: Baldwin and Cradock, 1829).
Ellis, William, *Education as a Means of Preventing Destitution; With Exemplifications from the Teaching at the Birkbeck Schools* (London: Smith, Elder, and Co., 1851).
Engels, Friedrich, *Condition of the Working Class in England*, 1st pub. 1844 (London: Panther, 1969).
Engels, Friedrich, *The Housing Question* (Moscow: Co-operative Publishing Society of Foreign Workers, 1872).
'Eva Germaine Rimington Taylor', *Transactions of the Institute of British Geographers*, 45 (September 1968).
Evans, Richard J., *Eric Hobsbawm: A Life in History* (London: Little, Brown, 2019).
Evans, Richard J., 'History, Memory, and the Law: The Historian as Expert Witness', *History and Theory*, 41.3 (October 2002).
Evans, Richard, *In Defence of History* (London: Granta Books, 1997).
Evans, Richard J., 'Introduction: Redesigning the Past: History in Political Transitions', *Journal of Contemporary History*, 38.1 (2003).

Extance, Andy, 'The Forgotten Female Crystallographer Who Discovered C-H···O Bonds', *Chemistry World* (8 July 2019).
Fairbairn, Ben, 'Louis Joel Mordell's Time in London', *BSHM Bulletin: Journal of the British Society for the History of Mathematics*, 32.2 (2017).
Feinstein, Leon, Tashweka M. Anderson, Cathie Hammond, Anne Jamieson, and Alan Woodley, 'The Social and Economic Benefits of Part-Time, Mature Study at Birkbeck College and the Open University' (London: Open University and Birkbeck College, 2007).
Flexner, Helen Hudson, 'The London Mechanics' Institution: Social and Cultural Foundations', PhD thesis (London: University College London, 2014).
Floud, Roderick and Sean Glynn (eds), *London Higher: The Establishment of Higher Education in London* (London: Athlone Press, 1998).
For Those Who Would be Sisters: Uncovering Lesbian History (London: Centre for Extra-Mural Studies, 1986).
Foster, R. F., *Modern Ireland, 1600–1972* (London: Allen Lane, 1988).
Foucault, Michel, 'The Order of Discourse', 1st pub. 1970, in Robert Young (ed.), *Untying the Text: A Post-Structuralist Reader* (London: Routledge, 1981).
Freeman, T. W., 'Geography Then and Now', *L'Espace géographique*, 14.1 (January/March 1985).
Freire, Olival, 'Science and Exile: David Bohm, the Cold War, and a New Interpretation of Quantum Mechanics', *Historical Studies in the Physical and Biological Sciences*, 36.1 (2005).
Freud, Sigmund, *The Joke and its Relation to the Unconscious*, ed. James Strachey, 1st pub. 1905 (New York: Norton, 1963).
Freud, Sigmund, 'On the Teaching of Psychoanalysis in Universities', in *Standard Edition of the Complete Psychological Works of Sigmund Freud*, vol. 17, 1st pub. 1919 (London: Hogarth Press, 1953–74).
Frosh, Stephen, 'Psychosocial Studies and Psychology: Is a Critical Approach Emerging?', *Human Relations*, 56.12 (2003).
Furth, Reinhold, *The Physics Department of Birkbeck College (University of London)* (London: Institute of Physics, July 1954).
Fyfe, Hamilton, *Sir Arthur Pinero's Plays and Players* (London: Ernest Benn Ltd, 1930).
Gamble, Andrew, 'Paul Hirst: An Appreciation', *Renewal*, 11.4 (2003).
Games, Stephen, *Pevsner: The Complete Broadcast Talks—Architecture and Art on Radio and Television, 1945–1977* (London: Ashgate, 2014).
Games, Steven, *Pevsner: The Early Life—Germany and Art* (London: Continuum, 2010).
Gann, Lewis H., 'Ex Africa: An Africanist's Intellectual Autobiography', *Journal of Modern African Studies*, 31.3 (1993).
Gardner, Martin, *Science: Good, Bad and Bogus* (Buffalo: Prometheus Books, 1989).
Garnett, Olive, 'John Frederick Unstead', *Geography*, 51.2 (April 1966).
Garnett, William, 'The Work of the Polytechnics', *Journal of the Society of Arts* (23 July 1897).
Garvey, Marcus, 'The British West Indies in the Mirror of Civilization: History Making by Colonial Negroes', *African Times and Orient Review*, 2 (October 1913).
'George Bernard Shaw on Education', *Journal of Education*, 89.11 (13 March 1919).
Gilbert, Edmund W., 'Professor J. F. Unstead', *Geographical Journal*, 132.2 (June 1966).
Glennie, Paul and Nigel Thrift, *Shaping the Day: A History of Time Keeping in England and Wales, 1300–1800* (Oxford: Oxford University Press, 2009).
Godard, John George, *George Birkbeck: The Pioneer of Popular Education—A Memoir and a Review* (London: Bemrose and Sons, 1884).
Goldsmith, Maurice, *Sage: Life of J. D. Bernal* (London: Hutchinson, 1980).

Goldstein, Sheldon, 'Review: Bohmian Mechanics and the Quantum Revolution', *Synthese*, 107.1 (April 1996).
Goodrich, Peter, Costas Douzinas, and Yifat Hachamovitch, 'Introduction: Politics, Ethics, and the Legality of the Contingent', in Goodrich, Douzinas, and Hachamovitch (eds), *Politics, Postmodernity, and Critical Legal Studies: The Legality of the Contingent* (London: Routledge, 1994).
Grant, Colin, *Negro with a Hat: The Rise and Fall of Marcus Garvey and His Dream of Mother Africa* (London: Jonathan Cape, 2008).
Greaves, Robert, 'Penson, Dame Lillian Margery', in H. C. G. Matthew and Brian Harrison (eds), *Oxford Dictionary of National Biography*, vol. 43 (Oxford: Oxford University Press, 2004).
Griffin, Emma, 'The Making of the Chartists: Popular Politics and Working-Class Autobiography in Early Victorian Britain', *English Historical Review*, 129.538 (June 2014).
Grinfield, Edward William, *A Reply to Mr. Brougham's 'Practical Observations Upon the Education of the People; Addressed to the Working Classes and Their Employers'* (London: C. & J. Rivinton, 1825).
Grossmith, George, *See Me Dance the Polka: Humorous Song Written, Composed, and Sung by George Grossmith* (London: J. Bath, 1886).
Grove, J. W., 'Rationality at Risk: Science Against Pseudoscience', *Minerva*, 23.2 (June 1985).
Haldane, John, 'A Memorial Address', in I. G. McFetridge, *Logical Necessity and Other Essays*, ed. John Haldane and Roger Scruton (London: Aristotelian Society, 1990).
Halsey, A. L., 'The Decline of Donnish Domination?', *Oxford Review of Education*, 8.3 (1982).
Hamilton, Robert, 'Dr Joad and the Angels', *Irish Ecclesiastical Review* (December 1955).
Hannam, June, 'Women and the ILP, 1890–1914', in David James, Tony Jowitt, and Keith Laybourne (eds), *The Centenary History of the Independent Labour Party* (Edinburgh: Edinburgh University Press, 1992).
Harries, Susie, *Nikolaus Pevsner* (London: Vintage Digital, 2011).
Harries, Susie, *Nikolaus Pevsner: The Life* (London: Chatto and Windus, 2011).
Harris, Peter J. F., 'Rosalind Franklin's Work on Coal, Carbon, and Graphite', *Interdisciplinary Science Reviews*, 26.3 (autumn 2001).
Harrison, J. F. C., 'The Victorian Gospel of Success', *Victorian Studies*, 1.2 (December 1957).
Harrison, Royden J., *The Life and Times of Sidney and Beatrice Webb: 1858–1905—The Formative Years* (Basingstoke: Macmillan, 1999).
Hasted, John, *Alternative Memoirs* (Itchenor, West Sussex: Greengates Press, 1992).
Hasted, John, *The Metal-Benders* (London: Routledge and Kegan Paul, 1981).
Hawes, Frances, *Henry Brougham* (London: Jonathan Cape, 1957).
Haydon, Benjamin Robert, *The Autobiography and Journals of Benjamin Robert Haydon*, ed. Malcolm Elwin, 1st pub. 1853 (London: MacDonald, 1950).
Haydon, Benjamin Robert, *The Diary of Benjamin Robert Haydon*, ed. William Bissell Pope, vol. 1 (Cambridge, MA: Harvard University Press, 1960).
Hayhoe, Barney, 'Birkbeck College. A New Structure. The Report of the Committee on Restructuring the College. February 1987' (London: Birkbeck College, 1987).
Herrin, Judith, 'Robert Browning', *Past and Present*, 156 (August 1997).
Heyck, Thomas William, 'The Idea of a University in Britain, 1870–1970', *History of European Ideas*, 8.2 (1987).
Higgins, David, 'Art, Genius, and Racial Theory in the Early Nineteenth Century: Benjamin Robert Haydon', *History Workshop Journal*, 58 (autumn 2004).
Hiley, Basil J., 'David Joseph Bohm, 20 December 1917–27 October 1992', *Biographical Memoirs of Fellows of the Royal Society*, 43 (November 1997).

Hiley, Basil J., 'The Early History of the Aharonov–Bohm Effect', *History and Philosophy of Physics* (7 April 2013).

Hill, Robert A., 'The First England Years and After, 1912–1916', in John Henrik Clarke with the assistance of Amy Jacques Garvey (eds), *Marcus Garvey and the Vision of Africa* (New York: Random House, 1974).

Hind, C. Lewis, *Naphtali: Being Influences and Adventures While Earning a Living by Writing* (London: John Lane, 1926).

Hindess, Barry and Paul Q. Hirst, *Pre-Capitalist Modes of Production* (London: Routledge and Kegan Paul, 1975).

Hines, A. G., *On the Reappraisal of Keynesian Economics: A Revised and Extended Version of a University Special Lecture Delivered at Queen Mary College in the University of London on 7th December 1970* (London: Martin Robertson and Co. Ltd, 1971).

Hirst, Paul, 'The Future of Political Studies', *European Political Science*, 3.1 (2003).

Hirst, Paul, *Marxism and Historical Writing* (London: Routledge, 1985).

Hobsbawm, Eric, 'Bernal at Birkbeck', in Brenda Swann and Francis Aprahamian (eds), *J. D. Bernal: A Life in Science and Politics* (London: Verso, 1999).

Hobsbawm, Eric, 'Birkbeck and the Left', *Times Change: Quarterly Political and Cultural Review*, 21 (spring/summer 2001).

Hobsbawm, Eric J., *How to Change the World: Marx and Marxism, 1840–2011* (London: Little, Brown, 2011).

Hobsbawm, Eric J., *The Jazz Scene*, 1st pub. 1959 (New York: Pantheon Books, 1993).

Hobsbawm, Eric J., *Uncommon People: Resistance, Rebellion, and Jazz* (London: Weidenfeld and Nicolson, 1998).

Hodgkin, Dorothy M. C., 'John Desmond Bernal, 10 May 1901–15 September 1971', *Biographical Memoirs of Fellows of the Royal Society*, 26 (November 1980).

Hodgskin, Thomas, *An Essay on Naval Discipline, Shewing Part of its Evil Effects on the Minds of Officers, on the Minds of Men, and on the Community; with an Amended System by which Pressing be Immediately Abolished* (London: The Author, 1813).

Hodgskin, Thomas, *Travels in the North of Germany; Describing the Present State of the Social and Political Institutions, the Agriculture, Manufactures, Commerce, Education, Arts and Manners in that Country, Particularly in the Kingdom of Hannover*, vol. 2 (Edinburgh: Archibald Constable and Co., 1820).

Hodgson, E. M., 'John—or Charles—Wesley?', *Proceedings of the Wesley Historical Society*, 7.41 (October 1977).

Holland, Merlin and Rupert Hart-Davis (eds), *The Complete Letters of Oscar Wilde* (London: Fourth Estate, 2000).

Hollow, Matthew, 'Strategic Inertia, Financial Fragility and Organisational Failure: The Case of the Birkbeck Bank, 1870–1911', *Business History*, 56.5 (2014).

Holmes, Colin, *Searching for Lord Haw-Haw: The Political Lives of William Joyce* (London: Routledge, 2015).

Holroyd, Stuart, *PSI and the Consciousness Explosion* (London: The Bodley Head, 1977).

Hoskin, Keith W. and Richard H. Macve, 'Accounting and the Examination: A Genealogy of Disciplinary Power', *Accounting, Organizations and Society*, 11.2 (1986).

Huch, Ronald K., *Henry, Lord Brougham: The Later Years, 1830–1868—The 'Great Actor'* (Lewiston: Lampeter, 1993).

Hudson, James William, *The History of Adult Education, in Which it Comprised a Full and Complete History of the Mechanics' and Literary Institutions, Athenæums, Philosophical, Mental and Christian Improvement Societies, Literary Unions, Schools of Design, Etc., of Great Britain, Ireland, America, Etc. Etc.* (London: Longman, Brown, Green and Longmans, 1851).

Hudson, Richard, 'A History of the LAGB: The First Fifty Years', *Journal of Linguistics*, 45.1 (March 2009).
Hughes, Mary and Mary Kennedy, 'Breaking Out: Women in Adult Education', *Women's Studies International*, 6.3 (1983).
Hughson, David, *London: Being an Accurate History and Description of the British Metropolis and Its Neighbourhood, to Thirty Miles Extent, from an Actual Perambulation*, vol. 4 (London: J. Stratford, 1807).
Hume, C. W., *The Status of Animals in the Christian Religion* (London: Universities Federation for Animal Welfare, 1956).
Hunt, Karen, *Equivocal Feminists: The Social Democratic Federation and the Woman Question* (Cambridge: Cambridge University Press, 1996).
Hutchins, John, 'Milestones in Machine Translation', *Language Today* (13 October 1998).
Ives, D. J. G., 'Fred Barrow, 1882–1964', *Proceedings of the Chemical Society* (November 1964).
Jaki, Stanley, 'One Hundred Years of the Two Cultures', *University of Windsor Review*, 11 (fall–winter 1975).
Jenkins, Alan, *Stephen Potter: Inventor of Gamemanship* (London: Weidenfeld and Nicolson, 1980).
Jill, Robert A. (ed.), *The Marcus Garvey and Universal Negro Improvement Association Papers, Volume XI: The Caribbean Diaspora 1910–1920* (Durham: Duke University Press, 2011).
Joad, C. E. M., *Essays in Common-Sense Philosophy* (London: The Swarthmore Press, 1919).
Joad, C. E. M., *Guide to Modern Wickedness* (London: Faber and Faber, 1939).
Joad, C. E. M., *More Opinions by Joad* (London: Westhouse, 1947).
Joad, C. E. M., *The Pleasure of Being Oneself* (London: George Weidenfeld and Nicolson, 1951).
Joad, C. E. M., *A Year More or Less* (London: Victor Gollancz, 1948).
J. O. I. 'The UFAW Handbook on the Care and Management of Laboratory Animals', *Journal of the Royal Statistical Society*, 111.1 (1948).
'John Frederick Unstead', *Transactions of the Institute of British Geographers*, 38 (June 1966).
Johnson, Richard, 'Educational Policy and Social Control in Early Victorian England', *Past and Present*, 49 (November 1970).
Johnson, Roger, 'School of Computer Science and Information Systems' (London: Birkbeck College, 2008).
Joyce, William, 'A Note on the Mid Back Slack Unrounded Vowel [a] in the English of To-Day', *Review of English Studies*, 4.15 (1928).
Judge, Tony, *Radio Philosopher: The Radical Life of Cyril Joad* (Charleston: Alpha House, 2012).
Kaiser, David, *How the Hippies Saved Physics: Science, Counterculture, and the Quantum Revival* (New York: W. W. Norton and Company, 2011).
Keating, P. J., *The Working Classes in Victorian Fiction* (London: Routledge and Kegan Paul, 1971).
Keller, Evelyn Fox, 'Fractured Images of Science, Language, and Power: A Postmodern Optic, or Just Bad Eyesight?', *Poetics Today*, 12.2 (summer 1991).
Kelly, Thomas, *George Birkbeck: Pioneer of Adult Education* (Liverpool: Liverpool University Press, 1957).
Kenny, Mary, *Germany Calling: A Personal Biography of William Joyce, Lord Haw-Haw* (Dublin: New Island, 2003).
Knox, Robert, *The Races of Men: A Fragment* (London: Henry Renshaw, 1850).
Kojevnikov, Alexei, 'David Bohm and Collective Movement', *Historical Studies in the Physical and Biological Sciences*, 33.1 (2002).
Kundnani, A., *Spooked! How Not to Prevent Violent Terrorism* (London: Institute of Race Relations, 2015).

Laiou, Angeliki E. Laiou and Alice-Mary Talbot, 'Robert Browning, 1914–1997', *Dumbarton Oak Papers*, 51(1997).
Lanchester, Elsa *Elsa Lanchester Herself* (New York: St Martin's Press, 1983).
Lane-Petter, W., 'The Ethics of Animal Experimentation', *Journal of Medical Ethics*, 2 (1976).
Lavington, Simon, *Early British Computers: The Story of Vintage Computers and the People Who Built Them* (Manchester: Manchester University Press, 1980).
Leake, Bernard Elgey, 'The Life and Work of Professor J. W. Gregory FRS (1864–1932): Geologist, Writer and Explorer' (London: Geological Society Memoir No. 34, Geological Society, 2011).
Leatherby, James Norman, 'William McFee: Writing Engineer', *Prairie Schooner*, 23.2 (summer 1949).
Ledger, Sally, 'Ibsen, the New Woman, and the Actress', in Angelique Richard and Chris Willis (eds), *The New Woman in Fiction and in Fact: Fin-de-Siècle Feminisms* (New York: Palgrave, 2001).
Lennard, Fiennes Barrett, 'Some Aspects of Colonial Law', *Transactions of the Grotius Society*, 19 (1933).
Levison, Michael, 'The Application of the Ferranti Mercury Computer to Linguistic Problems', *Information and Control*, 3 (1960).
Levison, Michael, 'The Computer in Literary Studies', in A. D. Booth (ed.), *Machine Translation* (New York: John Wiley, 1967).
Levison, Michael, 'The Computer in Literary Studies', *IFIP Congress '68*, 1 (1968).
'London Mechanics' Institution' (London: London Mechanics' Institution, 1839).
'The London Mechanics' Institution' (London: London Mechanics' Institution, 1848).
'London Mechanics' Institution… The Following Lectures Will Be Delivered During the Present Quarter' (London: London Mechanics' Institution, 1853).
Lord Russell of Killowen, *Address by the Right Honorable Lord Russell of Killowen, Lord Chief Justice of England, to the Students of the Birkbeck Institution, on the Occasion of the Annual Distribution of Prizes and Certificates, January 14th, 1897* (London: J. C. Larrance Printer, 1897).
Lovell, Bernard, 'Patrick Maynard Stuart Blackett, Baron Blackett of Chelsea, 18 November 1897–13 July 1974', *Biographical Memoirs of Fellows of the Royal Society*, 21 (November 1975).
Lovelock, James, *Homage to Gaia: The Life of an Independent Scientist* (Oxford: Oxford University Press, 2000).
Lovenduski, Joni, 'Feminizing Politics', *Women: A Cultural Review*, 13.2 (2002).
Lowe, Roy, 'The Expansion of Higher Education in England', in Konrad H. Jarausch (ed.), *The Transformation of Higher Learning 1860–1930: Expansion, Diversification, Social Opening, and Professionalization in England, Germany, Russia, and the United States* (Chicago: University of Chicago Press, 1983).
McGovern, Mark, 'The University, Prevent, and Cultures of Compliance', *Prometheus*, 34.1 (March 2016).
McGucken, William, *Scientists, Society, and State: The Social Relations of Science Movement in Great Britain, 1931–1947* (Columbus: Ohio University State University Press, 1984).
MacInnes, Colin, 'The Englishness of Dr Pevsner', *Twentieth Century* (January 1960).
MacKay, A. L., 'Lucretius or the Philosophy of Chemistry', *Colloids and Surfaces A: Physicochemical and Engineering Aspects* (1997).
Mackenzie, Fred A., 'The Birkbeck Institution: The Story of London's Evening University', *The Windsor Magazine: An Illustrated Monthly for Men and Women*, 7 (December 1897).

Maddox, Brenda, *Rosalind Franklin: The Dark Lady of DNA* (London: Harper Collins, 2002).
Maddrell, Avril, 'The "Map Girls": British Women Geographers' War Work, Shifting Gender Boundaries and Reflections on the History of Geography', *Transactions of the Institute of British Geographers*, 33.1 (January 2008), 132.
Malik, Kenan, *The Meaning of Race: Race, History, and Culture in Western Society* (Houndmills: Macmillan, 1996).
Margolis, Jonathan, *Uri Geller: Magician or Mystic?* (London: Orion, 1998).
Margulis, Lynn, '[Review of] J. D. Bernal: A Life in Science and Politics by Brenda Swann and Francis Aprahamian', *Science, Technology and Human Values*, 25.2 (spring 2000).
Marx, Karl, *Capital: A Critique of Political Economy*, vol. 1, trans. Ben Fowkes (Harmondsworth: Penguin in association with the New Left Review, 1976).
Matos, T. Carlo, *Ibsen's Foreign Contagion: Henrik Ibsen, Arthur Wing Pinero, and Modernism on the London Stage, 1890–21900* (London: Academica Press, 2012).
Matthew, H. C. G. and Brian Harrison (eds), *Oxford Dictionary of National Biography*, vol. 43 (Oxford: Oxford University Press, 2004).
Mead, Margaret, 'Introduction', in Russell Targ and Harold E. Puthoff, *Mind-Reach: Scientists Look at Psychic Ability* (London: Jonathan Cape, 1977).
Mead, Matthew, 'Empire Windrush: Cultural Memory and Archival Disturbance', *Moveable Type*, 3 (2007).
Mead, W. R., 'Eila as Geographer', *Imago Mundi*, 47 (1995).
Mead, W. R., 'Obituary. William Gordon East, 1902–1998', *Journal of Historical Geography*, 24.3 (1998).
Moi, Toril, *Henrik Ibsen and the Birth of Modernism: Art, Theatre, Philosophy* (Oxford: Oxford University Press, 2006).
Moodie, Graeme, 'The Disintegrating Chair: Professors in Britain Today', *European Journal of Education*, 21.1 (1986).
Morrison, Herbert, 'Anniversary Dinner 1948', *Notes and Records of the Royal Society of London*, 6.2 (May 1949).
Mosley, Oswald, *The Greater Britain*, 2nd ed. (London: Jeff Coats, 1934).
Mulvey, Laura, 'Visual Pleasure and Narrative Cinema', *Screen*, 16.3 (autumn 1975).
Murphy, John A., *The College: A History of Queen's/University College Cork, 1845–1995* (Cork: Cork University Press, 1995).
Murray, Peter, 'Nikolaus Bernhard Leon Pevsner', 70 *Proceedings of the British Academy* (1984).
Musser, George, 'The Wholeness of Quantum Reality: An Interview with Physicist Basil Hiley', *Scientific American* (4 November 2013).
Myers, David Gershom, *The Elephants Teach: Creative Writing Since 1880* (Prentice Hall: Englewood Cliffs, 1996).
Neruda, Pablo, 'A Poem to J. D. Bernal', in *Tribute to John Desmond Bernal in his Seventieth Year, by Artists and Scientists* (Watford: Farleigh Press, 1971).
Newman, Ian, 'Civilizing Taste: "Sandman Joe", the Bawdy Ballad, and Metropolitan Improvement', *Eighteenth-Century Studies*, 48.4 (summer 2015).
Nicoll, Irena, 'A Statistical Profile of the London PhD in History 1921–1990', *Oxford Review of Education*, 22.3 (1996).
Nussbaum, Frederick L., 'Turgot and the Ancien Régime by Douglas Dakin', *American Historical Review*, 45.4 (July 1940).
Nye, Mary Jo, *Blackett: Physics, War, and Politics in the Twentieth Century* (Cambridge, MA: Harvard University Press, 1935).
Oldfield, Derek, *Slow to Begin With: A Memoir* (London: Privately Printed, 2004).
Olney, Clarke, 'John Keats and Benjamin Robert Haydon', *PMLA*, 49.1 (March 1934).

Olwell, Russell, 'Physical Isolation and Marginalization in Physics: David Bohm's Cold War Exile', *Isis*, 90.4 (December 1999).

Orczy, Baroness Emma, *The Old Man in the Corner* (London: Greening and Co., 1908).

Ostrande, Sheila and Lynn Schroeder, *PSI: Psychic Discoveries behind the Iron Curtain*, 1st pub. 1973 (London: Abacus, 1977).

Page, Lou Williams, 'A Student's Introduction to Geology (Mainly Physical) by George MacDonald Davies', *Journal of Geology*, 59.4 (July 1951).

Parolin, Christina, *Radical Spaces: Venues of Popular Politics in London, 1790–c.1845* (Canberra: ANU Press, 2010).

Parry, William, *The Last Days of Lord Byron; With His Lordship's Opinions on Various Subjects, Particularly on the State and Prospects of Greece* (Paris: The Author, 1826).

Paul, Diane B., 'A War on Two Fronts: J. B. S. Haldane and the Response to Lysentoism in Britain', *Journal of the History of Biology*, 161 (spring 1983).

Peacock, Kent A., '[Review] From Physics to Metaphysics by Michael Redhead', *Canadian Journal of Philosophy*, 28.2 (June 1998).

Penrose, Roger, *The Emperor's New Mind: Concerning Computers, Minds, and the Laws of Physics* (Oxford: Oxford University Press, 1989).

Penrose, Roger, 'Gravitational Collapse and Space-Time Singularities', *Physical Review Letters*, 14.3 (18 January 1965).

Penrose, Roger, 'Gravity and State Vector Reduction', in Roger Penrose and C. J. Isham (eds), *Quantum Concepts in Space and Time* (Oxford: Clarendon Press, 1986).

Penrose, Roger, *The Road to Reality: A Complete Guide to the Laws of the Universe* (London: Jonathan Cape, 2004).

Penrose, Roger, 'Space-Time Quantum Non Locality: Does Palatial Tristor Theory Suggest an Objective Mathematical Framework?', Fetzer Franklin Fund, at https://www.fetzer-franklin-fund.org/media/space-time-quantum-non-locality-roger-penrose-video/.

Penson, Lillian M., *The Colonial Agents of the British West Indies: A Study in Colonial Administration, Mainly in the Eighteenth Century* (London: University of London Press, 1924).

Penson, Lillian, 'University Ventures Old and New', *British Medical Journal*, 2.4683 (7 October 1950).

Peters, Ted, *Science, Theology, and Ethics* (Aldershot: Ashgate, 2003).

Pevsner, Nikolaus, *The Buildings of England: London I. The Cities of London and Westminster* (Harmondsworth: Penguin, 1973).

Pevsner, Nikolaus, *A History of Building Types* (London: Thames and Hudson, 1976).

Pevsner, Nikolaus, *Visual Pleasure from Everyday Things: An Attempt to Establish Criteria by which the Aesthetic Qualities of Design can be Judged* (London: B. T. Batsford, 1946).

Pinch, Trevor, 'Review: Karen Barad, Quantum Mechanics and the Paradox of Mutual Exclusivity', *Social Studies in Science*, 41.3 (June 2011).

Pinero, Arthur Wing, *The Collected Letters of Sir Arthur Pinero* (Minneapolis: University of Minnesota Press, 1984).

'A Pioneer Educator. W. Mattieu Williams', *The Character Builder: Devoted to Personal and Social Betterment*, ed. John T. Miller (February 1919).

Pritchard, Rosalind M. O., 'Has the Federation a Future? The Case of the University of London', *Oxford Review of Education*, 21.1 (March 1995).

Quester, George H., 'The Psychological Effects of Bombing on Civilian Populations: Wars of the Past', in Betty Glad (ed.), *Psychological Dimensions of War* (Newbury Park: Sage, 1990).

Rankin, George Claus, 'Democracy in Literature', MA dissertation (Edinburgh: University of Edinburgh, 1898).

Rankin, G. C., *Background to Indian Law* (Cambridge: Cambridge University Press, 1946).
Rankin, G. C., 'The Development of European Polity', *International Journal of Ethics*, 14.4 (July 1904).
Rankin, G. C., 'Hobbes by Lesley Stephen', *International Journal of Ethics*, 15.3 (April 1905).
Rankin, G. C., 'International Arbitration as a Substitute for War Between Nations by Russell Lowell Jones', *International Journal of Ethics*, 9.4 (July 1909).
Raymond, James C., *English as a Discipline: Or, Is there a Plot in this Play?* (Tuscaloosa: University of Alabama Press, 1996).
Rehman, Javaid, 'Islam, "War on Terror" and the Future of Muslim Minorities in the United Kingdom: Dilemmas of Multiculturalism in the Aftermath of the London Bombings', *Human Rights Quarterly*, 29.4 (November 2007).
Report of the Lord Mayor of London's National Hungarian and Central European Relief Fund Nov. 1956–Sept. 1958 (London: The Lord Mayor, 1958).
Richardson, Albert Edward, 'Scholarship and the Fine Arts' (London: Birkbeck College, 1955).
Ridge, W. Pett, *Three Women and Mr Frank Cardwell* (London: C. Arthur Pearson Ltd, 1898).
Roberts, Edwin A., *The Anglo-Marxists: A Study in Ideology and Culture* (Oxford: Rowman and Littlefield, 1997).
Roberts, Edwin A., 'From the History of Science to the Science of History: Scientists and Historians in the Shaping of British Marxist Theory', *Science and Society*, 69.4 (October 2005).
Rodger, Alec, *On Vocational Guidance* (Loughborough: The Author, 1936).
Rodger, Alec, 'The Work of the Admiralty Psychologists', *Occupational Psychology*, 19 (1945).
Rose, Hilary and Steven Rose, 'The Two Bernals', *Fundamental Scientia*, 1.2 (1981).
Rosenberg, Isaac, *The Collected Works of Isaac Rosenberg: Poetry, Prose, Letters, and Some Drawings*, ed. Gordon Bottomley and Denys Harding (London: Chatto and Windus, 1937).
Rossiter, Margaret W., 'Which Science? Which Women?', *Osiris*, 12 (1997).
Royle, Nicholas, *The Uncanny: An Introduction* (Manchester: Manchester University Press, 2002).
Rules and Orders of the Birkbeck Literary and Scientific Institution (London: J. C. Larrance, 1881).
Said, Edward, *Representations of the Intellectual: The Reith Lectures* (London: Vintage, 1996).
Sambrook, Stephen Curtis, 'The Optical Munitions Industry in Great Britain, 1888–1923', PhD thesis (Glasgow: University of Glasgow, 2005).
Samuel, Joseph, 'The Aharonov–Bohm Effect', *Current Science*, 66.10 (25 May 1994).
Samuel, Viscount, 'The World After the War', *Philosophy*, 18.62 (April 1943).
Sayre, Anne, *Rosalind Franklin and DNA*, 1st pub. 1975 (New York: W. W. Norton and Co., 2000).
Schippers, Joop, 'On the Need for Universities to Engage in Lifelong Learning', in Armand Heijnen and Rob van der Vaart (eds), *Places of Engagement: Reflections on Higher Education in 2040—A Global Approach* (Amsterdam: Amsterdam University Press, 2018).
Schofield, Michael, see Westwood, Gordon.
Schwalbe, Carl H., 'June Sutor and the C-H···O Hydrogen Bonding Controversy', *Crystallography Review*, 18.3 (July 2012).
Sebeok, Thomas A., assisted by Marcia E. Erickson (eds), *Carnival!* (New York: Mouton Publishers, 1984).
Shapin, Steven and Barry Barnes, 'Science, Nature and Control: Interpreting Mechanics' Institutes', *Social Studies of Science*, 7.1 (February 1977).
Sharma, C. S., 'The Role of Mathematics in Physics', *British Journal for the Philosophy of Science*, 33 (1982).

Sharpe, Kevin J., *David Bohm's World: New Physics and New Religion* (Lewisburg: Bucknell University Press, 1993).
Shaw, Robert A., 'The Bangalore–Birkbeck Phosphazene Project, 1971–1981: A Retrospective on This and Other International and Interdisciplinary Scientific Research Collaborations', *Current Science*, 107.11 (10 December 2014).
Shimmin, Sylvia and Don Wallis, *Fifty Years of Occupational Psychology in Britain* (Leicester: British Psychological Society, 1994).
Shumway, David R. and Ellen Messer-Davidow, 'Disciplinarity: An Introduction', *Poetics Today*, 12.2 (summer 1991).
'Sidney William Wooldridge, 1900–1963', *Biographical Memoirs of Fellows of the Royal Society*, 10 (November 1964).
'Sidney William Wooldridge: Biographical Memoirs' (London: Royal Society, 1944).
'The Situation and the Science of Biology: Report of a Conference Called to Discuss the Issues Raised by T. D. Lysenko's Address on Soviet Biology', *Transactions of the Engels Society* (April 1949).
Smith, A. H., 'Some Modern English Vowels', *Review of English Studies*, 5.7 (January 1929).
Snow, C. P., 'The Age of Rutherford', *Atlantic Monthly*, 102 (1958), 79–80.
Snow, C. P., *Recent Thoughts on the Two Cultures: An Oration Delivered at Birkbeck College, London, 12th December, 1961, in Celebration of the 138th Anniversary of the Foundation of the College* (London: Birkbeck College, 1961).
Snow, C. P., *Recent Thoughts on the Two Cultures* (London: Birkbeck College, 1962).
Snow, C. P., *The Two Cultures and the Scientific Revolution: The Rede Lecture 1959* (Cambridge: Cambridge University Press, 1959).
Snow, C. P., 'The Two Cultures and the Scientific Revolution', *Encounter*, 12 (June 1959).
Spearman, C., 'Obituary Notice. Francis Aveling, 1875–1941', *British Journal of Psychology. General Section*, 32.1 (1 July 1941).
Spurzheim, Johann Caspar, *A View of the Philosophical Principles of Phrenology*, 3rd ed. (London: Charles Knight, 1825).
Statement by the Council of the University of London, Explanatory of the Nature and Objects of the Institution (London: Longman, Rees, Orme, and Green and John-Murray, 1927).
Steadman-Jones, Richard, *Colonialism and Grammatical Presentation: John Gilchrist and the Analysis of the 'Hindustani' Language in the Late Eighteenth and Early Nineteenth Centuries* (Oxford: Berg, 2007).
Steel, Robert W., 'Harry Cyril Knapp Henderson 1903–1983', *Transactions of the Institute of British Geographers*, 9.2 (1984).
Stewart, Robert, *Henry Brougham 1778–1868: His Public Career* (London: The Bodley Head, 1985).
Stone, Lawrence, 'Literacy and Education in England, 1640–1900', *Past and Present*, 42 (February 1969).
Story, A. M. Somerville, *Twenty Years in Paris with a Pen* (London: Alston Rivers, 1927).
Strunk, William, *The Elements of Style* (New York: Macmillan, 1979).
Surridge, Christopher, '50 Years of Biomolecular Structure at Birkbeck: Bernal's Legacy', *Nature Structural Biology*, 6.1 (January 1999).
Sutor, D. J. [Dorothy June], 'The C-H···O Hydrogen Bond in Crystals', *Nature*, 195 (1962), 68–9.
Sutor, D. J., 'Evidence for the Existence of C-H···O Hydrogen Bonds in Crystals', *Journal of the Chemistry Society* (1963).
Sutton, Graham, 'The Centenary of the Birth of W. H. Young (20th October 1863)', *Mathematical Gazette*, 49.367 (February 1965).

Tapper, Richard and Sami Zudaida, 'Introduction', in Zubaida and Tapper (eds), *Culinary Cultures of the Middle* East (London: I. B. Tauris, 1994).
Taylor, Becky, '"Their Only Words in English were "Thank You": Rights, Gratitude and "Deserving" Hungarian Refugees to Britain in 1956', unpublished paper (2018).
Taylor, E. G. R., 'Geography in War and Peace', *Geographical Review*, 38.1 (1948).
Taylor, John Robert, 'Letter to the Right Honorable Lord Brougham and Vaux on Instituting Special Evening Classes, In Connection with the London Mechanics' and Other Similar Institutes' (London: n.p., 1857).
Taylor, John Robert, *The Rise and Progress of Mechanics' Institutes in England: An Address Delivered at St. Pierres-Les-Calais, France, to The St. Pierre's Young Men's Mutual Improvement Society on Saturday Evening, the 15th December, 1860* (London: Simpkin, Marshall, and Co., 1860).
Taylor, Nicholas, 'Ceramic Extravagance', *Architectural Review*, 138 (1965).
Thomas, John Meurig, *J. D. Bernal and the World of Catalysis* (London: Birkbeck College, 1997).
Thompson, Edward, *The Poverty of Theory, and Other Essays* (London: Merlin Press, 1978).
Trevelyan, G. O., *The Life and Letters of Lord Macaulay* (London: Longman, Green, and Co., 1881).
Trilling, Lionel, 'Science, Literature, and Culture: A Comment on the Snow–Leavis Controversy', *Commentary*, 33 (June 1962).
Trowler, Paul, 'Academic Tribes and Territories: The Theoretical Trajectory', *Österreichische Zeitschrift für Geschichtswissenschaften*, 25.3 (January 2014).
Universities Federation for Animal Welfare and the Royal Society, *Guidelines on the Care of Laboratory Animals and their Use for Scientific Purposes: I—Housing and Care* (London: Royal Society and UFAW, 1987).
University of London Animal Welfare Society, *Animal Welfare: Its Dependence on Accurate Information. Report of a Meeting Held at the Seventh Annual Congress of the Association of Special Libraries and Information Bureaux, Oxford, September 20, 1930* (London: ULAWS, 1930).
'The Urbanization of the Shetland Islands: Discussion', *Geographical Journal*, 81.6 (June 1933).
Vaughan, William, 'Higher Education and the Visual Arts', in Roderick Floud and Sean Glynn (eds), *London Higher: The Establishment of Higher Education in London* (London: Athlone Press, 1998).
Wallace, A. R., *The Wonderful Century: Its Successes and Failures* (London: Swan Sonnenschein and Co., 1898).
Warden, A. N. and W. Lane-Petter (eds), 'The UFAW Handbook on the Care and Management of Laboratory Animals', *Journal of Animal Ecology*, 27.2 (November 1958).
Warmington, E. H., *A History of Birkbeck College University of London during the Second World War* (London: Birkbeck College, 1954).
Watermeyer, Richard and Mark Olssen, ' "Excellence" and Exclusion: The Individual Costs of Institutional Competitiveness', *Minerva*, 54.2 (2016).
Watson, Hewett C., *Statistics of Phrenology: Being a Sketch of the Progress and Present State of that Science in the British Isles* (London: n.p., 1836).
Watson, James D. and Gunther Siegmund Stent, *The Double Helix: A Personal Account of the Discovery of the Structure of DNA* (New York: Scribner, 1998).
Webb, Katherine, *Birkbeck under Tessa Blackstone: A Brief History* (London: Birkbeck College, 1997).
Webb, Katherine, 'A Tribute to Tessa Blackstone. Master of Birkbeck College 1987–1997' (7 March 1998).

Wells, G. G., *Experiment in Autobiography: Discoveries and Conclusions of a Very Ordinary Brain, Since 1866* (London: Victor Gollancz, 1934).
Wells, H. G., *The Outline of History: Being a Plain History of Life and Mankind*, vol. 2 (New York: The Macmillan Company, 1920).
Westwood, Gordon [pseudo. Michael Schofield], *A Minority: A Report on the Life of the Male Homosexual in Great Britain* (London: Longmans, Green and Co., 1960).
Westwood, Gordon [pseudo. Michael Schofield], *Society and the Homosexual* (London: Victor Gollancz, 1952).
Wilk, Stephen R., *How the Ray Gun Got Its Zap: Odd Excursions into Optics* (Oxford: Oxford University Press, 2013).
Williams, William Mattieu, 'The Birkbeck School, London Mechanics' Institution. Under the Patronage of the Right Hon. The Earl of Radnor' (Edinburgh: n.p., 1848).
Williams, William Mattieu, *The Intellectual Destiny of the Working Man; An Address Delivered on the 28th May, 1863, to the Members of the 'Institute Chemical Society'* (Birmingham: Cornish Brothers, 1863).
Williams, William Mattieu, *A Vindication of Phrenology* (London: Chatto and Windus, 1894).
Willingham, Robert Allen II, 'Jews in Leipzig: Nationality and Community in the 20th Century', PhD thesis (Austin: University of Texas, 2005).
'Windsor House, Bream's Buildings & Cursitor Street', plans (London: Cuthbert Lake and Sutton, n.d., *c.*1880s).
Winnington-Ingram, R. P., 'Amy Marjorie Dale, 1902–1967', *Proceedings of the British Academy*, 53 (1967).
Woolf, Virginia, *A Room of One's Own/Three Guineas*, 1st pub. 1929 (Harmondsworth: Penguin, 1993).
Woolf, Virginia, *Three Guineas* (London: Harcourt, Brace, and Co., 1938).
World Economic Forum, *The Future of Jobs* (Geneva: WEF, 2016).
Wozniak, Heather Anne, 'The Play with a Past: Arthur Wing Pinero's New Drama', *Victorian Literature and Culture*, 37 (2009).
Wyndham-Goldie, Grace, 'The Story Behind the Challenge of our Time', in Arthur Koestler, E. L. Woodward, J. D. Bernal, et al., *The Challenge of our Time: A Series of Essays* (London: Percival Marshall, 1948).
Zagorski, Nick, 'Profile of Janet Thornton', *Proceedings of the National Academy of Sciences of the United States*, 102.35 (30 August 2005).
Žižek, Slavoj, *The Ticklish Subject: The Absent Centre of Political Ontology* (London: Verso, 1999).

Acknowledgements

David Latchman, Birkbeck's Vice Chancellor, had the original idea for a book celebrating the college's bicentenary. His commitment to the Birkbeck community has been crucial, as has the support of Matt Innes (Deputy Vice Chancellor), Keith Harrison (College Secretary), and other officers of the college. True to their word, they never attempted to edit a single sentence of the text.

I have been blessed by a large community of collaborators, colleagues, scholars, and friends, without whom this book could not have been written. Most of all, I am grateful to librarians and archivists at Birkbeck and throughout the country. The archive in Birkbeck's Malet Street building, looked after by the super-helpful Emma Illingworth, has been invaluable. Sarah Hall has been incredible in advising me about the visual images in the Birkbeck History section of the Birkbeck Image Collections. An extraordinary part of Birkbeck's archive is held at the Bishop's Move storage facility just outside of Ely. It is difficult to convey the importance of this archive to non-historians. While the archive in Malet Street contains vital *institutional* papers as well as student documents (such as student newsletters and magazines), the archive in Ely is packed with more everyday college papers. For anyone interested in the history of education or the social and political lives of Londoners more broadly, please take a look. It tells the history of Britain in the past 200 years, in terms of sociability, sport, diet, war, sex, gender, architecture, collegiate interactions, disciplinarity, and—well—*life*. It is a treasure trove. While writing this book, accessing this material required the heavy (literally) labour of Paul Colledge, who employed a forklift to transport the massive shipping containers from their perch in the warehouse to a busy, fume-filled lorry-park outside. That was where I worked, in winter winds and summer suns. Thanks so much, Paul and branch manager Michala Burnell. I am thrilled that the college is now committed to bringing this archive to Birkbeck's central building.

Special mention must go to the anonymous reviewers for Oxford University Press who gave wise advice, and to OUP's Cathryn Steele, Stephanie Ireland, Sarah Posner, and Bhavani Govindasamy. Guidance was generously provided by Jen Baird, Antony Bale, Ollie Berman, Sean Brady, Laurel Brake, Carolyn Burdett, Richard Clarke, Steven Connor, Christy Constantakopoulou, Matt Cook, Catharine Edwards, Richard Evans, Alan Forth, Stephen Frosh, Kayleigh Woods Harley, Briony Harmer, Sarah Hart, Basil Hiley, Dermot Hodson, Diane Houston, Jessica Jeske, Roger Johnson, Nicholas Keep, Fraser Keir, Niki Lacey, Marjorie Lorch, Almuth McDowall, Lesley Mcfadyen, Alan MacKay, Carmen Mangion, Carolyn Moores, Hannah Mullarky, Greg Neale, Tim Reynolds, Helen Shaw, Michael Slater, Naomi Smith, Rhea Sookdeosingh, Julian Swann, Becky Taylor, William Vaughan, Alison Watson, Jonathan Woodhead, and Sami Zubaida. Many others are acknowledged in footnotes. Thanks also to my agent, James Pullen of The Wylie Agency. This book was written over many years, so I fear that there are people I have omitted: please forgive me if I don't name you. Your help and encouragement spurred me on.

My journey through the history of Birkbeck was shared by two early career scholars who were simultaneously researching the College for our bicentenary. Jonny Matfin and Ciarán O'Donohue have been a joy to work with and have been diplomatic assessors of some of my hypotheses. Sasha Dovzhyk took time out from her own research to provide excellent research assistance and fact-checking. My family in New Zealand, Australia, Switzerland, and Greece were a barometer of what was an interested story, or not. I was sitting with Louise Hide and Sarah Weir in a fish taverna in Koukaki, Athens, when I made the decision to write this history. They have delicately nudged this book in important directions.

Finally, this book is dedicated to Costas Douzinas, who shares my passion for Birkbeck's radical historical mission and its unique students. He is my constant companion, inspiration, and joy.

Index

Note: Figures are indicated by an italic '*f*' following the page number.

For the benefit of digital users, indexed terms that span two pages (e.g., 52–53) may, on occasion, appear on only one of those pages.

Aason, Chas. 70–1
Academic Assistance Council 363
Academic Board 111
Academic gowns 507–8
Adler, Nathan Marcus 5, 191–2
Administrating Staff, *see* Secretaries
Adult Education 2, 80, 224, 388–9, 512, 520, 527, 530, 540–1, 547–50, 553, 555–6, 560, 563, 576, 588*f And throughout*
Aesthetics 394–5, 401
Aharonov-Bohm 418–19, 429–30
Ali, Dusé Mohammed 205–6
Alison, Archibald 4
Allen, Grant 183–7
Allen, Mike 157
Allot, Miriam 172*f*
Althusser/Althusserianism 384–6, 393, 402
Alumni 118–19, 139–40, 139*f*, 151, 258–9, 294*f*, 553, 556–7, 579, 581
Alvesson, Mats 450–1
Amschewitz, John Henry 149
Anatomy classes 58–60, 145, 176, 187–8
Anderson, John/Anderson Institution 2, 19–20, 366
Anderson, Perry 388
Angel, Moses 191–2
Angell, John 70–1
Animal Experimentation, *see* Animals
Animal Liberation Front 300
Animals 49, 64, 175, 286–303, 446–7, 461
Anthem, College's 134, 135*f*, 317
Anthropology, *see* Politics and Sociology
Anti-Semitism 228–9, 263–4, 274, 341, 373, 395–6, 409
Aprahamian, Hovhannes Francis 373, 377–9, 417, 543
Architecture 30, 90–1, 143–59, 228–9, 345, 386, 509–10
Archaeology 386, 393, 453–4, 454*f*, 577
Archive 286
Arlen, Michael 275

Armitage-Smith, George 97, 102, 108, 111–12, 114–15, 119, 126–32, 134, 150–1, 192, 197–8, 256, 322, 330–1, 336, 389–90, 436–7, 590–3
Armstrong, Isobel 113*f*
Arnold, Matthew 536
Art 57, 136, 143–59, 195, 238–9, 345, 522–3, 579
Art History, Department 151, 153–5, 159, 339, 345, 394–5, 401
Arts and Humanities 43, 52–3, 156–8, 171–2, 201, 218, 272, 309, 371, 383, 389–90, 431–55, 463–4, 501–2, 508, 516, 528, 531–8
Ashby, Eric 540–1
Ashley, William 136
Association of Scientific Workers 366
Astronomy 5, 34, 43, 436
Attendants 234–5, 238, 284, 286, 288, 300–1, 312, 344–5, 578, 593
Attlee, Clement 367
Austerity 314, 467–8
Aveling, Francis Arthur Powell 444–5
Aveling, Edward Bibbins 185–6, 193, 445–6

Baby Lab/Centre for Brain and Cognitive Development 450–1
Back, Les 204
Bacon, Francis 30–1
Baillie, Joanna 144
Baker, Kenneth 553–4, 556–7
Bakewell, Joan 118
Balfour, Arthur 136, 207
Balfour, Lord of Burleigh 254–5, 305
Balfour, Clara Lucas 188–91
Baldwin, Stanley 136–40, 491
Bancroft, Squire 164–5
Barnard, George Alfred 349
Bars/Pubs 241–5, 280–1
Baring, Thomas 117
Barnes, Barry 52–3
Barr, Hazel Kathleen 273–4
Barret-Lennard, Fiennes 206–7

620 INDEX

Barrett, Arthur 470–1
Barrett, Elizabeth 144
Barrow, Fred 407, 425
Barton Derek 424–5
Bastin, Edward 'Ted' 469–70, 472, 482, 488–9
Bateson, William 136
'Battle for Birkbeck' 547–69
Becher, Tony 432
Becker, Bernard H. 147–9, 163–4, 195
Bedford College 200
Behaviourism 301–2, 398, 444, 446–7
Bell, Charles 145
Bell, John S. 488
Bell, Lily 180–1
Bender, Hans 469–70
Benjamin, Walter 395
Bennett, Georgiana 188, 190–1
Bennett, John G. 340
Bentham, Jeremy 21, 250, 589
Berlin, Mike 233
Bernal, J. D. 197–8, 301–2, 343, 359–80, 407, 409–10, 412–13, 414*f*, 415–16, 415*f*, 417*f*, 425–9, 457–8, 464–5, 467–8, 488, 509, 509*f*, 514, 533–4, 537–8, 542–6
Berridge, John 277–80
Besant, Annie 192–6
Beveridge, William 585–7
Beyer, Ralph 356–8
Bigham, John Charles (Lord Mersey) 317–18
Biology 91–2, 103–4, 136, 192–3, 269, 276, 288, 290, 292, 296–9, 301–2, 336–7, 365, 407–8, 411–12, 415–16, 426–7, 429–30, 436, 498, 501–2, 522–3, 531, 536, 564–6, 577
Birch, Derek 171
Birkbeck Bank 44*f*, 78–94, 96, 147, 252–3
Birkbeck Building and Freehold Land Society, *see* Birkbeck Bank
Birkbeck, George 1–2, 14, 19–27, 29–39, 44, 47–8, 50–1, 56–61, 80, 96, 143–4, 161–2, 187–8, 294*f*, 335–6, 549–50, 587, 590
Birkbeck Institute for the Humanities 513
Birkbeck Institute for Social Research (BISR) 452
Birkbeck (formerly, Pears) Institute for the Study of Antisemitism 263–4
Birkbeck Players 167, 171–3, 273
Birkbeck Schools 44*f*, 45, 67–77, 80–3, 582
Birkbeck, William Lloyd 80–2, 88, 90, 96–7, 117
Birkinshaw, Keith 472
Birth Control 16–17, 192–5
Bithell, Jethro 133, 351–2
Blackbourn, David 387
Blackstone, Tessa 112, 113*f*, 116, 244, 379–80, 390–2, 390*f*, 496, 518

Blackett, Patrick Maynard Stuart Patrick 360, 362–6, 378, 413–14, 428–9, 537
Blair, Robert 128
Blair, Tony 398–9
Blank, Michel 443–4
Blandford, George Fielding 178–9
Blanchot, Maurice 395
Bloomsbury/Bloomsbury Group 2, 136, 158, 227, 238–9, 242–4, 528–9
Blue Anchor Pub 242–4
Blundell, Tom 426–9
Bohm, David 362, 379, 417–18, 420–2, 429, 471–95
Bohr, Niels 424
Booth, Andrew Donald and Kathleen 415–16, 456–68
Bostock, A. Leslie 343–4
Botany 174–5, 274, 292–3, 327–30, 486–7, 533–4, 537
see also Sciences
Bourke, Joanna 387
Boyd-Carpenter, John 279
Boyle, Robert 387
Bragg, William 365, 428–9
Bragg, Lawrence 365, 416, 428–9
Brah, Avtar 204–5, 208
Brandram, Samuel 164–5
Bream's Building 88–90, 122, 123*f*, 259–60, 286, 305, 332–4, 332*f*, 413–14, 426*f*, 506, 521–2, 529*f*
Brexit 403, 576, 585
Britten, Kathleen Hylda Valerie, *see* Booth, Kathleen
British Brothers League 207–8
British Film Institute 157–8
British Union of Fascists 207–8, 271–6
Brooks, Harold Fletcher 512–13
Brooks, Roy 277
Broome, John 402–3
Brown, Andrew 378
Brougham, Henry 1, 6–7, 14, 17–19, 22–6, 31–9, 47–8, 51, 60–1, 146–7, 178–9, 250, 348, 587
Browning, Robert 285, 360–2, 364, 376, 379, 395–6, 515–17
Bukharin, Nikolai 372
Bull, William James 79–80, 98–102, 139–40, 149–51, 165, 238–9, 331
Bullough, William Sydney 295–9, 545–6
Bu'Lock, John D. 276
Bulwer-Lytton, Robert 252
Burne-Jones, Edward 345
Busk, Edward 128
Burdett, Francis 60–1
Burhop, E. H. S. 491–2
Burns, A. Gavin 88, 255–6

Burns, Cecil Delisle 126–7, 136
Burns, John 179
Burton, N. 299
Buss, Henry 125–6, 146–7, 519
Butler, R. A. 268, 270
Butler, Mrs S. 195
Butt, David Keith 340–1
Byron, Lord/Lady 50, 72

Cahn, Andrew 585–6
Cambridge House 585–6
Campaign for Nuclear Disarmament 367
Campbell, Archibald Bruce 498–9
Campbell, Eila 240–1, 440–1
Caraffi, Arnolfo John 116, 233, 245–6, 267–8, 280–1, 463–6, 504–5, 528
Carlile, Harry 379, 410–11, 414–16, 415f
Carlile, Richard 54, 64, 367
Carlyle, Thomas 272
Carroll, Lewis 381
Carter, H. F. 197–8
Carver, Vida 510–11
Cato Street conspiracy 13, 54–5, 60
Centenary Celebrations 134–40, 306f, 336
Chairman Mao 364
Che Guevara 364
Chadd, Elizabeth 16–17
Chaloner, George 496–7
Chamberlain, Neville 348
Chancery Lane 25, 90–2, 136–7, 153, 167, 235, 238–9, 242, 250, 263, 313, 344, 522
Chandler, Tony 516
Chapman, Mike 299
Chapman, Sydney 555–6
Chartism 25–6, 87
Charter 88 399–400
Chemistry 329–30, 336–7, 343, 408, 424–5, 426f, 427–8, 486, 496–7, 531, 533–5, 538, 544–5, 551, 582
  see also Sciences
Cheshire, Frederic John 503–4
Childcare 284
Chivers, Lena May 337–8, 337f, 347–8, 367
Chomsky, Noam 382, 403–4
Christie, Ian 157
Churchill, Winston Spencer 335, 348–9
Ciaccia, Benedetta 583–4
Cinema, Birkbeck 158–9
City Parochial Foundation 252–3
City Polytechnic 95, 102–3, 126, 128–31
Clarke, Arthur C. 472–3
Clarke, Richard 85
Classics 104, 111–12, 125, 244, 285, 292–3, 319, 343–4, 360–2, 364, 386, 515–17, 527, 531–3

Cleaners 577–8, 583
Cleaver, Arthur Valentine 473
Clee, Charles R. 294f
Clements, Reginald Francis 319–22, 322f, 334, 334f
Clive, Violet 293
Clore Lecture Theatre 565, 576–7, 587
Cobbett, William 21
Cold War, *see* Soviet Union/USSR
Coleridge, Samuel Taylor 144, 249
College Secretary 113f, 114, 116–17, 119, 194, 233, 235–6
Collins, Harry M. 483–4
Colonialism, *see* Empire
Combe, George 64–5, 73
Combination Laws 32
Common Rooms 122, 233–45, 247–86, 312–13, 330, 335, 344–5, 359–60, 364, 379–80, 409–10, 506, 579–80, 585
Common Wealth Party 313
Communism-Communist Party 273, 335–6, 338, 349, 359–80, 395–6, 409, 417–18, 442–3, 467–8, 471, 485, 488, 490, 492–3, 503–4, 542–3
Compass Project 592
Complaints 514
Computing 456–68, 522–3, 550, 574–5, 581–4
Congreve, William Henry 97–102, 116–17, 194
Connolly, James 174–5
Connor, Steve 172–3
Conservative Student Society 273
Conscription 323–5, 336–7, 341–2, 353, 497
Constructivism/Deconstruction 387, 392, 394–5, 400, 450, 455, 488
Continuing Education, *see* Extra Mural Studies Department
Converzational 256
Cooke, R. G. 349
Cooper, Gladys 164–5
Corporation of London 390–1
Council for At-Risk Academics 363
Council of Christians and Jews 341
COVID-19 569, 573–9, 581–2, 587
Coward, Barry 513
Coward, Nöel 275
Cox, David Roxbee 433
Creager, Angela 411–12
Creative Writing/Composition 43, 61, 69, 188, 194f, 386, 454–5, 582
Crenshaw, Kimberlé W. 204
Crick, Bernard 388–9, 394, 398–400, 402–3, 520, 554–5
Crick, Francis 413, 416–17, 427–8
Criminology, Department 390–1

622 INDEX

Critical Legal Studies 394–5
Critical Race Theory 394–5
Critical Theory 157–8, 400, 450
Crossley, Paul 151
Crown and Anchor Tavern 2, 11–31, 54–5
Crystallography (*see also* Physics) 113*f*, 343, 362, 364, 378, 408, 413, 415*f*, 421, 424–9, 457–8, 509, 509*f*, 542–6
Curriculum 43, 45–7, 58–66, 69, 73–4, 99, 102–3, 124–5, 127–8, 150–1, 155, 170

Dakin, Douglas 248–9, 343–4, 352–3
Dale, Army Marjorie 244
Dalton, Hugh 398–9
Darcus, Mrs John 188, 190
Darlington, Reginald Ralph 372, 386–7, 503–5
Daunt, Beatrice Marjorie 272, 342–3, 506, 509–10, 512–13, 520
Davies, George MacDonald 122–4, 503
De Bac, Pierre Barthelemy Guinebert 68–70
Deconstruction, *see* Constructionism
De László, Philip 328*f*
Deleuze, Gilles 395
Denning, Lord 117, 269, 555–6
Derbyshire, Mr. 236–7
Derrida, Jacques 387, 395
Descartes 419
Desmond, Adrian 51
De Witt, Bryce 477
Dickens, Charles, and Charles Dickens Jr. 67, 75, 145–6, 160, 164–5, 168, 172–3
Dickinson, Henry Douglas 368
Dienes, Paul 336–49, 360, 364, 379
Dimbleby, David 469–70, 479–80
Disability 7–8, 204, 226–8, 511, 575, 591
Disciplines 431–55
Disraeli, Benjamin 4
Diversity 228, 518
 see also LGBTQ, Minoritized Communities, Disabilities
DNA 408, 411
Dobson, Frank 556
Dobson, Paul 283
Dodds, Harold 418
Doern, Kristin G. 191
Dolphin, Philippa 113*f*
Donohue, Jerry 427–8
Douzinas, Costas 391–2, 394–5, 400–1, 518
Drama, *see* Theatre and Social Life
Dryden, John 272
Dutton, Brian 443–4

Eames, Hubert Wells 119, 323–4
Earth Sciences 365–6, 436, 441, 577
 see also Geology

East, Gordon W. 438–9
Economics, Department of 74, 114–15, 126, 132, 330, 338, 381–3, 386, 402–3, 515, 532, 555
Ede and Ravenscroft 79–80
Education Reform Act of 1988 515
Edwards, Catherine 387
Edwards, Peter Douglaw 390*f*
Ehrenberg, Werner E. 379, 415–16, 415*f*, 429, 543
Einstein, Albert 417–18, 421–2, 424, 477, 485, 488
Elementary Education 67–77
 see Birkbeck Schools
Elias, Norbert 388
Eller, Rev. Irvin 4
Elliott, Marianne 387–8, 396–7
Elliott, Walter 306–7
Ellis, William, *see* Birkbeck Schools
Ellison, Arthur 473
Elocution 46, 52–3, 97–8, 127–8, 163–4, 173, 190, 195–6, 386
Empire/Colonialism 6, 116–17, 161–3, 200–1, 206–8, 250–1, 283–4, 317–18, 329–30, 400–1, 450–1
Engels Society of CPGB 368
Engels, Friedrich 51, 85–6
English Composition, *see* Creative Writing
English, Department of 113*f*, 134–6, 173, 249, 272, 274, 277, 302–3, 342–3, 386, 453–4, 506, 512, 516, 537–40
EPR Paradox 477
Estates Department 95, 574, 577
Ethics 383, 394–5, 397–8, 400–1
Eurocommunism 377
European Union 399–400, 576, 585
Evans, John William 436, 509
Evans, Richard 115–16, 378, 384–7, 392, 397–9
Evening Teaching 131–2, 241–2, 248, 342, 354–5, 379, 496, 520, 522–4, 527–46, 548–9, 573, 581
Evison, Vera 453–4
Eward, William 81–2
Exhibition Movement 50
Extra Mural Studies Department 157–8, 222–6, 453–4, 549–50, 560, 582–3
External Relations 581
Eyles, H. 356

Faculty for Lifelong Learning, *see* Extra Mural Studies Department
Fancuchen, Isidor 414–15
Fascism 207–8, 271–6, 314, 368, 497
Federalism 95
Fees 45–6, 68, 76–7, 102, 125–31, 144, 283–4, 338, 506, 547, 557–8, 563, 568–9, 576, 583, 587, 592

INDEX 623

Feldman, David 263-4
Fells, John Manger 194*f*
Feminism 118, 139-40, 157-8, 174-204, 220-6, 228-9, 337-8, 379-80, 392, 394-5, 401, 450, 453, 497, 501, 509-10, 512-13
Fetter Lane 118-19, 139, 192-3, 234, 237-8, 242-3, 250, 304-8, 311-12, 314, 445-6, 528, 539-40
Film, *see* History of Film
Finances 95-6, 109
Fine, Ben 384
Finch, John Thomas 410
Figes, Orlando 387
Finsberg, Geoffrey 555-6
Fisher Act of 1918 519
Fisher, A. Ernest 109
Flather, James L. 116
Fletcher, Hanslip 149
Floud, Jean 338
Floud, Roderick 338, 387, 552-4, 557, 559, 563
Foggo, George 53-4
Food, *see* Refectory
Foote, Maria 144
Forbes, Archibald 164-5
Forster, E. M. 539-40
Foss, Brian 443-4, 446-7
Foster, Roy F. 387-8
Foster, Mrs Thomas Cooke 188
Foucault, Michel 392, 402, 432, 453
Fox, Charles 346-7, 352
Frampton, George 148-9
Francis 'Ma' and Alfred 233-8, 234*f*, 243, 245-6, 311-13, 346, 507-8, 579
Franklin, Rosalind 374-5, 407, 427-8, 457-8
Frege, Gottlob 433
Freud, Sigmund 392, 453
Friends of Birkbeck, *see* Alumni
Frisch, Otto Robert 413-14
Frosh, Stephen 449-52, 513-14
Furth, Reinhold 424

Gaia Hypothesis 336-7
Galbraith, John Kenneth 402
Galbraith, William 109
Gamesmanship 249-50
Gardner, Martin 480-1
Garstand, Walter 292-3
Garvey, Marcus 205-8
'Geller Kids', *see* Julie Knowles; *see* Stephen North
Geller, Uri 469-95
Gender 133-4, 158, 197-8, 200, 204-5, 216, 225-6, 228-9, 268, 290-1, 314, 318, 350, 399-401, 408, 426-30, 490, 496, 504, 512-13, 580-1, 591
 see Sex/Sexuality; *see* LGBTQ; *see* Women

Geography 43, 114, 151, 211-12, 240-1, 431-2, 434-42, 504, 516, 529*f*
Geology, Department of 5, 99, 122-4, 194, 434-42, 503, 508-9, 551*f*, 561
Geometry 5-6, 41, 43, 407
 see Mathematics
Giangrande, Giuseppe 515-17, 532-3
Gilchrist, John Borthwick 250-1
Gill, Eric 356
Girard, Jean-Pierre 469-70
Glennie, Paul 505
Godwin, William 16-17
Goldney, Kathleen M. 486-7
Goldschmidt, Victor 340
Gollan, John 377
Gooch, George Peabody 136
Goodfellow, Julia 113*f*, 426-7
Goodrich, Peter 391-2, 394-5, 518
Gordon Square 158, 238-9, 243, 577
Gossling, Frank 109, 331
Governors 99-100, 102, 104-12, 106*f*, 117, 131-3, 198, 240, 252-3, 258-9, 263, 267, 355, 390-1, 440-1, 496-7, 506-7, 543, 575, 585-6
Governance 95-121, 583
Gower Street 577
Gramsci, Ontonio 377
Gray, Mary 176, 178-9
Greaves, Jim and Kathleen 540-1
Greece 13-14, 248-9, 337-8, 352-3, 361-2, 415*f*
Green, J. Samuel 205
Green, Simon 301-2
Greenford, *see* Sports
Greenwood, Thomas 350-1
Gregory, John Walter 437
Gresse Street 238-9, 241-2, 384, 388-9, 389*f*
Griffin, Emma 53-4
Griffiths, Albert 104, 509
Griffith, Arthur 326
Griffiths, A. Phillips 535
Grimond, Jo 555-6
Grinfield, Edward William 3, 5-7
Grossmith, George and Grossmith Jr. 160-1
Grosvenor, Mrs E. F. 195
Grote, George 21
Groundsmen 281-3
Guthrie, Woody 343
Gwynne-Vaughan, David Thomas 327
Gwynn-Vaughan, Helen 133, 258-9, 274, 292-3, 327-9, 328*f*, 340-1, 350, 350*f*, 486-7

Habermas, Jurgen 395
Hadlow, Henry 305, 308
Haldane, John 511
Haldane, Richard 127-8, 136, 308-9, 317-18, 332

624   INDEX

Hall, John 549–50
Hall, Radclyffe 289
Hamlyn, David W. 516–17, 554
Hanlon, Joseph 479–80
Hampson, Keith 555–6
Hardie, Keir 181–2
Harding, Vanessa 387
Hare, F. Kenneth 115–16, 541
Harris, George F. 122–4, 437, 503
Harris, Jonathan 550
Harrison, J. F. C. 53
Harrison, Keith 116, 573–4, 585–6
Hardy, Barbara 172–3, 512–13, 537–9
Hasted, John Barrett 469–95
Haydon, Benjamin Robert 143–8, 156–7, 159
Hazlitt, William 144
Hawking, Stephen 423
Headlam, Arthur Cayley 128–9
Heads of Department 385*f*
Hearn, K. M. 105
Healey, Lord 118
Heath, Ted 279–80
Hegelism 493
Henderson H.C.K. 435, 438, 440–1
Hepworth, Barbara 371–2
Herman, Ros 556–7
Henstock, Ralph 349
Hess, Myra 343
Hessen, Boris 369–70, 372
Hetherton, Henry 25–6
Heyck, Thomas William 7–8
Hichens, William Lionel 139–40, 355
Higher Education Funding for England (HEFCE) 451–2
Hill, Christopher 376
Hiley, Basil 419–23, 428–9, 483
Hind, C. Lewis 160, 164, 520
Hines, Albert Gregorio (Bertie) 381–4
Hirst, Paul Quentin 384–6, 388, 393–4, 399–400
Historians Group of Communist Party of Great Britain 368, 375
History, Department of 133, 194*f*, 198–202, 248–9, 272, 343–5, 348, 352–3, 359, 364, 386, 392, 395–6, 453–4, 503–5, 513, 519, 552, 576, 583–4
History of Art, Department of 157–8, 514
History of Film, Media, and Cultural Studies, Department of 157–8
History Workshop Journal 228–9
HIV/AIDS 518
Hoare, Valerie 518
Hobhouse, John 6, 54–5
Hobhouse, L. T. 388

Hobsbawm, Eric 117–18, 152, 359–80, 395–6, 403–4, 503–4, 546, 553
Hodgkin, Dorothy Crawfoot 416–17, 428, 509
Hodgskin, Thomas 1, 14–16, 22–6, 33–4, 38–9, 47–8, 67, 382–3, 587
Holgate, Philip 433
Holliday, Billy 371–2
Holmes, Kenneth C. 410
Holocaust 341–2, 342*f*, 397–8
Homosexuality, *see* LGBTQ
Hood, S, W. 105
Hore-Belisha, Lesley 366
Horne, Barry 301
Horner, Francis 19–20
Horne, *see* George Francis Troup Horne
Hornsby, Jennifer 113*f*
Hoskin, Keith 431–2
Hudson, James William 41–3
Hugh, Nicolas 433
Human Rights 400–1
Humanities, *see* Arts and Humanities
Hume, Charles Wesley 104–8, 122, 125–7, 252–3, 261–2, 286–303, 539–40
Hume, John 21, 32
Hume, Joseph 35, 60–1
Hume, Ricardo 21
Hungary 276–80, 278*f*, 374–7
Hunt, Leigh 144
Hunter, Michael 387
Hurst, G. H. J. 205
Hurwitz, Harry 446–7
Huxley, Aldous 363
Huxley, Julian 498–9
Huxley, T. H. 536
Hyndman, H. M. 174–5

Ibsen, Henrik 169–70
Iddesleigh, Earl of 270
Imperialism, *see* Empire
Industrial Psychology, *see* Occupational Psychology
Influenza Epidemic 235
Informational Technology Services (ITS) 574–5
Inge, Dean 310
Innes, Matt 576, 585–6
Insanity/Asylum 178–80, 186–7
Institute of Justice and Crime Policy Research 390–1
Intellectuals 381–404, 410, 497, 499, 501–4, 514, 537 *And throughout*
Interdisciplinarity 371, 395, 438–9, 443–4, 450, 452–3
Internationalism 424–5
International Students 239, 284, 576, 592

INDEX 625

Intersectionality 204–5, 216
  see also Minoritized Communities; see LGBTQ;
  see Disabilities
Ireland 387–8, 396
Irving, Henry 164–5, 397–8
Ivanovich, Nikolai 373
Ives, David James Gibbs 534–5

Jackson, Harold Gordon 112–15, 171, 245,
  292–3, 336, 340, 353, 527–8, 548, 549f
Jamaica, see West Indies
Janis, Byron and Maria Cooper 473
Jazz 371–2
  see also Music/Singing
Jeffrey, J.W. 360, 362, 364, 374, 415f, 416–17
Jeger, Baroness, see Lena May Chivers
Jennings, John 240–1
Jerrold, Douglas 27–8
Jew/Jewish 7, 150, 152, 191–2, 223, 263–4, 273,
  275–6, 289, 338–42, 342f, 351–2, 359, 363,
  365, 373, 388, 397–8, 408–10
Joad, C. E. M. 249–50, 274, 292–3, 335–6, 345, 352,
  444–5, 486–7, 496–502, 502f, 511, 513, 524
Jodl, Alfred 353
Johnson, Boris 573
Johnson, Richard 51
Johnson, Roger 460
Joliot-Curie, Frederic 367, 414f
Joliot-Curie, Irene 414f
Jones, Arthur 133, 343–4, 348–9, 386
Joyce, William 207–8, 271–6
'Joy Night' 304–14

Kaiser, David 488
Keats, John 144
Keet, Hilda 119–21, 323–4
Keller, Evelyn Fox 301–2
Kelsey, Franklyn 171
Keynes, John Maynard 158, 384
Khrushchev, Nikita 374–5, 375f
King, Rickie 284
Kinnock, Neil 395–6
King, Martin Luther 367
King's College London 128–9, 311–13
King, Tricia 581
Kitz, Norman 456
Klug, Aaron 410–12, 457–8
Knowles, Julie 475–6, 481–2, 484, 490
Knox, Robert 207
Koestler, Arthur 472–3
Krishnamurti, Jiddu 484–5, 492

Levene, Sam 415f
Labanyi, Josephine 113f

Labour Party 118, 136, 181–2, 198, 337–8, 337f,
  388–9, 395–6, 402–3, 497
  see also Marxism and Social Democratic
  Federation
Lacan, Jacques 395
Lacey, Nicola 113f
Laclau, Ernesto 395
Lamb, Charles 144
Lanchester, Edith 174–87, 203
Lanchester, Elsa 187
Lanchester, Henry James 174–5
Lander, G. Druce 109
Lansbury, George 175, 193
Langdale, Charles 3
Language Research Centre 443–4, 466–7
Languages 97–8, 113f, 125, 133, 250–1, 351–2,
  442, 462–4, 466–7, 514, 516, 519, 527–8,
  533, 550, 573
Latchman, David 1, 77, 111–12, 115, 527, 575,
  585–7, 586f, 591–2
Latin/Greek, see Languages
Lauder, Harry 326
Laurence, Edna 295
Law, Bonar 328–9
Law, Department of 113f, 167–8, 205, 386,
  389–90, 401, 518, 522–3
Lazarus, Jack 273
League Tables 452–3, 583
Leavis, F. R. 535
Ledger, Sally 169–70
Lee, Ronald 300
Left/Leftists 359–404
Legendre, Pierre 395
Legge, Antony 453–4
Leighton, Frederic 345
Lenin Prize 366
Lessing, Doris 376
Levey, M. F. 109
Levin, Bernard 381
Levinas, Emmanuel 395
Levison, J. L. 63–4
Levison, Michael 463–4
Levy-Lawson, Harry 308
Lewis, Wyndham 537
Library 44–5, 62–3, 95–6, 113f, 114, 122–4, 123f,
  133, 144, 168–70, 284, 345, 346f, 347f, 389f,
  528, 532, 545, 549–50, 573, 575, 580f, 581–2
Liddell Hart, Lobban, Basil Henry 366
Lindemann, Frederick Alexander 485
Linguistics/Applied Linguistics 442–4, 460–1,
  463–4, 466–7, 554–5
Lintorn-Orman, Rotha 272

626 INDEX

Lipstad, Deborah 397–8
Lissauer, Frank 356–7
Literature 394–5
  see also English Department
Littlewood, Sydney 295
Hay, John 134–6
Lobban, John Hay 272
Locke, William Nash 460–1, 463
Lockwood, Betty 118
Lockwood, John F. 110–11, 115–16, 277, 279, 294f, 372, 464–5, 527–46
Lodestone 247–59, 257f, 267, 285
Lord Haw-Haw, *see* Joyce, William
Lovelock, James 336–7
Lovenduski, Joni 401
Logic 277, 383
London School of Economics (LSE) 99, 383, 530, 548–9
Lonsdale, Kathleen 428–9, 544
Lord Haw Haw, *see* William Joyce
Lovett, William 25–6
Lukacs, Gyorgy 402
Lurgan, Lord 311
Lysenko, Trofim Denishovic 372–3
Lucas, John Seymour 148–9
Luhmann, Niklas 395
Lyotard, Jean-Luc 395

Mabey, Christine 113f
Macaulay, Thomas Babington 145–6
MacDonald, Ramsay 136, 140, 258–9, 588–9, 588f
MacFarlane, Andrew 81–2, 96, 98–9, 116
MacFee, Andy 158
McFee, William 258
McFetridge, Ian 511–12
Machin, Trevor 527
MacKay, Alan 421–2
Mackay, Lindsay 360, 362, 364, 379
Mackworth, Margaret 139–40
Mace, Alec Cecil 444–8, 510–11, 510f
Macmillan, Lord 306, 337–8
McNulty, Bridget 238
Macve, Richard 431–2
Magnus, Albertus 258
Malet Street Building 132–3, 171–3
Management and Business, School of 449, 514, 522–3, 565, 568
Maoism 377
Marquis of Queensbury 181, 183–4
Marris, Robin 402–3, 555
Martin, Kingsley 362
Martin, William 205
Mary Poppins 92–3
Marx, Eleanor ('Tussy') 174–6, 185–6

Marx, Karl 15–16, 19, 51, 364–5, 382–4
Marxism 174–5, 337–8, 359–80, 393–4, 400, 402–3, 467–8, 488, 492–3, 533–4
Mascot 294f, 311–13
Mason, Alfred William 148–51, 156–7
Mason, Edith ('Emma') 504–5
Massey, Gerald 174, 180–1
Masters/Principals/Vice Chancellors 111–16, 121
Mathematics 43, 119, 194f, 198, 287, 349, 352, 360, 420–1, 423–5, 431, 433, 456–7, 460–1, 466, 486–7, 501–2, 514, 531, 533–4, 538
  see also Sciences
Maud, John Primatt Redcliffe 112–16, 336, 340, 342–3
Maybank, Thomas 149
Mayhew, Judith 390–1
McDonnell, John 388–9
Mead, Margaret 470
Meara, Paul 554–5
Mechanics 1–2, 19–25, 32–5, 38–42, 47, 57, 96–7, 122, 433, 590
Mechanics Institutes (general) 2–8, 38, 40–3, 80
Megau, Helen 415–16, 415f
Mendel, Gregor Johann 372
Michaelis, Ernst Gunther 275–6, 339–41
Mill, James 21
Mill, John Stuart 21
Millington, John 25
Mindszenty, Jozsef 376
Minerva 256
Minoritized Communities 204–29, 584, 591–2
Misogyny 395–6, 401, 411–12
Mitchell, David William 70–1
Mitford, Mary Russell 144
Moeran, Edward 313–14
Moi, Toni 169
Molecular Biology, *see* Biology
Moodle 574–5
Moore, Henry 356–7, 371–2
Mordell, Louis Joel 433
Morgan, Gregory J. 411–12
Morgan Thomas Hunt 372
Morice, Beaumont 205
Morley, Henry 75–6
Morrell, Ottoline 243
Morris, William 174–5, 179
Mosley, Oswald 207–8, 274
Mountbatten, Lord 366
Mulvey, Laura 157–8
Murray, Peter 157
Murray report 109
Music/Singing 43, 52–3, 57, 124, 160–73, 195, 310, 326, 343, 471, 481, 485, 490–1

INDEX 627

Mutual Instruction 56–7, 65, 582
Myers, David Gershom 454–5

Nabokov, Vladimir 454–5
Nandy, Lisa 389–90
Nass, Michael 481
National Repository, *see* Exhibition Movement
Nazi Germany 375
Nelson, Alec, *see* Edward Bibbins Aveling
Neruda, Pablo 407
Nettleton, Harold Redmayne 197–8, 248–9, 267–8
Neuroscience 301–2, 444, 450–2
Neuss, Paula 172–3, 172*f*
New Left 377, 379–80
Newman, Philip Harry 332
New Party 274
Newton, Francis 371–2
'New Managerialism' 95, 110–11
Nicholson, Ben 371–2
Nightingale, Florence 72
Nobel Prize 340–1, 411–12, 416–18, 420, 422, 424–5, 471, 485–6
Norris, George Morris 43, 45–7, 96–102, 108, 111–12, 114, 506, 519
North, Stephen 475–7, 484, 489–90
Northern Ireland 396
Northbrook, Lord 164–5
Nuclear Disarmament 367

Oakeshott, R. L. 121
Oakley, Ron and family 281–3
Oaksford, Mike 451–2
Occupational/Organizational Psychology 268, 431, 540–3, 574–5
  see also Psychology
Officer's Training Corps 273, 318, 326
Oldfield, Derek 512–13
Old Students' Association, *see* Alumni
Oppenheimer, Robert 417–18, 485
Opponents of Mechanics Institutes 2–8, 37–8
Orczy, Baroness 78–9, 82–3, 91–2
O'Regan, Brendan 472, 482, 488–9
Orwell, George 364, 398–9
O'Shaughnessy, Pat 245
O'Shea, Timothy M. M. 115–16
Overend, William George 112–13, 115–17, 372, 402–3, 516–17, 545–6, 551, 553
Owen, David 139–40
Owen, Wilfred 320

Pacifism/Peace Movement 335–6, 338, 363, 367, 375*f*, 377, 413, 471, 490–1, 497, 542–3
Pavlichenko, Lyudmila 343
Paine, Tom 16–17

Paranormal Sciences 469–95
Part-Time Education 227–8, 336–7, 390–1, 518–24, 527, 530–5, 537–44, 547–9, 552–4, 558–61, 563–4, 567–9, 579, 587, 591–2
Payne, James 238–9
Peace Campaigns, *see* Pacifism/Peace Movement
Pearson, Thomas J. 114, 116–17
Peat, David F. 419–20
Peltz Gallery 159
Penrose, Roger 420–3
Penson, Lillian 198–203
Percy, Eustace 304–5, 309
Peterloo massacre 54–5
Peiser, Herbert Stefan 415–16, 415*f*
Pett Ridge, William 99–101, 196–7, 331
Pevsner, Nikolaus 30, 90–1, 151–7, 159, 339, 345, 357–8, 509–10
Philosophy, Department of 113*f*, 136, 205, 249, 277, 292–3, 335–6, 350–1, 401, 444–6, 451, 486–7, 497–500, 511–12, 516–17, 522–3, 535, 554–5, 582
Phrenology 52–3, 60–6, 486, 582
Physics 104, 125, 197–8, 209, 240–1, 248–9, 267–8, 287, 340–1, 362, 364, 378, 408, 413, 417–18, 424–5, 434, 456, 464–6, 469–95, 503–4, 509, 535, 537, 542–6
  see also Crystallography
Picasso, Pablo 367, 371–2
Pierrepoint, Albert 276
Pimlott, Ben 398–9, 547, 552, 554–5, 569
Pinch, Trevor J. 483–4
Pinero, Arthur Wing 167–70, 186–7, 331
Pirani, Marcelli 340
Pitt, Geoffrey 415*f*
Place, Francis 1, 11, 14, 16–17, 22–6, 33, 41, 47–8, 348, 587, 590
Playfair, Lyon 45–7
Pleasure of Teaching 379 *And throughout*
Plummer, Desmond 555–6
Pocock, Childs 148–9
Podolsky, Boris 477
Poetry 67, 134–6, 144, 149–50, 155, 164–5, 177–91, 243–4, 258, 263–4, 320, 321*f*, 331
Politics/Political Economy 74, 330
Politics, Discussion of 53–7, 61–2
Politics and Sociology Department 240, 330, 336, 383–6, 388, 393, 398, 400–3, 437, 444, 520, 532, 555, 583–4
Polytechnic, *see* City Polytechnic
Potter, Stephen 249–50
Porter, Dorothy 392
Porter, Jeff 583–4
Porters, *see* Attendants
Portes, Richard 381–4, 554

Postcolonial/Postcolonialism 392, 394–5, 400–1
Postmodernism 393–5
Poststructuralism 391–2, 394–5, 401
Post-room 574
Pound, Ezra 537
Powell, C. F. 340–1
Presbyterianism 365
President of the College 117–18, 127–8, 164–5
Preston, Samuel 68–9
Price, Harry 486–7
Priestley, J. B. 352
Psychology, Department of 157–8, 249, 268, 301–2, 335, 444–51, 486–7, 497–500, 510–11, 517–18, 528, 529f, 539, 550, 573
Psychoanalysis 387, 394–5, 400, 450–1, 453–5
Psychosocial Studies, Department of 431, 444, 449–53, 513–14, 522–3
Public Engagement 581
Puharich, Andrija 469–70, 484

Quantum theory/mechanics 418–19, 477, 479, 481, 488, 493
Queens Park Rangers 282

Racism 161–2, 204–22, 250–2, 276, 304–5, 395–6, 401, 591–2
    see also Minoritized Communities
Radicalism/Radical theory xiii–xiv, 1–2, 6, 11, 13–14, 16–27, 32–4, 37–8, 47–8, 51–7, 60, 63–4, 66–7, 77, 87, 111, 145, 158, 174–203, 220, 222, 224, 228–9, 359–404, 485–94, 587–90
Radio 277–8, 497–9, 501, 540–1
Raemaeker, Louis 321f
'Ragging' 136–40, 137f, 285, 304–14
Ramon, C. V. 414f
Ramsey, William 486
Randall, John 408
Randi, James 481
Ranke von, Leopold 387
Rankin, G. C. 205
Ravenscroft, Clement A. 109
Ravenscroft, Francis 79–94
Ray, Mrs. 579
Raymond, James C 431
RAE/REF 432, 547, 553, 566–8, 581
Read, F. Oxley 275
Reception Desk 579
Refectory 233–47, 249, 261–2, 265, 278, 304–5, 311–13, 343–4, 346, 509–10, 512–13, 574, 578, 583
Reform Act of 1832 17–18, 21–2, 84–5, 144–5
Refugees 208, 275–80, 322, 323f, 338–41, 351–2, 485, 592

Reith, John 497–8
Religion 3, 5–7, 52–3, 58–60, 64–5, 72–4, 117, 150, 152, 188–9, 191–3, 194f, 261, 263–4, 287, 289, 292, 319, 321, 397, 462–4, 472, 499, 590–1
Rendle, Alfred B. 109
Research Assessment Exercises, see RAE/REF
Rhetoric 394–5
Ricardo, David 384
Richardson, Henry Gerald 104–8, 150
Ridge, William Pett 148f, 164–5
Rimington Taylor, Eva Germaine 435–6, 504–5
Rimmell, Anita 415f, 417
Robbins Report 448, 529–30
Roberts, Brian 116–17
Robertson, Forbes 164–5
Robertson, Joseph Clinton 1, 14, 22–6, 29–39, 47–8, 57, 587, 590
Robinson, Abraham 349
Rodger, Alec 268–9, 447–9
Roebuck, John Arthur 55
Rose, Gillian 395
Rose, Jacqueline 395
Rosen, Nathan 477
Rosenberg, Isaac 149–50
Roseneil, Sasha 452
Ross, David 550
Royal Society for the Prevention of Cruelty to Animals 286–8
Royalty/Royal Family 31, 35, 88–90, 117–19, 139–40, 162–3, 317, 350f, 353, 354f, 398–9, 498–9
Rowlandson, Jane 387
Rüntz, John, see Birkbeck School
Russell, Bertrand 196, 433, 500
Russell Square 528, 577
Rutherford, Ernest 362, 365, 537
Ryan, P. Loftus 275

Sadler, Michael 136
Salaries 234–5, 241, 506, 521–2
Salter, Arthur 366
Samnadan-Pillai, James Julian Ben 209–16, 209f, 238–9
Samuel, Herbert 348–9
Sapire, Hillary 387
Sarfatti, Jack 472–3, 481
Sarkar, Bikash Kusam 238
Sassoon, Siegfried 150, 320
Saunders, Andrew 172f
Saw, Ruth 500
Sayre, Anne 409
Sayre, David 409
Scarman, Lord 555–6

Schwalbe, Carl H. 427–8
Schiff, Kathe 379
Schofield, Michael 268–70
Schools, National 3
Sciences 43, 52–3, 58–66, 114–15, 119, 122–4, 133, 192–4, 324–5, 407–30, 522–3, 533–8, 582, 588*f*
Scoulaudi, Helen 415*f*
Scruton, Roger 401–2, 511, 554–5
Seccombe, Thomas 386
Secretaries 119, 238, 504–5, 510–11
Secretary and Clerk to the Governors, *see* College Secretary
Security Staff 284, 578, 583
Selbourne, David 401
Self-Help 53, 76, 85–7, 520, 550, 554–5, 557
Semiotics 394–5
Senter, George 43, 100, 111–12, 114–16, 119, 267, 280–1, 287, 292–3, 308, 310, 331
Sex/Sexuality 16–17, 177–8, 181–6, 264–71, 313–14, 328, 500–1
Seyton, Clara 188
Seaton, Jean 398–9
Shapin, Steven 52–3
Sharma, Chandra Shekhar 433
Shaw, George Bernard 166–7, 194*f*, 275
Shaw, Robert 424–5, 428–9
Shiner, Alfred M. 109
Shipley, Pat 448–9
Shorthand/Typing 34, 176–7, 194*f*
Shostakovich, Dmitri 367
Shum, Jon 517–18
Siddons, Sarah 144
Skinner, B. F. 446–7
Skoldberg, Kaj 450–1
Slater, Michael 172–3, 172*f*
Slater, William Kershaw 409
Slavery/Enslavers 4, 17–18, 97–8, 144–5, 205–6, 550
Slutz, Ralph 456
Small, James 197–8
Smiles, Samuel 283–4, 520, 550, 554, 557
Smith, Elizabeth Margaret 118
Smith, Ruth 539–40
Smith, Sydney 19–20
Smoking 261–3
Snow, C. P. 383–4, 535–7, 543
Soal, George 486–7
Social Control 51–8
Social Democratic Federation 174–5, 177–9, 181–2
Social Life 160–73, 247–85, 520–1
Social Mobility 41–2
Social Psychology 450

Social Sciences 383–4
    see also Politics and Sociology
Society for the Diffusion of Useful Knowledge 17
Sociology/Social Work 449–52, 532
    see also Politics and Sociology
Somers, Annie 198
Southampton Buildings 25, 29–39, 42, 68, 88, 167
Southey, Robert 144
Soviet Union/USSR 361–2, 367, 369–70, 373–8, 418, 442–4, 462, 470, 484–5, 490–3, 542–3
Spectrum 256
Spencer, Herbert 388
Spiritualism 486–7
Sports 209*f*, 247–85, 287, 325, 531
Spurgeon, Caroline 200
Spurzheim, Johann Caspar 62–4, 486
    see also Phrenology
Ste. Croix, Geoffrey 360–2, 379, 395–6
Stalin/Stalinism 374–6, 378–80, 492–3
    see also Soviet Union/USSR
Stanbrook, Ivor 555–6
Stanley, Henry Morton 164–5
Statistics 349, 433, 542–3
    see also Mathematics
Steadman-Jones, Richard 250–1
Stoker, Bram 165
Stone, Louise W. 345
Stopes, Marie 194–5
Strachey, Lytton 335
Student Central 284, 585–7
Student characteristics 518–24
Student Revolt of 1880s 95, 98–102
Students' Union/Representation 102, 104–8, 119, 134–6, 194, 197–8, 236, 239–40, 245, 247–85, 287, 310, 324*f*, 325, 336–8, 343–4, 497, 507–8, 520, 539–41, 547–8, 550
Strunk, William 501–2
Suburbanization 85
Suffield, Ruth 346–7
Suffrage and Suffragettes 84–7, 186–7
    see also Feminism
Sullivan, James 177, 181, 183, 187
Sutor, June 427–8
Swainson, Robert E. 116–17, 282–3, 516
Sweeting, Xenia 459*f*
Swinnerton-Dyer, Peter 551–4
Synagogue 413
Systems Theory 453

Taylor, Brenda 557
Taylor, Eva 438–41

Taylor, John 469, 474, 487–8
Taylor, John Robert 49, 64, 76–7
Taylor, Phyllis 510–11
Teacher Training 125, 176, 521–2
Teaching 496–524, 579–93 *And throughout*
Temperance 49–50, 82–3, 82*f*, 85, 114, 188–9, 191
Temple, William 117–18, 341
Tenure 515, 547, 583
Terrorism 300–1, 302*f*, 583–5
Terry, Ellen 165
Thatcher/Thatcherism 399–400, 547–8, 550–1, 551*f*, 554–6
Theatre 134–6, 160–73, 247–8, 273, 275, 304–5, 331, 344–5
Thirlwall, Connop 60–1
Thomas, Sidney Gilchrist 496–7
Thornton, Janet 426–7
Thompson, E. P. 57, 376, 393, 402
Thomson, Joseph John 136
Thorndike 521*f*
Thrift, Nigel 505
Tillotson, Geoffrey 512–13
Time/Timekeeping 505
Toddler Lab/Babylab 587
Topliss, Charles 42–3, 50
Torrington Square 172–3, 409–10, 416, 586–7
Travis, Phyllis 550
Tress, Ronald C. 115–16, 383–4, 388–90, 547–9, 551, 551*f*, 588–9
Troup Horne, George Francis 116, 119, 134, 153–4, 235–8, 248–9, 252–3, 273, 333–4, 339–47, 350–2, 351*f*, 528–9
Trowel, Paul 431–2, 453–4
Turner, Percy Moore 136
Two Cultures Debate 527–37, 543

Uganda 208
Unionist Party 329*f*
Universal Negro Improvement and Conservation Association and African Communities League 206–7
Universities and Colleges Admissions Service (UCAS) 542
Universities/Higher Education 7–8, 122–40, 201, 431–2
Universities Superannuation Scheme 583
University Grants Committee (UGC) 108–11, 241–2, 448, 547, 551–5
University of London 99, 102–10, 122–40, 201, 241, 282, 287, 330, 337–8, 354–5, 383, 431, 464–6, 506–7, 512–13, 518, 551, 582, 585–6, 592–3
University of London Animal Welfare Society 286–98

Unstead, John Frederick 435–6, 438
Uren, Ormond 442
Urry, William 519
Useful Knowledge 17–18, 29–32, 49–66, 202
USSR, *see* Soviet Union/USSR
Utilitarianism 16, 36, 55, 67, 185–6, 250, 589

Vallentine, Samuel 25, 42, 44
Varwell, M. G. 324*f*
Victorian Society 152
Vivat Academia 134, 135*f*
Vivisection, *see* Animals
Voelker, Carl 250, 251*f*
Vote, The, *see* Suffrage; *see* Reform Act

Wages, *see* Salaries
Walker, David 553, 555
Walsh, John 325–6
Warburton, David 446–7
Wardlaw, William 343
War Memorial 332–4, 332*f*, 356–8, 357*f*
Warmington, Eric 292–3, 531–2
Warrington, Ronnie 394–5
Watson, Anthony 550
Watson, James 408–9, 411–13, 416–17, 427–8
Way, A. G. 515
Webb, Beatrice 132
Webb, Sidney 99–101, 132, 194*f*, 383
Webster, Richard 117
Weisman, August 372
Weait, Matthew 518
Wellcome Trust 368
Wells, H. G. 196–7, 589
West Indies 205–9
Westwood, Gordon, *see* Schofield, Michael
White, James Charles Napoleon 43, 47, 87, 100–2, 109, 250
Wilde, Oscar 165, 166*f*, 181
Wilkins, Maurice 408–9, 413
Williams, Shirley 556
Williams, William Mattieu 5, 60–6, 70–1
Wilson, Harold 398–9, 550
Wittgenstein, Ludwig 500
Wolf, Leonard 363
Wolfenden Report 269
Wollstonecraft 182
Woodward, James 109
Woolf, Virginia 158, 243, 363, 494, 500
Woolridge, Sidney William 438–9
Women 22, 29, 31, 35, 57–60, 63, 82–3, 85, 98, 100–1, 112, 113*f*, 118, 124–5, 148–9, 158, 169–70, 174–203, 250, 254–5, 290–3, 324–9, 350, 407–10, 410*f*, 428–9, 438, 440–1, 504–5, 538, 544, 579, 591 *And throughout*

Women's Army Auxiliary Corps 327–9, 350
Woolridge, W. R. 166, 171, 440–1
Workers' Educational Association 497–8
World Federation of Scientific Workers 366
World Peace, World Peace Congress, Scientist for Peace 367
World War One 119, 132–6, 149–50, 195, 207–8, 234, 252, 280–1, 314, 317–34, 359, 362–3, 439–40, 486–7, 497, 505
World War Two 112–14, 133, 152–4, 208, 237–8, 275–6, 283–4, 287, 293, 314, 335–58, 366, 383, 408, 415–16, 440–2, 444–8, 497–9, 517–18, 522, 528, 529*f*, 548, 549*f*, 578–9
Worthsworth, William 144
Wright, Alice and Lilian 195
Wright, Frederick A. 104, 125–7, 248–9, 285, 319, 506
Wynn-Harris, Lynn 491
Wyon, Allan G. 333–4

Young, Baron of Dartington 118
Yugoslavia 362

Zetetical Society 194*f*
Zhukov, Yuri 375*f*
Zizek, Slavoj 395, 396*f*, 494, 513
'Zoo Group' 554
Zoology 171, 174–5, 194, 291*f*, 292–3, 295–9, 548
 see also Sciences
Zubaida, Sami 240–1, 244, 388, 400–1
Zuckerman, Solly 366